中国残疾人事业统计年鉴

China Statistical Yearbook on the Work for Persons with Disabilities

2014

（总第13期 No. 13）

中国残疾人联合会 编

China Disabled Persons' Federation

图书在版编目（CIP）数据

中国残疾人事业统计年鉴. 2014 / 中国残疾人联合会编. -- 北京 : 中国统计出版社, 2014.8
ISBN 978-7-5037-7091-3

Ⅰ. ①中… Ⅱ. ①中… Ⅲ. ①残疾人－社会福利事业－统计资料－中国－2014－年鉴 Ⅳ. ①D669.69-66

中国版本图书馆 CIP 数据核字(2014)第 112318 号

中国残疾人事业统计年鉴－2014

作　　者/中国残疾人联合会
责任编辑/王振宇
封面设计/王　鹏
出版发行/中国统计出版社
通信地址/北京市丰台区西三环南路甲 6 号　邮政编码/100073
电　　话/邮购（010）63376909　书店（010）68783171
网　　址/http://csp.stats.gov.cn
印　　刷/三河市双峰印刷有限公司
经　　销/新华书店
开　　本/880×1230mm　1/16
印　　张/20.5　8 彩页
字　　数/680 千字
版　　别/2014 年 9 月第 1 版
版　　次/2014 年 9 月第 1 次印刷
定　　价/180.00 元

如有印装差错，由本社发行部调换。

《中国残疾人事业统计年鉴-2014》
编委会和编辑工作人员

编者说明

《中国残疾人事业统计年鉴-2014》系统收录了全国和各省、自治区、直辖市2013年残疾人工作各方面的统计数据，是一部全面反映中国残疾人事业发展的资料性年刊。

本书内容由六部分组成：第一部分为主要指标数据图；第二部分为统计公报与专文，包括2013年中国残疾人事业发展统计公报和部分业务专题文章；第三部分为综合统计资料，是历年统计情况的综合反映；第四部分为2013年度分省统计资料，记录2013年各省任务指标执行情况和全国汇总情况；第五部分为分省统计报告，包括全国31个省（自治区、直辖市）、新疆生产建设兵团和黑龙江垦区的残疾人事业统计公报；第六部分为附录，介绍中国残疾人事业统计有关的政策法规文件。

本年鉴涉及的全国性统计数据均不包括香港、澳门特别行政区和台湾省数据。

本年鉴是根据各地残联报送的统计年报和部分专项业务项目统计结果编制而成。表格中“空格”表示该项统计指标数据不足本表最小单位数、数据不详或无该项数据。

2014年7月

目　　录

Contents

第一部分　主要数据图

Part Ⅰ　Charts

第二部分　统计公报与专文
Part Ⅱ　Communiqué and Reports

第三部分　综合统计资料
Part Ⅲ　Comprehensive Statistical Data

第四部分　分省统计资料
Part Ⅳ　Statistical Data of Provinces

康　复
Rehabilitation

扶　贫
Poverty Alleviation

专门协会
Special Associations

盲人按摩
Blind Massage

宣传文化
Publicity and Cultural Activities

体　育
Sports

维　权
Rights Protection

第六部分　附　　录

Part Ⅵ　Appendix

1

主要数据图

Charts

图-1 "十二五"期间累计得到不同程度康复的残疾人

Chart 1 PWDs Receiving Rehabilitation Service during the 12th Five-year Planning Period

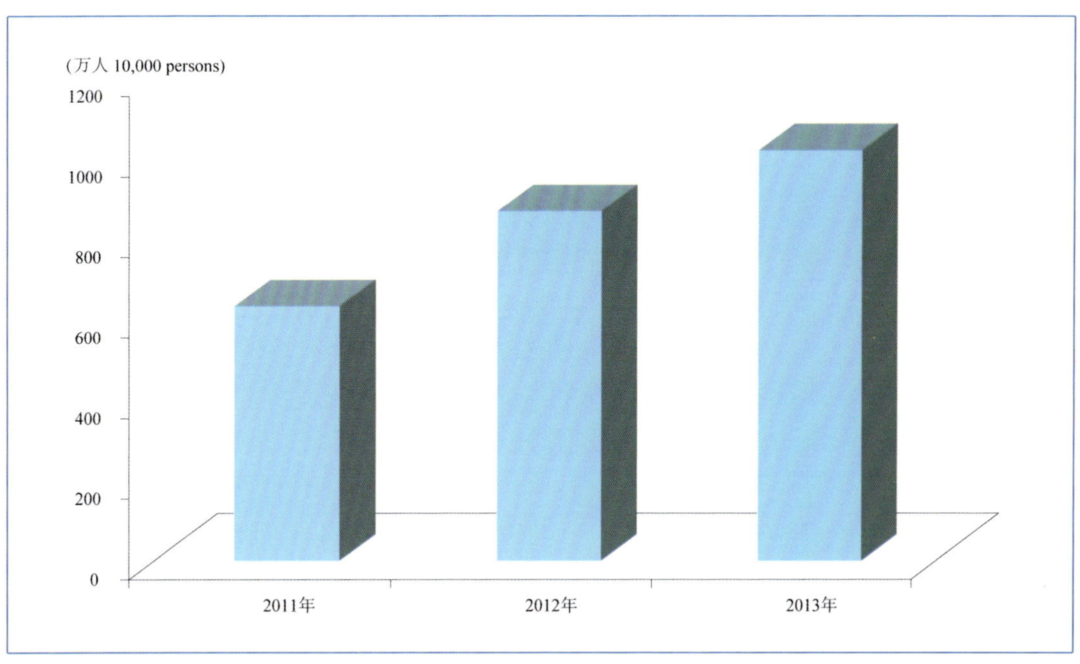

图-2 2010-2013年开展社区康复服务的县（市、区）

Chart 2 Counties and Cities Where CBR has been Conducted during 2010-2013

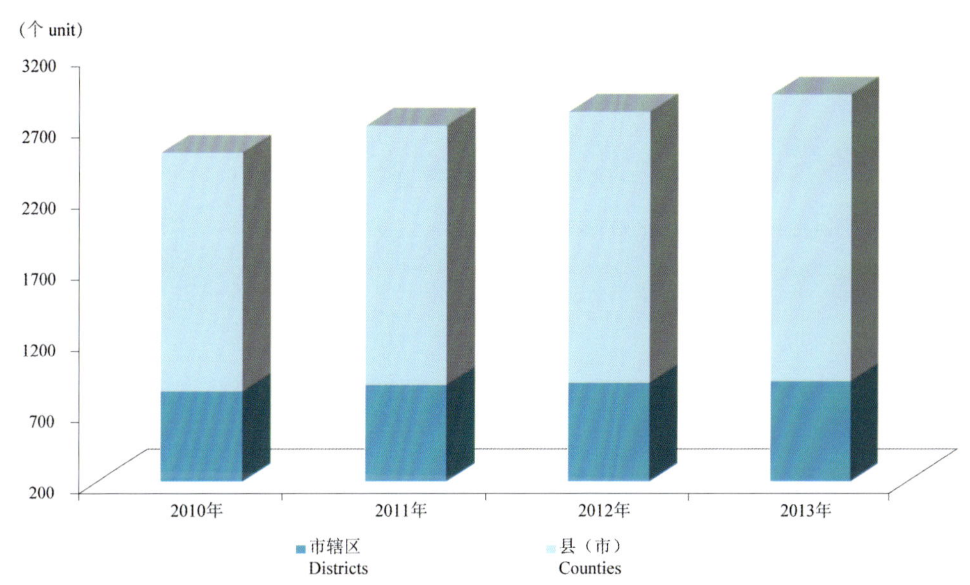

图-3 2010-2013年残疾儿童康复主要工作完成情况

Chart 3 Rehabilitation for Children with Disabilities during 2010-2013

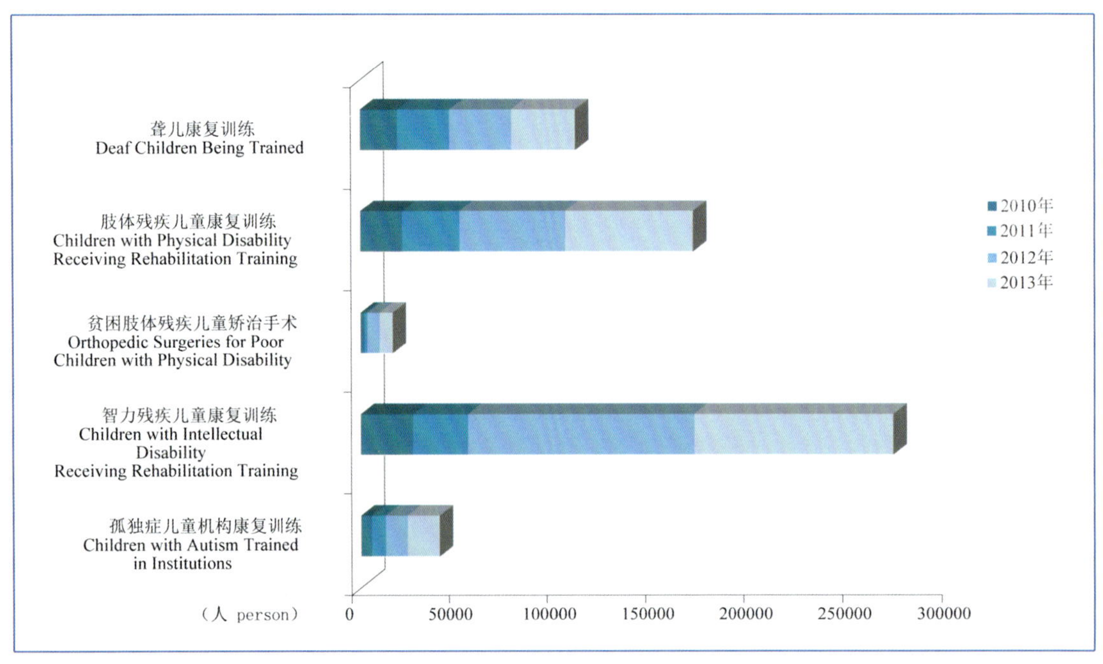

图-4 2010-2013年假肢与矫形器装配情况

Chart 4 Artificial Limbs and Orthotic Devices Fitted during 2010-2013

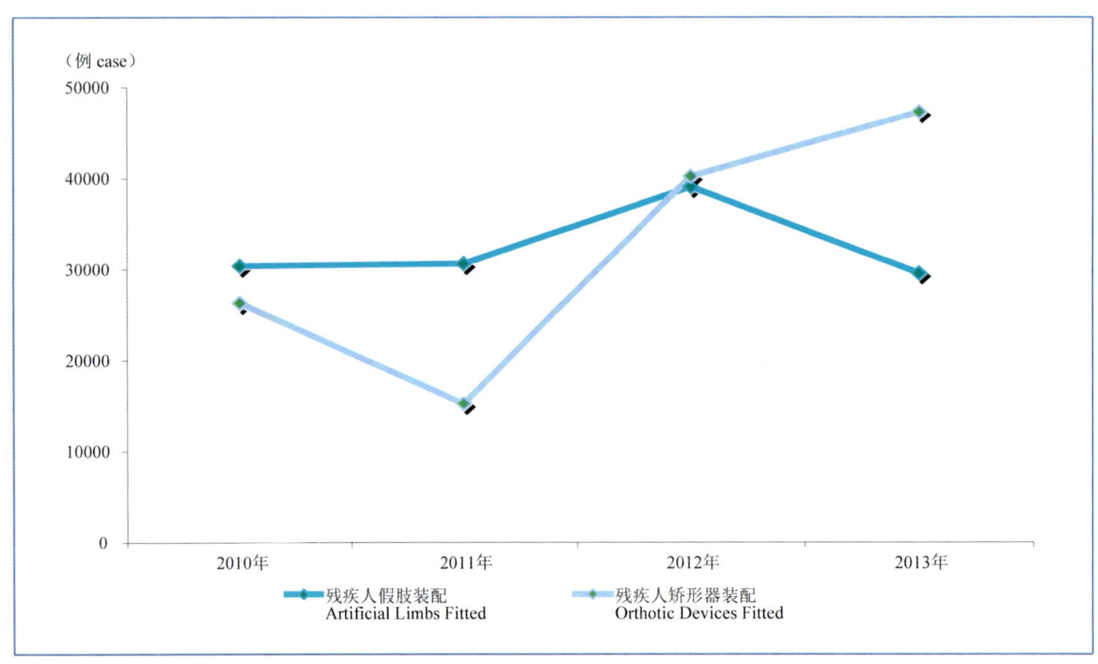

图-5　2010-2013年高等院校录取残疾考生情况

Chart 5 Admission of Disabled Students by Higher Educational Institution during 2010-2013

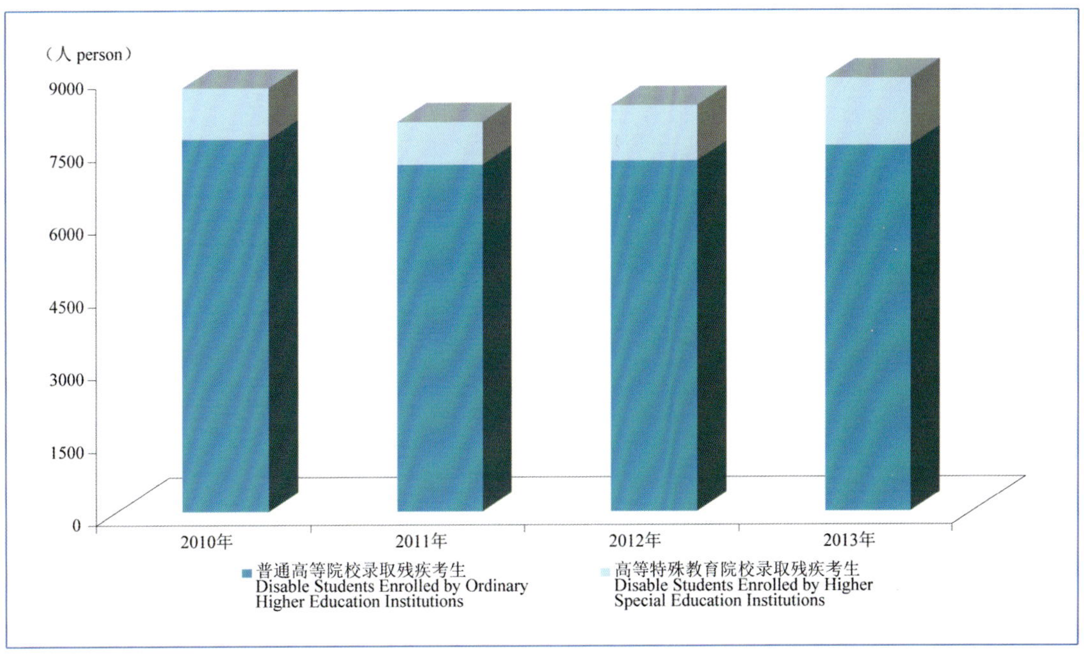

图-6　2013年未入学残疾儿童情况

Chart 6 Total Number of Unadmitted School Age Disabled Children in 2013

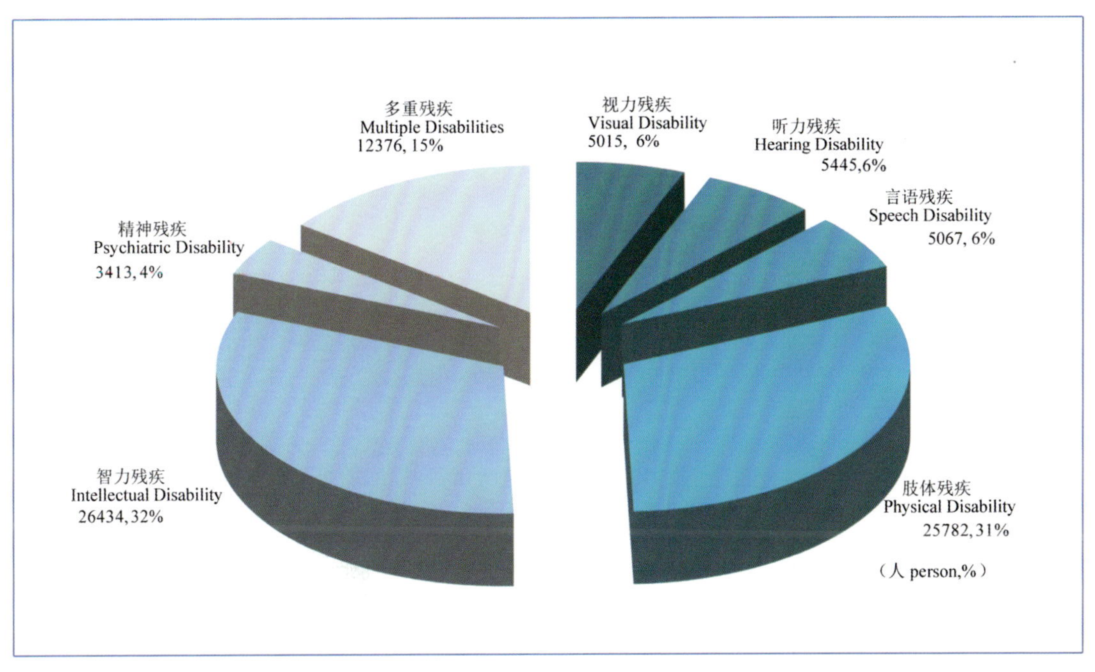

图-7　2010-2013年城镇残疾人新安排就业情况

Chart 7 Newly-added Employment of Disabled Persons in Urban Areas during 2010-2013

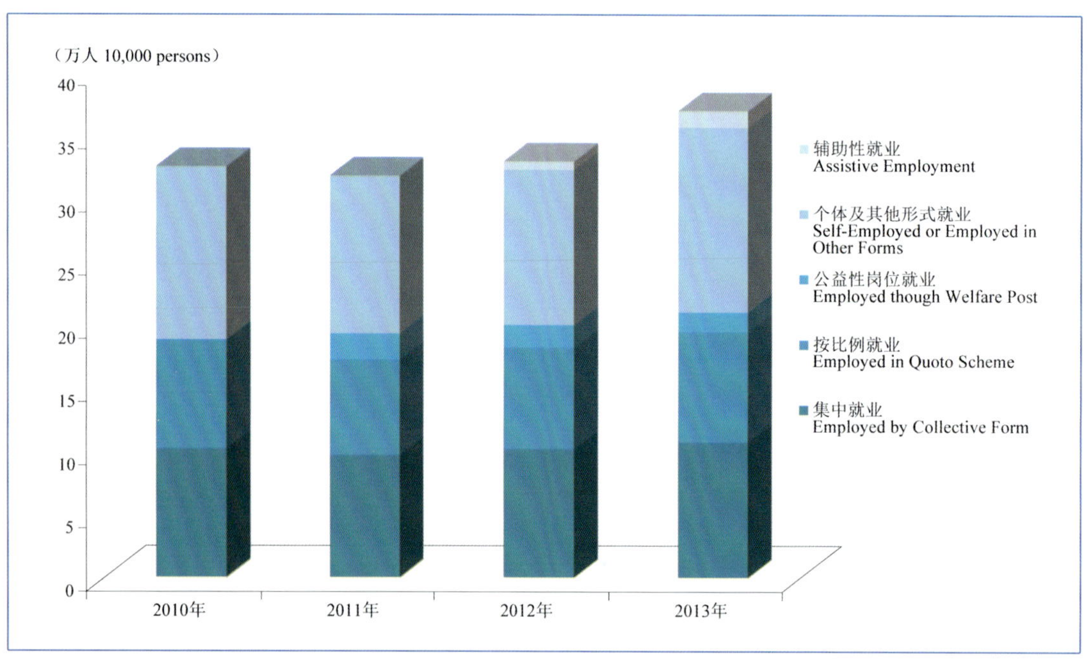

图-8　2010-2013年度盲人按摩人员培训情况

Chart 8 Massage Training for Blind Persons during 2010-2013

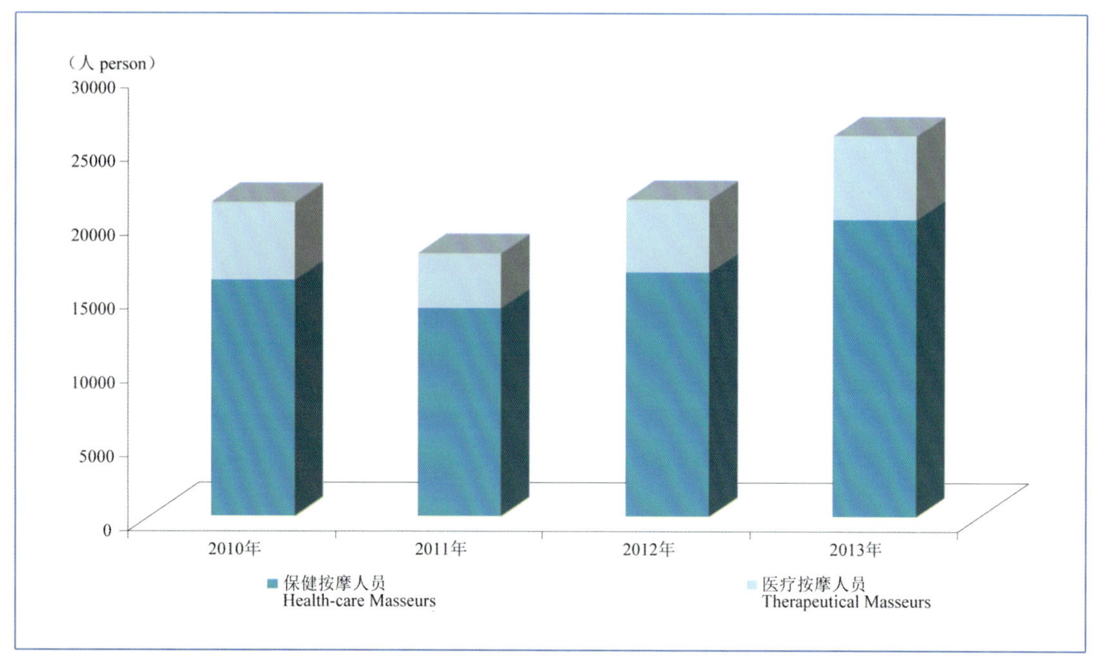

图-9　2010-2013年残疾人参加养老保险情况

Chart 9 PWDs Joining Endowment Insurance during 2010-2013

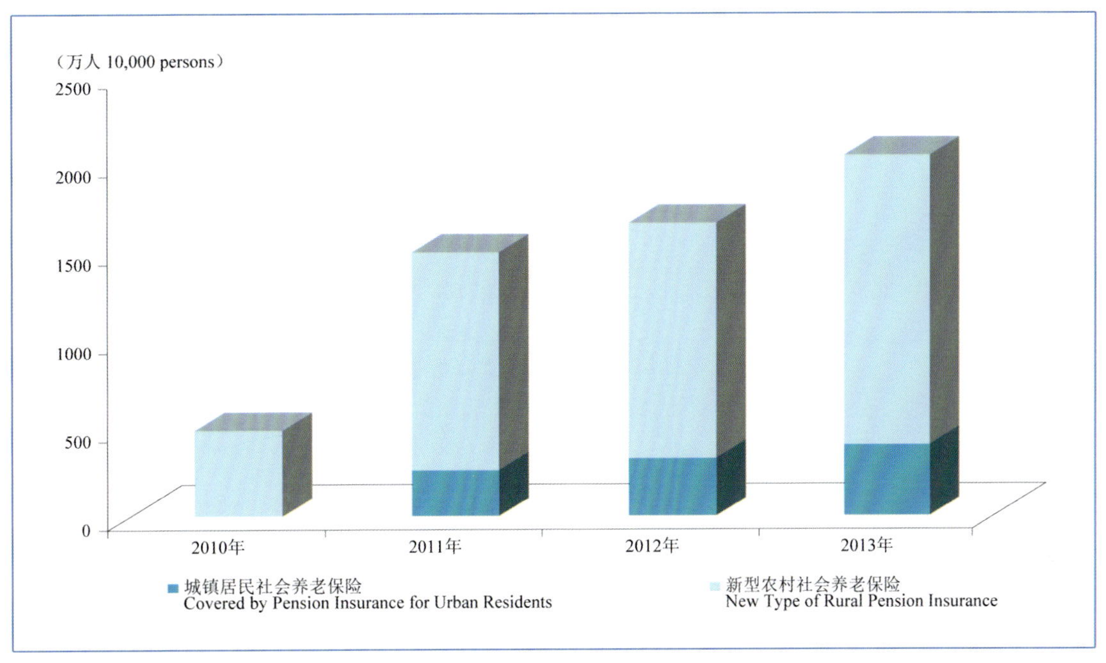

图-10　2011-2013年残疾人获得护理补贴和生活补贴情况

Chart 10 PWDs Receiving Care Subsidies and Living Allowances during 2010-2013

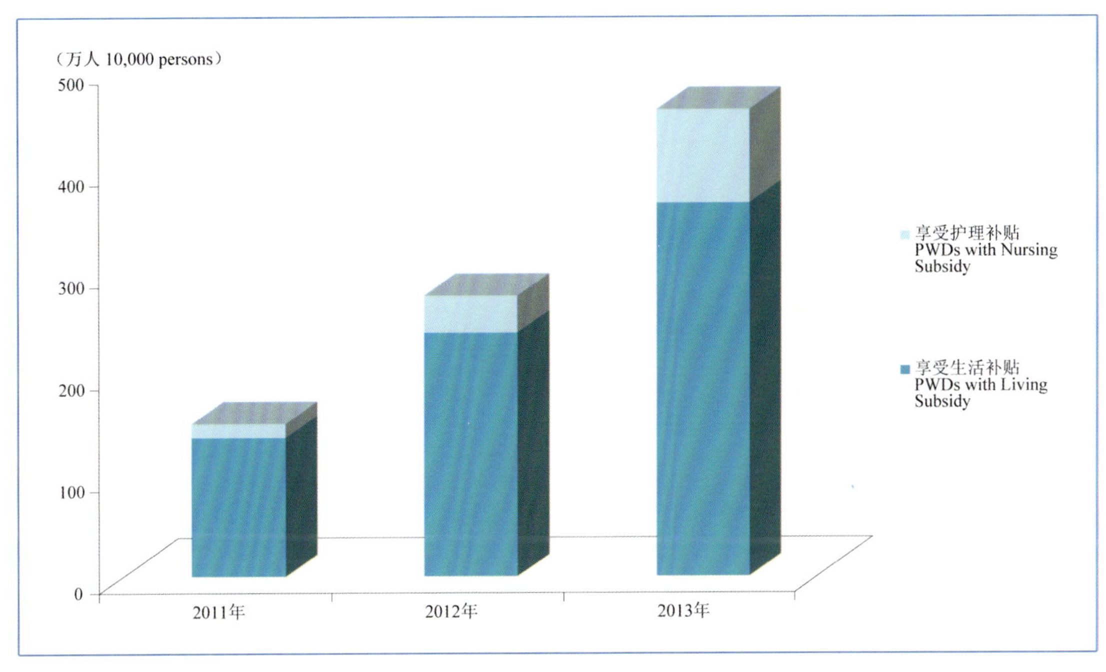

图-11　2010-2013年农村贫困残疾人危房改造情况

Chart 11　House Renovation for Poor PWDs in Rural Areas during 2011-2013

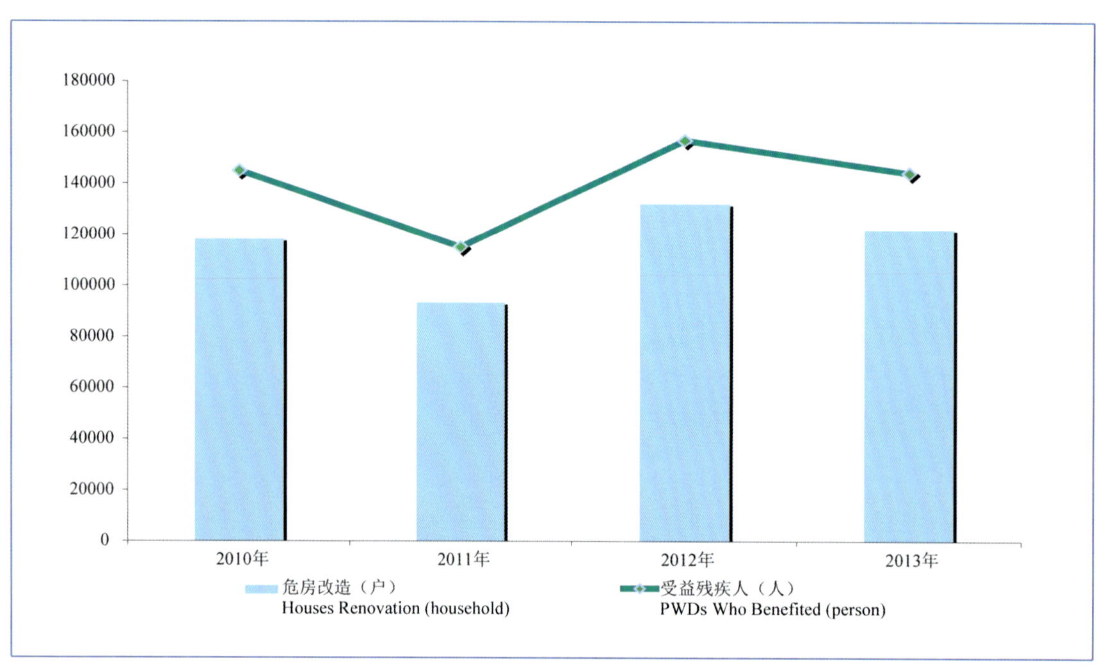

图-12　2010-2012年省、市两级残疾人宣传栏目开展情况

Chart 12　Propaganda Columns for PWDs at Provincial and City Level during 2010-2013

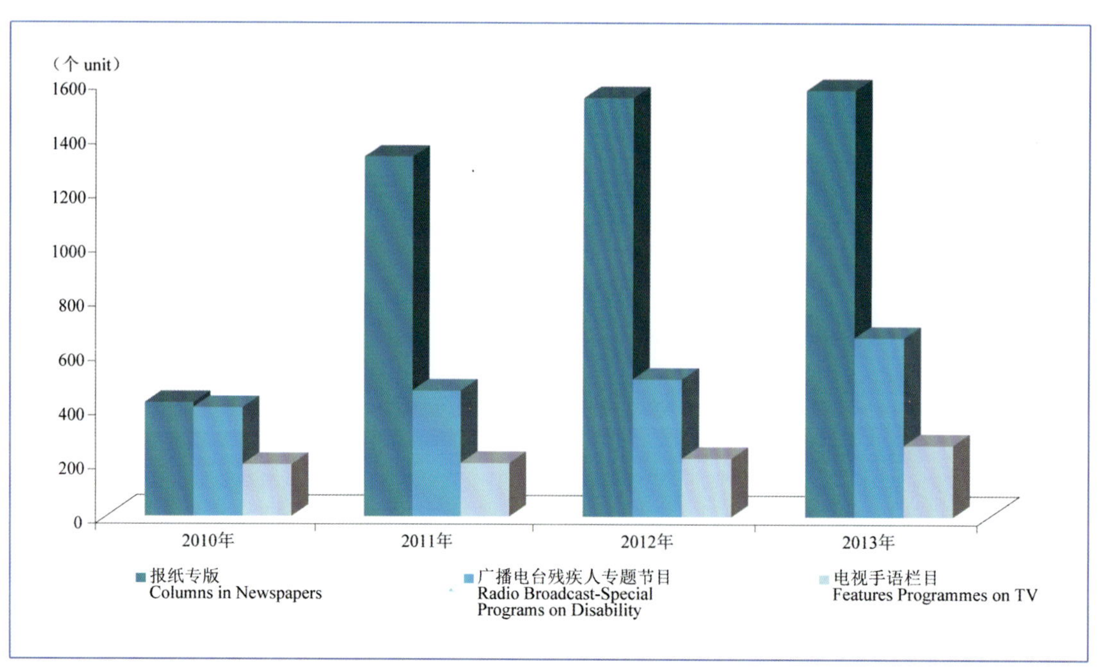

图–13 2011–2013年省、地市两级残疾人参加群众体育健身活动情况

Chart 13 PWDs Participating Mass Sports or Fitness Activities during 2010-2013

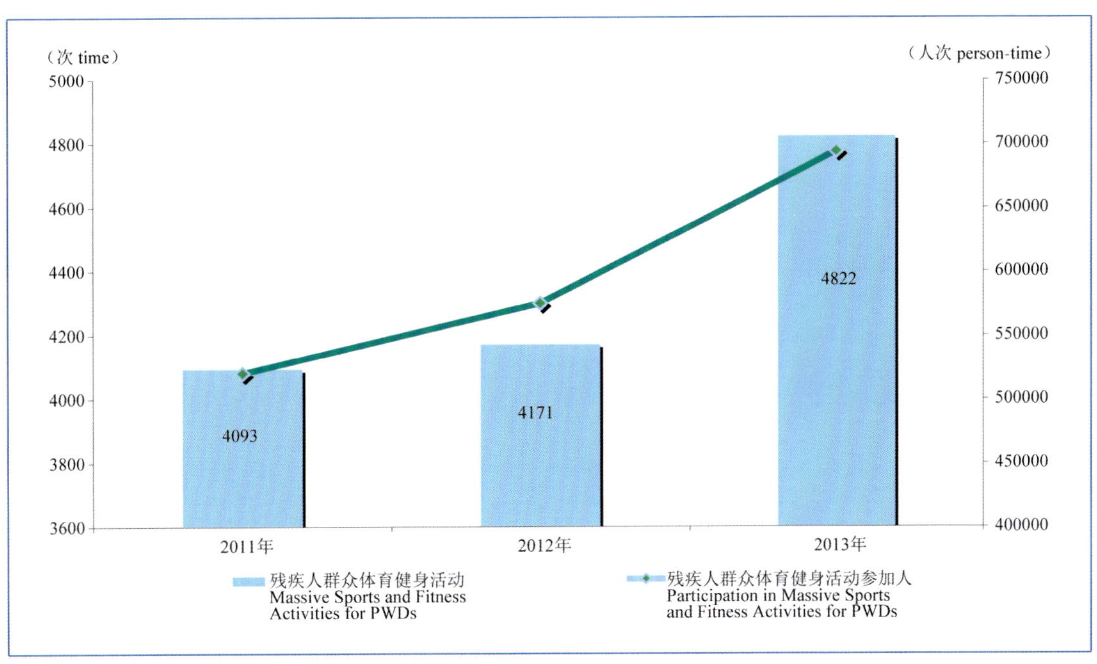

图–14 2010–2013年残疾人法律救助机构及服务情况

Chart 14 Legal Aid Centers (Stations) for PWDS and Their Service during 2010-2013

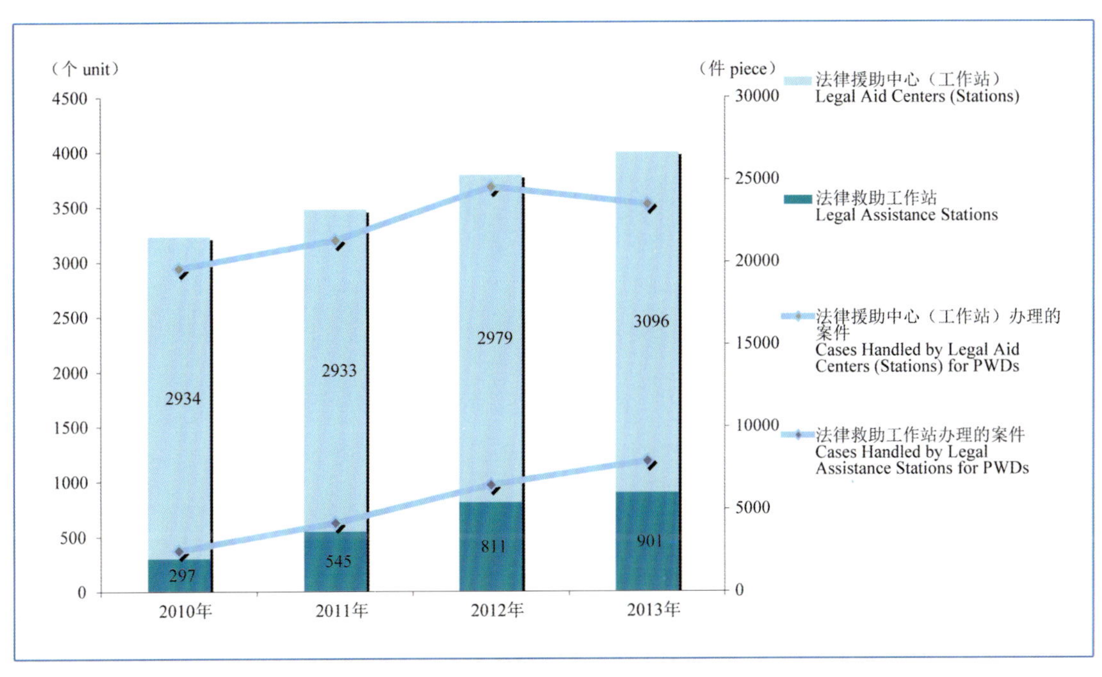

图-15 2010-2013年残疾人专职委员选聘情况

Chart 15 Full-time Workers on Disability at Grass-roots during 2010-2013

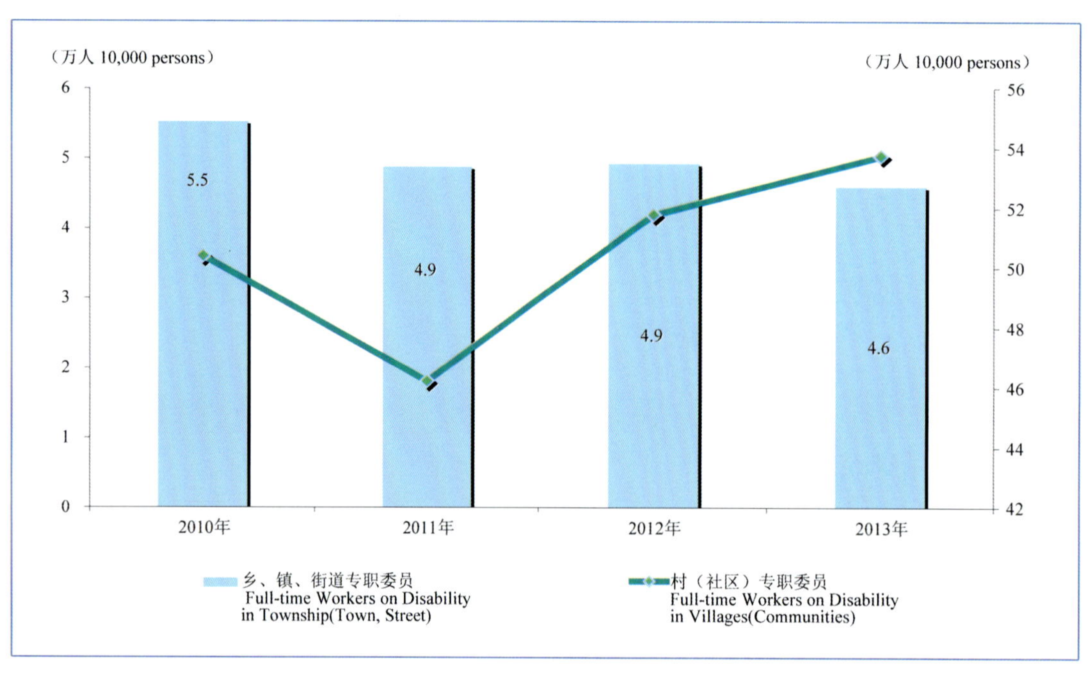

图-16 2013年残疾人服务设施建设情况

Chart 16 The Construction of Service Facilities for PWDs in 2013

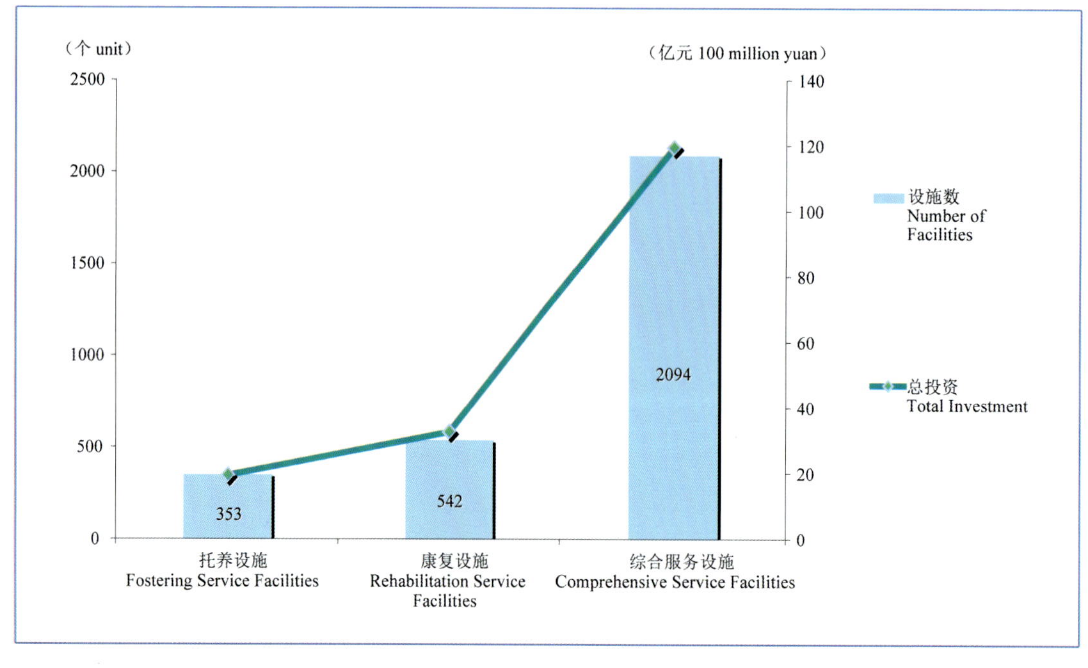

统计公报与专文

Communiqué and Reports

2013 年中国残疾人事业发展统计公报

2013 年中国残联第六次全国代表大会胜利召开，为在新的起点上推动创新发展提供了重要的思想和组织保障。在党中央、国务院正确领导和带领下，党政部门高度重视，残联组织辛勤工作，社会各界积极参与，广大残疾人自强不息，残疾人事业取得了新的进步。

一、康复

2013 年，通过实施一批重点康复工程，使 746.8 万残疾人得到不同程度的康复。开展全国残疾人社区康复示范区、县培育活动，积极推进残疾人社区康复工作；做好儿童残疾预防，尤其是 0-6 岁儿童残疾筛查工作；指导加强残疾人康复服务机构建设力度；实施《全国残联系统康复人才培养规划》，加强人才队伍建设；积极推动残疾人医疗康复保障政策的出台和落实；大力宣传和普及康复知识。

在 901 个市辖区和 2014 个县（市）开展了社区康复工作，累计已建社区康复站的社区总数 21.4 万个，配备 37.9 万名社区康复协调员。

1458 个县的 1844 个医疗卫生机构陆续开展残疾儿童筛查工作，年度新诊断 0-6 岁残疾儿童 5.0 万人。

开展视力残疾康复机构总数达到 805 个，完成白内障复明手术 74.6 万例；为 29.1 万名贫困白内障患者免费施行复明手术；为 12.9 万名低视力患者配用助视器，培训低视力儿童家长 3.8 万名，有效开展家庭康复训练。对 12.0 万名盲人进行定向行走训练。

推进听力语言康复机构规范化管理，完善基层服务网络。已建设省级听力语言康复机构 32 个，基层听力语言康复机构 1014 个。年度新收训聋儿 2.0 万名，在训聋儿 3.2 万名；规范聋儿家长学校，开展家庭训练，共培训聋儿家长 3.9 万名；开展各级各类听力语言康复专业技术人员培训，共培训专业人员 6448 人；实施贫困聋儿人工耳蜗、助听器抢救性康复项目，资助 4288 名聋儿免费植入人工耳蜗，资助 4500 名聋儿免费配戴助听器；开展彩票公益金成年听力残疾人（助听器）康复项目，为 1.0 万名贫困成年听力残疾人免费验配助听器，各级康复机构共为 3.2 万名成年听力残疾人提供技术服务。

开展肢体残疾康复训练服务机构达 1927 个，其中，省级康复机构 39 个，地市级、县级康复机构 1888 个；培训各级各类肢体残疾康复人员 3.5 万人次；全国共对 35.4 万肢体残疾者实施康复训练；实施救助项目资助 3.5 万名脑瘫儿童进行机构康复训练，资助 6721 名贫困肢体残疾儿童实施矫治手术。

为麻风畸残者实施矫治手术 418 例，开展宣传普及教育，为麻风患者回归社会营造良好社会氛围。

开展智力残疾康复训练服务的机构 1471 个，其中，省级康复机构 35 个，地市级、县级康复机构 1436 个；培训各级各类智力残疾康复人员 1.6 万人次；全国共对 13.1 万名智力残疾人进行康复训练；实施救助项目资助 2.4 万名智力残疾儿童进行机构康复训练，同时培训儿童家长。

大力推广“社会化、综合性、开放式”精神病防治康复工作。在 2627 个市县开展精神病防治康复工作，对 584.0 万重性精神病患者进行综合防治康复，监护率达到 79.1%，显好率达到 66.2%，社会参与率达到 51.4%，肇事率 0.17%；解除关锁 3702 人；对 46.9 万贫困精神病患者进行医疗救助。

建立了 34 个省级孤独症儿童康复训练机构；1.7 万名孤独症儿童在各级机构进行了康复训练。

加强残疾人辅助器具服务体系建设，深入开展辅助器具供应服务，为残疾人减免费用供应辅助器具 128.3 万件，其中装配假肢 2.9 万例、矫形器 4.7 万例，验配助视器 12.5 万件。

二、教育

2013 年，残疾人受教育权得到了更好保障，进一步提高了残疾人素质和平等参与社会的能力。

残疾人事业专项彩票公益金助学项目，为全国家庭经济困难的残疾儿童享受普惠性学前教育提供资助 1 万余人次。各地也积极多渠道争取资金支持，对 3489 名残疾儿童给予学前教育资助。

已开办特殊教育普通高中班（部）194 个，在校生 7313 人；其中聋高中 125 个，在校生 5704 人；盲高中 27 个，在校生 1609 人。残疾人中等职业学校（班）198 个，在校生 11350 人，毕业生 7772 人，其中 6200 人获得职业资格证书。全国有 7538 名残疾人被普通高等院校录取，1388 名残疾人进入特殊教育学院学习。

截至 2013 年底，全国有未入学适龄残疾儿童少年 8.4 万人，其中视力残疾儿童 0.5 万人，听力残疾儿童 0.5 万人，言语残疾儿童 0.5 万人，肢体残疾儿童 2.6 万人，智力残疾儿童 2.6 万人，精神残疾儿童 0.3 万人，多重残疾儿童 1.2 万人。

三、就业

2013 年，残疾人就业取得新进展。城镇新就业残疾人 36.9 万，其中，集中就业残疾人 10.7 万，按比例安排残疾人就业 8.7 万，公益性岗位就业 1.5 万，个体就业及其它形式灵活就业 14.6 万，辅助性就业 1.3 万。全国城镇就业人数 445.6 万；1757.2 万农村残疾人在业，其中 1385.4 万残疾人从事农业生产劳动。

全国残疾人职业培训基地达到 5357 个，其中残联兴办 2022 个，依托社会机构兴办 3335 个，37.8 万人次城镇残疾人接受了职业培训。

盲人按摩事业稳定发展，按摩机构迅速增长。2013 年度培训盲人保健按摩人员 20111 名、盲人医疗按摩人员 5694 名；保健按摩机构达到 14704 个，医疗按摩机构达到 936 个；在专业技术职务资格评审中，分别有 334 人和 1043 人通过医疗按摩人员中级和初级职称评审。

四、社会保障

2013 年新型农村和城镇居民社会养老保险进一步扩大覆盖面，已有 401.4 万城镇残疾人参加了城镇居民社会养老保险，参保率 65.1%。在 60 岁以下的参保残疾人中有 77.9 万重度残疾人，其中 73.1 万得到了政府的参保扶助，代缴补贴比例达到 93.8%。有 56.8 万非重度残疾人也享受了全额或部分代缴的优惠政策。领取养老金待遇的人数达到 162.0 万人。

新型农村社会养老保险方面，共有 1638.3 万残疾人参加了新型农村社会养老保险，参保率 71.2%。在 60 周岁以下的参保残疾人中有重度残疾人 314.0 万，其中 302.9 万得到了政府的参保扶助，代缴补贴比例达到 96.5%。有 175.2 万非重度残疾人也享受了全额或部分代缴的优惠政策。享受养老金待遇的人数达到 628.1 万人。

城镇残疾职工参加社会保险人数达到 296.7 万，城镇残疾居民参加基本医疗保险达到 547.3 万人，城镇 264.8 万和农村 828.2 万残疾人纳入最低生活保障范围；城镇集中供养残疾人和农村五保供养残疾人分别达到 11.7 万和 65.2 万；366.2 万和 92.0 万符合条件的城乡残疾人分别享受了稳定的生活补贴和护理补贴。266.0 万城乡残疾人得到了其他救助救济。

残疾人托养服务工作规范推进，残疾人托养服务机构达到 5677 个，共为 16.0 万残疾人提供了托养服务。其中寄宿制托养服务机构 1750 个；日间照料机构 2000 个；综合性托养服务机构 1927 个。接受居家托养服务的残疾人达到 78.4 万人。

五、扶贫开发

2013 年，残疾人扶贫开发成效显著，贫困残疾人生产生活状况得到进一步改善。238.7 万贫困残疾人得到扶持，其中 120.6 万人通过扶贫开发实际脱贫；接受实用技术培训的残疾人达到 85.6 万人次。

康复扶贫贴息贷款扶持 7.9 万农村残疾人，6.4 万个单位和 40.5 万个人对贫困残疾人开展结对帮扶。残疾人扶贫基地达到 6201 个，安置 16.4 万残疾人就业，扶持带动 24.6 万残疾人。

完成 12.2 万户农村贫困残疾人危房改造，各地投入危房资金 11.5 亿元，14.4 万残疾人受益。

基层党组织助残扶贫项目帮扶 76845 名农村贫困残疾人。“万村千乡市场工程”助残扶贫项目安置 6925 名贫困残疾人就业，帮扶贫困残疾人创办 2372 个村级农村店。

六、宣传文化

2013 年，“中国梦”、“走基层”等国家重点宣传栏目推出了多篇有关残疾人内容的报道；结合“帮扶贫困残疾人”第二十三次全国助残日活动，推出扶贫工作系列深度报道《农村残疾人扶贫应该怎么办》；

广泛开展典型宣传，组织媒体对全国11名优秀残疾人基层工作者事迹进行报道。全年中央电视台《新闻联播》播出残疾人题材报道40条，《朝闻天下》、《新闻直播间》等栏目播出88条，《人民日报》刊登相关社论、侧记和事业综述等80余篇。截至2013年底，全国共有省级残疾人专题广播节目120个，电视手语栏目36个；地市级残疾人专题广播节目539个，电视手语栏目227个。

残疾人文化生活更加丰富活跃，残疾人受到社会广泛关注并更加全面地参与到社会生活当中。以落实中宣部等11部委《关于加强残疾人文化建设的意见》为重点，全国26个省（区、市）出台了本地加强残疾人文化的意见，136个地市制定了本地实施意见；批准了全国32个残疾人文化体育示范市（区）和10个内地与澳门残疾人文化示范市（区）创建；组织第八届全国残疾人艺术汇演，全国31个省（区、市）和新疆兵团的5000余名演职员参加了声乐、器乐、舞蹈和戏剧小品四大类的比赛，少数民族节目超过20个，节目总数达348个，间接参与汇演的残疾人超过10万人，达历史之最；拍摄的残疾人题材电影《一生有爱》获蒙特利尔电影节优秀节目奖，联合摄制的电影《吴运铎》在俄罗斯举行的第十届尤•尼•奥泽罗夫国际军事电影节上荣获最佳视觉效果奖和最佳导演奖。

七、体育

2013年，残疾人体育工作以提高残疾人体育健身服务能力和残疾人体育运动水平为着力点，全面实施“自强健身工程”，不断提高竞技水平。

举办第三届残疾人健身周活动，全国27个省（区、市）开展了残疾人体育健身培训、比赛及体育进家庭等形式多样的活动6000多场次。全国累计培养审批了524名国家级残疾人体育健身指导员。在全国27个省（区、市）命名资助了90个自强健身示范点；为中西部地区配发了35套健身器材，并纳入示范点统一管理；累计共资助建设自强健身示范点203个。组织第七次全国特奥日活动、特奥足球比赛及家庭论坛等系列活动，特奥运动员达到115.9万人。

举办了18项全国单项赛事，2200名运动员参赛，涌现了一批优秀的年轻运动员。参加第22届世界夏季听障奥运会、第十届冬季特奥运动会等27项国际赛事交流活动。其中，参加第22届世界夏季听障奥运会获得12金、5银、8铜，位居金牌榜第四位。组织了27批次575人次的运动员集训，残疾人体育人才队伍和组织建设不断加强。注册登记的残疾人运动员达到6800人，审批的裁判员1188人、分级员45人。国家级残疾人体育培训基地达到31所。

各地深入开展残疾人体育工作。组织省级残疾人群众体育健身活动254次，5.8万多人次参加；建设省级残疾人群众体育活动示范点达到596个；培训省级残疾人体育健身指导员达到5352人；组织省级残疾人体育比赛114次，参赛运动员达1.3万人次；省级残疾人体育训练基地已达207个。组织地市级残疾人体育活动4568次，63.6万人次参加；设立地市级残疾人群众体育活动示范点1591个；培训地市级残疾人体育健身指导员1.2万人。

八、维权

各级残联维权组织建设得到加强，残疾人事业法律法规体系进一步完善，残疾人维权工作全面开展。

2013年，修订《残疾人保障法》地方实施办法4件；制定或修改了关于残疾人的专门法规、规章省级5件、地市级26件；制定或修改保障残疾人权益的规范性文件省级30件、地市级76件。全国县级以上人大进行《残疾人保障法》执法检查和专题调研799次；政协进行视察和专题调研746次。全国开展普法宣传教育活动6606次，105.2万人参加；举办法律培训班1670个，9.6万人参加。

截至2013年底，全国成立残疾人法律救助工作协调机构1306个，建立残疾人法律救助工作站901个，办理案件7905件，建立残疾人法律援助中心（工作站）3096个，办理案件2.3万件，有力地促进了法律救助和法律援助工作。

残疾人参政议政工作得到加强，各级残联协助人大代表、政协委员提出议案、建议、提案1743件，办理议案、建议、提案1464件。

无障碍建设法规、标准进一步完善。全国共出台了444个省、地市、县级无障碍建设与管理法规、规章和规范性文件；1419个市、县、区系统开展无障碍建设；全国开展无障碍建设检查3492次，无障碍培训3.6万人次；为13.6万个贫困残疾人家庭实施了无障碍改造；为 65.7 万残疾人发放了残疾人机动轮椅车燃油补贴。

全国各级残联共处理残疾人群众来信 5.4 万余件，接待残疾人群众来访 32.3 万人次，其中集体访 1145 批次、1.8 万人次。

九、组织建设

2013 年，30 个省级残联领导班子中配备了残疾人理事长或副理事长；251 个地市级残联在领导班子中配备了残疾人理事长或副理事长；1625 个县级残联机关配备了残疾人干部；已建乡镇（街道）残联 4.0 万个，已建率达到 98.0%，选聘残疾人专职委员 4.6 万名；已建社区（村）残协 58.1 万个，已建率达到 92.6%，选聘残疾人专职委员 53.8 万名。

全国省市县乡残联实有人员已达 11.1 万人。各级残联共举办培训班 3.2 万期，培训机关干部、协会干部及残疾人专职委员 76.5 万人次。

全国共建立省级以下各类残疾人专门协会 15410 个，市级专门协会已建比例为 97.6%，市辖区专门协会已建比例 96.3%；县（含县级市）级专门协会已建比例为 90.4%。

十、服务设施建设

残疾人服务设施建设得到全面发展。截至 2013 年底，全国已竣工并投入使用的各级残疾人综合服务设施 2094 个，总建设规模 424.1 万平方米，总投资 119.6 亿元；已竣工并投入使用的各级残疾人康复设施 542 个，总建设规模 100.7 万平方米，总投资 32.7 亿元；已竣工并投入使用的各级残疾人托养服务设施 353 个，总建设规模 78.2 万平方米，总投资 19.6 亿元。

十一、信息化建设

2013 年，中国残联网站年度访问量达到 6900 万次，刊发各地残联稿件超过 1.2 万篇，内容更新总量达到 1.6 万条。全国 33 个省级残联、277 个地市级残联和 1307 个县级残联开通网站，比 2012 年增加 77 个。33 个省、291 个地市、1779 个县级残联实现网上信息报送与审核。首次将网站无障碍纳入中国政府网站绩效评估范围，对 117 家部委和省政府等网站开展无障碍专项评估。

中国残疾人服务网连续第 3 年开展央视龙年春晚（文字+视频）网上无障碍直播服务，访问用户超过 28 万人。为盲人提供图形验证码网上识别服务达 127.4 万人次。加强与社会专业招聘信息网站合作，提供残疾人专属就业岗位信息超过 4000 余个。连续组织 7 期淘宝网“云客服”招募超过 1000 人报名。

截至 2013 年底，全国残疾人人口基础信息数据库累计采集、收录持证和非持证残疾人 4020 余万人。结合全国农村贫困残疾人扶贫调查，采集农村贫困残疾人扶贫需求信息 1500 余万条。作为国家权威的残疾人基础信息资源，残疾人人口基础数据库已取得较为明显的社会效益和经济效益。

Statistical Communiqué on the Development of the Work for Persons with Disabilities in 2013

The year of 2013 witnesses the 6th National Congress of China Disabled Persons' Federation (CDPF), which provides key ideaistic and organizational guarantee for the innovative development of work on disability from a new starting point. Under the proper leadership of CPC and the State Council, with strong support from the Communist Party and government authorities, through hard work by disabled persons' federations at all levels, active participation by all sectors of the society, and striving constantly for self-improvement by persons with disabilities (PWDs), the work on disabilities in China achieves new progress.

Ⅰ. Rehabilitation

In 2013, through implementation of some key projects, 7.468 million disabled persons received rehabilitation services at different degrees. The Campaign of Building Model Community or County was staged to vigorously promote community-based rehabilitation (CBR). Work on disability prevention were launched, especially the screening of disabled children aged 0-6 years old. Guidance was strengthened to the capacity building of rehabilitation institutions. The National Rehabilitation Personnel Training Program was implemented to further the work of personnel training. Measures were taken to push the promulgation and implementation of policies enabling PWDs to be covered by medical rehabilitation. Basic knowledge of rehabilitation was publicized and popularized.

Community-based rehabilitation was carried out in 901 districts under the jurisdiction of cities and 2,014 counties with 214,000 CBR stations set up and 379,000 CBR coordinators designated.

Number of institutions providing rehabilitation services for patients with visual impairment reached 805. 746,000 cases of cataract sight-restoring surgeries were conducted, including 291,000 free ones for poor cataract patients. 129,000 low-vision patients received vision aids. 38,000 parents of children with low vision got training for more effective family-based rehabilitation. 120,000 blind persons received orientation mobility trainings.

The hearing and speech training institutions were regularized and the grassroots service network became more perfect. There were 32 provincial-level rehabilitation centers for deaf children and 1,014 grassroots hearing and speech training institutions nationwide. 32,000 deaf children are receiving hearing and speech training, and 20,000 of them are newly enrolled in the past year. Parent schools were further regulated and trained 39,000 parents of deaf children. 6,448 various kinds of professionals in the field of hearing and speech training were trained. A rescuing rehabilitation project was implemented to provide 4228 poor deaf children with free cochlear and 4,500 ones with free hearing aids. The rehabilitation project for the adult with hearing disabilities (hearing aids) was also carry out supported by the public welfare lottery fund. 10,000 poor adult with hearing disability get free hearing aids and 32,000 poor adult with hearing disability get technical services by various levels of rehabilitation institutions.

The number of institutions able to provide rehabilitation and training services to persons with physical disability reached 1,927, including 39 provincial level rehabilitation institutions and 1,888 city level ones'. Skilled training was provided for 35,000 professionals on physical rehabilitation. Rehabilitation training was carried out for 354,000 persons with physical disability nationwide. With the support of some relieving projects, 35,000 children with cerebral palsy received rehabilitation training, and 6721 poor children with physical disability received corrective surgeries.

418 cases of corrective surgeries were conducted

on persons with leprosy-induced disabilities. Education campaigns were carried out to build a favorable social atmosphere for these patients to return to society.

The number of institutions providing rehabilitation and training services to persons with intellectual disability reached 1,471, including 35 provincial level rehabilitation institutions and 1,436 city level ones. 13,100 professionals on intellectual rehabilitation received rehabilitation skills training. Rehabilitation training was conducted for 160,000 persons with intellectual disability nationwide. With the support of some relieving projects, 34,000 children with intellectual disability as well as their parents were received rehabilitation training.

A "socialized, comprehensive and open" model was promoted for the prevention and rehabilitation of psychiatric diseases. The work of prevention and rehabilitation was carried out in 2,627 cities and counties, covering 5.84 million persons with severe mental illness. 79.1 % of the patients lived under guardianship, 66.2% of them showed signs of recovery, 51.4% participated in the society, and 0.17% caused incidents. 3,702 persons with mental illness were released from seclusion and 469,000 poor patients got medical assistance.

34 provincial-level autism rehabilitation institutions were set up and. 17,000 children with autism were provided with rehabilitation training.

The work of building a service system of assistive devices was strengthened to improve supply of assistive devices for PWDs. An accumulation of 1.283 million assistive devices, including 29,000 artificial limbs, 47,000 pieces of prosthetics and 125,000 were adapted and equipped for poor disabled persons at preferential rate or for free,.

II. Education

In 2013, disabled persons' right to education was better guaranteed. The quality of disabled persons and their ability to equally participate in social life were improved.

The education project funded by dedicated lottery fund provided more than 10,000 person/times of financial support to disabled children from poor families in their preschool education. Fund was also raised through various channels to support 3,489 disabled children in their preschool education.

There were 194 special education classes at senior high schools nationwide, with an enrollment of 7,313 students. Among these schools, 125 were for the deaf with 5,704 enrolled students, 27 were for the blind with 1,609 enrolled students. There were 198 medium-level vocational education institutions (classes) with 11,350 enrolled students, 7,772 graduates, of whom 6,200 were with vocational certification. In 2013, 7,538 students with disabilities were accepted by mainstream higher education institutions, and 1,388 disabled students entered special higher education institutions.

By the end of 2013, there were 84,000 disabled children and youth at school age who did not have access to education, including 5,000 with visual impairment, 5,000 with hearing impairment, 5,000 with speech impairment, 26,000 with physical disability, 26,000 with intellectual disability, 3,000 with psychiatric diseases and 12,000 with multiple disabilities.

III. Employment

In 2013, the work to promote employment of PWDs made new progress. 369,000 disabled persons in urban areas were newly employed, including 107,000 through concentrative placement, 87,000 through quota scheme, 15,000 through welfare job posts, 146,000 through individual business and other forms of employment, and 7,000 through supporting employment. 4.456 million disabled persons were in employment in the urban areas. 17.527 million rural PWDs had employment and 13.854 million of them took part in agricultural productive labor.

There were 5,357 special vocational training institutions nationwide, including 2,022 established by DPFs and 3,335 by social organizations. A total of 378,000 disabled persons in the urban areas received vocational training.

Massage business by the blind grew steadily with big increase of the number of massage institutions. In 2013, 20,111 health blind masseurs and 5,694 medical blind masseurs were trained. The number of healthcare massage institutions reached 14,704 and that of medical massage institutions amounted to 936. Through professional qualification evaluations, 551 and 1,655 medical blind masseurs passed secondary and elementary level qualification exams respectively.

IV Social Security

In 2013, the coverage of the new type of rural cooperative and urban social endowment insurance was further enlarged. 4.014 million or 65.1% of disabled persons in urban areas had joined in urban social endowment insurance, including 779,000 persons with severe disabilities under 60 years old, 731,000 of whom received governments' financial assistance. The percentage of government assistance or subsidy reached 93.8%. Also, 568,000 persons whose disabilities were not severe enjoyed the preferential treatment of all or part of the premium paid by governments. 1.62 million disabled persons are receiving old-age pension.

In 2013, 16.383 million or 71.2% of rural disabled persons were covered by the new type of rural social endowment insurance, including 3.14 million persons with severe disabilities under the age of 60. Among them, 3.029 million received governments' financial assistance. The percentage of government assistance or subsidy reached 96.5%. 1.752 million persons with disabilities received the full or partial financial assistance from the government. 6.281 million disabled persons are receiving old-age pension.

2.967 million urban workers with disabilities were covered by social endowment insurance. 5.473 million urban residents with disabilities were covered by basic medical insurance. 2.648 million urban disabled persons and 8.282 million rural disabled persons were covered by basic living insurance protection. The number of unban PWDs under centralized fostering and the number of full-guaranteed rural PWDs reached 122,000 and 685,000 respectively. After passing the assessment of conditions, 3.662 million urban PWDs and 0.92 million rural PWDs are receiving regular living allowances and care subsidies. Another 2.66 million urban and rural PWDs got other assistance or economic aid.

The fostering service for disabled persons made steady progress. The number of fostering service organizations for disabled persons amounted to 5,677, including 1,750 boarding service organizations, 2000 day-care organizations, and 1927 combined fostering service organizations. These organizations all together provided fostering service for 160000 PWDs. Another 784,000 persons with disabilities are receiving fostering services at home.

V. Poverty Alleviation

In 2013, the work of poverty alleviation made remarkable progress with the living and production conditions of poor disabled persons further improved. 2.387 million poor disabled persons were covered by poverty alleviation projects, including 1.206 million who actually got rid of poverty through these poverty alleviation projects. 856,000 persons/times of training of practical technology were provided for PWDs.

79,000 rural persons with disabilities were granted interest-subsidized loans under poverty alleviation through rehabilitation projects. 64,000 units and 405,000 individuals paired up with poor disabled persons to get them out of poverty. The number of poverty-alleviation bases increased to 6,201, employing 164,000 disabled persons, supporting and bringing along 246,000 disabled persons to join.

122,000 poor rural households with disabled persons had their houses renovated. 1.15 billion RMB Yuan were invested, benefiting 144,000 disabled persons.

Through a project "grassroots Party organizations assisting the disabled", 76,845 poor disabled persons in the rural areas got support. Another project called "Market program in ten thousand villages and one thousand townships" helped 6,925 disabled persons get employment, and 2059 village-level shops were set up by the disabled persons with the help of the project.

VI. Publicity and Cultural Activities

In 2013, some of the country's most influential TV programs such as "China Dream" and "Visiting the Grassroots" put forward a lot of reports relating to the work on disability. On the occasion of the 22nd National Day of Assisting Persons with Disabilities under the theme of "Assisting the poor rural PWDs", a series of in-depth poverty alleviation reports on "How to do poverty alleviation for rural PWDs" were aired. In order to promulgate the stories of some models of disabled persons, we organized some media to cover the stories of 11 outstanding grassroots workers in the field of disability. In this year, 40 news reports about people with disabilities were aired in CCTV's Evening News, and 88 news reports were aired by Morning News and News Live of CCTV. More than 80 editorials, reports and reviews were published on

People's Daily. By the end of 2013, at the provincial level, there were 120 radio programs specially designed on disability issues, and 36 TV news programs with sign language. At the district/city level, there were 539 radio programs specially designed on disability issues, and 227 TV news programs with sign language.

The cultural life of disabled persons became more active and colorful. PWDs received wide social attention and extensively participated in social life. Focusing on implementing The guideline on further promotion on the culture civilization for PWDs, jointly formulated and issued by Publicity department of central committee of CPC and CDPF, 26 provinces (municipalities or autonomous regions) issued their own guideline on further promotion on culture civilization for PWDs, and 136 cities/districts made their own implementation guidelines. 32 cities/districts nationwide were named as pilot model cities (districts) for culture and sports building for PWDs, and 11 cities were appointed as pilot model cities (districts) for culture building for PWDs jointly with Macao SAR. The 8th National Art Gala Show of PWDs was successfully organized. More than 5000 performers and staff participated the competition in 4 categories, i.e. vocal music, instrumental music, dancing and opera. There were 348 performances in total, among which more than 20 performances were given by minorities. More than 100,000 PWDs indirectly involved in the event, which is the most in history. The film "With Love for the Whole Life" about PWDs won the Award of Excellence during the Montreal Film Festival. The jointly produced film "Wu Yunduo" won the Best Visual Effect Award and Best Director Award in the 10th U. N. Ozerov International Military Films Festival in Russia.

VII. Sports

In 2013, the work of sport for PWDs was focused on improving the ability of providing fitness service for PWDs and enhancing the sports level of disabled athletes. Through implementation of "Self-improvement Fitness Program", the level of athletics was raised continuously.

The event of 3rd Fitness Week of Disabled Persons was organized. 27 provinces (municipalities or autonomous regions) organized more than 3000 various types of sports or fitness activities such as training on fitness for PWDs, sports games at home, etc.. In the whole country, 524 national level sports and fitness directors were appointed. 27 provinces (municipalities or autonomous regions) names 90 new demonstration sites of Self-improvement Fitness for PWDs. The number of such demonstration sites reached 203. 35 sets of fitness devices were donated to western China and were managed by the demonstration sites. A series of promotion events were organized, including the country's 7th "Day of Special Olympics", Special Olympic Competition of football matches and a forum of family members. The number of the athletes for Special Olympics has reaches 1.159 million.

18 sports competitions of disabled persons were organized and participated by 2,200 persons, among whom many were young and promising. CDPF participated 27 international games or sports matches, including the 22nd World Deaf Olympics, the 10th Winter Special Olympics. The delegation participating the 22nd World Deaf Olympics won 12 gold medals, 5 silver medals and 8 bronze medals, ranking number 4 on the result panel. We have also organized 27 times of training for a total of 575 athletes. The establishment of human resources team and organizations of sports for PWDs were further strengthened. The number of registered athlete reached 6800, with 1188 qualified judges and 45 professionals on classification. The number of country level bases of sports for PWDs reached 31.

The sports activity of disabled persons was extensively carried out in localities. 254 times of fitness activities were organized for disabled persons at provinces, with a participation of 58,000 person/times. 596 sports activity demonstration sites of disabled persons were established, training 5352 coaches for fitness activity of disabled persons. 114 sports competitions of disabled persons were organized at provincial level, participated by 13,000 persons. The number of provincial sports training base of disabled persons amounted to 207. At the city level, 4,568 times of sports activities of disabled persons were organized and participated by 636,000 person/times. 1591 sports activity demonstration sites of disabled persons were established, training 12,000 coaches for fitness activity of disabled persons.

VIII. Rights Protection

Disabled persons' federations at all levels further strengthened their work team in rights protection for disabled persons. The laws and regulations systems relating to the work on disability became more perfect. The work of rights protection was carried out in an all round way.

In 2013, 4 local implementation method of the Law of P.R.C. on the Protection of Persons with Disabilities were revised. 5 regulations especially for disabled persons at the province level and 26 ones at the city level were formulated or revised. 30 regulations directly related with disabled persons at the province level and 76 ones at the city level were formulated or revised. People's congress at and above the county levels carried out inspections on enforcement of the Law of P.R.C. on the Protection of Persons with Disabilities for 799 times. The Political Consultative Conferences at all levels carried out inspections and studies for 746 times. 6,606 times of law publicity and education activities for 1.052 million participants and 1,670 education courses for legal professionals were organized for 960,000 participants.

By the end of 2013, 1,306 coordination organizations of legal assistance for disabled persons and 901 legal aid stations were set up, handling 7,905 cases of rights violation against disabled persons. 3,096 legal aid stations were set up, handling 23,000 cases of rights violation against disabled persons. The work of legal aids and services for disabled persons were greatly promoted.

Disabled persons took a more active part in political consulting process. In 2013, 1,743 pieces of bills and proposals were raised by congress deputies and members of political consultative conferences from disabled persons' federation systems. 1,464 pieces of bills and proposals were dealt with.

Legislation and standards of accessibility were further improved. 444 regulations and administrative decrees on accessibility were issued in the provinces, cities and counties. Systematic accessibility construction was carried out in 1419 cities and counties. 3,492 times of special inspections on accessibility were carried out. 36,000 persons/times received trainings on accessibility. Accessibility renovation was made for 136,000 poor families with disabled persons. 657,000 persons with disabilities received subsidy for petrol used by their motorized wheelchairs.

The disabled persons' organizations at all levels received and handled over 54,000 compliant letters and 323,000 visitor/times in the year. Among the complaint visits, there are 1,145 group visits and 18,000 by individuals.

IX. Disabled Persons' Organizations

In 2013, 30 provincial DPFs had disabled persons as president or vice presidents. 251 city-level federations had disabled president or vice presidents in their offices. 1,625 county-level federations had disabled staffs in their offices. 40,000 towns (streets) had disabled persons' federations, accounting for 98% of the total and recruiting 46,000 disability commissioners. 581,000 communities (villages) had disabled persons' associations, accounting for 92.6% of the total and recruiting 538,000 disability commissioners.

Workers of city, county and township level disabled persons federations amounted to 111,000 persons. Personnel training made new progress. 32,000 training courses were organized for 765,000 person/times.

Nationwide, there are 15,410 special associations of disabled persons under the provincial level. 97.6 % of cities and 96.3% of districts under the jurisdiction of cities as well as 90.4% of the counties had special associations.

X. Service facilities

The construction of services facilities for disabled persons was developed in an all-around way. By the end of 2013, 2094 complicated services facilities at all levels were completed and put into use, with a total construction area of 4.241 million square meters. The total investment is 11.96 billion RMB. 542 complicated rehabilitation service facilities at all levels were completed and put into use, with the construction area of 1.007 million square meters. The total investment is 3.27 billion RMB. 353 combined fostering services facilities were completed and put into use, with the construction area of 782,000 square meters. The total investment is 1.96 billion RMB.

XI. Informationization

In 2013, the official website of China Disabled Persons' Federation recorded 69 million visits, publishing more than 120,000 pieces of new information from different levels of DPFs with 16,000 update in contents. 33 disabled persons' federations at the provincial level, 277 at the city level and 1,307 at the county level had built and opened their own websites, the number is 77 more than that of 2012. 33 disabled persons' federations at the provincial level, 291 at the city level and 1,779 at the county level can report and review their statistics on line. For the first time in China, accessibility became one of the aspects for evaluating government websites. The accessibility of 117 websites of government ministries or provincial government was evaluated.

For the third year in succession, the China Disabled Persons' Service Network (CDPSN) gave an accessible live broadcast on the Spring Festival Gala of CCTV through text and video on the eve of the Spring Festival, which recorded over 280,000 visits. The on-line graphical identification service helped blind people to identify graphical verification code for 1.274 million person/times. The network had strengthened cooperation with professional public recruiting information network, providing the information of more than 4000 job posts specially designed for PWDs. The recruitment "Taobao customer service cloud" was organized for 7 times, with more than 1000 applications by disabled persons.

By the end of 2013, the national basic database of persons with disabilities collected the basic data of 40.2 million disabled persons. The national survey on the poverty alleviation of disabled persons in the rural areas of China collected data on the poverty alleviation needs of more than 15 million disabled persons. As an authoritative basic information resource, the database has achieved obvious social and economic effect.

全国残疾人人口基础数据库主要数据简报

中国残联 2008 年启动建设全国残疾人人口基础数据库，结合第二代残疾人证核发工作进行持证残疾人的人口基础信息的收集与管理，并通过与公安部“全国公民身份信息服务系统”进行身份认证。

经过几年来的建设，通过残疾人证核发和开展康复需求调查、农村贫困残疾人状况摸底调查等工作，截至 2013 年底，全国残疾人人口基础数据库中共收集 4020 万残疾人数据，其中包括 2811.5 万持证残疾人信息和 1208.5 万非持证残疾人数据。按照全国残疾人口 8502 万计算，约占 46.6%，持证残疾人证比例为 33.1%。

一、人口库持证残疾人主要结构特征

持证残疾人的主要特征为：劳动年龄人口为主（16-59 岁占 60.2%），男性、中轻度、肢体残疾人各占到六成（分别为 60.1%、62.1%和 58.8%），四分之三为农业户口（75.3%），受教育程度以小学和初中为主体（70.3%）。

1.年龄结构

人口库中 2811.5 万持证残疾人的年龄构成为：0-14 岁 78.6 万人，占 2.8%；其中 0-6 岁残疾儿童 18.0 万人，占 0.6%；15-59 岁 1701.1 万人，占 60.5%；60 岁及以上 1031.8 万人，占 36.7%。

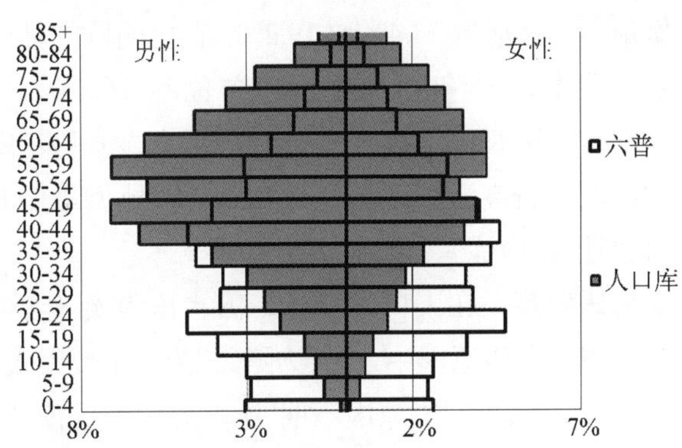

图 1　人口库持证残疾人与六普人口年龄金字塔比较

2. 性别结构

人口库中 2811.5 万持证残疾人的性别构成为：男性 1689.7 万人，占 60.1%；女性 1121.9 万人，占 39.9%。

3. 民族

人口库中汉族残疾人 2543.5 万人，占 90.5%；少数民族 268.0 万人，占 9.5%。

4. 户口性质

人口库中农业户口的持证残疾人 2115.7 万人，占 75.3%；非农业户口 695.8 万人，占 24.7%。

与第六次人口普查的全国人口中 50.3%居住在乡村相比，约四分之三的人口库持证残疾人仍然在农村，远远落后于全国的城镇化水平。

5. 受教育程度

人口库持证残疾人中 15 岁及以上文盲率为 18.4%，显著低于 2006 年调查的整体残疾人（43.3%[1]），但比 2010 年第六次全国人口普查的 4.1%高出 14.4 个百分点。

在人口库中的 2811.5 万持有二代残疾人证的残疾人中，具有大学及以上文化程度的有 40.3 万人，占 1.4%；具有高中（含中专）文化程度的有 230.4 万人，占 8.2%；具有初中文化程度的有 837.6 万人，占 29.8%；具有小学文化程度的有 1138.5 万人，占 40.5%。

人口库持证残疾人与 2010 年第六次全国人口普查分性别受教育程度的比较见下图。

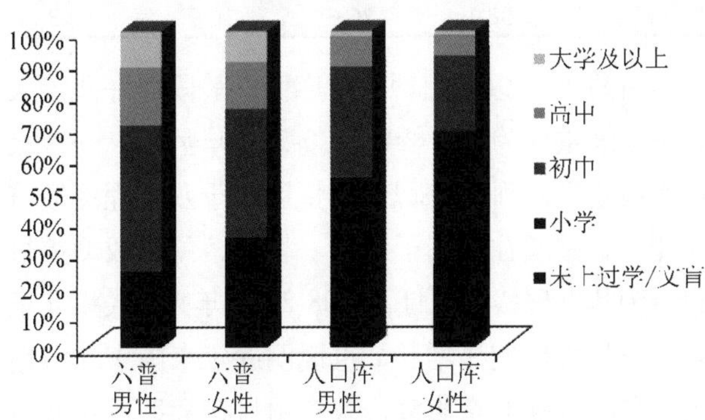

图 2　人口库持证残疾人与六普人口 15 岁及以上分性别受教育程度比较

[1] 2006 年调查残疾人的 43.3%指的是 15 岁及以上粗文盲率。

二、持证残疾人主要残疾特征

1. 残疾类别构成

人口库中 2811.5 万持证残疾人的类别构成为：视力残疾人 336.5 万人，占 12.0%；听力残疾人 221.1 万人，占 7.9%；言语残疾人 52.9 万人，占 1.9%；肢体残疾人 1653.5 人，占 58.8%；智力残疾人 230.8 万人，占 8.2%；精神残疾人 196.2 万人，占 7.0%；多重残疾人 120.5 万人，占 4.3%。

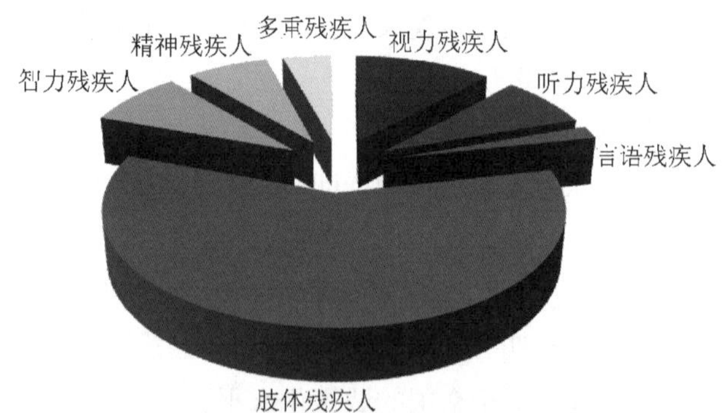

图 3　人口库持证残疾人残疾类别构成

2. 残疾等级构成

人口库中 2811.5 万持证残疾人的残疾等级构成为：残疾一级 381.5 万人，占 13.6%；残疾二级 682.7 万人，占 24.3%；残疾三级 779.6 万人，占 27.7；残疾四级 967.7 万人，占 34.4%。

表 1　人口库持证残疾人分类别残疾等级构成（%）

	残疾一级	残疾二级	残疾三级	残疾四级
合计	13.6	24.3	27.7	34.4
视力残疾人	27.7	19.4	16.7	36.2
听力残疾人	23.5	23.7	23.7	29.0
言语残疾人	46.1	23.5	15.0	15.4
肢体残疾人	5.3	20.0	31.8	42.8
智力残疾人	13.0	39.2	29.7	18.1
精神残疾人	12.1	50.5	28.2	9.2
多重残疾人	58.1	26.6	10.9	4.3

由图 5 可以看出，人口库低年龄段持证残疾人以一二级重度为主，特别是 0-5 岁年龄段，一二级重度残疾人占到 70%以上，说明对于残疾程度较重的儿童，家长往往出于康复、教育、项目救助等目的会为其办理残疾人证。2008-2013 年来，残疾儿童办证也呈现出明显增长，也说明近年来国家和各地区的各项残疾儿童康复、教育项目在救助残疾儿童的同时对于加强相应的办证管理和服务起到积极促进作用。残疾 16-59 劳动年龄段和 60 岁及以上老年残疾人的残疾等级构成基本一致。

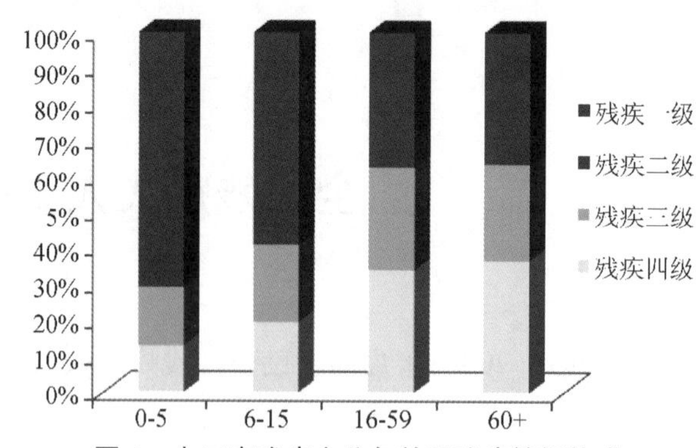

图 4　人口库残疾人分年龄段残疾等级构成

3. 主要致残原因

视力残疾　人口库 351.1 万视力残疾（含多重）的主要致残原因中，“其他”和“原因不明”占到较大比例，共计 23.7%。在已明确的具体致残原因中，“白内障”排在第一位，占 13.5%，其次为“视网膜、色素膜病变”11.9% 和“遗传、先天异常或发育障碍”10.5%，“外伤”、“视神经病变”、“角膜病”和“青光眼”分别为 8.7%、8.2%、7.2%和 6.2%，比例最小的是“中毒”，仅为 0.3%。

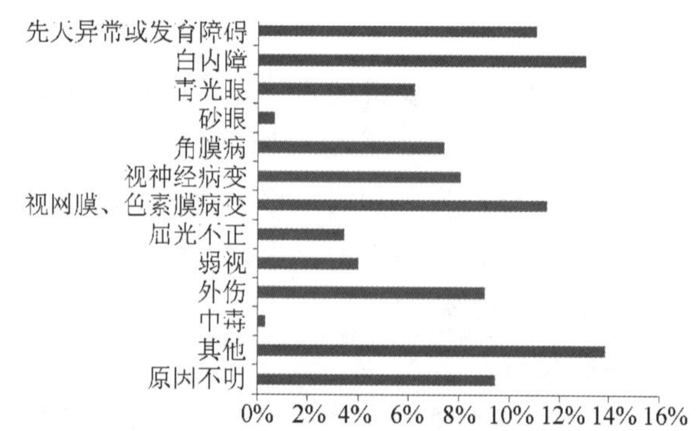

图 5　人口库持证残疾人视力残疾主要致残原因构成

听力残疾　在人口库 302.5 万听力残疾（含多重）的主要致残原因中，“原因不明”和“其他”所占比例最高，分别为 24.4%和 19.2%。在已明确的具体致残原因中，“老年性耳聋”排在首位占 16.2%，其次为“遗传”10.8%，此外，“药物中毒”、“中耳炎”所占的比例也较高，分别是 7.3%和 6.6%，比例最低的是“高胆红素血症”，仅占 0.08%。

言语残疾　在人口库 131.3 万言语残疾（含多重）的主要致残原因中，“听力障碍”为最主要因素，占 37.1%，“其他”和“原因不明”所占的比例也较高，分别占 18.3%和 17.2%，其余各种原因所占的比例较低，均在 5%以下。

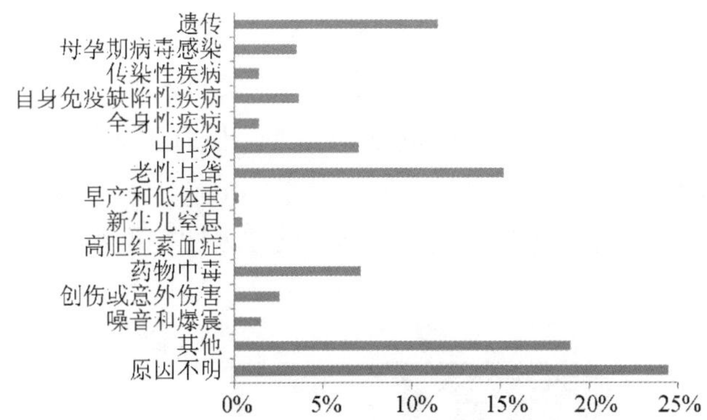

图 6 人口库持证残疾人听力残疾主要致残原因构成

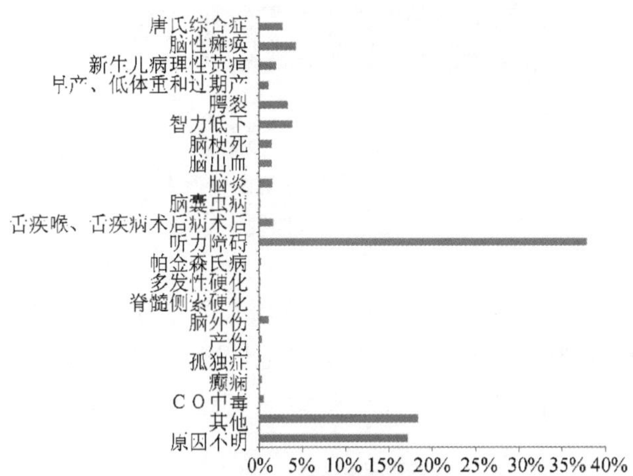

图 7 人口库持证残疾人言语残疾主要致残原因构成

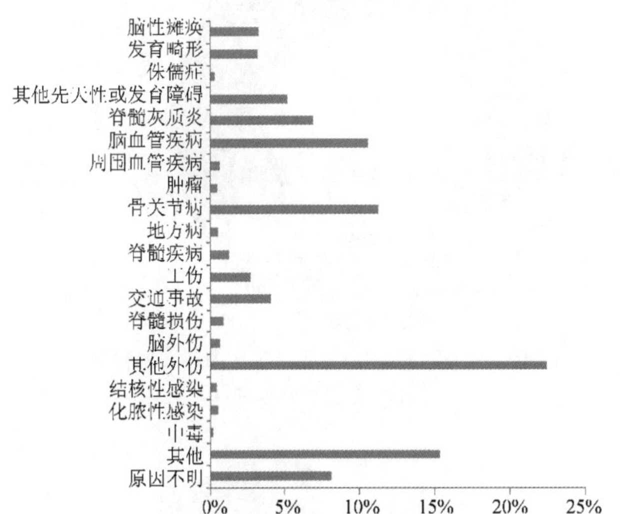

图 8 人口库持证残疾人肢体残疾主要致残原因构成

肢体残疾 在人口库 1690.2 万肢体残疾（含多重）的主要致残原因中，“其他外伤”排在首位，占 22.2%，其次为“其他”，占 15.5%，“骨关节病”、“脑血管疾病”、“脊髓灰质炎”分别占 11.8%、11.3%和 6.5%，“原因不明”占 8.2%，“其他先天性或发育障碍”占 4.9%，“交通事故”占 4.0%，其余各类原因所占比例均很小。

智力残疾 在人口库 252.4 万智力残疾（含多重）的主要致残原因中，“原因不明”和“其他”同样占较大比例，分别为 19.8%和 16.5%。在已明确的具体致残原因中，“脑疾病”所占比例最高，占 31.7%，其次为“遗传”11.9%，“发育畸形”占 4.8%，其余各类原因所占的比例均很小。

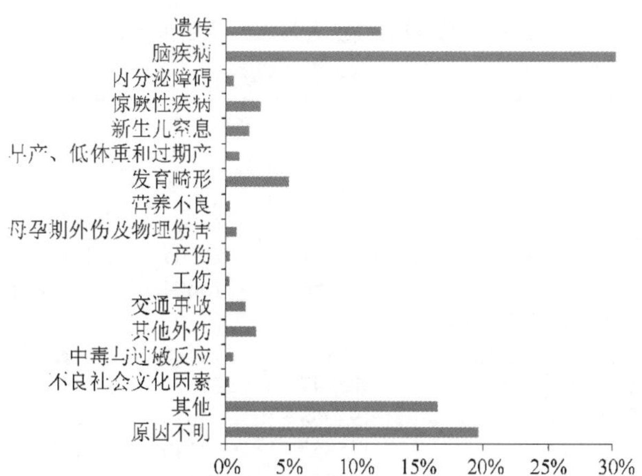

图 9 人口库持证残疾人智力残疾主要致残原因构成

精神残疾 在人口库 202.4 万精神残疾（含多重）的主要致残原因中，“精神分裂症”是最主要的原因，占 60.5%，其次为“其他”、“癫痫”和“原因不明”，分别为 8.1%、6.8%和 5.5%，其余各种原因所占的比例较小，均在 4%以下。

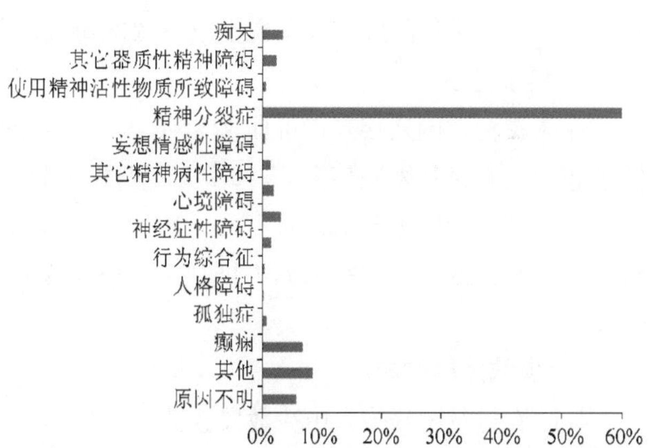

图 10 人口库持证残疾人精神残疾主要致残原因构成

三、集中连片特困地区贫困残疾人基本状况

2014 年 1 月，中共中央办公厅、国务院办公厅印发《关于创新机制扎实推进农村扶贫开发工作的意见》，要求各地区各部门结合实际认真贯彻执行。集中连片特困地区（以下简称“片区”）是国家新一轮扶贫开发攻坚战的主战场。片区内集中生活着大量贫困残疾人，是扶贫开发工作中的难中之难、重中之重。

截至 2013 年底，农村贫困残疾人（户）信息调查系统采集到 1503.6 万贫困残疾人数据，其中片区贫困残疾人 506.0 万，占 33.7%。片区贫困残疾人中，持证残疾人 282.7 万，占 55.9%; 非持证残疾人 223.4 万，占 44.1%。

表 2　片区持证残疾人与农村贫困残疾人

单位：人

集中连片特困地区	人口库持证残疾人	农村贫困残疾人（户）信息调查系统	
		持证贫困残疾人	非持证贫困残疾人
合计	5401161	2826505	2233801
大别山区	628856	315604	422766
大兴安岭南麓山区	175168	61107	15883
滇桂黔石漠化区	629470	414526	548329
滇西边境山区	385747	221679	41868
罗霄山区	194068	111073	28128
吕梁山区	115857	77149	16788
秦巴山区	900451	412446	369746
四省藏区	142568	49701	15633
乌蒙山区	520528	269834	137635
武陵山区	660280	377453	433581
西藏区	68026		
新疆南疆三地州	151594	71418	3562
燕山-太行山区	243883	109532	41650
六盘山地区	584665	334983	158232

根据农村贫困残疾人（户）信息调查系统采集到的数据，片区贫困残疾人呈现出以下状况特征:

1. 持证比例

片区农村贫困残疾人持证比例为 55.9%，显著低于非片区农村贫困残疾人的 73.7%，可能与片区社会保障制度和优惠政策相对不足、交通相对不便、基层组织有待健全、残疾人对办证缺乏了解等因素有关。

2. 少数民族构成

片区农村贫困残疾人中少数民族共有 117.1 万人，占 30.2% ，远高于非片区 5.9%的比重。其中，贫困残疾人较多的少数民族有壮族、苗族、土家族、回族、彝族、维吾尔族。

3. 残疾状况

片区农村贫困残疾人的残疾类别和残疾等级构成与非片区没有非常明显的差异，与全国残疾人人口基础库中持证残疾人的构成也基本一致。

4. 家庭状况

90.6%的片区农村贫困残疾人家庭年人均纯收入低于国家贫困标准，显著高于非片区的 78.3%。说明片区农村贫困残疾人家庭的确更加困难。

0.8%的片区农村贫困残疾人填报了其个人年工资收入，其中 58.8%的个人年工资收入低于 1000 元，30.8%介于 1001-2000 元之间，仅有 10.4%高于 2000 元。

与非片区农村贫困残疾人的收入比较见图 12。

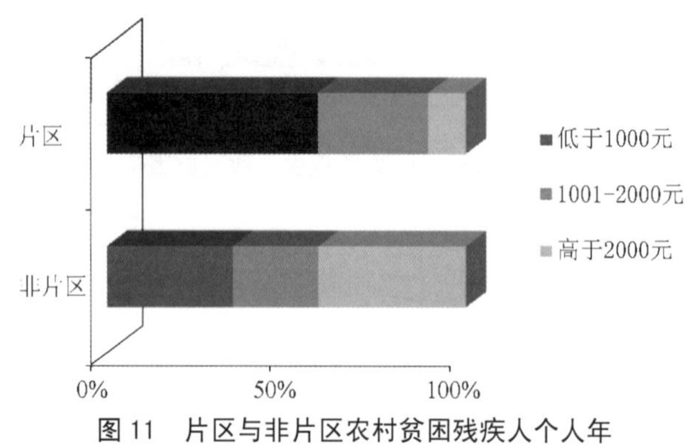

图 11　片区与非片区农村贫困残疾人个人年工资收入比较

34.4%的片区农村贫困残疾人家庭为老残一体，6.5%为一户多残，61.4%为其他情况。状况构成与非片区农村贫困残疾人家庭基本一致。

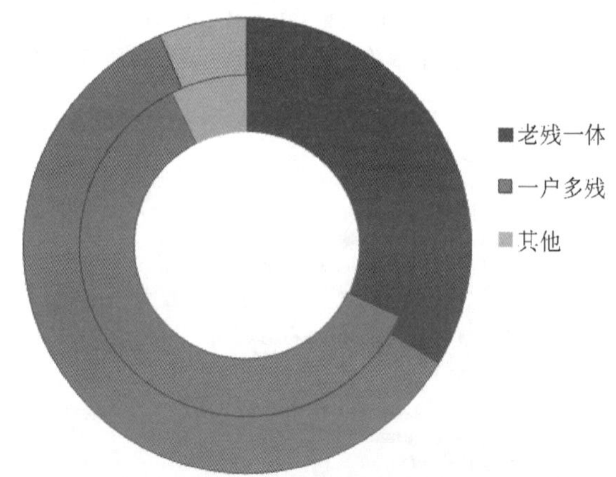

图 12　片区（外环）与非片区（内环）农村贫困残疾人家庭状况比较

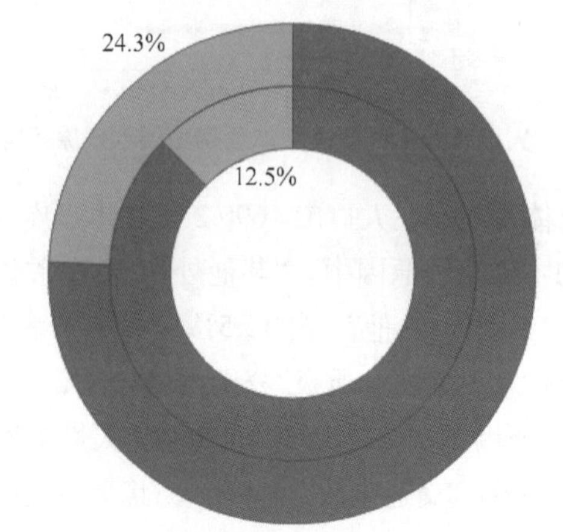

图 13　片区（外环）与非片区（内环）农村贫困残疾人危房情况比较

5. 住房情况

96.0%的片区农村贫困残疾人有住房，与非片区一致；其中 24.3%的住房为危房，接近非片区（12.5%）的两倍。

6. 致贫原因

数据显示，53.6%的片区农村贫困残疾人为因病致贫，24.7%为因缺劳力致贫，28.1%因缺资金致贫，14.4%因缺技术致贫，5.2%为因灾致贫，2.3%为因学致贫，23.2%因其他原因致贫。

与非片区农村贫困残疾人致贫原因的差异见下图。

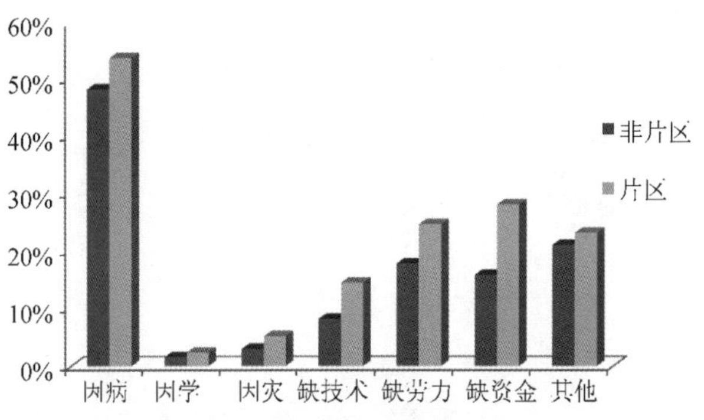

图 14　片区与非片区农村贫困残疾人致贫原因比较

7. 生活保障

片区农村贫困残疾人中，78.3%参加了新型农村社会医疗保险，96.9%了参加新型新学农村合作医疗保险，均率高于非片区农村贫困残疾人。没有参加任何养老保险和医疗保险的比例分别为 19.3%和 1.4%，分别低于非片区 5.4 和 1.2 个百分点。

数据显示，45.4%的片区农村贫困残疾人纳入最低生活保障，40.0%为接受亲属供养，6.9%得到政府部门提供的生活补助，2.6%享受五保供养，0.8%得到集中供养，还有 16.4%没有任何形式的生活保障。

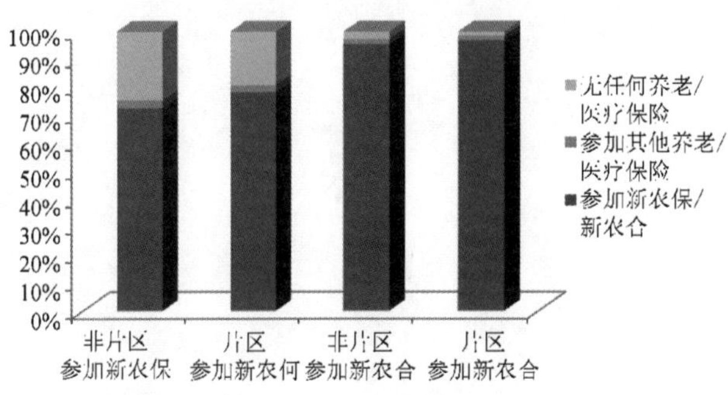

图 15　片区与非片区农村贫困残疾人参加社会保险情况比较

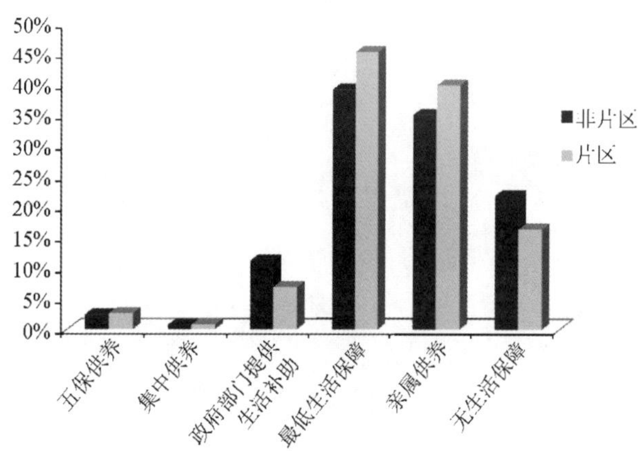

图 16　片区与非片区农村贫困残疾人生活保障情况比较

整体来看，与非片区农村贫困残疾人相比，片区农村贫困残疾人的生活保障情况基本持平并略好一点。除得到政府部门生活补助的比例低了 4.3 个百分点外，纳入低保和亲属供养的比例都出 4-6 个百分点，没有任何生活保障的比例也比非片区农村贫困残疾人低了 5.5 个百分点。

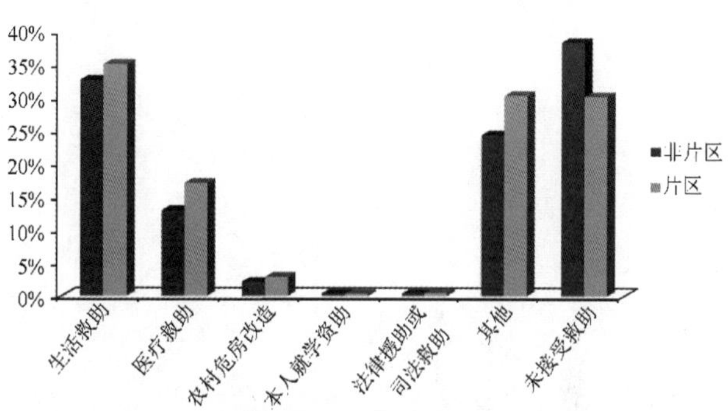

图 17　片区与非片区农村贫困残疾人接受救助扶持情况比较

8. 救助扶持情况

数据显示，35.1%的农村贫困残疾人接受到生活救助；17.1%接受到医疗救助；2.9%接受了危房改造；0.3%接受了法律援助或司法救助；0.4%接受了本人就学资助；30.4%接受到其他方面的救助；各项救助扶持比例均高于非片区农村贫困残疾人；30.3%的未接受救助比例比非片区农村贫困残疾人低了 8.1 个百分点。

3

综合统计资料

Comprehensive Statistical Data

中国残疾人事业“十二五”发展纲要执行简要情况
(2011－2013)

指 标 名 称		Item	
康 复		**Rehabilitation**	
得到不同程度康复残疾人	**(万人)**	**PWDs Received Rehabilitation Services of Different Degrees**	**(10,000 persons)**
1. 社区康复		**Community-based Rehabilitation (CBR)**	
开展社区康复服务的县、区	(个)	Counties and Districts Where CBR Has Been Conducted	(unit)
接受社区康复服务的残疾人	(万人)	Disabled Persons Who Began to Get CBR Service	(10,000 persons)
社区康复协调员	(万人)	CBR Coordinators at Communties	(10,000 persons)
2. 视力残疾康复		**Rehabilitation of Persons with Visual Disability**	
白内障复明手术	(万例)	Sight-restoring Surgeries for Cataract Patients	(10,000 cases)
其中：贫困患者免费手术	(万例)	Free Surgeries for Poor Catarat Patients	(10,000 cases)
低视力配用助视器	(万人)	Persons with Low Vision Fitted with Vision-aids	(10,000 persons)
培训低视力儿童家长	(万人)	Trained Parents of Children with Low Vison	(10,000 persons)
盲人定向行走训练	(万人)	Blind Persons Receiving Orientation Skills Training	(10,000 persons)
3. 听力语言残疾康复		**Rehabilitation of Persons with Hearing/Speech Disabilities**	
聋儿康复训练	(万人)	Deaf Children Trained	(10,000 persons)
聋儿家长培训	(万人)	Parents Trained	(10,000 persons)
4. 肢体残疾康复		**Rehabilitation of Persons with Physical Disability**	
肢体残疾(脑瘫)儿童机构康复训练	(万人)	Children with Physical Disability Receiving Rehabilitation Training in Institutions	(10000 persons)
肢体残疾人社区、家庭康复训练	(万人)	Persons with Physical Disability Receiving Rehabilitation Training in Communities and Families	(10000 persons)
贫困肢体残疾儿童矫治手术	(例)	Orthopedic Surgeries Conducted for Poor Children with Physical Disability	(case)
麻风畸残矫治手术	(例)	Orthopedic Surgeries Conducted for Persons with Leprosy- induced Disability	(case)
5. 智力残疾康复		**Rehabilitation of Persons with Intellectual Disability**	
智力残疾儿童康复训练	(万人)	Children with Intellectual Disability Receiving Rehabilitation Training	(10000 persons)
成年智力残疾人社区、家庭康复训练	(万人)	Adults with Physical Disability Receiving Rehabilitation Training in Communities and Families	(10000 persons)
6. 精神病防治康复		**Prevention and Rehabilitation of Mental Illness (PRMI)**	
监护精神病人	(万人)	People with Mental Illness under Guardianship	(10000 persons)
接受医疗救助的贫困精神病患者	(万人)	People with Mental Illness in Poverty Who Have Gotten Medical Assistance	(10000 persons)
孤独症儿童康复训练机构	(个)	Rehabilitation Institutions for Children with Autism	(unit)
孤独症儿童康复训练	(人)	Children with Autism Trained in Institutions	(person)

Brief Summary on Development of the Work for Persons with Disabilities during the 12th Five-year Plan Period (2011 – 2013)

"十一五" 完成/达到 the 11th Five-year Accomplishment	"十二五" 任务 the 12th Five-year Plan	"十二五" 完成情况 the 11th Five-year Accomplishment (2011 – 2013)			
		累计完成/达到 Total	2011	2012	2013
1037.9	**1300**	**867.9**	**631.8**	**760.2**	**746.8**
2507	2860	2915	2697	2794	2915
1036	—	801.3	303.5	328.8	169.0
32.9	30	37.9	31.4	35.3	37.9
423.6	328	229.9	75.8	79.6	74.6
127.6	—	93.5	31.0	33.4	29.1
17.3	50	28.2	3.6	11.7	12.9
6.5	20	8.2	0.7	3.7	3.8
6.3	50	26.5	2.5	12.0	12.0
9.8	10	5.8	1.8	2.0	2.0
12.2	10	10.8	2.9	3.9	3.9
7.8	3	8.3	1.8	3.0	3.5
41.6	85	79.5	14.9	32.8	31.8
10535	12000	14253	1311	6221	6721
8254	1000	1035	159	458	418
13.2	41.0	14.3	2.8	11.5	10.1
—	—	5.6	—	2.5	3.1
416.2	780	461.9	421.2	449.0	461.9
36.6	20	126.8	35.6	44.4	46.9
426	—	1108	839	929	1108
13743	50000	34685	6910	11119	16656

续表 1

指 标 名 称		Item	
7. **残疾人辅助器具供应服务**		**Provision of Assistive Devices**	
辅助器具供应	(万件)	Assistive Devices Provided	(10,000 pieces)
其中：贫困残疾人免费发放	(万件)	Assistive Devices Provided to Disabled Persons Free of Charge	(10,000 pieces)
残疾人普及型假肢装配	(万例)	Low-cost Artificial Limbs Fitted	(10,000 case)
残疾人矫形器装配	(万例)	Orthotic Devices Fitted	(10,000 case)
教 育		**Education**	
1. **学前教育**		**Pre-school Rehabilitation and Education**	
残疾人事业专项彩票公益金助学项目资助	(人)	Support of Educational Project Funded by Dedicated Welfare Lottery Fund	(person)
其他残疾儿童学前教育助学项目资助	(人)	Support of Other Pre-School Educational Project for Disabled Children	(person)
2. **残疾人高级中等教育**		**Senior Secondary Education for PWDs**	
特教普通高中	(个)	Special Education Senior High Schools	(unit)
特教普通高中在校学生	(人)	Students at Special Education Senior High Schools	(person)
中等职业教育机构	(个)	Secondary Vocational Schools	(unit)
中等职业教育在校学生	(人)	Students at Secondary Vocational Schools	(person)
3. **残疾人高等教育**		**Higher Education for PWDs**	
高等特殊教育院校	(个)	Ordinary Higher Education Institutions	(unit)
普通高等院校录取残疾考生	(人)	Disable Students Enrolled by Ordinary Higher Education Institutions	(person)
高等特殊教育院校录取残疾考生	(人)	Disable Students Enrolled by Higher Special Education Institutions	(person)
就 业		**Employment**	
1. **城镇残疾人就业状况**		**Employment of PWDs in Urban Areas**	
在业	(万人)	Employed Disabled Persons	(10,000 persons)
新增安排就业	(万人)	Newly Employed	(10,000 persons)
其中：集中就业	(万人)	Employed by Collective Form	(10,000 persons)
按比例就业	(万人)	Employed in Quoto Scheme	(10,000 persons)
公益性岗位就业	(万人)	Employed though Welfare Post	(10,000 persons)
个体及其他形式就业	(万人)	Self-Employed or Employed in Other Forms	(10,000 persons)
辅助性就业	(万人)	Assistive Employment	(10,000 persons)
2. **农村残疾人就业状况**		**Employment of PWDs in Rural Areas**	
已就业	(万人)	Employed Disabled Persons	(10,000 persons)
3. **残疾人职业培训**		**Vocational Education and Training for PWDs**	
残疾人职业培训基地	(个)	Vocational Training Bases for PWDs	(unit)
城镇残疾人职业培训	(万人次)	Vocational Training for Urban PWDs	10,000 person-time)
4. **盲人按摩**		**Blind Massage**	
按摩人员培训		**Massage Training**	
保健按摩人员	(人)	Training for Health-care Masseurs	(person)
医疗按摩人员	(人)	Training for Blind Therapeutical Masseurs	(person)
按摩机构		**Institutions of Blind Massage**	
医疗按摩机构	(个)	Therapeutical Blind Massage Clinics	(unit)
保健按摩机构	(个)	Health-care Blind Massage Houses	(unit)

Continued 1

"十一五"完成/达到 the 11th Five-year Accomplishment	"十二五"任务 the 12th Five-year Plan	"十二五"完成情况 the 11th Five-year Accomplishment (2011 - 2013)			
		累计完成/达到 Total	2011	2012	2013
514.7	500	317.1	74.3	114.5	128.3
242.3	50	111.2	41.2	33.8	36.2
12.1	7	9.9	3.1	3.9	2.9
7.7	5	10.2	1.5	4.0	4.7
—	51400	31028	10280	10280	10468
—		14545	6627	4429	3489
99	—	194	179	186	194
6067	—	7313	7207	7043	7313
147	—	198	131	152	198
11506	—	11350	11572	10442	11350
—	—	15	18	20	15
29915	—	21917	7150	7229	7538
5357	—	3399	877	1134	1388
	—				
	—				
441.2	—	445.6	440.5	444.8	445.6
179.7	100	101.6	31.8	32.9	36.9
53.4	—	30.6	9.7	10.2	10.7
49.6	—	24.3	7.5	8.0	8.7
—	—	5.4	2.1	1.8	1.5
76.8	—	39.4	12.5	12.3	14.6
—	—	2.0	—	0.7	1.3
1749.7	1800	1757.2	1748.8	1770.3	1757.2
—	—	5357	5254	5271	5357
137.9	180	97.6	29.9	29.9	37.8
61147	30000	50692	14067	16514	20111
28357	20000	14355	3736	4925	5694
1152	—	936	1031	848	936
11616	—	14704	12170	12887	14704

续表 2

指 标 名 称		Item	
社会保障		**Social Security**	
1. 城镇残疾人社会保障状况		**Social Security in Urban Area**	
(1)参加社会保险		Disabled Persons Covered by Social Insurance	
残疾职工参加社会保险	(万人)	Urban Workers with Disabilities Covered by Social Insurance	(10,000 persons)
参加养老保险	(万人)	Covered by Pension Insurance	(10,000 persons)
参加医疗保险	(万人)	Covered by Medical Care Insurance	(10,000 persons)
残疾居民参加城镇居民医疗保险	(万人)	Urban Residents with Disabilities Covered by Medical Care Insurance	(10,000 persons)
(2)接受社会救助		Disabled Persons Covered by Social Relief	
已纳入最低生活保障	(万人)	Covered by the Basic Living Allowance System	(10,000 persons)
集中供养及其他救助救济	(万人次)	Linving in Institutions or with Other Assistance and Relief	(10,000 person-time)
2. 农村残疾人社会保障状况		**Social Security in Rural Areas**	
参加新型农村社会养老保险	(万人)	Covered by New Type of Rural Pension Insurance	(10,000 persons)
接受社会救助		Disabled Persons Covered by Social Relief	
已纳入最低生活保障	(万人)	Covered by the Basic Living Allowance System	(10,000 persons)
五保供养及其他救助救济	(万人次)	Supported with Five Guarantees or Provided with	(10,000 person-time)
3. 托养服务		**Fostering Service**	
寄宿制托养服务机构	(个)	Boarding Fostering Institutions	(unit)
日间照料托养服务机构	(个)	Day-Care Fostering Service	(unit)
综合托养服务机构	(个)	Combined Fosteving Services Facilities	(unit)
机构内托养残疾人	(万人)	PWDs in Boarding and Day-Care Fostering Institutions	(10,000 persons)
享受居家托养服务	(万人)	PWDs Recieving Fostering Service an Home	(10,000 persons)
扶贫		**Poverty Alleviation**	
1. 农村贫困残疾人状况		**Impoverished PWDs in Rural Areas**	
农村贫困残疾人	(万人)	Impoverished PWDs in Rural Areas	(10,000 persons)
当地低收入残疾人	(万人)	PWDs with Low Income	(10,000 persons)
2. 扶贫效果		**Outcome of Poverty Alleviation**	
扶持贫困残疾人	(万人次)	Impoverished PWDs Assisted	(10,000 person-time)
实际脱贫	(万人次)	Out of Poverty	(10,000 person-time)
实用技术培训	(万人次)	Training on Applied Technologies for PWDs	(10,000 person-time)
3. 残疾人扶贫资金落实情况		**Poverty Alleviation Fund for PWDs**	
中央安排康复扶贫贴息贷款	(亿元)	Interest-subsidized Loans for Rehabilitation from the Central Fiscal Budget	(100 million yuan)
项目贷款扶持贫困残疾人	(人)	Poor Disabled Persons Supported by Loans for Project	(person)
到户贷款扶持贫困残疾人	(人)	Poor Disabled Persons Supported by Loans to Households	(person)

Continued 2

"十一五"完成/达到 the 11th Five-year Accomplishment	"十二五"任务 the 12th Five-year Plan	"十二五"完成情况 the 11th Five-year Accomplishment (2011－2013)			
		累计完成/达到 Total	2011	2012	2013
283.2	—	296.7	299.3	280.9	296.7
198.5	—	186.9	156.8	173.4	186.9
155.5	—	182.4	142.2	164.9	182.4
355.9	—	547.3	433.1	498.6	547.3
246.3	—	—	257.8	266.5	264.8
557.2	—	233.4	71.8	80.3	81.3
487.1	—	1638.3	1232.5	1333.8	1638.3
680.8	—	—	773.6	804.0	828.2
1704.7	—	764.1	240.9	261.6	261.6
—	—	1750	3921	3903	1750
—	—	2000	2368	3372	2000
—	—	1927	—	—	1927
33.3	—	51.2	16.5	18.7	16.0
43.5	—	178.6	44.2	56.0	78.4
1089.1	—	—	1097.0	1393.7	1457.2
715.4	—	—	758.0	825.6	812.8
932.2	1000	680.4	211.8	229.9	238.7
618.4	—	350.2	92.3	137.3	120.6
414.3	100	264.0	92.3	86.1	85.6
40.0	—	31.4	11.0	10.3	10.1
12.0	—	9.2	4.2	2.4	2.6
7.3	—	11.3	2.9	3.1	5.3

续表 3

指 标 名 称		Item	
4. **残疾人扶贫基地建设**		**Poverty Alleviation Bases for PWDs in Rural Areas**	
残疾人扶贫基地	(个)	Poverty Alleviation Bases for PWDs	(unit)
安置残疾人就业	(万人)	Providing Employment for PWDs	(10,000 persons)
扶持带动贫困残疾人	(万户)	Supporting and Leading Households with PWDs	(10,000 households)
5. **农村贫困残疾人危房改造**		**House Renovation for Poor PWDs in Rural Areas**	
危房改造	(万户)	Houses Renovated for PWDs	(10,000 households)
受益残疾人	(万人)	PWDs Who Benefited	(10,000 persons)
宣传文化		**Publicity and Culture**	
1. **宣传**		**Publicity at Provincial and Prefectural/City Level**	
省、市级报纸专版	(个)	Features in Newspapers	(unit)
省、市级广播电台残疾人专题节目	(个)	Radio Broadcast-Special Programs on Disability	(unit)
省、市级电视手语栏目	(个)	Programmes with Sign Language on TV	(unit)
2. **文化**		**Culture at Provincial and Prefectural/City Level**	
省、市级盲文及盲人有声读物阅览室	(个)	Reading Rooms with Braille and Audio Reading Materials	(unit)
残疾人文化周	(个)	Culture Week for PWDs	(unit)
残疾人文化艺术类比赛及展览	(个)	Culture or Art Competitions and Exhibitions for PWDs	(unit)
体 育		**Sports**	
1. **残疾人群众体育健身**		**Massive Sports and Fitness for PWDs at Provincial and Prefectural/City Level**	
省、市级残疾人群众体育健身活动	(次)	Massive Sports and Fitness Activities for PWDs	(time)
省、市级残疾人群众体育健身活动参加人	(万人次)	Participations in Massive Sports and Fitness Activities for PWDs	(10,000 person-time)
省、市级残疾人群众体育活动示范点	(个)	Sports Activity Demonstration Sites for PWDs	(unit)
省、市级残疾人体育健身指导员	(人)	Coaches for Fitness Activity for PWDs	(person)
2. **残疾人体育比赛**		**Sports Events for PWDs at Provincial Level**	
省级残疾人体育比赛	(次)	Sports Events for PWDs	(time)
参加省级残疾人体育比赛运动员	(人次)	Disabled Athletes Who Participated in Sports Events for PWDs	(person-time)
省级残疾人体育训练基地	(个)	Sports Trainong Bases for PWDs	(unit)
维 权		**Safeguarding the Rights of PWDs**	
1. **法规体系和政策文件**		**Legal System**	
制定或修改关于残疾人的专门法规、规章	(个)	Regulations Enacted or Reviewed for Assisting PWDs	(unit)
制定或修改保障残疾人权益的规范性文件	(个)	Policies Enacted for Protecting the Rights of PWDs	(unit)
2. **执法检查**		**Inspections on Law Enformance**	
人大执法检查	(次)	Inspections by Officials of People's Congresses	(time)
政协视察或专题调研	(次)	Inspections and Investigations by Officials of People's Political Consultative Conferences	(time)

Continued 3

"十一五"完成/达到 the 11th Five-year Accomplishment	"十二五"任务 the 12th Five-year Plan	"十二五"完成情况 the 11th Five-year Accomplishment (2011－2013)			
		累计完成/达到 Total	2011	2012	2013
—	—	6201	3985	5226	6201
—	—	35.3	8.7	10.2	16.4
—	—	66.0	15.6	25.8	24.6
49.4		34.8	9.4	13.2	12.2
68.1	—	41.7	11.5	15.7	14.4
418	—	1572	1325	1543	1572
400	—	659	463	506	659
523	—	263	196	214	263
441	—	596	438	479	596
—	—	2212	1426	1782	2212
3164	—	1399	1085	1125	1399
—	—	13086	4093	4171	4822
—	—	178.9	52.0	57.5	69.4
—	1200	2187	799	1391	2187
—	30000	16926	4150	9452	16926
519	—	294	100	80	114
74962	—	37868	12155	12574	13139
221	—	207	220	200	207
36	—	31	40	30	31
849	—	2120	871	706	543
5375	—	1747	824	923	799
5243	—	1655	845	810	746

续表 4

指 标 名 称		Item	
3. 法律救助		**Legal Aid**	
残疾人法律救助工作站	(个)	Legal Assistance Stations for PWDs	(unit)
残疾人法律救助工作站办理的案件	(件)	Cases Handled by Legal Assistance Stations for PWDs	(case)
残疾人法律援助中心(工作站)	(个)	Legal Aid Centers (Stations) for PWDs	(unit)
残疾人法律援助中心(工作站)办理的案件	(件)	Cases Handled by Legal Aid Centers (Stations) for PWDs	(case)
4. 参政议政		**PWDs Participating in the Administration and Discussion of State Affairs**	
协助人大、政协代表提出议案、建议、提案	(件)	Proposals Put forward at People's Congresses with Assistance of PWDs	(case)
办理人大政协交办的议案、建议、提案	(件)	Handling Proposals of Peoples'Congresses and Motions of People's Political Consultative Conferences	(case)
5. 无障碍设施建设		**Accessible Environment Building**	
无障碍设施建设法规、政府令	(个)	Regulations and Decrees on Accessible Environment Building and Management	(unit)
贫困残疾人家庭无障碍改造	(万户)	Accessibility Renovation for Homes of Poor PWDs	(10,000 households)
6. 残疾人机动轮椅车燃油补贴	**(万人)**	**Subsidy for Petrol Used by Motorized Wheelchairs of PWDs**	**(10,000 persons)**
7. 残疾人信访		**Complaint Letter and Visit**	
来信	(万件)	Complaint Letter	(10,000 cases)
来访	(万人次)	Complaint Visit	(10,000 person-time)
组织建设		**Organizational Structure**	
1. 省市县乡残联实有人员	**(万人)**	**Staff of Disabled Persons'Federations at Provincial, City, County and Township Level**	**(10,000 persons)**
2. 市(地)级残联		**Disabled Persons'Federations at Cities and Prefectures Level**	
配备残疾人领导干部的残联	(个)	Disabled Persons' Federations Whose Leadership Include PWDs	(unit)
残疾人干部	(人)	Staff with Disability	(person)
3. 县(市、区)级残联		**Disabled Persons' Federations at County Level**	
配备残疾人干部的残联	(个)	Disabled Persons' Federations Whose Leadership Include PWDs	(unit)
残疾人干部	(人)	Staff with Disability	(person)
4. 乡、镇、街道残联与村(社区)残疾人协会		**Disabled Persons' Federations in Township(Town, Street) and Villages(Communities)**	
已建乡、镇、街道残联	(万个)	Disabled Persons' Federation Established	(10,000 units)
其中：已配专兼职理事长	(万人)	Full-time(part-time) Presidents	(10,000 persons)
已建村(社区)残疾人协会	(万个)	Associations of Disabled Persons Established in Villages(Communities)	(10,000 units)
已选聘残疾人专职委员	(万人)	Full-time Workers on Disability	(10,000 persons)

Continued 4

"十一五"完成/达到 the 11th Five-year Accomplishment	"十二五"任务 the 12th Five-year Plan	"十二五"完成情况 the 11th Five-year Accomplishment (2011－2013)			
		"十二五"完成情况 the 11th Five-year Accomplishment (2011－2013)	2011	2012	2013
—	500	901	545	811	901
—	—	18511	4153	6453	7905
2934	—	3096	2933	2979	3096
19607	—	69354	21306	24550	23498
10580	—	5387	1873	1771	1743
7548	—	4269	1370	1435	1464
385	—	444	426	438	444
—	8	37.9	10.2	14.1	13.6
—	—	163.1	41.9	55.4	65.7
30.2	—	17.0	6.0	5.5	5.4
204.2	—	101.6	34.9	34.4	32.3
9.9	—	11.1	10.9	12	11.1
227	—	251	222	232	251
328	—	433	375	376	433
1744	—	1624	1599	1624	1625
2133	—	2221	2114	2207	2221
4.0	—	3.9	3.7	3.9	4.0
3.7	—	3.3	2.3	3.3	3.1
60.4	—	60.7	61.1	60.7	58.1
55.9	70	56.7	51.1	56.7	58.4

续表 5

指 标 名 称		Item	
5. 省级以下各类专门协会		**Special Associations below Provincial Level**	
盲人协会	(个)	Associations of Persons with Visual Disability	(unit)
聋人协会	(个)	Associatinss of Persons with Hearing Disability	(unit)
肢残人协会	(个)	Associations of Persons with Physical Disability	(unit)
智力残疾人及亲友协会	(个)	Associations of Persons with Intellectual Disability and Their Relatives and Friends	(unit)
精神残疾人及亲友协会	(个)	Associations of Persons with Psychiatric Disability and Their Relatives and Friends	(unit)
智力残疾人及亲友协会和精神残疾人及亲友协会合一的协会	(个)	Joint Associations of people with Mental or Psychiatric Disability and Their Relatives and Friends	(unit)
残疾人服务设施建设		**Service Facilities for PWDs**	
1. 残疾人综合服务设施		**Comprehensive Service Facilities for PWDs**	
建设完成已投入使用项目	(个)	Accumulated Projects in Operation	(unit)
总建设规模	(万平米)	Construction Area	(10,000 sq.m)
2. 残疾人康复设施		**Rehabilitation Service Facilities for PWDs**	
建设完成已投入使用项目	(个)	Accumulated Projects in Operation	(unit)
总建设规模	(万平米)	Construction Area	(10,000 sq.m)
3. 残疾人托养设施		**Fostering Service Facilities for PWDs**	
建设完成已投入使用项目	(个)	Accumulated Projects in Operation	(unit)
总建设规模	(万平米)	Construction Area	(10,000 sq.m)
信息化建设		**Informatization**	
1. 残疾人人口库综合数据	**(万人)**	**Data of the National Basic Database of Persons with Disabilities**	**(10,000 persons)**
2. 信息化专业人才	**(人)**	**IT Professionals**	**(person)**
3. 省、市、县各级残联网站	**(个)**	**Websites at Provincial, City, County Level**	**(unit)**

Continued 5

"十一五"完成/达到 the 11th Five-year Accomplishment	"十二五"任务 the 12th Five-year Plan	"十二五"完成情况 the 11th Five-year Accomplishment (2011－2013)			
		累计完成/达到 Total	2011	2012	2013
3132	—	3110	3095	3089	3110
3113	—	3097	3077	3073	3097
3168	—	3117	3127	3113	3117
3011	—	3001	2973	2983	3001
3013	—	3003	2973	2985	3003
63	—	82	90	78	82
	—				
2544	—	2094	1935	1971	2094
487.7	—	424.1	334.0	355.8	424.1
—	—	542	224	231	542
—	—	100.7	60.7	67.0	100.7
—	—	353	130	155	353
—	—	78.2	34.2	43.1	78.2
1793.7	3000	2811.5	2195.1	2527.2	2811.5
869	—	5019	4770	4948	5019
1241	—	1617	1411	1540	1617

全国残疾人人口基础数据库主要数据

Brief Data of the National Basic Information Database of Persons with Disabilities

单位：人　　(截止时间：2013年12月31日)　　(person)

地区	入库残疾人 PWDs in the Database	已办理证件 PWDs with Disabled Persons Certificate	0-14岁 Age 0-14	15-64岁 Age 15-64	65岁及以上 Age 65 and above
全国	**40200177**	**28115076**	**785544**	**17011318**	**10318214**
北京	494047	458944	5085	268863	184996
天津	264079	242344	3969	165973	72402
河北	2387321	1522870	41314	910749	570807
山西	1097873	789164	20589	512164	256411
内蒙古	1138767	692535	13057	474256	205222
辽宁	1172569	833181	14285	603525	215371
吉林	786614	645015	12932	467037	165046
黑龙江	902964	806933	15337	604242	187354
上海	566243	391233	1509	224329	165395
江苏	2866083	1347603	23547	826213	497843
浙江	1011025	1009512	18611	597946	392955
安徽	2084382	1385813	36956	791318	557539
福建	1100004	1046560	23586	458001	564973
江西	1072595	885518	32248	566640	286630
山东	2327207	1903818	50823	1094231	758764
河南	3871485	1674670	64675	1064803	545192
湖北	1620840	1053218	23726	706207	323285
湖南	2274293	1141832	34792	743755	363285
广东	1577700	1129643	50083	692629	386931
广西	2023939	1398029	39420	562035	796574
海南	149408	134572	6011	86698	41863
重庆	853838	764347	22646	467688	274013
四川	2673523	2026815	58896	1174943	792976
贵州	1375057	822092	37128	508921	276043
云南	1242600	1090733	42585	690407	357741
西藏	69036	68026	6144	45592	16290
陕西	1427167	1336749	20298	699873	616578
甘肃	705315	617556	21802	394350	201404
青海	146798	137894	7596	95554	34744
宁夏	279292	219205	8564	127842	82799
新疆	534698	441853	25355	310065	106433
新疆兵团	33507	32128	496	25190	6442
黑龙江垦区	69908	64671	1479	49279	13913

续表 1 Continued 1

单位：人 (person)

地 区	已办理证件残疾人 PWDs with Disabled Persons Certificate					
	性 别 Gender		残疾等级 Disability Grading			
	男 性 Male	女 性 Female	残疾一级 Grade-1	残疾二级 Grade-2	残疾三级 Grade-3	残疾四级 Grade-4
全 国	**16896534**	**11218549**	**3815179**	**6827024**	**7796378**	**9676506**
北 京	260433	198511	56190	109944	122587	170223
天 津	143275	99069	31039	67289	82700	61316
河 北	914024	608846	184402	300988	363075	674405
山 西	500233	288931	90587	186555	205549	306473
内蒙古	423591	268944	79807	162964	210047	239717
辽 宁	525598	307588	105616	193396	263392	270782
吉 林	402133	242882	86541	154550	205659	198265
黑龙江	510244	296691	97560	195829	255210	258336
上 海	215400	175833	51350	69220	104829	165834
江 苏	757632	589971	214848	397354	425003	310398
浙 江	616308	393204	153747	188670	313014	354081
安 徽	802896	582918	217834	620160	303607	244213
福 建	580519	466040	113417	272832	244924	415387
江 西	543652	341865	103973	208541	245457	327547
山 东	1177360	726458	282372	478825	532663	609958
河 南	1022942	651728	258406	461703	442763	511798
湖 北	645873	407345	174788	283269	273210	321951
湖 南	734073	407759	172510	274609	297092	397621
广 东	686653	442990	206580	294702	324093	304268
广 西	783249	614780	122171	229307	350780	695771
海 南	79729	54843	48983	23548	32409	29632
重 庆	468105	296243	95543	194035	206293	268477
四 川	1229771	797043	264078	433188	575446	754103
贵 州	521886	300206	86431	133770	218388	383503
云 南	660525	430207	137515	204314	265201	483703
西 藏	35869	32157	10470	13434	16586	27536
陕 西	756374	580375	148511	257108	484922	446208
甘 肃	367964	249592	97958	153760	174753	191085
青 海	80830	57064	24505	50340	32718	30331
宁 夏	122189	97016	28871	70336	58236	61762
新 疆	267872	173983	57991	117382	136613	129869
新疆兵团	20268	11860	3956	6141	9939	12092
黑龙江垦区	39064	25607	6629	18961	19220	19861

续表 2 Continued 2

单位：人 (person)

地 区	已办理证件残疾人 PWDs with Disabled Persons Certificate				
	残疾类别 Disability Category				
	视力残疾人 Persons with Visual Disability	听力残疾人 Persons with Hearing Disability	言语残疾人 Persons with Speech Disability	肢体残疾人 Persons with Physical Disability	智力残疾人 Persons with Intellectual Disability
全 国	**3365337**	**2211383**	**529320**	**16534708**	**2307855**
北 京	49020	30840	2805	261184	50830
天 津	22360	15750	3538	147479	27461
河 北	140397	109660	39877	1001991	114741
山 西	82880	62085	17905	495189	70392
内蒙古	72495	63355	15971	423239	55550
辽 宁	89064	62646	8688	465005	101201
吉 林	72589	52388	11919	379574	58744
黑龙江	85462	63323	11288	505766	65657
上 海	72812	36872	4338	172673	57336
江 苏	166323	82128	9090	756166	172033
浙 江	111480	118459	16246	539812	101352
安 徽	159749	89678	29053	746478	128383
福 建	171483	166601	12620	500653	80055
江 西	99390	70471	13548	514254	70049
山 东	159934	123672	24820	1211403	167830
河 南	157332	126329	48784	1086447	140536
湖 北	138673	65094	29623	578633	86811
湖 南	144647	57279	23741	682520	85158
广 东	112823	79222	20984	604200	111556
广 西	193471	134672	22514	850694	64380
海 南	15065	4580	2634	77730	11200
重 庆	124247	43559	12712	428533	61369
四 川	303922	145115	35749	1222104	135870
贵 州	104889	45118	17642	543564	37691
云 南	147583	77783	27627	668168	59781
西 藏	11348	7137	3534	33461	2121
陕 西	167523	149518	30064	777530	69719
甘 肃	68375	46580	11050	363634	48389
青 海	17389	16681	3240	75913	10827
宁 夏	27656	21375	4213	125208	17778
新 疆	63159	36861	12096	243062	33432
新疆兵团	3539	2237	576	17681	3290
黑龙江垦区	8258	4315	831	34760	6333

续表 3 Continued 3

单位：人 (person)

地区	已办理证件残疾人 PWDs with Disabled Persons Certificate			
	残疾类别 Disability Category		户口性质 Household Register Type	
	精神残疾人 Persons with Psychiatric Disability	多重残疾人 Persons with Multiple Disabilities	农业 Rural	非农业 Non-Rural
全国	**1961785**	**1204699**	**21157459**	**6957622**
北京	46829	17436	198671	260273
天津	22754	3002	101477	140867
河北	63981	52223	1291717	231153
山西	35338	25375	640164	149000
内蒙古	35448	26477	462029	230506
辽宁	78277	28305	450253	382933
吉林	48949	20852	364758	280256
黑龙江	49762	25677	392332	414603
上海	46491	711	82474	308759
江苏	121089	40774	230737	1116866
浙江	93336	28827	826815	182697
安徽	143299	89174	1146324	239490
福建	68803	46345	857335	189225
江西	72591	45215	707123	178395
山东	132536	83623	1670254	233563
河南	67259	47983	1458893	215777
湖北	99884	54500	826036	227182
湖南	82029	66458	955471	186361
广东	137570	63288	843434	286209
广西	62050	70248	1247833	150196
海南	16619	6744	100282	34290
重庆	65973	27955	602653	161693
四川	124371	59684	1707179	319635
贵州	25366	47822	723275	98817
云南	61596	48195	962346	128386
西藏	4034	6391	62579	5447
陕西	67215	75180	1151772	184977
甘肃	30064	49464	520359	97197
青海	3556	10288	107821	30073
宁夏	13105	9870	160942	58263
新疆	29476	23769	302222	139633
新疆兵团	3973	832	546	31582
黑龙江垦区	8162	2012	1353	63318

续表 4 Continued 4

单位：人 (person)

地 区	已办理证件残疾人 PWDs with Disabled Persons Certificate					
	15岁及以上受教育程度 Education of Age 15 and above					
	文 盲 Illiterate	小 学 Primary School	初 中 Junior High School	高中及中专 Senior High School	大学专科及以上 Junior College and above	其 他 Other
总 计	**5404346**	**11384689**	**8376143**	**2303732**	**402621**	**243552**
北 京	67415	87742	169608	86013	33894	14272
天 津	32457	61344	92477	42912	10834	2320
河 北	186876	645371	529965	123339	18806	18513
山 西	106010	279759	314362	69963	12215	6855
内蒙古	123402	236881	241960	74328	12825	3139
辽 宁	96036	258928	371549	87748	15034	3891
吉 林	72384	207131	259211	94398	9579	2312
黑龙江	68986	260891	347684	106712	15997	6665
上 海	32876	85519	167145	78431	21886	5376
江 苏	465110	424638	347066	90893	18742	1154
浙 江	220296	450513	262575	48525	12382	15221
安 徽	360520	614669	331295	65449	11890	1991
福 建	217501	522641	218130	61859	10400	16029
江 西	130716	387611	280633	66018	8087	12452
山 东	363413	724526	614174	167586	21479	12639
河 南	405195	527572	548788	150811	20608	21696
湖 北	219372	341703	353072	119218	15740	4113
湖 南	172795	479559	351962	119839	11664	6013
广 东	193744	474735	320985	91426	15375	33378
广 西	196760	767702	336406	70928	9089	17144
海 南	29969	43038	46474	12884	1637	570
重 庆	91552	405663	206807	43258	6377	10690
四 川	326796	1101904	481996	97110	15653	3355
贵 州	242763	353616	182358	32079	8228	3048
云 南	304627	514976	204853	48964	12926	4387
西 藏	38924	24989	2744	777	306	286
陕 西	274369	512586	415597	112041	17478	4678
甘 肃	201039	225605	133749	47445	7778	1940
青 海	32169	71007	22162	9279	2677	600
宁 夏	63355	82349	52078	15637	4362	1424
新 疆	59506	184610	127401	49376	14276	6686
新疆兵团	1945	6996	15342	6744	887	214
黑龙江垦区	5468	17915	25535	11742	3510	501

分省统计资料

Statistical Data of Provinces

1-1　社区康复

Community-Based Rehabilitation(CBR)

地　区	Region	开展社区康复服务的市辖区 Districts Where CBR Has Been Conducted	本年度新开展 Counties and Cities where CBR was Introduced in 2013	开展社区康复服务的县(市) Counties and Cities Where CBR Has Been Conducted	本年度新开展 Counties and Cities Where CBR Was Introduced in 2013
		个 unit	个 unit	个 unit	个 unit
全　国	**Total**	**901**	**20**	**2014**	**118**
北　京	Beijing	14		2	
天　津	Tianjin	13		3	
河　北	Hebei	37		138	
山　西	Shanxi	23		90	3
内蒙古	Inner Mongolia	22		81	
辽　宁	Liaoning	62		44	
吉　林	Jilin	30		40	
黑龙江	Heilongjiang	57		62	
上　海	Shanghai	16		1	
江　苏	Jiangsu	58	1	46	
浙　江	Zhejiang	32	2	56	2
安　徽	Anhui	44	2	56	
福　建	Fujian	26	1	58	
江　西	Jiangxi	23		79	2
山　东	Shandong	56	2	90	1
河　南	Henan	59	2	104	1
湖　北	Hubei	39		59	
湖　南	Hunan	37	1	88	
广　东	Guangdong	59	1	67	
广　西	Guangxi	36		75	
海　南	Hainan	3		10	2
重　庆	Chongqing	21		19	
四　川	Sichuan	31	4	100	4
贵　州	Guizhou	10	1	75	13
云　南	Yunnan	11		108	14
西　藏	Tibet	1		11	4
陕　西	Shaanxi	28	2	83	
甘　肃	Gansu	18		69	
青　海	Qinghai	4		42	
宁　夏	Ningxia	9		13	
新　疆	Xinjiang	11	1	80	1
新疆兵团	Xinjiang Corps	11		127	54
黑龙江垦区	Heilongjiang Land Reclamation			38	17

1-1 续表 1 Continued 1

地 区	Region	开展社区康复服务的社区(村) Communities (villages) Where CBR Has Been Conducted	社区康复协调员累计 Accumulative CBR Coordinators at Communties	本年度新增社区康复协调员 CBR Coordinators Who Were Engaged in 2013
		个 unit	人 person	人 person
全 国	**Total**	**319231**	**379386**	**38402**
北 京	Beijing	5656	5791	212
天 津	Tianjin	4571	4392	114
河 北	Hebei	29492	38785	2638
山 西	Shanxi	10217	18153	1153
内蒙古	Inner Mongolia	4795	10760	1541
辽 宁	Liaoning	11820	12626	1133
吉 林	Jilin	6631	8411	250
黑龙江	Heilongjiang	3037	3864	398
上 海	Shanghai	456	5519	287
江 苏	Jiangsu	16787	19188	629
浙 江	Zhejiang	16095	11457	1472
安 徽	Anhui	6454	9049	2747
福 建	Fujian	9722	10065	513
江 西	Jiangxi	8525	13125	1564
山 东	Shandong	51520	49607	322
河 南	Henan	38904	34666	4246
湖 北	Hubei	9146	8875	411
湖 南	Hunan	13270	15001	2611
广 东	Guangdong	14612	18414	1283
广 西	Guangxi	6276	12039	3128
海 南	Hainan	565	1373	11
重 庆	Chongqing	6126	8310	1205
四 川	Sichuan	15791	15330	2556
贵 州	Guizhou	3814	8552	1956
云 南	Yunnan	7652	11649	1743
西 藏	Tibet	10	16	3
陕 西	Shaanxi	5389	8769	2845
甘 肃	Gansu	4955	7863	272
青 海	Qinghai	2107	2120	141
宁 夏	Ningxia	824	1478	545
新 疆	Xinjiang	3795	3665	419
新疆兵团	Xinjiang Corps	174	313	50
黑龙江垦区	Heilongjiang Land Reclamation	43	161	4

1-1 续表 2 Continued 2

地 区	Region	接受过培训的社区康复协调员 Trained CBR Coordinators	已建社区康复站的社区累计 Accumulative Communities Where CBR Stations Have Been Established	本年度新建社区康复站的社区 Communities Where CBR Stations Were Established in 2013	已建社区康复服务档案的残疾人 PWDs who have been Established Files of CBR Service	本年度新增接受社区康复服务残疾人 PWDs Who Began to Get CBR Service in 2013
		人 person	个 unit	个 unit	万人 10,000 persons	万人 10,000 persons
全 国	**Total**	**362421**	**214264**	**9484**	**2071.8**	**169.0**
北 京	Beijing	5775	3626	48	41.8	3.7
天 津	Tianjin	3161	1658	47	26.4	3.8
河 北	Hebei	34655	16733	731	162.4	6.0
山 西	Shanxi	17371	5031	60	47.2	3.2
内蒙古	Inner Mongolia	10579	2063	46	30.8	2.5
辽 宁	Liaoning	12328	10280	183	116.4	8.7
吉 林	Jilin	8280	2849	105	103.8	12.5
黑龙江	Heilongjiang	3858	1357	99	29.8	1.3
上 海	Shanghai	5398	218		34.9	1.8
江 苏	Jiangsu	19147	14790	350	184.8	11.0
浙 江	Zhejiang	11353	10149	251	71.2	5.8
安 徽	Anhui	8739	4190	379	60.3	4.5
福 建	Fujian	9843	3887	127	72.0	8.6
江 西	Jiangxi	12700	3767	145	67.6	6.4
山 东	Shandong	47664	42038	1606	170.6	8.5
河 南	Henan	32967	52059	4067	178.0	17.4
湖 北	Hubei	8740	4683	133	86.6	4.1
湖 南	Hunan	14671	5368	123	78.4	3.6
广 东	Guangdong	17610	7892	198	121.3	7.1
广 西	Guangxi	11507	2366	13	33.8	1.7
海 南	Hainan	1030	623	8	3.0	0.1
重 庆	Chongqing	8302	3172	133	67.9	7.6
四 川	Sichuan	15040	6953	183	97.5	11.7
贵 州	Guizhou	7476	903	15	19.9	0.9
云 南	Yunnan	10501	2420	72	42.9	3.2
西 藏	Tibet	16	8	5	0.2	
陕 西	Shaanxi	8677	1282	85	35.0	4.5
甘 肃	Gansu	7629	1249	50	45.6	8.0
青 海	Qinghai	1943	484	23	4.4	0.5
宁 夏	Ningxia	1459	524	47	5.1	0.4
新 疆	Xinjiang	3529	1493	119	25.8	9.2
新疆兵团	Xinjiang Corps	312	131	32	2.7	0.4
黑龙江垦区	Heilongjiang Land Reclamation	161	18	1	3.8	

1-1 续表 3 Continued 3

地 区	Region	开展家长学校工作的残疾人康复机构 Rehabilitation Institutions for Parents Training of PWDs	省级 at Provincial Level	地市级 at Prefectural/ City Level	县级 at County Level	参加培训的家长 Parents Trained	省级 at Provincial Level	地市级 at Prefectural/ City Level	县级 at County Level
		个 unit	个 unit	个 unit	个 unit	人次 person-time	人次 person-time	人次 person-time	人次 person-time
全 国	**Total**	**1131**	**23**	**142**	**966**	**99450**	**15690**	**12828**	**70932**
北 京	Beijing	62	1		61	10870	4732		6138
天 津	Tianjin	2			2	143			143
河 北	Hebei	41	1	5	35	1424	180	254	990
山 西	Shanxi	46	3	15	28	2409	800	911	698
内蒙古	Inner Mongolia	9	1	3	5	698	350	57	291
辽 宁	Liaoning	18		3	15	564		415	149
吉 林	Jilin	39	2	21	16	3749	1475	1008	1266
黑龙江	Heilongjiang	3			3	26			26
上 海	Shanghai	325	3		322	23196	458		22738
江 苏	Jiangsu	64	1	6	57	6691	474	909	5308
浙 江	Zhejiang	43	2	7	34	12095	1360	1053	9682
安 徽	Anhui	36	1	1	34	5863	2021	440	3402
福 建	Fujian	9	1		8	1295	800		495
江 西	Jiangxi	26			26	1239		20	1219
山 东	Shandong	112		4	108	4281		195	4086
河 南	Henan	70		29	41	3913	15	2325	1573
湖 北	Hubei	5			5	552	2	23	527
湖 南	Hunan	45	1	14	30	5176	1650	1874	1652
广 东	Guangdong	33		10	23	6270	5	1763	4502
广 西	Guangxi	7		1	6	151		7	144
海 南	Hainan					8		8	
重 庆	Chongqing	30	1		29	1246	200		1046
四 川	Sichuan	22		6	16	1629		644	985
贵 州	Guizhou	6			6	325		62	263
云 南	Yunnan	5	1	1	3	485	60	239	186
西 藏	Tibet								
陕 西	Shaanxi								
甘 肃	Gansu					5			5
青 海	Qinghai	7			7	93			93
宁 夏	Ningxia	14	3	4	7	1603	950	212	441
新 疆	Xinjiang	52	1	12	39	3451	158	409	2884
新疆兵团	Xinjiang Corps								
黑龙江垦区	Heilongjiang Land Reclamation								

1-2 视力残疾康复

Rehabilitation of Persons with Visual Disability

地区	Region	白内障复明 Sight-restoring of Persons with Cataract-induced Blindness		低视力康复 Rehabilitation of Persons with Low Vision		盲人定向行走训练 Skills Training for Blind Persons	
		白内障复明手术 Sight-restoring Surgeries for Cataract Victims	贫困白内障患者免费手术 Free Surgeries for Poor Catarat Victims	低视力者配用助视器 Persons Fitted with Vision-aids	培训低视力儿童家长 Trained Parents of Children with Low Vison	盲人定向行走训练 Blind Persons Who Have Gotten Orientation Skills Training	盲人定向行走训练指导师 Orientation Skills Trainers for Blind Persons
		例 case	例 case	人 person	人 person	人 person	人 person
全国	**Total**	**745905**	**290721**	**129436**	**38070**	**119793**	**5253**
北京	Beijing	11124	1197	1514	17	1447	167
天津	Tianjin	5296	1536	1300	501	1071	21
河北	Hebei	30414	3367	6054	2047	6005	197
山西	Shanxi	23612	5012	103	2390	6089	171
内蒙古	Inner Mongolia	10538	5346	2445	1053	2519	114
辽宁	Liaoning	19800	5873	7979	1126	4656	334
吉林	Jilin	15441	2812	3756	1400	4250	149
黑龙江	Heilongjiang	11216	3148	4172	239	4145	68
上海	Shanghai	51381	3989	10938	1348	1817	469
江苏	Jiangsu	57879	14578	5911	1310	7514	201
浙江	Zhejiang	33297	16954	1560	523	3879	363
安徽	Anhui	34438	11804	4752	993	6732	459
福建	Fujian	16178	10734	4245	1833	4478	24
江西	Jiangxi	19312	3526	1752	706	4750	29
山东	Shandong	54291	19701	3602	906	6169	391
河南	Henan	19519	9903	9120	3952	8644	423
湖北	Hubei	30428	12576	6074	10170	6080	351
湖南	Hunan	29456	14242	6605	2313	5567	210
广东	Guangdong	91901	27747	2769	918	6838	251
广西	Guangxi	23172	11775	7697	305	2493	74
海南	Hainan	2894	1651	2927	11	997	19
重庆	Chongqing	17429	7320	2611	381	1141	91
四川	Sichuan	37773	24410	5640	565	6878	164
贵州	Guizhou	15686	9220	3807	228	2275	104
云南	Yunnan	35327	32179	6126	1289	2910	160
西藏	Tibet	909	290	20		281	
陕西	Shaanxi	14302	9020	2497	55	3764	55
甘肃	Gansu	10755	7331	3127	580	2126	22
青海	Qinghai	3613	3505	1927	87	1157	39
宁夏	Ningxia	2780	2120	1077	261	1219	6
新疆	Xinjiang	13550	7009	6163	309	1641	125
新疆兵团	Xinjiang Corps	1750	694	1026	194	121	2
黑龙江垦区	Heilongjiang Land Reclamation	444	152	140	60	140	

1-3 视力残疾康复机构

Rehabilitation Institutions for Persons with Visual Disability

地区	Region	开展视力残疾康复训练服务机构 Rehabilitation Institutions for Persons with Visual Disability	省级 at Provincial Level	地市级 at Prefectural/ City Level	县级 at County Level	本年度新建机构 Established in 2013	本年度注销机构 Cancelled Registration in 2013
		个 unit	个 unit	个 unit	个 unit	个 unit	个 unit
全　国	**Total**	**805**	**23**	**184**	**598**	**120**	**20**
北　京	Beijing	7			7		
天　津	Tianjin	5	1		4	1	
河　北	Hebei	18		6	12		
山　西	Shanxi	41	1	15	25	3	3
内蒙古	Inner Mongolia	17		9	8	3	
辽　宁	Liaoning	28	1	8	19	2	
吉　林	Jilin	53	3	18	32	4	
黑龙江	Heilongjiang	23	2	7	14	3	
上　海	Shanghai	41	1		40	12	
江　苏	Jiangsu	60	1	7	52	11	
浙　江	Zhejiang	16	1	4	11		4
安　徽	Anhui	9	1	4	4	1	1
福　建	Fujian	30		6	24	8	1
江　西	Jiangxi	10		4	6		
山　东	Shandong	91		16	75	10	
河　南	Henan	24	1	11	12	1	
湖　北	Hubei	17		4	13	5	1
湖　南	Hunan	32		8	24	10	
广　东	Guangdong	72	1	27	44	6	4
广　西	Guangxi	6		1	5		
海　南	Hainan						
重　庆	Chongqing	35			35	5	2
四　川	Sichuan	23	1	2	20	12	
贵　州	Guizhou	15		5	10	2	
云　南	Yunnan	31	2	8	21	3	1
西　藏	Tibet	1	1				
陕　西	Shaanxi	49	2	3	44	10	
甘　肃	Gansu	15	1	4	10		2
青　海	Qinghai	4	1		3	2	
宁　夏	Ningxia	4	1	1	2		
新　疆	Xinjiang	28		6	22	6	1
新疆兵团	Xinjiang Corps						
黑龙江垦区	Heilongjiang Land Reclamation						

1-3　续表　Continued

地　区	Region	视力残疾康复机构在岗人员 Staff of Rehabilitation Institutions for Persons with Visual Disability			
		在岗人员总数 Total Staff	专业技术人员 Technicians and Professionals	管理人员 Managerial Personnels	其他 Other Staff Members
		人 person	人 person	人 person	人 person
全　国	**Total**	**14493**	**9602**	**2338**	**2553**
北　京	Beijing	145	101	20	24
天　津	Tianjin	26	15	8	3
河　北	Hebei	134	85	33	16
山　西	Shanxi	3452	2705	384	363
内蒙古	Inner Mongolia	299	185	67	47
辽　宁	Liaoning	191	101	47	43
吉　林	Jilin	716	476	154	86
黑龙江	Heilongjiang	244	176	35	33
上　海	Shanghai	434	249	49	136
江　苏	Jiangsu	781	486	138	157
浙　江	Zhejiang	142	103	28	11
安　徽	Anhui	66	35	17	14
福　建	Fujian	403	242	89	72
江　西	Jiangxi	122	53	43	26
山　东	Shandong	2511	1679	344	488
河　南	Henan	310	209	62	39
湖　北	Hubei	193	105	34	54
湖　南	Hunan	829	448	164	217
广　东	Guangdong	970	611	111	248
广　西	Guangxi	18	7	6	5
海　南	Hainan				
重　庆	Chongqing	610	390	110	110
四　川	Sichuan	268	160	62	46
贵　州	Guizhou	355	232	72	51
云　南	Yunnan	441	202	79	160
西　藏	Tibet	3	2	1	
陕　西	Shaanxi	400	230	100	70
甘　肃	Gansu	258	210	36	12
青　海	Qinghai	9	5	3	1
宁　夏	Ningxia	15	8	5	2
新　疆	Xinjiang	148	92	37	19
新疆兵团	Xinjiang Corps				
黑龙江垦区	Heilongjiang Land Reclamation				

1-4 听力语言残疾康复

Rehabilitation of Persons with Hearing and Speech Disabilities

地 区	Region	新收训聋儿 Newly Trained Deaf Children	机构训练 Deaf Children Trained in Institutions	家庭训练 Deaf Children Trained in Families	在训聋儿 Deaf Children Being Trained	培训家长 Parents Trained
		人 person	人 person	人 person	人 person	人 person
全 国	**Total**	**20365**	**17065**	**3300**	**32284**	**39376**
北 京	Beijing	182	181	1	302	330
天 津	Tianjin	69	68	1	125	99
河 北	Hebei	2077	1183	894	2791	2452
山 西	Shanxi	435	435		793	1218
内蒙古	Inner Mongolia	418	307	111	584	803
辽 宁	Liaoning	601	489	112	1121	930
吉 林	Jilin	378	243	135	465	994
黑龙江	Heilongjiang	410	322	88	605	747
上 海	Shanghai	140	82	58	352	354
江 苏	Jiangsu	1064	1025	39	2700	2670
浙 江	Zhejiang	583	576	7	941	1016
安 徽	Anhui	1924	1900	24	2513	4978
福 建	Fujian	467	447	20	820	1014
江 西	Jiangxi	630	510	120	808	899
山 东	Shandong	1390	1301	89	2208	2794
河 南	Henan	2388	1881	507	3498	3137
湖 北	Hubei	833	811	22	1053	1178
湖 南	Hunan	917	776	141	1618	1780
广 东	Guangdong	1019	960	59	2350	3723
广 西	Guangxi	545	430	115	919	1099
海 南	Hainan	108	108		160	157
重 庆	Chongqing	334	266	68	443	714
四 川	Sichuan	859	736	123	1305	1563
贵 州	Guizhou	381	332	49	578	759
云 南	Yunnan	573	357	216	675	1135
西 藏	Tibet	13	13		15	13
陕 西	Shaanxi	626	496	130	951	1264
甘 肃	Gansu	396	304	92	571	454
青 海	Qinghai	132	110	22	180	196
宁 夏	Ningxia	80	78	2	167	199
新 疆	Xinjiang	220	206	14	349	449
新疆兵团	Xinjiang Corps	31	6	25	78	100
黑龙江垦区	Heilongjiang Land Reclamation	16		16	16	32

1-4 续表 1 Continued 1

地 区	Region	本年度接受国家项目救助 Subsidized by State Projects in 2013		本年度接受地方项目救助 Subsidized by Local Projects in 2013	专业人员培训 Professionals Trained		
		接受人工耳蜗救助 Poor Deaf Children Subsidized by CDPF Rescuing Project through Cochlear Implantation	接受助听器救助 Poor Deaf Children Subsidized by CDPF Hearing Aids Rescuing Project			培训省级机构专业人员 Professionals of Institutions at Provincial Level	培训地市级机构专业人员 Professionals of Institutions at Prefectual/City Level
		人 person	人 person	人 person	人 person	人 person	人 person
全 国	**Total**	**4500**	**4288**	**7353**	**6448**	**2201**	**1905**
北 京	Beijing		32	58	277	103	
天 津	Tianjin	22	15	250	34	16	15
河 北	Hebei	240	225	74	148	8	101
山 西	Shanxi	120	143	328	445	251	165
内蒙古	Inner Mongolia	95	85	164	62	27	19
辽 宁	Liaoning	140	160	50	312	163	149
吉 林	Jilin	110	108	36	308	62	185
黑龙江	Heilongjiang	150	150	4	25	5	2
上 海	Shanghai		16	118	159	65	
江 苏	Jiangsu	160	158	916	469	193	47
浙 江	Zhejiang	100	100	305	152	26	68
安 徽	Anhui	250	244	519	593	357	168
福 建	Fujian	100	105	312	121	43	15
江 西	Jiangxi	160	160	256	91	38	28
山 东	Shandong	320	310	582	409	29	149
河 南	Henan	360	385	153	379	34	76
湖 北	Hubei	210	220	598	50	12	20
湖 南	Hunan	240	250	177	311	84	141
广 东	Guangdong	188	200	1142	1058	391	456
广 西	Guangxi	200	200	147	68	42	14
海 南	Hainan	30	26	46	2		1
重 庆	Chongqing	130	130	68	380	86	
四 川	Sichuan	300	220	467	168	22	41
贵 州	Guizhou	180	122	140	96	4	4
云 南	Yunnan	200	110	47	68	3	12
西 藏	Tibet	15	12				
陕 西	Shaanxi	160	150	181	108	86	16
甘 肃	Gansu	130	110	50	6	1	1
青 海	Qinghai	25	20	80	64	4	1
宁 夏	Ningxia	30	25	6	40	40	
新 疆	Xinjiang	100	85	59	45	6	11
新疆兵团	Xinjiang Corps	10	10	20			
黑龙江垦区	Heilongjiang Land Reclamation	25	2				

1-4 续表 2 Continued 2

地 区	Region	培训县级机构专业人员 Professionals of Institutions at County Level	成年听力语言康复技术服务 Adults Received Hearing and Speech Rehabilitation Services	训练后走向 Directions in which Children have gone After Rehabilitation			
				普小 Ordinary Primary Schools	普幼 Ordinary Kindergartens	特殊教育学校(聋校) Special Education Schools (Schools for Deaf Students)	其他 Other Directions
		人 person	人次 person-time	人 person	人 person	人 person	人 person
全 国	**Total**	**2342**	**31738**	**1447**	**1526**	**2209**	**2012**
北 京	Beijing	174	276	4	16	3	52
天 津	Tianjin	3	1049	7	9	2	136
河 北	Hebei	39	1152	44	87	129	198
山 西	Shanxi	29	2711	25	30	25	29
内蒙古	Inner Mongolia	16	115	6	18	24	19
辽 宁	Liaoning		806	51	37	13	8
吉 林	Jilin	61	397	13	42	15	15
黑龙江	Heilongjiang	18	183	9	7	30	24
上 海	Shanghai	94	4748	43	24	13	9
江 苏	Jiangsu	229	2423	68	98	77	129
浙 江	Zhejiang	58	2865	66	75	41	85
安 徽	Anhui	68	1519	227	77	282	124
福 建	Fujian	63	677	16	55	18	69
江 西	Jiangxi	25	431	15	12	13	4
山 东	Shandong	231	1598	87	111	192	40
河 南	Henan	269	1630	106	148	167	150
湖 北	Hubei	18	649	47	45	62	53
湖 南	Hunan	86	880	154	155	264	197
广 东	Guangdong	211	1339	107	135	102	175
广 西	Guangxi	12	400	16	60	65	72
海 南	Hainan	1				2	
重 庆	Chongqing	294	1123	7	51	16	37
四 川	Sichuan	105	515	63	56	243	54
贵 州	Guizhou	88	266	39	8	75	22
云 南	Yunnan	53	271	51	44	200	198
西 藏	Tibet		615				
陕 西	Shaanxi	6	518	67	74	87	70
甘 肃	Gansu	4	76	27	9	12	23
青 海	Qinghai	59	120	5		9	
宁 夏	Ningxia			2	19		
新 疆	Xinjiang	28	1300	67	21	17	11
新疆兵团	Xinjiang Corps		1056	8	3	11	9
黑龙江垦区	Heilongjiang Land Reclamation		30				

1-5 听力语言康复机构

Rehabilitation Institutions of Hearing and Speech

地 区	Region	机构概况 Rehabilitation Institutions					
		累计建设 Rehab-institutions Established	省级 at Provincial Level	地市级 at Prefectural/ City Level	县级 at County Level	本年新建 Established in 2013	本年注销 Rehab-institutions Cancelled Registration in 2013
		个 unit	个 unit	个 unit	个 unit	个 unit	个 unit
全 国	**Total**	**1047**	**32**	**358**	**656**	**109**	**88**
北 京	Beijing	20	1		19	2	
天 津	Tianjin	8	1	4	3	1	1
河 北	Hebei	95	1	14	80	5	3
山 西	Shanxi	47	1	15	31	2	7
内蒙古	Inner Mongolia	24	1	17	6	2	1
辽 宁	Liaoning	45	1	22	22	1	
吉 林	Jilin	20	1	9	10		
黑龙江	Heilongjiang	29	1	15	13		1
上 海	Shanghai	19	1		18	2	1
江 苏	Jiangsu	65	1	10	54	5	1
浙 江	Zhejiang	30	1	10	19	4	1
安 徽	Anhui	59	1	26	32	9	1
福 建	Fujian	28	1	11	16	7	5
江 西	Jiangxi	25	1	9	15	6	12
山 东	Shandong	83	2	26	55	11	10
河 南	Henan	80	1	27	52	1	2
湖 北	Hubei	36	1	14	21	9	8
湖 南	Hunan	55	1	16	38	1	
广 东	Guangdong	78	1	30	47	9	7
广 西	Guangxi	29	1	9	19	5	2
海 南	Hainan	4	1		3	3	3
重 庆	Chongqing	13	1		12	1	
四 川	Sichuan	32	1	16	15	7	4
贵 州	Guizhou	21	1	7	13	8	9
云 南	Yunnan	18	1	14	3	3	4
西 藏	Tibet	1	1				
陕 西	Shaanxi	36	1	11	24	3	3
甘 肃	Gansu	18	1	11	6	1	1
青 海	Qinghai	6	1	4	1		
宁 夏	Ningxia	6	1	3	2	1	1
新 疆	Xinjiang	16	1	8	7		
新疆兵团	Xinjiang Corps						
黑龙江垦区	Heilongjiang Land Reclamation						

1-5 续表 1 Continued 1

地 区	Region	机构概况 Rehabilitation Institutions 机构康复功能 Rehabilitation Services Provided by the Institutions					
		开展助听器验配 Providing the Service of Fitting Hearing-aids	开展人工耳蜗术后调试 Providing Adjustments After Cochlear Implantation Surgery	开展听力语言训练 Providing Training of Hearing and Speech	开展社区指导 Providing Guidance at Communities	开展听觉口语法 Providing Implementation of Hearing and Speech Training	开展成年听力语言康复服务 Providing Hearing and Speech Rehabilitation Service to Adults
		个 unit	个 unit	个 unit	个 unit	个 unit	个 unit
全 国	**Total**	**341**	**143**	**946**	**402**	**345**	**206**
北 京	Beijing	3		17	11	6	5
天 津	Tianjin	5	1	7	4	3	3
河 北	Hebei	15	4	95	35	23	22
山 西	Shanxi	10	2	45	24	13	7
内蒙古	Inner Mongolia	7	2	21	5	10	3
辽 宁	Liaoning	18	3	37	16	14	12
吉 林	Jilin	9	6	20	16	9	9
黑龙江	Heilongjiang	9	5	25	9	10	4
上 海	Shanghai	5	3	18	15	11	5
江 苏	Jiangsu	23	10	60	32	30	13
浙 江	Zhejiang	13	7	25	8	9	6
安 徽	Anhui	9	8	58	13	21	10
福 建	Fujian	18	7	20	10	11	3
江 西	Jiangxi	14	5	21	10	7	5
山 东	Shandong	29	11	79	31	28	14
河 南	Henan	34	18	70	29	24	15
湖 北	Hubei	12	2	31	13	13	10
湖 南	Hunan	17	9	48	17	12	12
广 东	Guangdong	23	9	69	34	29	13
广 西	Guangxi	11	5	27	12	9	5
海 南	Hainan	3	1	4	4	3	4
重 庆	Chongqing	1	1	11	7	5	2
四 川	Sichuan	15	6	29	11	10	6
贵 州	Guizhou	7	6	18	4	7	4
云 南	Yunnan	8	3	15	3	2	2
西 藏	Tibet	1	1	1	1	1	1
陕 西	Shaanxi	6	3	33	12	9	4
甘 肃	Gansu	5	2	14	8	5	3
青 海	Qinghai	3		5	1	1	
宁 夏	Ningxia	1	1	6	2	2	1
新 疆	Xinjiang	6	1	16	4	7	2
新疆兵团	Xinjiang Corps						
黑龙江垦区	Heilongjiang Land Reclamation						

1-5　续表 2　Continued 2

地　区	Region	在岗专业人员 On-the-job Professionals				
		教师 Teachers	其中：个别化教师 Individualized Teachers	医技 Doctors and Technicians	其中：助听器验配师 Technicians That Check and Fit Hearing Aids	管理 Managerial Personnels
		人 person	人 person	人 person	人 person	人 person
全　国	**Total**	**9586**	**3705**	**1695**	**717**	**2325**
北　京	Beijing	219	104	38	10	53
天　津	Tianjin	51	19	10	6	17
河　北	Hebei	838	267	132	46	258
山　西	Shanxi	405	124	39	15	101
内蒙古	Inner Mongolia	280	78	57	20	60
辽　宁	Liaoning	435	129	51	26	103
吉　林	Jilin	214	84	31	18	49
黑龙江	Heilongjiang	315	77	47	16	67
上　海	Shanghai	96	48	6	4	25
江　苏	Jiangsu	665	264	101	47	146
浙　江	Zhejiang	196	94	54	25	44
安　徽	Anhui	504	244	31	14	98
福　建	Fujian	294	96	84	29	59
江　西	Jiangxi	161	67	31	18	40
山　东	Shandong	736	343	215	66	199
河　南	Henan	939	370	178	74	177
湖　北	Hubei	269	114	78	41	81
湖　南	Hunan	435	162	64	27	127
广　东	Guangdong	649	327	78	48	109
广　西	Guangxi	221	94	34	20	50
海　南	Hainan	53	18	11	6	10
重　庆	Chongqing	135	55	11	8	28
四　川	Sichuan	362	109	84	31	84
贵　州	Guizhou	178	70	41	16	75
云　南	Yunnan	213	49	24	17	28
西　藏	Tibet	6	4	2	2	1
陕　西	Shaanxi	410	142	55	14	97
甘　肃	Gansu	97	57	47	21	33
青　海	Qinghai	20	9	7	6	4
宁　夏	Ningxia	41	13	2	1	6
新　疆	Xinjiang	97	44	32	11	28
新疆兵团	Xinjiang Corps					
黑龙江垦区	Heilongjiang Land Reclamation					

1-6 肢体残疾康复

Rehabilitation of Persons with Physical Disability

地 区	Region	肢体残疾康复 Rehabilitation of Persons with Physical Disability				贫困肢体残疾儿童矫治手术 Orthopedic Surgeries Conducted for Poor Children with Physical Disability	麻风畸残矫治手术 Orthopedic Surgeries Conducted for Persons with Leprosy-induced Disability
		肢体残疾康复训练 Persons with Physical Disability Receiving Rehabilitation Training	脑瘫儿童机构康复训练 Systematic Rehabilitation Training in Institutions for Children with Cerebral Palsy	肢体残疾儿童社区、家庭康复训练 Children with Physical Disability Receiving Rehabilitation Training in Communities and Families	肢体残疾人社区、家庭康复训练 Persons with Physical Disability Receiving Rehabilitation Training in Communities and Families		
		人 person	人 person	人 person	人 person	人 person	例 case
全 国	**Total**	**353726**	**35399**	**29866**	**288461**	**6721**	**418**
北 京	Beijing	5954	267	103	5584		
天 津	Tianjin	3433	150	153	3130	19	
河 北	Hebei	10638	400	1351	8887	515	
山 西	Shanxi	5579	570	415	4594	321	
内蒙古	Inner Mongolia	6260	442	614	5204	113	
辽 宁	Liaoning	15004	799	1111	13094	331	
吉 林	Jilin	4937	473	167	4297	174	
黑龙江	Heilongjiang	5421	346	326	4749	133	
上 海	Shanghai	5438	650	531	4257	6	
江 苏	Jiangsu	36223	5163	1661	29399	196	
浙 江	Zhejiang	7834	572	509	6753	96	
安 徽	Anhui	17625	1381	743	15501	266	84
福 建	Fujian	10389	1404	1264	7721	103	
江 西	Jiangxi	10784	822	670	9292	173	110
山 东	Shandong	53908	3301	1531	49076	421	
河 南	Henan	15363	2850	3768	8745	464	
湖 北	Hubei	12328	2058	1132	9138	275	
湖 南	Hunan	12788	1338	967	10483	378	100
广 东	Guangdong	32972	3381	2697	26894	57	108
广 西	Guangxi	7845	614	1519	5712	203	
海 南	Hainan	1152	50	418	684		
重 庆	Chongqing	7301	283	606	6412	211	
四 川	Sichuan	22314	5285	2662	14367	556	16
贵 州	Guizhou	1813	398	341	1074	218	
云 南	Yunnan	11409	492	1735	9182	406	
西 藏	Tibet	504	90	116	298	25	
陕 西	Shaanxi	9422	421	697	8304	323	
甘 肃	Gansu	5176	439	865	3872	414	
青 海	Qinghai	1261	147	159	955	93	
宁 夏	Ningxia	5238	175	233	4830	71	
新 疆	Xinjiang	4972	586	555	3831	78	
新疆兵团	Xinjiang Corps	2124	25	247	1852	54	
黑龙江垦区	Heilongjiang Land Reclamation	317	27		290	28	

1-6 续表 Continued

地 区	Region	肢体残疾康复、管理技术人员培训 Training for Managerial and Technical Personnel on Physical Disability Rehabilitation	国家级 at State Level	省级 at Provincial Level	地市级 at Prefectural/ city Level	县级 at County Level
		人 person	人 person	人 person	人 person	人 person
全 国	**Total**	**35361**	**91**	**1522**	**7921**	**25827**
北 京	Beijing	2908	1	682		2225
天 津	Tianjin	249	2			247
河 北	Hebei	484	3		3	478
山 西	Shanxi	240	4	80	102	54
内蒙古	Inner Mongolia	132	3			129
辽 宁	Liaoning	4031	3		1285	2743
吉 林	Jilin	771	3		180	588
黑龙江	Heilongjiang	353	3		152	198
上 海	Shanghai	2651		200		2451
江 苏	Jiangsu	4485	2		112	4371
浙 江	Zhejiang	4723	3		4122	598
安 徽	Anhui	157	2		43	112
福 建	Fujian	280	2	75	27	176
江 西	Jiangxi	200	3		18	179
山 东	Shandong	5152	5		559	4588
河 南	Henan	443	5			438
湖 北	Hubei	291	4		4	283
湖 南	Hunan	351	4		85	262
广 东	Guangdong	1973	3	165	957	848
广 西	Guangxi	324	3		12	309
海 南	Hainan	10	2		4	4
重 庆	Chongqing	654	3	70		581
四 川	Sichuan	1360	3		182	1175
贵 州	Guizhou	207	2			205
云 南	Yunnan	1996	3	220		1773
西 藏	Tibet	16	2		3	11
陕 西	Shaanxi	52	4	30	2	16
甘 肃	Gansu	87	3		7	77
青 海	Qinghai	222	2		2	218
宁 夏	Ningxia	148	2			146
新 疆	Xinjiang	406	2		60	344
新疆兵团	Xinjiang Corps	2	2			
黑龙江垦区	Heilongjiang Land Reclamation	3	3			

1-7 肢体残疾康复训练服务机构

Rehabilitation Institutions for Persons with Physical Disability

地 区	Region	机构合计 Rehabilitation Institutions	省级 at Provincial Level	残联办 Run by Disabled Persons' Federations	其他办 Run by Others
		个 unit	个 unit	个 unit	个 unit
全 国	**Total**	**1927**	**39**	**29**	**10**
北 京	Beijing	14	1	1	
天 津	Tianjin	7	2	1	1
河 北	Hebei	117	1	1	
山 西	Shanxi	39	2	2	
内蒙古	Inner Mongolia	27			
辽 宁	Liaoning	64	3	1	2
吉 林	Jilin	118	1	1	
黑龙江	Heilongjiang	43	1	1	
上 海	Shanghai	124	2	2	
江 苏	Jiangsu	111			
浙 江	Zhejiang	43	1	1	
安 徽	Anhui	64	1	1	
福 建	Fujian	79	1	1	
江 西	Jiangxi	24	1	1	
山 东	Shandong	260			
河 南	Henan	59	1	1	
湖 北	Hubei	47	1	1	
湖 南	Hunan	54	2	1	1
广 东	Guangdong	243	1	1	
广 西	Guangxi	19	1	1	
海 南	Hainan	1	1		1
重 庆	Chongqing	33	1	1	
四 川	Sichuan	57	1	1	
贵 州	Guizhou	10	1	1	
云 南	Yunnan	32	2	2	
西 藏	Tibet	2	1	1	
陕 西	Shaanxi	97	4	1	3
甘 肃	Gansu	24	1	1	
青 海	Qinghai	10	1	1	
宁 夏	Ningxia	13	1	1	
新 疆	Xinjiang	73			
新疆兵团	Xinjiang Corps	1	1		1
黑龙江垦区	Heilongjiang Land Reclamation	18	1		1

1-7　续表 1　Continued 1

地　区	Region	开展肢体残疾康复训练机构 Rehabilitation Institutions					
		地市级 at Prefectural/ City Level	残联办 Run by Disabled Persons' Federations	其他办 Run by Others	县级 at County Level	残联办 Run by Disabled Persons' Federations	其他办 Run by Others
		个 unit	个 unit	个 unit	个 unit	个 unit	个 unit
全　国	**Total**	**316**	**146**	**170**	**1572**	**679**	**893**
北　京	Beijing				13	1	12
天　津	Tianjin				5	3	2
河　北	Hebei	15	4	11	101	28	73
山　西	Shanxi	13	9	4	24	14	10
内蒙古	Inner Mongolia	6	1	5	21	15	6
辽　宁	Liaoning	16	9	7	45	18	27
吉　林	Jilin	11	7	4	106	25	81
黑龙江	Heilongjiang	21	2	19	21	5	16
上　海	Shanghai				122	9	113
江　苏	Jiangsu	23	10	13	88	35	53
浙　江	Zhejiang	8	8		34	22	12
安　徽	Anhui	14	5	9	49	12	37
福　建	Fujian	14	5	9	64	18	46
江　西	Jiangxi	5	2	3	18	5	13
山　东	Shandong	31	9	22	229	72	157
河　南	Henan	20	7	13	38	15	23
湖　北	Hubei	14	6	8	32	25	7
湖　南	Hunan	13	5	8	39	21	18
广　东	Guangdong	40	25	15	202	157	45
广　西	Guangxi	2	1	1	16	13	3
海　南	Hainan						
重　庆	Chongqing				32	5	27
四　川	Sichuan	10	10		46	38	8
贵　州	Guizhou	3		3	6	1	5
云　南	Yunnan	9	4	5	21	17	4
西　藏	Tibet	1	1				
陕　西	Shaanxi	4	1	3	89	39	50
甘　肃	Gansu	6	4	2	17	13	4
青　海	Qinghai	2	2		7	6	1
宁　夏	Ningxia	5	5		7	7	
新　疆	Xinjiang	8	3	5	65	25	40
新疆兵团	Xinjiang Corps						
黑龙江垦区	Heilongjiang Land Reclamation	2	1	1	15	15	

1-7 续表 2 Continued 2

地 区	Region	残联办机构在岗人员 Staff of Rehabilitation Institutions Owned by PWDs' Federations	省级 at Provincial Level	医技 Doctors and Technicians	教师 Teachers	管理 Managerial Personnels	其他 Other Staff Members
		人 person	人 person	人 person	人 person	人 person	人 person
全 国	**Total**	**8721**	**1069**	**735**	**64**	**149**	**121**
北 京	Beijing	19	17	13	3	1	
天 津	Tianjin	41	29	26		1	2
河 北	Hebei	382	4	2	1	1	
山 西	Shanxi	218	31	26		5	
内蒙古	Inner Mongolia	83					
辽 宁	Liaoning	150	19	11	5	2	1
吉 林	Jilin	472	24	18	2	4	
黑龙江	Heilongjiang	45	6	1	3	1	1
上 海	Shanghai	507	410	258	2	72	78
江 苏	Jiangsu	680					
浙 江	Zhejiang	607	2	2			
安 徽	Anhui	111	31	22	5	2	2
福 建	Fujian	167	26	18	4	1	3
江 西	Jiangxi	123	22	12	5	3	2
山 东	Shandong	765					
河 南	Henan	476	27	21	3	2	1
湖 北	Hubei	356	7	1	5	1	
湖 南	Hunan	282	77	54	5	11	7
广 东	Guangdong	1604	11	5	5	1	
广 西	Guangxi	97	19	16		2	1
海 南	Hainan						
重 庆	Chongqing	35	11	5	2	1	3
四 川	Sichuan	515	90	71		19	
贵 州	Guizhou	9	8	7		1	
云 南	Yunnan	151	48	32		9	7
西 藏	Tibet	19	17	16		1	
陕 西	Shaanxi	382	75	55	5	3	12
甘 肃	Gansu	188	33	29		3	1
青 海	Qinghai	33	10	1	8	1	
宁 夏	Ningxia	81	15	13	1	1	
新 疆	Xinjiang	98					
新疆兵团	Xinjiang Corps						
黑龙江垦区	Heilongjiang Land Reclamation	25					

1-7 续表 3 Continued 3

地 区	Region	残联办机构在岗人员 Staff of Institutions Run by PWDs' Federations				
		地市级 at Prefectural/ City Level	医技 Doctors and Technicians	教师 Teachers	管理 Managerial Personnels	其他 Other Staff Members
		人 person	人 person	人 person	人 person	人 person
全 国	**Total**	**2664**	**1278**	**389**	**360**	**637**
北 京	Beijing					
天 津	Tianjin					
河 北	Hebei	225	141	2	24	58
山 西	Shanxi	92	46	20	16	10
内蒙古	Inner Mongolia	12	3	3	2	4
辽 宁	Liaoning	51	19	13	12	7
吉 林	Jilin	54	13	21	10	10
黑龙江	Heilongjiang	16	10	1	3	2
上 海	Shanghai					
江 苏	Jiangsu	169	55	43	26	45
浙 江	Zhejiang	352	246	7	23	76
安 徽	Anhui	39	12	15	5	7
福 建	Fujian	80	38	26	12	4
江 西	Jiangxi	10	4	2	3	1
山 东	Shandong	117	63	15	12	27
河 南	Henan	229	167	23	26	13
湖 北	Hubei	75	38	5	13	19
湖 南	Hunan	83	54	18	7	4
广 东	Guangdong	769	225	144	108	292
广 西	Guangxi	9	7		1	1
海 南	Hainan					
重 庆	Chongqing					
四 川	Sichuan	123	45	20	25	33
贵 州	Guizhou					
云 南	Yunnan	15	4		4	7
西 藏	Tibet	2	2			
陕 西	Shaanxi	2	1		1	
甘 肃	Gansu	95	74	1	13	7
青 海	Qinghai	2	1	1		
宁 夏	Ningxia	27	8	9	8	2
新 疆	Xinjiang	9	2		4	3
新疆兵团	Xinjiang Corps					
黑龙江垦区	Heilongjiang Land Reclamation	7			2	5

1-7 续表 4 Continued 4

地 区	Region	残联办机构在岗人员 Staff of Institutions Run by PWDs' Federations				
		县级 at County Level	医技 Doctors and Technicians	教师 Teachers	管理 Managerial Personnels	其他 Other Staff Members
		人 person	人 person	人 person	人 person	人 person
全 国	**Total**	**4988**	**1729**	**693**	**1137**	**1429**
北 京	Beijing	2	2			
天 津	Tianjin	12	3	3	4	2
河 北	Hebei	153	27	18	54	54
山 西	Shanxi	95	38	13	18	26
内蒙古	Inner Mongolia	71	24	13	17	17
辽 宁	Liaoning	80	8	2	45	25
吉 林	Jilin	394	62	15	55	262
黑龙江	Heilongjiang	23	7	4	8	4
上 海	Shanghai	97	63		13	21
江 苏	Jiangsu	511	288	72	65	86
浙 江	Zhejiang	253	84	22	40	107
安 徽	Anhui	41	7	10	14	10
福 建	Fujian	61	16	4	25	16
江 西	Jiangxi	91	40	8	6	37
山 东	Shandong	648	262	65	144	177
河 南	Henan	220	115	34	46	25
湖 北	Hubei	274	112	40	60	62
湖 南	Hunan	122	30	41	29	22
广 东	Guangdong	824	191	190	191	252
广 西	Guangxi	69	24	8	15	22
海 南	Hainan					
重 庆	Chongqing	24	2	6	15	1
四 川	Sichuan	302	88	48	84	82
贵 州	Guizhou	1			1	
云 南	Yunnan	88	6	20	39	23
西 藏	Tibet					
陕 西	Shaanxi	305	153	29	65	58
甘 肃	Gansu	60	22	14	13	11
青 海	Qinghai	21	10	2	8	1
宁 夏	Ningxia	39	13	8	10	8
新 疆	Xinjiang	89	31	4	38	16
新疆兵团	Xinjiang Corps					
黑龙江垦区	Heilongjiang Land Reclamation	18	1		15	2

1-8　智力残疾康复
Rehabilitation of Persons with Intellectual Disability

地区	Region	智力残疾儿童康复训练 Children with Intellectual Disability Receiving Rehabilitation Training	机构康复训练 Trained in Institutions	社区、家庭康复训练 Trained in Communities and Families	成年智力残疾人社区、家庭康复训练 Adults with Intellectual Disability Trained in Communities and Families
		人 person	人 person	人 person	人 person
全　国	**Total**	**100663**	**23859**	**76804**	**30789**
北　京	Beijing	616	477	139	2134
天　津	Tianjin	896	139	757	5
河　北	Hebei	4931	526	4405	747
山　西	Shanxi	2391	260	2131	39
内蒙古	Inner Mongolia	2151	457	1694	160
辽　宁	Liaoning	3304	697	2607	1018
吉　林	Jilin	1844	197	1647	36
黑龙江	Heilongjiang	2415	278	2137	464
上　海	Shanghai	2615	1156	1459	7871
江　苏	Jiangsu	7184	2532	4652	4280
浙　江	Zhejiang	3102	659	2443	692
安　徽	Anhui	6202	1245	4957	1105
福　建	Fujian	3102	999	2103	450
江　西	Jiangxi	3303	695	2608	203
山　东	Shandong	7860	2261	5599	2060
河　南	Henan	7944	1479	6465	111
湖　北	Hubei	4479	899	3580	958
湖　南	Hunan	4745	1069	3676	2717
广　东	Guangdong	7397	3177	4220	2341
广　西	Guangxi	3437	559	2878	145
海　南	Hainan	554	70	484	208
重　庆	Chongqing	2191	285	1906	363
四　川	Sichuan	5915	1100	4815	195
贵　州	Guizhou	739	370	369	138
云　南	Yunnan	3097	521	2576	703
西　藏	Tibet	107	5	102	69
陕　西	Shaanxi	2775	610	2165	582
甘　肃	Gansu	1889	392	1497	80
青　海	Qinghai	471	112	359	136
宁　夏	Ningxia	611	152	459	35
新　疆	Xinjiang	1954	410	1544	211
新疆兵团	Xinjiang Corps	272	19	253	533
黑龙江垦区	Heilongjiang Land Reclamation	170	52	118	

1-8 续表 Continued

地区	Region	智力残疾康复、管理技术人员培训 Training for Managerial and Technical Personnel on Intellectual Disabilities Rehabilitation	国家级 at State Level	省级 at Provincial Level	地市级 at Prefectural/ City Level	县级 at County Level
		人次 person-time	人次 person-time	人次 person-time	人次 person-time	人次 person-time
全 国	**Total**	**16074**	**116**	**1213**	**2513**	**12232**
北 京	Beijing	1767	2	570		1195
天 津	Tianjin	57	3			54
河 北	Hebei	461	3		25	433
山 西	Shanxi	183	4	70	99	10
内蒙古	Inner Mongolia	185	3			182
辽 宁	Liaoning	1257	3	1	140	1113
吉 林	Jilin	243	4		18	221
黑龙江	Heilongjiang	107	3			104
上 海	Shanghai	1174	3			1171
江 苏	Jiangsu	1984	5		36	1943
浙 江	Zhejiang	1750	3		1363	384
安 徽	Anhui	206	4	146	2	54
福 建	Fujian	512	3	320	13	176
江 西	Jiangxi	115	2		13	100
山 东	Shandong	1103	6		329	768
河 南	Henan	156	6			150
湖 北	Hubei	246	7		2	237
湖 南	Hunan	236	6		43	187
广 东	Guangdong	678	5	72	152	449
广 西	Guangxi	143	4		40	99
海 南	Hainan	28	2			26
重 庆	Chongqing	192	11	30		151
四 川	Sichuan	1008	3		58	947
贵 州	Guizhou	165	1			164
云 南	Yunnan	1562	3	4	10	1545
西 藏	Tibet	1	1			
陕 西	Shaanxi	256	3		167	86
甘 肃	Gansu	55	2		1	52
青 海	Qinghai	192	3		2	187
宁 夏	Ningxia	8	4			4
新 疆	Xinjiang	44	4			40
新疆兵团	Xinjiang Corps					
黑龙江垦区	Heilongjiang Land Reclamation					

1-9　智力残疾康复训练服务机构

Rehabilitation Institutions for Persons with Intellectual Disability

地　区	Region	机构合计 Rehabilitation Institutions for Persons with Intellectual Disability	省级 at Provincial Level	残联办 Run by Disabled Persons' Federations	其他办 Run by Others
		个 unit	个 unit	个 unit	个 unit
全　国	**Total**	**1471**	**35**	**29**	**6**
北　京	Beijing	35	1	1	
天　津	Tianjin	9	1	1	
河　北	Hebei	50	1	1	
山　西	Shanxi	37	2	2	
内蒙古	Inner Mongolia	23			
辽　宁	Liaoning	57	2	1	1
吉　林	Jilin	29	1	1	
黑龙江	Heilongjiang	29	1	1	
上　海	Shanghai	222	1	1	
江　苏	Jiangsu	89	1	1	
浙　江	Zhejiang	38	1	1	
安　徽	Anhui	40	1	1	
福　建	Fujian	58	1	1	
江　西	Jiangxi	20	1	1	
山　东	Shandong	107			
河　南	Henan	45	1	1	
湖　北	Hubei	49	1	1	
湖　南	Hunan	50	1	1	
广　东	Guangdong	251	1	1	
广　西	Guangxi	20	1	1	
海　南	Hainan	2	2		2
重　庆	Chongqing	36	1	1	
四　川	Sichuan	50	1	1	
贵　州	Guizhou	11			
云　南	Yunnan	21	2	2	
西　藏	Tibet	2	1	1	
陕　西	Shaanxi	21	2	1	1
甘　肃	Gansu	22	1	1	
青　海	Qinghai	9	1	1	
宁　夏	Ningxia	14	1	1	
新　疆	Xinjiang	23	1	1	
新疆兵团	Xinjiang Corps	1	1		1
黑龙江垦区	Heilongjiang Land Reclamation	1	1		1

1-9 续表 1 Continued 1

地 区	Region	机构 Intellectual Disability Rehabilitation Institutions					
		地市级 at Prefectural/ City Level	残联办 Run by PWDs' Federations	其他办 Run by Others	县级 at County Level	残联办 Run by PWDs' Federations	其他办 Run by Others
		个 unit	个 unit	个 unit	个 unit	个 unit	个 unit
全 国	**Total**	**258**	**121**	**137**	**1178**	**613**	**565**
北 京	Beijing				34		34
天 津	Tianjin				8	3	5
河 北	Hebei	13	5	8	36	9	27
山 西	Shanxi	9	7	2	26	8	18
内蒙古	Inner Mongolia	6	1	5	17	10	7
辽 宁	Liaoning	14	8	6	41	16	25
吉 林	Jilin	10	6	4	18	9	9
黑龙江	Heilongjiang	9	3	6	19	4	15
上 海	Shanghai				221	158	63
江 苏	Jiangsu	10	7	3	78	26	52
浙 江	Zhejiang	7	7		30	15	15
安 徽	Anhui	17	3	14	22	4	18
福 建	Fujian	6	4	2	51	10	41
江 西	Jiangxi	9	1	8	10	3	7
山 东	Shandong	19	7	12	88	19	69
河 南	Henan	15	6	9	29	10	19
湖 北	Hubei	11	2	9	37	26	11
湖 南	Hunan	10	3	7	39	17	22
广 东	Guangdong	33	17	16	217	176	41
广 西	Guangxi	9	6	3	10	5	5
海 南	Hainan						
重 庆	Chongqing				35	6	29
四 川	Sichuan	10	10		39	34	5
贵 州	Guizhou	4		4	7		7
云 南	Yunnan	8	3	5	11	6	5
西 藏	Tibet	1	1				
陕 西	Shaanxi	5	1	4	14	7	7
甘 肃	Gansu	9	2	7	12	7	5
青 海	Qinghai	2	2		6	6	
宁 夏	Ningxia	5	5		8	8	
新 疆	Xinjiang	7	4	3	15	11	4
新疆兵团	Xinjiang Corps						
黑龙江垦区	Heilongjiang Land Reclamation						

1-9 续表 2 Continued 2

地 区	Region	残联办机构在岗人员 Staff of Rehabilitation Institutions Owned by PWDs' Federations	省级 at Provincial Level	医技 Doctors and Technicians	教师 Teachers	管理 Managerial Personnels	其他 Other Staff Members
		人 person	人 person	人 person	人 person	人 person	人 person
全 国	**Total**	**6026**	**419**	**152**	**156**	**69**	**42**
北 京	Beijing	12	12	5	6	1	
天 津	Tianjin	27	9		5	1	3
河 北	Hebei	162	4	1	2	1	
山 西	Shanxi	146	32	20	8	4	
内蒙古	Inner Mongolia	53					
辽 宁	Liaoning	138	13	4	8	1	
吉 林	Jilin	106	8	4		4	
黑龙江	Heilongjiang	75	11	1	8	1	1
上 海	Shanghai	667	5	4		1	
江 苏	Jiangsu	331	11		9	1	1
浙 江	Zhejiang	187	2	2			
安 徽	Anhui	49	10	1	6	1	2
福 建	Fujian	83	2		2		
江 西	Jiangxi	51	26	12	5	2	7
山 东	Shandong	349					
河 南	Henan	506	23	1	16	1	5
湖 北	Hubei	320	10		9	1	
湖 南	Hunan	209	21		10	9	2
广 东	Guangdong	1545	11		8	1	2
广 西	Guangxi	117	29		16	12	1
海 南	Hainan						
重 庆	Chongqing	64	7	3	3	1	
四 川	Sichuan	425	82	66		16	
贵 州	Guizhou						
云 南	Yunnan	70	8	4	4		
西 藏	Tibet	4	3	1		1	1
陕 西	Shaanxi	92	30	14	2	2	12
甘 肃	Gansu	68	28	8	11	5	4
青 海	Qinghai	28	6	1	4		1
宁 夏	Ningxia	65	9		8	1	
新 疆	Xinjiang	77	7		6	1	
新疆兵团	Xinjiang Corps						
黑龙江垦区	Heilongjiang Land Reclamation						

1-9 续表 3 Continued 3

地 区	Region	残联办机构在岗人员 Staff of Rehabilitation Institutions Run by PWDs' Federations				
		地市级 at Prefectural/ City Level	医技 Doctors and Technicians	教师 Teachers	管理 Managerial Personnels	其他 Other Staff Members
		人 person	人 person	人 person	人 person	人 person
全 国	**Total**	**1927**	**561**	**665**	**289**	**412**
北 京	Beijing					
天 津	Tianjin					
河 北	Hebei	108	15	36	29	28
山 西	Shanxi	69	32	15	12	10
内蒙古	Inner Mongolia	7	1	3	1	2
辽 宁	Liaoning	51	3	29	13	6
吉 林	Jilin	53	8	27	8	10
黑龙江	Heilongjiang	49	4	25	8	12
上 海	Shanghai					
江 苏	Jiangsu	121	15	59	25	22
浙 江	Zhejiang	53	1	39	5	8
安 徽	Anhui	14	3	7	1	3
福 建	Fujian	41		20	11	10
江 西	Jiangxi	8	2	3	2	1
山 东	Shandong	80	8	43	14	15
河 南	Henan	276	157	38	31	50
湖 北	Hubei	19	11	1	3	4
湖 南	Hunan	25	11	10	4	
广 东	Guangdong	689	246	192	74	177
广 西	Guangxi	75	9	35	10	21
海 南	Hainan					
重 庆	Chongqing					
四 川	Sichuan	120	20	67	17	16
贵 州	Guizhou					
云 南	Yunnan	9	1		3	5
西 藏	Tibet	1	1			
陕 西	Shaanxi	7	1		1	5
甘 肃	Gansu	8	2	2	2	2
青 海	Qinghai	2	1	1		
宁 夏	Ningxia	22	5	9	7	1
新 疆	Xinjiang	20	4	4	8	4
新疆兵团	Xinjiang Corps					
黑龙江垦区	Heilongjiang Land Reclamation					

1-9　续表 4　Continued 4

地　区	Region	残联办机构在岗人员 Staff of Rehabilitation Agencies Run by Disabled Persons' Federations				
		县级 at County Level	医技 Doctors and Technicians	教师 Teachers	管理 Managerial Personnels	其他 Other Staff Members
		人 person	人 person	人 person	人 person	人 person
全　国	**Total**	**3680**	**632**	**1054**	**877**	**1117**
北　京	Beijing					
天　津	Tianjin	18		8	8	2
河　北	Hebei	50	11	6	14	19
山　西	Shanxi	45	17	12	9	7
内蒙古	Inner Mongolia	46	16	8	12	10
辽　宁	Liaoning	74	3	24	16	31
吉　林	Jilin	45	7	13	15	10
黑龙江	Heilongjiang	15	6	3	4	2
上　海	Shanghai	662		133	171	358
江　苏	Jiangsu	199	49	74	33	43
浙　江	Zhejiang	132	26	47	22	37
安　徽	Anhui	25	5	13	4	3
福　建	Fujian	40	9	7	15	9
江　西	Jiangxi	17	7	4	4	2
山　东	Shandong	269	71	92	39	67
河　南	Henan	207	104	43	35	25
湖　北	Hubei	291	71	74	66	80
湖　南	Hunan	163	18	49	34	62
广　东	Guangdong	845	112	268	210	255
广　西	Guangxi	13	3	5	4	1
海　南	Hainan					
重　庆	Chongqing	57	1	37	17	2
四　川	Sichuan	223	36	69	75	43
贵　州	Guizhou					
云　南	Yunnan	53	1	19	26	7
西　藏	Tibet					
陕　西	Shaanxi	55	19	9	10	17
甘　肃	Gansu	32	8	9	7	8
青　海	Qinghai	20	6	6	7	1
宁　夏	Ningxia	34	11	10	7	6
新　疆	Xinjiang	50	15	12	13	10
新疆兵团	Xinjiang Corps					
黑龙江垦区	Heilongjiang Land Reclamation					

1-10 精神病防治康复

Prevention and Rehabilitation of Mental Illness

地 区	Region	开展精防康复工作县(市、区) Counties/Cities/Districts where Prevention and Rehabilitation of Mental Illness have been Conducted	精神病人 People with Mental Illness	监护病人 People with Mental Illness under Guardianship	监护率 Guardian-ship Rate
		个 unit	万人 10,000 persons	万人 10,000 persons	%
全 国	**Total**	**2627**	**584.0**	**461.9**	**79.1**
北 京	Beijing	16	6.9	6.0	86.3
天 津	Tianjin	16	6.3	6.0	95.4
河 北	Hebei	170	26.0	22.7	87.3
山 西	Shanxi	64	9.9	8.1	81.9
内蒙古	Inner Mongolia	84	7.1	5.8	81.7
辽 宁	Liaoning	107	27.1	24.4	89.9
吉 林	Jilin	63	16.0	15.5	96.8
黑龙江	Heilongjiang	124	18.3	15.0	82.0
上 海	Shanghai	17	11.4	11.1	98.2
江 苏	Jiangsu	104	52.8	42.4	80.4
浙 江	Zhejiang	75	19.0	17.4	91.3
安 徽	Anhui	88	27.2	22.3	82.0
福 建	Fujian	84	12.2	10.7	87.5
江 西	Jiangxi	101	18.4	14.7	80.3
山 东	Shandong	138	38.6	32.3	83.7
河 南	Henan	156	43.9	20.4	46.5
湖 北	Hubei	92	34.7	22.6	65.1
湖 南	Hunan	120	33.3	31.8	95.6
广 东	Guangdong	129	38.9	30.6	78.6
广 西	Guangxi	92	12.4	9.6	77.4
海 南	Hainan	13	1.6	1.1	69.9
重 庆	Chongqing	40	18.0	14.6	81.1
四 川	Sichuan	143	40.1	31.7	78.9
贵 州	Guizhou	86	7.8	6.5	83.9
云 南	Yunnan	123	15.2	10.0	65.7
西 藏	Tibet				
陕 西	Shaanxi	110	20.3	11.8	58.2
甘 肃	Gansu	60	12.0	10.3	86.2
青 海	Qinghai	34	0.4	0.2	60.4
宁 夏	Ningxia	21	3.6	3.2	90.7
新 疆	Xinjiang	69	2.3	1.6	66.6
新疆兵团	Xinjiang Corps	6	1.0	0.7	71.2
黑龙江垦区	Heilongjiang Land Reclamation	82	1.4	0.7	45.1

1-10　续表 1　Continued 1

地　区	Region	显好病人 People with Mental Illness who have gotten Effective Treatment	显好率 Significant Improvement Rate	参与社会总人数 People with Mental Illness who have Participated into Social Life after Rehabilitation	参与率 Social Involvement Rate	肇事人次 People with Mental Illness who Caused Serious Troubles	肇事率 Violent Events Rate
		万人 10,000 persons	%	万人 10,000 persons	%	人次 person-time	%
全　国	**Total**	**305.6**	**66.2**	**237.5**	**51.4**	**7940**	**0.17**
北　京	Beijing	3.5	57.9	2.6	42.8	11	0.02
天　津	Tianjin	4.8	79.7	4.2	69.0	2	0.00
河　北	Hebei	14.9	65.6	11.9	52.7	125	0.06
山　西	Shanxi	5.6	69.2	4.2	52.1	41	0.05
内蒙古	Inner Mongolia	3.6	63.2	3.1	53.8	132	0.23
辽　宁	Liaoning	16.5	67.5	12.9	52.8	27	0.01
吉　林	Jilin	10.7	68.9	8.9	57.4	46	0.03
黑龙江	Heilongjiang	9.7	64.4	6.1	40.5	76	0.05
上　海	Shanghai	11.0	98.3	9.6	86.4	4	
江　苏	Jiangsu	31.6	74.6	26.5	62.5	65	0.02
浙　江	Zhejiang	12.1	69.6	10.3	59.4	391	0.23
安　徽	Anhui	12.9	57.8	10.5	47.0	50	0.02
福　建	Fujian	7.7	72.0	5.7	53.6	105	0.10
江　西	Jiangxi	8.4	57.1	6.2	42.2	1947	1.32
山　东	Shandong	23.7	73.6	19.8	61.3	115	0.04
河　南	Henan	10.8	52.9	8.0	39.2	566	0.28
湖　北	Hubei	14.1	62.3	10.6	47.0	427	0.19
湖　南	Hunan	15.5	48.6	11.5	36.1	216	0.07
广　东	Guangdong	20.8	67.8	15.3	49.9	636	0.21
广　西	Guangxi	6.6	68.5	5.1	53.3	459	0.48
海　南	Hainan	0.2	20.9	0.1	12.0	14	0.13
重　庆	Chongqing	12.1	82.4	9.6	65.5	284	0.19
四　川	Sichuan	19.5	61.7	11.0	34.9	1346	0.43
贵　州	Guizhou	4.5	68.1	3.7	56.2	316	0.48
云　南	Yunnan	6.1	60.6	5.0	49.7	227	0.23
西　藏	Tibet						
陕　西	Shaanxi	7.9	66.7	6.5	55.2	141	0.12
甘　肃	Gansu	7.2	69.7	5.6	54.6	68	0.07
青　海	Qinghai	0.1	50.2	0.1	34.2		
宁　夏	Ningxia	2.3	70.5	1.9	57.6	92	0.28
新　疆	Xinjiang	0.8	49.9	0.5	32.6	1	0.01
新疆兵团	Xinjiang Corps	0.5	65.3	0.4	51.4	10	0.14
黑龙江垦区	Heilongjiang Land Reclamation	0.2	36.4	0.1	12.0		

1-10 续表 2 Continued 2

地 区	Region	接受治疗的精神病患者 People with Mental Illness who have gotten Medical Treatment	接受康复训练 People with Mental Illness who have gotten Rehabilitation Training	精神康复机构 Rehabilitation Institutions for People with Mental Illness	其中：精神病人 People with Mental Illness who have gotten Rehabilitation Training in Those Institutions
		人 person	人 person	个 unit	人 person
全 国	**Total**	**1845920**	**1057254**	**2270**	**520784**
北 京	Beijing	24972	10993	15	3547
天 津	Tianjin	14457	10742	13	8171
河 北	Hebei	91469	57288	83	7649
山 西	Shanxi	26998	13810	56	15373
内蒙古	Inner Mongolia	21740	7824	36	2060
辽 宁	Liaoning	63577	38966	154	20082
吉 林	Jilin	35005	42064	56	12708
黑龙江	Heilongjiang	23093	6588	40	5264
上 海	Shanghai	65417	18616	192	3247
江 苏	Jiangsu	178313	136591	110	42437
浙 江	Zhejiang	99347	74432	37	13656
安 徽	Anhui	80774	34525	51	9138
福 建	Fujian	54551	39394	63	14726
江 西	Jiangxi	67074	32359	81	28936
山 东	Shandong	203151	115712	234	42635
河 南	Henan	96057	69394	91	34321
湖 北	Hubei	114585	55279	92	49321
湖 南	Hunan	105844	53646	110	19786
广 东	Guangdong	120036	57580	372	50198
广 西	Guangxi	66448	21289	29	18018
海 南	Hainan	3804	560	1	250
重 庆	Chongqing	88253	55117	41	21136
四 川	Sichuan	78387	43467	103	39721
贵 州	Guizhou	13675	14468	28	5359
云 南	Yunnan	32089	10920	43	19119
西 藏	Tibet			1	5
陕 西	Shaanxi	46101	25866	59	24149
甘 肃	Gansu	13753	3260	32	2060
青 海	Qinghai	632	18	3	110
宁 夏	Ningxia	6093	2600	8	1047
新 疆	Xinjiang	4618	2278	27	3892
新疆兵团	Xinjiang Corps	3051	1608	6	2036
黑龙江垦区	Heilongjiang Land Reclamation	2556		3	627

1-10　续表 3　Continued 3

地　区	Region	贫困患者 People with Mental Illness Living in Poverty	接受医疗救助的贫困患者 Those who have gotten Medical Assistance	接受国家专项彩金免费服药项目医疗救助的贫困患者 Poor Patients who Received Free Medicines Funded by National Lottery Medical Assistance Project	接受国家专项彩金免费住院项目医疗救助的贫困患者 Poor Patients who Received Free Treatment in Hospital Funded by National Lottery Medical Assistance Project	接受其他项目医疗救助的贫困患者 Poor Patients who Received Medical Assistance Funded by Other Projects
		人 person	人 person	人 person	人 person	人 person
全　国	**Total**	**1467040**	**468750**	**148392**	**24901**	**295457**
北　京	Beijing	11018	7398			7398
天　津	Tianjin	7912	3635			3635
河　北	Hebei	24359	6190	4906	1027	257
山　西	Shanxi	16593	5519	4401	538	580
内蒙古	Inner Mongolia	22547	3160	2381	429	350
辽　宁	Liaoning	75173	23973	4975	840	18158
吉　林	Jilin	54483	17998	6160	1520	10318
黑龙江	Heilongjiang	26169	6730	5657	870	203
上　海	Shanghai	15893	13146			13146
江　苏	Jiangsu	89982	39470	5000	1060	33410
浙　江	Zhejiang	29735	17264	2264	258	14742
安　徽	Anhui	100466	73273	8625	1328	63320
福　建	Fujian	73688	10847	4971	843	5033
江　西	Jiangxi	75737	20793	8529	534	11730
山　东	Shandong	97190	24402	8221	1550	14631
河　南	Henan	56607	20390	6500	1500	12390
湖　北	Hubei	91176	15905	11290	1285	3330
湖　南	Hunan	75887	13244	4800	1000	7444
广　东	Guangdong	103142	46722	8027	909	37786
广　西	Guangxi	60610	11238	7226	1232	2780
海　南	Hainan	5761	1886	1410	125	351
重　庆	Chongqing	80102	11610	4307	656	6647
四　川	Sichuan	104847	18815	9403	1634	7778
贵　州	Guizhou	21819	5134	2383	537	2214
云　南	Yunnan	44305	15271	5901	1892	7478
西　藏	Tibet					
陕　西	Shaanxi	51335	16543	7976	1416	7151
甘　肃	Gansu	21061	3502	2696	570	236
青　海	Qinghai	1699	1500	941	354	205
宁　夏	Ningxia	11158	4438	4038	400	
新　疆	Xinjiang	8405	4820	2706	429	1685
新疆兵团	Xinjiang Corps	2996	2033	797	165	1071
黑龙江垦区	Heilongjiang Land Reclamation	5185	1901	1901		

1-10 续表 4 Continued 4

地 区	Region	发现关锁病人 People with Mental Illness who were Found being Locked-up	解除关锁病人 Freed from Locked-up	培训精防康复管理、技术人员 Trained Managerial Personnels and Technicians of Prevention and Rehabilitation
		人 person	人 person	人 person
全 国	**Total**	**6779**	**3702**	**41749**
北 京	Beijing			1188
天 津	Tianjin			1307
河 北	Hebei	226	109	2717
山 西	Shanxi	480	261	393
内蒙古	Inner Mongolia	314	108	139
辽 宁	Liaoning	50	36	1273
吉 林	Jilin	8	6	1275
黑龙江	Heilongjiang	21	8	129
上 海	Shanghai	47	47	4933
江 苏	Jiangsu	64	59	4120
浙 江	Zhejiang	52	23	6508
安 徽	Anhui	38	32	327
福 建	Fujian	164	78	704
江 西	Jiangxi	320	213	240
山 东	Shandong	116	73	5250
河 南	Henan	984	626	237
湖 北	Hubei	381	218	649
湖 南	Hunan	337	262	686
广 东	Guangdong	1549	537	4492
广 西	Guangxi	35	30	230
海 南	Hainan	215	65	
重 庆	Chongqing	114	99	1481
四 川	Sichuan	403	316	1937
贵 州	Guizhou	293	256	129
云 南	Yunnan	157	71	678
西 藏	Tibet			
陕 西	Shaanxi	293	138	393
甘 肃	Gansu	102	23	14
青 海	Qinghai	7	3	89
宁 夏	Ningxia	3	1	60
新 疆	Xinjiang	6	4	123
新疆兵团	Xinjiang Corps			48
黑龙江垦区	Heilongjiang Land Reclamation			

1-11 孤独症儿童康复训练
Rehabilitation Training for Children with Autism

地 区	Region	孤独症儿童康复训练机构 Rehabilitation Institutions for Children with Autism	省级机构 at Provincial Level	地市级及以下其他机构 at Prefectual/City Level and Lower	机构内教师 Teachers Working in Those Institutions	省级机构内教师 at Provincial Level	地市级及以下其他机构内教师 at Prefectual/City Level and Lower
		个 unit	个 unit	个 unit	人 person	人 person	人 person
全 国	**Total**	**1108**	**34**	**1074**	**7660**	**347**	**7313**
北 京	Beijing	24	1	23	248	23	225
天 津	Tianjin	13	2	11	257	19	238
河 北	Hebei	32	1	31	133		133
山 西	Shanxi	14	2	12	99	20	79
内蒙古	Inner Mongolia	30		30	136		136
辽 宁	Liaoning	47	1	46	300	38	262
吉 林	Jilin	39	1	38	479	26	453
黑龙江	Heilongjiang	35	1	34	255	15	240
上 海	Shanghai	30	1	29	194	7	187
江 苏	Jiangsu	88	1	87	622	5	617
浙 江	Zhejiang	39	1	38	322	10	312
安 徽	Anhui	52	1	51	300	7	293
福 建	Fujian	56	1	55	449	22	427
江 西	Jiangxi	28	1	27	89	5	84
山 东	Shandong	101		101	806		806
河 南	Henan	100	1	99	523	9	514
湖 北	Hubei	32	1	31	222	9	213
湖 南	Hunan	44	1	43	294	12	282
广 东	Guangdong	118	1	117	1033	6	1027
广 西	Guangxi	15	1	14	161	13	148
海 南	Hainan	2	2		15	15	
重 庆	Chongqing	18	1	17	166	3	163
四 川	Sichuan	46	1	45	184	6	178
贵 州	Guizhou	18	1	17	87	27	60
云 南	Yunnan	22	1	21	43	9	34
西 藏	Tibet						
陕 西	Shaanxi	20	2	18	99	8	91
甘 肃	Gansu	15	1	14	62	10	52
青 海	Qinghai	7	1	6	8	4	4
宁 夏	Ningxia	15	1	14	43	8	35
新 疆	Xinjiang	6	1	5	25	5	20
新疆兵团	Xinjiang Corps	1	1		5	5	
黑龙江垦区	Heilongjiang Land Reclamation	1	1		1	1	

1-11 续表 1 Continued 1

地 区	Region	机构内在训儿童 Children with Autism Trained in Those Institutions	省级机构在训儿童 at Provincial Level	地市级及以下其他机构在训儿童 at City Level and Lower	贫困孤独症儿童救助 Poor Children with Autism Supported
		人 person	人 person	人 person	人 person
全 国	**Total**	**16656**	**2020**	**14636**	**8732**
北 京	Beijing	420	201	219	38
天 津	Tianjin	105	50	55	117
河 北	Hebei	409		409	245
山 西	Shanxi	311	70	241	222
内蒙古	Inner Mongolia	449		449	382
辽 宁	Liaoning	664	172	492	277
吉 林	Jilin	612	80	532	541
黑龙江	Heilongjiang	385	62	323	179
上 海	Shanghai	298	1	297	261
江 苏	Jiangsu	940	20	920	399
浙 江	Zhejiang	358		358	206
安 徽	Anhui	755	42	713	288
福 建	Fujian	907	65	842	438
江 西	Jiangxi	471	45	426	20
山 东	Shandong	1402	53	1349	741
河 南	Henan	1158	110	1048	340
湖 北	Hubei	586	117	469	440
湖 南	Hunan	501	60	441	423
广 东	Guangdong	3000	20	2980	1581
广 西	Guangxi	399	49	350	143
海 南	Hainan	7	7		25
重 庆	Chongqing	329	15	314	360
四 川	Sichuan	459	171	288	135
贵 州	Guizhou	309	90	219	255
云 南	Yunnan	161	25	136	85
西 藏	Tibet				
陕 西	Shaanxi	419	282	137	430
甘 肃	Gansu	68	7	61	84
青 海	Qinghai	161	65	96	25
宁 夏	Ningxia	163	36	127	45
新 疆	Xinjiang	406	61	345	7
新疆兵团	Xinjiang Corps	24	24		
黑龙江垦区	Heilongjiang Land Reclamation	20	20		

1-11 续表 2 Continued 2

地区	Region	儿童训练后走向 Directions in which Children have gone After Rehabilitation					
		省级 at Provincial Level			地市级及以下 at Prefectual/ City Level and Lower		
		普幼及普小 Ordinary Kindergartens or Primary Schools	特殊教育学校 Special Education Schools	其他 Other Directions	普幼及普小 Ordinary Kindergartens or Primary Schools	特殊教育学校 Special Education Schools	其他 Other Directions
		人 person	人 person	人 person	人 person	人 person	人 person
全 国	**Total**	**121**	**51**	**164**	**930**	**624**	**1304**
北 京	Beijing			1	50	62	16
天 津	Tianjin				5	2	
河 北	Hebei				19	6	32
山 西	Shanxi		10	17	8		5
内蒙古	Inner Mongolia				52	30	48
辽 宁	Liaoning				10	80	17
吉 林	Jilin	1			42	60	42
黑龙江	Heilongjiang	2		8	61	2	32
上 海	Shanghai			1	25	59	47
江 苏	Jiangsu	1	4	1	59	61	40
浙 江	Zhejiang				24	28	16
安 徽	Anhui	1			47	17	46
福 建	Fujian	6	12	1	11	2	50
江 西	Jiangxi				8	4	
山 东	Shandong	32		1	48	63	70
河 南	Henan	9	1	84	175	33	268
湖 北	Hubei				16		40
湖 南	Hunan		4	9	49	6	47
广 东	Guangdong	1			132	54	222
广 西	Guangxi			2	6	6	83
海 南	Hainan				1		
重 庆	Chongqing			11	7		3
四 川	Sichuan	53			4	33	27
贵 州	Guizhou				33	11	85
云 南	Yunnan				4	3	32
西 藏	Tibet						
陕 西	Shaanxi	7	2	13	11	1	11
甘 肃	Gansu				9	1	10
青 海	Qinghai			3	1		14
宁 夏	Ningxia	7		4	13		
新 疆	Xinjiang	1					1
新疆兵团	Xinjiang Corps		17				
黑龙江垦区	Heilongjiang Land Reclamation		1	8			

1–12 辅助器具供应服务
Provision of Assistive Devices

地 区	Region	辅助器具供应 Assistive Devices Provided	辅助器具供应品种 Categories of Assistive Devices Provided	矫形器装配 Orthotic Devices Fitted	国家彩金项目装配 Fitted for PWDs by the National	上肢矫形器 Orthoses for Upper Limbs	脊柱矫形器 Orthoses for Spinal Cord	下肢矫形器 Orthoses for Lower Limbs
		件 piece	种 category	例 case	例 case	例 case	例 case	例 case
全 国	**Total**	**1283422**	**1606**	**47159**	**11762**	**713**	**299**	**10750**
北 京	Beijing	9872	39	283	212	14	11	187
天 津	Tianjin	33608	106	318	196	11		185
河 北	Hebei	28872	60	639	639	22	11	606
山 西	Shanxi	17967	137	172	3			3
内蒙古	Inner Mongolia	17065	39	78	59	6	2	51
辽 宁	Liaoning	39238	414	426	344	8	6	330
吉 林	Jilin	9978	38	373	188	10	3	175
黑龙江	Heilongjiang	13474	130	92	61	10	2	49
上 海	Shanghai	195304	400	29432				
江 苏	Jiangsu	94021	202	2022	1391	37	16	1338
浙 江	Zhejiang	27613	364	152	32		3	29
安 徽	Anhui	19704	70	836	613	40	1	572
福 建	Fujian	19786	680	406	366	38	2	326
江 西	Jiangxi	14794	100	258	258	42	6	210
山 东	Shandong	97433	697	624	296	19	3	274
河 南	Henan	119910	140	787				
湖 北	Hubei	43117	282	786	683	30	17	636
湖 南	Hunan	66752	1058	1062	793	36	29	728
广 东	Guangdong	54505	720	3834	2233	31	1	2201
广 西	Guangxi	29332	200	213	201	25		176
海 南	Hainan	5866	250	6	6	2		4
重 庆	Chongqing	14500	546	104	77		1	76
四 川	Sichuan	80906	1606	608	223	62	19	142
贵 州	Guizhou	19289	104	223	204	4	1	199
云 南	Yunnan	46816	232	874	765	91	20	654
西 藏	Tibet	275						
陕 西	Shaanxi	55396	202	782	414	1	19	394
甘 肃	Gansu	18385	104	349	347	52	28	267
青 海	Qinghai	20909	500	591	546	61	35	450
宁 夏	Ningxia	23558	450	183	152	4	10	138
新 疆	Xinjiang	37829	216	506	322	33	5	284
新疆兵团	Xinjiang Corps	4996	14	36	34	1		33
黑龙江垦区	Heilongjiang Land Reclamation	2352	11	104	104	23	48	33

1-12　续表 1　Continued 1

地 区	Region	假肢装配 Artificial Limbs Fitted	国家彩金项目装配 Fitted for PWDs by the National Lottery Project	大腿 Upper-knee Artificial Limbs Fitted	小腿 Lower-knee Artificial Limbs Fitted
		例 case	例 case	例 case	例 case
全　国	**Total**	**29447**	**21285**	**7810**	**9949**
北　京	Beijing	592	357	100	182
天　津	Tianjin	290	290	88	117
河　北	Hebei	896	837	336	388
山　西	Shanxi	395	90	35	55
内蒙古	Inner Mongolia	856	595	199	329
辽　宁	Liaoning	2097	1353	474	577
吉　林	Jilin	386	380	100	100
黑龙江	Heilongjiang	705	509	223	230
上　海	Shanghai	552			
江　苏	Jiangsu	1659	1070	395	459
浙　江	Zhejiang	1146	648	282	333
安　徽	Anhui	827	738	279	303
福　建	Fujian	480	332	131	116
江　西	Jiangxi	950	587	278	257
山　东	Shandong	1722	1123	449	590
河　南	Henan	92			
湖　北	Hubei	1311	1247	504	658
湖　南	Hunan	2373	1431	554	615
广　东	Guangdong	2599	1502	473	680
广　西	Guangxi	1224	1136	420	602
海　南	Hainan	464	374	72	143
重　庆	Chongqing	232	221	96	94
四　川	Sichuan	1597	1123	460	576
贵　州	Guizhou	813	734	284	359
云　南	Yunnan	1228	1016	308	538
西　藏	Tibet	60	8		8
陕　西	Shaanxi	1371	1196	497	500
甘　肃	Gansu	726	725	228	292
青　海	Qinghai	719	678	189	349
宁　夏	Ningxia	285	281	117	148
新　疆	Xinjiang	523	427	139	203
新疆兵团	Xinjiang Corps	102	102	42	60
黑龙江垦区	Heilongjiang Land Reclamation	175	175	58	88

1-12 续表 2 Continued 2

地 区	Region	膝离断 Knee From off	髋离断 Hip From off	功能性上肢 Functional Upper Limbs	装饰假手 Artificial Hands for Decoration Purpose
		例 case	例 case	例 case	例 case
全 国	**Total**	**764**	**481**	**786**	**1495**
北 京	Beijing	7	2	44	22
天 津	Tianjin	12	7	6	60
河 北	Hebei	31	10	22	50
山 西	Shanxi				
内蒙古	Inner Mongolia	31	13	10	13
辽 宁	Liaoning	35	17	168	82
吉 林	Jilin	34	46	36	64
黑龙江	Heilongjiang	8	5	35	8
上 海	Shanghai				
江 苏	Jiangsu	31	25	61	99
浙 江	Zhejiang	16	17		
安 徽	Anhui	40	24	33	59
福 建	Fujian	20	13	3	49
江 西	Jiangxi	15	7	5	25
山 东	Shandong	39	35	8	2
河 南	Henan				
湖 北	Hubei	29	18	11	27
湖 南	Hunan	60	45	45	112
广 东	Guangdong	38	32	38	241
广 西	Guangxi	6	9	11	88
海 南	Hainan	7	10	43	99
重 庆	Chongqing	26	5		
四 川	Sichuan	29	22	21	15
贵 州	Guizhou	70	21		
云 南	Yunnan	35	15	42	78
西 藏	Tibet				
陕 西	Shaanxi	55	36	23	85
甘 肃	Gansu	19	23	96	67
青 海	Qinghai	42	8	8	82
宁 夏	Ningxia	8	8		
新 疆	Xinjiang	13	3	12	57
新疆兵团	Xinjiang Corps				
黑龙江垦区	Heilongjiang Land Reclamation	8	5	5	11

1-12　续表 3　Continued 3

地区	Region	其他辅助器具供应 Other Assistive Devices Provided	国家彩金项目免费发放 Assistive Devices Provided to PWDs by the National Lottery Project				
				助视器 Vision-Aids	免费发放 Free of Charge	重度残疾人适配 Fitted for PWDs with Severe Disabilities	就学、就业适配 Fitted for PWDs of Schooling and Employment
		件 piece	件 piece	件 piece	件 piece	件 piece	件 piece
全　国	**Total**	**1206816**	**328984**	**125045**	**148667**	**49605**	**5667**
北　京	Beijing	8997	3988	1708	844	874	562
天　津	Tianjin	33000	5608	2012	1715	1378	503
河　北	Hebei	27337	21477	6442	12336	1882	817
山　西	Shanxi	17400	708	66	116	526	
内蒙古	Inner Mongolia	16131	4747	2370	1908	442	27
辽　宁	Liaoning	36715	23949	7988	5948	9827	186
吉　林	Jilin	9219	6654	4433	1407	726	88
黑龙江	Heilongjiang	12677	5914	3639	1759	479	37
上　海	Shanghai	165320					
江　苏	Jiangsu	90340	15845	6518	5797	2519	1011
浙　江	Zhejiang	26315	1821	989	832		
安　徽	Anhui	18041	12223	9320	1814	959	130
福　建	Fujian	18900	8181	4329	2544	1065	243
江　西	Jiangxi	13586	7563	1873	4643	848	199
山　东	Shandong	95087	14549	5956	8169	418	6
河　南	Henan	119031					
湖　北	Hubei	41020	20651	5863	13298	1275	215
湖　南	Hunan	63317	15131	5646	8059	1377	49
广　东	Guangdong	48072	7108	3831	2353	805	119
广　西	Guangxi	27895	22285	9674	7397	4821	393
海　南	Hainan	5396	3773	2387	1088	263	35
重　庆	Chongqing	14164	6998	4501	2497		
四　川	Sichuan	78701	18531	5532	11847	1096	56
贵　州	Guizhou	18253	8836	5527	3183	112	14
云　南	Yunnan	44714	20988	7318	11657	1880	133
西　藏	Tibet	215	80	20	60		
陕　西	Shaanxi	53243	21450	3100	7356	10955	39
甘　肃	Gansu	17310	8895	3235	3939	1043	678
青　海	Qinghai	19599	7004	1741	4773	487	3
宁　夏	Ningxia	23090	7458	831	6242	385	
新　疆	Xinjiang	36800	22374	6662	12605	3010	97
新疆兵团	Xinjiang Corps	4858	2122	1284	666	145	27
黑龙江垦区	Heilongjiang Land Reclamation	2073	2073	250	1815	8	

1-13 辅助器具供应服务机构
Assistive Devices Provision and Service Centers

地 区	Region	地市级机构 Assistive Devices Provision and Service Centers at Prefectural/city Level	本年度新建 Established in 2013	县级机构 Assistive Devices Provision and Service Centers at County Level	本年度新建 Established in 2013
		个 unit	个 unit	个 unit	个 unit
全 国	**Total**	**214**	**27**	**913**	**116**
北 京	Beijing			7	
天 津	Tianjin			11	3
河 北	Hebei	11	3	53	2
山 西	Shanxi	7		34	1
内蒙古	Inner Mongolia	6	2	27	3
辽 宁	Liaoning	14		93	3
吉 林	Jilin	8		35	2
黑龙江	Heilongjiang	6		9	1
上 海	Shanghai			15	2
江 苏	Jiangsu	10	3	49	1
浙 江	Zhejiang	8		29	5
安 徽	Anhui	5		5	3
福 建	Fujian	10	2	34	11
江 西	Jiangxi	5		16	1
山 东	Shandong	17	3	63	8
河 南	Henan	12	2	30	4
湖 北	Hubei	7	1	29	8
湖 南	Hunan	14	1	82	11
广 东	Guangdong	19		63	5
广 西	Guangxi	7	1	12	2
海 南	Hainan				
重 庆	Chongqing			27	3
四 川	Sichuan	7	1	23	9
贵 州	Guizhou	3	1	13	5
云 南	Yunnan	10	1	41	3
西 藏	Tibet	1	1		
陕 西	Shaanxi	7	2	19	6
甘 肃	Gansu	8	1	58	7
青 海	Qinghai	3	1	7	3
宁 夏	Ningxia	1	1	4	1
新 疆	Xinjiang	5		21	3
新疆兵团	Xinjiang Corps	1			
黑龙江垦区	Heilongjiang Land Reclamation	2		4	

1-14　儿童残疾预防
Disability Prevention for Children

地　区	Region	残疾儿童筛查 Screening for Children with Disabilities						
		开展残疾儿童筛查工作县 Counties Which has Developed the Screening for Children with Disabilities	开展残疾儿童筛查工作的医疗卫生机构 Medical Care Institutions Which has Developed the Screening for Children with Disabilities	省级 at Provincial Level	地市级 at Prefectural/City Level	县级 at County Level	本年度新诊断0-6岁残疾儿童 Children with Disabilities Newly Diagnosed from 0-6 Years Old in 2013	视力残疾儿童 Children with Visual Disability
		个 unit	个 unit	个 unit	个 unit	个 unit	人 person	人 person
全　国	**Total**	**1458**	**1844**	**12**	**146**	**1686**	**50037**	**4912**
北　京	Beijing	14	26			26	443	9
天　津	Tianjin	16	15	1	0	14	311	19
河　北	Hebei	37	41		3	38	1485	81
山　西	Shanxi	87	106	8	15	83	1374	136
内蒙古	Inner Mongolia	22	25		0	25	271	22
辽　宁	Liaoning	42	25		10	15	1019	53
吉　林	Jilin	25	25		3	22	466	62
黑龙江	Heilongjiang	55	33		1	32	780	52
上　海	Shanghai	17	274	2	0	272	1191	412
江　苏	Jiangsu	104	140		4	136	4525	775
浙　江	Zhejiang	49	114		2	112	982	22
安　徽	Anhui	70	38		4	34	4759	312
福　建	Fujian	11	11		1	10	980	28
江　西	Jiangxi	19	36			36	2461	908
山　东	Shandong	108	133		1	132	5696	235
河　南	Henan	10	2		0	2	230	20
湖　北	Hubei	48	70		10	60	1835	102
湖　南	Hunan	64	88		9	79	3056	465
广　东	Guangdong	41	169		51	118	3175	118
广　西	Guangxi	48	32		0	32	2373	114
海　南	Hainan	3	0		0	0	209	9
重　庆	Chongqing	40	125			125	2777	140
四　川	Sichuan	71	82		1	81	4256	410
贵　州	Guizhou	19	8		1	7	534	42
云　南	Yunnan	79	51		1	50	2146	170
西　藏	Tibet	10	2		0	2	78	2
陕　西	Shaanxi	23	29		3	26	1018	88
甘　肃	Gansu	63	33		1	32	613	63
青　海	Qinghai	16	42		2	40	255	17
宁　夏	Ningxia	9	10		2	8	210	8
新　疆	Xinjiang	8	9			9	134	9
新疆兵团	Xinjiang Corps	127	42	1	13	28	385	9
黑龙江垦区	Heilongjiang Land Reclamation	103	8		8		10	

1-14 续表 1 Continued 1

地 区	Region	本年度新诊断0-6岁残疾儿童 Children with Disabilities Newly Diagnosed from 0-6 Years Old in 2013					
		听力残疾儿童 Children with Hearing Disability	言语残疾儿童 Children with Speech Disability	肢体残疾儿童 Children with Physical Disability	智力残疾儿童 Children with Intellectual Disability	精神残疾儿童 Children with Psychiatric Disability	多重残疾儿童 Children with Multiple Disability
		人 person	人 person	人 person	人 person	人 person	人 person
全 国	**Total**	**7538**	**3636**	**15518**	**9776**	**3470**	**5187**
北 京	Beijing	105	4	90	129	64	42
天 津	Tianjin	79	28	75	79	22	9
河 北	Hebei	391	154	482	250	33	94
山 西	Shanxi	218	149	420	238	49	164
内蒙古	Inner Mongolia	32	18	75	57	14	53
辽 宁	Liaoning	404	43	259	164	56	40
吉 林	Jilin	145	64	113	71	4	7
黑龙江	Heilongjiang	133	34	256	140	125	40
上 海	Shanghai	66	16	459	95	136	7
江 苏	Jiangsu	650	193	1037	533	300	1037
浙 江	Zhejiang	249	31	232	290	89	69
安 徽	Anhui	878	355	1564	723	362	565
福 建	Fujian	115	43	267	383	42	102
江 西	Jiangxi	229	266	441	406	91	120
山 东	Shandong	737	295	2113	1218	517	581
河 南	Henan	32	23	65	35	17	38
湖 北	Hubei	259	152	706	368	95	153
湖 南	Hunan	430	275	761	576	228	321
广 东	Guangdong	338	168	1059	732	358	402
广 西	Guangxi	385	214	782	522	81	275
海 南	Hainan	40	23	45	45	22	25
重 庆	Chongqing	362	193	1000	708	205	169
四 川	Sichuan	570	378	1362	951	312	273
贵 州	Guizhou	63	39	162	89	79	60
云 南	Yunnan	247	223	777	440	37	252
西 藏	Tibet	7	11	36	11	11	11
陕 西	Shaanxi	204	130	303	140	62	91
甘 肃	Gansu	86	56	163	111	28	106
青 海	Qinghai	28	23	73	80	9	25
宁 夏	Ningxia	17	16	46	69	26	28
新 疆	Xinjiang	13	8	49	42	3	10
新疆兵团	Xinjiang Corps	24	9	242	79	4	18
黑龙江垦区	Heilongjiang Land Reclamation	2	2	4	2		

1-14 续表 2 Continued 2

地 区	Region	儿童残疾预防宣传 Prevention of Children with Disability		残疾儿童家长学校 Schools for Training Parents of Children with Disabilities			
		发放儿童残疾预防宣传材料 Distributed Advocacy Materials	举办儿童残疾预防宣传活动 Advocacy Activities Holded	残疾儿童家长学校累计数 Total	省级 at Provincial Level	地市级 at Prefectural/ City Level	县级 at County Level
		份 piece	次 time	个 unit	个 unit	个 unit	个 unit
全 国	**Total**	**2694324**	**4168**	**1200**	**25**	**115**	**1060**
北 京	Beijing	35895	84	45	1		44
天 津	Tianjin	17133	23	5	4		1
河 北	Hebei	212884	199	41	1	10	30
山 西	Shanxi	75320	76	57	3	15	39
内蒙古	Inner Mongolia	9292	11	4	1		3
辽 宁	Liaoning	49627	47	33	2	16	15
吉 林	Jilin	8970	23	18	2	8	8
黑龙江	Heilongjiang	16897	67	10		1	9
上 海	Shanghai	154673	296	113	2		111
江 苏	Jiangsu	225219	308	64	1	4	59
浙 江	Zhejiang	78353	154	73		6	67
安 徽	Anhui	141458	282	43	1	2	40
福 建	Fujian	16315	65	5	1		4
江 西	Jiangxi	59304	18	5			5
山 东	Shandong	280358	533	89		9	80
河 南	Henan	1210	1	2		1	1
湖 北	Hubei	83150	111	7			7
湖 南	Hunan	129644	111	42		10	32
广 东	Guangdong	99523	116	41	1	24	16
广 西	Guangxi	95879	61	6		1	5
海 南	Hainan	200	2				
重 庆	Chongqing	198678	177	43	4		39
四 川	Sichuan	182879	200	426		1	425
贵 州	Guizhou	60934	346	2			2
云 南	Yunnan	148525	156	5		1	4
西 藏	Tibet	1120	7				
陕 西	Shaanxi	90700	90	2		2	
甘 肃	Gansu	141578	373				
青 海	Qinghai	16209	35	7			7
宁 夏	Ningxia	32150	25	11	1	4	6
新 疆	Xinjiang	8127	38	1			1
新疆兵团	Xinjiang Corps	20715	118				
黑龙江垦区	Heilongjiang Land Reclamation	1405	15				

1-14 续表 3 Continued 3

地 区	Region	残疾儿童家长学校 Schools for Training Parents of Children with Disabilities							
		本年度开展家长学校活动 Activities Holded for Parents of Children with Disabilities in 2013	省级 at Provincial Level	地市级 at Prefectural/ City Level	县级 at County Level	本年度残疾儿童家长参与人数 Parents of Children with Disabilities Participating in 2013	省级 at Provincial Level	地市级 at Prefectural/ City Level	县级 at County Level
		次 time	次 time	次 time	次 time	人次 person time	人次 person time	人次 person time	人次 person time
全 国	**Total**	**2137**	**291**	**319**	**1527**	**77061**	**19669**	**10320**	**47072**
北 京	Beijing	340	76		264	14994	4732		10262
天 津	Tianjin	31	30		1	1025	1000		25
河 北	Hebei	75	3	15	57	3389	180	1440	1769
山 西	Shanxi	158	30	55	73	2668	500	806	1362
内蒙古	Inner Mongolia	5	1		4	467	350		117
辽 宁	Liaoning	66	2	44	20	1487	362	834	291
吉 林	Jilin	45	12	14	19	3005	950	985	1070
黑龙江	Heilongjiang	10		1	9	113		55	58
上 海	Shanghai	230	7		223	7001	458		6543
江 苏	Jiangsu	189	5	27	157	6544	80	854	5610
浙 江	Zhejiang	180		34	146	4375		999	3376
安 徽	Anhui	105	35	3	67	6788	5000	98	1690
福 建	Fujian	49	30		19	960	800		160
江 西	Jiangxi	10			10	470			470
山 东	Shandong	186		9	177	4887		263	4624
河 南	Henan	1			1	50			50
湖 北	Hubei	16			16	844			844
湖 南	Hunan	118		60	58	4091		2294	1797
广 东	Guangdong	141	53	32	56	6016	3947	919	1150
广 西	Guangxi	7		1	6	325		7	318
海 南	Hainan								
重 庆	Chongqing	76	6		70	1854	360		1494
四 川	Sichuan	46		1	45	3267		126	3141
贵 州	Guizhou	2			2	42			42
云 南	Yunnan	9		3	6	350		100	250
西 藏	Tibet								
陕 西	Shaanxi	10		10		330		330	
甘 肃	Gansu					30		30	
青 海	Qinghai	4			4	223			223
宁 夏	Ningxia	27	1	10	16	1465	950	180	335
新 疆	Xinjiang	1			1	1			1
新疆兵团	Xinjiang Corps								
黑龙江垦区	Heilongjiang Land Reclamation								

1-15　康复人才

Rehabilitation Professionals

地　区	Region	康复机构在岗人员 Staff of Rehabilitation Institutions	省级 Staff of Rehabilitation Institutions at Provincial Level	业务人员 Professionals	管理人员 Managerial Personnels	其他人员 Other Staff Members
		人 person	人 person	人 person	人 person	人 person
全　国	**Total**	**216250**	**13903**	**9827**	**2135**	**1941**
北　京	Beijing	2999	86	61	18	7
天　津	Tianjin	2363	146	116	21	9
河　北	Hebei	7118	455	339	51	65
山　西	Shanxi	9095	271	163	53	55
内蒙古	Inner Mongolia	4091	1792	1073	438	281
辽　宁	Liaoning	11096	2912	2315	538	59
吉　林	Jilin	8379	778	539	125	114
黑龙江	Heilongjiang	6534	368	223	50	95
上　海	Shanghai	4160	499	304	89	106
江　苏	Jiangsu	10724	72	45	11	16
浙　江	Zhejiang	4000	160	80	15	65
安　徽	Anhui	5693	116	75	16	25
福　建	Fujian	7635	241	156	28	57
江　西	Jiangxi	4450	31	18	6	7
山　东	Shandong	24341	101	70	11	20
河　南	Henan	11357	102	40	28	34
湖　北	Hubei	9078	39	30	5	4
湖　南	Hunan	12030	475	385	35	55
广　东	Guangdong	22866	330	206	37	87
广　西	Guangxi	4746	120	92	22	6
海　南	Hainan	187	134	94	19	21
重　庆	Chongqing	5668	66	23	36	7
四　川	Sichuan	8874	993	677	166	150
贵　州	Guizhou	7075	333	244	40	49
云　南	Yunnan	4653	137	94	19	24
西　藏	Tibet	61	54	35	11	8
陕　西	Shaanxi	8940	1581	1013	136	432
甘　肃	Gansu	1988	565	516	29	20
青　海	Qinghai	136	38	23	9	6
宁　夏	Ningxia	360	71	56	8	7
新　疆	Xinjiang	4501	641	565	41	35
新疆兵团	Xinjiang Corps	703	33	12	6	15
黑龙江垦区	Heilongjiang Land Reclamation	349	163	145	18	

1-15 续表 1 Continued 1

地 区	Region	康复机构在岗人员 Staff of Rehabilitation Institutions			
		地市级康复机构在岗人员 Staff of Rehabilitation Institutions at Prefectural/City Level	业务人员 Professionals	管理人员 Managerial Personnels	其他人员 Other Staff Members
		人 person	人 person	人 person	人 person
全 国	**Total**	**71293**	**49613**	**9100**	**12580**
北 京	Beijing				
天 津	Tianjin	74	35	12	27
河 北	Hebei	3431	2415	520	496
山 西	Shanxi	4599	3407	537	655
内蒙古	Inner Mongolia	1233	840	170	223
辽 宁	Liaoning	2562	1653	377	532
吉 林	Jilin	4293	2806	831	656
黑龙江	Heilongjiang	4520	3208	714	598
上 海	Shanghai				
江 苏	Jiangsu	2337	1495	430	412
浙 江	Zhejiang	1420	818	275	327
安 徽	Anhui	2878	1523	430	925
福 建	Fujian	2187	1780	225	182
江 西	Jiangxi	1283	761	159	363
山 东	Shandong	7984	6058	898	1028
河 南	Henan	4588	3146	454	988
湖 北	Hubei	3713	2857	441	415
湖 南	Hunan	5768	3764	603	1401
广 东	Guangdong	4898	3333	565	1000
广 西	Guangxi	1956	1600	121	235
海 南	Hainan				
重 庆	Chongqing				
四 川	Sichuan	1507	874	248	385
贵 州	Guizhou	2623	1927	429	267
云 南	Yunnan	2518	1559	198	761
西 藏	Tibet	7	3	1	3
陕 西	Shaanxi	1790	1278	239	273
甘 肃	Gansu	515	373	72	70
青 海	Qinghai	29	15	5	9
宁 夏	Ningxia	117	80	12	25
新 疆	Xinjiang	2118	1770	103	245
新疆兵团	Xinjiang Corps	242	193	7	42
黑龙江垦区	Heilongjiang Land Reclamation	103	42	24	37

1-15 续表 2 Continued 2

地 区	Region	康复机构在岗人员 Staff of Rehabilitation Institutions			
		县级康复机构在岗人员 Staff of Rehabilitation Institutions at County Level	业务人员 Professionals	管理人员 Managerial Personnels	其他人员 Other Staff Members
		人 person	人 person	人 person	人 person
全 国	**Total**	**131054**	**83036**	**18077**	**29941**
北 京	Beijing	2913	2120	422	371
天 津	Tianjin	2143	1217	198	728
河 北	Hebei	3232	1981	716	535
山 西	Shanxi	4225	2799	455	971
内蒙古	Inner Mongolia	1066	648	185	233
辽 宁	Liaoning	5622	3149	723	1750
吉 林	Jilin	3308	1670	615	1023
黑龙江	Heilongjiang	1646	1104	211	331
上 海	Shanghai	3661	2300	703	658
江 苏	Jiangsu	8315	5525	1022	1768
浙 江	Zhejiang	2420	1513	314	593
安 徽	Anhui	2699	1412	518	769
福 建	Fujian	5207	2906	654	1647
江 西	Jiangxi	3136	1781	386	969
山 东	Shandong	16256	11990	1788	2478
河 南	Henan	6667	4512	853	1302
湖 北	Hubei	5326	3637	698	991
湖 南	Hunan	5787	3711	991	1085
广 东	Guangdong	17638	11831	2755	3052
广 西	Guangxi	2670	1761	305	604
海 南	Hainan	53	36	8	9
重 庆	Chongqing	5602	3805	855	942
四 川	Sichuan	6374	3037	762	2575
贵 州	Guizhou	4119	1601	323	2195
云 南	Yunnan	1998	1282	269	447
西 藏	Tibet				
陕 西	Shaanxi	5569	3768	773	1028
甘 肃	Gansu	908	466	163	279
青 海	Qinghai	69	39	17	13
宁 夏	Ningxia	172	98	37	37
新 疆	Xinjiang	1742	1055	225	462
新疆兵团	Xinjiang Corps	428	246	102	80
黑龙江垦区	Heilongjiang Land Reclamation	83	36	31	16

1-15 续表 3 Continued 3

地 区	Region	康复人才培训情况 Training for Staff of Rehabilitation Institutions					
		本年度举办康复管理人员培训班 Training Courses for Rehabilitation Managerial Staff in 2013	培训康复管理人员 Rehabilitation Managerial Staff Trained	本年度举办康复业务人员培训班 Training Courses for Rehabilitation Professionals in 2013	培训康复业务人员 Rehabilitation Professionals Trained	本年度举办社区康复协调员培训班 Training Courses for Community-Based Rehabilitation Coordinators in 2013	培训社区康复协调员 Community-Based Rehabilitation Coordinators Trained
		期 course	人 person	期 course	人 person	期 course	人 person
全 国	**Total**	**1760**	**24690**	**2241**	**54536**	**3217**	**177212**
北 京	Beijing	23	1966	23	1107	82	5780
天 津	Tianjin	12	262	9	165	16	1355
河 北	Hebei	111	990	113	1879	149	6555
山 西	Shanxi	48	689	51	1389	110	4533
内蒙古	Inner Mongolia	36	248	48	418	78	4981
辽 宁	Liaoning	111	1943	117	2605	182	9204
吉 林	Jilin	60	667	67	1093	81	5269
黑龙江	Heilongjiang	28	177	36	353	82	1737
上 海	Shanghai	98	761	127	4015	58	5613
江 苏	Jiangsu	92	1719	145	4997	191	14083
浙 江	Zhejiang	43	737	91	2467	74	7860
安 徽	Anhui	50	1622	67	3287	87	8371
福 建	Fujian	35	523	39	964	64	3384
江 西	Jiangxi	43	485	75	826	78	2775
山 东	Shandong	206	2684	252	6801	257	22230
河 南	Henan	30	289	31	1157	144	7156
湖 北	Hubei	38	277	43	611	262	4948
湖 南	Hunan	65	1001	90	2197	184	7297
广 东	Guangdong	129	2144	225	6167	117	11606
广 西	Guangxi	31	613	32	1208	60	4291
海 南	Hainan	23	94	6	20	21	760
重 庆	Chongqing	48	606	59	1805	76	6882
四 川	Sichuan	80	1024	126	2371	170	8614
贵 州	Guizhou	24	303	29	638	41	1926
云 南	Yunnan	105	1144	132	3093	128	9212
西 藏	Tibet	1	1	5	187	1	6
陕 西	Shaanxi	50	880	42	1183	96	4592
甘 肃	Gansu	38	155	46	390	147	2127
青 海	Qinghai	49	186	42	336	69	904
宁 夏	Ningxia	10	159	8	151	17	647
新 疆	Xinjiang	31	296	51	560	85	2167
新疆兵团	Xinjiang Corps			2	50	2	203
黑龙江垦区	Heilongjiang Land Reclamation	12	45	12	46	8	144

2-1　学前教育阶段

Pre-school Rehabilitation and Education

地　区	Region	残疾人事业专项彩票公益金助学项目资助 Support of Educational Project Funded by Dedicated Welfare Lottery Fund in 2013	视力残疾 Children with Visual Disability	听力残疾 Children with Hearing Disability	言语残疾 Children with Speech Disability	肢体残疾 Children with Physical Disability
		人 person	人 person	人 person	人 person	人 person
全　国	**Total**	**10468**	**350**	**2724**	**554**	**1724**
北　京	Beijing	143	1	23	4	16
天　津	Tianjin	100	3	42	4	4
河　北	Hebei	600	3	149	22	93
山　西	Shanxi	260	6	87	25	27
内蒙古	Inner Mongolia	292	23	42	17	110
辽　宁	Liaoning	472	19	93	9	92
吉　林	Jilin	260	13	17	15	33
黑龙江	Heilongjiang	300	6	51	9	72
上　海	Shanghai					
江　苏	Jiangsu	720	8	306	14	45
浙　江	Zhejiang	531	17	214	7	92
安　徽	Anhui	300		95	14	44
福　建	Fujian	400	14	108	8	72
江　西	Jiangxi	315	1	97	22	16
山　东	Shandong	895	34	169	38	171
河　南	Henan	710	59	188	85	57
湖　北	Hubei	500	13	75	33	100
湖　南	Hunan	400	5	155	22	22
广　东	Guangdong	550	20	79	24	181
广　西	Guangxi	393	15	96	24	35
海　南	Hainan	78	2	9	14	20
重　庆	Chongqing	200	8	36	20	24
四　川	Sichuan	758	40	205	26	145
贵　州	Guizhou	241	9	30	17	61
云　南	Yunnan	266	2	51	31	20
西　藏	Tibet	30	15	4	6	1
陕　西	Shaanxi	200		146	7	
甘　肃	Gansu	170	3	21	11	79
青　海	Qinghai	74	2	19	1	28
宁　夏	Ningxia	60	4	4	3	23
新　疆	Xinjiang	200	2	108	20	11
新疆兵团	Xinjiang Corps	30	3	5	2	13
黑龙江垦区	Heilongjiang Land Reclamation	20				17

2-1 续表 Continued

地 区	Region	智力残疾 Chidren with Intellectual Disability	精神残疾 Children with Psychiatric Disability	多重残疾 Children with Multi-disabilities	其他残疾儿童学前教育助学项目资助 Support of Other Pre-School Educational Project for Disabled Children in 2013
		人 person	人 person	人 person	人 person
全 国	**Total**	**2624**	**807**	**1685**	**3489**
北 京	Beijing	36	41	22	
天 津	Tianjin	46		1	40
河 北	Hebei	179	49	105	
山 西	Shanxi	57	6	52	
内蒙古	Inner Mongolia	46	15	39	13
辽 宁	Liaoning	141	80	38	23
吉 林	Jilin	89	78	15	
黑龙江	Heilongjiang	86	52	24	12
上 海	Shanghai				
江 苏	Jiangsu	184	51	112	27
浙 江	Zhejiang	104	73	24	399
安 徽	Anhui	50	13	84	61
福 建	Fujian	100	31	67	59
江 西	Jiangxi	78	4	97	3
山 东	Shandong	218	115	150	271
河 南	Henan	221	13	87	
湖 北	Hubei	182	14	83	25
湖 南	Hunan	85	17	94	96
广 东	Guangdong	115	57	74	444
广 西	Guangxi	118	4	101	94
海 南	Hainan	17	1	15	
重 庆	Chongqing	75	3	34	64
四 川	Sichuan	217	12	113	1107
贵 州	Guizhou	41	31	52	62
云 南	Yunnan	59	39	64	12
西 藏	Tibet			4	
陕 西	Shaanxi			47	67
甘 肃	Gansu	29	2	25	253
青 海	Qinghai	13		11	279
宁 夏	Ningxia	16	3	7	69
新 疆	Xinjiang	15	2	42	4
新疆兵团	Xinjiang Corps	6	1		5
黑龙江垦区	Heilongjiang Land Reclamation	1		2	

2-2 义务教育阶段未入学学龄残疾儿童少年

School-age Children with Disabilities Unable to Enter Schools

地 区	Region	未入学学龄残疾儿童少年 School-age Children with Disabilities Unable to Enter Schools	视力残疾 Children with Visual Disability	听力残疾 Children with Hearing Disability	言语残疾 Children with Speech Disability
		人 person	人 person	人 person	人 person
全 国	**Total**	**83532**	**5015**	**5445**	**5067**
北 京	Beijing	243	3	1	1
天 津	Tianjin	445	9	16	13
河 北	Hebei	1135	45	72	69
山 西	Shanxi	2481	122	181	163
内蒙古	Inner Mongolia	1576	56	62	83
辽 宁	Liaoning	2094	67	104	59
吉 林	Jilin	2896	78	133	148
黑龙江	Heilongjiang	1037	40	57	33
上 海	Shanghai	9			
江 苏	Jiangsu	1435	52	129	16
浙 江	Zhejiang	526	10	33	8
安 徽	Anhui	5034	153	262	217
福 建	Fujian	1474	44	95	33
江 西	Jiangxi	5234	538	563	449
山 东	Shandong	3752	262	154	126
河 南	Henan	7948	377	610	591
湖 北	Hubei	2461	178	204	125
湖 南	Hunan	5839	276	232	327
广 东	Guangdong	4303	154	160	180
广 西	Guangxi	4804	228	240	386
海 南	Hainan	443	18	13	35
重 庆	Chongqing	943	59	47	56
四 川	Sichuan	4436	381	310	322
贵 州	Guizhou	4427	666	564	424
云 南	Yunnan	4878	306	316	392
西 藏	Tibet	178	20	13	26
陕 西	Shaanxi	4017	316	398	216
甘 肃	Gansu	3137	194	186	170
青 海	Qinghai	928	61	61	51
宁 夏	Ningxia	1021	72	46	56
新 疆	Xinjiang	4183	224	177	279
新疆兵团	Xinjiang Corps	49	4	1	2
黑龙江垦区	Heilongjiang Land Reclamation	166	2	5	11

2-2 续表 Continued

地 区	Region	肢体残疾 Children with Physical Disability	智力残疾 Chidren with Intellectual Disability	精神残疾 Children with Psychiatric Disability	多重残疾 Children with Multi-disabilities
		人 person	人 person	人 person	人 person
全 国	**Total**	**25782**	**26434**	**3413**	**12376**
北 京	Beijing	72	112	18	36
天 津	Tianjin	150	230	1	26
河 北	Hebei	439	362	22	126
山 西	Shanxi	761	887	62	305
内蒙古	Inner Mongolia	482	516	67	310
辽 宁	Liaoning	716	805	145	198
吉 林	Jilin	907	1136	202	292
黑龙江	Heilongjiang	292	400	82	133
上 海	Shanghai	5	3		1
江 苏	Jiangsu	478	642	33	85
浙 江	Zhejiang	172	217	21	65
安 徽	Anhui	1429	1757	283	933
福 建	Fujian	392	682	76	152
江 西	Jiangxi	1176	1536	251	721
山 东	Shandong	1105	1408	210	487
河 南	Henan	2994	2619	98	659
湖 北	Hubei	799	654	102	399
湖 南	Hunan	2114	1595	163	1132
广 东	Guangdong	1123	1546	346	794
广 西	Guangxi	1395	1302	144	1109
海 南	Hainan	126	132	24	95
重 庆	Chongqing	312	389	33	47
四 川	Sichuan	1548	1295	105	475
贵 州	Guizhou	1026	1006	240	501
云 南	Yunnan	1577	1241	95	951
西 藏	Tibet	74	10	7	28
陕 西	Shaanxi	1201	1048	173	665
甘 肃	Gansu	1106	829	123	529
青 海	Qinghai	309	296	15	135
宁 夏	Ningxia	262	383	37	165
新 疆	Xinjiang	1171	1304	224	804
新疆兵团	Xinjiang Corps	16	14	5	7
黑龙江垦区	Heilongjiang Land Reclamation	53	78	6	11

2-3 高中教育阶段
Senior High Education

地 区	Region	特殊教育普通高中学校(班) Special Education Senior High Schools/classes	盲普通高中 Senior High Schools for Blind Students	聋普通高中 Senior High Schools for Deaf Students	其他 Others	学生 Students 招生 Newly Enrolled Studnets with Disabilities	盲 Students with Visual Disability	聋 Students with Hearing Disability
		个 unit	个 unit	个 unit	个 unit	人 person	人 person	人 person
全 国	**Total**	**194**	**27**	**125**	**42**	**2706**	**340**	**2366**
北 京	Beijing	2	1	1		1	1	
天 津	Tianjin	2	1	1		38	13	25
河 北	Hebei	13	2	11		233	50	183
山 西	Shanxi	5	1	4		217	40	177
内蒙古	Inner Mongolia	6		3	3	76	5	71
辽 宁	Liaoning	11	2	8	1	38	6	32
吉 林	Jilin	4		4		23		23
黑龙江	Heilongjiang	1		1				
上 海	Shanghai	1	1			9	9	
江 苏	Jiangsu	4		4		144	5	139
浙 江	Zhejiang	4		4		63		63
安 徽	Anhui	3		3		181	7	174
福 建	Fujian	26	6	13	7	204	10	194
江 西	Jiangxi	4		4		60		60
山 东	Shandong	23	1	16	6	371	22	349
河 南	Henan	5	1	3	1	105	10	95
湖 北	Hubei	8		7	1	170		170
湖 南	Hunan	14	2	9	3	245	8	237
广 东	Guangdong	8		5	3	51	4	47
广 西	Guangxi	11	3	7	1	44	5	39
海 南	Hainan	8			8			
重 庆	Chongqing	2	1	1		74	72	2
四 川	Sichuan	13	1	5	7	82	12	70
贵 州	Guizhou	6		5	1	73	11	62
云 南	Yunnan							
西 藏	Tibet							
陕 西	Shaanxi	3	1	2		30		30
甘 肃	Gansu	3	2	1		122	31	91
青 海	Qinghai	2		2		17	14	3
宁 夏	Ningxia	1	1			13	5	8
新 疆	Xinjiang	1		1		22		22
新疆兵团	Xinjiang Corps							
黑龙江垦区	Heilongjiang Land Reclamation							

2-3 续表 1 Continued 1

地区	Region	学生 Students					
		在校生 Students at Schools	盲 Students with Visual Disability	聋 Students with Hearing Disability	毕业生 Graduates	盲 Students with Visual Disability	聋 Students with Hearing Disability
		人 person	人 person	人 person	人 person	人 person	人 person
全国	**Total**	**7313**	**1609**	**5704**	**1826**	**286**	**1540**
北京	Beijing	114	16	98	33	1	32
天津	Tianjin	134	29	105	58	7	51
河北	Hebei	461	101	360	125	20	105
山西	Shanxi	391	32	359	124	35	89
内蒙古	Inner Mongolia	96	7	89	30	8	22
辽宁	Liaoning	166	22	144	38	7	31
吉林	Jilin	41		41	12		12
黑龙江	Heilongjiang						
上海	Shanghai	186	186		10	10	
江苏	Jiangsu	397	5	392	114		114
浙江	Zhejiang	182		182	50		50
安徽	Anhui	421	7	414	117		117
福建	Fujian	734	108	626	193	12	181
江西	Jiangxi	140		140	40	6	34
山东	Shandong	632	41	591	132	9	123
河南	Henan	243	26	217	113	10	103
湖北	Hubei	334		334	84	1	83
湖南	Hunan	335	16	319	160	7	153
广东	Guangdong	140	15	125	43	4	39
广西	Guangxi	261	40	221	38	2	36
海南	Hainan	610	610		103	103	
重庆	Chongqing	201	193	8	24	22	2
四川	Sichuan	219	58	161	61	12	49
贵州	Guizhou	212	14	198	45		45
云南	Yunnan						
西藏	Tibet						
陕西	Shaanxi	106	8	98	17		17
甘肃	Gansu	165	40	125	40	10	30
青海	Qinghai	54		54	2		2
宁夏	Ningxia	281	35	246	10		10
新疆	Xinjiang	57		57	10		10
新疆兵团	Xinjiang Corps						
黑龙江垦区	Heilongjiang Land Reclamation						

2-3　续表 2　Continued 2

地　区	Region	残疾人中等职业学校(班) Secondary Vocational Schools/classes for PWDs	教育部门办 Established by Education Administrative Departments	残联部门办 Established by Disabled Persons' Federations	其他 Others
		个 unit	个 unit	个 unit	个 unit
全　国	**Total**	**198**	**141**	**27**	**30**
北　京	Beijing	3	3		
天　津	Tianjin	1		1	
河　北	Hebei	3	2		1
山　西	Shanxi	1			1
内蒙古	Inner Mongolia	8	5	1	2
辽　宁	Liaoning	9	7	1	1
吉　林	Jilin	5	5		
黑龙江	Heilongjiang	7	4		3
上　海	Shanghai	2	2		
江　苏	Jiangsu	15	14	1	
浙　江	Zhejiang	16	9	4	3
安　徽	Anhui	6	5	1	
福　建	Fujian	7	6		1
江　西	Jiangxi	2	2		
山　东	Shandong	22	14	4	4
河　南	Henan	7	7		
湖　北	Hubei	8	2	1	5
湖　南	Hunan	21	10	8	3
广　东	Guangdong	8	6	2	
广　西	Guangxi	7	5		2
海　南	Hainan	2	2		
重　庆	Chongqing	5	4		1
四　川	Sichuan	10	9		1
贵　州	Guizhou	1	1		
云　南	Yunnan	5	4	1	
西　藏	Tibet				
陕　西	Shaanxi	8	5	1	2
甘　肃	Gansu	4	4		
青　海	Qinghai	2	2		
宁　夏	Ningxia	1	1		
新　疆	Xinjiang	2	1	1	
新疆兵团	Xinjiang Corps				
黑龙江垦区	Heilongjiang Land Reclamation				

2-3 续表 3 Continued 3

地 区	Region	残疾人中等职业学校(班)学生 Students of Secondary Vocational Schools/classes for PWDs			
		招生 Newly Enrolled Students	盲 Students with Visual Disability	聋 Students with Hearing Disability	肢残 Students with Physical Disability
		人 person	人 person	人 person	人 person
全 国	**Total**	**5355**	**1323**	**1905**	**2127**
北 京	Beijing	55	41	14	
天 津	Tianjin				
河 北	Hebei	101	40	10	51
山 西	Shanxi	115	100		15
内蒙古	Inner Mongolia	13	1	5	7
辽 宁	Liaoning	84	45	39	
吉 林	Jilin	216	160	56	
黑龙江	Heilongjiang	65	2	55	8
上 海	Shanghai	31		31	
江 苏	Jiangsu	414	49	321	44
浙 江	Zhejiang	218	14	181	23
安 徽	Anhui	288	82	111	95
福 建	Fujian	24	9	13	2
江 西	Jiangxi	44	8	16	20
山 东	Shandong	513	172	226	115
河 南	Henan	116	34	73	9
湖 北	Hubei	103	20	7	76
湖 南	Hunan	419	86	157	176
广 东	Guangdong	229	95	53	81
广 西	Guangxi	62	1	31	30
海 南	Hainan	4			4
重 庆	Chongqing	165	47	30	88
四 川	Sichuan	81		29	52
贵 州	Guizhou				
云 南	Yunnan	306	79	132	95
西 藏	Tibet				
陕 西	Shaanxi	1548	183	269	1096
甘 肃	Gansu	35		30	5
青 海	Qinghai				
宁 夏	Ningxia				
新 疆	Xinjiang	106	55	16	35
新疆兵团	Xinjiang Corps				
黑龙江垦区	Heilongjiang Land Reclamation				

2-3　续表 4　Continued 4

地　区	Region	残疾人中等职业学校(班)学生 Students of Secondary Vocational Schools/classes for PWDs			
		在校学生 Students at Schools	盲 Students with Visual Disability	聋 Students with Hearing Disability	肢残 Students with Physical Disability
		人 person	人 person	人 person	人 person
全　国	**Total**	**11350**	**2916**	**5101**	**3333**
北　京	Beijing	213	98	115	
天　津	Tianjin				
河　北	Hebei	91	38	8	45
山　西	Shanxi	286	256		30
内蒙古	Inner Mongolia	213	102	88	23
辽　宁	Liaoning	301	219	82	
吉　林	Jilin	483	319	164	
黑龙江	Heilongjiang	101	2	86	13
上　海	Shanghai	163		163	
江　苏	Jiangsu	1015	171	678	166
浙　江	Zhejiang	683	30	601	52
安　徽	Anhui	660	197	236	227
福　建	Fujian	42	11	29	2
江　西	Jiangxi	128	23	40	65
山　东	Shandong	1315	399	659	257
河　南	Henan	270	75	179	16
湖　北	Hubei	160	20	26	114
湖　南	Hunan	1091	288	428	375
广　东	Guangdong	855	221	300	334
广　西	Guangxi	169	3	77	89
海　南	Hainan	4			4
重　庆	Chongqing	247	42	81	124
四　川	Sichuan	249	30	49	170
贵　州	Guizhou	13		13	
云　南	Yunnan	580	70	308	202
西　藏	Tibet				
陕　西	Shaanxi	1399	141	576	682
甘　肃	Gansu	45	14	30	1
青　海	Qinghai	29		15	14
宁　夏	Ningxia	15			15
新　疆	Xinjiang	530	147	70	313
新疆兵团	Xinjiang Corps				
黑龙江垦区	Heilongjiang Land Reclamation				

2-3 续表 5 Continued 5

地 区	Region	残疾人中等职业学校(班)学生 Students of Secondary Vocational Schools/classes for PWDs			
		毕业生 Graduates	盲 Students with Visual Disability	聋 Students with Hearing Disability	肢残 Students with Physical Disability
		人 person	人 person	人 person	人 person
全 国	**Total**	**7772**	**2192**	**1543**	**4037**
北 京	Beijing	115	48	56	11
天 津	Tianjin				
河 北	Hebei	73	17	16	40
山 西	Shanxi	67	59		8
内蒙古	Inner Mongolia	187	160	14	13
辽 宁	Liaoning	41	28	13	
吉 林	Jilin	118	90	28	
黑龙江	Heilongjiang	9		9	
上 海	Shanghai	48		48	
江 苏	Jiangsu	294	45	155	94
浙 江	Zhejiang	211		205	6
安 徽	Anhui	178	61	76	41
福 建	Fujian	17	6	11	
江 西	Jiangxi	31	5	10	16
山 东	Shandong	569	163	277	129
河 南	Henan	128	58	55	15
湖 北	Hubei	76	19	7	50
湖 南	Hunan	381	121	135	125
广 东	Guangdong	224	73	40	111
广 西	Guangxi	77		38	39
海 南	Hainan	1			1
重 庆	Chongqing	3147	951	26	2170
四 川	Sichuan	65	8	32	25
贵 州	Guizhou				
云 南	Yunnan	245	83	99	63
西 藏	Tibet				
陕 西	Shaanxi	1223	120	131	972
甘 肃	Gansu	101	16	25	60
青 海	Qinghai				
宁 夏	Ningxia	2	2		
新 疆	Xinjiang	144	59	37	48
新疆兵团	Xinjiang Corps				
黑龙江垦区	Heilongjiang Land Reclamation				

2-3　续表 6　Continued 6

地 区	Region	残疾人中等职业学校(班)学生 Students of Secondary Vocational Schools/classes for PWDs			
		毕业生获得职业资格证书 Graduates Who were Issued Professional Qualification Certificates	盲 Students with Visual Disability	聋 Students with Hearing Disability	肢残 Students with Physical Disability
		人 person	人 person	人 person	人 person
全　国	**Total**	**6200**	**1876**	**853**	**3471**
北　京	Beijing	95	48	36	11
天　津	Tianjin				
河　北	Hebei	12	2	1	9
山　西	Shanxi	67	59		8
内蒙古	Inner Mongolia	157	154	3	
辽　宁	Liaoning	34	28	6	
吉　林	Jilin	90	90		
黑龙江	Heilongjiang				
上　海	Shanghai	28		28	
江　苏	Jiangsu	242	37	111	94
浙　江	Zhejiang	210		205	5
安　徽	Anhui	175	58	76	41
福　建	Fujian	17	6	11	
江　西	Jiangxi	31	5	10	16
山　东	Shandong	423	150	197	76
河　南	Henan	56	36	11	9
湖　北	Hubei	41		7	34
湖　南	Hunan	136	32	46	58
广　东	Guangdong	134	30	32	72
广　西	Guangxi				
海　南	Hainan	1			1
重　庆	Chongqing	3038	910		2128
四　川	Sichuan	9			9
贵　州	Guizhou				
云　南	Yunnan	90	70	12	8
西　藏	Tibet				
陕　西	Shaanxi	997	100	45	852
甘　肃	Gansu	4			4
青　海	Qinghai				
宁　夏	Ningxia	2	2		
新　疆	Xinjiang	111	59	16	36
新疆兵团	Xinjiang Corps				
黑龙江垦区	Heilongjiang Land Reclamation				

2-4 高等教育
Higher Education

地 区	Region	高等特殊教育学院 Higher Special Education Institutions							
		机构 Institutions	录取残疾考生 Newly Enrolled Students	本科 Under-graduates	盲 Students with Visual Disability	聋 Students with Hearing Disability	专科(高职) Postsecondary Specialised College Students (Vocational College Students)	盲 Students with Visual Disability	聋 Students with Hearing Disability
		个 unit	人 person	人 person	人 person	人 person	人 person	人 person	人 person
全 国	**Total**	**15**	**1388**	**596**	**106**	**490**	**792**	**149**	**643**
北 京	Beijing	1	163	106	42	64	57		57
天 津	Tianjin	1	123	123		123			
河 北	Hebei								
山 西	Shanxi								
内蒙古	Inner Mongolia								
辽 宁	Liaoning								
吉 林	Jilin	1	195	195	64	131			
黑龙江	Heilongjiang								
上 海	Shanghai								
江 苏	Jiangsu	3	232	25		25	207	29	178
浙 江	Zhejiang								
安 徽	Anhui								
福 建	Fujian	1	30				30		30
江 西	Jiangxi								
山 东	Shandong	1	25				25	20	5
河 南	Henan	3	413	127		127	286	100	186
湖 北	Hubei								
湖 南	Hunan	1	120				120		120
广 东	Guangdong	1	37				37		37
广 西	Guangxi								
海 南	Hainan								
重 庆	Chongqing	1	20	20		20			
四 川	Sichuan								
贵 州	Guizhou								
云 南	Yunnan								
西 藏	Tibet								
陕 西	Shaanxi	1	30				30		30
甘 肃	Gansu								
青 海	Qinghai								
宁 夏	Ningxia								
新 疆	Xinjiang								
新疆兵团	Xinjiang Corps								
黑龙江垦区	Heilongjiang Land Reclamation								

2-4 续表 1 Continued 1

地 区	Region	普通高等院校 Ordinary Higher Education Institutions					
		残疾考生达到录取分数线 Students who Passed the Admission Line	录取人数 Students Enrolled	本科 Undergraduates	盲 Students with Visual Disability	聋 Students with Hearing Disability	肢残 Students with Physical Disability
		人 person	人 person	人 person	人 person	人 person	人 person
全 国	**Total**	**11604**	**7538**	**3795**	**324**	**516**	**2955**
北 京	Beijing	70	70	29	4	8	17
天 津	Tianjin	102	97	51	4	6	41
河 北	Hebei	343	308	190	26	37	127
山 西	Shanxi	168	168	75			75
内蒙古	Inner Mongolia	770	445	214	10	25	179
辽 宁	Liaoning	272	269	136	15	35	86
吉 林	Jilin	151	151	101	14	20	67
黑龙江	Heilongjiang	189	189	117	9	34	74
上 海	Shanghai	55	55	32	2	17	13
江 苏	Jiangsu	426	426	222			222
浙 江	Zhejiang	1212	308	102	4	30	68
安 徽	Anhui	384	332	166	12	36	118
福 建	Fujian	326	317	141	17	25	99
江 西	Jiangxi	252	235	130	12	11	107
山 东	Shandong	362	353	203	32	42	129
河 南	Henan	388	388	220	22	15	183
湖 北	Hubei	308	305	140	15	16	109
湖 南	Hunan	744	268	178	15	17	146
广 东	Guangdong	377	342	62	2	5	55
广 西	Guangxi	429	201	89	10	13	66
海 南	Hainan	1090	54	33	1	1	31
重 庆	Chongqing	197	194	107	15	13	79
四 川	Sichuan	332	295	140	19	17	104
贵 州	Guizhou	378	339	169	1	2	166
云 南	Yunnan	429	413	224	17	27	180
西 藏	Tibet	266	8	4	2		2
陕 西	Shaanxi	291	291	168	4	16	148
甘 肃	Gansu	803	247	103	13	11	79
青 海	Qinghai	75	75	45	3	2	40
宁 夏	Ningxia	125	121	66	12	13	41
新 疆	Xinjiang	257	241	116	12	20	84
新疆兵团	Xinjiang Corps	33	33	22		2	20
黑龙江垦区	Heilongjiang Land Reclamation						

2-4 续表 2 Continued 2

地 区	Region	普通高等院校 Ordinary Higher Education Institutions 录取残疾考生 Students Enrolled 专科(高职) Postsecondary Specialised College Students (Vocational College Students) 人 person	盲 Students with Visual Disability 人 person	聋 Students with Hearing Disability 人 person	肢残 Students with Physical Disability 人 person
全 国	**Total**	**3743**	**339**	**581**	**2823**
北 京	Beijing	41	3	15	23
天 津	Tianjin	46	3	18	25
河 北	Hebei	118	13	22	83
山 西	Shanxi	93			93
内蒙古	Inner Mongolia	231	15	25	191
辽 宁	Liaoning	133	20	22	91
吉 林	Jilin	50	5	16	29
黑龙江	Heilongjiang	72	6	21	45
上 海	Shanghai	23	1	6	16
江 苏	Jiangsu	204			204
浙 江	Zhejiang	206	18	82	106
安 徽	Anhui	166	15	53	98
福 建	Fujian	176	18	30	128
江 西	Jiangxi	105	11	10	84
山 东	Shandong	150	19	41	90
河 南	Henan	168	19	13	136
湖 北	Hubei	165	8	35	122
湖 南	Hunan	90	5	12	73
广 东	Guangdong	280	66	29	185
广 西	Guangxi	112	8	19	85
海 南	Hainan	21	1		20
重 庆	Chongqing	87	8	20	59
四 川	Sichuan	155	20	20	115
贵 州	Guizhou	170	2	4	164
云 南	Yunnan	189	10	17	162
西 藏	Tibet	4	1		3
陕 西	Shaanxi	123	2	6	115
甘 肃	Gansu	144	17	17	110
青 海	Qinghai	30	2	3	25
宁 夏	Ningxia	55	9	10	36
新 疆	Xinjiang	125	13	13	99
新疆兵团	Xinjiang Corps	11	1	2	8
黑龙江垦区	Heilongjiang Land Reclamation				

3-1 城镇残疾人就业状况

Employment of PWDs in Urban Areas

地 区	Region	就业合计 Employed PWDs	集中就业 PWDs Employed in Collective Form	本年度新安排 Newly Employed in Collective Form in 2013	按比例就业 PWDs Employed by quota Scheme	本年度新安排 Newly Employed by Quota Scheme in 2013	公益性岗位就业 PWDs Employed through Welfare Post
		人 person	人 person	人 person	人 person	人 person	人 person
全 国	**Total**	**4455751**	**1200522**	**107244**	**1183198**	**87215**	**93180**
北 京	Beijing	72309	3088	75	42161	1221	2165
天 津	Tianjin	38227	7907	562	25560	1596	399
河 北	Hebei	202582	54648	4865	84925	3377	5839
山 西	Shanxi	120803	38626	2323	23698	1050	1966
内蒙古	Inner Mongolia	116518	16787	1517	18828	1196	3384
辽 宁	Liaoning	315069	100182	2532	82009	2222	2302
吉 林	Jilin	159153	39998	1949	26019	863	3243
黑龙江	Heilongjiang	125602	33286	4139	21150	1881	8215
上 海	Shanghai	67419	15445	721	37209	1480	4909
江 苏	Jiangsu	306911	107671	8328	91913	7205	4255
浙 江	Zhejiang	206371	89249	5406	70201	3592	4810
安 徽	Anhui	172256	27570	6187	26637	4280	1777
福 建	Fujian	123416	46513	1987	25463	1694	2333
江 西	Jiangxi	152566	32557	5113	16109	975	5921
山 东	Shandong	247362	75530	5422	81176	8345	1883
河 南	Henan	315461	109385	15136	56662	7195	7795
湖 北	Hubei	229978	57781	9774	43231	8169	4563
湖 南	Hunan	278823	58527	4110	68413	2330	4089
广 东	Guangdong	201791	23924	3048	79766	8655	3317
广 西	Guangxi	77329	17904	1106	23592	1794	1817
海 南	Hainan	12356	1715	309	4762	1114	104
重 庆	Chongqing	137604	52319	2659	31352	1391	1312
四 川	Sichuan	269092	60418	10683	52889	6692	4452
贵 州	Guizhou	80543	27768	1149	13083	1379	402
云 南	Yunnan	76222	28681	1850	23417	880	475
西 藏	Tibet	1530	876	77	143	53	127
陕 西	Shaanxi	106263	23385	2135	34623	2289	2924
甘 肃	Gansu	106012	24599	1219	20183	1337	5853
青 海	Qinghai	6467	2256	602	1332	157	427
宁 夏	Ningxia	23602	5054	218	6475	425	439
新 疆	Xinjiang	72393	15021	1787	33279	1876	1167
新疆兵团	Xinjiang Corps	17920	1800	255	11478	460	221
黑龙江垦区	Heilongjiang Land Reclamation	15801	52	1	5460	42	295

3-1 续表 Continued

地 区	Region	本年度新安排 Newly Employed in 2013	个体及其他形式就业 PWDs Self-employed or Employed in Other Forms	本年度新安排 Newly Employed in 2013	辅助性就业 PWDs of Assistive Employment	本年度新安排 Newly Employed in 2013
		人 person	人 person	人 person	人 person	人 person
全 国	**Total**	**15471**	**1938472**	**146078**	**40379**	**13295**
北 京	Beijing	193	18786	1233	6109	522
天 津	Tianjin	13	4354	323	7	7
河 北	Hebei	303	56958	3533	212	141
山 西	Shanxi	103	55639	3524	874	527
内蒙古	Inner Mongolia	488	76739	3384	780	217
辽 宁	Liaoning	516	130435	3881	141	54
吉 林	Jilin	590	89893	5986		
黑龙江	Heilongjiang	901	62846	6839	105	89
上 海	Shanghai	366	7211	-79	2645	978
江 苏	Jiangsu	354	101756	5366	1316	900
浙 江	Zhejiang	449	38045	2937	4066	1044
安 徽	Anhui	490	113424	22316	2848	628
福 建	Fujian	256	48062	3945	1045	577
江 西	Jiangxi	321	96130	6686	1849	511
山 东	Shandong	249	87897	6533	876	434
河 南	Henan	705	139420	14006	2199	216
湖 北	Hubei	1525	122324	11946	2079	1908
湖 南	Hunan	955	147388	6091	406	249
广 东	Guangdong	1119	92653	6207	2131	755
广 西	Guangxi	574	33177	1456	839	348
海 南	Hainan	12	5595	678	180	20
重 庆	Chongqing	157	49034	2354	3587	376
四 川	Sichuan	1082	148232	12633	3101	871
贵 州	Guizhou	176	39275	3214	15	10
云 南	Yunnan	86	23406	1521	243	148
西 藏	Tibet	11	373	23	11	
陕 西	Shaanxi	680	44903	2710	428	52
甘 肃	Gansu	2273	54602	3572	775	589
青 海	Qinghai	109	2266	439	186	108
宁 夏	Ningxia	128	11604	679	30	12
新 疆	Xinjiang	216	22628	1833	298	170
新疆兵团	Xinjiang Corps	70	3468	195	953	789
黑龙江垦区	Heilongjiang Land Reclamation	1	9949	114	45	45

3-2　农村残疾人就业状况
Employment of PWDs in Rural Areas

地　区	Region	实际就业 Employed PWDs	从事农业生产劳动 PWDs Engaged in Farming	从事其他形式就业 PWDs Employed in Other Forms
		万人 10,000 persons	万人 10,000 persons	万人 10,000 persons
全　国	**Total**	**1757.2**	**1385.4**	**371.7**
北　京	Beijing	6.4	4.0	2.4
天　津	Tianjin	6.8	4.8	2.0
河　北	Hebei	89.1	70.3	18.7
山　西	Shanxi	40.0	28.8	11.2
内蒙古	Inner Mongolia	27.8	22.6	5.2
辽　宁	Liaoning	39.9	29.1	10.9
吉　林	Jilin	30.5	25.4	5.1
黑龙江	Heilongjiang	24.2	19.7	4.5
上　海	Shanghai	2.5	0.5	2.0
江　苏	Jiangsu	68.3	51.9	16.4
浙　江	Zhejiang	32.3	21.3	11.0
安　徽	Anhui	83.5	67.9	15.6
福　建	Fujian	32.4	25.0	7.4
江　西	Jiangxi	55.9	42.0	14.0
山　东	Shandong	139.4	110.3	29.2
河　南	Henan	190.8	154.0	36.8
湖　北	Hubei	90.3	68.6	21.6
湖　南	Hunan	93.1	68.3	24.8
广　东	Guangdong	61.4	50.2	11.2
广　西	Guangxi	64.0	50.9	13.0
海　南	Hainan	6.7	5.6	1.0
重　庆	Chongqing	50.1	40.5	9.5
四　川	Sichuan	180.5	143.7	36.8
贵　州	Guizhou	79.2	62.5	16.7
云　南	Yunnan	97.3	84.2	13.1
西　藏	Tibet	1.9	1.9	0.1
陕　西	Shaanxi	70.5	53.4	17.1
甘　肃	Gansu	53.9	44.7	9.1
青　海	Qinghai	4.7	4.0	0.7
宁　夏	Ningxia	11.0	9.5	1.5
新　疆	Xinjiang	23.0	20.0	3.0
新疆兵团	Xinjiang Corps			
黑龙江垦区	Heilongjiang Land Reclamation			

3-3 城镇残疾人登记失业与职业培训

Unemployment Registration of PWDs in Urban Areas and Vocational Training

地区	Region	本年度城镇残疾人新登记失业 PWDs in Urban Areas who Registered as being Unemployed Newly Added in 2013	残疾人职业培训 Vocational Training for PWDs			
			职业培训基地 Vocational Training Base	残联兴办 Established by Disabled Persons' Federations	依托社会机构兴办 Established by Social Organizations	本年度城镇职业培训 PWDs in Urban Areas Receiving Vocational Training in 2013
		人 person	个 unit	个 unit	个 unit	人 person
全 国	**Total**	**50237**	**5357**	**2022**	**3335**	**378247**
北 京	Beijing	809	62	8	54	10471
天 津	Tianjin		30	6	24	2837
河 北	Hebei	814	386	267	119	20775
山 西	Shanxi	445	512	282	230	8422
内蒙古	Inner Mongolia	1002	66	20	46	12213
辽 宁	Liaoning	1011	158	60	98	14869
吉 林	Jilin	8382	180	52	128	13823
黑龙江	Heilongjiang	1151	94	32	62	12399
上 海	Shanghai	1084	16	6	10	11666
江 苏	Jiangsu	2766	216	71	145	23208
浙 江	Zhejiang	1749	291	104	187	14397
安 徽	Anhui	521	86	23	63	12114
福 建	Fujian	1015	201	79	122	8799
江 西	Jiangxi	1580	227	44	183	3802
山 东	Shandong	1993	683	103	580	22642
河 南	Henan	1686	230	49	181	51062
湖 北	Hubei	1806	269	205	64	10749
湖 南	Hunan	1504	185	75	110	6368
广 东	Guangdong	7997	130	56	74	13117
广 西	Guangxi	424	65	28	37	6327
海 南	Hainan	3	12	3	9	2322
重 庆	Chongqing	953	32	5	27	4762
四 川	Sichuan	4210	517	240	277	31184
贵 州	Guizhou	3499	40	10	30	4423
云 南	Yunnan	369	111	36	75	8451
西 藏	Tibet	60	5	3	2	193
陕 西	Shaanxi	1125	80	21	59	12337
甘 肃	Gansu	984	42	19	23	19494
青 海	Qinghai	91	28	15	13	2131
宁 夏	Ningxia	311	31	3	28	2861
新 疆	Xinjiang	743	370	96	274	9257
新疆兵团	Xinjiang Corps	150	2	1	1	772
黑龙江垦区	Heilongjiang Land Reclamation					

4-1　城镇残疾人参加社会保险
Urban PWDs Covered by Social Insurance

地　区	Region	城镇残疾职工参加社会保险合计 Urban Workers with Disabilities Covered by Social Insurance	参加养老保险 Covered by Pension Insurance	参加医疗保险 Covered by Medical Insurance	残疾居民参加社会保险 Disabled Residents Covered by Social Insurance	参加城镇居民医疗保险 Covered by Medical Insurance for Urban Residents	参加城镇居民社会养老保险 Covered by Pension Insurance for Urban Residents
		万人 10,000 persons	万人 10,000 persons	万人 10,000 persons	万人 10,000 persons	万人 10,000 persons	万人 10,000 persons
全　国	**Total**	**296.7**	**186.9**	**182.4**	**1184.5**	**547.3**	**401.4**
北　京	Beijing	6.6	6.6	6.6	4.9	4.9	2.6
天　津	Tianjin	4.0	3.3	3.1	10.4	7.2	2.0
河　北	Hebei	9.8	5.5	4.8	52.7	15.2	13.4
山　西	Shanxi	10.2	4.6	5.5	52.9	22.7	20.1
内蒙古	Inner Mongolia	6.4	2.8	3.5	34.9	13.5	6.2
辽　宁	Liaoning	19.5	11.7	10.0	41.9	19.2	18.8
吉　林	Jilin	6.7	3.5	3.3	27.0	21.3	8.6
黑龙江	Heilongjiang	7.0	3.2	3.1	32.9	15.7	12.5
上　海	Shanghai	7.4	7.4	7.4	4.4	2.9	2.4
江　苏	Jiangsu	27.7	20.2	19.1	107.9	41.1	30.6
浙　江	Zhejiang	16.4	13.8	13.9	16.3	12.7	7.9
安　徽	Anhui	8.4	5.6	4.6	49.3	30.0	17.8
福　建	Fujian	5.0	2.8	2.6	24.0	13.4	10.4
江　西	Jiangxi	10.9	4.0	4.1	71.2	22.9	11.4
山　东	Shandong	20.4	13.3	12.1	63.7	16.6	22.5
河　南	Henan	25.0	12.3	11.4	162.6	38.4	29.2
湖　北	Hubei	16.5	8.1	8.4	54.9	30.3	22.5
湖　南	Hunan	20.1	12.7	10.8	54.3	30.1	32.1
广　东	Guangdong	13.7	9.0	10.8	40.4	30.6	9.2
广　西	Guangxi	4.6	2.4	3.0	26.8	16.9	17.9
海　南	Hainan	0.8	0.4	0.5	6.0	5.0	5.2
重　庆	Chongqing	7.3	5.3	4.8	21.8	17.5	13.3
四　川	Sichuan	13.3	9.6	9.6	66.5	33.7	26.4
贵　州	Guizhou	3.9	2.0	2.1	20.6	10.8	9.4
云　南	Yunnan	5.8	3.8	3.5	21.0	11.5	12.2
西　藏	Tibet	0.7	0.4	0.5	0.5	0.4	0.2
陕　西	Shaanxi	6.7	4.2	4.2	51.7	20.0	8.9
甘　肃	Gansu	2.9	1.8	1.9	25.6	19.2	12.6
青　海	Qinghai	0.5	0.3	0.3	1.8	1.3	0.8
宁　夏	Ningxia	0.9	0.8	0.6	8.7	4.8	4.9
新　疆	Xinjiang	5.6	3.4	4.1	18.8	9.5	8.2
新疆兵团	Xinjiang Corps	1.4	1.4	1.4	2.4	2.3	0.9
黑龙江垦区	Heilongjiang Land Reclamation	0.8	0.8	0.8	5.6	5.6	

4-1 续表 1 Continued 1

地 区	Region	残疾居民参加城镇居民社会养老保险 PWDs Covered by Payment in New Types of Pension Insurance						
		享受养老保金 PWDs Covered by the Insurance Pension	重度残疾人 Persons with Severe Disability	60周岁以下参保残疾人 PWDs under Age 60	重度残疾人 Persons with Severe Disability	全部或部分代缴 Paid by Subsidy Totally or Partially	其他残疾人 Other PWDs	全部或部分代缴 Paid by Subsidy Totally or Partially
		万人 10,000 persons	万人 10,000 persons	万人 10,000 persons	万人 10,000 persons	万人 10,000 persons	万人 10,000 persons	万人 10,000 persons
全 国	**Total**	**161.97**	**46.81**	**239.47**	**77.89**	**73.07**	**161.58**	**56.75**
北 京	Beijing	0.32	0.12	2.29	1.39	1.32	0.90	0.65
天 津	Tianjin	0.99	0.29	1.00	0.84	0.84	0.16	0.16
河 北	Hebei	4.40	1.42	9.03	2.08	2.05	6.95	1.98
山 西	Shanxi	11.46	1.79	8.68	2.35	2.18	6.33	1.63
内蒙古	Inner Mongolia	2.41	0.90	3.83	1.56	1.43	2.27	0.85
辽 宁	Liaoning	6.31	1.71	12.52	4.01	3.70	8.51	5.67
吉 林	Jilin	1.88	0.84	6.68	2.64	2.64	4.04	2.53
黑龙江	Heilongjiang	5.77	1.17	6.77	1.77	1.39	5.00	1.44
上 海	Shanghai	0.03	0.03	2.39	2.39	2.39	0.00	0.00
江 苏	Jiangsu	17.33	3.09	13.25	4.72	4.51	8.53	3.14
浙 江	Zhejiang	3.37	1.01	4.49	1.80	1.63	2.69	1.45
安 徽	Anhui	7.84	4.01	9.97	4.64	4.01	5.33	0.86
福 建	Fujian	5.13	1.69	5.30	1.70	1.49	3.61	2.51
江 西	Jiangxi	5.86	0.74	5.58	1.45	1.45	4.14	2.93
山 东	Shandong	9.06	2.44	13.47	4.55	4.36	8.92	2.57
河 南	Henan	12.63	3.22	16.60	5.64	5.39	10.96	0.48
湖 北	Hubei	6.49	2.34	16.05	5.61	5.48	10.44	6.96
湖 南	Hunan	13.23	5.21	18.84	5.86	5.70	12.98	2.17
广 东	Guangdong	3.27	1.65	5.96	2.18	1.96	3.77	1.32
广 西	Guangxi	9.14	2.52	8.72	1.53	1.37	7.19	1.23
海 南	Hainan	1.80	0.44	3.41	0.81	0.74	2.60	0.07
重 庆	Chongqing	5.33	1.90	7.95	2.44	2.44	5.51	3.95
四 川	Sichuan	7.15	2.21	19.27	4.41	4.37	14.85	2.08
贵 州	Guizhou	5.92	0.96	3.48	1.22	1.14	2.26	0.71
云 南	Yunnan	2.04	0.84	10.18	2.11	2.01	8.07	2.16
西 藏	Tibet	0.13	0.06	0.07	0.03	0.03	0.04	0.04
陕 西	Shaanxi	3.33	0.73	5.61	1.73	1.73	3.87	2.69
甘 肃	Gansu	4.11	1.12	8.54	3.91	2.95	4.63	1.64
青 海	Qinghai	0.58	0.10	0.24	0.13	0.13	0.11	0.01
宁 夏	Ningxia	2.26	1.32	2.63	1.10	1.04	1.53	1.02
新 疆	Xinjiang	2.08	0.66	6.08	0.98	0.95	5.10	1.70
新疆兵团	Xinjiang Corps	0.30	0.27	0.60	0.31	0.26	0.28	0.14
黑龙江垦区	Heilongjiang Land Reclamation							

4-1 续表 2 Continued 2

地 区	Region	城镇个体就业参加社会保险 PWDs in Urban Areas Self-employed and Covered by Social Insurance				
		参加社会保险 Self-employed and Covered by Social Insurance	参加养老保险 Self-employed and Covered by Pension Insurance	参加城镇职工养老保险 Covered by Pension Insurance for Urban Workers	参加城镇居民养老保险 Covered by Pension Insurance for Urban Residents	参加医疗保险 Self-employed and Covered by Medical Insurance
		万人 10,000 persons	万人 10,000 persons	万人 10,000 persons	万人 10,000 persons	万人 10,000 persons
全 国	**Total**	**110.48**	**60.07**	**18.97**	**41.10**	**47.03**
北 京	Beijing	2.32	1.70	1.38	0.33	1.13
天 津	Tianjin	0.03	0.01	0.01	0.00	0.02
河 北	Hebei	2.92	1.72	0.34	1.38	1.68
山 西	Shanxi	3.32	2.12	0.62	1.49	1.15
内蒙古	Inner Mongolia	2.20	1.50	0.60	0.90	1.03
辽 宁	Liaoning	3.63	1.59	0.82	0.77	1.67
吉 林	Jilin	2.89	1.31	0.57	0.74	1.57
黑龙江	Heilongjiang	3.41	1.21	0.40	0.81	1.14
上 海	Shanghai	0.16	0.09	0.09		0.15
江 苏	Jiangsu	11.98	4.63	1.47	3.17	3.57
浙 江	Zhejiang	1.93	1.65	1.17	0.48	1.45
安 徽	Anhui	9.21	3.77	0.76	3.01	2.78
福 建	Fujian	1.48	1.00	0.33	0.67	0.52
江 西	Jiangxi	3.44	1.73	0.42	1.31	1.74
山 东	Shandong	5.55	3.07	1.52	1.55	2.23
河 南	Henan	9.38	3.78	1.21	2.57	3.31
湖 北	Hubei	7.92	3.17	0.87	2.30	4.13
湖 南	Hunan	6.89	4.10	1.05	3.05	2.75
广 东	Guangdong	5.05	3.06	1.12	1.94	3.03
广 西	Guangxi	1.57	0.87	0.25	0.62	0.88
海 南	Hainan	0.28	0.20	0.06	0.14	0.22
重 庆	Chongqing	2.35	1.94	0.54	1.40	1.72
四 川	Sichuan	6.39	4.49	1.10	3.40	3.92
贵 州	Guizhou	1.46	0.48	0.11	0.37	0.92
云 南	Yunnan	1.28	0.92	0.23	0.69	0.73
西 藏	Tibet					
陕 西	Shaanxi	8.04	6.30	0.77	5.53	1.24
甘 肃	Gansu	1.63	1.18	0.15	1.03	0.73
青 海	Qinghai	0.14	0.10	0.04	0.05	0.07
宁 夏	Ningxia	0.51	0.45	0.10	0.35	0.20
新 疆	Xinjiang	2.32	1.40	0.48	0.93	0.83
新疆兵团	Xinjiang Corps	0.23	0.19	0.08	0.11	0.13
黑龙江垦区	Heilongjiang Land Reclamation	0.58	0.34	0.34		0.38

4–2 残疾人参加新型农村社会养老保险

PWDs Covered by New Type of Rural Pension Insurance

地 区	Region	参保残疾人 PWDs Covered by the Insurance	享受养老保金 PWDs Covered by the Insurance Pension	重度残疾人 Persons with Severe Disability	60周岁以下参保残疾人 PWDs under Age 60
		万人 10,000 persons	万人 10,000 persons	万人 10,000 persons	万人 10,000 persons
全 国	**Total**	**1638.33**	**628.11**	**178.52**	**1010.22**
北 京	Beijing	7.85	1.33	0.68	6.52
天 津	Tianjin	3.77	2.49	0.87	1.28
河 北	Hebei	115.11	35.33	9.03	79.79
山 西	Shanxi	74.08	37.17	4.93	36.91
内蒙古	Inner Mongolia	21.66	9.90	3.84	11.76
辽 宁	Liaoning	33.18	8.54	2.65	24.64
吉 林	Jilin	12.07	3.51	1.22	8.56
黑龙江	Heilongjiang	12.65	6.30	0.70	6.35
上 海	Shanghai	2.61	1.06	0.25	1.55
江 苏	Jiangsu	52.03	18.04	6.84	33.99
浙 江	Zhejiang	34.75	18.09	4.91	16.67
安 徽	Anhui	82.09	31.60	11.05	50.49
福 建	Fujian	44.38	22.45	8.43	21.93
江 西	Jiangxi	46.74	24.78	3.88	21.95
山 东	Shandong	112.70	42.55	14.01	70.15
河 南	Henan	199.96	85.85	15.74	114.10
湖 北	Hubei	84.90	35.70	8.91	49.21
湖 南	Hunan	130.47	49.89	17.66	80.58
广 东	Guangdong	49.12	19.00	8.29	30.12
广 西	Guangxi	72.73	33.97	10.64	38.77
海 南	Hainan	12.77	4.49	1.27	8.29
重 庆	Chongqing	30.13	13.18	4.05	16.94
四 川	Sichuan	145.76	33.89	11.51	111.88
贵 州	Guizhou	42.74	20.63	5.00	22.11
云 南	Yunnan	63.88	18.57	6.24	45.30
西 藏	Tibet	1.49	0.70	0.15	0.78
陕 西	Shaanxi	34.52	9.67	3.50	24.85
甘 肃	Gansu	79.29	25.44	6.61	53.84
青 海	Qinghai	4.18	2.83	0.28	1.35
宁 夏	Ningxia	13.97	5.78	3.84	8.18
新 疆	Xinjiang	16.75	5.38	1.57	11.37
新疆兵团	Xinjiang Corps				
黑龙江垦区	Heilongjiang Land Reclamation				

4-2 续表 Continued

地 区	Region	参保残疾人 PWDs Covered by the Insurance			
		60周岁以下参保残疾人 PWDs under Age 60			
		重度残疾人 Persons with Severe Disability	全部或部分代缴 Paid by Subsidy Totally or Partially	其他残疾人 Other PWDs	全部或部分代缴 Paid by Subsidy Totally or Partially
		万人 10,000 persons	万人 10,000 persons	万人 10,000 persons	万人 10,000 persons
全 国	**Total**	**314.02**	**302.91**	**696.20**	**175.16**
北 京	Beijing	3.00	3.00	3.52	2.48
天 津	Tianjin	0.89	0.88	0.40	0.40
河 北	Hebei	16.08	16.05	63.70	17.67
山 西	Shanxi	11.60	11.09	25.31	4.49
内蒙古	Inner Mongolia	4.01	3.53	7.75	2.77
辽 宁	Liaoning	5.71	5.47	18.94	14.48
吉 林	Jilin	2.83	2.83	5.73	3.43
黑龙江	Heilongjiang	1.59	1.56	4.76	0.86
上 海	Shanghai	1.00	0.99	0.55	0.53
江 苏	Jiangsu	8.32	8.18	25.68	10.57
浙 江	Zhejiang	5.89	5.63	10.78	5.67
安 徽	Anhui	17.92	17.09	32.57	2.86
福 建	Fujian	10.42	10.22	11.51	7.26
江 西	Jiangxi	5.98	5.94	15.97	2.93
山 东	Shandong	21.59	20.60	48.56	17.40
河 南	Henan	49.19	48.03	64.91	1.53
湖 北	Hubei	15.32	13.83	33.89	11.16
湖 南	Hunan	23.03	22.73	57.54	4.94
广 东	Guangdong	11.92	11.49	18.20	5.96
广 西	Guangxi	11.30	10.52	27.47	5.34
海 南	Hainan	2.65	2.56	5.63	0.08
重 庆	Chongqing	6.13	6.13	10.82	6.72
四 川	Sichuan	24.82	24.80	87.06	8.25
贵 州	Guizhou	6.77	6.77	15.34	2.29
云 南	Yunnan	12.07	11.63	33.23	11.13
西 藏	Tibet	0.15	0.13	0.64	0.50
陕 西	Shaanxi	7.87	7.37	16.98	10.62
甘 肃	Gansu	17.56	16.01	36.29	4.97
青 海	Qinghai	1.05	1.05	0.31	0.03
宁 夏	Ningxia	3.71	3.65	4.47	2.54
新 疆	Xinjiang	3.66	3.15	7.71	5.30
新疆兵团	Xinjiang Corps				
黑龙江垦区	Heilongjiang Land Reclamation				

4-3 社会救助与社会福利

Social Relief and Welfare

地区	Region	社会救助 Social Relief			
		城镇 in Urban Areas			农村 in Rural Areas
		已纳入最低生活保障范围 PWDs Covered by Basic Living Allowance System	集中供养 PWDs Living in Welfare Institutions	其他救助救济 Other Assistance and Relief	已纳入最低生活保障范围 PWDs Covered by Basic Living Allowance System
		万人 10,000 persons	万人 10,000 persons	万人 10,000 persons	万人 10,000 persons
全国	**Total**	**264.80**	**11.67**	**69.68**	**828.24**
北京	Beijing	1.99	0.01	0.73	2.20
天津	Tianjin	3.36	0.01	1.09	2.30
河北	Hebei	6.77	0.37	1.13	34.72
山西	Shanxi	6.70	0.13	1.68	23.77
内蒙古	Inner Mongolia	9.30	0.25	4.83	20.91
辽宁	Liaoning	15.87	0.45	2.00	18.45
吉林	Jilin	13.27	0.65	1.64	15.23
黑龙江	Heilongjiang	16.23	0.35	1.67	13.97
上海	Shanghai	1.53	0.01	5.72	0.28
江苏	Jiangsu	9.16	0.77	4.62	22.65
浙江	Zhejiang	2.79	0.32	1.46	14.99
安徽	Anhui	11.48	0.57	0.95	39.67
福建	Fujian	3.81	0.15	1.23	19.29
江西	Jiangxi	10.75	1.08	1.52	25.85
山东	Shandong	7.77	0.78	2.09	35.17
河南	Henan	19.63	0.89	4.28	67.48
湖北	Hubei	18.46	1.23	2.47	53.03
湖南	Hunan	20.95	0.78	4.48	65.72
广东	Guangdong	9.19	0.38	3.30	27.84
广西	Guangxi	7.04	0.20	0.75	40.60
海南	Hainan	1.44	0.03	0.88	4.61
重庆	Chongqing	6.26	0.37	2.77	12.80
四川	Sichuan	15.97	0.81	5.73	73.80
贵州	Guizhou	5.39	0.18	0.99	44.69
云南	Yunnan	8.07	0.28	1.81	57.28
西藏	Tibet	0.09		0.06	1.57
陕西	Shaanxi	7.19	0.31	5.70	31.69
甘肃	Gansu	11.37	0.10	1.25	33.35
青海	Qinghai	0.57	0.07	0.07	2.28
宁夏	Ningxia	1.47	0.03	0.61	7.31
新疆	Xinjiang	5.79	0.09	0.93	14.73
新疆兵团	Xinjiang Corps	2.08	0.02	0.81	
黑龙江垦区	Heilongjiang Land Reclamation	3.06	0.01	0.42	

4-3 续表 Continued

地 区	Region	社会救助 Social Relief		社会福利 Social Welfare	
		农村 in Rural Areas			
		五保供养 PWDs Living in Welfare Institutions	其他救助救济 Other Assistance and Relief	享受生活补贴 PWDs with Living Subsidy	享受护理补贴 PWDs with Nursing Subsidy
		万人 10,000 persons	万人 10,000 persons	万人 10,000 persons	万人 10,000 persons
全 国	**Total**	**65.24**	**196.32**	**366.18**	**91.98**
北 京	Beijing	0.09	1.39	12.38	
天 津	Tianjin	0.37	0.93	5.87	0.74
河 北	Hebei	2.40	4.08	1.79	0.00
山 西	Shanxi	2.54	4.81	1.01	1.49
内蒙古	Inner Mongolia	1.32	8.34	20.60	19.87
辽 宁	Liaoning	2.33	3.16	0.15	0.19
吉 林	Jilin	1.03	1.44		
黑龙江	Heilongjiang	1.02	3.00	0.60	0.78
上 海	Shanghai	0.01	1.96	4.19	4.19
江 苏	Jiangsu	2.22	10.39	28.08	11.65
浙 江	Zhejiang	0.66	8.07	20.09	7.36
安 徽	Anhui	3.76	5.22	27.43	0.67
福 建	Fujian	1.12	5.49	25.24	1.71
江 西	Jiangxi	2.61	3.87		
山 东	Shandong	3.09	6.73	21.40	1.23
河 南	Henan	5.54	13.58	30.96	0.14
湖 北	Hubei	4.15	6.83	20.14	0.31
湖 南	Hunan	6.80	11.58	12.17	0.01
广 东	Guangdong	2.41	4.44	36.28	29.94
广 西	Guangxi	4.17	5.57	0.53	0.02
海 南	Hainan	0.21	1.11	0.17	3.04
重 庆	Chongqing	1.81	5.70	0.76	0.81
四 川	Sichuan	5.29	16.26	4.44	1.23
贵 州	Guizhou	1.27	7.01		
云 南	Yunnan	4.46	9.79	2.08	0.06
西 藏	Tibet	0.04	0.08	0.26	
陕 西	Shaanxi	2.12	34.03	76.92	0.04
甘 肃	Gansu	1.83	8.87	1.91	5.70
青 海	Qinghai	0.17	0.57	1.93	
宁 夏	Ningxia	0.15	1.05	7.78	
新 疆	Xinjiang	0.27	0.97	1.03	0.79
新疆兵团	Xinjiang Corps				
黑龙江垦区	Heilongjiang Land Reclamation				

4-4 托养服务
Fostering Service

地 区	Region	托养服务机构合计 Fostering Institutions	寄宿制托养服务 Boarding Fostering Services	日间照料托养服务机构 Day-Care Fostering Service	综合托养服务机构 Combined Fostering Services Facilities	托养残疾人 PWDs in the Institutions	寄宿制机构中托养残疾人 PWDs Fostered in the Form of Boarding
		个 unit	个 unit	个 unit	个 unit	人 person	人 person
全 国	**Total**	**5677**	**1750**	**2000**	**1927**	**944081**	**50061**
北 京	Beijing	80	29		51	99748	256
天 津	Tianjin	84	14	68	2	16352	232
河 北	Hebei	147	54	12	81	22937	1847
山 西	Shanxi	88	51	6	31	16654	593
内蒙古	Inner Mongolia	110	68	8	34	21031	1797
辽 宁	Liaoning	218	77	104	37	31421	4334
吉 林	Jilin	15	6	1	8	16238	479
黑龙江	Heilongjiang	101	39	2	60	22429	2074
上 海	Shanghai	781	365	416		38357	5443
江 苏	Jiangsu	1122	40	299	783	98216	1276
浙 江	Zhejiang	757	451	132	174	83465	8138
安 徽	Anhui	81	12	15	54	18641	683
福 建	Fujian	110	15	49	46	27526	726
江 西	Jiangxi	21	10	3	8	15861	978
山 东	Shandong	440	168	37	235	50555	5695
河 南	Henan	46	5	1	40	23397	296
湖 北	Hubei	209	62	124	23	21914	1049
湖 南	Hunan	111	20	50	41	23352	754
广 东	Guangdong	385	20	328	37	32420	881
广 西	Guangxi	30	3	24	3	20593	172
海 南	Hainan	6	6			12162	410
重 庆	Chongqing	97	19	52	26	16590	591
四 川	Sichuan	177	39	106	32	52560	1453
贵 州	Guizhou	14	4	4	6	14145	318
云 南	Yunnan	43	17	3	23	21822	674
西 藏	Tibet					6733	
陕 西	Shaanxi	128	61	20	47	25737	5917
甘 肃	Gansu	47	21	7	19	27535	925
青 海	Qinghai	41	24	4	13	15925	369
宁 夏	Ningxia	44	5	34	5	15688	204
新 疆	Xinjiang	110	16	88	6	25120	586
新疆兵团	Xinjiang Corps	27	23	2	2	7034	540
黑龙江垦区	Heilongjiang Land Reclamation	7	6	1		1923	371

4-4 续表 1 continued 1

地 区	Region	智力残疾人 Persons with Intellectual Disability	精神残疾人 Persons with Psychiatric Disability	重度肢体残疾人 Persons with Severe Physical Disability	日间照料机构中托养残疾人 PWDs Fostered in the Form of Day Care	智力残疾人 Persons with Intellectual Disability	精神残疾人 Persons with Psychiatric Disability	重度肢体残疾人 Persons with Severe Physical Disability	综合托养服务机构中托养残疾人 PWDs in Combined Fostering Services Facilities
		人 person	人 person	人 person	人 person	人 person	人 person	人 person	人 person
全 国	**Total**	**12546**	**17174**	**7644**	**56833**	**27715**	**14934**	**3620**	**52874**
北 京	Beijing	126	33	11					951
天 津	Tianjin	69	44	22	981	606	127	150	32
河 北	Hebei	367	916	366	319	85	5	164	2215
山 西	Shanxi	198	212	86	679	177	129	302	692
内蒙古	Inner Mongolia	383	144	558	128	49	29	9	845
辽 宁	Liaoning	1089	1731	1195	2257	1832	130	53	1168
吉 林	Jilin	48	325	14	20	15	3	2	313
黑龙江	Heilongjiang	500	891	200	80	45	35		2183
上 海	Shanghai	2312	1942		13394	8005	3000		
江 苏	Jiangsu	400	94	268	5440	2310	1258	732	17193
浙 江	Zhejiang	1662	2473	2081	3550	1552	1269	208	3975
安 徽	Anhui	84	370	186	301	140	58	13	1654
福 建	Fujian	173	374	60	1134	465	209	55	2168
江 西	Jiangxi	674	192		71	43	9	6	214
山 东	Shandong	1803	1776	1207	3645	1676	1363	200	6237
河 南	Henan	30	97	9	30	6	9	15	2532
湖 北	Hubei	398	322	59	6620	3089	2320	221	275
湖 南	Hunan	268	199	109	1216	608	359	110	1529
广 东	Guangdong	240	311	128	9684	4021	2986	569	2263
广 西	Guangxi	2	170		906	462	182	73	73
海 南	Hainan	109	238	1					
重 庆	Chongqing	68	338	102	466	106	78	162	977
四 川	Sichuan	164	866	88	2216	1416	313	129	909
贵 州	Guizhou	33	248	37	38	29			164
云 南	Yunnan	67	556	35	63	23	21	18	703
西 藏	Tibet								
陕 西	Shaanxi	663	1320	382	340	142	121	25	1935
甘 肃	Gansu	216	100	173	543	83	42		1210
青 海	Qinghai	87	101	11	45	4	4	25	189
宁 夏	Ningxia	47	105	11	1197	170	584	129	160
新 疆	Xinjiang	161	75	174	1390	542	240	245	55
新疆兵团	Xinjiang Corps	64	335	48	70	14	51	5	60
黑龙江垦区	Heilongjiang Land Reclamation	41	276	23	10				

4-4 续表 2 continued 2

地 区	Region	以寄宿制方式托养的残疾人 PWDs Fostered in the Form of Boarding	智力残疾人 Persons with Intellectual Disability	精神残疾人 Persons with Psychiatric Disability	重度肢体残疾人 Persons with Severe Physical Disability	以日间照料方式托养的残疾人 PWDs Fostered in the Form of Day Care	智力残疾人 Persons with Intellectual Disability	精神残疾人 Persons with Psychiatric Disability	重度肢体残疾人 Persons with Severe Physical Disability	享受居家托养服务残疾人 PWDs Recieving Fostering Service at Home
		人 person	人 person	人 person	人 person	人 person	人 person	人 person	人 person	人 person
全 国	**Total**	**33644**	**8782**	**6599**	**7555**	**19230**	**5642**	**2294**	**3558**	**784313**
北 京	Beijing	700	223	61	173	251	170	49	20	98541
天 津	Tianjin	27	13	6	8	5			5	15107
河 北	Hebei	1685	367	716	468	530	187	60	97	18556
山 西	Shanxi	527	82	103	134	165	42	11	48	14690
内蒙古	Inner Mongolia	631	180	33	204	214	32	10	47	18261
辽 宁	Liaoning	675	189	119	222	493	197	34	72	23662
吉 林	Jilin	166	11	18	119	147			15	15426
黑龙江	Heilongjiang	1766	542	348	522	417	61	85	82	18092
上 海	Shanghai									19520
江 苏	Jiangsu	8877	3383	1246	2169	8316	3165	1011	1711	74307
浙 江	Zhejiang	3142	366	788	701	833	142	67	149	67802
安 徽	Anhui	1323	158	36	222	331	7	4	11	16003
福 建	Fujian	2012	801	265	465	156	70	11	15	23498
江 西	Jiangxi	138	25	47	23	76	15	4	7	14598
山 东	Shandong	4011	1347	802	714	2226	507	434	513	34978
河 南	Henan	1718	255	279	366	814	99	102	158	20539
湖 北	Hubei	150				125	13	16	21	13970
湖 南	Hunan	796	123	223	222	733	184	166	91	19853
广 东	Guangdong	1288	22	66	198	975	253	51	296	19592
广 西	Guangxi	73		50						19442
海 南	Hainan									11752
重 庆	Chongqing	840	91	665	47	137	50	25	6	14556
四 川	Sichuan	558	92	150	70	351	110	49	29	47982
贵 州	Guizhou	152	25	25	22	12	7		5	13625
云 南	Yunnan	526	137	292	58	177	6	41	1	20382
西 藏	Tibet									6733
陕 西	Shaanxi	1177	213	175	261	758	233	16	37	17545
甘 肃	Gansu	447	93	29	114	763	49	25	58	24857
青 海	Qinghai	96	17	21	14	93	2		30	15322
宁 夏	Ningxia	41				119	41	23	21	14127
新 疆	Xinjiang	42	6	2	34	13			13	23089
新疆兵团	Xinjiang Corps	60	21	34	5					6364
黑龙江垦区	Heilongjiang Land Reclamation									1542

5-1　农村贫困残疾人扶持效果
Poverty Alleviation for PWDs in Rural Areas

地　区	Region	贫困残疾人扶持效果 Results of Assisting PWDs to Get Rid of Poverty				残疾人实用技术培训 Training on Applied Technologies for PWDs	
		本年扶持贫困残疾人户 Poor Households with Disabled Member Assisted in 2013	本年扶持贫困残疾人 PWDs Assisted in 2013	本年实际脱贫 Rural PWDs who Got Rid of Poverty in 2013	本年返贫 Reimpoverished PWDs in 2013	本年度培训残疾人 Training on Applied Technologies for PWDs in 2013	本年度培训投入经费 Fund for Training on Applied Technologies for PWDs in 2013
		万户 10,000 households	万人次 10,000 person-times	万人 10,000 persons	万人 10,000 persons	万人次 10,000 person-times	万元 10,000 yuan
全　国	**Total**	**155.03**	**238.72**	**120.61**	**19.42**	**85.59**	**26639.2**
北　京	Beijing	0.92	0.92	0.40		0.43	28.6
天　津	Tianjin	2.01	2.37			0.27	68.7
河　北	Hebei	17.03	20.56	12.55	1.03	4.25	1549.6
山　西	Shanxi	6.21	9.82	4.14	1.19	2.00	845.0
内蒙古	Inner Mongolia	1.97	4.14	3.91	0.76	1.77	720.9
辽　宁	Liaoning	5.50	6.90	3.68	0.43	1.56	490.5
吉　林	Jilin	1.83	2.95	2.14	0.14	3.17	697.9
黑龙江	Heilongjiang	1.76	1.87	1.37	0.13	3.23	577.3
上　海	Shanghai	0.36	0.52	0.01		0.35	185.3
江　苏	Jiangsu	2.21	3.14	2.23	0.12	1.76	1118.9
浙　江	Zhejiang	7.16	10.46	2.44	0.48	2.22	1613.1
安　徽	Anhui	11.33	15.79	2.89	0.71	2.30	654.4
福　建	Fujian	2.45	3.04	1.54	0.14	9.19	1057.0
江　西	Jiangxi	2.57	4.06	6.77	0.44	0.79	400.0
山　东	Shandong	8.19	11.92	5.64	0.35	5.03	1539.5
河　南	Henan	5.82	16.77	8.42	0.66	5.59	1607.5
湖　北	Hubei	5.85	11.17	5.96	0.49	5.50	866.1
湖　南	Hunan	5.26	8.69	4.36	0.90	1.49	1125.3
广　东	Guangdong	2.49	4.66	2.11	0.07	1.73	697.6
广　西	Guangxi	2.41	4.84	3.55	0.59	3.22	845.3
海　南	Hainan	0.37	0.70	0.16	0.05	0.52	255.3
重　庆	Chongqing	4.13	4.67	2.27	1.28	1.34	620.6
四　川	Sichuan	15.93	25.39	12.12	2.56	11.15	3438.4
贵　州	Guizhou	6.88	10.69	6.89	1.19	1.37	590.7
云　南	Yunnan	5.95	8.42	3.30	1.59	4.37	1530.3
西　藏	Tibet	0.03	0.04	0.01		0.02	360.6
陕　西	Shaanxi	13.79	23.72	8.62	1.44	1.67	844.1
甘　肃	Gansu	7.94	11.56	9.69	2.24	4.50	960.5
青　海	Qinghai	1.07	1.32	0.70	0.04	0.67	96.1
宁　夏	Ningxia	1.42	1.55	1.26	0.17	0.66	429.4
新　疆	Xinjiang	2.76	3.53	1.12	0.20	2.03	387.1
新疆兵团	Xinjiang Corps	1.01	2.00	0.22	0.04	1.24	389.5
黑龙江垦区	Heilongjiang Land Reclamation	0.43	0.53	0.15		0.21	48.1

5-2 扶贫资金与残疾人扶贫贷款
Poverty Alleviation Fund and Loans

地区	Region	扶贫资金 Poverty Alleviation Fund		残疾人扶贫贷款 Poverty Alleviation Fund and Loans		
				康复扶贫贴息贷款 Interest-subsidized Loans for Rehabilitation		
		省级财政投入 Poverty Alleviation Fund from the Provincial Budget	社会募集 Fund Raised From Society	本年度贷款实际落实 Actually Allocated Loans in 2013	本年度项目贷款扶持贫困残疾人 Poor PWDs Supported by Loans for Project in 2013	本年度到户贷款扶持贫困残疾人 Poor PWDs Supported by Loans to the Households in 2013
		万元 10,000 yuan	万元 10,000 yuan	万元 10,000 yuan	人 person	人 person
全国	**Total**	**25356.9**	**1520.6**	**101253.4**	**25913**	**52674**
北京	Beijing	316.2				
天津	Tianjin	2138.6				
河北	Hebei			6000.0	1538	1923
山西	Shanxi	250.0	102.0	4989.0	667	1968
内蒙古	Inner Mongolia	39.1	36.0	4757.0	812	17029
辽宁	Liaoning	500.0	5.0	5600.0	1399	863
吉林	Jilin		64.6	3546.0		1681
黑龙江	Heilongjiang	1337.6	3.8	4420.1	1900	1208
上海	Shanghai					
江苏	Jiangsu	811.3	69.0	2109.0	395	942
浙江	Zhejiang	6830.5	167.0	1925.1	410	505
安徽	Anhui	236.3		4491.4	1601	371
福建	Fujian	1739.8	23.8	3189.0	1261	
江西	Jiangxi	43.0	28.6	4989.0	2527	981
山东	Shandong	514.3	244.0	3980.0	1300	350
河南	Henan	700.0	0.5	5315.0	1227	764
湖北	Hubei	308.5	14.0	4800.0	518	2955
湖南	Hunan	220.0	161.0	4900.0	350	1609
广东	Guangdong	67.2	32.0	1989.0	870	230
广西	Guangxi	2833.7	183.6	1542.9	84	503
海南	Hainan	528.9		428.6	76	2
重庆	Chongqing	1900.0	32.8	3000.0	1044	308
四川	Sichuan	912.3	12.6	5506.3	1283	1748
贵州	Guizhou	37.5		2184.0	236	218
云南	Yunnan	187.3	103.0	3497.0	736	493
西藏	Tibet	0.1				
陕西	Shaanxi	1395.0	139.8	5503.0	1720	12030
甘肃	Gansu	363.3	53.0	3702.0	870	696
青海	Qinghai			2091.0	201	345
宁夏	Ningxia	120.0	4.2	1800.0	653	472
新疆	Xinjiang	181.6	16.0	3576.0	1925	2154
新疆兵团	Xinjiang Corps	845.0		1303.0	280	326
黑龙江垦区	Heilongjiang Land Reclamation		24.3	120.0	30	

5-3 社会帮扶与残疾人扶贫基地建设
Social Assistance and Construction of Poverty Alleviation Bases

地 区	Region	社会帮扶 Social Assistance for Needy PWDs		残疾人扶贫基地建设 Poverty Alleviation bases for PWDs		
		结对帮扶单位 Companies or Units who Assisted PWDs in One-to-one way	结对帮扶个人 Individuals who Assisted PWDs in One-to-one way	残疾人扶贫基地 Poverty Alleviation Bases for PWDs	安置残疾人就业 Providing Employment for Disabled Persons	扶持带动贫困残疾人 Supporting and Leading Disabled Persons
		个 unit	人 person	个 unit	人 person	户 household
全 国	**Total**	**64113**	**404615**	**6201**	**164155**	**246017**
北 京	Beijing	177	577	128	4575	4444
天 津	Tianjin	147	255	165	2149	3010
河 北	Hebei	1202	7143	128	2296	6906
山 西	Shanxi	938	6969	312	5019	6721
内蒙古	Inner Mongolia	2852	5962	98	2213	3154
辽 宁	Liaoning	3730	20927	50	1491	2143
吉 林	Jilin	1964	5021	236	3915	10476
黑龙江	Heilongjiang	2999	3592	171	5335	8875
上 海	Shanghai	687	893	58	2174	1776
江 苏	Jiangsu	1963	11321	446	11608	16951
浙 江	Zhejiang	2469	13738	1262	9786	25738
安 徽	Anhui	847	9060	90	1752	3396
福 建	Fujian	2336	3995	174	4772	10595
江 西	Jiangxi	2601	12288	164	2251	2922
山 东	Shandong	5523	16567	821	16073	28007
河 南	Henan	2272	76084	273	9797	15944
湖 北	Hubei	1526	8301	100	2665	11169
湖 南	Hunan	1631	9636	184	4529	10878
广 东	Guangdong	1584	7652	82	3506	5158
广 西	Guangxi	5654	9128	133	2315	13471
海 南	Hainan	273	285	9	127	644
重 庆	Chongqing	1209	13904	100	1378	2097
四 川	Sichuan	4962	26882	343	52991	23184
贵 州	Guizhou	585	18442	134	975	3548
云 南	Yunnan	2199	24839	107	1301	4415
西 藏	Tibet	56	169			
陕 西	Shaanxi	1166	6167	198	3632	10022
甘 肃	Gansu	6637	72815	44	1745	2124
青 海	Qinghai	340	954	29	350	390
宁 夏	Ningxia	244	957	26	686	2950
新 疆	Xinjiang	2040	6521	114	2263	4029
新疆兵团	Xinjiang Corps	1192	2876	18	328	808
黑龙江垦区	Heilongjiang Land Reclamation	108	695	4	158	72

5-4 农村贫困残疾人危房改造

House Renovation for Poor PWDs in Rural Areas

地 区	Region	本年度危房改造实际完成 Houses Renovated for PWDs in 2013	本年度危房改造项目受益贫困残疾人 Poor PWDs who Benefited by House Renovation Project in 2013	本年度投入资金 Fund Input in Houses Renovation in 2013	省级投入资金 Fund from the Provincial Budgets	地市级投入资金 Fund from the Prefectural/ City Level Budgets	县级投入资金 Fund from the County Level Budgets
		户 household	人 person	万元 10,000 yuan	万元 10,000 yuan	万元 10,000 yuan	万元 10,000 yuan
全 国	**Total**	**122280**	**144359**	**114756.8**	**54044.7**	**14810.2**	**45901.9**
北 京	Beijing	731	803	592.4	71.4	197.1	323.9
天 津	Tianjin	109	109	176.4	75.3		101.1
河 北	Hebei	3468	4389	4095.4	1749.9	1171.9	1173.6
山 西	Shanxi	1805	2351	2069.0	990.0	566.0	513.0
内蒙古	Inner Mongolia	7473	9152	8064.1	1280.1	2530.0	4254.0
辽 宁	Liaoning	1486	1484	867.2		186.0	681.3
吉 林	Jilin	1226	1408	1527.5	847.7	180.6	499.2
黑龙江	Heilongjiang	2392	2659	1636.5	1200.0	265.0	171.5
上 海	Shanghai	388	388	100.7	6.2	25.3	69.3
江 苏	Jiangsu	992	1133	285.2	138.0	2.0	145.2
浙 江	Zhejiang	4030	4864	3632.2	149.8	134.9	3347.5
安 徽	Anhui	11029	13942	7195.3	2942.9		4252.4
福 建	Fujian	3905	5678	4895.1	1203.8	1047.5	2643.8
江 西	Jiangxi	4788	5433	1248.6	917.8	131.4	199.4
山 东	Shandong	3721	4719	4416.8	1542.3	1522.9	1351.6
河 南	Henan	2233	3135	463.5		88.5	375.0
湖 北	Hubei	1200	1525	946.8	720.0	16.0	210.8
湖 南	Hunan	7639	8430	5241.6	1065.8	1039.4	3136.4
广 东	Guangdong	1486	1655	1691.9	510.7	729.7	451.5
广 西	Guangxi	7853	9303	6225.6	3786.4	893.8	1545.4
海 南	Hainan	2622	2724	1950.5	899.0	55.4	996.1
重 庆	Chongqing	3355	3655	5772.8	1600.0		4172.8
四 川	Sichuan	3046	3660	5238.4	2691.4	93.9	2453.1
贵 州	Guizhou	2306	3226	1224.7	501.6	15.0	708.2
云 南	Yunnan	6435	7270	8612.3	6388.3	627.5	1596.6
西 藏	Tibet	74	69	34.3	28.3		6.0
陕 西	Shaanxi	4432	5675	4042.7		2014.8	2028.0
甘 肃	Gansu	9932	13045	11730.2	9114.4	596.0	2019.8
青 海	Qinghai	2554	2621	3178.6	2207.0	13.3	958.3
宁 夏	Ningxia	283	311	140.8	70.0	9.0	61.8
新 疆	Xinjiang	15280	15490	6748.1	1956.2	531.6	4260.3
新疆兵团	Xinjiang Corps	3407	3428	9617.5	9325.5	126.0	166.0
黑龙江垦区	Heilongjiang Land Reclamation	600	625	1094.3	64.9		1029.4

6-1　地、州、盟(不含地级市)专门协会建立情况
Establishment of Special Associations in Prefectures

地区	Region	盲人协会 Associations of Persons with Visual Disability Established	聋人协会 Associatins of Persons with Hearing Disability Established	肢残人协会 Association of Persons with Physical Disability Established	智力残疾人及亲友协会 Associations of Persons with Intellectual Disability and Their Relatives and Friends Established	精神残疾人及亲友协会 Associations of Persons with Ppsychiatric Disability and Their Relatives and Friends Established	备注 Remarks
		个 unit	个 unit	个 unit	个 unit	个 unit	个 unit
全　国	**Total**	**56**	**55**	**57**	**52**	**52**	**2**
北　京	Beijing						
天　津	Tianjin						
河　北	Hebei						
山　西	Shanxi						
内蒙古	Inner Mongolia	3	3	3	3	3	
辽　宁	Liaoning						
吉　林	Jilin	1	1	1	1	1	
黑龙江	Heilongjiang	1	1	1	1	1	
上　海	Shanghai						
江　苏	Jiangsu						
浙　江	Zhejiang						
安　徽	Anhui						
福　建	Fujian						
江　西	Jiangxi						
山　东	Shandong						
河　南	Henan						
湖　北	Hubei	1	1	1	1	1	
湖　南	Hunan	2	2	2	2	2	
广　东	Guangdong						
广　西	Guangxi						
海　南	Hainan						
重　庆	Chongqing						
四　川	Sichuan	3	3	3	3	3	
贵　州	Guizhou	4	4	4	4	4	
云　南	Yunnan	8	8	8	8	8	
西　藏	Tibet	2	1	2	1	1	
陕　西	Shaanxi						
甘　肃	Gansu	3	3	3	3	3	
青　海	Qinghai	7	7	7	7	7	
宁　夏	Ningxia						
新　疆	Xinjiang	11	11	11	10	10	1
新疆兵团	Xinjiang Corps	10	10	11	8	8	1
黑龙江垦区	Heilongjiang Land Reclamation						

备注：指智力残疾人及亲友协会和精神残疾人及亲友协会合一的协会。

6-2 市(含地级市)专门协会建立情况

Establishment of Special Associations in Cities

地 区	Region	盲人协会 Associations of Persons with Visual Disability Established	聋人协会 Associatins of Persons with Hearing Disability Established	肢残人协会 Association of Persons with Physical Disability Established	智力残疾人及亲友协会 Associations of Persons with Intellectual Disability and Their Relatives and Friends Established	精神残疾人及亲友协会 Associations of Persons with Ppsychiatric Disability and Their Relatives and Friends Established	备注 Remarks
		个 unit	个 unit	个 unit	个 unit	个 unit	个 unit
全 国	**Total**	**288**	**288**	**288**	**281**	**281**	**6**
北 京	Beijing						
天 津	Tianjin						
河 北	Hebei	11	11	11	11	11	
山 西	Shanxi	10	10	10	10	10	
内蒙古	Inner Mongolia	9	9	9	7	7	2
辽 宁	Liaoning	14	14	14	14	14	
吉 林	Jilin	8	8	8	8	8	
黑龙江	Heilongjiang	12	12	12	12	12	
上 海	Shanghai						
江 苏	Jiangsu	12	12	12	12	12	
浙 江	Zhejiang	10	10	10	7	7	3
安 徽	Anhui	16	16	16	16	16	
福 建	Fujian	9	9	9	9	9	
江 西	Jiangxi	11	11	11	11	11	
山 东	Shandong	17	17	17	15	15	1
河 南	Henan	18	18	18	18	18	
湖 北	Hubei	12	12	12	12	12	
湖 南	Hunan	12	12	12	12	12	
广 东	Guangdong	21	21	21	21	21	
广 西	Guangxi	14	14	14	14	14	
海 南	Hainan	2	2	2	2	2	
重 庆	Chongqing						
四 川	Sichuan	18	18	18	18	18	
贵 州	Guizhou	5	5	5	5	5	
云 南	Yunnan	8	8	8	8	8	
西 藏	Tibet						
陕 西	Shaanxi	10	10	10	10	10	
甘 肃	Gansu	12	12	12	12	12	
青 海	Qinghai	1	1	1	1	1	
宁 夏	Ningxia	4	4	4	4	4	
新 疆	Xinjiang	3	3	3	3	3	
新疆兵团	Xinjiang Corps						
黑龙江垦区	Heilongjiang Land Reclamation	9	9	9	9	9	

备注：指智力残疾人及亲友协会和精神残疾人及亲友协会合一的协会。

6-3　市辖区专门协会建立情况

Establishment of Special Associations in Districts under Cities

地　区	Region	盲人协会 Associations of Persons with Visual Disability Established	聋人协会 Associatins of Persons with Hearing Disability Established	肢残人协会 Association of Persons with Physical Disability Established	智力残疾人及亲友协会 Associations of Persons with Intellectual Disability and Their Relatives and Friends Established	精神残疾人及亲友协会 Associations of Persons with Ppsychiatric Disability and Their Relatives and Friends Established	备注 Remarks
		个 unit	个 unit	个 unit	个 unit	个 unit	个 unit
全　国	**Total**	**846**	**845**	**847**	**815**	**818**	**25**
北　京	Beijing	14	14	14	14	14	
天　津	Tianjin	16	16	16	16	16	
河　北	Hebei	37	37	37	36	36	1
山　西	Shanxi	20	20	20	18	18	2
内蒙古	Inner Mongolia	18	18	18	18	18	
辽　宁	Liaoning	60	60	60	60	60	
吉　林	Jilin	23	22	23	22	22	
黑龙江	Heilongjiang	68	68	68	68	68	
上　海	Shanghai	16	16	16	16	16	
江　苏	Jiangsu	53	53	53	52	53	
浙　江	Zhejiang	28	28	28	17	18	9
安　徽	Anhui	38	38	39	37	37	
福　建	Fujian	24	24	24	20	20	5
江　西	Jiangxi	13	13	13	13	13	
山　东	Shandong	53	53	53	52	52	
河　南	Henan	50	50	50	50	50	
湖　北	Hubei	35	35	35	30	31	4
湖　南	Hunan	37	37	37	36	36	1
广　东	Guangdong	54	54	54	53	53	1
广　西	Guangxi	35	35	35	35	35	
海　南	Hainan	3	3	3	3	3	
重　庆	Chongqing	20	20	20	19	19	1
四　川	Sichuan	45	45	45	44	44	1
贵　州	Guizhou	10	10	10	10	10	
云　南	Yunnan	12	12	12	12	12	
西　藏	Tibet						
陕　西	Shaanxi	25	25	25	25	25	
甘　肃	Gansu	17	17	17	17	17	
青　海	Qinghai	4	4	4	4	4	
宁　夏	Ningxia	7	7	7	7	7	
新　疆	Xinjiang	11	11	11	11	11	
新疆兵团	Xinjiang Corps						
黑龙江垦区	Heilongjiang Land Reclamation						

备注：指智力残疾人及亲友协会和精神残疾人及亲友协会合一的协会。

6-4 县(含县级市)专门协会建立情况
Establishment of Special Associations in Counties

地 区	Region	盲人协会 Associations of Persons with Visual Disability Established	聋人协会 Associatins of Persons with Hearing Disability Established	肢残人协会 Association of Persons with Physical Disability Established	智力残疾人及亲友协会 Associations of Persons with Intellectual Disability and Their Relatives and Friends Established	精神残疾人及亲友协会 Associations of Persons with Ppsychiatric Disability and Their Relatives and Friends Established	备注 Remarks
		个 unit	个 unit	个 unit	个 unit	个 unit	个 unit
全 国	**Total**	**1920**	**1909**	**1925**	**1853**	**1852**	**49**
北 京	Beijing	2	2	2	2	2	
天 津	Tianjin	3	3	3	3	3	
河 北	Hebei	135	135	135	134	134	1
山 西	Shanxi	76	76	76	75	74	2
内蒙古	Inner Mongolia	83	83	83	77	77	6
辽 宁	Liaoning	44	44	44	44	44	
吉 林	Jilin	40	40	40	40	40	
黑龙江	Heilongjiang	64	64	64	64	64	
上 海	Shanghai	1	1	1	1	1	
江 苏	Jiangsu	43	43	43	43	43	
浙 江	Zhejiang	54	53	55	39	39	12
安 徽	Anhui	55	54	56	52	51	1
福 建	Fujian	58	58	58	50	50	8
江 西	Jiangxi	61	61	61	60	60	
山 东	Shandong	89	84	87	81	81	2
河 南	Henan	108	108	108	108	108	
湖 北	Hubei	63	62	63	57	57	2
湖 南	Hunan	81	81	81	79	79	2
广 东	Guangdong	69	69	69	69	69	
广 西	Guangxi	75	75	75	75	75	
海 南	Hainan	12	12	12	12	12	
重 庆	Chongqing	19	18	19	17	17	1
四 川	Sichuan	121	121	121	120	120	1
贵 州	Guizhou	71	71	73	70	70	1
云 南	Yunnan	107	107	109	102	102	5
西 藏	Tibet	3	2	2	2	3	
陕 西	Shaanxi	83	83	83	81	82	
甘 肃	Gansu	67	67	67	67	67	
青 海	Qinghai	42	42	42	42	42	
宁 夏	Ningxia	8	8	8	7	7	1
新 疆	Xinjiang	81	81	81	78	78	3
新疆兵团	Xinjiang Corps	3	2	5	3	2	1
黑龙江垦区	Heilongjiang Land Reclamation	99	99	99	99	99	

备注：指智力残疾人及亲友协会和精神残疾人及亲友协会合一的协会。

7-1　盲人按摩

Blind Massage

地　区	Region	保健按摩人员本年度培训 Blind Health-care Masseurs Trained in 2013	医疗按摩人员本年度培训 Blind Therapeutical Masseurs Trained in 2013	按摩机构 Institutions of Blind Massage	
				医疗按摩机构 Therapeutical Blind Massage Clinics	保健按摩机构 Health-care Blind Massage Houses
		人 person	人 person	人 person	人 person
全　国	**Total**	**20111**	**5694**	**936**	**14704**
北　京	Beijing	1115	23	2	409
天　津	Tianjin	36	22	4	164
河　北	Hebei	1100	1076	56	426
山　西	Shanxi	656	151	51	383
内蒙古	Inner Mongolia	332	155	42	262
辽　宁	Liaoning	541	152	26	1108
吉　林	Jilin	1092	321	40	287
黑龙江	Heilongjiang	280	50	40	230
上　海	Shanghai	341	16		113
江　苏	Jiangsu	775	86	26	946
浙　江	Zhejiang	643	257	29	1060
安　徽	Anhui	1013	69	90	305
福　建	Fujian	523	472	7	262
江　西	Jiangxi	619	295	70	532
山　东	Shandong	800	275	77	1236
河　南	Henan	2092	674	90	517
湖　北	Hubei	671	286	49	790
湖　南	Hunan	1302	194	17	531
广　东	Guangdong	896	282	8	752
广　西	Guangxi	609	64	7	155
海　南	Hainan	195	30	2	146
重　庆	Chongqing	298	143	9	703
四　川	Sichuan	1064	58	42	1381
贵　州	Guizhou	467	27	4	370
云　南	Yunnan	597	88	11	656
西　藏	Tibet	13	13		17
陕　西	Shaanxi	1016	85	79	304
甘　肃	Gansu	371	112	28	209
青　海	Qinghai	266	68	3	203
宁　夏	Ningxia	174	60	1	117
新　疆	Xinjiang	196	90	18	102
新疆兵团	Xinjiang Corps	18		7	26
黑龙江垦区	Heilongjiang Land Reclamation			1	2

7-1 续表 Continued

地区	Region	盲人医疗按摩人员专业技术职务任职资格评审 Vocational Qualification Appraisal for the Blind Therapeutical Masseurs		盲人保健按摩人员就业 Employed Blind Health-care Masseurs	盲人医疗按摩人员就业 Employed Blind Therapeutical Masseurs	扶持特困盲人按摩师就业 Employed Blind Masseurs in Poverty Assisted in 2013
		中级 Middle Level Blind Therapeutical Masseurs	初级 Junior Level Blind Therapeutical Masseurs			
		人 person	人 person	人 person	人 person	人 person
全 国	**Total**	**334**	**1043**	**25787**	**2590**	**7375**
北 京	Beijing	34	32	1368	168	22
天 津	Tianjin			475	21	23
河 北	Hebei	26	184	914	256	337
山 西	Shanxi	16	81	446	86	181
内蒙古	Inner Mongolia	4	11	608	63	350
辽 宁	Liaoning	26	48	502	59	98
吉 林	Jilin	11	13	947	156	239
黑龙江	Heilongjiang	37	60	370	48	118
上 海	Shanghai			373	21	
江 苏	Jiangsu	43	98	1054	33	224
浙 江	Zhejiang	1	32	1846	74	296
安 徽	Anhui	6	29	1161	144	237
福 建	Fujian	37	68	1069	82	232
江 西	Jiangxi	29	58	750	58	200
山 东	Shandong		78	1009	265	256
河 南	Henan	9	12	1003	141	900
湖 北	Hubei		14	1429	208	656
湖 南	Hunan		41	1008	194	613
广 东	Guangdong			1815	70	246
广 西	Guangxi		9	853	16	175
海 南	Hainan	9	26	169		119
重 庆	Chongqing			282	143	161
四 川	Sichuan			3247	60	562
贵 州	Guizhou		14	1184	40	207
云 南	Yunnan	8	56	501	1	373
西 藏	Tibet	8		8		
陕 西	Shaanxi		15	619	78	153
甘 肃	Gansu	6	16	227	56	144
青 海	Qinghai	9	17	231	6	187
宁 夏	Ningxia	4	6	186	20	27
新 疆	Xinjiang		15	121	22	35
新疆兵团	Xinjiang Corps	7	5	7	1	4
黑龙江垦区	Heilongjiang Land Reclamation	4	5	5		

8-1　宣传文化
Publicity and Culture

地　区	Region	宣传 Publicity					
		省级 at Provincial Level					
		中央级媒体采用稿件 Articles Used by Central Media	主要新闻媒体刊播稿件 Articles Used by Major Media	报纸专版 Features in Newspapers	广播电台残疾人专题栏目 Radio Broadcast Special Programs on Disability	电视手语栏目 Sign Language TV Programmes	电视公益广告片 Advertisement for Public Interest on TV
		件 piece	件 piece	个 unit	个 unit	个 unit	个 unit
全　国	**Total**	**1024**	**12443**	**284**	**120**	**36**	**67**
北　京	Beijing	339	972	60	1	1	19
天　津	Tianjin	5	1960	6	1	1	1
河　北	Hebei	22	829	7	2	1	5
山　西	Shanxi		310	5	1	1	
内蒙古	Inner Mongolia		10	23		1	1
辽　宁	Liaoning	23	410	18	1	1	1
吉　林	Jilin	30	511	6	1	1	1
黑龙江	Heilongjiang	11	55	3	1	1	1
上　海	Shanghai	12	80	33	1	2	5
江　苏	Jiangsu	12	282	8	1	2	3
浙　江	Zhejiang	17	88	3	1	1	
安　徽	Anhui	31	525	3	1	1	1
福　建	Fujian	4	5	8	1	1	2
江　西	Jiangxi	65	56	5	2	1	
山　东	Shandong	7	550	4	1	1	1
河　南	Henan	5	240	3	1	1	1
湖　北	Hubei	24	1450	22	2	1	
湖　南	Hunan	12	20	2		1	3
广　东	Guangdong	3	85	4	1	1	
广　西	Guangxi		112	4	1	1	
海　南	Hainan		176	3	3	1	
重　庆	Chongqing	40	280	8	1	1	1
四　川	Sichuan	15	100	15	5	5	
贵　州	Guizhou						
云　南	Yunnan		237	14	1	1	1
西　藏	Tibet		20				
陕　西	Shaanxi	214	403			1	2
甘　肃	Gansu	60	600	7	1	1	6
青　海	Qinghai	12	765		1	1	5
宁　夏	Ningxia	1	560	2	1	1	
新　疆	Xinjiang	60	260	7	1	1	3
新疆兵团	Xinjiang Corps		485	1		1	4
黑龙江垦区	Heilongjiang Land Reclamation		7				

8-1 续表 1 Continued 1

地 区	Region	宣传 Publicity					
		省级 at Provincial Level		地市级 at Prefectural/City Level			
		报纸公益广告 Advertisement for Public Interest on Newspaper	新促会 Societies for Promoting News Relating to PWDs	主要新闻媒体刊播稿件 Articles Used by Major Media	报纸专版 Features in Newspapers	广播电台残疾人专题栏目 Radio Broadcast Special Programs on Disability	电视手语栏目 Sign Language TV Programmes
		个 unit	个 unit	件 piece	个 unit	个 unit	个 unit
全 国	**Total**	**59**	**27**	**50513**	**1288**	**539**	**227**
北 京	Beijing		1	786	55	11	3
天 津	Tianjin		1	222	5	10	4
河 北	Hebei	3		3012	71	20	12
山 西	Shanxi			1362	22	12	1
内蒙古	Inner Mongolia		1	1784	17	19	8
辽 宁	Liaoning	2	1	6013	35	11	9
吉 林	Jilin	1	1	1545	15	17	9
黑龙江	Heilongjiang		1	495	15	26	7
上 海	Shanghai		1	227	40	12	12
江 苏	Jiangsu	11	1	2414	161	28	16
浙 江	Zhejiang		1	4194	31	16	14
安 徽	Anhui	3	1	2650	44	13	12
福 建	Fujian	1	1	883	45	8	11
江 西	Jiangxi		1	620	7	3	4
山 东	Shandong		1	3044	51	16	8
河 南	Henan	2	1	680	27	11	3
湖 北	Hubei		1	1840	120	15	4
湖 南	Hunan	8	1	3585	135	55	1
广 东	Guangdong		1	2564	37	24	9
广 西	Guangxi		1	524	18	12	4
海 南	Hainan		1	20		1	2
重 庆	Chongqing	1	1	800	66	12	10
四 川	Sichuan		1	2294	94	62	5
贵 州	Guizhou			282	3	3	3
云 南	Yunnan		1	1179	42	14	7
西 藏	Tibet			2	17		
陕 西	Shaanxi	1	1	1088	11	8	9
甘 肃	Gansu	4	1	2945	34	44	9
青 海	Qinghai	2	1	172	35	15	
宁 夏	Ningxia		1	413	15	6	3
新 疆	Xinjiang	5	1	1472	15	35	5
新疆兵团	Xinjiang Corps	15		1196	5		
黑龙江垦区	Heilongjiang Land Reclamation			206			

8-1　续表 2　Continued 2

地　区	Region	宣传 Publicity			文化 Culture		
		地市级 at Prefectural/City Level			省级 at Provincial Level		
		电视公益广告片 Advertisement for Public Interest on TV	报纸公益广告 Advertisement for Public Interest on Newspaper	新促会 Societies for Promoting News Relating to PWDs	公共图书馆盲文及盲人有声读物图书室 Reading Rooms with Braille and Audio Reading Materials in Public Library	残疾人文化周 Culture Week for PWDs	残疾人文化艺术类比赛及展览 Cultural or Art Competitions and Exhibitions of PWDs
		个 unit	个 unit	个 unit	个 unit	场次 time	次 time
全　国	**Total**	**305**	**529**	**135**	**69**	**155**	**228**
北　京	Beijing	7	6	1	6	19	45
天　津	Tianjin	1	2	2	2	5	5
河　北	Hebei	23	23	6	1	21	19
山　西	Shanxi	2	3	3	2	1	2
内蒙古	Inner Mongolia	5	3	3	1	1	
辽　宁	Liaoning	26	22	3	1	3	3
吉　林	Jilin	9	14	6	5	3	2
黑龙江	Heilongjiang	12	24	4	1	1	2
上　海	Shanghai		4	2	1	15	3
江　苏	Jiangsu	42	161	9	1	5	16
浙　江	Zhejiang	18	30	10	1	1	5
安　徽	Anhui	11	32	4	1	1	1
福　建	Fujian	4	5	7	2	1	1
江　西	Jiangxi	6	3		1	2	3
山　东	Shandong	15	20	9	1	1	4
河　南	Henan	2	11	13	3	1	1
湖　北	Hubei	10	28		20	17	18
湖　南	Hunan	19	65	5	6	3	5
广　东	Guangdong	24	7	22	2	8	3
广　西	Guangxi	2	1	1	1	1	2
海　南	Hainan				1	2	4
重　庆	Chongqing	10	8	1	1	1	1
四　川	Sichuan	22	29			27	52
贵　州	Guizhou	2	5	3			
云　南	Yunnan	1	1	9	1	1	2
西　藏	Tibet					3	
陕　西	Shaanxi	13	10	3	1	2	2
甘　肃	Gansu	8	6	6	1	1	20
青　海	Qinghai				1	2	2
宁　夏	Ningxia	6	5		1	1	1
新　疆	Xinjiang	5	1	3	3	2	3
新疆兵团	Xinjiang Corps					2	1
黑龙江垦区	Heilongjiang Land Reclamation					1	

8-1 续表 3 Continued 3

地 区	Region	文化 Culture				
		省级 at Provincial Level	地市级 at Prefectural/City Level			
		残疾人艺术团 PWDs' Performing Art Troupes	公共图书馆盲文及盲人有声读物图书室 Reading Rooms with Braille and Audio Reading Materials in Public Library	残疾人文化周 Culture Week for PWDs	残疾人文化艺术类比赛及展览 Cultural or Art Competitions and Exhibitions of PWDs	残疾人艺术团 PWDs' Performing Art Troupes
		个 unit	个 unit	场次 time	次 time	个 unit
全 国	**Total**	**59**	**527**	**2057**	**1171**	**297**
北 京	Beijing	1	18	277	151	48
天 津	Tianjin	3	22	17	35	14
河 北	Hebei		18	108	47	6
山 西	Shanxi		13	23	28	6
内蒙古	Inner Mongolia	1	19	26	30	7
辽 宁	Liaoning	1	22	101	48	9
吉 林	Jilin	5	9	64	16	6
黑龙江	Heilongjiang	1	27	31	50	13
上 海	Shanghai	1	41	192	96	31
江 苏	Jiangsu	1	17	75	77	16
浙 江	Zhejiang	2	14	30	26	16
安 徽	Anhui		23	81	29	12
福 建	Fujian	1	33	16	66	5
江 西	Jiangxi	1	9	13	11	6
山 东	Shandong	1	23	34	27	12
河 南	Henan	1	17	82	37	3
湖 北	Hubei	19	11	56	54	6
湖 南	Hunan		26	112	107	29
广 东	Guangdong	1	39	90	24	11
广 西	Guangxi		6	26	7	4
海 南	Hainan	1	1	27	4	
重 庆	Chongqing		19	108	37	9
四 川	Sichuan	1	38	43	27	3
贵 州	Guizhou		8	68	9	1
云 南	Yunnan	14	12	72	12	11
西 藏	Tibet			3		
陕 西	Shaanxi	1	17	34	14	4
甘 肃	Gansu	1	10	40	29	2
青 海	Qinghai		4	15	4	1
宁 夏	Ningxia		5	11	30	2
新 疆	Xinjiang	1	5	63	22	4
新疆兵团	Xinjiang Corps		1	20	5	
黑龙江垦区	Heilongjiang Land Reclamation			99	12	

9-1 体　育

Sports

地　区	Region	省级 at Provincial Level					
		残疾人群众体育健身活动 Massive Sports and Fitness Activities for PWDs	残疾人群众体育健身活动参加人数 Participation in Massive Sports and Fitness Activities for PWDs	残疾人群众体育活动示范点 Sports Activity Demonstration Sites for PWDs	残疾人体育健身指导员 Coaches for Fitness Activity for PWDs	残疾人体育比赛 Sports Events for PWDs	参赛残疾人运动员 Disabled Athletes who Participated in the Sports Events
		次 time	人次 person-time	个 unit	人 person	次 time	人次 person-time
全　国	**Total**	**254**	**58239**	**596**	**5352**	**114**	**13139**
北　京	Beijing	25	15200	51	1050	15	392
天　津	Tianjin	11	4860	28	415	8	2500
河　北	Hebei	16	650	27	112	20	700
山　西	Shanxi	4	350	3	392	2	294
内蒙古	Inner Mongolia	5	150	1	9		
辽　宁	Liaoning				137		
吉　林	Jilin	3	2000	38	183	2	300
黑龙江	Heilongjiang	2	480	28	280	2	200
上　海	Shanghai	27	4200	203	130	21	4500
江　苏	Jiangsu	8	3210	11	150	2	532
浙　江	Zhejiang	4	1000	5	219	2	350
安　徽	Anhui				285	5	182
福　建	Fujian	30	2800	30	50	1	200
江　西	Jiangxi	3	620	6	40	1	210
山　东	Shandong			11	78		
河　南	Henan	3	1500	5	50		
湖　北	Hubei	24	2500	25	480	1	100
湖　南	Hunan	7	345	6	54	3	512
广　东	Guangdong	8	1130	22	123	8	430
广　西	Guangxi	1	92	2	46	1	272
海　南	Hainan	3	180		40	1	167
重　庆	Chongqing	3	1780	10	85	1	65
四　川	Sichuan	5	4000	5	31	1	72
贵　州	Guizhou	1	30	15	50		
云　南	Yunnan	2	1237	8	95		
西　藏	Tibet	1	10		1		
陕　西	Shaanxi	43	3800	25	189	8	213
甘　肃	Gansu	2	3000	18	401	4	148
青　海	Qinghai	8	2000	4	70	5	800
宁　夏	Ningxia	1	750	9	104		
新　疆	Xinjiang	2	200				
新疆兵团	Xinjiang Corps	2	165		3		
黑龙江垦区	Heilongjiang Land Reclamation						

9-1 续表 Continued

地 区	Region	省级 at Provincial Level			地市级 at Prefectural/City Level			
		残疾人体育训练基地 Sports Training Bases for PWDs	残疾人体育训练基地在编人员 Full-time Staff at Sports Training Bases for PWDs	聘任教练员 Stable Coaches	残疾人体育活动 Sports Activity of PWDs	残疾人体育活动参加残疾人 Participants with Disabilities in Sports Activity of PWDs	残疾人群众体育活动示范点 Sports Activity Demonstration Sites for PWDs	残疾人体育健身指导员 Coaches for Fitness Activity for PWDs
		个 unit	人 person	人 person	次 time	人次 person-time	个 unit	人 person
全 国	**Total**	**207**	**542**	**700**	**4568**	**635535**	**1591**	**11574**
北 京	Beijing	10	65	30	1350	88696	79	528
天 津	Tianjin	5	42	18	176	7209	39	356
河 北	Hebei	16	50	53	129	14600	121	1280
山 西	Shanxi			18	67	1923	32	273
内蒙古	Inner Mongolia	2	18	5	17	3052	19	37
辽 宁	Liaoning	28	50	25	107	45132	54	612
吉 林	Jilin	16	46	10	100	8539	170	598
黑龙江	Heilongjiang	3	3	8	21	4293	5	237
上 海	Shanghai	5	16	160	1044	272821	202	469
江 苏	Jiangsu	1	20	31	96	7772	95	68
浙 江	Zhejiang	6	60	25	71	7843	135	984
安 徽	Anhui	1	6	15	92	4934	49	349
福 建	Fujian	15	38	58	60	4134	38	611
江 西	Jiangxi	2	8	13	11	715	4	12
山 东	Shandong	4	36	12	104	8526	56	288
河 南	Henan	6	6	10	56	7425	19	974
湖 北	Hubei	10	10	24	211	13165	63	191
湖 南	Hunan	8	8	16	121	8675	51	584
广 东	Guangdong	12		27	96	10806	42	373
广 西	Guangxi	1		11	30	3554	13	192
海 南	Hainan				2	100	3	2
重 庆	Chongqing	5	5	15	336	31795	104	427
四 川	Sichuan	5	5	33	74	4976	113	1604
贵 州	Guizhou	4	8	11	10	1064	3	31
云 南	Yunnan			18	39	1469	12	43
西 藏	Tibet							
陕 西	Shaanxi	25	25	12	64	3149	28	83
甘 肃	Gansu	9	9	17	36	63975	16	202
青 海	Qinghai	1	1	6	5	220	1	2
宁 夏	Ningxia	2	2	5	9	458	19	51
新 疆	Xinjiang	5	5	12	18	2973	4	26
新疆兵团	Xinjiang Corps			2	16	1542	2	87
黑龙江垦区	Heilongjiang Land Reclamation							

10-1　法规体系

Legal System

地　区	Region	省级修订《残疾人保障法实施办法》Revision of the Implementation Method of the Law on the Protection of PWDs	制定或修改关于残疾人的专门法规、规章 Laws and Regulations Enacted or Reviewed Specially for PWDs			制定或修改保障残疾人权益的规范性文件 Regulations Enacted Or Reviewed Directly Related to PWDs			
				省级 at Provincial Level	地市级 at Prefectural/ City Level		省级 at Provincial Level	地市级 at Prefectural/ City Level	县级 at County Level
		个 unit	个 unit	个 unit	个 unit	个 unit	个 unit	个 unit	个 unit
全　国	**Total**	**4**	**31**	**5**	**26**	**543**	**30**	**76**	**437**
北　京	Beijing								
天　津	Tianjin					15	12		3
河　北	Hebei		3	1	2	51	5	7	39
山　西	Shanxi		1		1	12		2	10
内蒙古	Inner Mongolia					5			5
辽　宁	Liaoning		2		2	7		1	6
吉　林	Jilin	1	1		1	17		3	14
黑龙江	Heilongjiang		1		1	1			1
上　海	Shanghai	1				4			4
江　苏	Jiangsu					34		2	32
浙　江	Zhejiang		3	1	2	51	2	7	42
安　徽	Anhui					9		4	5
福　建	Fujian					7		7	
江　西	Jiangxi	1	2		2	22		5	17
山　东	Shandong		4	1	3	67	1	8	58
河　南	Henan		1		1	17	1	6	10
湖　北	Hubei		2		2	13		2	11
湖　南	Hunan					20		2	18
广　东	Guangdong					12		5	7
广　西	Guangxi					11		2	9
海　南	Hainan								
重　庆	Chongqing					19	1		18
四　川	Sichuan		2	1	1	47	3	4	40
贵　州	Guizhou		1		1	8	1		7
云　南	Yunnan					7		1	6
西　藏	Tibet	1				2			2
陕　西	Shaanxi					2			2
甘　肃	Gansu		5	1	4	70		8	62
青　海	Qinghai					6	4		2
宁　夏	Ningxia		2		2	4			4
新　疆	Xinjiang		1		1	3			3
新疆兵团	Xinjiang Corps								
黑龙江垦区	Heilongjiang Land Reclamation								

10-2 执法检查
Inspections on Law Enforcement

地　区	Region	人大执法检查或专题调研 Inspections and Investigations by Officials of People's Congresses	省级 at Provincial Level	地市级 at Prefectural/City Level	县级 at County Level
		次 time	次 time	次 time	次 time
全　国	**Total**	**799**	**16**	**114**	**669**
北　京	Beijing	5			5
天　津	Tianjin	11	1		10
河　北	Hebei	67	1	8	58
山　西	Shanxi	42		7	35
内蒙古	Inner Mongolia	14		1	13
辽　宁	Liaoning	24		4	20
吉　林	Jilin	13			13
黑龙江	Heilongjiang	15		4	11
上　海	Shanghai	8	5		3
江　苏	Jiangsu	45	1	6	38
浙　江	Zhejiang	58		7	51
安　徽	Anhui	30	1	4	25
福　建	Fujian	26		4	22
江　西	Jiangxi	25	1	3	21
山　东	Shandong	76		14	62
河　南	Henan	29	1	9	19
湖　北	Hubei	39	1	10	28
湖　南	Hunan	36		2	34
广　东	Guangdong	19		5	14
广　西	Guangxi	8		2	6
海　南	Hainan	4		2	2
重　庆	Chongqing	21			21
四　川	Sichuan	41	1	5	35
贵　州	Guizhou	19	1	2	16
云　南	Yunnan	26		4	22
西　藏	Tibet	1	1		
陕　西	Shaanxi	12		1	11
甘　肃	Gansu	56		8	48
青　海	Qinghai	9			9
宁　夏	Ningxia	6		1	5
新　疆	Xinjiang	14	1	1	12
新疆兵团	Xinjiang Corps				
黑龙江垦区	Heilongjiang Land Reclamation				

10-2 续表 Continued

地 区	Region	政协视察或专题调研 Inspections and Investigations by Officials of People's Political Consultative Conferences	省级 at Provincial Level	地市级 at Prefectural/City Level	县级 at County Level
		次 time	次 time	次 time	次 time
全 国	**Total**	**746**	**12**	**102**	**632**
北 京	Beijing	4			4
天 津	Tianjin	2			2
河 北	Hebei	56	1	5	50
山 西	Shanxi	29		3	26
内蒙古	Inner Mongolia	11			11
辽 宁	Liaoning	22		4	18
吉 林	Jilin	10			10
黑龙江	Heilongjiang	16	2	3	11
上 海	Shanghai	2	1		1
江 苏	Jiangsu	45		6	39
浙 江	Zhejiang	84	1	11	72
安 徽	Anhui	39	1	8	30
福 建	Fujian	32		4	28
江 西	Jiangxi	23	2	3	18
山 东	Shandong	56		7	49
河 南	Henan	28		6	22
湖 北	Hubei	36	1	9	26
湖 南	Hunan	33		3	30
广 东	Guangdong	14		10	4
广 西	Guangxi	4		1	3
海 南	Hainan	2			2
重 庆	Chongqing	29			29
四 川	Sichuan	60	1	9	50
贵 州	Guizhou	7		1	6
云 南	Yunnan	21			21
西 藏	Tibet				
陕 西	Shaanxi	12	1		11
甘 肃	Gansu	43	1	5	37
青 海	Qinghai	9		2	7
宁 夏	Ningxia	6		1	5
新 疆	Xinjiang	11		1	10
新疆兵团	Xinjiang Corps				
黑龙江垦区	Heilongjiang Land Reclamation				

10-3 法制宣传
Publicity on Laws

地 区	Region	普法宣传教育活动 Activities for Laws Publicity and Education	省级 at Provincial Level	地市级 at Prefectural/ City Level	县级 at County Level	普法宣传教育活动参加人数 Participients of Activities for Laws Publicity and Education	省级 at Provincial Level	地市级 at Prefectural/ City Level	县级 at County Level
		次 time	次 time	次 time	次 time	人 person	人 person	人 person	人 person
全 国	**Total**	**6606**	**121**	**762**	**5723**	**1051629**	**23721**	**131503**	**896405**
北 京	Beijing	109	48		61	18628	9000		9628
天 津	Tianjin	48	2		46	2447	225		2222
河 北	Hebei	317	1	32	284	45043	1700	6928	36415
山 西	Shanxi	194	2	25	167	43158	130	21593	21435
内蒙古	Inner Mongolia	211		24	187	19409		2006	17403
辽 宁	Liaoning	229	2	38	189	21283	150	3629	17504
吉 林	Jilin	172	1	19	152	20736	300	2239	18197
黑龙江	Heilongjiang	146	3	22	121	14317	79	3820	10418
上 海	Shanghai	120	7		113	13348	750		12598
江 苏	Jiangsu	383	1	31	351	40480	91	3941	36448
浙 江	Zhejiang	220	2	22	196	22190	101	2254	19835
安 徽	Anhui	309	1	38	270	19682	50	3143	16489
福 建	Fujian	221		14	207	16812		1615	15197
江 西	Jiangxi	138	1	18	119	12596	76	870	11650
山 东	Shandong	269	1	42	226	22855	140	5143	17572
河 南	Henan	237		33	204	48516		6198	42318
湖 北	Hubei	182	2	36	144	38159	300	4684	33175
湖 南	Hunan	222		25	197	15305		1619	13686
广 东	Guangdong	258	2	98	158	24186	3000	8730	12456
广 西	Guangxi	235	16	14	205	111494	2000	4676	104818
海 南	Hainan	17	2	2	13	2375	321	380	1674
重 庆	Chongqing	191	2		189	71010	230		70780
四 川	Sichuan	644	5	63	576	113696	320	2867	110509
贵 州	Guizhou	242	2	16	224	32281	2000	1177	29104
云 南	Yunnan	261		9	252	27997		536	27461
西 藏	Tibet	65	4	9	52	8237	570	2530	5137
陕 西	Shaanxi	144	1	24	119	20122	83	4062	15977
甘 肃	Gansu	191	2	40	149	67127	100	3722	63305
青 海	Qinghai	87	3	8	76	7664	110	146	7408
宁 夏	Ningxia	40	1	10	29	2388	30	327	2031
新 疆	Xinjiang	238	1	22	215	60906	230	8209	52467
新疆兵团	Xinjiang Corps	205	4	13	188	64044	648	23381	40015
黑龙江垦区	Heilongjiang Land Reclamation	61	2	15	44	3138	987	1078	1073

10-3 续表 Continued

地区	Region	残疾人工作者法律培训班 Training Courses for Laws	省级 at Provincial Level	地市级 at Prefectural/ City Level	县级 at County Level	法律培训班参加人数 Trainees of Laws Courses	省级 at Provincial Level	地市级 at Prefectural/ City Level	县级 at County Level
		次 time	次 time	次 time	次 time	人 person	人 person	人 person	人 person
全国	**Total**	**1670**	**31**	**229**	**1410**	**96153**	**2485**	**20953**	**72715**
北京	Beijing	36	1		35	4507	200		4307
天津	Tianjin	20	2		18	1206	155		1051
河北	Hebei	74	1	13	60	4431	65	1634	2732
山西	Shanxi	74	1	23	50	4014	120	1101	2793
内蒙古	Inner Mongolia	61		2	59	2619		66	2553
辽宁	Liaoning	75	2	22	51	8008	200	4190	3618
吉林	Jilin	44	1	6	37	2132	130	487	1515
黑龙江	Heilongjiang	31		8	23	1057		275	782
上海	Shanghai	33	1		32	1954	45		1909
江苏	Jiangsu	87		9	78	5315		706	4609
浙江	Zhejiang	81	1	9	71	5804	39	1265	4500
安徽	Anhui	91		20	71	4027		2044	1983
福建	Fujian	35		4	31	1759		460	1299
江西	Jiangxi	46	1	6	39	2009	62	102	1845
山东	Shandong	151	7	12	132	6015	750	661	4604
河南	Henan	80		11	69	5385		1689	3696
湖北	Hubei	64	2	8	54	3219	150	1159	1910
湖南	Hunan	65	1	4	60	3035	32	361	2642
广东	Guangdong	64		21	43	4022		1839	2183
广西	Guangxi	49	2	4	43	3177	110	384	2683
海南	Hainan	5	1	1	3	409	52	150	207
重庆	Chongqing	43	1		42	3594	80		3514
四川	Sichuan	121	2	15	104	6630	4	1191	5435
贵州	Guizhou	29		2	27	1900		120	1780
云南	Yunnan	46		1	45	2574		22	2552
西藏	Tibet								
陕西	Shaanxi	27	1	7	19	2169	83	500	1586
甘肃	Gansu	56	1	9	46	2549	50	261	2238
青海	Qinghai	24		3	21	578		30	548
宁夏	Ningxia	18		3	15	451		104	347
新疆	Xinjiang	37	1	6	30	1434	48	152	1234
新疆兵团	Xinjiang Corps								
黑龙江垦区	Heilongjiang Land Reclamation	3	1		2	170	110		60

10-4 法律救助

Legal Aid

地区	Region	建立残疾人法律救助协调组织 Legal Assistance and Coordination Organization for PWDs			
		建立残疾人法律救助工作协调机构 Legal Assistance and Coordination Organization for PWDs	省级 at Provincial Level	地市级 at Prefectural/City Level	县级 at County Level
		个 unit	个 unit	个 unit	个 unit
全　国	**Total**	**1306**	**44**	**215**	**1047**
北　京	Beijing	17	1		16
天　津	Tianjin	18	1		17
河　北	Hebei	134	1	11	122
山　西	Shanxi	24	1	7	16
内蒙古	Inner Mongolia	41		2	39
辽　宁	Liaoning	64	1	13	50
吉　林	Jilin	36	1	6	29
黑龙江	Heilongjiang	10	1	3	6
上　海	Shanghai	6	1		5
江　苏	Jiangsu	69	1	9	59
浙　江	Zhejiang	74	1	17	56
安　徽	Anhui	13	1	4	8
福　建	Fujian	44	1	7	36
江　西	Jiangxi	18	1	2	15
山　东	Shandong	48	1	8	39
河　南	Henan	69	1	17	51
湖　北	Hubei	100	17	18	65
湖　南	Hunan	71	1	12	58
广　东	Guangdong	42	1	8	33
广　西	Guangxi	18	1	7	10
海　南	Hainan				
重　庆	Chongqing	41	1		40
四　川	Sichuan	86	1	15	70
贵　州	Guizhou	37	1	6	30
云　南	Yunnan	2	1	1	
西　藏	Tibet				
陕　西	Shaanxi	25		9	16
甘　肃	Gansu	77	1	15	61
青　海	Qinghai	55	1	8	46
宁　夏	Ningxia	8		2	6
新　疆	Xinjiang	50	1	2	47
新疆兵团	Xinjiang Corps	4	1	3	
黑龙江垦区	Heilongjiang Land Reclamation	5	1	3	1

10-4 续表 1 Continued 1

地 区	Region	残疾人法律救助工作站 Legal Assistance Station for PWDs			
		残疾人法律救助工作站 Legal Assistance Station for PWDs	省级 at Provincial Level	地市级 at Prefectural/City Level	县级 at County Level
		个 unit	个 unit	个 unit	个 unit
全 国	**Total**	**901**	**16**	**145**	**740**
北 京	Beijing	4			4
天 津	Tianjin	17	1		16
河 北	Hebei	133	1	11	121
山 西	Shanxi	30		6	24
内蒙古	Inner Mongolia	31		3	28
辽 宁	Liaoning	43	1	14	28
吉 林	Jilin	14		4	10
黑龙江	Heilongjiang	7		2	5
上 海	Shanghai	5	1		4
江 苏	Jiangsu	66	1	10	55
浙 江	Zhejiang	43	1	7	35
安 徽	Anhui	9			9
福 建	Fujian	37		5	32
江 西	Jiangxi	23	1	2	20
山 东	Shandong	48	1	8	39
河 南	Henan	51		9	42
湖 北	Hubei	38	1	7	30
湖 南	Hunan	72	1	12	59
广 东	Guangdong	16	1	5	10
广 西	Guangxi	26	1	7	18
海 南	Hainan	2			2
重 庆	Chongqing	15			15
四 川	Sichuan	44	1	9	34
贵 州	Guizhou	15		2	13
云 南	Yunnan	2	1	1	
西 藏	Tibet				
陕 西	Shaanxi	4			4
甘 肃	Gansu	77	1	15	61
青 海	Qinghai				
宁 夏	Ningxia	5		1	4
新 疆	Xinjiang	21	1	2	18
新疆兵团	Xinjiang Corps	3		3	
黑龙江垦区	Heilongjiang Land Reclamation				

10-4 续表 2 Continued 2

地 区	Region	残疾人法律救助工作站 Legal Assistance Station for PWDs			
		残疾人法律救助工作站办理的案件 Cases Handled by the Legal Assistance Stations for PWDs	省级 at Provincial Level	地市级 at Prefectural/City Level	县级 at County Level
		件 case	件 case	件 case	件 case
全 国	**Total**	**7905**	**739**	**1746**	**5420**
北 京	Beijing	69			69
天 津	Tianjin	474	114		360
河 北	Hebei	1771	20	610	1141
山 西	Shanxi	205		116	89
内蒙古	Inner Mongolia	61		6	55
辽 宁	Liaoning	215	11	85	119
吉 林	Jilin	56		6	50
黑龙江	Heilongjiang	43		32	11
上 海	Shanghai	43			43
江 苏	Jiangsu	205	3	35	167
浙 江	Zhejiang	513	6	34	473
安 徽	Anhui	81			81
福 建	Fujian	259		34	225
江 西	Jiangxi	104	12	13	79
山 东	Shandong	463	2	250	211
河 南	Henan	227		48	179
湖 北	Hubei	698	310	113	275
湖 南	Hunan	368	24	57	287
广 东	Guangdong	166	5	83	78
广 西	Guangxi	149	8	66	75
海 南	Hainan	2			2
重 庆	Chongqing	676			676
四 川	Sichuan	240	4	52	184
贵 州	Guizhou	29		2	27
云 南	Yunnan	10	9	1	
西 藏	Tibet				
陕 西	Shaanxi	5			5
甘 肃	Gansu	504	209	33	262
青 海	Qinghai				
宁 夏	Ningxia	61		39	22
新 疆	Xinjiang	178	2	1	175
新疆兵团	Xinjiang Corps	30		30	
黑龙江垦区	Heilongjiang Land Reclamation				

10-4　续表 3　Continued 3

地　区	Region	残疾人法律援助中心(工作站) Legal Aid Centers (Station) for PWDs			
		残疾人法律援助中心（工作站）Legal Aid Centers (Station) for PWDs	省级 at Provincial Level	地市级 at Prefectural/City Level	县级 at County Level
		个 unit	个 unit	个 unit	个 unit
全　国	**Total**	**3096**	**28**	**332**	**2736**
北　京	Beijing	17	1		16
天　津	Tianjin				
河　北	Hebei	186	1	11	174
山　西	Shanxi	120		10	110
内蒙古	Inner Mongolia	102	1	12	89
辽　宁	Liaoning	115	1	14	100
吉　林	Jilin	66	1	8	57
黑龙江	Heilongjiang	119	1	13	105
上　海	Shanghai	18	1		17
江　苏	Jiangsu	111	1	13	97
浙　江	Zhejiang	98	1	11	86
安　徽	Anhui	115	1	15	99
福　建	Fujian	93	1	9	83
江　西	Jiangxi	94	1	9	84
山　东	Shandong	152	1	17	134
河　南	Henan	165	1	17	147
湖　北	Hubei	95	1	13	81
湖　南	Hunan	118	1	13	104
广　东	Guangdong	124	1	20	103
广　西	Guangxi	119	1	14	104
海　南	Hainan	17		2	15
重　庆	Chongqing	41	1		40
四　川	Sichuan	139	1	15	123
贵　州	Guizhou	85	1	7	77
云　南	Yunnan	134	1	14	119
西　藏	Tibet	8	1	7	
陕　西	Shaanxi	107	1	9	97
甘　肃	Gansu	95	1	15	79
青　海	Qinghai	55	1	8	46
宁　夏	Ningxia	25		5	20
新　疆	Xinjiang	87	1	9	77
新疆兵团	Xinjiang Corps	166	1	14	151
黑龙江垦区	Heilongjiang Land Reclamation	110		8	102

10-4 续表 4 Continued 4

地 区	Region	残疾人法律法律援助中心(工作站) Legal Aid Center(Station) for PWDs			
		残疾人法律援助中心(工作站)办理的案件 Cases Handled by Legal Aid Centers(Stations)	省级 at Provincial Level	地市级 at Prefectural/City Level	县级 at County Level
		件 case	件 case	件 case	件 case
全 国	**Total**	**23498**	**433**	**5708**	**17357**
北 京	Beijing	337	6		331
天 津	Tianjin				
河 北	Hebei	2471	29	1177	1265
山 西	Shanxi	674		357	317
内蒙古	Inner Mongolia	359	1	52	306
辽 宁	Liaoning	989	2	252	735
吉 林	Jilin	396	10	48	338
黑龙江	Heilongjiang	857	20	221	616
上 海	Shanghai	210			210
江 苏	Jiangsu	948	3	132	813
浙 江	Zhejiang	1009	5	159	845
安 徽	Anhui	1132	12	184	936
福 建	Fujian	993	8	217	768
江 西	Jiangxi	804	13	161	630
山 东	Shandong	1453	1	508	944
河 南	Henan	712	7	219	486
湖 北	Hubei	1369	195	231	943
湖 南	Hunan	753	9	72	672
广 东	Guangdong	624	5	247	372
广 西	Guangxi	606	1	93	512
海 南	Hainan	75		16	59
重 庆	Chongqing	1271			1271
四 川	Sichuan	1074	4	101	969
贵 州	Guizhou	200	1	12	187
云 南	Yunnan	836	8	100	728
西 藏	Tibet	2		2	
陕 西	Shaanxi	646	11	411	224
甘 肃	Gansu	939	2	72	865
青 海	Qinghai	154	3	19	132
宁 夏	Ningxia	372		284	88
新 疆	Xinjiang	751	2	171	578
新疆兵团	Xinjiang Corps	339	75	180	84
黑龙江垦区	Heilongjiang Land Reclamation	143		10	133

10-5　参政议政

PWDs Participating in the Administration and Discussion of State Affairs

地　区	Region	人大代表和政协委员 Disabled deputies of People's Congresses and Committee Members of People's Political Consultative Conferences			
		人大代表 Disabled Deputies of the People's Congresses	省级 at Provincial Level	地市级 at Prefectural/City Level	县级 at County Level
		人 person	人 person	人 person	人 person
全　国	**Total**	**1886**	**37**	**239**	**1610**
北　京	Beijing	29	1		28
天　津	Tianjin	7	1		6
河　北	Hebei	102	4	14	84
山　西	Shanxi	79	2	5	72
内蒙古	Inner Mongolia	87		6	81
辽　宁	Liaoning	81	2	11	68
吉　林	Jilin	59	1	6	52
黑龙江	Heilongjiang	54	3	5	46
上　海	Shanghai	7	1		6
江　苏	Jiangsu	87	1	14	72
浙　江	Zhejiang	139	5	19	115
安　徽	Anhui	74	2	7	65
福　建	Fujian	21		6	15
江　西	Jiangxi	36	1	3	32
山　东	Shandong	81	1	7	73
河　南	Henan	60		9	51
湖　北	Hubei	125	1	38	86
湖　南	Hunan	131	1	13	117
广　东	Guangdong	50	1	15	34
广　西	Guangxi	28	1	5	22
海　南	Hainan	5	1		4
重　庆	Chongqing	60			60
四　川	Sichuan	145	2	9	134
贵　州	Guizhou	67	2	6	59
云　南	Yunnan	80		5	75
西　藏	Tibet	4		3	1
陕　西	Shaanxi	51		11	40
甘　肃	Gansu	45	1	12	32
青　海	Qinghai	43	1	2	40
宁　夏	Ningxia	10		2	8
新　疆	Xinjiang	35	1	3	31
新疆兵团	Xinjiang Corps	4		3	1
黑龙江垦区	Heilongjiang Land Reclamation				

10-5 续表 1 Continued 1

地 区	Region	人大代表和政协委员 Disabled Deputies of People's Congresses and Committee Members of People's Political Consultative Conferences			
		政协委员 Disabled Committee Members of People's Political Consultative Conferences	省级 at Provincial Level	地市级 at Prefectural/City Level	县级 at County Level
		人 person	人 person	人 person	人 person
全 国	**Total**	**3720**	**83**	**479**	**3158**
北 京	Beijing	25	1		24
天 津	Tianjin	18	1		17
河 北	Hebei	255	6	21	228
山 西	Shanxi	161	1	12	148
内蒙古	Inner Mongolia	119	2	16	101
辽 宁	Liaoning	185	2	33	150
吉 林	Jilin	103	1	13	89
黑龙江	Heilongjiang	146	3	19	124
上 海	Shanghai	23	2		21
江 苏	Jiangsu	168	1	22	145
浙 江	Zhejiang	213	7	22	184
安 徽	Anhui	138	4	24	110
福 建	Fujian	116	3	9	104
江 西	Jiangxi	137	4	33	100
山 东	Shandong	183	2	20	161
河 南	Henan	183	4	24	155
湖 北	Hubei	174	4	49	121
湖 南	Hunan	181	4	19	158
广 东	Guangdong	131	2	33	96
广 西	Guangxi	72	1	8	63
海 南	Hainan	26			26
重 庆	Chongqing	92	1		91
四 川	Sichuan	209	5	24	180
贵 州	Guizhou	106	5	9	92
云 南	Yunnan	163	1	13	149
西 藏	Tibet	7	3	4	
陕 西	Shaanxi	113	3	10	100
甘 肃	Gansu	119	5	17	97
青 海	Qinghai	51	2	5	44
宁 夏	Ningxia	27	1	7	19
新 疆	Xinjiang	71	2	10	59
新疆兵团	Xinjiang Corps	5		3	2
黑龙江垦区	Heilongjiang Land Reclamation				

10-5　续表 2　Continued 2

地　区	Region	协助提出建议、议案和提案 PWDs Assisting to Put Forward Proposals and Motions		办理人大政协建议、提案 Handling Proposals of Peoples' Congresses and Motions of People's Political Consultative Conferences	
		协助人大代表提出议案、建议 Proposals Put Forward at People's Congresses with Assistance of PWDs	协助政协委员提出提案 Motions Put forward at People's Political Consultative Conferences with Participation of PWDs	办理人大建议 Proposals of Peoples' Congresses Handled	办理政协提案 Motions of People's Political Consultative Conferences Handled
		件 case	件 case	件 case	件 case
全　国	**Total**	**566**	**1177**	**496**	**968**
北　京	Beijing		3		3
天　津	Tianjin	2	2	3	9
河　北	Hebei	23	47	22	34
山　西	Shanxi	33	68	12	29
内蒙古	Inner Mongolia	20	52	5	31
辽　宁	Liaoning	19	40	19	32
吉　林	Jilin	16	28	6	18
黑龙江	Heilongjiang	10	26	11	24
上　海	Shanghai	1	3	1	6
江　苏	Jiangsu	31	53	48	87
浙　江	Zhejiang	84	123	78	108
安　徽	Anhui	11	45	19	43
福　建	Fujian	10	37	11	42
江　西	Jiangxi	29	40	18	31
山　东	Shandong	29	73	43	67
河　南	Henan	16	38	14	27
湖　北	Hubei	50	78	33	48
湖　南	Hunan	21	58	23	30
广　东	Guangdong	24	35	37	42
广　西	Guangxi	5	27	3	17
海　南	Hainan	2	6	5	5
重　庆	Chongqing	30	41	23	41
四　川	Sichuan	32	70	22	51
贵　州	Guizhou	15	28	4	16
云　南	Yunnan	9	40	5	25
西　藏	Tibet		2	1	2
陕　西	Shaanxi	11	17	11	22
甘　肃	Gansu	21	45	10	47
青　海	Qinghai	4	8	3	6
宁　夏	Ningxia		13	1	13
新　疆	Xinjiang	8	31	5	12
新疆兵团	Xinjiang Corps				
黑龙江垦区	Heilongjiang Land Reclamation				

10-6 无障碍环境建设

Accessible Environment Building

地 区	Region	无障碍建设与管理法规、政府令 Regulations and Decrees on Accessible Environment Building and Management	无障碍建设领导协调组织 Leading and Coordinating Bodies for Building Accessible Environment	系统开展无障碍建设市、县 Cities and Counties that Systematic Accessibitity Construction has been Carried out	地市级 at Prefectural/City Level	县级 at County Level
		个 unit	个 unit	个 unit	个 unit	个 unit
全 国	**Total**	**444**	**1263**	**1419**	**210**	**1209**
北 京	Beijing	2	14	16		16
天 津	Tianjin	9	17	16	16	
河 北	Hebei	44	131	183	11	172
山 西	Shanxi	9	41	68	11	57
内蒙古	Inner Mongolia	5	23	62	6	56
辽 宁	Liaoning	6	39	5	4	1
吉 林	Jilin	12	24	12	4	8
黑龙江	Heilongjiang	4	12	27	4	23
上 海	Shanghai	5	28	17		17
江 苏	Jiangsu	22	74	61	13	48
浙 江	Zhejiang	24	35	26	2	24
安 徽	Anhui	10	23	77	16	61
福 建	Fujian	24	50	48	9	39
江 西	Jiangxi	7	29	58	11	47
山 东	Shandong	32	69	56	5	51
河 南	Henan	29	36	58	5	53
湖 北	Hubei	6	20	76	17	59
湖 南	Hunan	22	31	6	6	
广 东	Guangdong	30	35	65	10	55
广 西	Guangxi	11	32	125	14	111
海 南	Hainan		4	2	2	
重 庆	Chongqing	6	32	38		38
四 川	Sichuan	23	182	35	7	28
贵 州	Guizhou	14	17	26	2	24
云 南	Yunnan	18	37	74	5	69
西 藏	Tibet		4			
陕 西	Shaanxi	13	30	43	3	40
甘 肃	Gansu	39	62	101	15	86
青 海	Qinghai	1	53	11	3	8
宁 夏	Ningxia	5	16	23	5	18
新 疆	Xinjiang	10	47	2	2	
新疆兵团	Xinjiang Corps		4			
黑龙江垦区	Heilongjiang Land Reclamation	2	12	2	2	

10-6　续表　Continued

地　区	Region	贫困残疾人家庭无障碍改造 Accessibility Renovation for Homes of Poor Disabled Persons	省级 at Provincial Level	地市级 at Prefectural/City Level	县级 at County Level	无障碍建设检查 Inspections on Accessibility	无障碍培训 Training on Accessibility
		户 household	户 household	户 household	户 household	次 time	人次 person-time
全　国	**Total**	**135838**	**10786**	**8174**	**116878**	**3492**	**36329**
北　京	Beijing	15825			15825	253	5024
天　津	Tianjin	1584			1584	65	531
河　北	Hebei	1983		319	1664	135	831
山　西	Shanxi	1989			1989	45	922
内蒙古	Inner Mongolia	6873		200	6673	84	136
辽　宁	Liaoning	8533		120	8413	215	3355
吉　林	Jilin	890		120	770	36	474
黑龙江	Heilongjiang	3490		20	3470	25	156
上　海	Shanghai	2921	666		2255	289	4865
江　苏	Jiangsu	16525			16525	153	4525
浙　江	Zhejiang	7131		1761	5370	213	1176
安　徽	Anhui	1271		220	1051	162	766
福　建	Fujian	3853		45	3808	120	1155
江　西	Jiangxi	1131		72	1059	32	190
山　东	Shandong	18613	8300	545	9768	162	1475
河　南	Henan	2003		272	1731	153	468
湖　北	Hubei	2467	1000	519	948	189	263
湖　南	Hunan	1861		50	1811	52	373
广　东	Guangdong	6560	200	2332	4028	100	2165
广　西	Guangxi	3780		11	3769	182	510
海　南	Hainan	551		115	436	47	55
重　庆	Chongqing	3952			3952	64	1152
四　川	Sichuan	12688		545	12143	263	4015
贵　州	Guizhou	1185	600	50	535	44	113
云　南	Yunnan	1241			1241	145	306
西　藏	Tibet	202		87	115	4	37
陕　西	Shaanxi	1091		200	891	30	80
甘　肃	Gansu	1218		40	1178	72	282
青　海	Qinghai	1198		38	1160	22	33
宁　夏	Ningxia	1162		343	819	36	148
新　疆	Xinjiang	1717		75	1642	97	525
新疆兵团	Xinjiang Corps	200		75	125		6
黑龙江垦区	Heilongjiang Land Reclamation	150	20		130	3	217

10-7 残疾人机动轮椅车燃油补贴
Subsidy for Petrol Used by Motorized Wheelchairs of Disabled Persons

地 区	Region	残疾人机动轮椅车燃油补贴 Subsidy for Petrol Used by Motorized Wheelchairs of Disabled Persons	省级 at Provincial Level	地市级 at Prefectural/City level	县级 at County Level
		人 person	人 person	人 person	人 person
全 国	**Total**	**656664**	**52479**	**34430**	**569755**
北 京	Beijing	22553			22553
天 津	Tianjin	16618			16618
河 北	Hebei	15594		42	15552
山 西	Shanxi	15947		13	15934
内蒙古	Inner Mongolia	25002		383	24619
辽 宁	Liaoning	15383		6	15377
吉 林	Jilin	14801		372	14429
黑龙江	Heilongjiang	15130		1054	14076
上 海	Shanghai	14672			14672
江 苏	Jiangsu	31306		509	30797
浙 江	Zhejiang	12309		1862	10447
安 徽	Anhui	27210		6312	20898
福 建	Fujian	14197			14197
江 西	Jiangxi	22383		1387	20996
山 东	Shandong	27384	1986	1876	23522
河 南	Henan	55921		11434	44487
湖 北	Hubei	45654	45654		
湖 南	Hunan	50150		749	49401
广 东	Guangdong	29087		1725	27362
广 西	Guangxi	18765		52	18713
海 南	Hainan	9015		2385	6630
重 庆	Chongqing	4258			4258
四 川	Sichuan	28344	35	1399	26910
贵 州	Guizhou	16731	4785		11946
云 南	Yunnan	19376			19376
西 藏	Tibet	2421		648	1773
陕 西	Shaanxi	19697			19697
甘 肃	Gansu	15866		509	15357
青 海	Qinghai	7703			7703
宁 夏	Ningxia	16193		731	15462
新 疆	Xinjiang	20488		498	19990
新疆兵团	Xinjiang Corps	4888		462	4426
黑龙江垦区	Heilongjiang Land Reclamation	1618	19	22	1577

10-8 残疾人信访

Complaints by Letter and Visit

地 区	Region	来信 Complaint Letter					
		总计 Subtotal	涉法涉诉类 Complaints Related with Legal Lawsuit	康复类 Rehabilitation	教育类 Education	就业类 Employment	扶贫类 Poverty Alleviation
		件 case	件 case	件 case	件 case	件 case	件 case
全 国	**Total**	**54176**	**2166**	**7754**	**3182**	**6890**	**10382**
北 京	Beijing	6921	323	369	156	458	1731
天 津	Tianjin	135	22	5	2	16	10
河 北	Hebei	1499	204	205	108	345	303
山 西	Shanxi	1408	49	262	106	271	191
内蒙古	Inner Mongolia	1308	17	148	157	218	338
辽 宁	Liaoning	1010	93	128	24	187	141
吉 林	Jilin	672	96	103	43	146	149
黑龙江	Heilongjiang	1338	68	247	83	314	286
上 海	Shanghai	2344	55	144	39	120	185
江 苏	Jiangsu	1061	59	120	33	161	116
浙 江	Zhejiang	2637	89	435	341	276	505
安 徽	Anhui	2274	62	371	101	280	366
福 建	Fujian	1065	81	194	57	184	145
江 西	Jiangxi	638	24	134	40	139	65
山 东	Shandong	829	42	168	82	104	183
河 南	Henan	1109	30	148	67	188	137
湖 北	Hubei	2509	124	303	81	347	357
湖 南	Hunan	3701	118	758	271	710	716
广 东	Guangdong	3208	68	611	287	315	915
广 西	Guangxi	1916	40	402	105	368	329
海 南	Hainan	191	2	25	9	23	36
重 庆	Chongqing	279	33	12	20	23	17
四 川	Sichuan	5569	167	520	197	623	846
贵 州	Guizhou	2052	35	329	57	193	510
云 南	Yunnan	3699	55	630	336	266	1008
西 藏	Tibet	394	3	4	1	13	151
陕 西	Shaanxi	447	19	76	26	70	104
甘 肃	Gansu	1793	151	377	159	241	209
青 海	Qinghai	183	5	40	29	24	39
宁 夏	Ningxia	124	7	14	10	22	18
新 疆	Xinjiang	1383	22	417	97	159	188
新疆兵团	Xinjiang Corps	347	3	45	24	56	56
黑龙江垦区	Heilongjiang Land Reclamation	133		10	34	30	32

10-8 续表 1 Continued 1

地区	Region	来信 Complaint Letter				
		社会保障类 Social Security	文化体育类 Culture and Sports	机动车轮椅类 Motor Vehicle and Wheelchair	意见建议类 Opinions and Suggestions	其他类 Others
		件 case	件 case	件 case	件 case	件 case
全国	**Total**	**9770**	**731**	**4081**	**1869**	**7351**
北京	Beijing	1678	115	376	38	1677
天津	Tianjin	52			1	27
河北	Hebei	154	19	88	37	36
山西	Shanxi	172	26	175	47	109
内蒙古	Inner Mongolia	206	6	58	90	70
辽宁	Liaoning	189	1	78	34	135
吉林	Jilin	89	10	19	13	4
黑龙江	Heilongjiang	179	13	96	19	33
上海	Shanghai	467	18	147	395	774
江苏	Jiangsu	226	14	35	83	214
浙江	Zhejiang	340	20	135	97	399
安徽	Anhui	663	56	136	80	159
福建	Fujian	220	13	88	24	59
江西	Jiangxi	101	6	68	22	39
山东	Shandong	134	12	29	27	48
河南	Henan	191	9	186	65	88
湖北	Hubei	451	13	147	112	574
湖南	Hunan	526	78	229	113	182
广东	Guangdong	606	34	143	50	179
广西	Guangxi	220	29	179	136	108
海南	Hainan	35	1	16	6	38
重庆	Chongqing	53	4	19	15	83
四川	Sichuan	1274	50	459	161	1272
贵州	Guizhou	203	13	262	15	435
云南	Yunnan	628	52	385	30	309
西藏	Tibet	170	45	4	2	1
陕西	Shaanxi	63	2	41	3	43
甘肃	Gansu	218	28	266	19	125
青海	Qinghai	9		11	1	25
宁夏	Ningxia	35		12	3	3
新疆	Xinjiang	104	34	174	112	76
新疆兵团	Xinjiang Corps	87	10	20	19	27
黑龙江垦区	Heilongjiang Land Reclamation	27				

10-8 续表 2 Continued 2

地 区	Region	来访 Complaint Visit 总计 Subtotal	涉法涉诉类 Complaints Related with Legal Lawsuit	康复类 Rehabilitation	教育类 Education	就业类 Employment	扶贫类 Poverty Alleviation
		人次 person-time	人次 person-time	人次 person-time	人次 person-time	人次 person-time	人次 person-time
全 国	**Total**	**323433**	**11839**	**57361**	**18317**	**44805**	**54038**
北 京	Beijing	4617	743	279	138	459	702
天 津	Tianjin	2198	323	167	103	182	227
河 北	Hebei	7796	824	1680	549	1587	1237
山 西	Shanxi	16314	364	3166	653	1856	2345
内蒙古	Inner Mongolia	4220	47	703	281	523	1249
辽 宁	Liaoning	14042	934	1550	508	1878	2875
吉 林	Jilin	4923	213	638	256	862	833
黑龙江	Heilongjiang	4412	150	851	229	1010	624
上 海	Shanghai	3439	232	310	129	357	501
江 苏	Jiangsu	5813	168	768	387	969	992
浙 江	Zhejiang	11533	514	1588	561	1545	1709
安 徽	Anhui	15869	280	2161	864	2093	3082
福 建	Fujian	8386	255	2699	923	1142	1115
江 西	Jiangxi	5753	220	1124	369	1183	946
山 东	Shandong	6517	329	672	321	1041	1187
河 南	Henan	6435	185	884	379	1034	964
湖 北	Hubei	24561	1442	2632	898	3239	3353
湖 南	Hunan	29317	1203	4839	1780	4696	3844
广 东	Guangdong	11579	154	2021	702	1667	1467
广 西	Guangxi	17030	179	4107	810	2830	2472
海 南	Hainan	2658	47	303	223	266	1011
重 庆	Chongqing	4291	165	391	156	487	410
四 川	Sichuan	35944	1718	6075	1978	4963	6937
贵 州	Guizhou	8468	164	2774	321	1106	1506
云 南	Yunnan	22756	291	4670	1693	2571	4390
西 藏	Tibet	411		55	49	37	120
陕 西	Shaanxi	17635	260	4093	942	2109	2975
甘 肃	Gansu	6672	281	1283	414	828	1652
青 海	Qinghai	440	14	61	24	56	99
宁 夏	Ningxia	2559	31	528	226	227	543
新 疆	Xinjiang	12873	97	3251	979	1468	1735
新疆兵团	Xinjiang Corps	2750	12	376	191	435	812
黑龙江垦区	Heilongjiang Land Reclamation	1222		662	281	99	124

10-8 续表 3 Continued 3

地区	Region	来访 Complaint Visit				
		社会保障类 Social Security	文化体育类 Culture and Sports	机动车轮椅类 Motor Vehicle and Wheelchair	意见建议类 Opinions and Suggestions	其他类 Others
		人次 person-time	人次 person-time	人次 person-time	人次 person-time	人次 person-time
全　国	**Total**	**58670**	**4315**	**36175**	**3998**	**33915**
北　京	Beijing	702	57	359	56	1122
天　津	Tianjin	630	51	80	6	429
河　北	Hebei	971	105	617	83	143
山　西	Shanxi	2757	312	3340	203	1318
内蒙古	Inner Mongolia	707	37	373	27	273
辽　宁	Liaoning	2324	191	2355	329	1098
吉　林	Jilin	534	25	1083	21	458
黑龙江	Heilongjiang	676	65	507	105	195
上　海	Shanghai	560	49	298	143	860
江　苏	Jiangsu	905	22	829	105	668
浙　江	Zhejiang	2576	127	1472	153	1288
安　徽	Anhui	4235	264	1070	228	1592
福　建	Fujian	1171	80	516	108	377
江　西	Jiangxi	848	76	661	119	207
山　东	Shandong	1212	111	305	85	1254
河　南	Henan	1454	110	779	122	524
湖　北	Hubei	5067	163	3740	253	3774
湖　南	Hunan	6916	327	3041	330	2341
广　东	Guangdong	2185	143	1920	142	1178
广　西	Guangxi	2457	134	2386	89	1566
海　南	Hainan	251	15	380	12	150
重　庆	Chongqing	1352	30	373	95	832
四　川	Sichuan	5936	472	2887	385	4593
贵　州	Guizhou	914	127	971	72	513
云　南	Yunnan	3896	332	2424	96	2393
西　藏	Tibet	126	2	5		17
陕　西	Shaanxi	3668	464	1309	107	1708
甘　肃	Gansu	999	164	734	54	263
青　海	Qinghai	73	1	51	2	59
宁　夏	Ningxia	544	14	280	35	131
新　疆	Xinjiang	1365	235	915	354	2474
新疆兵团	Xinjiang Corps	605	10	115	79	115
黑龙江垦区	Heilongjiang Land Reclamation	54				2

11-1 省(自治区、直辖市)级残联

Disabled Persons' Federations in Provinces, Autonomous Regions and Municipalities

地 区	Region	省市县乡残联实有人员 Actual Total Staff of Disabled Persons' Federations at Provincial,City, County and Township Level	省级残联机关 Disabled Persons' Federations at Provincial Level		省级残联事业单位 Affiliated Institutions at Provincial Level		
			实有人员 Actual Staff	残疾人干部 Staff with Disability	单位 Institu-tions	实有人员 Actual Total Staff	残疾人 Persons with Disability
		人 person	人 person	人 person	个 unit	人 person	人 person
全 国	**Total**	**110870**	**1588**	**138**	**155**	**6209**	**257**
北 京	Beijing	1202	65	12	11	252	
天 津	Tianjin	962	47	5	9	179	31
河 北	Hebei	5529	55	4	4	143	5
山 西	Shanxi	4750	59	5	8	235	7
内蒙古	Inner Mongolia	3015	32	4	4	73	2
辽 宁	Liaoning	4171	47	6	6	345	14
吉 林	Jilin	2857	43	5	4	208	14
黑龙江	Heilongjiang	2864	42	5	2	55	2
上 海	Shanghai	1108	45	4	7	179	13
江 苏	Jiangsu	4978	53	4	6	146	7
浙 江	Zhejiang	4319	44	5	6	404	
安 徽	Anhui	3453	49	3	4	137	6
福 建	Fujian	2404	40	4	4	78	8
江 西	Jiangxi	4268	65	1	6	118	
山 东	Shandong	6006	53	3	2	169	6
河 南	Henan	8048	54	6	3	132	5
湖 北	Hubei	3507	46	2	4	46	1
湖 南	Hunan	5519	47	4	6	114	3
广 东	Guangdong	6850	51	6	5	326	40
广 西	Guangxi	3028	62	4	5	121	5
海 南	Hainan	632	46	3	2	81	3
重 庆	Chongqing	1966	37	1	3	150	5
四 川	Sichuan	8811	50	5	2	600	
贵 州	Guizhou	3098	45	3	2	78	2
云 南	Yunnan	3532	57	9	8	224	25
西 藏	Tibet	202	28	3	2	79	3
陕 西	Shaanxi	4640	60	3	7	720	9
甘 肃	Gansu	3993	103	6	10	538	20
青 海	Qinghai	1196	39	2	2	22	2
宁 夏	Ningxia	689	51	5	2	75	
新 疆	Xinjiang	2779	53	5	5	164	17
新疆兵团	Xinjiang Corps	284	13	1	3	14	1
黑龙江垦区	Heilongjiang Land Reclamation	210	7		1	4	1

11-1 续表 Continued

地 区	Region	干部队伍综合培训情况 Training of Staff						志愿者助残情况 Volunteer	
		省级举办综合培训班 Provincial-level General Training Courses	参加省级综合培训人次 Trainees on Provincial-level Training Courses	省级举办残疾人干部培训班 Provincial-level Training Courses for Staff with Disability	参加省级残疾人干部培训人次 Trainees on Provincial-level Training Courses for Staff with Disability	参加全国培训人次 Trainees on State-level Training Courses	参加全国残疾人干部培训人次 Trainees on Stats-level Training Courses for Staff with Disability	志愿者登记在册 Registered Volunteer	受助残疾人 PWDs Helped by Volunteers
		期 course	人次 person-time	期 course	人次 person-time	人次 person-time	人次 person-time	人 persons	人 persons
全 国	**Total**	**127**	**16207**	**31**	**2339**	**881**	**120**	**5824**	**272451**
北 京	Beijing	5	450	3	120				
天 津	Tianjin	1	42	2	137	7	2		
河 北	Hebei	2	49						
山 西	Shanxi						1	1	1
内蒙古	Inner Mongolia								
辽 宁	Liaoning	5	130						
吉 林	Jilin	2	50	1	10			315	31280
黑龙江	Heilongjiang	1	132						
上 海	Shanghai	45	7445	4	510			4773	238650
江 苏	Jiangsu	2	100	1	60				
浙 江	Zhejiang	3	150	1	50	20	60		
安 徽	Anhui	4	1430	1	70	462	17		
福 建	Fujian	11	200					627	1275
江 西	Jiangxi	1	206	2	62	69	20		
山 东	Shandong					11			
河 南	Henan	3	195				4	108	1245
湖 北	Hubei	2	150	2	80				
湖 南	Hunan	5	432	1	140				
广 东	Guangdong	5	700	1	40	28	2		
广 西	Guangxi	10	800	2	150	150			
海 南	Hainan	1	1						
重 庆	Chongqing	1	80						
四 川	Sichuan	6	1050	6	463				
贵 州	Guizhou					90	10		
云 南	Yunnan	1	40						
西 藏	Tibet								
陕 西	Shaanxi	2	1240	3	300				
甘 肃	Gansu								
青 海	Qinghai	3	540						
宁 夏	Ningxia		80		22	20			
新 疆	Xinjiang	4	268	1	125	8	3		
新疆兵团	Xinjiang Corps								
黑龙江垦区	Heilongjiang Land Reclamation	2	247			16	1		

11-2　地市级残联

Disabled Persons' Federations in Cities and Prefectures

地　区	Region	残联 Disabled Persons' Federations	配备了残疾人领导干部的残联 Disabled Persons' Federations whose Leadership Include PWDs	残联机关 Disabled Persons' Federations				
				实有人员 Actual Staff	残疾人领导干部 Leaders with Disability	残疾人干部 Ordinary Staff with Disability	建立残疾人人才库的残联 Disabled Persons' Federations that have Established Data base of Talents with Disabilities	残疾人人才库入库 PWDs Enrolled in the Data Base of Talents with Disabilities
		个 unit	个 unit	人 person	人 person	人 person	个 unit	人 person
全　国	**Total**	**360**	**251**	**5444**	**274**	**433**	**238**	**14722**
北　京	Beijing							
天　津	Tianjin							
河　北	Hebei	11	11	226	11	11	11	721
山　西	Shanxi	11	9	171	9	11	7	620
内蒙古	Inner Mongolia	12	11	220	12	30	11	273
辽　宁	Liaoning	14	14	317	15	24	14	1617
吉　林	Jilin	10	5	166	5	11	9	537
黑龙江	Heilongjiang	13	9	175	9	12	13	611
上　海	Shanghai							
江　苏	Jiangsu	13	8	369	9	20	10	772
浙　江	Zhejiang	11	9	181	12	17	8	790
安　徽	Anhui	16	10	211	10	9	10	639
福　建	Fujian	9	9	128	9	12	6	324
江　西	Jiangxi	11	8	142	9	12	7	804
山　东	Shandong	17	14	365	14	24	12	1421
河　南	Henan	18	12	307	14	17	18	1049
湖　北	Hubei	13	5	169	6	14	4	289
湖　南	Hunan	14	11	238	11	14	8	820
广　东	Guangdong	21	13	332	17	27	10	173
广　西	Guangxi	15	14	140	15	18	9	93
海　南	Hainan	3	2	31	2	4	1	19
重　庆	Chongqing							
四　川	Sichuan	21	10	258	11	25	13	1101
贵　州	Guizhou	9	8	124	8	10	4	109
云　南	Yunnan	16	15	210	18	24	9	157
西　藏	Tibet	7	2	72	3	6		
陕　西	Shaanxi	10	9	219	9	17	3	456
甘　肃	Gansu	15	14	280	14	33	15	431
青　海	Qinghai	8	2	70	2	3	6	183
宁　夏	Ningxia	5	4	65	5	2	2	36
新　疆	Xinjiang	14	12	187	14	24	6	561
新疆兵团	Xinjiang Corps	14	1	49	1	2	6	108
黑龙江垦区	Heilongjiang Land Reclamation	9		22			6	8

11-2 续表 Continued

地 区	Region	事业单位 Affiliated Institutions			干部队伍综合培训情况 Training of Cadre				志愿者助残情况 Volunteer	
		单位 Institutions	实有人员 Actual Total of Staff	残疾人 Persons with Disability	地市级举办综合培训班 City-level General Training Courses	参加地市级培训人次 Trainees on City-level General Training Courses	地市级举办残疾人干部培训班 City-level Training Courses for Staff with Disability	参加地市级残疾人干部培训人次 Trainees on City-level Training Courses for Staff with Disability	志愿者登记在册 Registered Volunteer	受助残疾人 PWDs Helped by Volunteers
		个 unit	人 person	人 person	期 course	人次 person-time	期 course	人次 person-time	人 persons	人 persons
全 国	**Total**	**688**	**8374**	**499**	**979**	**66972**	**484**	**23918**	**32016**	**179381**
北 京	Beijing									
天 津	Tianjin									
河 北	Hebei	22	368	18	32	2527	15	701	2333	4625
山 西	Shanxi	36	447	33	26	2108	18	1134	28	280
内蒙古	Inner Mongolia	18	112	8	16	995	9	1514		
辽 宁	Liaoning	37	464	41	105	10286	91	3692	1671	10448
吉 林	Jilin	23	266	13	30	1691	18	710		
黑龙江	Heilongjiang	23	202	10	23	4279	11	308	15	141
上 海	Shanghai									
江 苏	Jiangsu	32	449	14	20	1575	7	370	1088	13264
浙 江	Zhejiang	24	426	20	17	1584	12	683	73	602
安 徽	Anhui	27	207	10	64	2902	21	2481	465	6335
福 建	Fujian	25	204	12	27	3234			1561	1481
江 西	Jiangxi	20	95	7	21	825	11	356	53	335
山 东	Shandong	42	662	69	46	2345	19	1272	12312	9109
河 南	Henan	43	738	23	31	1213	17	766	6843	58672
湖 北	Hubei	28	204	12	22	605	8	384	1239	23120
湖 南	Hunan	30	167	8	32	1491	18	882	118	3802
广 东	Guangdong	75	1917	89	141	9393	24	1684	833	4912
广 西	Guangxi	28	180	6	34	1494	6	128	157	962
海 南	Hainan	4	38	2	1	61		8	445	22250
重 庆	Chongqing									
四 川	Sichuan	34	296	17	141	9626	116	4257	1672	16941
贵 州	Guizhou	13	50	4	5	276	2	160	50	430
云 南	Yunnan	24	103	11	26	1848	6	455	101	142
西 藏	Tibet	4	13		1	100	1	11		
陕 西	Shaanxi	17	145	9	37	3277	14	504	25	200
甘 肃	Gansu	24	439	48	34	2213	15	750	27	48
青 海	Qinghai	6	35		7	242	7	328	20	
宁 夏	Ningxia	6	46	4	10	210	3	147	865	1225
新 疆	Xinjiang	15	77	8	29	559	14	222	19	51
新疆兵团	Xinjiang Corps	8	24	3					3	6
黑龙江垦区	Heilongjiang Land Reclamation				1	13	1	11		

11-3　县(县级市、市辖区)级残联

Disabled Persons' Federations in Counties, County-Level Cities and Districts under Cities

地　区	Region	残　联 Disabled Persons' Federations	残联机关 Disabled Persons' Federations				
			配备了残疾人干部的残联 Disabled Persons' Federations with Disabled Staff	实有人员 Actual Staff	残疾人干部 Ordinary Staff with Disability	建立残疾人人才库的残联 Disabled Persons' Federations that have Established Data base of Talents with Disabilities	残疾人人才库入库 PWDs Enrolled in the Data Base of Talents with Disabilities
		个 unit	个 unit	人 person	人 person	个 unit	人 person
全　国	**Total**	**3126**	**1625**	**26976**	**2221**	**1802**	**79613**
北　京	Beijing	16	12	174	22	10	519
天　津	Tianjin	19	14	153	21	18	466
河　北	Hebei	172	172	1429	186	134	7462
山　西	Shanxi	119	96	1479	125	98	3288
内蒙古	Inner Mongolia	106	56	935	95	62	1174
辽　宁	Liaoning	103	100	764	112	99	2932
吉　林	Jilin	70	28	756	47	49	1330
黑龙江	Heilongjiang	132	36	635	40	129	3921
上　海	Shanghai	17	7	188	8	13	225
江　苏	Jiangsu	102	58	1307	73	73	6463
浙　江	Zhejiang	91	63	988	74	56	2163
安　徽	Anhui	112	29	790	34	53	5650
福　建	Fujian	84	33	442	34	52	1351
江　西	Jiangxi	108	52	917	92	58	1927
山　东	Shandong	155	55	1735	77	99	11668
河　南	Henan	167	90	2366	119	125	3032
湖　北	Hubei	103	47	910	66	34	966
湖　南	Hunan	125	73	1461	94	48	2370
广　东	Guangdong	133	49	1096	61	20	331
广　西	Guangxi	111	42	783	59	34	775
海　南	Hainan	20	8	141	9	4	10
重　庆	Chongqing	40	21	315	25	23	2088
四　川	Sichuan	185	96	1417	127	113	4451
贵　州	Guizhou	88	70	796	107	51	1786
云　南	Yunnan	129	91	1195	153	102	1969
西　藏	Tibet	7	1	10	1		
陕　西	Shaanxi	111	61	1125	99	38	5570
甘　肃	Gansu	86	77	1058	134	50	2351
青　海	Qinghai	46	14	281	18	18	137
宁　夏	Ningxia	21	10	187	13	11	301
新　疆	Xinjiang	95	58	793	90	63	2678
新疆兵团	Xinjiang Corps	150	3	174	3	22	172
黑龙江垦区	Heilongjiang Land Reclamation	103	3	176	3	43	87

11-3 续表 Continued

地区	Region	事业单位 Affiliated Institutions			干部队伍综合培训情况 Training of Cadre		志愿者助残情况 Volunteer	
		单位 Institutions	实有人员 Actual Total of Staff	残疾人 Persons with Disability	县级举办综合培训班累计 County-level General Training Courses	参加县级培训 Trainees on County-level General Training Courses	志愿者登记在册 Registered Volunteer	受助残疾人 PWDs Helped by Volunteers
		个 unit	人 person	人 person	期 course	人次 person-time	人 persons	人 persons
全国	**Total**	**2307**	**12518**	**938**	**6139**	**296502**	**472899**	**3968797**
北京	Beijing	34	328	32	64	5531	48	1240
天津	Tianjin	26	203	22	74	3676	11880	71303
河北	Hebei	94	676	39	365	16647	23345	150553
山西	Shanxi	153	672	33	273	10073	2101	24759
内蒙古	Inner Mongolia	44	190	30	182	12160	2253	32593
辽宁	Liaoning	89	481	36	295	15689	14749	71877
吉林	Jilin	64	365	15	158	7640	57660	405741
黑龙江	Heilongjiang	69	261	36	178	5840	48986	354298
上海	Shanghai	20	170	20	45	1720	660	168570
江苏	Jiangsu	127	848	49	357	20651	9463	88348
浙江	Zhejiang	124	731	54	355	15409	5948	205228
安徽	Anhui	45	262	32	234	14884	5135	71593
福建	Fujian	125	329	43	197	7957	34256	123388
江西	Jiangxi	58	302	23	187	6750	1490	9914
山东	Shandong	92	579	38	446	20421	20351	187682
河南	Henan	160	1246	49	252	12781	75424	687751
湖北	Hubei	103	500	31	162	5811	30189	93464
湖南	Hunan	127	729	26	206	8886	9405	76151
广东	Guangdong	179	1025	54	162	9384	1791	27204
广西	Guangxi	91	313	48	198	11905	5808	106577
海南	Hainan	10	60	6	24	1431	3574	30392
重庆	Chongqing	44	189	21	116	7514	8519	171773
四川	Sichuan	79	444	30	509	26788	22494	334461
贵州	Guizhou	42	186	19	125	6333	2122	14950
云南	Yunnan	97	260	37	229	11201	2057	47856
西藏	Tibet					132	43	159
陕西	Shaanxi	77	570	31	322	10277	8269	112052
甘肃	Gansu	50	149	28	190	10775	60133	247953
青海	Qinghai	24	91	7	55	2367	801	4089
宁夏	Ningxia	5	39	3	40	1328	1404	6125
新疆	Xinjiang	54	317	45	139	4541	1429	14877
新疆兵团	Xinjiang Corps	1	3	1			1112	25876
黑龙江垦区	Heilongjiang Land Reclamation							

11-4 乡(镇、街道)残联

Disabled Persons' Federations in Townships (Towns, Streets)

地 区	Region	乡(镇、街道)已建残联 Disabled Persons' Federations Established in Townships (Towns, Streets)	残联机关 Disabled Persons' Federation			
			实有人员 Actual Staff	专职残联理事长 Full-time Presidents	兼职残联理事长 Part-time Presidents	残疾人专职委员 Full-time Workers on Disability
		个 unit	人 person	人 person	人 person	人 person
全 国	**Total**	**39666**	**49761**	**12923**	**18562**	**46038**
北 京	Beijing	323	383	253	61	505
天 津	Tianjin	242	380	242		240
河 北	Hebei	2271	2632	793	1478	2272
山 西	Shanxi	1459	1687	500	687	1769
内蒙古	Inner Mongolia	1102	1453	287	662	1156
辽 宁	Liaoning	1513	1753	515	943	1603
吉 林	Jilin	911	1053	192	677	867
黑龙江	Heilongjiang	1319	1494	158	709	1950
上 海	Shanghai	218	526	9	150	1592
江 苏	Jiangsu	1337	1806	1133	204	1463
浙 江	Zhejiang	1309	1545	923	342	1321
安 徽	Anhui	1478	1797	338	593	1476
福 建	Fujian	1077	1183	236	562	1402
江 西	Jiangxi	1556	2629	481	898	3357
山 东	Shandong	1805	2443	759	416	2003
河 南	Henan	2355	3205	1027	1061	2387
湖 北	Hubei	1251	1632	143	635	1872
湖 南	Hunan	2407	2763	750	1303	2421
广 东	Guangdong	1605	2103	503	790	1612
广 西	Guangxi	1237	1429	170	702	1456
海 南	Hainan	227	235	46	95	255
重 庆	Chongqing	1012	1275	455	364	946
四 川	Sichuan	4302	5746	880	2319	4026
贵 州	Guizhou	1425	1819	387	562	1443
云 南	Yunnan	1360	1483	608	510	1311
西 藏	Tibet					
陕 西	Shaanxi	1543	1801	382	454	1663
甘 肃	Gansu	1369	1426	603	532	1405
青 海	Qinghai	404	658	45	162	528
宁 夏	Ningxia	225	226	13	131	240
新 疆	Xinjiang	1016	1188	92	560	1379
新疆兵团	Xinjiang Corps	7	7			9
黑龙江垦区	Heilongjiang Land Reclamation	1	1			109

11-4 续表 Continued

地区	Region	干部队伍综合培训情况 Training of Staff		志愿者助残情况 Volunteer	
		乡镇级举办综合培训班 Township-level General Training Courses	参加乡镇级培训人次 Trainees on Township-level Training	志愿者登记在册 Registered Volunteer	受助残疾人 PWDs Helped by Volunteers
		期 course	人次 person-time	万人 10,000 persons	万人 10,000 persons
全 国	**Total**	**24441**	**358031**	**155.6**	**746.3**
北 京	Beijing	659	19177	0.4	22.0
天 津	Tianjin	226	4780	7.6	20.3
河 北	Hebei	1088	15164	15.3	59.3
山 西	Shanxi	985	19713	1.6	4.9
内蒙古	Inner Mongolia	334	5072	0.9	5.5
辽 宁	Liaoning	963	18586	1.8	9.5
吉 林	Jilin	385	5393	6.1	28.1
黑龙江	Heilongjiang	308	2490	14.6	21.5
上 海	Shanghai	212	20881	0.4	29.8
江 苏	Jiangsu	1251	26321	4.9	50.7
浙 江	Zhejiang	992	20569	1.7	16.2
安 徽	Anhui	908	17402	0.7	5.4
福 建	Fujian	355	5989	4.9	10.2
江 西	Jiangxi	906	9690	2.6	8.5
山 东	Shandong	2194	34032	12.5	31.5
河 南	Henan	882	7770	17.9	204.9
湖 北	Hubei	802	5429	3.4	10.0
湖 南	Hunan	368	6258	8.8	22.5
广 东	Guangdong	811	10620	22.2	5.9
广 西	Guangxi	658	8038	0.8	6.1
海 南	Hainan	80	683	0.6	2.5
重 庆	Chongqing	712	8711	0.9	24.1
四 川	Sichuan	4829	36736	7.0	32.6
贵 州	Guizhou	398	7734	3.1	3.8
云 南	Yunnan	576	10975	0.6	6.2
西 藏	Tibet				
陕 西	Shaanxi	1343	10509	2.9	14.9
甘 肃	Gansu	620	11465	9.0	81.6
青 海	Qinghai	69	1167	0.1	0.7
宁 夏	Ningxia	97	1958	2.0	2.0
新 疆	Xinjiang	430	4719	0.3	4.7
新疆兵团	Xinjiang Corps			0.1	0.2
黑龙江垦区	Heilongjiang Land Reclamation				

11-5 村(社区)残疾人组织
Disabled Persons' Federations in Villages and Communities

地 区	Region	已建残协 Associations of PWDs Established		残协情况 Associations		
		村 in Villages	社区 in Communities	已建残疾人活动室 Entertainment Rooms for PWDs Established	村 in Villages	社区 in Communities
		个 unit	个 unit	个 unit	个 unit	个 unit
全 国	**Total**	**514622**	**66609**	**385628**	**327537**	**58091**
北 京	Beijing	3594	2039	4047	2337	1710
天 津	Tianjin	3352	1259	4717	3477	1240
河 北	Hebei	48413	3006	51419	48413	3006
山 西	Shanxi	20678	1620	13624	12393	1231
内蒙古	Inner Mongolia	10891	1835	8398	5416	2982
辽 宁	Liaoning	11536	3866	15137	11291	3846
吉 林	Jilin	9355	1507	7234	6026	1208
黑龙江	Heilongjiang	6981	2154	4635	3010	1625
上 海	Shanghai	1274	2778	3891	1285	2606
江 苏	Jiangsu	15676	4701	18783	14378	4405
浙 江	Zhejiang	17700	2396	15374	12898	2476
安 徽	Anhui	13034	2116	6979	5688	1291
福 建	Fujian	12743	1756	7949	6804	1145
江 西	Jiangxi	15451	2216	10518	8812	1706
山 东	Shandong	60886	4468	46355	42483	3872
河 南	Henan	43407	3310	28428	25416	3012
湖 北	Hubei	20390	2786	11083	9172	1911
湖 南	Hunan	36618	3070	22882	20329	2553
广 东	Guangdong	18082	5014	7761	4136	3625
广 西	Guangxi	14279	1428	6946	5961	985
海 南	Hainan	2367	276	571	419	152
重 庆	Chongqing	8734	1862	7201	5557	1644
四 川	Sichuan	39855	3765	33114	29317	3797
贵 州	Guizhou	12363	842	6988	6160	828
云 南	Yunnan	12615	1397	5941	4980	961
西 藏	Tibet					
陕 西	Shaanxi	26353	1803	13601	12302	1299
甘 肃	Gansu	16089	1125	13951	12828	1123
青 海	Qinghai	4165	350	1565	1374	191
宁 夏	Ningxia	1660	339	833	583	250
新 疆	Xinjiang	6081	1519	5700	4292	1408
新疆兵团	Xinjiang Corps		3			
黑龙江垦区	Heilongjiang Land Reclamation		3	3		3

11-5 续表 Continued

地 区	Region	残协情况 Associations			志愿者助残情况 Volunteers	
		残疾人专职委员选聘情况 Full-time Workers on Disability				
		残疾人专职委员 Full-time Workers on Disability	村 in Villages	社区 in Communties	志愿者登记在册 Registered Volunteers	受助残疾人 PWDs Assisted by Volunteers
		人 person	人 person	人 person	万人 10,000 person	万人 10,000 person
全 国	**Total**	**537511**	**480170**	**57341**	**139.4**	**644.0**
北 京	Beijing	5322	3669	1653	1	19
天 津	Tianjin	4515	3323	1192	7	10
河 北	Hebei	51419	48413	3006	11	44
山 西	Shanxi	24365	22814	1551	2	5
内蒙古	Inner Mongolia	12391	10544	1847		3
辽 宁	Liaoning	15391	11602	3789	3	23
吉 林	Jilin	10539	9020	1519	7	27
黑龙江	Heilongjiang	5868	2864	3004	10	12
上 海	Shanghai	3456	1953	1503		2
江 苏	Jiangsu	19399	15157	4242	7	52
浙 江	Zhejiang	17975	15947	2028	2	18
安 徽	Anhui	15415	13459	1956	2	25
福 建	Fujian	15286	13621	1665	3	12
江 西	Jiangxi	13184	11563	1621	2	6
山 东	Shandong	60916	57381	3535	6	20
河 南	Henan	48803	45472	3331	20	209
湖 北	Hubei	13942	12256	1686	4	14
湖 南	Hunan	34420	32009	2411	11	26
广 东	Guangdong	22869	19141	3728	13	2
广 西	Guangxi	15846	14373	1473	1	8
海 南	Hainan	2664	2457	207		2
重 庆	Chongqing	10255	8320	1935	1	22
四 川	Sichuan	31823	29717	2106	8	26
贵 州	Guizhou	12717	12001	716	1	2
云 南	Yunnan	13132	11825	1307		3
西 藏	Tibet					
陕 西	Shaanxi	28746	26994	1752	7	15
甘 肃	Gansu	17220	16161	1059	7	33
青 海	Qinghai	2975	2835	140		
宁 夏	Ningxia	1668	1381	287	1	1
新 疆	Xinjiang	4987	3898	1089		2
新疆兵团	Xinjiang Corps	3		3		
黑龙江垦区	Heilongjiang Land Reclamation					

12-1　残疾人综合服务设施
Comprehensive Service Facilities for PWDs

地　区	Region	已投入使用项目 Projects in Operation		
		本年度新投入使用项目 Projects Getting into Operation in 2013		
		项目个数 Number of Projects	建设规模 Construction Area	总投资 Total Investment
		个 unit	平方米 square meter	万元 10,000 yuan
全　国	**Total**	**141**	**493467**	**194672.4**
北　京	Beijing	3	50268	26764.7
天　津	Tianjin	2	7800	7250.0
河　北	Hebei	2	1069	100.0
山　西	Shanxi	5	6867	1307.0
内蒙古	Inner Mongolia	6	4714	270.0
辽　宁	Liaoning	1	200	12.0
吉　林	Jilin	6	18002	5248.0
黑龙江	Heilongjiang	4	45800	21700.0
上　海	Shanghai			
江　苏	Jiangsu	11	58374	23326.5
浙　江	Zhejiang	8	33612	9833.8
安　徽	Anhui	9	31298	22495.0
福　建	Fujian	2	13109	4255.0
江　西	Jiangxi	1	3600	2320.0
山　东	Shandong	4	6632	1733.6
河　南	Henan	3	5028	555.0
湖　北	Hubei	8	26277	4066.0
湖　南	Hunan	6	9584	1589.0
广　东	Guangdong	10	34332	13660.8
广　西	Guangxi	1	21600	5530.0
海　南	Hainan	2	1155	847.0
重　庆	Chongqing	3	6157	1688.0
四　川	Sichuan	10	26984	11180.0
贵　州	Guizhou	2	2351	460.0
云　南	Yunnan	4	10750	2047.5
西　藏	Tibet			
陕　西	Shaanxi	3	7286	1661.0
甘　肃	Gansu	6	8814	5504.3
青　海	Qinghai	3	3748	1425.0
宁　夏	Ningxia			
新　疆	Xinjiang	16	48057	17843.1
新疆兵团	Xinjiang Corps			
黑龙江垦区	Heilongjiang Land Reclamation			

12-1 续表 1 Continued 1

地 区	Region	已投入使用项目 Projects in Operation 累计已投入使用项目 Accumulated Projects in Operation 项目个数 Number of Projects		
		项目个数 Number of Projects	建设规模 Construction Area	总投资 Total Investment
		个 unit	平方米 square meter	万元 10,000 yuan
全 国	**Total**	**2094**	**4241338**	**1195573.4**
北 京	Beijing	4	55621	29679.5
天 津	Tianjin	24	88532	46817.3
河 北	Hebei	146	145790	28347.7
山 西	Shanxi	52	108182	28489.8
内蒙古	Inner Mongolia	65	54516	8906.8
辽 宁	Liaoning	126	249023	81402.2
吉 林	Jilin	45	77648	19854.4
黑龙江	Heilongjiang	101	108296	36933.9
上 海	Shanghai	6	11497	6738.5
江 苏	Jiangsu	73	405092	139575.1
浙 江	Zhejiang	71	429389	158245.1
安 徽	Anhui	71	142314	44092.1
福 建	Fujian	78	152741	50529.7
江 西	Jiangxi	20	29213	7367.0
山 东	Shandong	136	333071	66015.9
河 南	Henan	134	178147	28293.8
湖 北	Hubei	68	107958	22566.5
湖 南	Hunan	93	121628	23428.9
广 东	Guangdong	85	342616	109419.6
广 西	Guangxi	94	129906	21962.4
海 南	Hainan	7	6306	1731.0
重 庆	Chongqing	28	85417	25116.2
四 川	Sichuan	82	185735	52203.4
贵 州	Guizhou	59	52786	8872.2
云 南	Yunnan	126	158312	25964.2
西 藏	Tibet			
陕 西	Shaanxi	76	146942	31195.3
甘 肃	Gansu	92	97181	30511.2
青 海	Qinghai	31	17911	4011.2
宁 夏	Ningxia	17	29792	6957.1
新 疆	Xinjiang	68	177847	48768.6
新疆兵团	Xinjiang Corps	10	6983	968.0
黑龙江垦区	Heilongjiang Land Reclamation	6	4949	608.6

12-1　续表 2　Continued 2

地　区	Region	在建项目 Projects under Construction 项目个数 Number of Projects	建设规模 Construction Area	总投资 Total Investment
		个 unit	平方米 square meter	万元 10,000 yuan
全　国	**Total**	**183**	**1207816**	**389065.4**
北　京	Beijing	3	33239	30568.7
天　津	Tianjin			
河　北	Hebei	6	10409	2030.0
山　西	Shanxi	10	50587	8828.3
内蒙古	Inner Mongolia	8	71505	26567.0
辽　宁	Liaoning	2	17500	5280.0
吉　林	Jilin	2	8792	1834.0
黑龙江	Heilongjiang	3	2642	385.0
上　海	Shanghai	1	5541	4100.0
江　苏	Jiangsu	6	58650	22500.0
浙　江	Zhejiang	18	112054	59190.3
安　徽	Anhui	13	54096	7722.0
福　建	Fujian	6	22167	6620.0
江　西	Jiangxi	3	12182	2100.0
山　东	Shandong	9	79815	21834.0
河　南	Henan	12	175292	41365.0
湖　北	Hubei	13	53305	18299.0
湖　南	Hunan	1	2983	460.0
广　东	Guangdong	11	152193	49002.5
广　西	Guangxi	9	17551	3608.8
海　南	Hainan	4	10022	5950.0
重　庆	Chongqing	3	23135	10829.3
四　川	Sichuan	10	50709	11217.0
贵　州	Guizhou	4	59270	21350.4
云　南	Yunnan	5	20362	4430.0
西　藏	Tibet			
陕　西	Shaanxi	3	19800	4550.0
甘　肃	Gansu	4	4672	1288.5
青　海	Qinghai	2	38000	8880.0
宁　夏	Ningxia	1	3000	555.0
新　疆	Xinjiang	11	38342	7720.7
新疆兵团	Xinjiang Corps			
黑龙江垦区	Heilongjiang Land Reclamation			

12-1 续表 3 Continued 3

地区	Region	筹建项目 Projects under Discussion and Preparation		
		项目个数 Number of Projects	建设规模 Construction Area	总投资 Total Investment
		个 unit	平方米 square meter	万元 10,000 yuan
全国	**Total**	**136**	**688673**	**275045.4**
北京	Beijing			
天津	Tianjin	1	13456	4200.0
河北	Hebei	2	974	362.2
山西	Shanxi	10	26765	7666.0
内蒙古	Inner Mongolia	2	30500	440.0
辽宁	Liaoning	1	3000	570.0
吉林	Jilin			
黑龙江	Heilongjiang	3	1600	383.0
上海	Shanghai			
江苏	Jiangsu	3	22800	25000.0
浙江	Zhejiang	7	116471	54651.0
安徽	Anhui	5	16600	1810.0
福建	Fujian	5	14038	2818.0
江西	Jiangxi	3	31956	4886.0
山东	Shandong	3	11282	1186.0
河南	Henan	9	26700	7100.0
湖北	Hubei	12	50504	12692.8
湖南	Hunan	6	21000	4190.0
广东	Guangdong	12	116277	60672.9
广西	Guangxi			
海南	Hainan	6	4900	8890.0
重庆	Chongqing	3	34000	928.0
四川	Sichuan	11	38295	14216.0
贵州	Guizhou	9	48300	39275.6
云南	Yunnan	4	9827	968.0
西藏	Tibet			
陕西	Shaanxi	5	22286	13921.2
甘肃	Gansu	3	5567	1259.0
青海	Qinghai	6	8939	4280.0
宁夏	Ningxia	2	3540	1059.8
新疆	Xinjiang	3	9096	1620.0
新疆兵团	Xinjiang Corps			
黑龙江垦区	Heilongjiang Land Reclamation			

12-2　残疾人康复设施
Rehabilitation Service Facilities for PWDs

地　区	Region	已投入使用项目 Projects in Operation		
		本年度新投入使用项目 Projects Getting into Operation in 2013		
		项目个数 Number of Projects	建设规模 Construction Area	总投资 Total Investment
		个 unit	平方米 square meter	万元 10,000 yuan
全　国	**Total**	**76**	**196611**	**59613.7**
北　京	Beijing	1	8721	6900.0
天　津	Tianjin			
河　北	Hebei	2	21883	6500.0
山　西	Shanxi	1	3300	600.0
内蒙古	Inner Mongolia			
辽　宁	Liaoning	2	17586	4842.0
吉　林	Jilin	2	4242	1217.0
黑龙江	Heilongjiang			
上　海	Shanghai			
江　苏	Jiangsu	6	21404	4956.0
浙　江	Zhejiang	2	9036	2900.0
安　徽	Anhui	2	8500	1584.0
福　建	Fujian	13	1190	74.3
江　西	Jiangxi			
山　东	Shandong	10	36450	10412.4
河　南	Henan			
湖　北	Hubei	4	11200	2700.0
湖　南	Hunan	3	9300	2071.5
广　东	Guangdong	5	10314	2965.0
广　西	Guangxi			
海　南	Hainan			
重　庆	Chongqing	1	800	70.0
四　川	Sichuan	6	17152	6787.0
贵　州	Guizhou			
云　南	Yunnan			
西　藏	Tibet			
陕　西	Shaanxi	7	6174	1606.0
甘　肃	Gansu			
青　海	Qinghai	2	285	173.0
宁　夏	Ningxia			
新　疆	Xinjiang	5	2500	1127.0
新疆兵团	Xinjiang Corps	2	6574	2128.5
黑龙江垦区	Heilongjiang Land Reclamation			

12-2 续表 1 Continued 1

地 区	Region	已投入使用项目 Projects in Operation 累计已投入使用项目 Accumulated Projects in Operation 项目个数 Number of Projects (个 unit)	建设规模 Construction Area (平方米 square meter)	总投资 Total Investment (万元 10,000 yuan)
全 国	**Total**	**542**	**1007332**	**327475.1**
北 京	Beijing	3	13221	8273.7
天 津	Tianjin	8	9550	1966.0
河 北	Hebei	7	33979	8178.1
山 西	Shanxi	32	71946	17293.4
内蒙古	Inner Mongolia	2	4005	430.0
辽 宁	Liaoning	13	57927	11813.9
吉 林	Jilin	8	27941	10356.0
黑龙江	Heilongjiang	3	4246	307.0
上 海	Shanghai	1	49734	45000.0
江 苏	Jiangsu	47	119259	30456.0
浙 江	Zhejiang	21	136598	40983.4
安 徽	Anhui	4	11932	2318.0
福 建	Fujian	208	26808	3935.3
江 西	Jiangxi	7	11520	6406.0
山 东	Shandong	27	78168	27728.0
河 南	Henan	6	44942	9304.0
湖 北	Hubei	11	22737	4445.0
湖 南	Hunan	18	16645	3245.5
广 东	Guangdong	49	90618	25771.8
广 西	Guangxi	1	660	125.0
海 南	Hainan			
重 庆	Chongqing	4	4613	1200.0
四 川	Sichuan	25	112549	55821.0
贵 州	Guizhou	3	11397	2519.9
云 南	Yunnan			
西 藏	Tibet			
陕 西	Shaanxi	19	29026	4492.7
甘 肃	Gansu	2	1300	347.0
青 海	Qinghai	3	4088	973.0
宁 夏	Ningxia			
新 疆	Xinjiang	8	5350	1657.0
新疆兵团	Xinjiang Corps	2	6574	2128.5
黑龙江垦区	Heilongjiang Land Reclamation			

12-2　续表 2　Continued 2

地　区	Region	在建项目 Projects under Construction 项目个数 Number of Projects	建设规模 Construction Area	总投资 Total Investment
		个 unit	平方米 square meter	万元 10,000 yuan
全　国	**Total**	**120**	**1073688**	**328689.8**
北　京	Beijing			
天　津	Tianjin			
河　北	Hebei	1	5778	1599.0
山　西	Shanxi	7	20746	6163.0
内蒙古	Inner Mongolia	3	31823	6900.0
辽　宁	Liaoning	2	10747	3341.0
吉　林	Jilin	1	8000	1600.0
黑龙江	Heilongjiang			
上　海	Shanghai			
江　苏	Jiangsu	13	117069	57349.5
浙　江	Zhejiang	6	81467	42495.0
安　徽	Anhui	5	48510	7650.0
福　建	Fujian	2	6940	1300.0
江　西	Jiangxi	1	8000	1700.0
山　东	Shandong	10	181182	60066.6
河　南	Henan	4	26536	6500.0
湖　北	Hubei	5	72536	19382.0
湖　南	Hunan	4	21656	1690.0
广　东	Guangdong	10	45905	10494.2
广　西	Guangxi	4	15061	2578.0
海　南	Hainan			
重　庆	Chongqing	4	25260	6451.3
四　川	Sichuan	2	8000	3996.0
贵　州	Guizhou	4	46536	11402.0
云　南	Yunnan	3	24000	5800.0
西　藏	Tibet			
陕　西	Shaanxi	11	58380	12382.0
甘　肃	Gansu	5	95119	22763.0
青　海	Qinghai	3	520	229.1
宁　夏	Ningxia	3	41321	20758.0
新　疆	Xinjiang	3	36097	7500.0
新疆兵团	Xinjiang Corps	2	20000	3300.0
黑龙江垦区	Heilongjiang Land Reclamation	2	16500	3300.0

12-2 续表 3 Continued 3

地 区	Region	筹建项目 Projects under Discussion and Preparation		
		项目个数 Number of Projects	建设规模 Construction Area	总投资 Total Investment
		个 unit	平方米 square meter	万元 10,000 yuan
全 国	**Total**	**63**	**481221**	**166908.7**
北 京	Beijing			
天 津	Tianjin			
河 北	Hebei	1	63000	39000.0
山 西	Shanxi	4	9860	2408.0
内蒙古	Inner Mongolia			
辽 宁	Liaoning			
吉 林	Jilin			
黑龙江	Heilongjiang	4	44000	10940.0
上 海	Shanghai			
江 苏	Jiangsu	1	3000	300.0
浙 江	Zhejiang	1	2700	1962.0
安 徽	Anhui	2	11000	2900.0
福 建	Fujian	1	8916	3225.0
江 西	Jiangxi	2	3100	1200.0
山 东	Shandong	5	33500	11230.0
河 南	Henan	8	44128	9837.0
湖 北	Hubei	5	25779	3360.3
湖 南	Hunan	2	14600	3200.0
广 东	Guangdong	6	62583	40265.5
广 西	Guangxi	5	48955	8643.0
海 南	Hainan	2	1700	731.8
重 庆	Chongqing	6	42500	13717.0
四 川	Sichuan	1	8000	2984.0
贵 州	Guizhou			
云 南	Yunnan			
西 藏	Tibet			
陕 西	Shaanxi	5	38000	7005.0
甘 肃	Gansu			
青 海	Qinghai	2	15900	4000.0
宁 夏	Ningxia			
新 疆	Xinjiang			
新疆兵团	Xinjiang Corps			
黑龙江垦区	Heilongjiang Land Reclamation			

12-3　残疾人托养设施

Fostering Service Facilities for PWDs

地　区	Region	已投入使用项目 Projects in Operation		
		本年度新投入使用项目 Projects Getting into Operation in 2013		
		项目个数 Number of Projects	建设规模 Construction Area	总投资 Total Investment
		个 unit	平方米 square meter	万元 10,000 yuan
全　国	**Total**	**105**	**217688**	**50123.7**
北　京	Beijing			
天　津	Tianjin	2	2073	1246.0
河　北	Hebei	5	20915	3235.1
山　西	Shanxi			
内蒙古	Inner Mongolia	1	630	200.0
辽　宁	Liaoning	1	3286	485.0
吉　林	Jilin			
黑龙江	Heilongjiang			
上　海	Shanghai			
江　苏	Jiangsu	14	57937	15450.0
浙　江	Zhejiang	4	32711	11509.0
安　徽	Anhui			
福　建	Fujian	12	12722	3686.4
江　西	Jiangxi			
山　东	Shandong	3	5500	1150.0
河　南	Henan			
湖　北	Hubei	11	10428	2316.5
湖　南	Hunan	18	16398	1288.6
广　东	Guangdong	1	100	10.0
广　西	Guangxi	2	920	70.2
海　南	Hainan			
重　庆	Chongqing			
四　川	Sichuan	4	8800	1530.0
贵　州	Guizhou	1	1640	252.0
云　南	Yunnan			
西　藏	Tibet			
陕　西	Shaanxi	10	22093	2282.0
甘　肃	Gansu	1	1200	620.0
青　海	Qinghai			
宁　夏	Ningxia			
新　疆	Xinjiang	6	7279	1438.0
新疆兵团	Xinjiang Corps	9	13056	3355.0
黑龙江垦区	Heilongjiang Land Reclamation			

12-3 续表 1 Continued 1

地 区	Region	已投入使用项目 Projects in Operation 累计已投入使用项目 Accumulated Projects in Operation 项目个数 Number of Projects 个 unit	建设规模 Construction Area 平方米 square meter	总投资 Total Investment 万元 10,000 yuan
全 国	**Total**	**353**	**782398**	**195743.5**
北 京	Beijing			
天 津	Tianjin	16	10613	3866.0
河 北	Hebei	8	31219	5550.1
山 西	Shanxi	1	2000	400.0
内蒙古	Inner Mongolia	4	4496	500.0
辽 宁	Liaoning	16	22898	10368.5
吉 林	Jilin	1	3345	1452.0
黑龙江	Heilongjiang	3	10817	3346.0
上 海	Shanghai			
江 苏	Jiangsu	40	174136	54361.0
浙 江	Zhejiang	12	89766	32383.0
安 徽	Anhui			
福 建	Fujian	40	54247	10362.2
江 西	Jiangxi	2	650	65.0
山 东	Shandong	25	74631	20986.0
河 南	Henan	2	5400	1500.0
湖 北	Hubei	28	32938	5079.5
湖 南	Hunan	32	28568	3384.1
广 东	Guangdong	33	45321	8842.1
广 西	Guangxi	2	920	70.2
海 南	Hainan			
重 庆	Chongqing	1	68	197.9
四 川	Sichuan	9	20732	4214.7
贵 州	Guizhou	1	1640	252.0
云 南	Yunnan			
西 藏	Tibet			
陕 西	Shaanxi	37	93257	12396.3
甘 肃	Gansu	4	10575	1864.0
青 海	Qinghai			
宁 夏	Ningxia			
新 疆	Xinjiang	7	10302	2326.0
新疆兵团	Xinjiang Corps	27	45338	6629.9
黑龙江垦区	Heilongjiang Land Reclamation	2	8521	5347.0

12-3　续表 2　Continued 2

地　区	Region	在建项目 Projects under Construction		
		项目个数 Number of Projects	建设规模 Construction Area	总投资 Total Investment
		个 unit	平方米 square meter	万元 10,000 yuan
全　国	**Total**	**83**	**405231**	**127283.1**
北　京	Beijing			
天　津	Tianjin			
河　北	Hebei	2	21900	5838.0
山　西	Shanxi	2	5000	1000.0
内蒙古	Inner Mongolia	3	7585	2400.0
辽　宁	Liaoning	8	56551	30315.0
吉　林	Jilin	2	6800	1400.0
黑龙江	Heilongjiang	1	10000	2000.0
上　海	Shanghai			
江　苏	Jiangsu	16	146834	45276.2
浙　江	Zhejiang	6	18348	5750.0
安　徽	Anhui	1	3000	450.0
福　建	Fujian	3	5550	1000.0
江　西	Jiangxi	1	1800	35.0
山　东	Shandong	4	11500	4405.0
河　南	Henan	7	24621	4909.0
湖　北	Hubei	3	11000	2100.0
湖　南	Hunan	3	20439	8859.9
广　东	Guangdong	3	11678	3067.0
广　西	Guangxi	2	3600	700.0
海　南	Hainan			
重　庆	Chongqing	1	3860	1200.0
四　川	Sichuan	1	2000	300.0
贵　州	Guizhou	1	2000	330.0
云　南	Yunnan			
西　藏	Tibet			
陕　西	Shaanxi	4	7313	1550.0
甘　肃	Gansu	2	6052	750.0
青　海	Qinghai	4	8200	2210.0
宁　夏	Ningxia			
新　疆	Xinjiang	3	9601	1438.0
新疆兵团	Xinjiang Corps			
黑龙江垦区	Heilongjiang Land Reclamation			

12-3 续表 3 Continued 3

地 区	Region	筹建项目 Projects under Discussion and Preparation		
		项目个数 Number of Projects	建设规模 Construction Area	总投资 Total Investment
		个 unit	平方米 square meter	万元 10,000 yuan
全 国	**Total**	**59**	**277928**	**63177.8**
北 京	Beijing			
天 津	Tianjin			
河 北	Hebei	2	4000	580.0
山 西	Shanxi	5	16400	4270.0
内蒙古	Inner Mongolia	1	3800	480.0
辽 宁	Liaoning	2	2800	900.0
吉 林	Jilin			
黑龙江	Heilongjiang			
上 海	Shanghai			
江 苏	Jiangsu	1	5000	100.0
浙 江	Zhejiang	4	35150	14091.0
安 徽	Anhui			
福 建	Fujian	2	33150	3529.0
江 西	Jiangxi			
山 东	Shandong	5	13957	3460.0
河 南	Henan	6	22316	2750.0
湖 北	Hubei	4	18320	2080.0
湖 南	Hunan	2	12788	3720.0
广 东	Guangdong	5	34850	11399.0
广 西	Guangxi	6	24807	2814.1
海 南	Hainan	1	1800	497.7
重 庆	Chongqing	4	16500	6217.0
四 川	Sichuan			
贵 州	Guizhou			
云 南	Yunnan	1	2082	330.0
西 藏	Tibet			
陕 西	Shaanxi	6	26200	5090.0
甘 肃	Gansu			
青 海	Qinghai	1	2008	570.0
宁 夏	Ningxia			
新 疆	Xinjiang	1	2000	300.0
新疆兵团	Xinjiang Corps			
黑龙江垦区	Heilongjiang Land Reclamation			

13-1　残疾人事业信息化建设
Informationzation on the Work for PWDs

地　区	Region	门户网站 Websites	省级 at Provincial Level	地市级 at Prefectural/ City Level	县级 at County Level	省级网站本年度发稿量 Articles Published by Provincial-level Websites of Disabled Persons' Federations	各级信息化专业人才 IT Professionals
		个 unit	个 unit	个 unit	个 unit	篇 sheet	人 person
全　国	**Total**	**1617**	**33**	**277**	**1307**	**71024**	**5019**
北　京	Beijing	17	1		16	2185	44
天　津	Tianjin	16	1		15	969	56
河　北	Hebei	37	1	10	26	3328	285
山　西	Shanxi	87	1	11	75	1403	197
内蒙古	Inner Mongolia	40	1	8	31	900	147
辽　宁	Liaoning	67	1	14	52	4710	193
吉　林	Jilin	43	1	9	33	1337	130
黑龙江	Heilongjiang	29	1	7	21	854	174
上　海	Shanghai	18	1		17	2782	50
江　苏	Jiangsu	109	1	13	95	5835	212
浙　江	Zhejiang	97	1	12	84	6000	162
安　徽	Anhui	90	1	16	73	10000	182
福　建	Fujian	94	1	9	84	2450	163
江　西	Jiangxi	43	1	6	36	479	166
山　东	Shandong	88	1	17	70	1350	216
河　南	Henan	28	1	10	17	904	235
湖　北	Hubei	52	1	12	39	4587	147
湖　南	Hunan	74	1	13	60	2300	193
广　东	Guangdong	81	1	21	59	2838	281
广　西	Guangxi	117	1	14	102	1500	202
海　南	Hainan	2	1	1		51	36
重　庆	Chongqing	38	1		37	1350	86
四　川	Sichuan	109	1	17	91	370	283
贵　州	Guizhou	23	1	3	19	829	103
云　南	Yunnan	48	1	11	36	2200	217
西　藏	Tibet	1	1			23	18
陕　西	Shaanxi	64	1	10	53	1760	160
甘　肃	Gansu	45	1	14	30	2414	127
青　海	Qinghai	8	1	4	3	499	70
宁　夏	Ningxia	13	1	4	8	1800	37
新　疆	Xinjiang	36	1	10	25	1610	137
新疆兵团	Xinjiang Corps	2	1	1		507	184
黑龙江垦区	Heilongjiang Land Reclamation	1	1			900	126

13-1 续表 Continued

地区	Region	本年度信息工作培训情况 Training for Web Technology and Management in 2013			
		省级 at Provincial Level		地市级 at Prefectural/City Level	
		举办信息工作培训班 Training Course for Web Technology and Management	参加信息工作培训班 Participants of Training Course	举办信息工作培训班 Training Course for Web Technology and Management	参加信息工作培训班 Participants of Training Course
		期 course	人次 person-time	期 course	人次 person-time
全 国	**Total**	**43**	**3222**	**652**	**9675**
北 京	Beijing	3	150		
天 津	Tianjin	1	1		
河 北	Hebei	2	85	18	461
山 西	Shanxi			7	138
内蒙古	Inner Mongolia	1	130	9	137
辽 宁	Liaoning	2	110	21	1000
吉 林	Jilin	2	90	11	434
黑龙江	Heilongjiang			3	67
上 海	Shanghai	6	500		
江 苏	Jiangsu	1	50	26	1318
浙 江	Zhejiang	1	35	7	671
安 徽	Anhui	1	140	19	367
福 建	Fujian	2	260	8	256
江 西	Jiangxi	1	260	13	217
山 东	Shandong			20	400
河 南	Henan			19	381
湖 北	Hubei	3	500	334	673
湖 南	Hunan			10	174
广 东	Guangdong	1	36	22	649
广 西	Guangxi	1	150	11	138
海 南	Hainan	1	50		
重 庆	Chongqing	1	55		
四 川	Sichuan			30	892
贵 州	Guizhou	2	90	2	250
云 南	Yunnan	1	50	13	256
西 藏	Tibet	1	20	1	20
陕 西	Shaanxi	4	128	9	197
甘 肃	Gansu	1	130	15	180
青 海	Qinghai	1	80	10	154
宁 夏	Ningxia	1	87	5	122
新 疆	Xinjiang	1	20	5	73
新疆兵团	Xinjiang Corps				
黑龙江垦区	Heilongjiang Land Reclamation	1	15	4	50

分省统计报告

Statistical Report of Provinces

2013 年北京市残疾人事业发展统计公报

2013 年，在中国残联指导下，在各区县、各部门和社会各界的共同支持下，北京市全面加快残疾人社会保障和服务体系建设，努力推动残疾人事业科学发展、融合发展、创新发展，残疾人康复、教育、就业、社会保障、文化体育、法律维权和无障碍环境建设等工作得到有效落实，残疾人保障和服务水平进一步提高，首都残疾人事业迈上了新台阶。

一、康复

2013 年，康复服务质量有了新提升。以扩面、提标为着力点，注重康复人群全覆盖，37 万名残疾人得到不同程度的康复。为 2.4 万名重残无业残疾人进行健康体检，为 3000 名重度残疾人提供居家康复服务。重视精神残疾人康复，会同北京市卫生局开展精神残疾人居家与社区康复试点工作，规范精神卫生服务，支持海淀区试点建成 10 个精神残疾人融入社会的“中途宿舍”。规范残疾儿童少年康复服务标准，确保免费康复项目政策顺利实施。北京康复中心建设有序推进，全市 16 所家庭康复培训学校全部投入使用，为 2 万名家长提供了康复基本知识和技能培训，有效提高了康复服务水平。

在全市 16 个区县开展了社区康复工作，累计已建社区康复站的社区总数 3626 个，配备 5775 名社区康复协调员。14 个区县的 26 个医疗卫生机构陆续开展残疾儿童筛查工作，年度新诊断 0-6 岁残疾儿童 443 人。

开展视力残疾康复机构总数达到 7 个，完成白内障复明手术 1.11 万例，为 1197 名贫困白内障患者免费施行复明手术，为 1514 名低视力患者配用助视器，培训低视力儿童家长 17 名，有效开展家庭康复训练，对 1447 名盲人进行定向行走训练。

推进听力语言康复机构规范化管理，完善基层服务网络。已建设市级听力语言康复机构 1 个，基层听力语言康复机构 19 个。年度新收训聋儿 182 名，在训聋儿 302 名；规范聋儿家长学校，开展家庭训练，共培训聋儿家长 330 名；开展各级各类听力语言康复专业技术人员培训，共培训专业人员 277 人。

开展肢体残疾康复训练服务机构达 14 个，其中，市级康复机构 1 个，区县级康复机构 13 个。培训各级各类肢体残疾康复人员 2908 人次；对 5954 名肢体残疾者实施康复训练；实施救助项目资助 267 名脑瘫儿童进行机构康复训练。

开展智力残疾康复训练服务机构 35 个，其中，市级康复机构 1 个，区县级康复机构 34 个。培训各级各类智力残疾康复人员 1767 人次；共对 2750 名智力残疾人进行康复训练；实施救助项目资助 477 名智力残疾儿童进行机构康复训练，同时对儿童家长进行培训。

大力推广“社会化、综合性、开放式”精神病防治康复工作。在 16 个区县开展精神病防治康复工作，对 6.94 万重性精神病患者进行综合防治康复，监护率达到 86.32%，显好率达到 57.9%，社会参与率达到 42.75%，肇事率 0.02%；对 7398 名贫困精神病患者进行医疗救助。

建立了 1 个市级孤独症儿童康复训练机构，420 名孤独症儿童在各级机构进行了康复训练。

加强残疾人辅助器具服务体系建设，深入开展辅助器具供应服务。为残疾人减免费用供应辅助器具 9872 件，其中装配假肢 592 例、矫形器 283 例、验配助视器 1708 件。

二、教育

2013 年，北京市政府办公厅印发《北京市中小学融合教育行动计划》，配合教育部门出台随班就读工作意见、送教上门指导意见，制定北京市残疾人融合教育示范区、示范校评选标准，举办残疾人融合教育研讨会，从制度上保障了残疾儿童少年平等接受教育的权利。对全市 7461 名 15—50 岁残疾人青壮年文盲进行扫盲需求调查；以房山区和平谷区为试点开展残疾人青壮年扫盲工作，分类制定扫盲工作方案，从源头提高残疾人素质。

市残联积极从多渠道争取资金支持，为残疾儿童给予学前教育资助。为家庭经济困难的残疾儿童享受普惠性学前教育提供资助 101 人次。

已开办特殊教育普通高中班（部）2 个，在校生 114 人。其中聋高中 1 个，在校生 98 人；盲高中 1 个，在校生 16 人。残疾人中等职业学校（班）3 个，在校生 213 人，毕业生 115 人，其中 95 人获得职业资格证书。有 70 名残疾人被普通高等院校录取，163 名残疾人进入特殊教育学院学习。

截止到 2013 年底，有未入学适龄残疾儿童少年 243 人。其中视力残疾儿童 3 人，听力残疾儿童 1 人，言语残疾儿童 1 人，智力残疾儿童 112 人，肢体残疾儿童 72 人，精神残疾儿童 18 人，多重残疾儿童 36 人。

三、就业

2013 年，我市坚持把实现就业作为残疾人增收的关键措施。依法推动按比例就业工作，会同市人力社保局和市国资委分别制定了《关于进一步推进市属事业单位安排残疾人就业工作的指导意见》，成功举办首届国有企业面向残疾人专场招聘会，全市按比例就业的残疾人达到 4 万人。出台促进残疾人毕业生就业“六项措施”，应届残疾人大中专毕业生就业率保持在 98%以上。全市建设职业康复站 511 个，13 个区县已经或者规划建设了职业康复中心，智力残疾人和稳定期精神残疾人的职业康复劳动项目得到进一步开发。助残日期间举行全市性残疾人就业招聘会，各区县分别设立招聘会场。

城镇新就业残疾人 3244 人。其中，集中就业 75 人、按比例安排就业 1221 人、公益性岗位就业 193 人、个体就业及其它形式灵活就业 1233 人、辅助性就业 522 人。

残疾人职业培训基地达到 62 个，其中残联兴办 8 个，依托社会机构兴办 54 个，1.05 万人次城镇残疾人接受了职业培训。

培训盲人保健按摩人员 1115 名，盲人医疗按摩人员 23 名；保健按摩机构达到 409 个，医疗按摩机构达到 2 个；在专业技术职务资格评审中，分别有 34 人和 32 人通过医疗按摩人员中级和初级职称评审。

四、社会保障

截止到 2013 年底，全市有 6.56 万城镇残疾职工参加社会保险。有 2.61 万城镇残疾人参加了城镇居民社会养老保险，在 60 岁以下的参保残疾人中有 1.39 万重度残疾人，其中 1.32 万人得到了政府的参保扶助，有 6525 名非重度残疾人享受了全额或部分代缴的优惠政策，领取养老金待遇的人数达到 3230 人。

新型农村社会养老保险方面，共有 7.85 万残疾人参加了新型农村社会养老保险。在 60 周岁以下的参保残疾人中有重度残疾人 3 万人，全部得到了政府的参保扶助。有 2.48 万非重度残疾人也享受了全额或部分代缴的优惠政策。享受养老金待遇的人数达到 1.33 万人。

城镇残疾居民参加基本医疗保险达到 4.90 万人，农村居民参加新型农村合作医疗达到 11.63 万人；12.38 万符合条件的城乡残疾人享受了稳定的生活补贴；城镇 1.99 万和农村 2.20 万残疾人纳入最低生活保障范围；2.13 万城乡残疾人得到了其他救助救济。

残疾人托养服务工作规范推进，残疾人托养服务机构达到 80 个，共为 1207 名残疾人提供了托养服务。其中寄宿制托养服务机构 29 个，综合性托养服务机构 51 个，接受居家托养服务的残疾人达到 9.85 万人。

五、扶贫开发

2013 年，我市农村残疾人扶贫开发工作多渠道发展，科技扶贫效能显著，农村低收入贫困残疾人生产生活状况得到较大改善。与市商委合作，开展“万村千乡市场工程”助残扶贫项目，安置农村残疾人或家庭成员就业，帮扶农村残疾人家庭创办村级店；结合“融合就业六大工程”，协助农村基层党组织开展助残扶贫活动，督促落实各项帮扶措施。

全年共扶持 9197 名低收入贫困残疾人增收，其中通过 128 个残疾人扶贫基地安置 4575 名，辐射带动 4444 名残疾人就业，年均收入过万。全年农村种养殖实用技术培训 4309 人次；177 个单位和 577 名个人对低收入贫困残疾人开展结对帮扶；完成 731 户农村贫困残疾人危房改造，各地投入危房资金 592.35 万元，803 名残疾人受益。

六、维权

2013 年，我市扎实开展残疾人法律维权，配合市人大内司委、市政协社法委对残疾人保障法本市实施办法两年来的执行情况进行专题调研和视察活动。同时，加强了政策法规宣传，向持证残疾人、残疾人工作者及基层社区统一发放了 60 万册政策口袋书。与市司法局联合举办法律大讲堂，通过易行热线、12348 热线、温馨家园法律服务工作站向残疾人提供日常法律服务，保障残疾人的合法权益。重视残疾人信访工作，信访结案率达到 98%，确保了残疾人群体稳定。

各级残联维权组织建设得到加强，残疾人事业法律法规体系进一步完善，残疾人维权工作全面开展。

市和区县人大进行《残疾人保障法》执法检查和专题调研 5 次，政协进行视察和专题调研 4 次。开展普法宣传教育活动 109 次，1.86 万人参加；举办法律培训班 36 个，4507 人参加。

截止 2013 年底，成立残疾人法律救助工作协调机构 17 个，建立残疾人法律救助工作站 317 个，建立残疾人法律援助中心（工作站）17 个，办理案件 337 件，有力地促进了法律救助和法律援助工作。

残疾人参政议政工作得到加强，各级残联协助人大代表、政协委员提出议案、建议、提案 3 件，办理议案、建议、提案 3 件。

无障碍建设成效显著。启动了无障碍区县创建工作，积极促进无障碍环境建设城乡均衡发展。以需求为导向，推进公共交通无障碍，研究制定无障碍出租车发展方案，以老旧小区综合整治为契机，推进小区无障碍改造工作，加强对残疾人家庭无障碍改造工作力度，累计改造完成 9 万户。

16 个区县大力加强无障碍建设。开展无障碍建设检查 253 次，无障碍培训 5024 人次；为 1.58 万个贫困残疾人家庭实施了无障碍改造；为 2.26 万残疾人发放了残疾人机动轮椅车燃油补贴。

各级残联共处理残疾人群众来信 6921 余件，接待残疾人群众来访 4617 人次。

七、宣传文化

2013 年，我市 11 部门联合出台《关于加强北京市残疾人文化建设的意见》，有力推动了残疾人群众性文化体育活动广泛开展。出色承办第八届残疾人艺术汇演北京赛区比赛，北京赛区组委会获组织奖，北京市获团体金奖。继续组织残疾人走入高雅艺术殿堂，让广大残疾人共享高品质文化生活。

中央及市级媒体采用稿件 339 件，主要新闻媒体刊播稿件 972 件，报刊专版 60 个，残疾人专题广播节目 1 个，电视手语新闻栏目 1 个，市级残疾人事业新闻宣传促进会 1 个。各区县主要新闻媒体刊播稿件 786 件，报刊专版 55 个，残疾人专题广播节目 11 个，电视手语新闻栏目 3 个，建立市级新促会 1 个。

市在公共图书馆设立盲文及盲人有声读物阅览室 6 个，各区县在公共图书馆设立盲文及盲人有声读物阅览室 18 个；市和区县举办残疾人文化周分别为 19 个和 277 个；举办残疾人文化艺术类比赛及展览分别为 45 个和 151 个；市和区县分别成立残疾人艺术团队 1 个和 48 个。

八、体育

我市启动了残疾人运动员落户北京、辅具适配等方面优待政策，在国际重大体育赛事中获奖的残疾人运动员享受到与健全运动员同等奖励标准。

市级残疾人体育健身活动 25 次，参加人数 1.52 万人；残疾人体育示范点 51 个，残疾人体育健身指导员 1050 人；残疾人体育比赛 15 次，参与的残疾人运动员 392 人次；残疾人体育训练基地 10 个，聘任教练员 30 人。

区县级别残疾人体育健身活动 1350 次，参加人数 8.87 万人；残疾人体育示范点 79 个；残疾人体育健身指导员 528 人。

九、组织建设

2013 年，我市下大力气推进基层组织建设。为乡镇（街道）残联全部配齐了专兼职理事长，实现了职责、机构、人员、经费“四个单列”；加强了对 403 个温馨家园日常管理，制定服务规范，进一步完善了常态化工作机制。

2013 年，市残联领导班子中配备 3 名残疾人领导干部；12 个区县残联机关配备了残疾人干部；已建乡镇（街道）残联 323 个，已建率达到 100%；选聘残疾人专职委员 505 名；已建社区（村）残协 5633 个，已建率达到 89.06%；选聘残疾人专职委员 5322 名。

市、区（县）、乡镇（街道）残联实有人员 1202 人。各级残联共举办培训班 728 期，培训机关干部、协会干部及残疾人专职委员 2.53 万人次。

全市各区县共建立各类残疾人专门协会 80 个，专门协会已建比例 100%。

十、服务设施

截至2013年底，全市已竣工并投入使用的各级残疾人综合服务设施4个，总建设规模5.56万平方米，总投资29679.54万元；已竣工并投入使用的各级残疾人康复设施3个，总建设规模1.32万平方米，总投资8273.73万元。各类服务设施的投入使用，为残疾人服务提供了可靠的基础保障。

十一、信息化

“残疾人服务一卡通”作为2013年北京市政府折子工程，受到全社会特别是残疾人的高度关注。一期工程已于2013年底投入试运行，为实现“一卡在手、服务全有，一卡连接、身份了然，一卡管理、统一终端，一卡通用、畅游京城”的目标奠定了扎实基础。

市残联网站加大对残疾人各项政策、残疾人事业的宣传，年度访问量达到5115万次，完成2185条信息更新。

北京市残联系统已全部开通了公众服务网站，1个市级残联网站和16个区县级残联网站。2013年，市级残联开设网站技术培训班3期，培训各级残联信息员达150人次。

统计队伍建设进一步加强。各级残联共有20名专、兼职统计人员从事残疾人事业统计工作，市级残联举办统计培训班1期，参加培训的人员达到100人次。

市、区（县）两级残联共有44名专业技术人员从事信息化工作；建立市级残联局域网和网上办公（OA）系统，为协同办公提供了保障。

2013年天津市残疾人事业发展统计公报

2013年，在市委、市政府的领导和中国残联的指导以及全社会的大力支持下，天津市全面完成了残疾人事业各项工作的年度任务，加快健全残疾人社会保障和服务体系，积极推进残疾人社会保障、康复、教育、就业、扶贫、维权、托养、重残护理、文化体育、福利基金、组织建设、服务设施和信息化建设等工作，取得了新的成效和新的突破，残疾人物质和文化生活状况得到进一步改善。现根据2013年度残疾人事业统计数据和实际情况，进行分析，并公报如下：

一、残疾人康复工作稳步提高

积极推进残疾人社区康复工作。截至2013年底，在13个市辖区和3个县开展了社区康复工作，有1658个社区已建立康复站。目前，有社区康复协调员4392人，比2012年增加8.3%；为264000名生活在社区的残疾人建立了社区康复服务档案，到2013年底，累计有229656人接受了社区康复服务，比2012年增加19.8%。从图1-1看，"十二五"以来，社区康复工作水平显著提高。

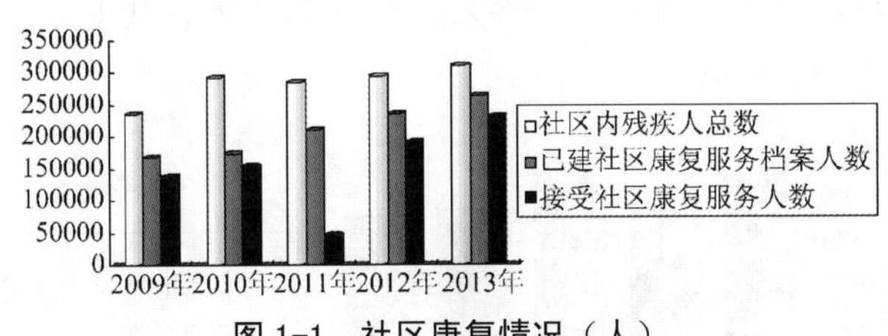

图1-1　社区康复情况（人）

2013年，通过实施一批重点康复工程，使各类别残疾人得到不同程度的康复。全年完成白内障复明手术5296例，为1536例贫困白内障患者免费施行复明手术，比2012年增加31.5%。全年为1300名低视力患者配用助视器。培训低视力儿童家长501名，是2012年的3.6倍。加大了开展家庭康复训练的力度。对1071名盲人进行定向行走训练，康复范围不断扩大。

加强市级聋儿康复机构建设，完善聋儿康复网络。2013年对新收训69名聋儿进行了听力语言训练，比2012年增加23.2%。其中机构康复训练人数68名，比2012年增加38.8%。家庭康复训练人数1名。共对125名聋儿进行了听力语言康复训练。规范聋儿家长学校，开展家庭训练，共培训聋儿家长99名；培训各类专业人员34人，是2012年的2倍。受训聋儿有16名进入普幼普小，有2名进入聋校；开展成年听力语言康复技术服务，聋人接受服务1049人次。机构康复功能主要集中在听力语言训练和社区指导上；助听器验配、人工耳蜗术后调试、听觉口语法、成年听力语言康复等由于技术含量较大，主要集中在市聋儿康复中心开展。

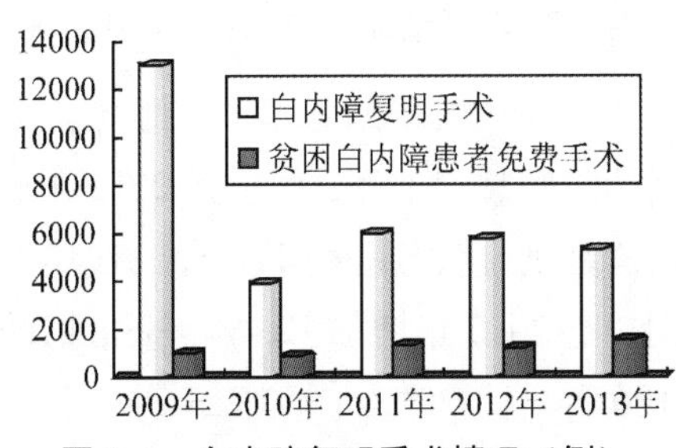

图1-2　白内障复明手术情况（例）

大力推广"社会化、综合性、开放式"精神病防治康复工作。2013年，在16个区县开展精神病防治康复工作，覆盖总人口数达到1005.1万人。对63411名精神病患者进行综合防治康复，监护率达到95.4%，显好率达到76%，社会参与率达到65.8%，无关锁病人。接受治疗的精神病患者14457人。接受康复训练的精神病人数10742人，其中在精神康复机构训练的8171人。对3635名贫困精神病患者进行医疗救助，占贫困患者的45.9%。建立了2个市级孤独症儿童康复训练机构，有50名孤独症儿童进行了康复训练。

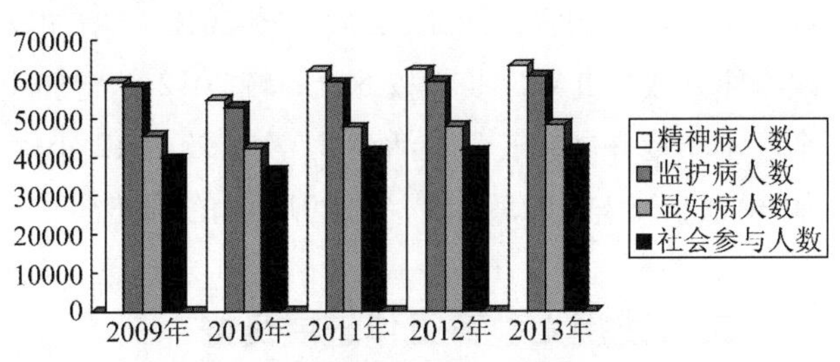

图1-3　精神病防治康复工作情况（人）

全年开展肢体残疾康复训练服务的机构达到7个，完成19例贫困肢体残疾儿童矫治手术、装配了矫形器等辅助器具，进行了术后康复训练。对3433名肢体残疾人进行了康复训练，其中：脑瘫儿童机构康复训练150人，比2012年增加51.5%，肢体残疾儿童社区、家庭康复153人，成年肢体残疾人社区、家庭康复3130人。

全年开展智力残疾康复训练服务的机构达到9个，对901名智力残疾儿童进行了康复训练，不同程度地开展了智力残疾儿童早期康复训练与服务。

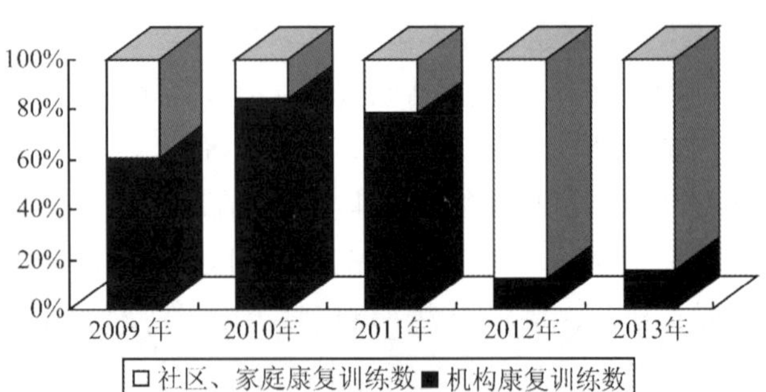

图1-4　智力残疾康复机构训练与社区、家庭训练对比

深入开展残疾人辅助器具供应服务，全面推进普及型辅助假肢装配工作，截止到2013年底，累计建立辅助器具供应服务机构11个，为残疾人装配假肢290例，比2012年增加12.4%。全市辅助器具供应品种106种，比2012年增加21种，各类辅助器具供应数达到33608件，装配矫形器318例。国家彩金项目为残疾人免费发放5608件，比2012年增加1642件。残疾人辅助器具管理水平和供应服务水平有所提高，使更多贫困残疾人得以恢复和改善肢体功能，生活自理。从2013年与近几年辅助器具各个指标对比上看，辅助器具供应呈增加趋势。

2013年，大力开展儿童残疾预防工作，与上年相比有较大幅度提高。开展残疾儿童筛查工作区县16个，较2012年增加2个。开展残疾儿童筛查工作的医疗卫生机构15个，较2012年增加9个。本年度新诊断0-6岁残疾儿童311人，发放儿童残疾预防宣传材料17133份，将近是2012年的2倍。举办儿童残疾预防宣传活动23次，较2012年增加9次；建立残疾儿童家长学校5个，较2012年增加4个；本年度开展家长学校活动31次，较2012年增加30次；参与1025人次，是2012年的41倍。

二、残疾人教育工作进展良好

2013年，为接受各阶段教育的残疾学生发放助学金，残疾人整体素质有所提高。全市各特教学校义务教育阶段对残疾学生继续实施“三免一补”（免交杂费、教科书费、住宿费，补贴生活费）政策，实现义务教育阶段免费教育。未入学学龄残疾儿童少年总数445人，其中视力残疾9人，听力残疾16人，言语残疾13人，智力残疾230人，肢体残疾150人，精神残疾1人，多重残疾26人。

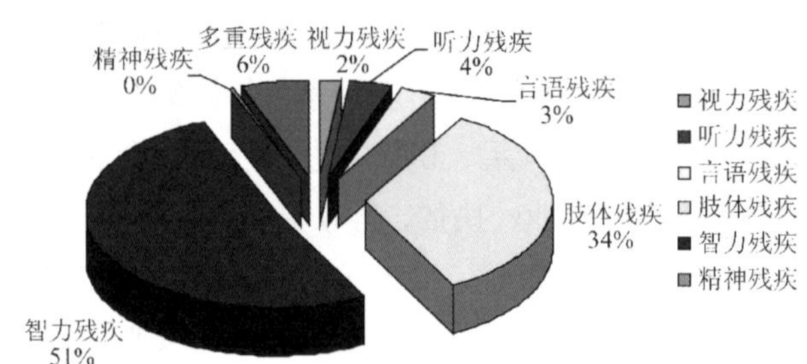

图2-1　2013年度未入学学龄残疾儿童少年分类

2013年，残疾人特殊教育事业发展较稳定。开办特殊教育普通高中2所，在校生134人；其中聋高中1所，在校生105人；盲高中1所，在校生29人。残疾人中等职业教育机构有1个。高等特殊教育学院1所，有97名残疾人被普通高等院校录取。

三、残疾人就业工作稳步推进

2013年，各区县残疾人城镇集中就业人数有所增加，本年度新增562人；按比例就业依然是残疾人主要就业形式，2013年新增1596人；个体就业及其他形式就业2013年新增323人。到2013年底，全市城镇累计安排残疾人就业38227人，其中公益性岗位就业399人。

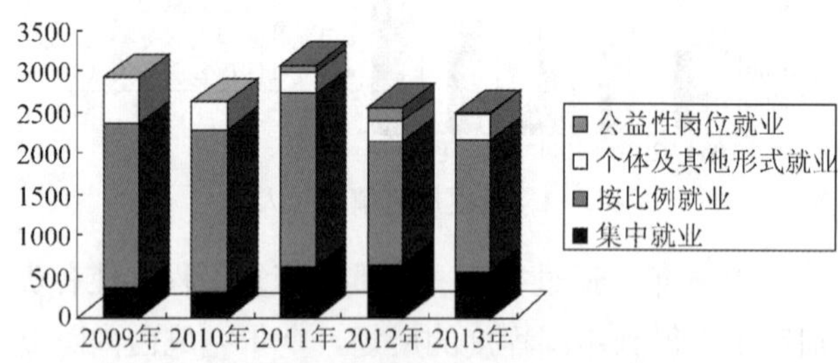

图3-1　近几年城镇残疾人本年度新增就业状况（人）

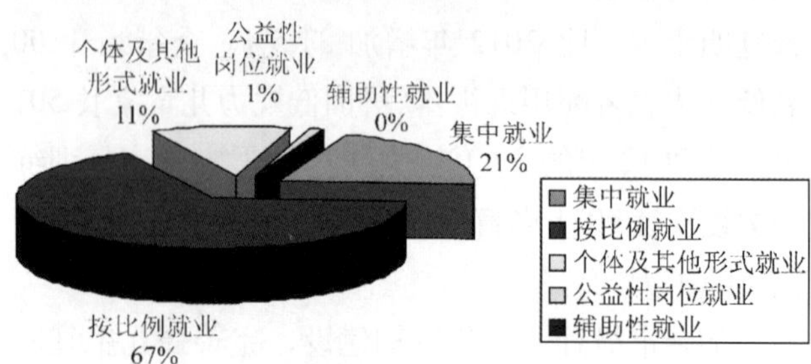

图3-2　2013年城镇残疾人五种就业形式本年度新增就业情况

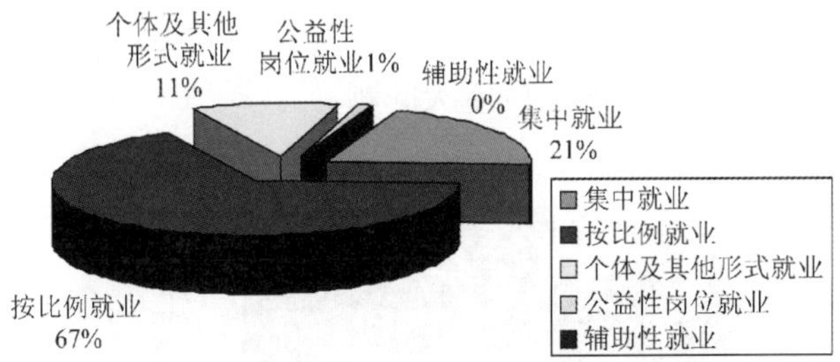

图 3-3　2013 年城镇残疾人五种就业形式累计就业情况

到 2013 年底，农村残疾人实际就业 67634 人。农村残疾人主要从事农业生产劳动，有 47800 人，占总数的 71%，较 2012 年有所增加。

截止 2013 年底，全市城乡残疾人就业合计 105861 人，较 2012 年增加 3608 人。

职业培训基地 30 个，其中残联兴办 6 个，依托社会机构兴办 24 个，较 2012 年有所增加。本年度城镇职业培训 2837 人次。培训盲人保健按摩 36 人，医疗按摩人员 22 人，保健按摩机构达到 164 个，医疗按摩机构达到 4 个，较 2012 年有所增加。

四、残疾人社会保障工作切实加强

随着我市生活保障制度的不断规范和完善，更多的残疾人得到扶助，2013 年，城乡 56632 名残疾人纳入最低生活保障范围，实现了“应保尽保”；为进一步改善残疾人家庭的生活状况，在低保这一最基本的保障措施基础上给予生活救助，城镇已纳入最低生活保障 33587 人，城镇集中供养和其他救助救济 10916 人；农村已纳入最低生活保障 23045 人，农村五保供养和其他救助救济 12921 人。在城镇，残疾人参加社会保险的人数较 2012 年有所增加，2013 年城镇残疾职工参加社会保险人数达到 39612 人，其中参加养老保险人数 32871 人，参加医疗保险人数 31141 人；城镇残疾居民参加城镇居民医疗保险达到 72101 人，农村居民参加新型农村合作医疗人数 84490 人。

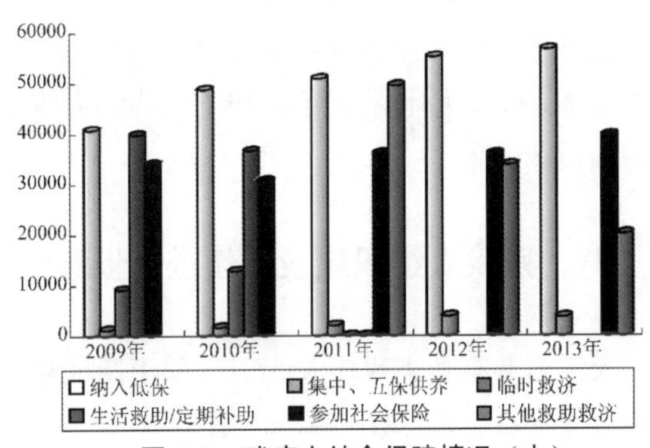

图 4-1　残疾人社会保障情况（人）

截止 2013 年，建立了寄宿制托养服务机构 14 个，托养残疾人 232 人，比 2012 年增加 70 人；日间照料托养服务机构合计 68 个，托养残疾人 981 人；综合托养服务机构 2 个，托养残疾人 32 人；本年度享受居家托养服务残疾人 15107 人。

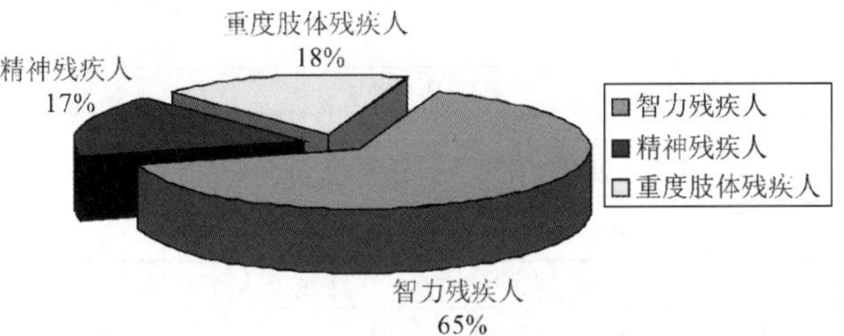

图 4-2　2013 年在托养服务机构中托养的残疾人情况

五、残疾人扶贫工作成效显著

加大农村残疾人扶持力度，加强实用技术培训，扩大扶贫成果，切实改善农村贫困残疾人生活状况。2013 年，扶持贫困残疾人户 20131 户，扶持贫困残疾人 23683 人次，无返贫人员。接受实用技术培训的残疾人 2684 人次，投入培训经费 68.7 万元。积极动员机关、企事业单位、志愿者组织及党员、干部、学生、街坊邻里等社会各界，采取多种形式，进行“帮、包、带、扶”，并充分发挥工会、共青团、妇联等团体和组织在残疾人扶贫工作中的作用，结对帮扶单位 147 个，结对帮扶个人 255 人；建立残疾人扶贫基地 165 个，安置残疾人就业 2149 人，扶持带动残疾人户 3010 户。

农村贫困残疾人危房改造成绩显著。2013 年完成 109 户农村贫困残疾人危房改造，投入危房改造资金 176 万元，受益残疾人 109 人。

六、残疾人维权工作逐步完善

继续完善残疾人事业法律法规，加大执法检查和监督力度，开展法律服务、法律援助，维护残疾人权益，推动无障碍设施建设。2013 年，制定或修改保障残疾人权益的规范性文件 15 个，其中省级 12 个、县级 3 个；各级人大、政协的检查或专题调研 13 次，对残疾人保障法的贯彻实施起到了重要的推动作用。

已建立残疾人法律救助工作协调机构 18 个；建立残疾人法律救助工作站 17 个，2013 年办理案件 474 件，其中，省级 114 件、区县级 360 件。2013

年残联协助人大代表、政协委员提出议案、建议、提案4件，办理建议、提案12件，残疾人参政议政工作得到加强。

表1　2013年残疾人执法检查情况表

级　别	人大执法检查或专题调研	政协视察或专题调研
省　级	1	0
区县级	10	2

表2　2013年残疾人法制宣传教育和法律工作者培训班情况表

级 别	法制宣传教育		残疾人工作者法律培训	
	普法宣传教育活动		法律培训班	
	次数	人数	个数	人数
省 级	2	225	2	155
县 级	46	2222	18	1051

截止2013年底，市和区县颁布无障碍建设与管理法规、政府令9个；建立无障碍建设领导协调组织17个；系统开展无障碍建设的区县16个。本年度进行无障碍建设检查65次，有531人次参加了无障碍培训，对1584户贫困残疾人家庭进行了无障碍改造。本年度对16618人发放了残疾人机动轮椅车燃油补贴。全市大多数新建主要城市道路、公共建筑物、居住建筑大都建设了相应的无障碍设施，同时加强了无障碍改造和对已建无障碍设施的管理，我市城市无障碍设施建设得到进一步加强，大大方便了广大残疾人、老年人、妇女、儿童、伤病人和全体社会成员参与社会生活。

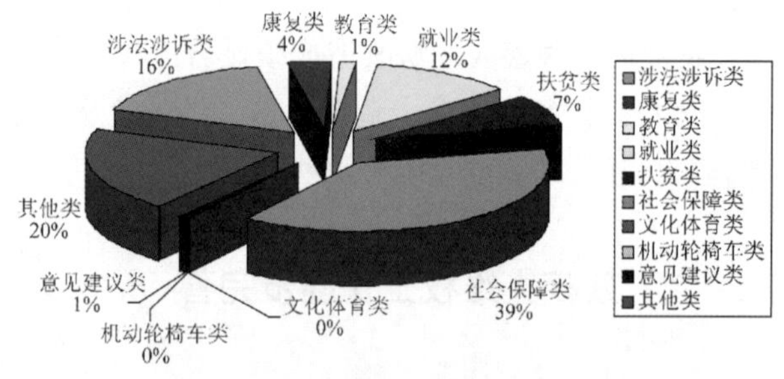

图6-1　2013年残疾人来信（件）情况

2013年，全市各级残联信访部门共处理来信135件，主要集中在涉法涉诉22件、扶贫10件、就业16件、社会保障52件四类；接待来访2198人次，同样集中在涉法涉诉323人次、扶贫227人次、就业182人次、社会保障630人次四类。整体来看，2013年较前几年来信来访总量有所减少，其中，涉法涉诉、扶贫、就业、社会保障四类分别占总的来信量的16.3%、7.4%、11.9%、38.5%，占来访量的14.7%、10.3%、8.3%、28.7%；残疾人基本生活、就业、维护权利等问题，尤其是残疾人生活，仍然是我们迫切要解决的重大问题。

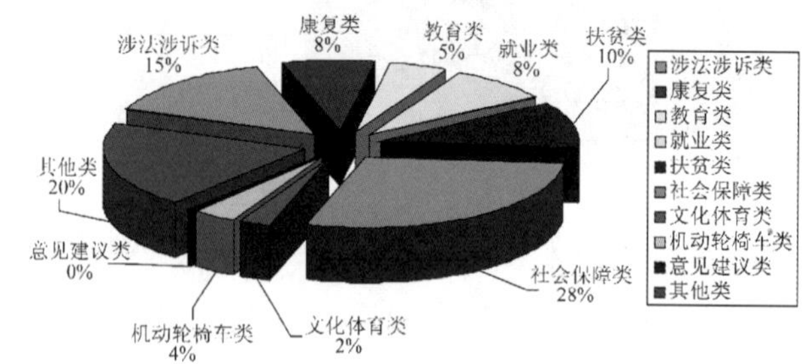

图6-2　2013年残疾人来访（人次）情况

七、宣传文化体育工作广泛深入

2013年，中央级媒体采用稿件5件，省级主要新闻媒体刊播稿件数1960件，省级报纸专版6个，省级广播电台残疾人专题节目1个，省级电视手语栏目1个，省级电视公益广告片1个，省级残疾人事业新闻宣传促进会1个；地市级主要新闻媒体刊播稿件数222件，地市级报纸专版5个，地市级广播电台残疾人专题节目10个，地市级电视手语栏目4个，地市级电视公益广告片1个，地市级报纸公益广告2个，建立地市级新促会2个。

省级公共图书馆设立盲文及盲人有声读物图书室已达到2个，举办残疾人文化周5场次，举办残疾人文化艺术类比赛及展览5次，已成立残疾人艺术团队3个。

地市级公共图书馆设立盲文及盲人有声读物阅览室已达到22个，举办残疾人文化周17场次，举办残疾人文化艺术类比赛及展览35次，已成立残疾人艺术团队14个。

省级开展残疾人群众体育健身活动11次，有4860人次参加，残疾人群众体育活动示范点28个，残疾人体育健身指导员415人，残疾人体育比赛8次，参与的残疾人运动员2500人次，残疾人体育训练基地5个，聘任教练员18人。

地市级残疾人体育健身活动176次，有7209人次参加，残疾人体育示范点39个，残疾人体育健身指导员356人。

八、残疾人组织建设工作进一步健全

天津市共有各类残疾人57万，其中持证残疾人23.4万，占残疾人总数的41%。截至2013年底，全市残联系统实有人员共有962人，其中：市残联机关工作人员47名、事业单位工作人员179名，区县残联机关工作人员153名、事业单位工作人员203名，乡镇（街道）残联工作人员380名。全市街道（乡镇）已建残联242个，配备残疾人专职委员240人，有专职理事长242名，无兼职理事长，基本建立了“一办三站一岗”（残联办公室、残疾人康复站、服务站（社）、志愿者助残联络站、残疾人维权岗），形成了多层次、多项目的残疾人服务载体和服务工作网络，为残疾人服务的能力显著增强。市及区县残联全部建立了残疾人人才库，有589名残疾人入库，其中，市级123人，区县级466人。目前，村（含农村社区）已建立3352个残协，建立了3477个残疾人活动室，选聘了3323个残疾人专职委员；城市社区已建立1259个残协，建立了1240个残疾人活动室，选聘了1192个残疾人专职委员。随着志愿者队伍的不断壮大，越来越多的残疾人得到不同程度的帮助。

九、残疾人信息化建设工作力度加大

残疾人信息化建设队伍不断壮大，市及区县残联至少配备了一名统计人员，全系统共有统计人员26人，其中7人获得了统计从业资格证书；有信息化专业技术人才56人，全系统工作人员计算机知识水平较往年有所提高。目前，市残联及15个区县残联建立了门户网站。市残联门户网站全年发稿969篇。加大信息化基础设施建设和技术保障工作，提高信息化安全投入。2013年，全系统计算机拥有量533台；全年信息化建设投入193.4万元。其中：硬件投入137万元，软件投入21.7万元，系统运行维护费34.7万元；用于信息化安全的投入7.7万元。

总之，2013年是全面完成残疾人事业“十二五”中期任务的关键一年。各项保障残疾人民生的政策措施加快实施，市20项民心工程扶残项目和市政府2013年为残疾人办实事安排全面落实。各级残联认真组织开展了残疾人事业“十二五”规划中期检查评估，“十二五”中期任务和年度任务圆满成功，残疾人事业实现了又好又快发展。制定实施了有关抢救性康复项目实施方案，进一步加大了对孤独症儿童的救助力度，组织实施了各项重点康复工程和社区康复，进一步健全和落实0-7岁残疾儿童抢救性康复救助政策。残疾儿童学前教育补贴和残疾人教育助学金政策全面落实。大力实施促进残疾人就业政策，扶持残疾人多渠道、多种形式就业和自主创业。建设残疾人培训基地，努力提高残疾人技术技能、就业层次和收入水平。加大扶贫保障力度，多种形式扶持贫困残疾人增收，全市各级党委、政府及社会各界爱心人士广泛深入开展了多种形式公益助残活动。扩大了住房保障覆盖面，农村贫困残疾人老旧危陋住房改造纳入了全市农村危房改造工程统一组织实施。深入落实了基本医疗和养老保险补贴，将非低保重度残疾人纳入医疗救助范围，提高了生活救助金补贴标准，扎实做好低保、特困残疾人生活救助金补贴发放工作，重度残疾人护理补贴工作在全市启动。全市残疾人托养服务水平进一步提高，滨海新区和河东区被中国残联命名为“全国阳光家园示范区”。全市进一步完善了残疾人法律救助标准和信访工作机制，认真办理市和区县“两会”涉残建议、提案，认真做好无障碍“进社区进家庭”设施改造，积极配合市政府做好治理残疾人机动三轮车前期工作。进一步加强残疾人事业宣传，天津电视台公共频道《新说法》全程加配手语。组织开展了丰富多彩的残疾人文化体育活动和比赛，在第八届全国残疾人艺术汇演中，我市取得了团体总分名列赛区第二名和全国团体银奖的好成绩，成功承办有24支代表队400余人参加的全国特奥足球比赛。市残联政务微博正式开通，开辟了服务残疾人、引导舆论、宣传残疾人事业的新途径。进一步推动了各区县基层残疾人组织建设。对残疾人证管理系统进行了升级，积极做好基础数据库资源共享，进一步提升了政务信息公开工作效率和水平，市残联获得2012年度全国残疾人状况及小康进程监测工作第一名和残疾人事业统计工作第三名。一年来，全市残疾人工作取得了较好成绩，但还存在一些差距和问题，我们将深入学习贯彻十八届三中全会精神和市委十届四次全会精神，按照全面深化改革的总要求，认真研究，采取措施，切实加以解决，推动我市残疾人工作再上新的水平。

2013年河北省残疾人事业发展统计公报

2013年，在省委、省政府的坚强领导、中国残联的有力指导的社会各界的大力支持下，全省各级残联深入学习贯彻党的十八大、十八届三中全会和省委八届五次、六次全会精神，坚持解放思想，改革创新，求真务实，围绕夯实基础和打开局面、重点突破、进步赶超，扎实推进各项工作，使我省残疾人事业发展呈现出新气象、新局面。

一、康复工作

社区康复服务覆盖面稳步扩大：在37个市辖区和138个县（市）的2.9万个社区（村）开展了社区康复服务工作，占社区（村）总数的58.2%；累计已建社区康复服务站的社区总数达16733个，配备社区康复协调员38785人，接受过培训的社区康复协调员累计达34655人；为162.4万名残疾人建立了社区康复服务档案，占社区残疾人总数的41.1%，截止2013年底，接受过社区康复服务的残疾人累计达36万人，比2012年增加了20%。

积极开展视力残疾康复工作：开展视力残疾康复机构总数达到18个，全年完成白内障复明手术30414例，为3367名贫困白内障患者免费施行复明手术；为6054名低视力患者配用助视器，培训低视力儿童家长2047名，有效开展家庭康复训练；有盲人定向行走训练师197名，对6005名盲人进行定向行走训练。

认真做好听力语言、肢体和智力残疾康复工作：推进康复机构规范化管理，完善基层服务网络。建设省级听力语言残疾康复机构1个，市级机构14个，县级机构80个；年度新收训聋儿2077名，在训聋儿2791名；规范聋儿家长学校，开展家庭训练，共培训聋儿家长2452名；74名聋儿接受了地方项目救助；积极开展听力语言康复专业技术人员培训，共培训各级专业人员148名；各级康复训练机构共为1152人次成年听力残疾人提供康复技术服务。截止2013年底，开展肢体残疾康复训练服务机构达117个，其中省级1个，市级15个，县级101个；对1.06万名肢体残疾患者实施康复训练；实施国家救助项目，资助400名脑瘫儿童进行机构康复训练，资助515名贫困肢体残疾儿童实施矫治手术；培训各级肢体残疾康复管理、技术人员484人次。开展智力残疾康复训练服务机构50个，其中省级1个，市级13个，县级36个；5678名智力残疾儿童得到康复训练，培训各级智力残疾康复人员461人次。

大力推广“社会化、综合性、开放式”精神病防治康复工作：在170个县（市、区）开展精神病防治康复工作，覆盖总人口5515.6万人，对26万名精神病患者进行综合防治康复，监护率达到87.3%，显好率达到57.2%，社会参与率达到46%；解除关锁109人；91469名精神病患者接受治疗，57288名精神病患者接受康复训练；全省共有精神病康复机构83个，机构内精神病人7649名；对12380名贫困精神病患者进行医疗救助，占贫困精神病患者的50.8%。建立孤独症儿童康复机构32个，409名孤独症儿童在各级机构接受康复训练；245名贫困孤独症儿童得到康复救助。

加强残疾人辅助器具供应服务，全面推进普及型假肢装配工作：截止2013年底，累计建立辅助器具供应机构64个，其中市级11个，县级53个；全省各类辅助器具供应2.9万件，其中装配普及型假肢896例，矫形器装配639例，为贫困残疾人免费发放其他辅助器具2.2万件。

积极做好残疾预防工作：截止2013年底，全省在37个县（市、区）的41个医疗卫生机构开展残疾儿童筛查工作，本年度新诊断0-6岁残疾儿童1485人。发放残疾预防宣传材料21.3万份，举办儿童残疾预防宣传活动199次。有残疾儿童家长学校41个，本年度开展家长学校活动75次，残疾儿童家长参与人数达3389人次。

加强康复人才培养：截止2013年底，各级康复机构在岗人员总数为7118人，其中省级455人、市级3431人、县级3232人。2013年共举办康复管理人员培训班111期，培训康复管理人员990人；举办康复业务人员培训班113期，培训康复业务人员

1879 人；举办社区康复协调员培训班 149 期，培训社区康复协调员 6555 人。

二、教育工作

积极发展残疾人教育：2013 年 12 月，河北省残疾人远程教育项目正式启动，河北省广播电视大学特殊教育学院正式揭牌，该学院将为一些不能走进校门的重度残疾人提供网络教育，使残疾人受教育权得到更好保障，残疾人素质和平等参与社会的能力得到进一步提高。专项彩票公益金助学项目资助 600 名学前残疾儿童，专项彩票公益金助学项目资助新入园 225 名学前残疾儿童。

开办特殊教育普通高中学校（班）13 个，在校生 461 人，毕业生 125 人；其中聋普通高中 11 个，在校生 360 人，毕业生 105 人；盲普通高中 2 个，在校生 101 人，毕业生 20 人。残疾人中等职业学校（班）3 个，在校生 91 人，毕业生 73 人，其中 12 人获得职业资格证书。全省有 308 名残疾人被普通高等院校录取。

截止 2013 年底，全省有未入学适龄残疾儿童少年总数 1135 人，其中视力残疾儿童 45 人，听力残疾儿童 72 人，言语残疾儿童 69 人，肢体残疾儿童 439 人，智力残疾儿童 362 人，精神残疾儿童 22 人，多重残疾儿童 126 人。

三、就业工作

残疾人就业状况稳定：2013 年，城镇新增 1.2 万残疾人就业，其中集中就业 4865 人、按比例就业 3377 人、公益性岗位就业 303 人、个体及其他形式就业 3533 人，辅助性就业 141 人。到 2013 年底，城镇残疾人实际在业人数 20.3 万人，仍有 2.3 万城镇残疾人未就业；本年度城镇新登记失业残疾人 814 人。89.1 万农村残疾人实现稳定就业，其中从事农业生产劳动 70.3 万人，其他形式就业 18.7 万人，仍有 16.6 万农村残疾人未就业。

全省残疾人职业培训基地达到 386 个，其中残联兴办 267 个，依托社会机构兴办 119 个，2.1 万名城镇残疾人接受了职业培训。

盲人按摩事业稳步发展：2013 年度，培训盲人保健按摩人员 1100 名、盲人医疗按摩人员 1076 名；医疗按摩机构达到 56 个，保健按摩机构达到 426 个；在盲人医疗按摩人员专业技术职务任职资格评审中，26 人通过中级、184 人通过初级职称评审；1170 名盲人按摩人员就业，扶持 337 名特困盲人按摩师实现就业。

四、社会保障工作

2013 年残疾人社会保障状况保持平稳。城镇居民社会养老保险符合参保条件 16.6 万人，实际参保 13.4 万人，参保率 80.7%；在 60 周岁以下的参保残疾居民中有 20806 名重度残疾人，其中 20515 人得到了政府的参保扶助，有 19828 名非重度残疾人也享受了全额或部分代缴的优惠政策。领取社会养老金待遇人数达 44016 人，其中 14213 人为重度残疾人。

新型农村社会养老保险方面，符合参保条件的农村残疾人达 133.1 万人，实际参保 115.1 万人，参保率 86.5%。在 60 周岁以下的参保残疾人中有 160841 人重度残疾人，160474 人得到了政府的参保扶助，其中 72857 人全额代缴，87617 人部分代缴；在 63.7 万参保非重度残疾人中，17.7 万也享受了全额或部分代缴的优惠政策。享受养老保险金待遇的人数达到 35.3 万人。

城镇残疾职工参加社会保险人数达 9.8 万人，比上年度增长 4.8%，其中参加养老保险 5.5 万人，比上年度增长 4.1%，参加医疗保险 4.8 万人，比上年度增长 4.6%；城镇残疾居民参加基本医疗保险 15.2 万人；城镇个体就业参加社会保险 2.9 万人。城乡 41.5 万名残疾人纳入最低生活保障范围，城镇集中供养和农村五保供养残疾人分别达到 3722 人和 2.4 万人；5.2 万名城乡残疾人获得其他救助救济。1.8 万名符合条件的城乡残疾人享受了稳定的生活补贴。

到 2013 年底，残疾人寄宿制托养服务机构 54 个，托养残疾人 1847 人；残疾人日间照料机构 12 个，为 319 名残疾人提供托养服务；综合托养服务机构 81 个，托养残疾人 2215 人；接受居家托养服务的残疾人达到 1.9 万人。

五、残疾人扶贫工作

2013 年，残疾人扶贫开发成效显著，贫困残疾人生产生活状况得到进一步改善。20.6 万贫困残疾人得到扶持，其中12.6万通过扶贫开发实际脱贫；接受实用技术培训的残疾人达到4.3万人次。

康复扶贫贴息贷款扶持3461名农村残疾人，1202个单位和7143名个人对贫困残疾人开展结对帮扶。残疾人扶贫基地达到128个，安置2296名残疾人就业，扶持带动6906残疾人户。2013年，全省各级共投入4095.4万元，对3468户农村贫困残疾人实施了危房改造，4389名残疾人受益。

六、残疾人宣传文体工作

2013年，中央级媒体采用稿件22件，省级主要新闻媒体刊播稿件3841件；报纸专版78个，其中省级7个、市级71个；广播电台残疾人专题节目22个，其中省级2个、市级20个；电视手语栏目13个，其中省级1个、市级12个；电视公益广告片28个，其中省级5个、市级23个；报纸公益广告26个，其中省级3个、市级23个；建立市级新促会6个。

公共图书馆设立盲文及盲人有声读物图书室19个，其中省级1个、市级18个；全省共举办残疾人文化活动周129场次；举办残疾人文化艺术类比赛及展览66次，其中省级19次、市级47次；有6个市级残疾人艺术团队。

2013年，举办省级残疾人群众体育健身活动16次，参加体育健身活动的残疾人达650人次。省级残疾人群众体育活动示范点27个，残疾人体育健身指导员112人，残疾人体育训练基地16个，残疾人体育训练基地在编人员50人，聘任教练员53人。举办省级体育比赛20次，参赛残疾人运动员700人次。组织市级残疾人体育活动129次，参加体育活动的残疾人达1.5万人次。有市级残疾人群众体育活动示范点121个，残疾人体育健身指导员1280人。

七、残疾人维权工作

继续完善残疾人法规和规章：制定或修改了关于残疾人的专门法规、规章省级1件、地市级2件；制定或修改保障残疾人权益的规范性文件省级5件、地市级7件、县级39件。

加大执法力度和法制宣传：2013年，各级人大进行执法检查或专题调研67次；各级政协进行视察或专题调研56次。各级残联开展普法宣传教育活动317次，4.5万人参加；举办残疾人工作者法律培训班74期，4431人参加培训。

积极开展法律服务和法律援助工作，维护残疾人合法权益：截止2013年底，成立残疾人法律救助工作协调机构134个；建立残疾人法律救助工作站133个，办理法律救助案件1771件；建立残疾人法律援助中心（工作站）186个，办理法律援助案件2471件。

各级残联积极发挥参政议政作用：截止2013年底，残联系统共有各级人大代表102人，其中省级4人、市级14人、县级84人；政协委员255人，其中省级6人、市级21人、县级228人；残疾人参政议政工作得到加强，各级残联协助人大代表、政协委员提出议案、建议、提案70件，其中省级2件、市级9件、县级59件；办理议案、建议、提案56件，其中省级5件、市级20件、县级31件。

无障碍工作继续推进：全省11个设区市、172个县（市、区）全部系统开展了无障碍建设工作。出台无障碍建设与管理法规、政府令45个，其中省级1个、市级6个、县级38个；成立无障碍建设领导协调组织128个，其中省级1个、市级11个、县级119个；全省各级开展无障碍建设检查135次，无障碍培训831人次；为1983户贫困残疾人家庭实施了无障碍改造；为15594名残疾人发放了残疾人机动轮椅车燃油补贴。

各级残联派出大量人员下访，把问题解决在基层，确保了社会稳定。2013年各级残联共处理残疾人群众来信1499件；接待残疾人群众来访7796人次，其中集体访14批次、214人次，有效地维护了残疾人的合法权益。

八、残疾人组织更加健全

2013年市、县两级残联全部配备了残疾人领导干部；172个县（市、区）残联全部规范化达标；全省2271个乡（镇、街道）全部建立残联，其中有专职残联理事长793人，占乡（镇、街道）残联总数的34.9%，兼职理事长1478人，选聘残疾人专职委员2272人。全省各级各类残疾人专门协会全部建立。省市县乡残联实有人员已达5529人。

截止2013年底，全省48413个村(含农村社区)、3006个城市社区全部建立了残疾人协会，配备了残疾人专职委员，建立了残疾人活动室。积极开展志愿者助残活动，助残志愿者登记在册人数达到 29.1 万人，受助残疾人达 118.6 万人。

为提高残联干部队伍素质，2013 年各级残联共举办培训班 1497 期，35088 人次参加了培训。

九、综合服务设施建设

残疾人综合服务设施建设得到全面发展。截止到 2013 年底，全省已竣工并投入使用的各级残疾人综合服务设施 146 个，总建设规模 14.6 万平方米，总投资 2.8 亿元；已竣工并投入使用的各级残疾人康复服务设施 7 个，总建设规模 33979 平方米，总投资 8178.1 万元；已竣工并投入使用的各级托养服务设施 8 个，总建设规模 31219 平方米，总投资 5550 万元。

十、信息化建设

残疾人信息化建设队伍不断壮大，各级残联至少配备了一名统计员，全系统共有专、兼职统计人员 244 名，其中 147 人获得了统计从业资格证书，占统计人员总数的 60.2%；统计人员业务素质培养普遍得到重视，省级残联举办统计培训班 1 期，50 名统计人员参加了培训，市级举办统计培训班 15 期，参加培训的人员达到 514 人。

全面推进信息化建设，全省各级残联共有 285 名专业技术人员从事信息化工作，举办信息化工作培训班 20 期，546 人次参加了培训；全省残联系统共建成 37 个，其中省级 1 个、市级 10 个、县级 26 个；省级网站当年发稿 3328 篇。各级残联本年度信息化建设投入各种经费 281.9 万元，其中硬件投入 168.3 万元，软件投入 71.5 万元，系统运行维护费 42.1 万元；用于信息化安全的投入 26.1 万元。全省各级残联拥有计算机 1226 台。

2013 年山西省残疾人事业发展统计公报

2013 年，全省各级残联按照省委、省政府的部署和中国残联的要求，以残联换届和开展党的群众路线教育实践活动为契机，全面加强残疾人组织建设；以制定特惠政策为突破，加快推进残疾人社会保障和服务体系建设；以强化宣传为抓手，营造发展残疾人事业的良好环境，圆满完成了各项工作任务。

一、康复工作

2013 年，康复工作紧紧围绕残疾人“人人享有康复服务”目标这一主线，不断推进康复机构规范化建设，康复救助政策不断完善，国家“七彩梦行动计划”、“国家彩票公益金”和省彩票公益金贫困残疾人康复救助项目顺利实施，大批残疾人得到康复救助。

（一）社区康复。在 23 个市辖区和 90 个县（市）开展了社区康复工作，已建社区康复站的社区总数 5031 个，配备了 18153 名社区康复协调员。

（二）视力残疾康复。开展视力残疾康复机构总数达到 41 个，完成白内障复明手术 23612 例；为 5012 名贫困白内障患者免费施行复明手术；为 103 名低视力患者配用助视器；培训低视力儿童家长 2390 名，有效开展家庭康复训练；对 6089 名盲人进行定向行走训练。

（三）听力语言残疾康复。推进听力语言康复机构规范化管理，完善基层服务网络。全省共建立听力语言康复机构 47 个。年度新收训聋儿 435 名，在训聋儿 793 名；规范聋儿家长学校，开展家庭训练，共培训聋儿家长 1218 名；组织开展各级各类听力语言康复专业技术人员培训，共培训专业人员 445 人。

（四）肢体残疾康复。全年开展肢体残疾康复训练服务机构达 39 个，其中：省级康复机构 2 个，地市级、县级康复机构 37 个；培训各级各类肢体残疾康复人员 240 人次；全省共对 5579 名肢体残疾者实施康复训练；实施救助项目资助 570 名脑瘫儿童进行机构康复训练，资助 321 名贫困肢体残疾儿童实施矫治手术。

（五）智力残疾康复。全年开展智力残疾康复训练服务的机构 37 个，其中：省级康复机构 2 个，地市级、县级康复机构 35 个；培训各级各类智力残疾康复人员 183 人次；全省共对 2430 名智力残疾人进行康复训练；实施救助项目资助 260 名智力残疾儿童进行机构康复训练，同时培训儿童家长。

（六）精神病防治康复和孤独症儿童康复。大力推广“社会化、综合性、开放式”精神病防治康复工作。在全省 64 个市县开展精神病防治康复工作，对 99112 名重性精神病患者进行综合防治康复，监护率达到 81.95%，显好率达到 69.22%，社会参与率达到 52.07%，肇事率 0.05%；解除关锁 261 人；对 5519 名贫困精神病患者进行医疗救助。

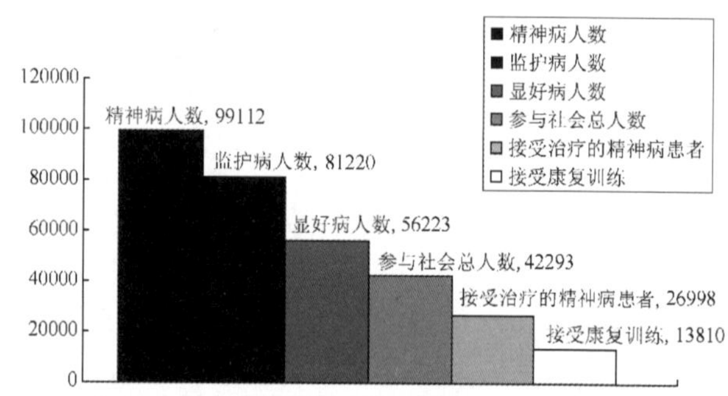

图表 1　2013 年精神病防治康复情况（单位：人）

311 名孤独症儿童在 2 个省级孤独症儿童康复训练机构、12 个地市级及以下其他机构进行了康复训练。

（七）辅助器具供应服务。加强残疾人辅助器具服务体系建设，深入开展辅助器具供应服务，为残疾人减免费用供应辅助器具 17967 件，其中装配假肢 395 例、矫形器 172 例，验配助视器 66 件。

（八）儿童残疾康复。全省 87 个县的 106 个医疗卫生机构陆续开展残疾儿童筛查工作，年度新诊断 0-6 岁残疾儿童 1374 人。

（九）康复人才。全省各级康复机构在岗人员 9095 人。全年培训康复管理人员 689 人、业务人员 1389 人、社区康复协调员 4533 人。

二、教育工作

为家庭经济困难的残疾儿童享受普惠性学前教

育提供资助 260 人次。

全省已开办特殊教育普通高中学校（班）5 个，在校生 391 人；其中：聋高中 4 个，在校生 359 人；盲高中 1 个，在校生 32

人。残疾人中等职业学校（班）1 个，在校生 286 人，毕业生 67 人，其中 67 人获得职业资格证书。168 名残疾人被普通高等院校录取。

截止到 2013 年底，全省未入学适龄残疾儿童少年 2481 人，其中：视力残疾儿童 122 人、听力残疾儿童 181 人、言语残疾儿童 163 人、智力残疾儿童 887 人、肢体残疾儿童 761 人、精神残疾儿童 62 人、多重残疾儿童 305 人。

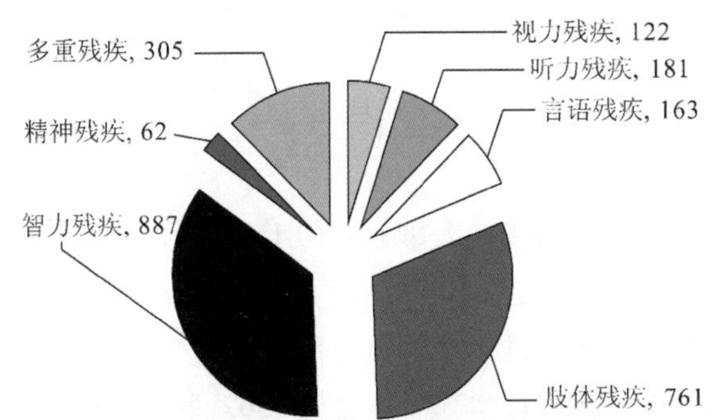

图 2　2013 年未入学学龄残疾儿童少年情况（单位：人）

三、就业工作

（一）就业。2013 年，城镇新就业残疾人 7527 人，其中：集中就业 2323 人、按比例安排就业 1050 人、公益性岗位就业 103 人、个体就业及其它形式灵活就业 3524 人、辅助性就业 527 人。城镇就业人数达到了 120803 人；农村在业残疾人 399808 名，其中 287751 名残疾人从事农业生产劳动。

（二）职业培训。全省残疾人职业培训基地达到 512 个，其中：残联兴办 282 个、依托社会机构兴办 230 个，8422 人次城镇残疾人接受了职业培训。

（三）盲人按摩。盲人按摩事业稳定发展，按摩机构迅速增长。2013 年度培训盲人保健按摩人员 656 名、盲人医疗按摩人员 151 名；全省盲人保健按摩机构达到 383 个，医疗按摩机构达到 51 个；在专业技术职务资格评审中，分别有 16 人和 81 人通过医疗按摩人员中级和初级职称评审。

四、社会保障工作

2013 年，201346 名城镇残疾人参加了城镇居民社会养老保险，参保率 81.30%。在 60 岁以下的参保残疾人中有 23476 名重度残疾人，其中 21842 名得到了政府的参保扶助，代缴补贴比例达到 93.04%。有 16304 名非重度残疾人也享受了全额或部分代缴的优惠政策。领取养老金待遇的人数达到 114585 人。

新型农村社会养老保险方面，共有 740756 名残疾人参加了新型农村社会养老保险，参保率 76.86%。在 60 周岁以下的参保残疾人中有重度残疾人 116006 名，其中 110910 名得到了政府的参保扶助，代缴补贴比例达到 95.61%。有 44911 名非重度残疾人也享受了全额或部分代缴的优惠政策。享受养老金待遇的人数达到 371684 人。

城镇残疾职工参加社会保险人数达到 101500 人，城镇残疾居民参加基本医疗保险达到 227074 人，城镇 67034 名和农村 237686 名残疾人纳入最低生活保障范围；城镇集中供养残疾人和农村五保供养残疾人分别达到 1289 人和 25407 人；10072 名和 14855 名符合条件的城乡残疾人分别享受了稳定的生活补贴和护理补贴。664891 名城乡残疾人得到了其他救助救济。

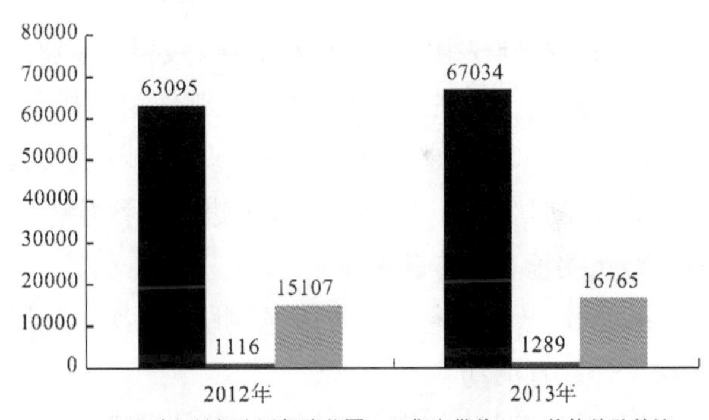

图 3　2012 年与 2013 年城镇残疾人社会救助对比表（单位：人）

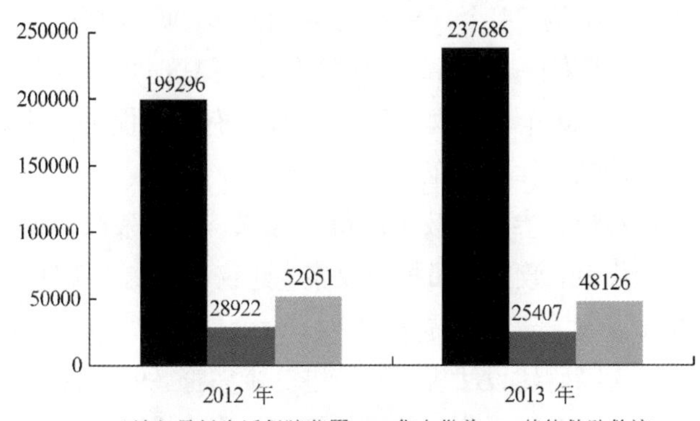

图 4　2012 年与 2013 年农村残疾人社会救助对比表（单位：人）

残疾人托养服务工作规范推进。全省 88 个残疾人托养服务机构共为 1964 名残疾人提供了托养服务。其中：寄宿制托养服务机构 51 个，托养残疾人 593 人；日间照料机构 6 个，托养残疾人

679 人；综合性托养服务机构 31 个，托养残疾人 692 人。14690 名残疾人享受居家托养服务。

五、扶贫工作

2013 年，全省 98185 名贫困残疾人得到扶持，其中 41363 名通过扶贫开发实际脱贫；接受实用技术培训的残疾人达到 19990 人次。

康复扶贫贴息贷款扶持 2635 名农村残疾人，938 个单位和 6969 名个人对贫困残疾人开展结对帮扶。残疾人扶贫基地达到 312 个，安置 5019 名残疾人就业，扶持带动 6721 名残疾人。

全年为 1805 户农村贫困残疾人实施危房改造，各地共投入危房改造资金 2069.03 万元，2351 名残疾人受益。

六、维权工作

各级残联维权组织建设得到加强，残疾人事业法律法规体系进一步完善，残疾人维权工作全面开展。

2013 年，两个地市级制定或修改了保障残疾人权益的规范性文件。县级以上人大进行《残疾人保障法》执法检查和专题调研

42 次；政协进行视察和专题调研 29 次。开展普法宣传教育活动

194 次，43158 人参加；举办法律培训班 74 个，4014 人参加。

截至 2013 年底，全省共成立残疾人法律救助工作协调机构 24 个，建立残疾人法律救助工作站 30 个，办理案件 205 件；建立残疾人法律援助中心（工作站）120 个，办理案件 674 件，有力地促进了法律救助和法律援助工作。

残疾人参政议政工作得到加强，各级残联协助人大代表、政协委员提出议案、建议、提案 101 件，办理议案、建议、提案 41 件。

无障碍建设法规、标准进一步完善。9 个地市、县级共出台了无障碍建设与管理法规、规章；68 个市、县（市、区）开展了无障碍建设；全省开展无障碍建设检查 45 次，组织无障碍培训 922 人次；全年为 1989 个贫困残疾人家庭实施了无障碍改造；为 15934 名残疾人发放了残疾人机动轮椅车燃油补贴。

各级残联共处理残疾人群众来信 1408 余件，接待残疾人群众来访 16314 人次，其中集体访 43 批次、1729 人次。

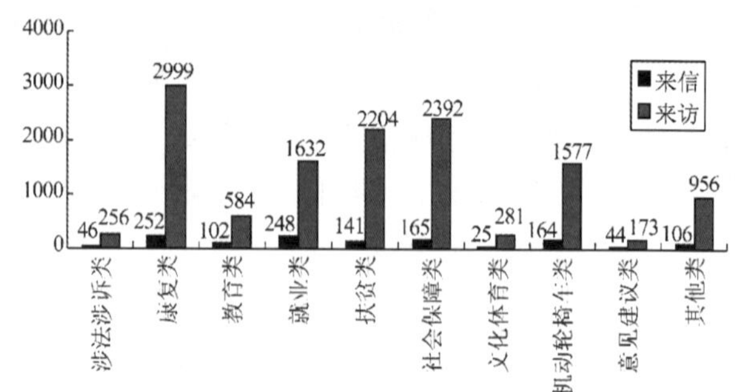

图 5　2013 年残疾人来信来访（县级）情况
（单位：人、件）

七、宣传文化工作

积极开展残疾人事业宣传工作，省级主要新闻媒体刊播稿件数 310 件，设立报刊专版 5 个、残疾人专题广播节目 1 个，电视手语新闻栏目 1 个。地市级主要新闻媒体刊播稿件数 1362 件，设立报刊专版 22 个、残疾人专题广播节目 12 个、电视手语新闻栏目 1 个，建立地市级新促会 3 个。

省级和地市级公共图书馆设立盲文及盲人有声读物阅览室分别达到 2 个和 13 个，举办残疾人文化周 1 个和 23 个，举办残疾人文化艺术类比赛及展览分别是 2 个和 28 个。

八、体育工作

组织参加全国第八届残疾人艺术汇演北京赛区比赛，举办省第四届特殊奥林匹克运动会，254 名特奥运动员参加了 9 个大项的比赛。

省级组织残疾人体育健身活动 4 次，参加人数 350 人，残疾人体育示范点 3 个，残疾人体育健身指导员 392 人，残疾人体育比赛 2 次，参与的残疾人运动员 294 人次。

地市级残疾人体育健身活动 67 次，参加人数 1923 人，残疾人体育示范点 32 个，残疾人体育健身指导员 273 人。

九、组织建设工作

2013 年，省残联领导班子中配备了残疾人副理

事长；9 个地市级残联在领导班子中配备了残疾人理事长或副理事长；96 个县级残联机关配备了残疾人干部；已建乡镇（街道）残联 1459 个，已建率达到 99.32%，选聘残疾人专职委员 1769 名；已建社区（村）残协 22298 个，已建率达到 82.78%，选聘残疾人专职委员 24365 名。

省市县乡残联实有人员已达 4750 人。各级残联共举办培训班 1302 期，培训机关干部、协会干部及残疾人专职委员 33028 人次。共建立省级以下各类残疾人专门协会 527 个，市级专门协会已建比例为 90.91%，市辖区专门协会已建比例 85.22%；县（含县级市）级专门协会已建比例为 79.79%。

十、信息化建设工作

统计队伍建设进一步加强，各级残联共有 137 名专、兼职统计人员从事残疾人事业统计工作，统计人员业务素质培养普遍得到重视，省级残联举办培训班 1 期，参加培训的人员达到 83 人次；地市级举办培训班 10 期，参加培训的人员达到 194 人次。

地方残联全面推进网站建设，目前省残联已开通了公众服务网站，11 个地市级残联网站和 75 个县级残联网站也已开通。2013 年，省级及地市级残联开设网站技术培训班 7 期，培训各级残联信息员达 138 人次。

省残联建立了 1 个局域网，各级残联共有 197 名专业技术人员从事信息化工作。

十一、基础设施建设工作

截至 2013 年底，全省已竣工并投入使用的各级残疾人综合服务设施 52 个，总建设规模 10.82 万平方米，总投资 28489.83 万元；已竣工并投入使用的各级残疾人康复设施 32 个，总建设规模 7.19 万平方米，总投资 17293.35 万元；已竣工并投入使用的各级残疾人托养服务设施 1 个，总建设规模 0.20 万平方米，总投资 400.00 万元。

十二、各级残联工作积极创新，锐意进取，扎实推进，特色突出

（一）建立“两个补贴”特惠政策，残疾人社会保障实现新突破。在省委、省政府的亲切关怀下，在相关厅局的积极配合下，在省残联党组、理事会高度重视和机关相关部（室）通力协作下，我省建立了重度残疾人护理补贴和贫困残疾人生活补贴制度。省政府第 31 次常务会议决定：从 2014 年起对未纳入城乡低保的一级重度残疾人每人每年发放护理补贴 480 元，对纳入城乡低保的贫困一级重度残疾人在享受低保的基础上每人每年再给予生活补贴 480 元。该内容已写入 2014 年省政府工作报告。我省成为中国残联六代会后第 1 家、中部第 1 个建立了“两个补贴”制度的省份。

（二）各市残联结合实际，发挥优势，积极创新工作，努力为残疾人搞好服务。太原市残联积极推进残疾人免费乘坐公共汽车工作，2013 年 5 月 10 日起，持有第二代残疾人证的太原市残疾人，可以免费乘坐市内公交车，各县（市、区）残联同时推行残疾人证和乘车证一站式服务。阳泉市残联实施了“普惠加特惠，残疾人得实惠”工作思路，全市投入 813.6 万元，对 9980 名重度残疾人进行了特殊救助。晋中市残联大力开展“需求调查访进门、康复服务送进门、帮扶救助找进门、参与社会走出门”的“三进一出”活动，初步建立市县乡三级残疾人服务信息网络平台，惠及 7 万余名残疾人；吕梁市汾阳市申报创建内地与澳门残疾人文化建设示范市取得成功，成为全国首批 10 个城市之一和全省唯一一家参加创建残疾人文化建设的示范市。大同市残联紧紧围绕“帮扶贫困残疾人”主体，帮助他们摆脱贫困，并积极动员社会力量为残疾人进行捐助。晋城市残疾人职业教育中心确立了“以市场为导向、以培训为核心、以就业为目标”的工作思路，采取培训与市场需求相结合、培训与残疾人自身特点相结合、培训与就业服务相结合的培训方式，多形式、多渠道、多层次的开展残疾人职业培训工作，逐步形成摸底评估、分类培训、推荐就业、动态反馈的就业服务体系。长治市残联农村基层党组织助残扶贫工作成效显著，积极协调政府职能部门，加大帮扶力度，根据地区产业结构，确定扶持项目，发动基层组织，扩大帮扶面积，增加帮扶资金，提高扶持效果，使帮扶户平均增加 2000 元收入。朔州市残联结合朔州市创建国家文化达标示范区建设，将残疾人文化体育工作纳入统一规划，启动了“残疾人精神文化生活圈”建设。忻州市残联广泛利用各类

新闻媒体深入基层，对我市部分创业成功的残疾人及助残工作先进企业、残疾朋友艰辛创业励志历程感悟爱心人士的助残真情故事进行了深入地报道，唤醒全社会都来关心贫困残疾人，支持残疾人事业。运城市市本级及所属13个县（市、区）残联都建立了设计超前、规划科学、较为完善的残疾人基础设施，全市设施总占地225亩，总建筑面积39301平方米，总价值近3亿元。临汾市残联在借鉴考察四川省“量体裁衣”式个性化服务模式的基础上，结合本市工作实际，提出了“亲情一家人”优质化服务新思路，计划用三年时间打造临汾残疾人服务新品牌。

我省残疾人事业虽然得到了快速发展，但残疾人事业滞后于经济社会发展的局面尚未根本改变，残疾人生活保障水平还比较低，就业形势依然严峻；有的地方执行政策力度不够，市县之间发展不平衡；基础服务设施建设滞后，专业人才匮乏；基础工作薄弱，管理不到位，操作不规范，残疾人的基本服务需求掌握得不准不实，信息化建设滞后。

2014年是深入贯彻党的十八届三中全会精神，全面落实中国残联和省残联“六代会”部署的开局之年。总体要求是：高举中国特色社会主义伟大旗帜，以邓小平理论、“三个代表”重要思想、科学发展观为指导，认真落实《残疾人保障法》，不断健全残疾人权益保障制度，有力促进残疾人服务托住底、补短板工作，有效落实残疾人同步小康年度任务，加快推进残疾人社会保障和服务体系建设，扎实提升残联组织的服务能力和管理水平，努力以改革创新精神推进残疾人事业科学发展，为实现残疾人与全省人民同步小康目标做出新贡献。

2013 年内蒙古自治区残疾人事业发展统计公报

2013 年，内蒙古残疾人工作在自治区党委、政府的领导和中国残联的指导下，以自治区“8337”发展思路为指导，以加快残疾人社会保障和服务体系建设为主线，以全面实施残疾人工作五个专项工程为重点，残疾人工作呈现出创新发展、加快发展的良好局面，残疾人和残疾人家庭生活状况得到进一步改善。

一、残疾人康复工作

全区在 22 个市辖区和 81 个旗县（市）开展了社区康复工作，累计已建社区康复站 2063 个，配备 1.1 万名社区康复协调员。有 22 个县的 25 个医疗卫生机构陆续开展残疾儿童筛查工作，年度新诊断 0-6 岁残疾儿童 271 人。

全区视力残疾康复机构共 17 个，完成白内障复明手术 1.1 万例；为 5346 名贫困白内障患者免费施行复明手术；为 2445 名低视力患者配用助视器，培训低视力儿童家长 1053 名，对 2519 名盲人进行定向行走训练。

全区现有省级听力语言康复机构 1 个，基层听力语言康复机构 23 个。年度新收训聋儿 418 名，在训聋儿 584 名，培训聋儿家长 803 名；开展各级各类听力语言康复专业技术人员培训，共培训专业人员 62 人。

全区肢体残疾康复训练服务机构 27 个；培训各级各类肢体残疾康复人员 132 人次；全区共对 6260 名肢体残疾人实施康复训练；资助 442 名脑瘫儿童进行机构康复训练，资助 113 名贫困肢体残疾儿童实施矫治手术。

全区智力残疾康复训练服务机构 23 个，培训各级各类智力残疾康复人员 185 人次；资助 457 名智力残疾儿童进行机构康复训练，同时培训儿童家长。

大力推广“社会化、综合性、开放式”精神病防治康复工作。在 84 个旗县（市、区）开展精神病防治康复工作，对 7.1 万名重性精神病患者进行综合防治康复，监护率达到 81.7%，显好率达到 63.3%，社会参与率达到 53.8%，肇事率 0.2%；解除关锁 108 人；对 3160 名贫困精神病患者进行医疗救助。为 449 名孤独症儿童进行了康复训练。

加强残疾人辅助器具服务体系建设，努力提高辅助器具供应服务水平，为残疾人供应各类辅助器具 17065 件，其中装配假肢 856 例、矫形器 78 例、其他辅助器具 16131 件，为残疾人免费发放辅具器具 4747 件。

二、残疾人教育工作

为家庭经济困难的残疾儿童享受普惠性学前教育提供资助 204 人次。开办特殊教育普通高中班（部）6 个，在校生 96 人。残疾人中等职业学校（班）8 个，在校生 213 人，毕业生 187 人，其中 157 人获得职业资格证书。有 445 名残疾人被普通高等院校录取。

未入学适龄残疾儿童少年 1576 人，其中视力残疾儿童 56 人，听力残疾儿童 62 人，言语残疾儿童 83 人，智力残疾儿童 516 人，肢体残疾儿童 482 人，精神残疾儿童 67 人，多重残疾儿童 310 人。

三、残疾人就业工作

城镇新增就业残疾人 6802 人，其中，集中就业 1517 人，按比例安排就业 1196 人，公益性岗位就业 488 人，个体就业及其它形式灵活就业 3384 人，辅助性就业 217 人。城镇就业人数 11.7 万；27.8 万农村残疾人在业，其中 22.6 万残疾人从事农业生产劳动。

全区建立残疾人职业培训基地 66 个，其中残联兴办 20 个，依托社会机构兴办 46 个，1.2 万人次城镇残疾人接受了职业培训。

2013 年度培训盲人保健按摩人员 332 名、盲人医疗按摩人员 155 名；保健按摩机构达到 262 个，医疗按摩机构达到 42 个。

四、残疾人社会保障工作

全区城镇残疾职工参加社会保险人数达到 6.4 万,城镇残疾居民参加基本医疗保险达到 13.5 万人,城镇 9.3 万和农村 20.9 万残疾人纳入最低生活保障范围;城镇集中供养残疾人和农村五保供养残疾人分别达到 2474 人和 13168 人;20.6 万名和 19.8 万名残疾人分别享受到稳定的生活补贴和护理补贴。13.2 万名城乡贫困残疾人得到了其他救助救济。

残疾人托养服务机构达到 110 个,共为 2770 名残疾人提供了托养服务。其中寄宿制托养服务机构 68 个;日间照料机构 8 个;综合性托养服务机构 34 个。接受居家托养服务的残疾人达到 1.8 万名。

五、残疾人扶贫工作

扶持残疾人 4.1 万人,其中 3.9 万残疾人实现脱贫;接受实用技术培训的残疾人达到 1.8 万人次。康复扶贫贴息贷款扶持贫困残疾人 17841 名,2852 个单位和 5962 个人对贫困残疾人开展结对帮扶。残疾人扶贫基地达到 98 个,安置 2213 名残疾人就业,扶持带动 3154 户残疾人家庭。完成 7473 户农村贫困残疾人危房改造任务,各地投入危房资金 8,064 万元,9152 名残疾人受益。

六、残疾人宣传、文化、体育工作

在主要新闻媒体刊播稿件数 10 件,报刊专版 23 个,电视手语新闻栏目 1 个;地市级主要新闻媒体刊播稿件数 1784 件,报刊专版 17 个,残疾人专题广播节目 19 个,电视手语新闻栏目 8 个,建立地市级新促会 3 个。各级公共图书馆设立盲文及盲人有声读物阅览室已达到 20 个。举办残疾人文化周活动 27 场次,成立残疾人艺术团队 8 个。举办残疾人文化艺术类展览 30 场次。各地开展残疾人体育健身活动 22 次,参加人数 3202 人。建成残疾人体育示范点 20 个,培养残疾人体育健身指导员 46 人。建成残疾人体育训练基地 2 个,聘任教练员 5 人。

七、残疾人维权工作

各级残联维权组织建设得到加强,残疾人事业法律法规体系进一步完善,残疾人维权工作全面开展。县级以上人大进行《残疾人保障法》执法检查和专题调研 14 次;政协进行视察和专题调研 11 次。开展普法宣传教育活动 211 次,1.9 万人参加宣传活动;举办法律培训班 61 个,0.26 万人参训。建立残疾人法律救助工作协调机构 41 个,建立残疾人法律救助工作站 31 个,办理案件 61 件。建立残疾人法律援助中心(工作站)102 个,办理案件 359 件。各级残联协助人大代表、政协委员提出议案、建议、提案 72 件,办理议案、建议、提案 36 件。

无障碍建设法规、标准进一步完善。62 个旗县(市、区)开展无障碍建设;开展无障碍建设检查 84 次,无障碍培训 136 人次;为 6873 个贫困残疾人家庭实施了无障碍改造;为 2.5 万残疾人发放了残疾人机动轮椅车燃油补贴。

各级残联共处理残疾人群众来信 1308 余件,接待残疾人群众来访 4220 人次。

八、残疾人组织建设工作

各级残联实有工作人员 3015 人。11 个盟市残联在领导班子中配备了残疾人干部;56 个县级残联机关配备了残疾人干部;已建乡镇(街道)残联 1102 个,已建率达到 99.3%,选聘残疾人专职委员 1156 名;已建社区(村)残协 1.3 万个,已建率达到 93.9%,选聘残疾人专职委员 1.2 万名。省级以下各类残疾人专门协会 557 个,市级专门协会已建比例为 93.5%,市辖区专门协会已建比例 85.7%;县(含县级市)级专门协会已建比例为 99.2%。

九、残疾人事业信息化建设工作

全区残疾人事业统计队伍建设进一步加强,各级残联共有 122 名专、兼职统计人员,自治区残联举办培训班 1 期,参加培训的人员达到 180 人次;盟市举办培训班 12 期,参加培训的人员达到 271 人次。

各级残联全面推进网站建设,除自治区级残联开通了门户网站外,有 8 个盟市残联网站和 31 个县级残联网站也已开通。2013 年各级残联开设网站技术培训班 10 期,培训各级残联信息员达 267 人次。各级残联共有 147 名专业技术人员从事信息化工作。

2014 年,自治区残联将按照自治区党委、政府和中国残联的总体部署,认真落实党的十八大、十八届三中全会、习近平总书记系列讲话和中国残联第六次代表大会精神，认真贯彻自治区“8337”发展思路，全面实施残疾人工作专项工程，不断完善残疾人社会保障和服务体系，促进残疾人事业在新的起点上加快发展，为残疾人“同步全面小康”目标的实现做出应有贡献。

2013年辽宁省残疾人事业发展统计公报

2013年，辽宁省残疾人事业在省委、省政府高度重视和中国残联悉心指导下，紧紧围绕全省工作大局，牢牢抓住国家加快社会建设，着力保障和改善民生及高度重视残疾人事业的战略机遇期，以组织实施全省“残疾人十大民生工程”为载体，圆满完成年度任务指标。残疾人生活状况进一步改善，残疾人“两个体系”建设取得显著成果，残疾人幸福指数不断提升。

一、康复

2013年，全省有62个市辖区、44个县（市）开展了社区康复服务，已开展康复服务的社区（村）11820个，占社区（村）总数的86%。社区康复协调员12626名，本年新增1133名。已建社区康复站的社区10280个，本年新增183个。全省共1164478人建立了社区康复服务档案，占全省残疾人总数的56.7%，比上年度增长2.8%。404100人次的残疾人接受了社区康复服务，比上年度增长27.3%。

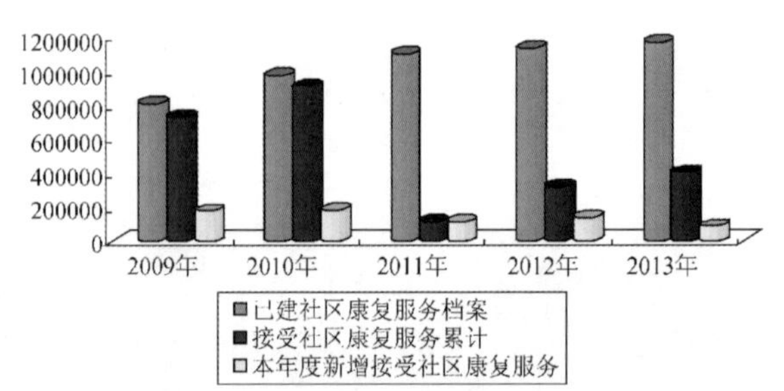

图1　2013年度与2009-2012年度全省社区康复情况（单位：人）

全省实施白内障复明手术19800例，其中，免费施行白内障复明手术的贫困患者5873名，占全年白内障手术总数的29.7%。低视力患者配用助视器人数为7979名，比上年度增长34.6%，培训低视力儿童家长1126名，对4656名盲人进行定向行走训练。

全省新收训聋儿601名，其中，机构训练489名，占新收训聋儿总数的81.4%，家庭训练112名，占新收训聋儿18.6%。在训聋儿数1121名，培训聋儿家长930名，培训专业人员312人，比上年度增长17.3%。接受地方项目救助50人，为806名成年人提供康复语言技术服务。听力语言康复机构45个，在岗专业人员共589名。

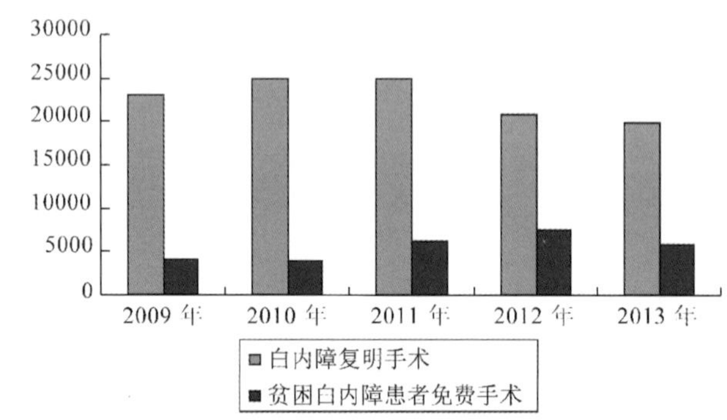

图2　2013年度与2009-2012年度白内障复明手术情况（单位：例）

全省107个县（市、区）开展精神病防治康复工作，对271425名精神病患者进行综合防治康复，监护率89.9%，显好率67.5%，社会参与率52.8%，肇事率0.01%，接受治疗的精神病患者63577人，接受康复训练38966人，对23973贫困精神病患者进行医疗救助。全省精神康复机构154个，其中，精神病人数为20082名。培训精防康复管理、技术人员1273名。全省孤独症儿童康复训练机构47个，在训儿童664名，比去年增长16.9%。

肢体残疾康复训练服务机构64个，各级残联办机构在岗人员150名。肢体残疾康复训练15004人，其中，脑瘫儿童系统康复训练799人，肢体残疾儿童社区、家庭康复训练1111人，成年肢体残疾人社区、家庭康复训练13094名。

智力残疾儿童康复4322人，比上年度增长12.1%。培训康复管理、技术人员1257人。智力残疾康复训练服务机构57个，残联办机构在岗人员138人，比上年度增长24.3%。

深入开展辅助器具供应服务，全面推进普及型假肢装配。累计建立辅助器具供应服务机构107个，供应辅助器具414个品种，39238件各类辅助器具，装配矫形器426例，装配假肢2097例，装配其他辅助器具36715件，国家彩金项目为残疾人免费发放23949件辅助器具。

注重康复人才培养。举办康复管理人员培训班111期，培训1943人。举办康复业务人员培训班117期，培训2605人。举办社区康复协调员培训班182期，培训9204人。

二、教育

健全残疾人教育服务体系，提高残疾人受教育水平。全省残疾人事业专项彩票公益金助学项目资助500名家庭经济困难的残疾儿童，专项彩票公益金项目资助新入园儿童194人。

未入学学龄残疾儿童少年总数2094人，其中，视力残疾67人，听力残疾104人，言语残疾59人，智力残疾805人，肢体残疾716人，精神残疾145人，多重残疾198人。

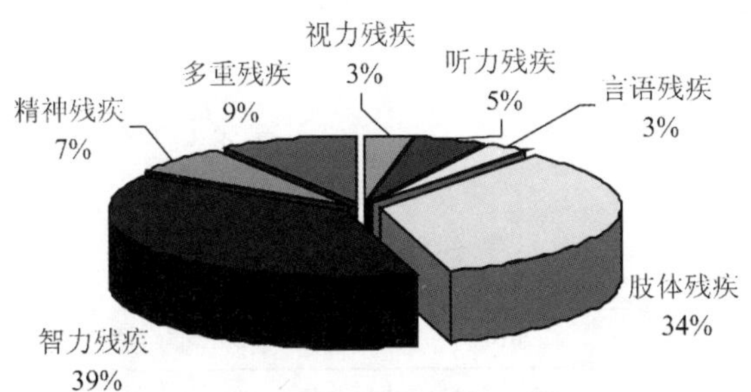

图3　2013年度未入学学龄残疾儿童少年分类

特殊教育普通高中学校（班）11个，在校生166人。残疾人中等职业学校（班）9个，招生84名，在校生301人，毕业生41人，获得职业资格证书34人。272名达到录取分数线的残疾人被普通高等院校录取。

三、就业

2013年，我省强化了残疾人职业技能培训，促进更多的残疾人稳定就业。城镇315069残疾人实现就业，其中，集中就业残疾人100182人，按比例就业残疾人82009人，个体及其他形式就业130435人，公益性岗位就业2302人，辅助性就业141人。据综上所述，残疾人个体及其他形式就业为城镇残疾人就业的主要形式，占整个就业比例的41.4%。农村残疾人就业人数稳定增长， 有399223名残疾人实际就业，其中，从事农业生产劳动290611人，其他形式就业为108612人。

残疾人职业培训基地158个，其中，残联开办60个，依托社会机构开办98个，培训城镇残疾人14869人次。盲人医疗按摩人员专业技术职务任职资格评审中，26人通过中级、48人通过初级评审。盲人保健按摩人员和医疗按摩人员就业人数分别为502人和59人，扶持98名特困盲人按摩师就业。

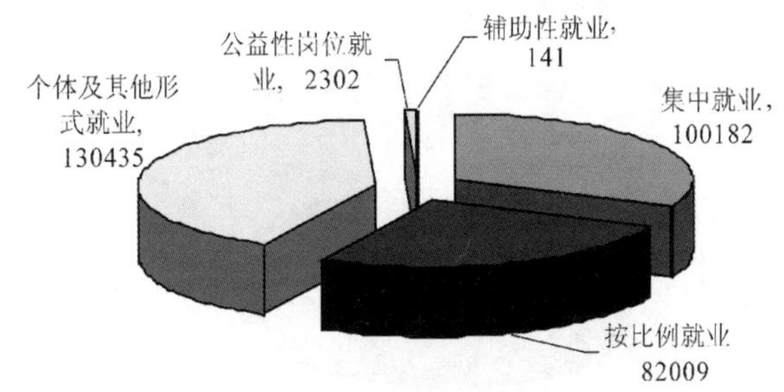

图4　2013年度全省城镇残疾人就业情况（单位：人）

四、社会保障

2013年，全省残疾人随着社会保障制度不断改善，残疾人社会保障水平进一步提高。城镇残疾职工参加社会保险已达194533人，其中，参加养老保险人数为117170名，比上年度增长5%，参加医疗保险人数100444人，比上年度增长12.3%。城镇残疾居民参加社会保险419482人，其中，参加城镇居民医疗保险192026人，比上年度增长4.5%。城镇个体就业参加社会保险36308人，其中，参加养老保险15898人，参加医疗保险16714人。农村居民参加社会保险587794人，其中，参加新型农村合作医疗500148人。

城镇纳入最低生活保障残疾人158744名，比去年减少3%。农村纳入最低生活保障残疾人184467名，其中，五保供养23317人，其他救助救济31574人。全省享受生活补贴的人数为1470名，享受护理补贴的人数为1862名。

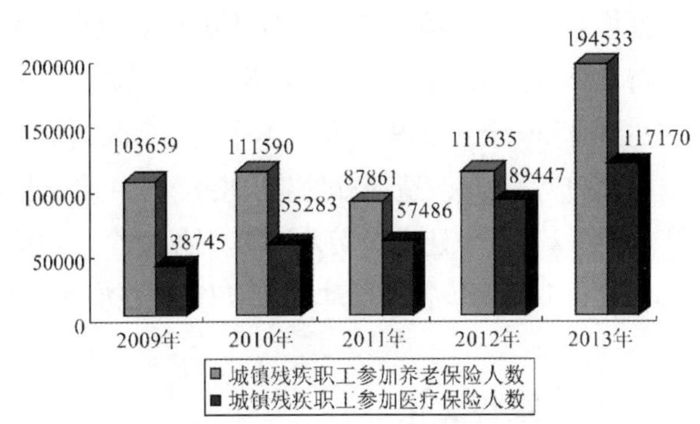

图5　2013年度与2009-2012年度全省城镇残疾职工参加社会保险情况（单位：人）

残疾人托养服务机构日趋完善。全省共有托养机构 218 个，31421 名残疾人享受托养服务。其中，寄宿制托养服务机构 77 个，为 4334 人提供托养服务。日间照料机构 104 个，为 2257 人提供托养服务。综合托养服务机构 37 个，为 1168 人提供托养服务。共有 23662 名残疾人享受居家托养服务。

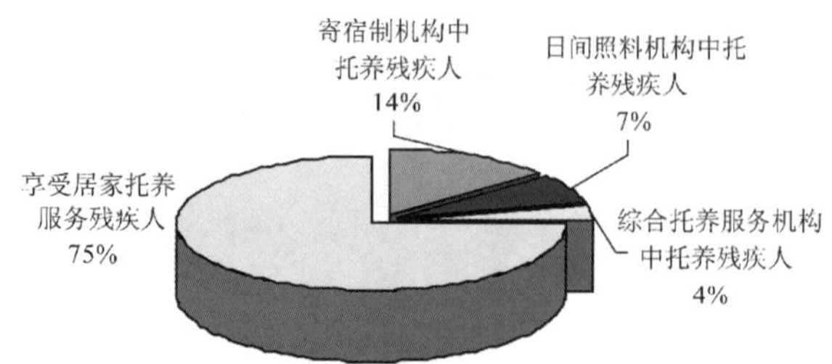

图 6　2013 年度全省残疾人托养服务情况

五、扶贫开发

2013 年，全省共有 68974 名贫困残疾人得到扶持，其中，36752 人通过扶贫开发实际脱贫，接受实用技术培训的残疾人 15574 名，地方投入培训经费 490.5 万元。

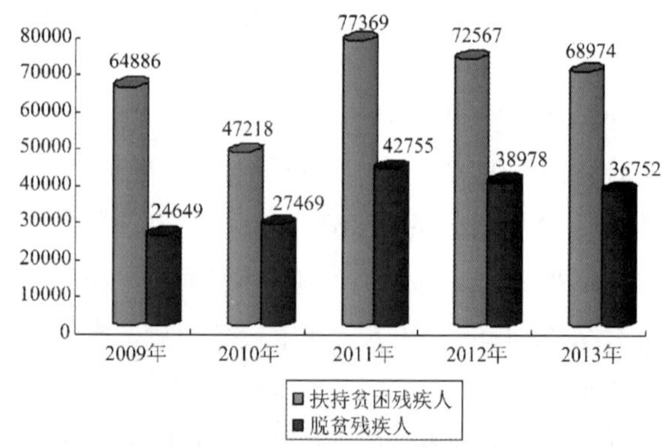

图 7　2013 年度与 2009-2012 年度全省贫困残疾人扶持情况（单位：人次）

省级财政投入扶贫资金 500 万元，社会募集 5 万元。康复扶贫贴息贷款实际落实 5600 万元，比上年度增长 1.8%，项目贷款扶持 1399 人，到户贷款扶持 863 人。结对帮扶贫困残疾人的单位和个人分别达到 3730 个和 20927 人。本年度危房改造实际完成 1486 户，危房改造项目受益残疾人 1484 名，投入资金 867.2 万元。建立残疾人扶持基地 50 个，安排残疾人就业 1491 名，扶持带动 2143 户贫困残疾人就业。

六、宣传文化

2013 年，全省进一步丰富残疾人文化服务，取得显著成绩。中央级媒体采用稿件 23 件，省级主要新闻媒体刊播稿件 410 件，报纸专版有 18 个，广播电台残疾人专题节目 1 个，电视手语栏目 1 个，电视公益广告片 1 个，报纸公益广告 2 个。市级主要新闻媒体刊播稿 6013 件，报纸专版 35 个，广播电台残疾人专题节目 11 个，电视手语栏目 9 个，电视公益广告片 26 个，报纸公益广告 22 个。

已建省级公共图书馆盲文及盲人有声读物图书室 1 个，举办省级残疾人文化周活动 3 场次，残疾人文化艺术类的比赛及展览 3 次，建立残疾人艺术团队 1 个。已建市级公共图书馆盲文及盲人有声读物图书室 22 个，举办残疾人文化周 101 场次，残疾人文化艺术类的比赛及展览 48 次，建立残疾人艺术团队 9 个。

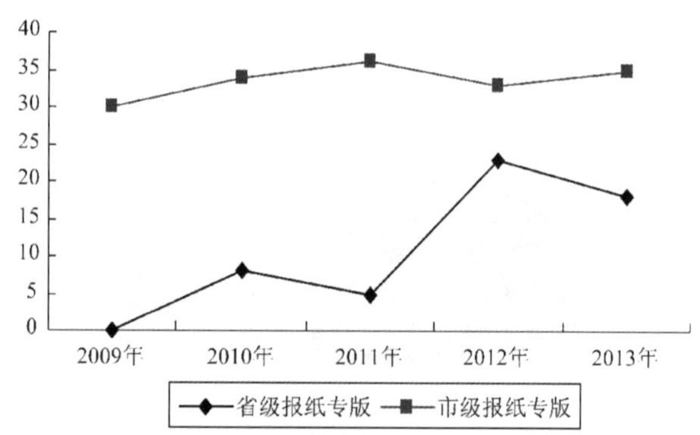

图 8　2013 年度与 2009-2012 年度全省报纸专版情况（单位：个）

七、体育

2013 年，全省建立省级残疾人体育训练基地 28 个，在编工作人员 50 人，聘任教练员 25 人。市级组织残疾人体育活动 107 次，45132 人次参加，残疾人群众体育活动示范点 54 个，比上年度增长 35%，体育健身指导员 612 人，比上年度增长 70.9%。

八、维权

我省残疾人法规体系建设逐步完善。省级举办普法宣传教育活动 2 次，150 人参加。举办残疾人工作者法律培训班 2 个，200 人参加。建立残疾人法律救助工作协调机构 1 个，残疾人法律救助工作站 1 个，办理案件 11 件。残疾人法律援助中心（工作站）1 个，办理案件 2 件。

市级举办普法宣传教育活动 38 次，3629 人参加。举办残疾人工作者法律培训班 22 个，4190 人参加。建立残疾人法律救助工作协调机构 13 个，残疾人法律救助工作站 14 个，办理案件 85 件。残疾人援助中心（工作站）14 个，办理案件 252 件。

县级举办普法宣传教育活动 189 次，17504 人参加。举办法律培训班 51 次，3618 人参加。建立残疾人法律救助工作协调机构 50 个，残疾人法律救助工作站 28 个，办理案件 119 件。残疾人法律援助中心（工作站）100 个，办理案件 735 件。

省级人大代表 2 人，政协委员 2 人。残联协助人大代表提出议案、建议 1 件，协助政协委员提出提案 3 件。残联办理人大建议 3 件，办理政协提案 6 件。

表 1　2013 年度全省残疾人法律救助情况

级别	法律救助协调机构（个）	法律救助		法律援助	
		工作站（个）	办理案件（件）	工作站（个）	办理案件（件）
省　级	1	1	11	1	1
地市级	13	14	85	14	252
县　级	50	28	119	100	735
总　计	64	43	215	115	989

市级人大代表 11 人，政协委员 33 人，残联协助人大代表提出议案、建议 9 件，协助政协委员提出提案 17 件。残联办理人大建议 11 件，办理政协提案 19 件。

表 2　2013 年度全省残疾人参政议政情况

级　别	人大		
	人大代表（人）	协助人大代表提出议案、建议（件）	办理人大建议（件）
省　级	2	1	3
地市级	11	9	11
县　级	68	9	5
总　计	81	19	19
级　别	政协		
	政协委员（人）	协助政协委员提出议案、建议（件）	办理政协提案（件）
省　级	2	3	6
地市级	33	17	19
县　级	150	20	7
总　计	185	40	32

县级人大代表 68 人，政协委员 150 人，残联协助人大代表提出议案、建议 9 件，协助政协委员提出提案 20 件，残联办理人大建议 5 件，办理政协提案 7 件。

2013 年，无障碍建设法规、标准进一步完善。我省系统开展无障碍建设市、县 5 个。省、市、县（市、区）无障碍建设检查分别是 7 次、111 次、97 次，无障碍培训分别为 280 人次、1661 人次、1414 人次。市级完成贫困残疾人家庭无障碍改造 120 户，县级完成 8413 户。全省各级残联共处理残疾人来信 1010 件，接待来访 14042 人次，其中个人访为 11760 人次，集体访 115 批次 2282 人次。

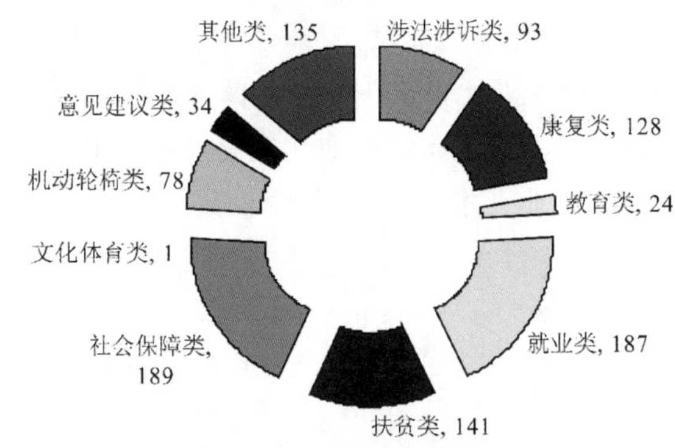

图 9　2013 年度全省残疾人维权（来信）情况（单位：件）

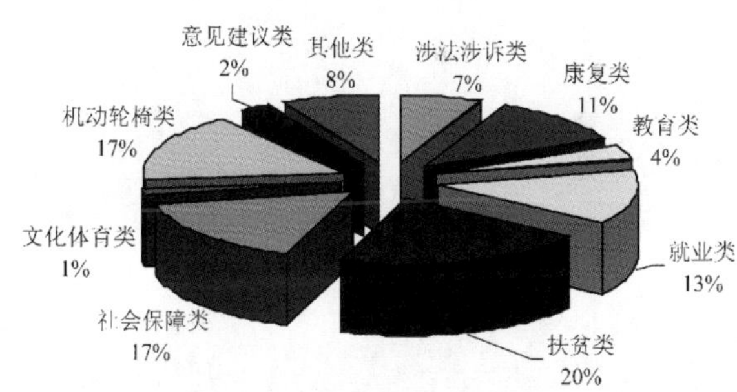

图 10　2013 年度全省残疾人维权（来访）情况

九、组织建设

省及 14 个市残联理事会已配备残疾人领导干部 21 人，县（市、区）配备残疾人干部 112 人。全省已建乡镇（街道）残联 1513 个，村（含农村社区）已建残协 11536 个，城市社区已建残协 3866 个。全省街道、乡镇残联配备专职理事长 515 人、兼职理事长 943 人，配备残疾人专职委员 1603 人。村（社区）配备残疾人专职委员 15391 人，其中，村（含农村社区）11602 人，城市社区 3789 人。全省各级残联助残志愿者登记在册的总数为 67645 人，受助残疾人 411682 名。

十、信息化建设

2013 年，全省有 129 名专、兼职统计人员从事残疾人事业统计工作。各级残联非常重视统计人员业务培养工作，省级举办 1 期培训班，20 人参训，市级举办 16 期培训班，336 人参训 。

2013 年，我省加大残联网站的建设力度，已建立省级门户网站 1 个，市级 14 个，县级 52 个。省及各市举办信息工作培训班 23 期，1110 人参训。省级网站全年发稿量 4710 篇。

全省信息化建设投入 338.2 万元。其中，硬件投入 188.9 万元，软件投入为 62.1 万元，系统运行维护费近 87.3 万元。信息化安全投入为 18.8 万元。信息化专业人才 193 名，计算机数量 1689 台，省级服务器 14 台。

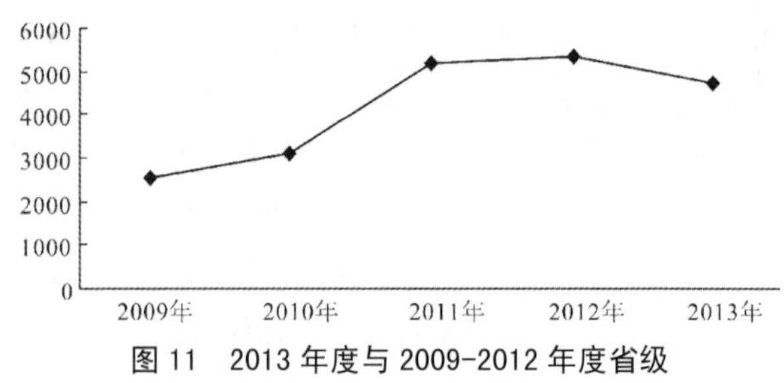

图 11　2013 年度与 2009-2012 年度省级网站发稿量（单位：件）

从整体统计数据分析，2013 年全省残疾人事业各项任务指标基本完成，呈现积极向上的发展态势和卓有成效的工作局面。城乡残疾人参加社会保障的数量和范围明显扩大，残疾人教育基础设施明显改善，残疾人家庭无障碍改造数量和质量明显提高，残疾人社会保障水平提高，残疾人服务持续改善。新的一年，我省残联将围绕残疾人保障体系和服务体系建设的工作主线，继续实施好“残疾人十大民生工程”，以提高残疾人满意度和幸福指数为出发点和落脚点，切实加大保障和改善残疾人民生工作，让更多的残疾人得到实实在在的利益。

2013 年吉林省残疾人事业发展统计公报

2013 年，吉林省残疾人工作认真贯彻落实党的十八大、省十次党代会精神，以保障残疾人的生存权、发展权和参与权为中心，以加快残疾人“两个体系”建设为主线，认真落实省政府确定的民生实事任务，深入实施各类助残工程（项目），不断加强残疾人基本公共服务，着力改善残疾人的生产生活状况，全面完成了年度各项任务，残疾人事业发展成绩显著，亮点纷呈。

一、康复工作

围绕残疾人“人人享有康复服务”目标，继续推进康复服务体系建设，组织实施国家残疾人事业专项彩票公益金康复项目和“七彩梦行动计划”及吉林省“互助关爱助残工程”，等各类康复救助工程（项目），推进残疾人康复工作全面开展。

（一）视力残疾康复。全年完成白内障复明手术 1.5 万例；为 2812 名贫困白内障患者免费施行复明手术，全年为 3756 名低视力患者配用助视器，培训低视力儿童家长 1400 名，有效开展家庭康复训练。对 4250 名盲人进行定向行走训练。

（二）听力语言康复。加强省级聋儿康复机构建设，完善聋儿康复网络。共对 465 名聋儿进行了听力语言康复训练，规范聋儿家长学校，开展家庭训练，共培训聋儿家长 994 名；培养各类专业人员 308 人。

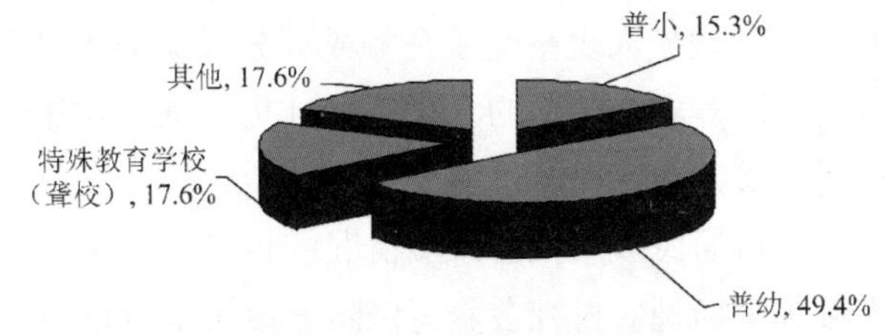

图 1　2013 年吉林省听力语言残疾儿童训练后走向

本年度接受国家人工耳蜗项目救助 73 人，接受国家助听器项目救助 315 人，接受地方听力康复项目救助 36 人。

听力语言残疾儿童训练后走向所占比例为普小 15.3 %，普幼 49.4 %，特教学校（聋校）17.6 %，其他 17.6 %。

（三）精防康复和孤独症儿童康复。大力推广“社会化、综合性、开放式”精神病防治康复工作。2013 年，在全省范围内开展精神病防治康复工作，对 16.0 万精神病患者进行综合防治康复，监护率达到 96.8 %，显好率达到 66.7 %，社会参与率达到 55.6 %，肇事率 2.9‰；解除关锁 6 人；对 17998 名贫困精神病患者进行医疗救助。

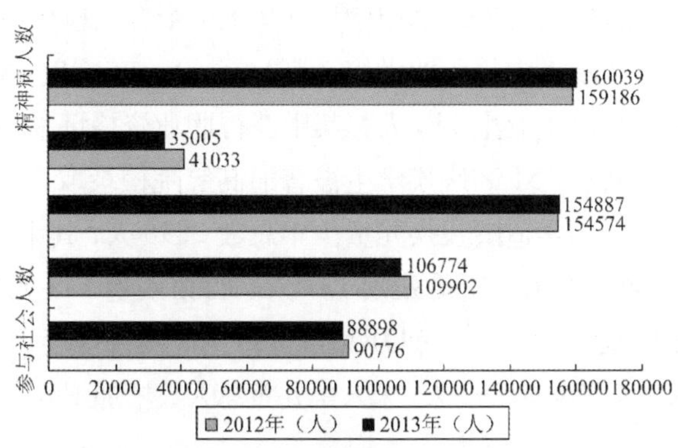

图 2　2013 年与 2012 年吉林省精防康复情况对比

全省共有孤独症儿童康复训练机构 39 个，其中本年度新增 3 个，在训儿童 612 名。有 541 名贫困孤独症儿童得到了康复救助。据测算，还有大量贫困家庭孤独症儿童没有条件接受正规机构训练。

（四）肢体与智力残疾康复。全年开展肢体残疾康复训练服务的机构达到 118 个，其中本年度新增 6 个，对 174 名贫困肢体残疾儿童实施矫治手术、装配了矫形器等辅助器具，进行了术后康复训练；对 4，937 名肢体残疾人进行了康复训练，其中：脑瘫儿童系统康复训练 473 人，肢体残疾儿童社区、家庭康复 167 人，成年肢体残疾人社区、家庭康复 4297 人。

全年开展智力残疾康复训练服务的机构达到 29 个，其中本年度新增 2 个；对 1880 名智力残疾儿童进行了康复训练，不同程度地开展了智力残疾儿童早期康复训练与服务。

（五）辅助器具供应服务。深入开展辅助器具供应服务，全面推进普及型假肢装配，截止到 2013

年底，累计建立辅助器具供应服务机构 43 个，为残疾人减免费用装配普及型假肢 386 例，供应各类辅助器具 9978 件。

（六）社区康复服务。在 30 个市辖区（含开发区）和 40 个县（市）开展了社区康复工作，累计建立社区康复站 2849 个，配备 8411 名社区康复协调员。开展家长学校工作的残疾人康复机构达到 39 家，培训家长 3749 人次。

（七）康复人才。截止 2013 年底，全省康复机构在岗人数为 8379 人，全年由各地残联主办的各类培训班 208 期，培训 7029 名各类康复人才。

二、教育情况

特殊教育普通高中学校（班）4 个，在校生 41 人；残疾人中等职业学校（班） 5 个，在校生 483 人，当年毕业生 118 人，其中获得职业资格证书 90 人。共有 151 名残疾学生被普通高等院校录取。

未入学适龄残疾儿童少年总数 2896 人，其中视力残疾 78 人，听力残疾 133 人，言语残疾 148 人，肢体残疾 907 人，智力残疾 1136 人，精神残疾 202 人，多重残疾 292 人。未入学儿童总人数增加 186 人。

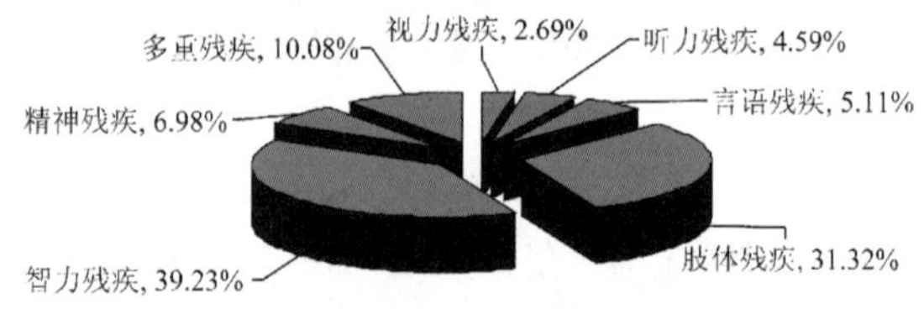

图 3　2013 年吉林省残疾未入学儿童少年情况

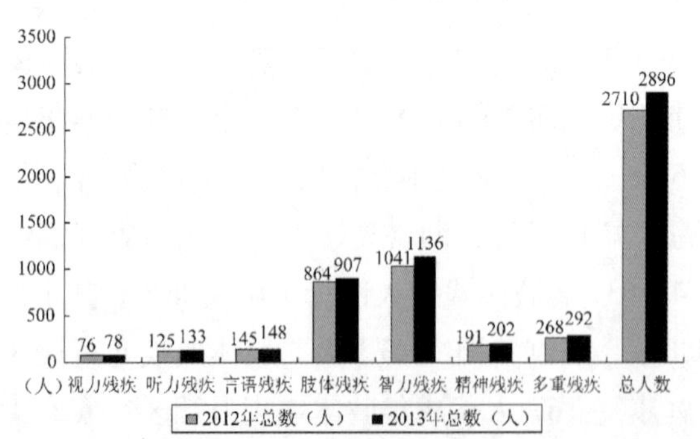

图 4　2013 年与 2012 年残疾儿童少年未入学情况对比

三、就业培训

（一）城乡残疾人就业情况。2013 年城镇新安排 9388 名残疾人就业。其中，集中就业残疾人 1，949 人，按比例安排残疾人就业 863 人，公益性岗位就业 590 人，个体及其它形式就业 5986 人，全省城镇实际在业残疾人 15.9 万人。30.5 万农村残疾人实现稳定就业，其中从事农业生产劳动 25.4 万人。全省共建立残疾人职业培训基地 180 个，其中残联兴办 52 个，依托社会机构兴办 128 个，本年度城镇职业培训人数 1.4 万人。

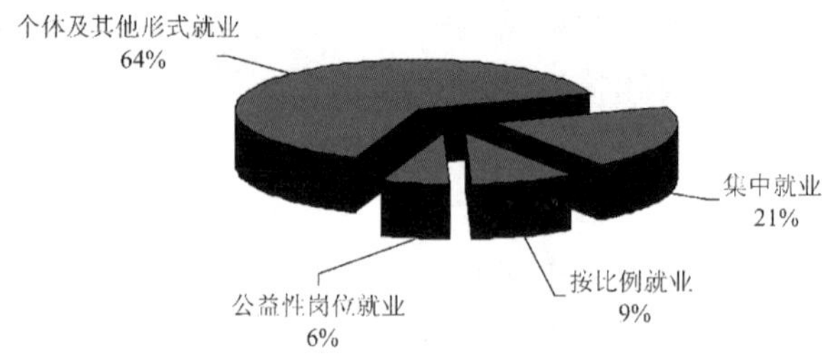

图 5　2013 年城镇残疾人新增就业情况

（二）盲人按摩。本年度培训盲人保健按摩人员 1092 人；培训医疗按摩人员 321 人，医疗按摩机构达到 40 个，保健按摩机构达到 287 个；有 1，103 名盲人按摩人员实现就业，其中保健按摩人员 947 人，医疗按摩人员 156 人，全省各级残联扶持 239 名特困盲人按摩师实现就业。

四、社会保障

（一）社会保险。2013 年全省残疾人社会保障状况保持平稳。

城镇残疾职工参加社会保险情况：全省城镇残疾职工参加社会保险人数达到 6.7 万人，其中参加养老保险人数 3.5 万人，参加医疗保险人数 3.3 万人。

城镇残疾居民参加社会保险情况：已有 8.6 万城镇残疾人参加了城镇居民社会养老保险，参保率 88.6%。在 60 岁以下的参保残疾人中 2.6 万重度残疾人，全部由当地政府全额代缴养老保险费，有 2.5 万非重度残疾人也享受了全额或部分代缴的优惠政策。领取养老金待遇的人数达到 1.9 万人。城镇残疾居民参加医疗保险达到 21.3 万人。

农村居民残疾社会保险情况：共有 12.1 万残疾人参加了新型农村社会养老保险，参保率 92.0%。在 60 周岁以下的参保残疾人中重度残疾人 2.8 万，全部由当地政府全额代缴养老保险费，有 5.7 万非重度残疾人也享受了全额或部分代缴的优惠政策。享受养老金待遇的人数达到 3.5 万人。参加新型农村合作医疗达到 31.9 万人。

（二）社会救助。2013 年全省城乡共有 28.5 万名残疾人纳入最低生活保障范围；城镇已纳入最低生活保障 13.3 万人，城镇集中供养 6495 人，其他救助救济 1.6 万人。

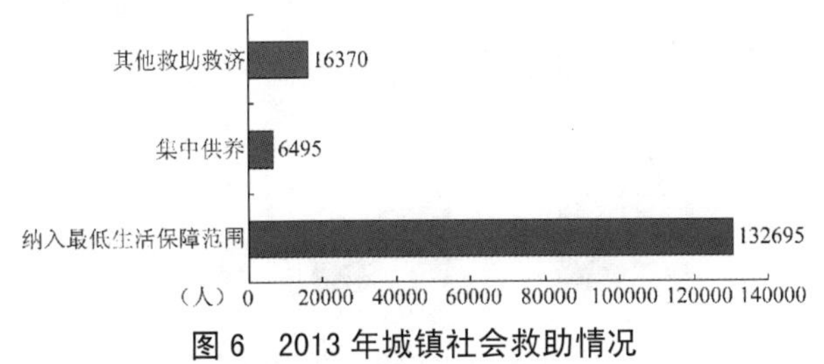

图 6 2013 年城镇社会救助情况

农村已纳入最低生活保障 15.2 万人，农村五保供养 1.0 万人，其他救助救济 1.4 万人。

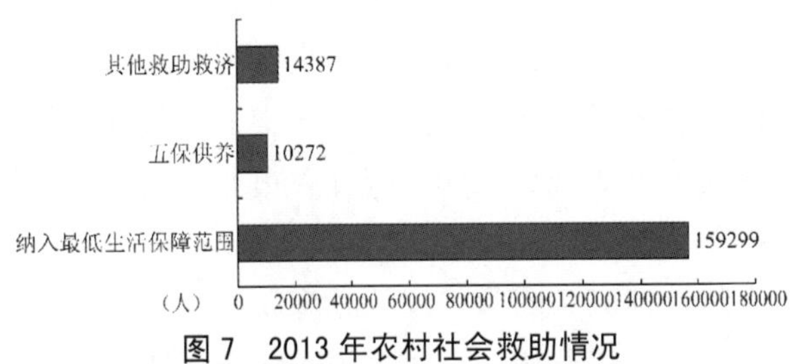

图 7 2013 年农村社会救助情况

（三）托养服务。全省享受托养服务的残疾人共 1.6 万人，其中寄宿制托养机构全年托养残疾人 479 人；日间照料机构托养残疾人 20 人，综合托养服务机构托养残疾人 313 人；实现居家托养残疾人 1.5 万人。目前全省共有残疾人托养服务机构 15 个，远远满足不了残疾人托养服务的需求。

五、扶贫情况

本年度全省各级残联扶持贫困残疾人 1.8 万户，3.0 万人，其中脱贫 2.1 万人，接受实用技术培训的残疾人达 3.2 万人次，投入培训经费 697.9 万元。

开展社会帮扶活动，其中结对帮扶单位 1964 个，结对帮扶个人 5021 人；建立残疾人扶贫基地 236 个，安置残疾人就业 3915 人，扶持带动 10476 户残疾人脱贫致富。

六、法律维权

（一）残疾人法规政策及执法检查。2013 年 5 月 30 日，省第十二届人大常委会第二次会议通过《吉林省残疾人保障条例》（简称“《条例》”），并于 8 月 1 日起正式实施，为我省残疾人事业发展和残疾人民生改善提供了重要的法制保障；全年共有 4 个市（州），14 个县（区）制定或修改了保障残疾人权益的专门法规或规范性文件；县级以上人大执法检查或专题调研 13 次，政协视察和专题调研 10 次。

（二）残疾人法制宣传与法律救助。全年开展普法宣传教育活动 172 次，参加人数 2.1 万人；开办法律培训班 44 次，参加人数 2132 人；建立残疾人法律救助协调机构 36 个；建立残疾人法律救助工作站 14 个，办理案件 56 件；建立残疾人法律援助中心（工作站）66 个，办理案件 396 件。

（三）残疾人参政议政。全省残联协助各级人大代表、政协委员提出议案、建议、提案 44 件，办理议案、建议、提案 24 件。

（四）无障碍建设与残疾人机动轮椅车燃油补贴。截止 2013 年底，全省各级政府成立无障碍建设领导协调组织 24 个；贫困残疾人家庭无障碍改造 890 户，无障碍检查 36 次，无障碍培训 474 人次，残疾人机动轮椅车燃油补贴 1.5 万人。

（五）残疾人信访。2013 年，全省各级残联共处理残疾人群众来信 672 件，接待残疾人群众来访 4923 人次，其中集体访 42 批次，807 人次，办结率达到 98%。

七、组织建设

（一）残联组织。全省各级残联实有人员 2，857 人，通过培训教育使干部素质得到进一步提高。残疾人干部配备工作进一步加强，全省 10 个市（州）残联领导班子中已有 5 个配备了残疾人领导干部。全省各级残联残疾人人才库得到进一步充实和完善。

（二）残疾人专职委员。全省有 911 个乡镇（街道）选聘残疾人专职委员 867 名；9355 个社区（村）选聘残疾人专职委员 10539 名。选聘残疾人专职委员不仅为广大残疾人提供了大量就近服务的社会公益岗位，解决了部分人员的就业问题，还为基层推进“残疾人社会保障体系和服务体系”建设提供必要的人员保障。

（三）残疾人专门协会。全省共建立各类残疾人专门协会 357 个，其中盲人协会 72 个、聋人协会 71 个、肢残人协会 72 个、智力残疾人及亲友协会 71 个、精神残疾人及亲友协会 71 个。全省共有 55 个残疾人专门协会进行了社团登记注册。

（四）志愿者助残。全省助残志愿者活动蓬勃发展，涌现一大批扶残助残先进集体和个人。截止2013年底，全省助残志愿者登记数已达18.7万人，受助残疾人达到81.8万人次。

八、宣传文化

（一）宣传。各级新闻媒体采访报道了大量涉及残疾人等社会弱势群体的相关新闻、专题节目。省和地市级主要新闻媒体刊播稿件2056件，报刊专版21个，残疾人专题广播节目18个，电视手语新闻栏目10个，投放各类公益广告10个。

（二）文化。残疾人的文化事业发展势头良好。借助第九届东北亚博览会平台成功举办首届残疾人优秀作品（产品）展示（展销）活动，进一步营造了全社会关心、支持、帮助残疾人的良好社会氛围。

省和地市级公共图书馆设立盲文及盲人有声读物阅览室达到14个，举办残疾人文化周活动67场（次），举办残疾人文化艺术类比赛及展览18个，全省已成立11个残疾人艺术团队。

九、残疾人体育

积极开展残疾人体育活动。全省各地开展残疾人体育健身活动103次，参加人数为1.1万人；建立残疾人体育示范点208个，培训残疾人体育健身指导员781人；已建立省级残疾人体育训练基地16个。

十、服务设施

我省各类残疾人康复服务设施总计59个。

已竣工并投入使用的各级残疾人综合服务设施共计45个，在建项目共计2个。其中已竣工并投入使用的各级残疾人综合服务设施总建设规模 7.8 万平方米，累计投资2.0亿元。

已竣工并投入使用的各级康复设施共计8个，在建项目共计1个。其中已竣工并投入使用的各级康复设施总建设规模2.8万平方米，累计投资10，356万元.

已竣工并投入使用的各级托养设施共计1个，在建项目共计2个，其中已竣工并投入使用的各级托养设施总建设规模3352平方米，累计投资1452万元。

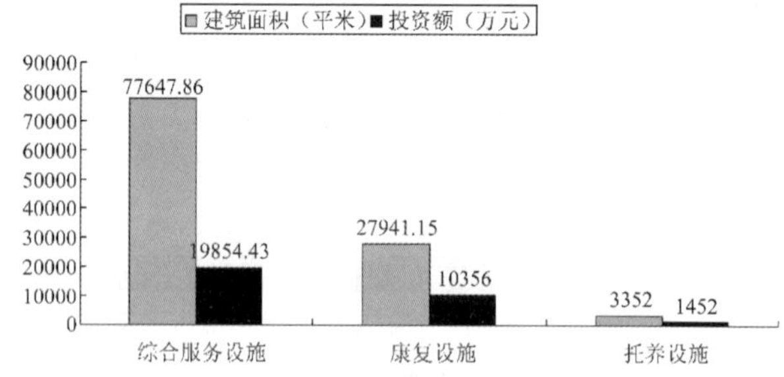

图8 吉林省残疾人综合服务设施建设情况

十一、统计与信息化

（一）残疾人事业统计。全省各级残联统计队伍建设进一步加强，共有90名专、兼职统计人员从事残疾人事业统计工作，统计人员业务素质培养普遍得到重视，统计数据质量逐年提高，全省举办统计人员培训班9期， 217人次参加培训。

（二）信息化。全省各级残联全面推进信息公开，目前省残联及各市州残联全面开通了公众网站，33个县级残联开通网站。全省各级残联共有130名专兼职技术人员从事信息化工作。举办信息工作培训班13期，培训各级残联信息员524人次。省残联网站全年发稿1337件，网站点击率逐年增加，网上信息服务能力逐年加强。

信息化手段的不断增强使我省残联组织管理残疾人事务的能力得到较大提升。但也应当看到长期以来我省残联信息化建设资金投入严重不足，还缺乏覆盖全省的残疾人基础数据库和综合服务系统，需要在今后的工作中加快推进。

一、备注解释

1. 本公报中数据均为初步统计数。部分数据因四舍五入的原因，存在着与分项合计不等的情况。

2. 残疾人"人人享有康复服务"，是指有康复需求的肢体、视力、听力、言语、智力、精神等各类残疾人有条件、有能力接受基本的康复服务，实现功能上的改善和能力上的提高。康复服务具体包括医疗康复、康复训练、日间照料、工（娱）疗、辅助器具服务、职业康复、心理支持、信息咨询与转介等，其中社区康复是实现残疾人"人人享有康复服务"的基础。

3. 残疾人的分类：残疾人分为视力残疾、听力残疾、言语残疾、肢体残疾、智力残疾、精神残疾和多重残疾七类。

二、吉林省残疾人事业重点项目介绍

1. 残疾人机动轮椅车燃油补贴：残疾人机动轮椅车燃油补贴是指用于补助城乡残疾人机动轮椅车车主，因成品油价格调整而增加的成品油消耗成本而设立的燃油补贴专项资金。城乡残疾人机动轮椅车车主，是指拥有符合国家标准（GB2995-2006）机动轮椅车辆、持有《中华人民共和国残疾人证》和购买机动轮椅车相关凭证的下肢残疾人。从2009年始，补贴资金由中央财政预算安排。

2. 贫困残疾人家庭无障碍改造项目：是指在“十二五”期间，中央财政安排专项彩票公益金支持各地实施贫困残疾人家庭无障碍改造的项目。项目资助对象为贫困残疾人家庭，优先安排一户多残、老残一体等困难家庭。实施项目改造的主要内容：地面平整及坡化、低位灶台（盲人家庭灶台有煤气泄露报警装置）、房门改造、坐便器改造、安装卫生间热水器、扶手或抓杆（洗手池扶手、座便器扶手、淋浴扶手）、浴凳及改善残疾人家居卫生条件的其他设施等。

3. 互助关爱助残工程：是2003年起经吉林省人民政府批准，在全省组织实施的一项助残工程。根据计划，“十二五”期间，项目将为全省贫困少年听力障碍者免费适配助听器、贫困肢残者免费装配普及型假肢和贫困苯丙酮尿症儿童提供特制奶粉补贴，并培训社区康复协调员及残疾人亲友。

4. 残疾人事业专项彩票公益金康复项目：是由中央财政安排专项彩票公益金组织实施的一项助残工程。资助对象为符合条件的城乡有康复需求的贫困残疾人，其中优先资助城乡低保家庭的贫困残疾人。内容具体包括：为贫困精神病患者实施医疗救助；为贫困残疾人配发和适配辅助器具；为贫困缺肢者装备假肢和矫形器；为贫困听力残疾人免费配戴助听器；为贫困智力残疾儿童进行系统康复训练。

5. 吉林省重性贫困精神病患者康复医疗救助项目：2004年起，省残联牵头与有关部门共同组织实施了重性贫困精神病患者康复医疗救助工作，为精神病患者免费提供康复医疗救助。救助条件：经具有资质的精神科医师确诊，持有残疾人证的重性贫困精神病患者，目前确实需要住院治疗或服用药物的精神病患者。患者本人或法定监护人自愿申请并书面同意接受住院或服药医疗救助。符合上述条件者中，处于关锁状态和城乡居民最低生活保证范围内的患者优先安排。

6. “七彩梦行动计划”残疾儿童康复救助项目：2011年至2015年，中央财政安排专项补助资金。优先开展残疾儿童抢救性治疗和康复，为符合条件的城乡有康复需求的贫困残疾儿童，其中优先资助城乡低保家庭的贫困残疾儿童实施康复救助。

——听力语言残疾儿童：为中低收入家庭聋儿购置配发人工耳蜗，并补助人工耳蜗手术、术后调机和术后康复训练经费；为贫困聋儿购置配发助听器并补助康复训练经费。

——肢体残疾儿童：为贫困肢体残疾儿童实施矫治手术、补助康复训练经费、装配矫形器。

——脑瘫儿童：为贫困脑瘫儿童康复训练、装配矫形器给予补助。

——孤独症儿童：为贫困孤独症儿童康复训练给予补助。

——辅助器具：为贫困残疾儿童装配假肢矫形器、适配辅助器具给予补助。

7. 吉林省贫困残疾儿童康复救助项目：项目由省财政厅和省残联共同牵头实施的脑瘫儿童、孤独症儿童救助项目。2014年将继续对具有家庭贫困持本省常住户口的0－6岁脑瘫、0-8岁孤独症儿童和0-3岁苯丙酮尿症儿童给予救助。

8. 吉林省省级专项彩票公益金“助行圆梦”行动（2013年）：总计投入省级专项彩票公益金一是用于购买小型康复器材及辅助器具，并通过借用的方式发放到全省40个县（市）的30余万名乡镇农村残疾人手中，供其居家使用；二是为县（市、区）配发残疾人流动康复服务车，将流动康复站建立在村屯，就近就便的为残疾人服务。

9. 农村残疾人“带传培训工程”：为了解决农村残疾人就业中遇到的生产技能低、经营能力差、经济收入少的问题，2009年起，省残联在全省范围内组织实施了农村残疾人“带传培训工程”。即在每个乡镇培养一名“一级带头人”，带领每个村一名“二级带头人”，向数百名残疾人面对面地传授种养殖生产技术，提高农村残疾人的生产能力，帮助残疾人实现脱贫致富。

10. “千家万户巧手工程”：主要目的是依托经济效益稳定、主导产品适合残疾人生产和经营的手工制作工艺品企业，开发适合残疾人创业就业的培训项目和产品，培育和建立残疾人就业实训基地，培训残疾人或重度残疾人家属学习工艺美术、手工制作等方面技能，通过采取送原料上门和登门取产品等服务，帮助残疾人足不出户实行创业、就业。

11. 彩票公益金助学项目："十二五"期间，中央财政进一步加大了对残疾人教育的支持力度，从彩票公益金中设立专项，实施"残疾人事业专项彩票公益金助学项目（学前教育）"，为家庭经济困难的残疾儿童享受普惠性学前教育提供资助。助学专款主要用于家庭经济困难的残疾儿童学前教育训练和生活费补贴。

12. "通向明天—交通银行残疾青少年助学计划"：是中国残联与交通银行2008年起共同组织实施的一项助学计划，资金主要用于资助家庭经济困难残疾学生完成学业，资助中西部地区新建特殊教育学校，资助残疾人中等职业学校建设实习实训基地和残疾人职业教育师资培训等。

13. 扶残助学金助学：为扶持残疾人学生及生活困难的残疾人子女接受中高等国民教育，省残联与省财政厅对原《吉林省助残奖学金管理使用暂行办法》进行了修改，制定印发了《吉林省扶残助学金管理使用暂行办法》。对我省当年考入大中专院校接受正规国民教育的残疾人学生和贫困残疾人子女，予以一次性学费资助。资助标准为：本科及本科以上层次每人3000元；专科层次每人2000元；中专层次每人1000元。对参加全国成人高考和高等教育自学考试等国家承认的大专以上学历的残疾人，在课程全部修完，取得学校颁发的毕业证书，当年给予一次性学费资助，资助标准为1000元。

14. 康复扶贫贷款：康复扶贫贷款是国家专项用于残疾人扶贫开发工作的信贷资金。中央财政在贴息期内，项目贷款按年利率5%给予贴息，到户贷款按年利率7%给予贴息。项目贷款重点投向促进农村贫困残疾人（户）快速增收，辐射带动贫困残疾人覆盖面大的种植业、养殖业、加工业等中小型扶贫企业项目。到户贷款主要用于扶持残疾人贫困户发展生产。

15. 残疾人实用技术培训项目：是中央财政安排专项补贴资金项目，要求我省"十二五"期间帮助5万名农村贫困残疾人接受实用技术培训，确保每个贫困残疾人掌握1-2项农村实用技能，切实提高自我发展和增收能力。具体实施对象为家庭年人均收入低于2800元、处于就业年龄段、有劳动意愿且具备接受培训的条件和能力的农村贫困残疾人。

16. "阳光助残扶贫基地"建设：是在中央和地方政府的扶持下，实施"阳光助残扶贫基地建设"项目，发挥地方龙头企业和农村经济合作组织等生产经营组织的辐射带动作用，帮扶贫困残疾人家庭就地就近发展设施农业、庭院经济和其他生产经营项目，有效提高家庭收入。

17. "阳光家园计划"：是2009年开始中国残联和财政部共同组织实施的为智力、精神和重度残疾人提供托养服务的项目。

2013年黑龙江省残疾人事业发展统计公报

2013年，在省委、省政府的领导下，在有关部门和社会各界的大力支持下，认真贯彻党的十八大、十八届三中全会和中国残联第六次代表大会精神，以残疾人同步小康为目标，积极推进残疾人康复、教育、就业、社会保障等工作，全面提升我省残疾人事业发展水平。现根据2013年度残疾人事业统计数据和实际情况，公报如下：

一、康复

在57个市辖区、62个县（市）、3037个社区（村）开展了社区康复工作，累计已建社区康复站的社区1357个，配备3864名社区康复协调员，本年度新增社区协调员398名。已建社区康复服务档案29.8万人，接受社区康复服务11.6万人，本年度新增1.3万人。

开展视力残疾康复机构总数达到23个。全年完成白内障复明手术1.1万例，为3148名贫困白内障患者免费施行复明手术，为4172名低视力患者配用助视器，培训低视力儿童家长239名，对4145名盲人进行定向行走训练。

推进听力语言康复机构规范化管理，完善基层服务网络。已建设听力语言康复机构29个。年度新收训聋儿410名，在训聋儿605名；规范聋儿家长学校，开展家庭训练，共培训聋儿家长747名；培训各类专业人员25名；各级康复机构共为183名成年听力残疾人提供技术服务。

开展肢体残疾康复训练服务机构达43个；资助133名贫困肢体残疾儿童实施矫治手术；对5421名肢体残疾人实施康复训练，其中：脑瘫儿童系统康复训练346人、肢体残疾儿童社区、家庭康复326人，成年肢体残疾人社区、家庭康复4749人。

开展智力残疾康复训练服务的机构29个，对2879名智力残疾人进行康复训练，其中，智力儿童系统康复训练278人，智力残疾儿童社区、家庭康复2137人，成年智力残疾人社区、家庭康复464人。

大力推广"社会化、综合性、开放式"精神病防治康复工作。在124个县（市、区）开展精神病防治康复工作，对18.3万重性精神病患者进行综合防治康复，监护率达到82%，显好率达到64.4%，社会参与率达到40.5%，肇事率0.1%；解除关锁8人；对6730名贫困精神病患者进行医疗救助。

全省共有孤独症儿童康复训练机构35个，385名孤独症儿童在各级机构进行了康复训练；对179名贫困孤独症儿童进行了康复救助。

加强残疾人辅助器具服务体系建设，深入开展辅助器具供应服务，为残疾人减免费用装配假肢705例，供应辅助器具13474件，装配矫形器92例，验配助视器3639件。

在55个县的33个医疗卫生机构陆续开展残疾儿童筛查工作，年度新诊断0-6岁残疾儿童780人。发放儿童残疾预防宣传材料16897份，举办儿童残疾预防宣传活动67次。

截至2013年底，各类康复机构在岗人员6534人，举办康复人才培训班146期，培训康复人才2267人。

二、教育

本年度接受残疾人事业专项彩票公益金助学项目资助的残疾儿童300人，接受残疾人事业专项彩票公益金助学项目资助新入园的残疾儿童102人，接受其他学前教育助学项目资助的残疾儿童12人。

截至2013年底，有未入学适龄残疾儿童少年1037人，其中视力残疾儿童40人，听力残疾儿童57人，言语残疾儿童33人，智力残疾儿童400人，肢体残疾儿童292人，精神残疾儿童82人，多重残疾儿童133人。

残疾人中等职业学校（班）7个，在校生101人。

参加全国普通高等教育统一考试达到分数线并被普通高等院（校）录取的各类残疾人高中毕业生189人，其中，本科117人，专科（高职）72人。

三、就业

2013年，城镇新安排残疾人就业13849人，其中，集中就业4139人，按比例安排就业1881人，公益性岗位就业 901 人，个体就业及其它形式灵活就业 6839 人，辅助性就业 89 人。城镇残疾人就业人数 12.6 万；24.2 万农村残疾人在业，其中 19.7 万残疾人从事农业生产劳动。残疾人职业培训基地 94 个，本年度有 1.2 万人次城镇残疾人接受各类职业培训机构（基地）培训。

2013 年，培训盲人保健按摩人员 280 名、盲人医疗按摩人员 50 名；医疗按摩机构达到 40 个，保健按摩机构达到 230 个；在专业技术职务资格评审中，有 37 人和 60 人通过医疗按摩人员中级和初级职称评审。

四、社会保障

截至 2013 年底， 12.5 万城镇残疾人参加了城镇居民社会养老保险，参保率 87%。在 60 岁以下的参保残疾人中有 1.8 万重度残疾人，其中 1.4 万得到了政府的参保扶助，代缴补贴比例达到 78.1%。有 1.4 万非重度残疾人也享受了全额或部分代缴的优惠政策。领取养老金待遇的人数达到 5.8 万人。

新型农村社会养老保险方面，共有 12.7 万残疾人参加了新型农村社会养老保险，参保率 50.1%。在 60 周岁以下的参保残疾人中，有 1.6 万重度残疾人得到了政府的参保扶助，代缴补贴比例达到 97.9%。有 0.9 万非重度残疾人也享受了全额或部分代缴的优惠政策。享受养老金待遇的人数达到 6.3 万人。

城镇残疾职工参加社会保险人数达到 7.0 万，城镇残疾居民参加基本医疗保险达到 15.7 万人，城镇 16.2 万和农村 14.0 万残疾人纳入最低生活保障范围；城镇集中供养残疾人和农村五保供养残疾人分别达到 3493 人和 10234 人；6007 人和 7807 人符合条件的城乡残疾人分别享受了稳定的生活补贴和护理补贴。4.7 万城乡残疾人得到了其他救助救济。

残疾人托养服务工作规范推进，残疾人托养服务机构达到 101 个，托养残疾人 4337 人。其中寄宿制托养服务机构 39 个；日间照料机构 2 个；综合性托养服务机构 60 个。接受居家托养服务的残疾人达到 1.8 万人。

五、扶贫

2013 年，扶持贫困残疾人户 1.8 万户，扶持贫困残疾人 1.9 万人次，1.4 万人通过扶贫开发实际脱贫；接受实用技术培训的残疾人达到 3.2 万人次，地方投入培训经费 577.3 万元。

康复扶贫贴息贷款扶持农村残疾人 3108 人，结对帮扶单位 2999 个，结对帮扶 3592 名残疾人。残疾人扶贫基地达到 171 个，安置 5335 名残疾人就业，扶持带动残疾人户 8875 户。

六、维权

2013 年，地市级制定或修改了关于残疾人的专门法规、规章 1 件；县级以上人大进行《残疾人保障法》执法检查和专题调研 15 次；政协进行视察和专题调研 16 次。开展普法宣传教育活动 146 次，1.4 万人参加；举办法律培训班 31 个，0.1 万人参加。

截至 2013 年底，成立残疾人法律救助工作协调机构 10 个，建立残疾人法律救助工作站 7 个，办理案件 43 件，建立残疾人法律援助中心（工作站）119 个，办理案件 857 件，有力地促进了法律救助和法律援助工作。

残疾人参政议政工作得到加强，各级残联协助人大代表、政协委员提出议案、建议、提案 36 件，办理议案、建议、提案 35 件。

无障碍建设法规、标准进一步完善。27 个市、县、区系统开展无障碍建设；开展无障碍建设检查 25 次，无障碍培训 156 人次；为 3490 户贫困残疾人家庭实施了无障碍改造；为 1.5 万残疾人发放了残疾人机动轮椅车燃油补贴。

各级残联共处理残疾人群众来信 1338 余件，接待残疾人群众来访 4412 人次，其中集体访 39 批次、261 人次。

七、宣传文化

2013 年，中央级媒体采用稿件数 11 件，省及地市级主要新闻媒体刊播残疾人事业稿件数 550 件，报刊专版 18 个，残疾人专题广播节目 27 个，电视手语新闻栏目 8 个，残疾人事业新闻宣传促进会 5 个。

省级和地市级公共图书馆设立盲文及盲人有声读物阅览室已达到 28 个，举办残疾人文化周 32 场（次），举办残疾人文化艺术类比赛及展览分别是 52 次，已成立残疾人艺术团队 14 个。

八、体育

2013 年举办残疾人体育健身活动 23 次，4，733 名残疾人参加活动。建设完成残疾人体育示范点 33 个，培养残疾人体育健身指导员 517 人，建有残疾人体育训练基地 3 个，聘任教练员 8 人。

九、组织建设

2013 年，9 个地市级残联在领导班子中配备了残疾人理事长或副理事长；36 个县级残联机关配备了残疾人干部；已建乡镇（街道）残联 1319 个，已建率达到 95.4%，选聘残疾人专职委员 1950 名；已建社区（村）残协 9135 个，已建率达到 90.1%，选聘残疾人专职委员 5868 名。

省、市、县乡残联实有人员 2864 人。各级残联共举办培训班 521 期，培训机关干部、协会干部及残疾人专职委员 1.3 万人次。

省、市（地）、县（市、区）三级专门协会均已建立健全，组建率达 100%。

十、信息化

全省各级残联共有 148 名专、兼职统计人员从事残疾人事业统计工作，其中 18 人有统计从业资格证书。2013 年全省残联系统共举办统计人员培训班 3 期，55 人参加培训。

全面推进网站建设，目前共开通 1 个省级残联、7 个地市级残联、21 个县级残联网站。2013 年全省各级残联开设网站技术培训班 3 期，培训各级残联信息员达 67 人次。

建有局域网 1 个、网上办公（OA）系统 1 个。全省各级残联系统拥有计算机 866 台。2013 年省级发稿量 854 篇，信息化建设投入 86.1 万元，信息化专业人才 174 人。

十一、综合服务设施

截至 2013 年底，已竣工并投入使用的各级残疾人综合服务设施 101 个，总建设规模 10.8 万平方米，总投资 36，933.9 万元；已竣工并投入使用的各级残疾人康复设施 3 个，总建设规模 0.4 万平方米，总投资 307 万元；已竣工并投入使用的各级残疾人托养服务设施 3 个，总建设规模 1.1 万平方米，总投资 3346 万元。

2013年上海市残疾人事业发展统计公报

2013年是全面推进"十二五"各项工作的重要一年。本年度，本市残疾人工作认真贯彻落实中央7号文件和市委10号文件精神，按照党的十八大和市十次党代会及中国残联、上海市残联第六次代表大会提出的工作要求，加快推进残疾人社会保障体系和服务体系建设，切实做好民生保障工作。圆满完成"十二五"发展纲要规定的各项阶段性目标任务，为携手残疾人全面建成小康社会的宏伟目标做出新的贡献。2013年，本市新领证残疾人21578人，持证残疾人总数合计385255人，其中视力残疾71367人，听力残疾36557人，言语残疾4015人，肢体残疾168092人，智力残疾56086人，精神残疾44945人，多重残疾4193人。

一、康复工作

本市再次将"为1万名残疾人补贴提供个性化辅助器具适配服务"纳入市政府实事项目。截至2013年底，该项目共完成适配人数18219人，适配辅助器具件数27500件。同时，为进一步完善本市残障人群康复辅助器具管理与保障机制，本市启动了国家科技部科技惠民项目《上海市残障人群康复辅助器具技术集成及应用示范》，在全市建立了3个示范区、20个示范点。

为满足残疾人日益增加的康复需求，本市积极协调市财政局，探索重度残疾人护理津贴、残疾人养护补贴标准政策调整等康复政策。根据残疾人个性化需求，开展常见遗传性耳聋致病基因检测试点工作，为育龄听障残疾人或听障残疾人直系亲属进行常见遗传性耳聋致病基因检测，并提供遗传咨询、婚育指导和产前诊断等服务，试点期间共检测252人。

上海市阳光康复中心顺利通过了省三级残疾人康复中心的检查验收，宝山区及嘉定区成为第二批全国"阳光家园"示范区，上海市示范型阳光心园、上海市残疾人示范型辅助器具服务社创建工作全面展开，本市残疾人康复机构建设有序推进，康复服务水平、服务能力不断提升。

2013年全市17个区（县）均开展残疾儿童筛查工作，建立各级残疾儿童家长学校113家。截至2013年底，累计建立社区康复服务档案348644人，接受社区康复服务累计达341753人。2013年度共完成白内障复明手术51381例，其中贫困白内障免费手术3989例。低视力者配用助视器10938名，培训低视力儿童家长1348人，盲人定向行走训练1817人。新收训聋儿140人，其中机构训练82人、家庭训练58人，在训聋儿352人，开展成年听力语言康复技术服务数4748人次。成年肢体残疾人社区、家庭康复4257人，脑瘫儿童康复训练650人。智力儿童机构康复训练1156人，成年智力残疾人社区、家庭康复7871人。监护精神病人111486人，其中显好病人数为109585人，医疗救助贫困精神病患者13146人、孤独症儿童康复救助261人。全年完成辅助器具适配服务195304件，其中假肢装配552例、矫形器装配29432例、其他辅助器具165320件。

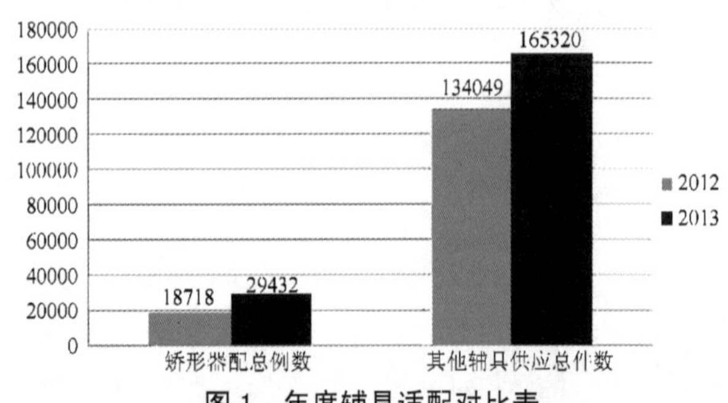

图1 年度辅具适配对比表

二、教育工作

2013年，本市继续开展未入学适龄残疾儿童少年调查工作，对发现的未入学适龄残疾儿童少年及时响应、及时妥善解决就学困难。据统计，2013年未入学适龄残疾儿童少年43人，同比2012年45人减少4.4%。全市特殊教育普通高中教育、中等职业教育相比2012年教育机构数未发生变化，在校残疾学生总数略有浮动。

三、就业培训工作

2013 年，本市的残疾人就业工作，已经形成以分散按比例就业和集中就业为主、以非正规就业和自主创业为辅，多种就业形式并存的格局。本市现有的残疾人就业保障政策主要包括：一是对分散就业中超比例的给予奖励，未按比例安排残疾人就业征收残疾人就业保障金；二是对集中安排残疾人就业的福利企业，根据国家税务总局规定实施退减税政策；三是对残疾人非正规就业和自主创业，分别实施阳光职业康复援助基地庇护性就业和个体工商户扶持等举措；四是残疾人职业技能培训等为提高残疾人就业竞争力的扶持政策。为强化残疾人就业扶持力度，相关特惠政策正在积极研究制定过程中，预计实施后将进一步稳定残疾人就业岗位。2013 年，本市残疾人就业主要数据与 2012 年相比呈现基本持平。城镇残疾人在业人数 67419 人，其中集中就业 15445 人，按比例就业 37209 人，个体及其他形式就业 7211 人，公益性岗位就业 4909 人，辅助性就业 2645 人。农村残疾人实际就业 24669 人，其中从事农业生产劳动 5011 人，其他形式就业 19658 人。

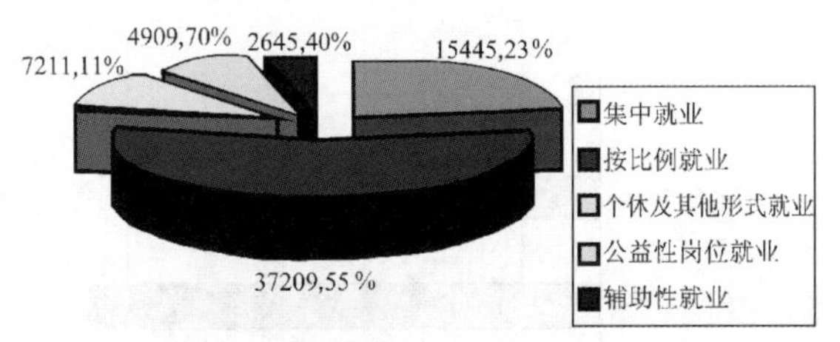

图 2 年度城镇残疾人各类型就业人数及比例（单位：人）

四、社会保障

2013 年，本市各类残疾人社会救助、社会保险和社会福利政策实施平稳。本市通过为重度残疾人代缴城镇居民社会养老保险和新型农村社会养老保险个人缴费、为重残人员代缴城镇居民基本医疗保险、为农村困难残疾人提供参加新型农村社会养老保险和新型农村合作医疗缴费补贴，保障了全市城乡残疾人的社会养老、医疗保险制度全覆盖。全市残疾人城乡最低生活保障、重残无业人员生活补助等社会救助政策应保尽保。城镇已纳入最低生活保障 15256 人，集中供养 138 人，其他救助救济 57235 人。农村已纳入最低生活保障 2802 人，五保供养 126 人，其他救助救济 19593 人。城镇重残无业生活困难补助总计救助 30268 人。

深入开展残疾人托养服务。机构托养残疾人 5443 人，日间照料机构托养智力残疾人 8005 人、精神残疾人 3000 人，居家托养服务残疾人 19520 人。

五、组织联络、维权工作

上海市残疾人联合会第六次代表大会于 2013 年 6 月 26 日召开，全市 360 名代表参加会议。大会成功选举产生了新一届市残联主席团、执行理事会以及市残疾人各专门协会的主席、副主席，并且选举产生了出席中国残疾人联合会第六次代表大会的代表，胜利地完成了换届选举任务。

截至 2013 年 6 月底，全市 17 个区县、217 个街道、乡镇残联也全部完成换届工作。10 个区县残联调整了理事长，10 名新调整的理事长有 9 名来自党委、政府及其相关职能部门，1 名来自群团部门。在 17 个区县残联中，有 6 名正副理事长由残联交流、提拔到了其它部门。17 个区县残联全部配备了残疾人干部。

市、区县残联各专门协会也顺利完成了换届工作，现任 188 名专门协会正副主席中，新任人数为 95 人，调整比例为 50.5%。其中盲人协会调整比例为 52.5%；聋人协会调整比例为 38.9%；肢残人协会调整比例为 51.2%；智力残疾人及亲友协会调整比例为 58.3%；精神残疾人及亲友协会调整比例为 51.5%。

2013 年，本市助残员队伍人数为 6472 人。市残联组织实施了全市残疾人专职委员三年轮训规划，对全市专职委员开展三年一轮（2011 年开始启动）的社会工作专业知识专题培训和网络在线学习培训工作，帮助残疾人专职委员进一步了解业务知识，提升工作能力。

维权工作着力规范初信初访办理，从源头上预防新增重复信访，在“事要解决”上下功夫，确保信访矛盾的有效化解，全年受理来信 1623 件，接待来访 367 人次。组织修订了《上海市实施<残疾人保障法>办法》，从立法层面上为保障残疾人权益提供依据。加强区县残疾人法律救助站建设，完善全市残疾人法律救助网络，推进残疾人法律援助和法律救助工作，降低残疾人享受法律救助服务的门槛，增加服务内容、扩大服务范围。积极开展残疾人法律援助、救助服务，先后为 330 人次提供法律服务，维护了残疾人的合法权益。从保障残疾人最直接的利益出发，认真做好惠及残疾人的实事项目，及时发放残疾人机动轮椅车人燃油补贴，惠及 14672 人；提高型家庭无障碍改造共惠及 666 户残疾人家庭。结合本市与市民生活密切相关的重大工程和民生工程，做到前期介入，开展现场检查，全年共组织市和区县督导队现场检查 107 次。为推动《无障碍环境建设条例》实施，提高督导队员素质，组织区县残联专职干部、督导队长及部分队员开展各类培训，共 2632 人次参加。

六、宣传文体

据不完全统计，全年本市各媒体共播出电视广播报道 50 余条，文字和图片报道共计 768 篇，约 124.4 万字，其中 29 篇出现在报纸头版。进一步加大了残疾人事业宣传，提升了残疾人事业的社会影响力。文化工作力求突破，会同市委宣传部等 12 家单位出台《关于推进本市残疾人文化建设的实施意见》。嘉定区、松江区获批开展“全国残疾人文化体育建设示范区”创建工作；黄浦区、徐汇区和奉贤区获批开展“上海市残疾人文化体育建设示范区”创建工作，以点带面推动全市残疾人文体建设。无障碍电影蓬勃发展，全市先后有 10 个商业影院开设无障碍电影专场，宝山、嘉定等 9 个区就近就便为残疾人提供无障碍公共文化服务，由著名播音员和主持人组成的电影志愿者解说员团队扩大到 100 多人。全年共为残疾人播放 70 多场无障碍电影，7500 多名残疾人感受到了电影艺术的魅力。信息无障碍建设不断发展，2013 年上海“两会”开幕式首次增配手语翻译，同步为听障观众“解读”会议内容，这是上海信息无障碍工作的又一重大突破。

2013 年，上海残疾人事业发展得到中央及市级媒体的关注，其中中央级媒体采用稿件数 12 件，本市各级主要新闻媒体刊播稿件数 307 件，其中专版及专题 33 个，刊播残疾人事业电视广播公益广告 5 个。2013 年“上海市残疾人文化月”期间，市级举办残疾人文化活动 15 场，区县级举办残疾人文化活动 192 场。

体育方面以举办上海市第八届残运会为重点，大力开展群众体育工作，做好国家队集训工作。进一步深入开展基层社区残疾人体育事业，借助社区残疾人体育训练点和阳光之家等平台，使残疾人能就近参与各类体育活动。在全社会关心支持下，全市常年参与体育活动的残疾人保持在 11 万余人，全年开展市级残疾人群众体育健身活动 27 次，残疾人群众体育健身活动参加人次 4200 次，残疾人群众体育活动示范点达到 58 个，聘任各类体育项目教练员 160 人，组织全市性残疾人体育赛事 21 次，参加各类残疾人体育赛事运动员达到 4500 人次，培养市级残疾人体育健身指导员 120 人。

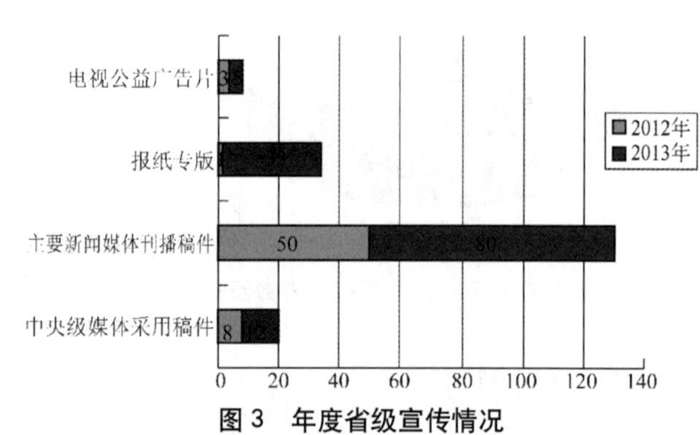

图 3　年度省级宣传情况

2013 年江苏省残疾人事业发展统计公报

2013 年，省残联第六次代表大会胜利召开，为在新的起点上推动创新发展提供了重要的思想和组织保障。全省残联系统认真贯彻省委、省政府决策部署，全面实施“残疾人幸福生活推进计划”，开拓进取、狠抓落实，全面完成了年初确定的各项工作任务，残疾人事业实现了新发展。

一、康复

2013 年，全省残疾人康复工作继续围绕残疾人“人人享有康复服务”目标，继续致力于完善“两个体系”—康复政策保障体系和康复服务体系，全力推进康复项目进医保政策贯彻落实，13 个市及所辖县（市）均制定出台了将部分康复项目纳入基本医疗保障范围的实施办法，其中 6 个市 26 个县已经实现报销。继续巩固实施专项救助政策，残疾人“人人享有康复服务”目标基本实现，全面完成了年度任务。

全省在 58 个市辖区和 46 个县（市）开展了社区康复工作；在 1.96 万个社区中，已开展社区康复服务的社区有 1.68 万个，占 85.71%；累计建立社区康复站 1.48 万个，配备 1.91 万名社区康复协调员；共有 64 个残疾人康复机构开展了家长学校工作，全年共培训家长 6691 人次。

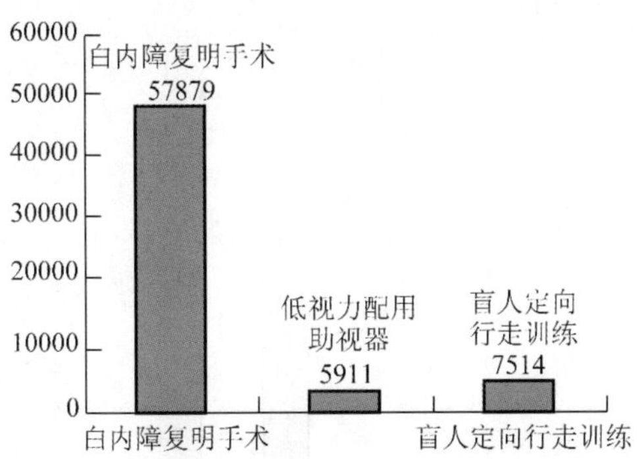

图 1 2013 年白内障复明手术、低视力康复、盲人定向行走训练开展情况（单位：例、人）

全省开展视力残疾康复机构总数达 60 个，巩固白内障无障碍省创建成果，全省白内障无障碍“发现一例、复明一例”机制成熟运行，全年完成白内障复明手术 5.79 万例，为 1.46 万名贫困白内障患者免费施行复明手术，为 5911 名低视力患者配用助视器，对 7514 名盲人进行定向行走训练。

推进听力语言康复机构规范化管理，完善基层服务网络；加强省级聋儿康复机构建设，完善聋儿康复网络；已建省级听力语言康复机构 1 个，基层听力语言康复机构 64 个；全省共对 2700 名聋儿进行了听力语言康复训练，接受地方项目救助的聋儿有 916 名。培训各类专业人员 469 人。实施贫困聋儿人工耳蜗救助项目，现已实施耳蜗植入手术 79 例并进行术后康复训练，共对 160 名听力残疾儿童免费验配助听器，为 900 名贫困听力障碍者配发助听器。

大力推广“社会化、综合性、开放式”精神病防治康复工作。2013 年在 104 个县（市、区）开展精神病防治康复工作，对 52.76 万名精神病患者进行综合防治康复，监护率达到 80.42%，显好率达到 59.98%，社会参与率达到 50.29%，肇事率 0.01%，解除关锁 59 人，对 3.95 万名贫困精神病患者进行医疗救助，截至 2013 年底全省共有 110 个精神康复机构。

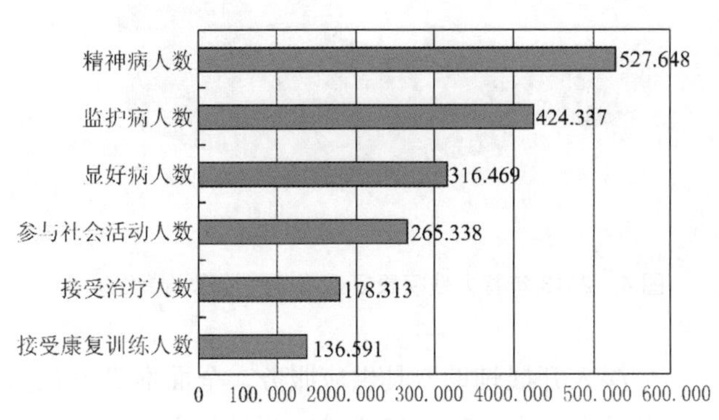

图 2 2013 年精神病人监护和救助情况（单位：人）

建立了 1 个省级孤独症儿童康复训练机构，20 名孤独症儿童在其中进行康复训练；基层共有 87 个孤独症儿童康复训练机构，在训孤独症儿童共计 920 人。

全年开展肢体残疾康复训练服务的机构达到 111 个，对 36223 名肢体残疾人进行了康复训练，其中：脑瘫儿童机构康复训练5163人，肢体残疾儿童社区、家庭康复训练1661人，成年肢体残疾人社区、家庭康复训练29399人，全年共完成贫困肢体残疾儿童矫治手术196例。

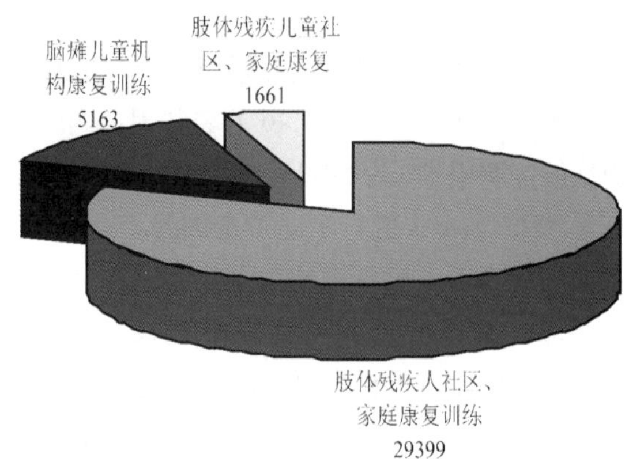

图3　2013年肢体残疾康复训练情况（单位：人）

全年开展智力残疾康复训练服务的机构达到89个，对11464名智力残疾儿童进行了康复训练，其中为2532名智力残疾儿童开展了机构康复训练，为4652名智力残疾儿童开展了社区、家庭康复，为4280名成年智力残疾人开展了社区、家庭康复，不同程度地开展了智力残疾儿童早期康复训练与服务；全年各类智力残疾康复管理、技术人员培训达1984人次。

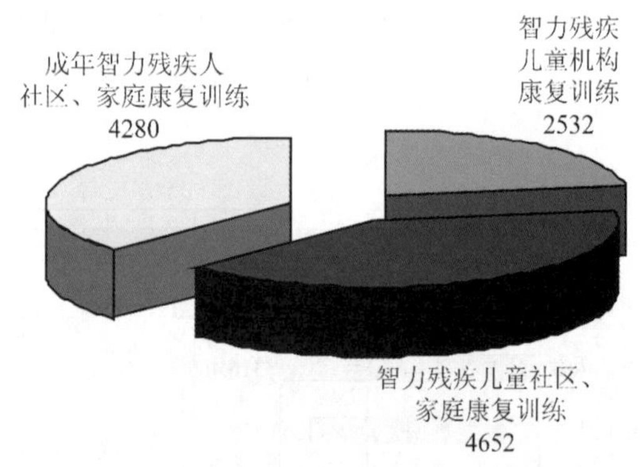

图4　2013年智力残疾康复训练开展情况（单位：人）

深入开展辅助器具供应服务，全面推进普及型假肢装配，截止到2013年底，累计建立辅助器具供应服务机构59个，为残疾人减免费用装配普及型假肢1659例，供应辅助器具达202种，供应各类辅助器具9.40万件，装配矫形器2022例；持续实施贫困残疾人辅助器具适配和家庭无障碍环境改造项目，共下拨省控经费2700万元，对全省5万名残疾人及其家庭适配辅助器具和家庭无障碍环境改造

全省共有104个县（市、区）和140个医疗卫生机构开展了残疾儿童筛查工作，2013年全年新诊断0-6岁残疾儿童4525名，全年共对近1.5万名0-6岁残疾儿童实施抢救性康复训练；全省共举办了308次儿童残疾预防宣传活动，发放儿童残疾预防宣传材料22.52万份；全省共有64个残疾儿童家长学校，全年共开展189次家长学校活动，残疾儿童家长参与人数达6544人次。

截至2013年底，我省共有康复机构在岗人员10724人，全省全年共举办康复管理人员培训班92期，培训康复管理人员1719人；举办康复业务人员培训班145期，培训康复业务人员4997人；举办康复社区康复协调员培训班191期，培训社区康复协调员14083人。

二、教育

2013年，残疾人受教育权进一步得到保障，残疾人义务教育免费和高中教育免学费、高中大学残疾学生教育专项补贴等全省性残疾人特殊保障普惠性政策得到全面落实，残疾人教育工作跨上新台阶。全年共有720名儿童接受了残疾人事业彩票公益金助学项目资助，其中204名儿童受资助新入园。我省各地多渠道争取资金支持，对27名残疾儿童给予学前教育资助。

全省已开办特殊教育普通高中4所，在校生397人。残疾人中等职业教育机构15个，在校生1015人，2013年度毕业生294人，其中获得职业资格证书242人。高等特殊教育学院3所，有426名残疾人被普通高等院校录取，232名残疾人进入特殊教育学院学习。

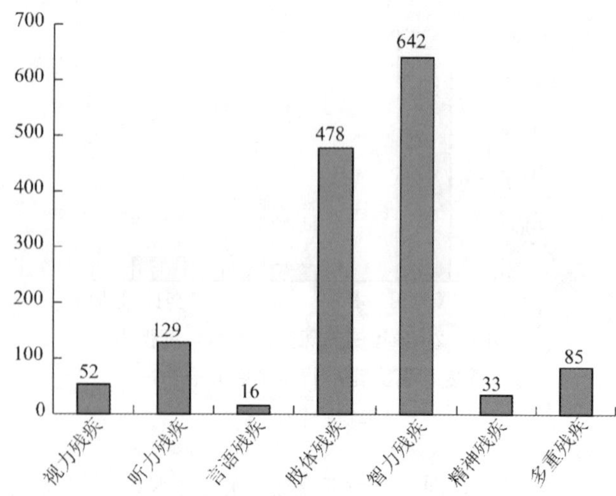

图5　2013年未入学学龄残疾儿童情况（单位：人）

截止到2013年底，全省有未入学适龄残疾儿童少年1435人，其中视力残疾52人，听力残疾129人，言语残疾16人，肢体残疾478人，智力残疾642人，精神残疾33人，多重残疾85人。

三、就业

全面促进《关于加快推进残疾人就业扶贫工作的意见》的贯彻落实。召开了全省残疾人就业扶贫工作电视电话会议，制定下发了《江苏省用人单位按比例安排残疾人就业补贴和超比例奖励办法》、《省级残疾人自主创业补贴资金管理办法》、《关于在全省推广使用江苏省残疾人就业保障金征缴工作信息交互平台的通知》等文件，积极实施“残疾人就业优先计划”，举办残疾人招聘会217场次。城镇新安排2.22万名残疾人就业，其中，集中就业残疾人8328人，按比例安排残疾人就业7205人，个体及其它形式就业5366人，公益性岗位就业354人，辅助性就业900人，全省城镇实际在业人数30.69万人；68.33万农村残疾人实现稳定就业，其中从事农业生产劳动51.94万人。

启动我省残疾人就业基地建设工作。草拟《江苏省省级残疾人就业星级基地申报与资金管理办法》，要求各地依托本地已有的各类残疾人培训、实习、转移就业基地，利用已实践成熟的培训、创业就业模式，开发就业岗位，积极安置残疾人就业，并在此基础上发展和新建基地，进一步推动残疾人在基地就业。全省残疾人职业培训基地达216个，其中残联兴办71个，依托社会机构兴办145个。抓好残疾人就业培训工作，全年共有2.32万城镇残疾人接受了职业培训。

进一步推动盲人保健按摩行业规范化管理。2013年度培训盲人保健按摩人员775名，盲人医疗按摩人员86名，保健按摩机构达到946个，医疗按摩机构达到26个；在专业技术职务资格评审中，分别有43人和98人通过医疗按摩人员中级和初级职称评审。

四、社会保障

全省残疾人保障水平持续提高。低保外重残及一户多残、依老养残生活救助、低保内重残补贴、保险补贴、无业重残人员护理补贴等政策得到全面落实，基本实现了全覆盖的目标。为加快推进残疾人社会保障体系和服务体系建设，进一步改善残疾人状况，促进残疾人平等参与社会生活、共享改革发展成果，残疾人参加新型农村和城镇居民社会养老保险工作继续推进。我省有52.03万残疾人参加了新型农村社会养老保险，在参保的残疾人中有6.84万重度残疾人领取养老金待遇，8.32万60岁以下重度残疾人参保，其中8.18万得到了政府的参保扶助（全部代缴6.90万人，部分代缴1.28万人），10.57万非重度残疾人享受了全额或部分代缴的优惠政策。在推行的城镇居民社会养老保险工作中我省有30.58万残疾人参保，享受养老金待遇的人数达到17.33万人。在参保的残疾人中有3.09万重度残疾人领取养老金待遇，60岁以下的重度残疾人中有4.50万得到了政府的参保扶助（全部代缴3.42万人，部分代缴1.08万人），3.14万非重度残疾人享受了全额或部分代缴的优惠政策。

城镇残疾职工参加社会保险人数达到27.73万人，其中参加养老保险人数20.19万人，参加医疗保险人数19.14万人；有41.07万残疾居民参加了城镇居民医疗保险，有128.93万残疾居民参加了新型农村合作医疗；城乡31.81万名残疾人纳入最低生活保障范围；城镇已纳入最低生活保障9.16万人，城镇集中供养和其他救助救济5.39万人；农村已纳入最低生活保障22.65万人，五保供养和其他救助救济12.60万人；2013年共有28.08万和11.65万符合条件的城乡残疾人分别享受了稳定的生活补贴和护理补贴。

2013年我省实施了托养机构服务床位补贴制度。省残联与省财政厅联合制定《江苏省残疾人托养服务补贴省补资金管理暂行办法》，明确对符合省补条件的托养机构给予省级补贴；残疾人托养中心建设有序推进，省残联会同省财政厅印发了《江苏省残疾人托养机构管理暂行办法》，市县残联累计组织残疾人托养机构工作人员培训90多次；安排专项资金支持200多个乡镇（街道）托养机构建设、支持146家托养机构开展残疾人劳动项目；2013年末全省已建成各类托养服务机构1122个，其中寄宿制托养服务机构40个，日间照料托养服务机构299个，综合托养服务机构783个；在托养服务机构中托养残疾人达9.82万人，享受居家托养服务残疾人达 7.43 万人。

五、扶贫开发

2013 年，我省残疾人扶贫工作紧紧围绕年初制定的扶贫工作目标，全面促进《关于加快推进残疾人就业扶贫工作的意见》的贯彻落实。继续做好残疾人扶贫基地建设、康复扶贫贷款、危房改造等残疾人扶贫工作，进一步完善扶贫措施，使贫困残疾人生活状况、收入水平、发展能力得到不断改善和提高。2013 年共扶持贫困残疾人户 2.21 万户，扶持残疾人 3.14 万人，脱贫 2.23 万人次，接受实用技术培训的残疾人达 1.76 万人次，投入培训经费 1118.90 万元。

2013 年全省共有结对帮扶单位 1963 个，结对帮扶个人 1.13 万人。建立残疾人扶贫基地 446 个，安置残疾人就业 11608 人，扶持带动残疾人 1.70 万人。完成 992 户农村贫困残疾人危房改造，投入危房资金 285.15 万元，受益残疾人 1133 人。

六、宣传文化

省残联会同省 12 个部门制定下发了《关于加强残疾人文化建设的意见》，举办“放飞梦想”全省残疾人摄影展；选送 12 个节目参加第八届全国残疾人艺术汇演，夺得表演特等奖 2 名、金奖 3 名、银奖 4 名，并荣获团体金奖。截至 2013 年底，省级宣传文化工作中，中央媒体采用稿件 12 件，主要新闻媒体刊播稿件数 282 件，省级共开辟报刊专版 8 个，残疾人专题广播节目 1 个，电视手语新闻栏目 2 个，电视公益广告片 3 个，省级残疾人事业新闻宣传促进会 1 个；地市级主要新闻媒体刊播稿件数 2414 件，共开辟地市级报刊专版 161 个，残疾人专题广播节目 28 个，电视手语新闻栏目 16 个，电视公益广告片 42 个，建立地市级新促会 9 个。

我省省级和地市级公共图书馆设立盲文及盲人有声读物阅览室分别达到 1 和 17 个，共举办 5 个省级和 75 个地市级残疾人文化周，共举办了 16 次省级和 77 次地市级残疾人文化艺术类比赛及展览。

七、体育

积极推进残疾人群众体育健身工作。组织省级残疾人群众体育健身活动 8 次，参加人数 3210 人，建设残疾人群众体育活动示范点 11 个，配备残疾人体育健身指导员 150 人，组织省级残疾人体育比赛 2 次，参与的残疾人运动员 532 人次，省级残疾人体育训练基地 1 个，聘任教练员达 31 人。

各地深入开展残疾人体育工作。地市级组织残疾人体育活动 96 次，参加人数 7772 人次，设立残疾人体育示范点 95 个，配备残疾人体育健身指导员 68 人。

八、维权

《江苏省残疾人保障条例》于 2013 年 3 月 1 日起正式施行。为推动条例宣传贯彻工作，省残联与省人大法工委共同召开条例新闻发布会；省残联印制了 4 万册《江苏省残疾人保障条例》单行本，向全省各级残联发放；出台专门文件，指导各市、县开展培训；深入基层，宣讲条例，对各地贯彻落实活动提出统一要求；协助人大及政府相关部门落实条例内容，使保障残疾人合法权益理念深入人心。

2013 年全省有 2 个地市制定或修改了保障残疾人权益的规范性文件； 全省县级以上人大执法检查或专题调研 45 次，政协视察和专题调研 45 次；全省开展普法宣传教育活动 383 次，参加人数 4.05 万人；举办法律工作者培训班 87 次，参加人数 5315 人。

截止到 2013 年底，我省建立残疾人法律救助协调机构 69 个； 建立残疾人法律救助工作站 66 个，办理案件 205 件；建立残疾人法律援助中心（工作站）111 个，办理案件 948 件，有力地促进了法律救助和法律援助工作。

残疾人参政议政工作得到加强，各级残联协助人大代表、政协委员提出议案、建议、提案 84 件，办理议案、建议、提案 135 件。

无障碍建设法规、标准进一步完善。全省共有 11 个地市、11 个县（市、区）出台了无障碍建设与管理办法；省本级、11 个市、62 个县（市、区）成立了无障碍建设领导协调组织；61 个县（市、区）系统开展无障碍建设；为 16525 户贫困残疾人家庭实施了无障碍改造，全省开展无障碍检查 153 次，无障碍培训 4525 人次；为 3.13 万残疾人发放了残疾人机动轮椅车燃油补贴。

各级残联共处理残疾人群众来信 1061 件，接待残疾人群众来访 5813 人次，其中集体来访 53 批次，911 人次。

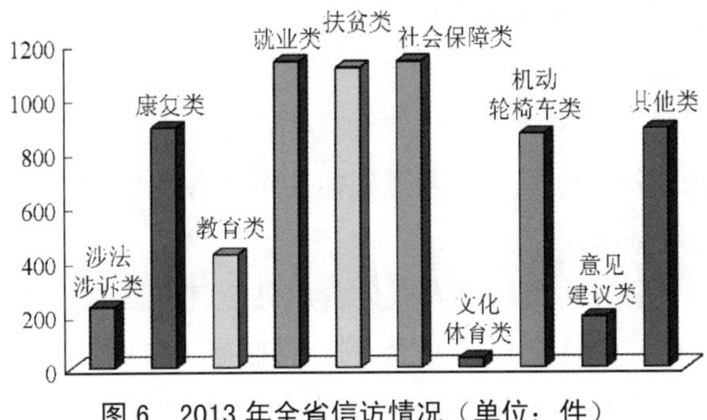

图 6 2013 年全省信访情况（单位：件）

九、组织建设

各级残联换届工作圆满完成。新调整理事长 43 名，配备残疾人领导干部及工作人员 100 余名，乡镇在编专职理事长配备率达 60%以上；完成各专门协会换届工作，启动全省志愿助残网上注册试点工作；隆重召开了省残联第六次代表大会；2013 年我省基层残疾人组织规范化建设进一步深入，残疾人工作者队伍建设力度进一步加大，城乡社区残疾人组织建设不断规范。

2013 年全省 13 个地市级残联中，8 个领导班子配备了残疾人理事长或副理事长；102 个县级残联中，58 个县级残联机关配备了残疾人干部；在残疾人专职委员选聘方面，1337 个乡镇（街道）选聘残疾人专职委员 1463 名；15676 个村（含农村社区）和 4701 个城市社区选聘残疾人专职委员 19399 名。

全省省、市、县乡残联实有人员已达 4978 人。干部培训工作取得新进展，各级残联共举办培训班 379 期，培训机关干部、协会干部及残疾人专职委员 2.23 万人次，对提高残联系统干部队伍素质起到了重要作用。

全省共建立省级以下各类残疾人专门协会 539 个，其中盲人协会 108 个、聋人协会 108 个、肢残人协会 108 个、智力残疾人及亲友协会 107 个、精神残疾人及亲友协会 108 个，各级各类残疾人专门协会活动日益活跃。

十、信息化建设

残疾人事业信息化建设得到加强。残疾人状况统计和监测工作科学规范，残疾人就业服务网、助残志愿者网站建设加快，残疾人工作业务信息数据库不断完善，为政策制定和执行评估提供了可靠依据；残疾人事业现代化研究取得新的成果。

2013 年全年省残联门户网站共录入信息 5835 条，加大“两个体系”建设、残疾人“人人享有康复服务”等重点工作的宣传报道，通过对省残联第六次代表大会的报道大力宣传残疾人事业发展成就。

残疾人事业统计队伍建设进一步加强，全省各级残联共有 136 名专、兼职统计人员从事残疾人事业统计工作，统计人员业务素质培养普遍得到重视，省级残联举办培训班 1 期，48 人参加培训；地市级举办培训班 15 期，416 人参加了培训。

地方残联全面推进网站建设，目前省级残联、13 个地市级残联和 95 个县级残联已全部开通了公众服务网站，为残联系统网站集群服务奠定了基础，残联系统网上信息服务正在逐步覆盖全省；地方残联也积极举办各类信息工作培训班，2013 年省级及地市级残联共开设网站技术培训班 26 期，培训各级残联信息员达 1318 人次，各级残联共有 212 名专业技术人员从事信息化工作。

2013 年浙江省残疾人事业发展统计公报

2013 年是我省残疾人事业确立新目标，全面推动残疾人事业又好又快发展的重要一年。全省残联认真贯彻落实中央和省委重大决策部署，围绕中国残联和省残联六代会目标，创新举措，扎实工作，落实任务，圆满完成“十二五”规划年度目标和 2013 年重点任务，残疾人的保障力度进一步加大，服务水平进一步提高，残疾人平等参与社会的环境进一步优化，残联组织服务能力明显增强。

一、康复

2013 年，通过实施康复工程，全省有 24.32 万残疾人得到不同程度的康复。

全省开展视力残疾康复机构共有 16 个，其中省级康复机构 1 个，地市级、县级康复机构 15 个。完成白内障复明手术 3.33 万例；为 16954 名贫困白内障患者免费施行复明手术；为 1560 名低视力患者配用助视器，培训低视力儿童家长 523 名，有效开展家庭康复训练。对 3879 名盲人进行定向行走训练。

全省开展听力语言康复机构共有 30 个，其中省级听力语言康复机构 1 个，地市、县级听力语言康复机构 29 个。年度新收训聋儿 583 名，在训聋儿 941 名；培训聋儿家长 1016 名；培训专业人员 152 人。

全省开展肢体残疾康复训练服务机构共有 43 个，其中，省级康复机构 1 个，地市级、县级康复机构 42 个；培训各级各类肢体残疾康复人员 4723 人次；共对 7834 名肢体残疾者实施康复训练；实施救助项目，资助 572 名脑瘫儿童进行机构康复训练，资助 96 名贫困肢体残疾儿童实施矫治手术。

全省开展智力残疾康复训练服务的机构共有 38 个，其中，省级康复机构 1 个，地市级、县级康复机构 37 个；培训各级各类智力残疾康复人员 1750 人次；共对 3794 名智力残疾人进行康复训练；实施救助项目，资助 659 名智力残疾儿童进行机构康复训练。

全省开展孤独症儿童康复训练机构共有 39 个，其中省级康复机构 1 个，地市级及以下康复机构 38 个；全省共有 443 名孤独症儿童在各级机构进行了康复训练。

全省共为残疾人减免费用供应辅助器具 27613 件，其中装配假肢 1146 例、矫形器 152 例。

此外，全省共有 49 个县（市、区）的 114 个医疗卫生机构陆续开展残疾儿童筛查工作，年度新诊断 0-6 岁残疾儿童 982 人。

二、教育

2013 年，全省共有 543 名家庭困难的学龄前残疾儿童享受专项彩票公益金助学项目资助；各地也积极多渠道争取资金支持，对 399 名残疾儿童给予学前教育资助。

全省已开办特殊教育普通高中班（部）4 个，在校生 182 人。残疾人中等职业学校（班）16 个，在校生 683 人，毕业生 211 人，其中 210 人获得职业资格证书。有 308 名残疾人被普通高等院校录取。

截止到 2013 年底，全省有适龄未入学的持证残疾儿童少年 526 人，其中视力残疾儿童 10 人，听力残疾儿童 33 人，言语残疾儿童 8 人，智力残疾儿童 217 人，肢体残疾儿童 172 人，精神残疾儿童 21 人，多重残疾儿童 65 人。

三、就业

2013 年，全省城镇残疾人新增就业 13428 人，其中，集中就业 5406 人，按比例安排就业 3592 人，公益性岗位就业 449 人，个体就业及其它形式灵活就业 2937 人，辅助性就业 1044 人。截止 2013 年底，全省城镇残疾人就业人数 20.64 万，有 21.30 万农村残疾人从事农业生产劳动。

截至 2013 年底，全省共有残疾人职业培训基地 291 个，其中残联兴办 104 个，依托社会机构兴办 187 个。

2013 年度共培训盲人保健按摩人员 643 名、盲人医疗按摩人员 257 名；保健按摩机构 1060 个，医疗按摩机构 29 个；在专业技术职务资格评审中，分别有 1 人和 32 人通过医疗按摩人员中级和初级职称评审。

四、社会保障

2013 年，全省有 7.85 万城镇残疾人参加了城乡居民社会养老保险，90.67%的重度残疾人享受了政府的参保补贴。有 1.45 万非重度残疾人也享受了全额或一定比例参保补贴的优惠政策。

农村残疾人参加城乡居民社会养老保险 34.75 万人，95.61%的重度残疾人享受政府的参保补贴；有 5.67 万非重度残疾人也享受了全额或一定比例参保补贴的优惠政策。

全省共有 16.36 万城镇残疾职工参加社会保险，44.26 万农村残疾人参加新型农村合作医疗保险。

全省有 2.79 万城镇残疾人和 14.99 万农村残疾人纳入最低生活保障范围；城镇集中供养残疾人和农村五保供养残疾人分别为 3213 人和 6609 人；20.09 万和 7.36 万符合条件的残疾人分别享受了稳定的生活补贴和护理补贴。有 9.54 万残疾人得到了无固定收入生活补助。

全省残疾人托养服务机构共有 757 个。其中综合性托养服务机构 174 个，为 1.57 万残疾人提供了寄宿制托养服务。1.37 万名残疾人享受日间照料服务，6.78 万名残疾人享受居家托养服务。

五、扶贫

2013 年，全省有 10.46 万贫困残疾人得到帮扶，接受实用技术培训的残疾人共 2.22 万人次。

全省共有2469个单位和13738名个人对贫困残疾人开展了结对帮扶。全省共有残疾人扶贫基地 1262 个，安置残疾人就业 9786 人。全省投入危房改造资金共计 3632.15 万元。

六、维权

2013 年，全省共制定或修改了关于残疾人的专门法规、规章 2 件；制定或修改保障残疾人权益的规范性文件 9 件。县级以上人大进行《残疾人保障法》执法检查和专题调研 58 次；政协进行视察和专题调研 84 次。开展普法宣传教育活动 220 次，2.22 万人参加；举办法律培训班 81 个，0.58 万人参加。

截至 2013 年底，成立残疾人法律救助工作协调机构 74 个，建立残疾人法律救助工作站 43 个，办理案件 513 件，建立残疾人法律援助中心（工作站）98 个，办理案件 1009 件，有力地促进了法律救助和法律援助工作。

各级残联协助人大代表、政协委员提出议案、建议、提案 207 件，办理议案、建议、提案 186 件。

26 个市、县、区系统开展无障碍设施建设；开展无障碍设施建设专项检查 213 次，无障碍培训 1200 人次；为 7100 个贫困残疾人家庭实施了无障碍改造；为 1.23 万残疾人发放了残疾人机动轮椅车燃油补贴。

各级残联共处理残疾人群众来信 2637 件，接待残疾人群众来访 11533 人次，其中集体来访 77 批次、1335 人次。

七、宣传文化

2013 年，中央级媒体采用我会稿件共 17 件，全省主要新闻媒体刊播稿件数 88 件，报刊专版 3 个，开设残疾人专题广播节目 1 个，电视手语新闻栏目 1 个，建有省级残疾人事业新闻宣传促进会 1 个；地市级主要新闻媒体刊播稿件数 4194 件，报刊专版 31 个，残疾人专题广播节目 16 个，电视手语新闻栏目 14 个，建立地市级新促会 10 个。

省级和地市级公共图书馆设立盲文及盲人有声读物阅览室分别为 1 和 14 个，省市两级分别举办残疾人文化周 1 和 30 个，举办残疾人文化艺术类比赛及展览分别是 5 和 26 个，全省各级已成立残疾人艺术团队共 18 个。

八、体育

2013 年共举办省级残疾人体育健身活动 4 次，参加人数 1000 人；建立省级残疾人体育示范点 5 个，培训残疾人体育健身指导员 219 人；举办省级残疾人体育比赛 2 次，参与的残疾人运动员 350 人次；建立省级残疾人体育训练基地 6 个，聘任教练员 25 人。

举办市级残疾人体育健身活动 71 次，参加人数 7843 人；建立残疾人体育示范点 135 个，残疾人体育健身指导员 984 人。

九、组织建设

2013 年，10 个地市级残联在领导班子中配备了残疾人领导干部；90 个县级残联中有 63 个县（市、区）残联配备了残疾人干部，其中有 24 个县级残联配备残疾人领导干部；已建乡镇（街道）残联 1309 个，其中 923 个配备专职理事长，专职配备率达 70.5%；选聘残疾人专职委员 1321 名；已建社区（村）残协 2.01 万个，已建率为 87.29%，选聘残疾人专职委员 1.8 万名。

我省各级残联有 87 位理事长担任同级人大、政协常委；全省残疾人、残疾人工作者有 332 人担任各级人大代表、政协委员。

省、市、县、乡残联实有人员 4300 人。各级残联共举办培训班 1400 余期，培训机关干部、协会主席及残疾人专职委员 3.85 万人次。

共建立省、市、县三级各类残疾人专门协会 427 个，市级专门协会已建比例为 83.93%，县（含市、区）级专门协会已建比例为 86.01%。

十、信息化建设

2013 年，各级残联共有 93 名专、兼职统计人员从事残疾人事业统计工作。省级残联举办培训班 2 期，参加培训的人员共 120 人次；地市级举办培训班 22 期，参加培训的人员共 681 人次。

全省已开通 11 个地市级残联网站和 84 个县级残联网站。2013 年省级及地市级残联开设网站技术培训班 8 期，培训各级残联信息员达 706 人次。

十一、残疾人综合服务设施

截至 2013 年底，全省已竣工并投入使用的各级残疾人综合服务设施 71 个，总建设规模 42.94 万平方米，总投资 15.82 亿元；已竣工并投入使用的各级残疾人康复设施 21 个，总建设规模 13.66 万平方米，总投资 4.10 亿元；已竣工并投入使用的各级残疾人托养服务设施 12 个，总建设规模 8.98 万平方米，总投资 3.24 亿元。

2013年安徽省残疾人事业发展统计公报

2013年，在省委、省政府的坚强领导下，在中国残联的有力支持下，我省残联深入学习贯彻党的十八大、十八届三中全会和中国残联六代会精神，紧紧围绕残疾人"两个体系"建设，着力保障和改善残疾人民生、维护残疾人合法权益、不断丰富残疾人精神文化生活，积极进取，扎实工作，各项工作取得了显著成效。

一、康复

2013年，我省残联深入开展残疾人康复工作，通过继续实施一批重点康复工程，使各类残疾人得到不同程度的康复；指导加强残疾人康复服务机构建设；积极推进残疾人社区康复工作；大力宣传和普及康复知识。

在44个市辖区和56个县（市）开展了社区康复工作，新增泗县、庐江等11个"社区康复示范县"；天长、南陵等8个"全国白内障无障碍县"。建立康复站的社区达4190个，配备社区康复协调员9049名。

38个县级医疗卫生机构陆续开展残疾儿童筛查工作，年度新确诊0-6岁残疾儿童4759人。

开展视力残疾康复工作机构9个，完成白内障复明手术3.4万例；为11，804名贫困白内障患者免费施行复明手术；为4752名低视力患者配用助视器，培训低视力儿童家长993名，有效开展家庭康复训练。对6732名盲人进行定向行走训练。

推进听力语言康复机构规范化管理，完善基层服务网络。已建立省级听力语言康复机构1个，基层听力语言康复机构58个。年度新收训聋儿1924名，在训聋儿2513名；规范聋儿家长学校，开展家庭训练，共培训聋儿家长4978名；开展各级各类听力语言康复专业技术人员培训，共培训专业人员593人。

开展肢体残疾康复训练服务机构达64个，其中，省级康复机构1个，地市级、县级康复机构63个；培训各级各类肢体残疾康复人员157人；共对17625肢体残疾者实施康复训练；实施救助项目资助1381名脑瘫儿童进行机构康复训练，资助266名贫困肢体残疾儿童实施矫治手术。

为麻风畸残者实施矫治手术84例，开展宣传普及教育，为麻风患者回归社会营造良好社会氛围。

开展智力残疾康复训练服务的机构达40个，其中，省级康复机构1个，地市级、县级康复机构39个；培训各级各类智力残疾康复人员206人次；共对7307名智力残疾人进行康复训练；实施救助项目资助1245名智力残疾儿童进行机构康复训练，同时培训儿童家长。

大力推广"社会化、综合性、开放式"精神病防治康复工作。在88个市（县、区）开展精神病防治康复工作，对27.2万重精神病患者进行综合防治康复，监护率达到82.0%，显好率达到57.8%，社会参与率达到47.0%，肇事率0.02%；解除关锁32人；对73273名贫困精神病患者进行医疗救助。

建立了1个省级孤独症儿童康复训练机构；755名孤独症儿童在各级机构进行了康复训练。

加强残疾人辅助器具服务体系建设，深入开展辅助器具服务工作。合肥、淮北、马鞍山、阜阳等9个市成立辅具器具服务机构，全省共计为贫困残疾人免费适配辅助器具19704件，其中装配假肢827例、矫形器836例，验配助视器9320件。

二、教育

2013年，残疾人教育工作平稳推进，受教育权得到了更好保障，残疾人素质和平等参与社会的能力得到进一步提高。

我省特教学校生均公用经费5倍于普通学校政策以及特教岗位津贴全面落实；省政府残工委成员单位继续开展结对慰问全省39所特教学校，全年捐款捐物合计超过100万元。

省级特教学校一期工程竣工并交付使用，开设盲人按摩、辅具适配等各类特色专业8个，试点与省内高校联合培养电子商务等高职专业。

实施残疾人事业专项彩票公益金助学项目，为家庭经济困难的残疾儿童享受普惠性学前教育提供资助达300人次。各地也积极争取资金支持，对61名残疾儿童给予学前教育资助。

已开办特殊教育普通高中班（部）3个，在校生421人；其中聋高中3个，在校生414人；残疾人中等职业学校（班）6个，在校生660人，毕业生178人，其中175人获得职业资格证书。有332名残疾人被普通高等院校录取。

截止到2013年底，有未入学适龄残疾儿童少年5034人，其中视力残疾儿童153人，听力残疾儿童262人，言语残疾儿童217人，智力残疾儿童1757人，肢体残疾儿童1429人，精神残疾儿童283人，多重残疾儿童933人。

三、就业

2013年，残疾人就业工作在保持稳定的基础上取得了新进展。

联合省委组织部、省人社厅等九部门印发《关于促进残疾人按比例就业的实施意见》，明确党政机关、事业单位及国有企业率先带头安置残疾人就业的职责，将按比例就业纳入各类评先。积极协商省文明办，将按比例安排残疾人就业工作纳入文明城市、县城评比考核指标体系；联合省财政厅制定《省级就业保障金使用管理暂行办法》，进一步加大直接补贴残疾人技能培训、就业创业扶持、公益岗位开发及社保缴费等力度；联合省人社厅在全国首个举办残疾人专场公务员招考，为各类残疾人提供无障碍考试服务，引起社会积极反响。

城镇新增就业残疾人33901人，其中，集中就业6187人，按比例安排就业4280人，公益性岗位就业490人，个体就业及其它形式灵活就业22316人，辅助性就业628人。城镇就业人数17.2万；83.5万农村残疾人在业，其中67.9万残疾人从事农业生产劳动。

残疾人职业培训基地共计86个，其中残联兴办23个，依托社会机构兴办63个，1.2万人次城镇残疾人接受了职业培训。

盲人按摩事业稳定发展。2013年度培训盲人保健按摩人员1013名、盲人医疗按摩人员69名；保健按摩机构达到305个，医疗按摩机构达到90个；在专业技术职务资格评审中，分别有6人和29人通过医疗按摩人员中级和初级职称评审。

四、社会保障

2013年我省继续将贫困重度残疾人救助纳入民生工程，城乡80多万贫困残疾人基本实现应保尽保，其中52.4万多人重度残疾人享受特别救助，人均年转移性收入千元以上，凸显了社保的兜底作用。

2013年新型农村和城镇居民社会养老保险进一步扩大覆盖面，已有17.8万城镇残疾人参加了城镇居民社会养老保险，参保率53.7%。60岁以下的参保残疾人中有4.6万名重度残疾人，其中4.0万人得到了政府的参保扶助，代缴补贴比例达到86.3%。有8633名非重度残疾人也享受了全额或部分代缴的优惠政策。领取养老金待遇的人数达到7.8万人。

参加新型农村社会养老保险的残疾人达到82.1万人，参保率71.3%。60周岁以下的参保残疾人中有17.9万名重度残疾人，其中17.1万人得到了政府的参保扶助，代缴补贴比例达到95.4%。有2.9万名非重度残疾人也享受了全额或部分代缴的优惠政策。享受养老金待遇的人数达到31.6万人。

城镇残疾职工参加社会保险人数达到8.4万人，城镇残疾居民参加基本医疗保险达到30.0万人，城镇11.5万和农村39.7万残疾人纳入最低生活保障范围；城镇集中供养残疾人和农村五保供养残疾人分别为5709人和37578人；27.4万和0.7万符合条件的城乡残疾人分别享受了稳定的生活补贴和护理补贴。6.2万名城乡残疾人得到了其他救助救济。

残疾人托养服务工作规范推进，残疾人托养服务机构达到81个，共为2638名残疾人提供了托养服务。其中寄宿制托养服务机构12个，日间照料机构15个，综合性托养服务机构54个。接受居家托养服务的残疾人达到1.6万人。

五、扶贫开发

2013年，残疾人扶贫开发成效显著，贫困残疾人生产、生活状况得到了进一步的改善。15.8万贫困残疾人得到扶持，其中2.9万人通过扶贫开发实际脱贫；接受实用技术培训的残疾人达到2.3万人次。

康复扶贫贴息贷款扶持1972个农村残疾人，847个单位和9060名个人对贫困残疾人开展结对帮扶。残疾人扶贫基地达到90个，安置1752名残疾人就业，扶持带动3396户残疾人。

投入危房改造资金7195.3万元，改造农村贫困残疾人危房1.1万户，1.4万名残疾人受益。

六、宣传文化

2013年，全省残疾人事业宣文工作成绩显著。

联合省委宣传部、省财政厅等12个部门，出台我省首个《关于加强残疾人文化建设的意见》，明确通过政府购买服务等方式，增加文化供给，并将残疾人文化产业纳入就业扶持范围。组织开展第四届全省残疾人文化周活动，成功举办第八届全省残疾人艺术汇演，在全国汇演中，我省参选的9个节目获奖。合肥市创建第一批“全国残疾人文化体育建设示范市”。

2013年，我省“两台一报一网”宣传报道份量进一步加重。省级中央媒体采用稿件31件，主要新闻媒体刊播稿件525件，报刊专版3个，残疾人专题广播节目1个，电视手语新闻栏目1个，省级残疾人事业新闻宣传促进会1个，省残联网站发布各类新闻稿件1万多条。

省辖市主要新闻媒体刊播稿件数2650件，报刊专版44个，残疾人专题广播节目13个，电视手语新闻栏目12个，建立地市级新闻宣传促进会4个。

省级和地市级公共图书馆设立盲文及盲人有声读物阅览室分别是1个和23个，举办残疾人文化周1个和81个，举办残疾人文化艺术类比赛及展览分别是1个和29个。地市级已成立残疾人艺术团队12个。

七、体育

2013年，残疾人体育工作以提高残疾人体育健身服务能力和残疾人体育运动水平为着力点，全面实施“自强健身工程”，积极开展群众性体育活动，以“特奥日”和“健身周”为载体，不断提高竞技水平和体能素质。

省级残疾人体育健身指导员285人，残疾人体育比赛5次，参与的残疾人运动员182人次，残疾人体育训练基地1个，聘任教练员15人。

地市级残疾人体育健身活动92次，参加人数4934人，残疾人体育示范点49个，残疾人体育健身指导员349人。

八、维权

2013年，各级残联维权组织建设得到加强，残疾人事业法律法规体系进一步完善，残疾人维权工作全面开展。省残联再次获得省委、省政府授予的“全省信访工作责任目标考核管理先进单位”称号。

联合省司法厅印发《关于进一步加强残疾人法律援助工作的通知》，扩大了残疾人法律援助范围，建立全省贫困重度残疾人法律援助信息库，明确了对听力、言语残疾的法律援助受援人免费提供手语翻译服务。

截至2013年底，我省共制定或修改保障残疾人权益的规范性文件地市级4件，县级5件。县级以上人大进行《残疾人保障法》执法检查和专题调研30次；政协进行视察和专题调研39次。开展普法宣传教育活动309次，19682人参加；举办法律培训班91个，4027人参加。

我省成立残疾人法律救助工作协调机构13个，建立残疾人法律救助工作站9个，办理案件81件，建立残疾人法律援助中心（工作站）115个，办理案件1132件，有力地促进了残疾人法律救助和法律援助工作。

残疾人参政议政工作得到加强，各级残联协助人大代表、政协委员提出议案、建议、提案56件，办理议案、建议、提案62件。

无障碍建设政策、标准进一步完善。共出台了10个省、地市、县级无障碍建设与管理规定；77个市、县、区系统开展无障碍建设；开展无障碍建设检查162次，无障碍培训766人次；为1271个贫困残疾人家庭实施了无障碍改造；为2.7万残疾人发放了残疾人机动轮椅车燃油补贴。

各级残联共处理残疾人群众来信2274件，接待残疾人群众来访1.6万人次，其中集体访8批次、82人次。

九、组织建设

2013年认真贯彻执行省委、省政府关于各级残联换届指导意见。截至2013年底，我省10个地市级残联配备了残疾人领导干部；29个县级残联机关配备了残疾人干部；已建乡镇（街道）残联1478个，已建率达到99.5%，选聘残疾人专职委员1476名；已建社区（村）残协1.5万个，已建率达到92.6%，选聘残疾人专职委员 1.5 万名。

全省、市、县、乡残联实有人员已达 3453 人。各级残联共举办培训班 1232 期，培训机关干部、协会干部及残疾人专职委员 4.0 万人次。

全省共建立省级以下各类残疾人专门协会 538 个，市级专门协会已建比例为 100.0%，市辖区专门协会已建比例 87.5%；县（含县级市）级专门协会已建比例为 85.4%。

十、服务设施建设

残疾人服务设施建设得到全面发展。截至 2013 年底，全省已竣工并投入使用的各级残疾人综合服务设施 71 个，总建设规模 14.2 万平方米，总投资 44092.1 万元；已竣工并投入使用的各级残疾人康复设施 4 个。

十一、信息化建设

2013 年统计队伍建设进一步加强，各级残联共有 138 名专、兼职统计人员从事残疾人事业统计工作，统计人员业务素质培养普遍得到重视，省级残联举办培训班 1 期，参加培训的人员 200 人次；地市级举办培训班 17 期，参加培训的人员 256 人次。

地方残联全面推进网站建设，目前 1 个省级残联已全部开通了公众服务网站，有 16 个地市级残联网站和 73 个县级残联网站也已开通。2013 年省级及地市级残联开设网站技术培训班 20 期，培训各级残联信息员 507 人次。

各级残联共有 182 名专业技术人员从事信息化工作；省级残联建有局域网 1 个，网上办公（OA）系统 1 个。

2013 年，省残联开始大力推行无纸化办公，建立的协同办公系统（OA）覆盖全省 16 个地市及其下辖县（区、市），进一步提升各级残联运用信息化技术手段的能力，提高系统内部公文管理效率。

截至 2013 年底，我省通过中国第二代残疾人证管理系统已核发第二代残疾人证 142 万本，省残联门户网站月浏览量 40 多万人次。全省残疾人综合业务管理系统已承载本省残疾人基本信息达 380 多万条，为省残联开展各项业务提供了数据支持。

2013年福建省残疾人事业发展统计公报

2013年，全省残疾人工作在省委、省政府的正确领导和中国残联的精心指导下，全面实施《福建省残疾人事业“十二五”发展纲要》，以改善残疾人生活、提高为残疾人服务能力为出发点和落脚点，开拓创新，扎实推进，残疾人事业科学发展、跨越发展取得明显成效。

一、残疾人康复工作

2013年，通过中央和省级重点康复项目的实施，以及各地实施的配套项目，使13.64万名残疾人得到康复服务，大力推进残疾人“人人享有康复服务”。

全年完成白内障复明手术1.62万例，其中为1.07万名贫困白内障患者免费施行复明手术。为4245名低视力患者配用助视器；培训低视力儿童家长1833名，比2012年增加1.9倍。对4478名盲人进行定向行走训练。

加强省级聋儿康复机构建设，完善聋儿康复网络。共对820名聋儿进行了听力语言康复训练；规范聋儿家长学校，开展家庭训练，共培训聋儿家长1014名；加强聋儿康复人才队伍建设，培养各类专业人员121人。

大力推广“社会化、综合性、开放式”精神病防治康复工作。2013年，在84个市县开展精神病防治康复工作，对12.25万名重性精神病患者进行综合防治康复，监护率达到87.53%，显好率达到72.00%，社会参与率达到53.63%，肇事率0.10%；解除关锁78人；对1.08万名贫困精神病患者进行医疗救助。

深入开展辅助器具供应服务，全面推进普及型假肢装配。截止到2013年底，累计建立县级以上辅助器具供应服务机构79个，为残疾人减免费用供应辅助器具19786件，其中装配假肢480例、矫形器406例，验配助视器4329件。为残疾人提供更趋个性化的服务。

全省开展肢体残疾康复训练服务的机构达79个，培训各级各类肢体残疾康复人员280人次；全省共对10389名肢体残疾者实施康复训练；实施救助项目资助1404名脑瘫儿童进行机构康复训练，资助103名贫困肢体残疾儿童实施矫治手术。

全年开展智力残疾康复训练服务的机构达58个；对3552名智力残疾儿童进行了康复训练，其中：智力残疾儿童机构康复训练999人，智力残疾儿童社区、家庭康复2103人。

在26个市辖区和58个县（市）开展了社区康复工作，累计建立社区康复站3887个，配备9722名社区康复协调员。

积极配合卫生等部门开展残疾儿童筛查工作。2013年，全省新诊断0-6岁残疾儿童980名。积极开展儿童残疾预防宣传，共发放宣传材料1.63万份。

二、残疾人教育工作

为家庭经济困难的残疾儿童享受普惠性学前教育提供资助400人次。已开办特殊教育普通高中班（部）26个，在校生734人；其中聋高中13个，在校生626人；盲高中6个，在校生108人。残疾人中等职业学校（班）7个，在校生42人，毕业生17人，其中17人获得职业资格证书。截止到2013年底，有未入学适龄残疾儿童少年1474人，其中以智力残疾、肢体残疾儿童人数居多，占总数的85%。

继续实施“双百扶残助学计划”等项目，残疾人教育扎实推进，131名残疾人考上大学。

三、残疾人就业工作

全省城镇新增就业15857人，其中按比例就业1294人，集中就业372人，个体就业5734人，其他渠道就业8457人。通过省委省政府为民办实事项目，落实资金3000万元，扶持就业6000人。

全省残保金申报总额达7.96亿元（其中厦门2.65亿元），安置残疾人就业9190人。

与省人社厅联合开展“就业援助月”活动，举办各类招聘会156场。

按照县级申报、市级验收、省级抽查的工作方式，全省已命名残疾人就业机构规范化建设达标单位 85 家，占全省机构总数的 90.4%。

盲人按摩事业稳定发展，按摩机构迅速增长。2013 年度培训盲人保健按摩人员 523 名、盲人医疗按摩人员 472 名；保健按摩机构达到 262 个，医疗按摩机构达到 7 个；在专业技术职务资格评审中，分别有 37 人和 68 人通过医疗按摩人员中级和初级职称评审。

四、残疾人社会保障工作

2013 年，全省残疾人社会保障状况进一步改善。城镇残疾职工参加社会保险人数达到 4.98 万人，其中参加养老保险人数 2.83 万人，参加医疗保险人数 2.56 万人；城镇残疾居民参加医疗保险达到 13.43 万人；城乡 23.1 万名残疾人纳入最低生活保障范围；城镇已纳入最低生活保障 3.8 万人，城镇集中供养和其他救助救济 1.38 万人；农村已纳入最低生活保障 19.29 万人，五保供养和其他救助救济 6.61 万人。继续实施"全省重度残疾人困难补助金制度"，23.5 万名贫困重度残疾人领取每月 30-50 元的补助。

进一步落实残疾人参加保险补助制度，参加城乡社会养老保险的残疾人达 57.8 万人，其中政府对重度残疾人、非重度残疾人参保最低档个人缴费分别给予补贴 100%和 50%。

残疾人托养服务工作规范推进，残疾人托养服务机构达到 110 个，共为 4028 残疾人提供了托养服务。其中寄宿制托养服务机构 15 个；日间照料机构 49 个；综合性托养服务机构 46 个。接受居家托养服务的残疾人达到 2.35 万人。

五、残疾人扶贫开发工作

落实中央康复扶贫贴息贷款金额 3200 万元，扶持 26 家企业，稳定就业 1261 人。争取省级康复扶贫资金 800 万元，扶持农村贫困残疾人 1588 人。

继续实施"造福工程"危房改造，扶助 12335 名残疾人（含家属人数）实施危房改造。继续实施"安居工程"危房改造，共计 1195 户。

继续开展"万村千乡市场工程"助残扶贫项目，全年新增安置 60 名农村贫困残疾人就业，帮扶 20 户农村贫困残疾人家庭创办村级店。开展"农村基层党组织助残扶贫工程"，全年新增帮扶 300 户。

六、残疾人宣传文化工作

成功举办第三届"闽台残疾人文化周"系列活动，38 位台湾嘉宾来闽参加，持续打响闽台残疾人文化交流合作的品牌。成功承办第八届全国残疾人艺术汇演（福建赛区）。8 个省（市）代表队选送的 88 个节目、920 多人参赛，我省共获得 22 个奖项及团体总分二等奖的历届最好成绩。

省级中央媒体采用稿件 4 件，主要新闻媒体刊播稿件数 5 件，报刊专版 8 个，残疾人专题广播节目 1 个，电视手语新闻栏目 1 个，省级残疾人事业新闻宣传促进会 1 个。地市级主要新闻媒体刊播稿件数 883 件，报刊专版 45 个，残疾人专题广播节目 8 个，电视手语新闻栏目 11 个，建立地市级新促会 7 个。省级公共图书馆设立盲文及盲人有声读物阅览室 2 个，市级已设立 33 个。在全省范围建设"福乐书屋"、逐步解决残疾人读书难的问题。省残疾人文化活动中心每周定期开放，为残疾人提供免费服务；省残疾人艺术团开展下基层、进高校等公益巡演 13 场。市级残联举办残疾人文化周 16 场次，举办残疾人文化艺术类比赛及展览 66 次，全省已建立市级残疾人艺术团队 5 个。

七、残疾人体育生活

参加残疾人体育赛事，屡获佳绩。选派运动员参加韩国第十届世界冬季特奥运动会、第五届亚洲盲人足球锦标赛、2013 年全国残疾人（25 岁以下）羽毛球锦标赛、2013 年全国坐式排球锦标赛等赛事，取得优异成绩；圆满承办 2013 年全国盲人足球锦标赛、2013 年全国残疾人（25 岁以下）田径锦标赛、2013 年国际特奥东亚区"融合杯"足球选拔赛等赛事，共有近 50 队（次）、1000 多人（次）参加，我省均获好成绩。成功举办了第五届全省特奥运动会。

在全省范围建设"福乐健身站"，残疾人体育健身指导员、分级员等队伍得到发展，全省残疾人体育工作新机制已初现端倪。省级举办残疾人体育健身活动 30 次，参加人数 2800 人；建立残疾人体育示范点30个，残疾人体育健身指导员50人；残疾人体育训练基地15个，聘任教练员58人。市级举办残疾人体育健身活动60次，参加人数4134人；建立残疾人体育示范点38个，残疾人体育健身指导员611人。

八、残疾人维权工作

各级残联维权组织建设得到加强，残疾人事业法律法规体系进一步完善，残疾人维权工作全面开展。

2013年，县级以上人大进行《残疾人保障法》执法检查和专题调研26次；政协进行视察和专题调研32次。开展普法宣传教育活动221次，1.68万人参加；举办法律培训班35个，0.18万人参加。

截至2013年底，成立残疾人法律救助工作协调机构44个，建立残疾人法律救助工作站37个，办理案件259件，建立残疾人法律援助中心（工作站）93个，办理案件993件，有力地促进了法律救助和法律援助工作。

残疾人参政议政工作得到加强，各级残联协助人大代表、政协委员提出议案、建议、提案47件，办理议案、建议、提案53件。

无障碍建设法规、标准进一步完善。共出台了24个地市、县级无障碍建设与管理法规、规章；48个市、县、区系统开展无障碍建设；开展无障碍建设检查120次，无障碍培训0.12万人次；为0.39万个贫困残疾人家庭实施了无障碍改造；为1.42万残疾人发放了残疾人机动轮椅车燃油补贴。

各级残联共处理残疾人群众来信1065余件，接待残疾人群众来访8386人次，其中集体访26批次、315人次。

九、残疾人组织建设

省残联第六次代表大会于2013年7月2日—3日在福州召开。尤权书记、苏树林省长等省四套班子领导和时任中国残联党组副书记、常务副理事长王乃坤出席大会开幕式，苏树林省长、王乃坤副理事长、洪捷序副省长作重要讲话。来自全省各行各业的300名正式代表参加大会。会议审议通过省残联第五届主席团作的工作报告，选举产生了福建省残联新一届领导机构，明确了今后五年全省残疾人工作的总体思路和主要任务。

2013年，我省各级残联通过政策推动、政府支持、残联争取，在机构建设、人员配置上实现了新的发展，全省新增残疾人就业中心、康复中心、辅具中心三个服务机构15个，新增“福乐家园”10个，新增人员编制机关5名，直属单位47名。

全省县级以上残联均成立五个残疾人专门协会，其中省级五个专门协会都进行了社团法人登记。积极探索残疾人社会组织管理与服务工作，开展残疾人社会组织调查，全省共成立各类残疾人服务机构530多家。

十、残疾人综合服务设施建设

制定省委、省政府为民办实事“福乐家园”建设项目实施方案，做好2013年10所省级公办“福乐家园”申报、评审工作。通过评选确定10个省级公办“福乐家园”建设项目，新增建筑面积49896.5平方米，新增收训规模近1000人，总投资9598万元（其中：中央及省级资金2660万元）。及时向有关市、县政府通报项目评审结果，按项目进度下达省级补助资金1580万元。

一批建设项目重大突破。总建筑面积8915m^{2}的省“福乐幼儿园”二期项目进展顺利，建成后将达到全国三级康复机构标准，招生可达500人，规模名列全国前茅。总建筑面积6928m^{2}的省残疾人游泳康复馆经省政府批准已正式立项建设，建成后可承接全国残疾人游泳比赛和我省残疾人运动员日常训练，将步入全国省级残疾人体育设施先进行列。

十一、信息化建设

重新整合、改造“海西助残”残疾人数据指标，提取既有项目指标数据整合到残疾人信息库；与中国残联二代证人口库建设实时数据接口，解决“海西助残”残疾人信息库与中国残联二代证数据不同步、数据不完整的问题。

继续推进“海西助残”综合业务管理系统的应用，目前残疾人基础库残疾人数据达106.5万人，比增22.13%，残疾人享受到各项优惠政策记录达26.5万条。

注重加强与纵向、横向部门（单位）的沟通协作，实现数据交换共享。2013 年，我省与省城乡居民养老保险中心实现了全省所有残疾人参加养老保险的数据交换，获得全省残疾人实际参保 24.7 万人的数据。

充分发挥省残联门户网站作用，省级发布信息 2420 条，网页浏览量逾 150.5 万人次，同比增长 72.3%，在残疾人事业新闻宣传、政务公开、信息服务等方面发挥了重要作用。推行电子政务的应用，发送政务短信 3426 条，通过政务邮箱向各级残联发送电子文件 4360 封。9 个地市级残联网站和 84 个县级残联网站已全部开通，残联系统网上信息服务逐步覆盖全省。省、市级残联共开办网站技术培训班 10 期，培训各级残联信息员达 516 人次。

统计队伍建设进一步加强，各级残联共有 111 名专、兼职统计人员从事残疾人事业统计工作，统计人员业务素质培养普遍得到重视，省级残联举办培训班 1 期，参加培训的人员达到 40 人次；地市级举办培训班 7 期，参加培训的人员达到 200 人次。

2013 年江西省残疾人事业发展统计公报

2013 年，在省委、省政府的坚强领导、中国残联的精心指导和社会各界的大力支持下，省残联新一届党组、理事会深入学习贯彻党的十八大、十八届三中全会和省委十三届七次、八次全会精神，坚持夯实基础、改革创新，重点突破、进位赶超，团结带领全省广大残疾人工作者，以良好的精神面貌和工作作风，扎实推进各项工作，我省残疾人事业发展呈现出一个崭新的局面，残疾人事业统计工作逐年推进，又上新台阶。

一、残疾人康复工作取得良好成效

在 23 个市辖区和 79 个县（市）开展了社区康复工作，累计已建社区康复站的社区总数 0.38 万个，配备 1.31 万名社区康复协调员。

19 个县的 36 个医疗卫生机构陆续开展残疾儿童筛查工作，年度新诊断 0-6 岁残疾儿童 2461 人。

开展视力残疾康复机构总数达到 10 个，完成白内障复明手术 1.93 万例；为 3，526.00 名贫困白内障患者免费施行复明手术；为 1752 名低视力患者配用助视器，培训低视力儿童家长 706 名，有效开展家庭康复训练。对 4750 名盲人进行定向行走训练。

推进听力语言康复机构规范化管理，完善基层服务网络。已建设省级听力语言康复机构 1 个，基层听力语言康复机构 24 个。年度新收训聋儿 630 名，在训聋儿 808 名；规范聋儿家长学校，开展家庭训练，共培训聋儿家长 899 名；开展各级各类听力语言康复专业技术人员培训，共培训专业人员 91 人。

开展肢体残疾康复训练服务机构达 24 个，其中，省级康复机构 1 个，地市级、县级康复机构 23 个；培训各级各类肢体残疾康复人员 200 人次；全国共对 10784 肢体残疾者实施康复训练；实施救助项目资助 822 名脑瘫儿童进行机构康复训练，资助 173 名贫困肢体残疾儿童实施矫治手术。

为麻风畸残者实施矫治手术 110 例，开展宣传普及教育，为麻风患者回归社会营造良好社会氛围。

开展智力残疾康复训练服务的机构 20 个，其中，省级康复机构 1 个，地市级、县级康复机构 19 个；培训各级各类智力残疾康复人员 115 人次；全国共对 3506 名智力残疾人进行康复训练；实施救助项目资助 695 名智力残疾儿童进行机构康复训练，同时培训儿童家长。

大力推广“社会化、综合性、开放式”精神病防治康复工作。在 101 个市县开展精神病防治康复工作，对 18.36 万重性精神病患者进行综合防治康复，监护率达到 80.26%，显好率达到 57.07%，社会参与率达到 42.19%，肇事率 1.32%；解除关锁 213 人；对 20793 名贫困精神病患者进行医疗救助。

建立了 1 个省级孤独症儿童康复训练机构；471 名孤独症儿童在各级机构进行了康复训练。

加强残疾人辅助器具服务体系建设，深入开展辅助器具供应服务，为残疾人减免费用供应辅助器具 14794 件，其中装配假肢 950 例、矫形器 258 例，验配助视器 1873 件。

二、残疾人教育工作全面深入开展

为家庭经济困难的残疾儿童享受普惠性学前教育提供资助 300 人次。各地也积极多渠道争取资金支持，对 3 名残疾儿童给予学前教育资助。

已开办特殊教育普通高中班（部）4 个，在校生 140 人；其中聋高中 4 个，在校生 140 人；盲高中 0 个，在校生 0 人。残疾人中等职业学校（班）2 个，在校生 128 人，毕业生 31 人，其中 31 人获得职业资格证书。有 235 名残疾人被普通高等院校录取。

截止到 2013 年底，有未入学适龄残疾儿童少年 5234 人，其中视力残疾儿童 538 人，听力残疾儿童 563 人，言语残疾儿童 449 人，智力残疾儿童 1536 人，肢体残疾儿童 1176 人，精神残疾儿童 251 人，多重残疾儿童 721 人。

三、残疾人就业工作稳定推进

2013 年，城镇新就业残疾人 13606 人，其中，集中就业 5113 人，按比例安排就业 975 人，公益性岗位就业 321 人，个体就业及其它形式灵活就业 6686 人，辅助性就业 511 人。城镇就业人数 15.26 万；55.92 万农村残疾人在业，其中 41.96 万残疾人从事农业生产劳动。

残疾人职业培训基地达到 227 个，其中残联兴办 44 个，依托社会机构兴办 183 个，0.38 万人次城镇残疾人接受了职业培训。

盲人按摩事业稳定发展，按摩机构迅速增长。2013 年度培训盲人保健按摩人员 619 名、盲人医疗按摩人员 295 名；保健按摩机构达到 532 个，医疗按摩机构达到 70 个；在专业技术职务资格评审中，分别有 29 人和 58 人通过医疗按摩人员中级和初级职称评审。

四、残疾人社会保障逐步完善

2013 年 11.45 万城镇残疾人参加了城镇居民社会养老保险，参保率 57.99%。在 60 岁以下的参保残疾人中有 1.45 万重度残疾人，其中 1.45 万得到了政府的参保扶助，代缴补贴比例达到 100%。有 2.93 万非重度残疾人也享受了全额或部分代缴的优惠政策。领取养老金待遇的人数达到 5.86 万人。

新型农村社会养老保险方面，共有 46.74 万残疾人参加了新型农村社会养老保险，参保率 78.47%。在 60 周岁以下的参保残疾人中有重度残疾人 5.98 万，其中 5.94 万得到了政府的参保扶助，代缴补贴比例达到 99.41%。有 2.93 万非重度残疾人也享受了全额或部分代缴的优惠政策。享受养老金待遇的人数达到 24.78 万人。

城镇残疾职工参加社会保险人数达到 10.87 万，城镇残疾居民参加基本医疗保险达到 22.92 万人，城镇 10.75 万和农村 25.85 万残疾人纳入最低生活保障范围；城镇集中供养残疾人和农村五保供养残疾人分别达到 10753 人和 26050 人；0 人和 0 人符合条件的城乡残疾人分别享受了稳定的生活补贴和护理补贴。5.39 万城乡残疾人得到了其他救助救济。

残疾人托养服务工作规范推进，残疾人托养服务机构达到 21 个，共为 1263 残疾人提供了托养服务。其中寄宿制托养服务机构 10 个；日间照料机构 3 个；综合性托养服务机构 8 个。接受居家托养服务的残疾人达到 1.46 万人。

五、残疾人扶贫工作成效突出

2013 年，4.06 万贫困残疾人得到扶持，其中 6.77 万人通过扶贫开发实际脱贫；接受实用技术培训的残疾人达到 0.79 万人次。

康复扶贫贴息贷款扶持 3508 农村残疾人，2601 个单位和 12288 个人对贫困残疾人开展结对帮扶。残疾人扶贫基地达到 164 个，安置 2251 残疾人就业，扶持带动 2922 残疾人。

完成 4788 户农村贫困残疾人危房改造，各地投入危房资金 1，248.63 万元，5433 名残疾人受益。

六、残疾人维权工作力度增大

各级残联维权组织建设得到加强，残疾人事业法律法规体系进一步完善，残疾人维权工作全面开展。

2013 年，修订《残疾人保障法》地方实施办法 1 件；制定或修改了关于残疾人的专门法规、规章地市级 2 件；制定或修改保障残疾人权益的规范性文件地市级 5 件。县级以上人大进行《残疾人保障法》执法检查和专题调研 25 次；政协进行视察和专题调研 23 次。开展普法宣传教育活动 138 次，1.26 万人参加；举办法律培训班 46 个，0.20 万人参加。

截至 2013 年底，成立残疾人法律救助工作协调机构 18 个，建立残疾人法律救助工作站 23 个，办理案件 104 件，建立残疾人法律援助中心（工作站）94 个，办理案件 804 件，有力地促进了法律救助和法律援助工作。

残疾人参政议政工作得到加强，各级残联协助人大代表、政协委员提出议案、建议、提案 69 件，办理议案、建议、提案 49 件。

无障碍建设法规、标准进一步完善。共出台了 7 个省、地市、县级无障碍建设与管理法规、规章；58 个市、县、区系统开展无障碍建设；开展无障碍建设检查 32 次，无障碍培训 0.02 万人次；为 0.11 万个贫困残疾人家庭实施了无障碍改造；为 2.24 万残疾人发放了残疾人机动轮椅车燃油补贴。

各级残联共处理残疾人群众来信 638 余件，接待残疾人群众来访 5753 人次，其中集体访 22 批次、222 人次。

七、宣传文化工作进一步加强

省级中央媒体采用稿件65件，主要新闻媒体刊播稿件数56件，报刊专版5个，残疾人专题广播节目2个，电视手语新闻栏目1个，省级残疾人事业新闻宣传促进会1个；

地市级主要新闻媒体刊播稿件数620件，报刊专版7个，残疾人专题广播节目3个，电视手语新闻栏目4个，建立地市级新促会0个。

省级和地市级公共图书馆设立盲文及盲人有声读物阅览室已达到1和9个，举办残疾人文化周2和13个，举办残疾人文化艺术类比赛及展览分别是3和11个，已成立残疾人艺术团队1和6个。

八、体育工作进一步提升

省级残疾人体育健身活动3次，参加人数0.06万人，残疾人体育示范点6个，残疾人体育健身指导员40人，残疾人体育比赛1次，参与的残疾人运动员210人次，残疾人体育训练基地2个，聘任教练员13人。

地市级残疾人体育健身活动11次，参加人数0.07万人，残疾人体育示范点4个，残疾人体育健身指导员12人。

九、残疾人组织建设进一步健全

2013年，残联领导班子中配备了残疾人理事长或副理事长；8个地市级残联在领导班子中配备了残疾人理事长或副理事长；52个县级残联机关配备了残疾人干部；已建乡镇（街道）残联1556个，已建率达到96.53%，选聘残疾人专职委员3357名；已建社区（村）残协1.77万个，已建率达到98.89%，选聘残疾人专职委员1.32万名。

省市县乡残联实有人员已达0.43万人。各级残联共举办培训班0.11万期，培训机关干部、协会干部及残疾人专职委员1.80万人次。

共建立省级以下各类残疾人专门协会423个，市级专门协会已建比例为100%，市辖区专门协会已建比例68.42%；县（含县级市）级专门协会已建比例为75.75%。

十、残疾人工作信息化建设扎实有效

统计队伍建设进一步加强，各级残联共有128名专、兼职统计人员从事残疾人事业统计工作，统计人员业务素质培养普遍得到重视，省级残联举办培训班1期，参加培训的人员达到29人次；地市级举办培训班11期，参加培训的人员达到200人次。

地方残联全面推进网站建设，目前1个省级残联已全部开通了公众服务网站，有6个地市级残联网站和36个县级残联网站也已开通。2013年省级及地市级残联开设网站技术培训班14期，培训各级残联信息员达477人次。

各级残联共有166名专业技术人员从事信息化工作；省级残联共建立局域网1个，网上办公（OA）系统1个。

十一、民生工程投入逐年增强

2013年，省政府进一步加大对我省残疾人民生工程的投入力度，全年共为16.38余万残疾人提供康复服务，其中为104655万名残疾人建立康复档案，为14566名残疾人配发了假肢等辅助器具，为21212名精神病患者提供了免费服药，为718名贫困残疾儿童提供了抢救性康复救助，为1038名残疾人提供了免费白内障复明手术；全年共为3793名残疾人提供了公益性岗位，8683名农家书屋残疾人管理员，为7054名残疾人提供了相应的职能技术培训服务。

2013 年山东省残疾人事业发展统计公报

2013 年，在省委、省政府的关心重视下，全省残联组织围绕大局、服务残疾人，以实现全省残疾人“整体赶平均、共同奔小康”为目标，以推动落实省政府为民办实事项目为重点，努力为残疾人解难事、办实事，全省残疾人工作取得显著成绩。

一、康复

残疾儿童康复。规范实施 0-6 岁残疾儿童免费抢救性康复。制定《山东省 0－6 岁残疾儿童抢救性康复救助实施办法》，实现了残疾儿童康复由项目化实施到制度性安排的根本性转变。全年完成聋儿听力语言康复训练 2208 人，脑瘫儿童机构康复训练 3301 人，智障儿童机构康复训练 2261 人。肢残儿童社区、家庭康复训练 1531 人，智障儿童社区、家庭康复训练 5599 人。对 421 名贫困肢残儿童实施矫治手术，孤独症儿童机构内在训 1402 人，救助贫困孤独症儿童 741 人。培训低视力儿童家长 906 人，聋儿家长 2794 人。全省 133 个医疗卫生机构开展了残疾儿童筛查工作，本年度新诊断 0-6 岁残疾儿童 5696 人。举办儿童残疾预防宣传活动 533 次，发放宣传材料 28.04 万份。残疾儿童家长学校 89 个，本年度开展各类活动 186 次，4887 名残疾儿童家长参与了活动。

各类残疾康复项目。全年完成白内障复明手术 5.43 万例，为 1.97 万贫困白内障患者免费实施复明手术。低视力患者配用助视器 3602 人，盲人进行定向行走训练 6169 人。成年听力残疾人康复服务 1598 人，成年肢体残疾人社区、家庭康复训练 4.91 万人，成年智力残疾人社区、家庭康复训练 2060 人。精神病患者通过服药、住院、家庭病床接受治疗 20.32 万人，其中 2.44 万贫困精神病患者得到医疗救助。供应各类辅助器具 9.74 万件，假肢装配 1722 例，矫形器装配 624 例。

康复机构和康复人才培养：截止 2013 年底，全省有视力残疾康复机构 91 个，听力语言康复机构 83 个，肢体残疾康复机构 260 个，智力残疾康复机构 107 个，孤独症儿童康复训练机构 101 个，辅助器具供应服务机构 80 个。全省 146 个县（市、区）（含开发区）开展社区康复工作，累计建立社区康复站 4.20 万个，配备社区康复协调员 4.96 万人。全省各级康复机构在岗人员 2.43 万人，本年度培训康复管理人员 2684 人，业务人员 6801 人，社区康复协调员 2.22 万人。

二、教育培训就业

义务教育：截止 2013 年底，全省未入学适龄残疾儿童少年总数 3752 人，其中视力残疾 262 人，听力残疾 154 人，言语残疾 126 人，肢体残疾 1105 人，智力残疾 1408 人，精神残疾 210 人，多重残疾 487 人。

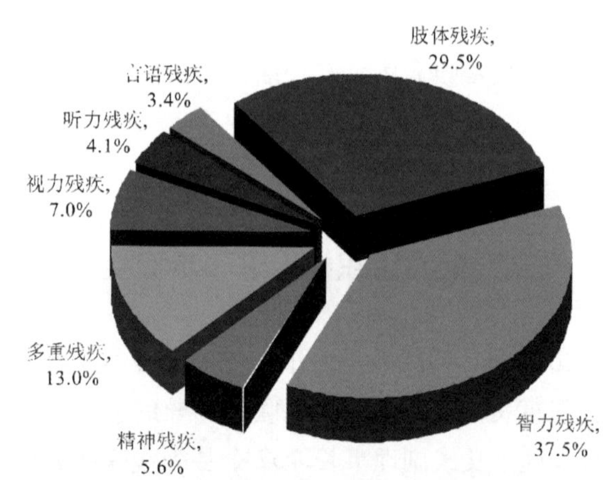

图 1　2013 年底全省未入学适龄各类残疾儿童分类

高中和高等教育：全省有特殊教育普通高中（班）23 所，其中：盲普通高中（班）1 所，聋普通高中（班）16 所，其他普通高中（班）6 所，在校生共 632 人。残疾人中等职业教育机构 22 个，在校生 1315 人，2013 年新招生 513 人，毕业 569 人，其中有 423 人获得职业资格证书。2013 年全省共有 362 名残疾学生高考达到大学录取分数线，被录取 353 人，其中：本科录取 203 人，专科（高职）录取 150 人。

就业：本年度全省城镇新安排残疾人就业 20983 人，其中：集中就业残疾人 5422 人，按比例安排残疾人就业 8345 人，个体及其它形式就业 6533 人，公益性岗位就业 249 人，辅助性就业 434 人。城镇实际在业残疾人 24.74 万人，农村 139.44 万残疾人实现稳定就业，其中从事农业生产劳动 110.27 万人。

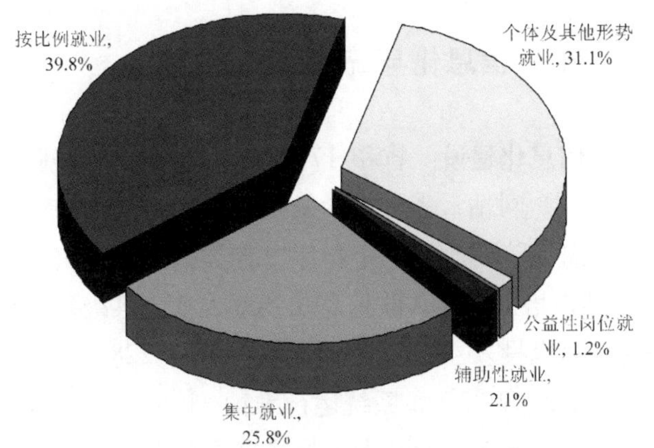

图 2 2013 年全省城镇新安排残疾人就业比例

职业培训：全省共有职业培训基地 683 个，其中残联兴办 103 个，依托社会机构兴办 580 个，本年度城镇职业培训 2.26 万人次。

盲人按摩：全省有盲人保健按摩机构 1236 个，医疗按摩机构 77 个。2013 年共培训盲人保健按摩人员 800 人、盲人医疗按摩人员 275 人。共有 78 人通过医疗按摩人员初级职称评审。

三、扶贫和社会保障

扶贫：2013 年全省共扶持贫困残疾人户 8.19 万户，扶持贫困残疾人 11.92 万人，脱贫 5.64 万人。组建结对帮扶单位 5523 个，结对帮扶 1.66 万人。已建残疾人扶贫基地 821 个，安置残疾人就业 1.61 万人，扶持带动了 2.80 万户残疾人。各级共投入经费 1539.45 万元，对 5.03 万残疾人进行实用技术培训。全年完成农村贫困残疾人危房改造 3721 户，受益残疾人 4719 人。

社会保障：全省城镇残疾职工参加养老保险 13.26 万人、医疗保险 12.12 万人。城镇残疾居民参加养老保险 22.53 万人、医疗保险 16.60 万人。城镇个体就业残疾人参加养老保险 3.07 万人、医疗保险 2.23 万人。7.77 万城镇残疾人纳入最低生活保障。农村居民参加新型农村社会养老保险 112.70 万人，参加新型农村合作医疗保险 167.60 万人，35.17 万农村残疾人纳入最低生活保障，五保供养和其他救助救济 9.82 万人。落实残疾人生活补贴政策制度，全省共有 21.40 万残疾人享受生活补贴，1.23 万人享受护理补贴。

托养：全省有残疾人托养服务机构 440 个，其中：寄宿制托养机构 168 个、日间照料托养机构 37 个、综合托养机构 235 个，共托养残疾人 1.56 万人。3.50 万残疾人享受居家托养服务。

四、政策法规与维权

法规、政策和执法：2013 年，市级制定或修改关于残疾人的专门法规、规章 3 个。市、县两级残联参与制定或修改保障残疾人权益的规范性文件 66 个。县级及以上人大开展执法检查或专题调研 76 次，政协视察和专题调研 56 次。

法制宣传：全省开展普法宣传教育活动 269 次，参加人数 2.29 万人次。开展法律培训班 151 次，培训 6015 人次。

法律救助：全省已建立残疾人法律救助协调机构 48 个。建立残疾人法律救助工作站 48 个，办理案件 463 件。 建立残疾人法律援助中心（工作站）152 个，办理案件 1453 件。

无障碍建设：全省累计出台 32 个无障碍建设与管理法规或政府令，56 个市、县系统开展无障碍建设，开展无障碍专项检查 162 次。完成贫困残疾人家庭无障碍改造 1.86 万户。发放残疾人机动轮椅车燃油补贴 2.74 万人。

信访：各级残联共处理残疾人来信 829 件次，接待残疾人来访 6517 人次，其中集体访 16 批、298 人次。

五、文化体育

宣传文化：截止 2013 年底，省、市两级共开播残疾人专题广播节目 17 个，电视手语新闻栏目 9 个，报刊专版 55 个，24 个公共图书馆设立盲文及盲人有声读物阅览室。全省举办残疾人文化周活动 35 次，残疾人文化艺术类比赛及展览 31 次。全省已成立残疾人艺术团 13 个，省级和 9 个市建立了残疾人事业新闻宣传促进会，各级主要新闻媒体共刊播与残疾人相关的稿件 3051 件。

体育：全省有残疾人体育训练基地 4 个，聘任教练员 12 人。市级组织残疾人体育活动 104 次，参加人数 8526 人次，残疾人体育示范点 56 个，残疾人体育健身指导员 288 人。

六、组织建设

组织队伍：截止 2013 年底，省、市、县、乡四级残联机关和事业单位共有编制 4247 个，实有人员 6006 人。14 个市级残联领导班子配备残疾人，55 个县级残联机关配备残疾人干部。选聘乡镇（街道）残疾人专职干事 2003 人、村（社区）残疾人专职委员 6.09 万人。

干部培训：省、市两级残联举办综合类培训班 46 期、培训 2345 人次，举办残疾人干部培训班 19 期、培训 1272 人次。县、乡两级残联举办各类培训班 2640 期、培训 5.45 万人次。

参政议政：在县级及以上残疾人及其亲友和残疾人工作者中，共有人大代表 81 人、政协委员 183 人。残联系统协助人大代表、政协委员提出议案、建议、提案 102 件，办理建议、提案 110 件。

专门协会：市、县两级共建立各类残疾人专门协会 767 个，其中：盲人协会 159 个、聋人协会 154 个、肢残人协会 157 个、智力残疾人及亲友协会 148 个、精神残疾人及亲友协会 148 个。

七、信息化与统计

信息化建设：省和 17 个市、70 个县级残联开通了门户网站，省、市两级残联全面完成门户网站的信息无障碍改造。全年举办各类信息工作培训班 20 期，培训各级残联信息员 400 人次。各级残联信息化建设投入 489.55 万元，其中：硬件 228.12 万元、软件 229.49 万元、系统运行维护 31.94 万元。各级残联有 216 名专业技术人员从事信息化工作。

统计工作：各级残联有从事残疾人事业统计工作的专、兼职人员 166 人，全年举办统计业务培训班 22 期，培训 485 人次。在全省的 38 个样本县（市、区）开展残疾人状况监测工作，对 1945 名残疾人进行了入户监测。

2013年河南省残疾人事业发展统计公报

2013年，在省委、省政府的高度重视、正确领导下，在全省各级残联的共同努力下，我省的残疾人事业在新的起点上实现了新的发展，圆满完成了各项年度目标任务，残疾人事业呈现出良好发展态势和发展趋势，整体迈上了一个新台阶。

一、康复

2013年全省康复工作进一步加强，为基层残疾人提供康复服务的能力和水平得到了明显提升。全省59个市辖区和104个县（市）开展了社区康复工作，累计已建社区康复站的社区总数5.2万个，配备社会康复协调员3.5万人。

省试点市10个县的2个医疗卫生机构陆续开展残疾儿童筛查工作，2013年新诊断0-6岁残疾儿童230人。

全省视力残疾康复机构总数达到24个，完成白内障复明手术2.0万例；为9900余名贫困白内障患者免费施行复明手术；为9120名低视力患者配用助视器，培训低视力儿童家长3952名；全省对8644名盲人进行定向行走训练。

全省听力语言康复机构进一步完善、规范。已建省级听力语言康复机构1个，基层听力语言康复机构79个。2013年新收训聋儿2388名，在训聋儿3498名；全省聋儿家长学校进一步规范，开展家庭训练，共培训聋儿家长3137名；全年培训各级各类听力语言康复专业技术人员379人。

全省开展肢体残疾康复训练服务机构达59个，其中，省级康复机构1个，地市级、县级康复机构58个；培训各级各类肢体残疾康复人员443人次；全省共对肢体残疾者实施康复训练15363人；实施救助项目资助2850名脑瘫儿童进行机构康复训练，资助464名贫困肢体残疾儿童实施矫治手术。

全省开展智力残疾康复训练服务的机构45个，其中，省级康复机构1个，地市级、县级康复机构44个；培训各级各类智力残疾康复师156人次；共对8055名智力残疾人进行康复训练；实施救助项目资助1479名智力残疾儿童进行机构康复训练，同时培训儿童家长。

大力推广"社会化、综合性、开放式"精神病防治康复工作。在156个市县开展精神病防治康复工作，对重性精神病患者进行综合防治康复监护率达到46.5%，显好率达到52.9%，社会参与率达到39.2%，肇事率0.3%；解除关锁626人；对20390名贫困精神病患者进行医疗救助。

全省1158名孤独症儿童在各级机构进行了康复训练。

全省残疾人辅助器具服务体系建设逐步完善，深入开展辅助器具供应服务，为残疾人减免费用供应辅助器具119910件。

二、教育

2013年，全省积极协调政府相关部门，不断加大财政投入力度，提高特殊教育保障水平和义务教育阶段残疾学生资助水平。全年资助家庭经济困难的残疾儿童享受普惠性学前教育710人次。全省已开办特殊教育普通高中班（部）5个，在校生243人；其中聋高中3个，在校生217人；盲高中1个，在校生26人。残疾人中等职业学校（班）7个，在校生270人，毕业生128人，其中56人获得职业资格证书。有388名残疾人被普通高等院校录取，413名残疾人进入特殊教育学院学习。

截止到2013年底，全省未入学适龄残疾儿童少年7948人，其中视力残疾儿童377人，听力残疾儿童610人，言语残疾儿童591人，智力残疾儿童2619人，肢体残疾儿童2994人，精神残疾儿童98人，多重残疾儿童659人。

三、就业

残疾人就业渠道不断拓展，尤其是近年来我省开展了"残疾人就业培训工程"，针对全省就业年龄段的残疾人提供免费培训和就业服务，取得了显著的成效。2013 年全省城镇新就业残疾人 37258 人，其中，集中就业 15136 人，按比例安排就业 7195 人，公益性岗位就业 705 人，个体就业及其它形式灵活就业 14006 人，辅助性就业 216 人。城镇就业人数 31.55 万；190.8 万农村残疾人在业，其中 154 万残疾人从事农业生产劳动。

全省建立残疾人职业培训基地 230 个，其中残联兴办 49 个，依托社会机构兴办 181 个，全年城镇残疾人接受职业培训 5.1 万人次。

盲人按摩事业稳定发展，按摩机构迅速增长。2013 年全省培训盲人保健按摩人员 2092 名、盲人医疗按摩人员 674 名；保健按摩机构达到 517 个，医疗按摩机构达到 90 个；在专业技术职务资格评审中，分别有 9 人和 12 人通过医疗按摩人员中级和初级职称评审。

四、社会保障

2013 年，全省参加城镇居民社会养老保险的残疾人 29.2 万人，参保率 42.4%。在 60 岁以下的参保残疾人中有 5.6 万重度残疾人，其中 5.39 万得到了政府的参保扶助，代缴补贴比例达到 95.6%。有 0.48 万非重度残疾人也享受了全额或部分代缴的优惠政策。领取养老金待遇的人数达到 12.6 万人。

新型农村社会养老保险方面，共有 199.96 万残疾人参加了新型农村社会养老保险，参保率 67.5%。在 60 周岁以下的参保残疾人中有重度残疾人 49.2 万，其中 48 万得到了政府的参保扶助，代缴补贴比例达到 97.6%。有 1.5 万非重度残疾人也享受了全额或部分代缴的优惠政策。享受养老金待遇的人数达到 85.9 万人。

城镇残疾职工参加社会保险人数达到 25.0 万，城镇残疾居民参加基本医疗保险达到 38.4 万人，城镇 19.6 万和农村 67.5 万残疾人纳入最低生活保障范围；城镇集中供养残疾人和农村五保供养残疾人分别达到 8877 人和 55392 人；309625 人和 1448 人符合条件的城乡残疾人分别享受了稳定的生活补贴和护理补贴。17.86 万城乡残疾人得到了其他救助救济。

全省残疾人托养服务工作规范推进，残疾人托养服务机构达到 46 个，共为 2858 残疾人提供了托养服务。其中寄宿制托养服务机构 5 个；日间照料机构 1 个；综合性托养服务机构 40 个。接受居家托养服务的残疾人达到 2.1 万人。

五、扶贫

2013 年，全省扶持贫困残疾人 16.8 万，其中 8.42 万人通过扶贫开发实际脱贫；接受实用技术培训的残疾人达到 5.6 万人次。

康复扶贫贴息贷款扶持农村残疾人 1991 人，2272 个单位和 76084 个人对贫困残疾人开展结对帮扶。残疾人扶贫基地达到 273 个，安置 9797 名残疾人就业，扶持带动 15944 名残疾人。

完成 2233 户农村贫困残疾人危房改造，各地投入危房资金 463.50 万元，3135 名残疾人受益。

六、维权

2013 年，全省各级残联维权组织建设得到加强，残疾人事业法律法规体系进一步完善，残疾人维权工作全面开展。制定或修改了关于残疾人的专门法规、规章地市级 1 件；制定或修改保障残疾人权益的规范性文件省级 1 件、地市级 6 件。县级以上人大进行《残疾人保障法》执法检查和专题调研 29 次；政协进行视察和专题调研 28 次。开展普法宣传教育活动 237 次，4.9 万人参加；举办法律培训班 80 个，5400 人参加了培训。

截至 2013 年底，全省各级残联成立残疾人法律救助工作协调机构 69 个，建立残疾人法律救助工作站 51 个，办理案件 227 件，建立残疾人法律援助中心（工作站）165 个，办理案件 712 件，有力地促进了法律救助和法律援助工作。

残疾人参政议政工作得到加强，各级残联协助人大代表、政协委员提出议案、建议、提案 54 件，办理议案、建议、提案 41 件。

无障碍建设法规、标准进一步完善。全省共出台了 29 个各级无障碍建设与管理法规、规章；58 个市、县、区系统开展无障碍建设；开展无障碍建设检查 153 次，无障碍培训 500 多人次；为 2000 多户贫困残疾人家庭实施了无障碍改造；为 5.6 万残疾人发放了残疾人机动轮椅车燃油补贴。

全省各级残联共处理残疾人群众来信 1109 余件，接待残疾人群众来访 6435 人次，其中集体访

29 批次、239 人次。

七、宣传文化

2013 年，省级中央媒体采用稿件 5 件，主要新闻媒体刊播稿件数 240 件，报刊专版 3 个，残疾人专题广播节目 1 个，电视手语新闻栏目 1 个，省级残疾人事业新闻宣传促进会 1 个；

地市级主要新闻媒体刊播稿件数 680 件，报刊专版 27 个，残疾人专题广播节目 11 个，电视手语新闻栏目 3 个，建立地市级新促会 13 个。

省级和地市级公共图书馆设立盲文及盲人有声读物阅览室已达到 3 和 17 个，举办残疾人文化周 1 和 82 个，举办残疾人文化艺术类比赛及展览分别是 1 和 37 个，已成立残疾人艺术团队 1 和 3 个。

八、体育

2013 年，开展省级残疾人体育健身活动 3 次，参加人数 0.2 万人，残疾人体育示范点 5 个，残疾人体育健身指导员 50 人，已建残疾人体育训练基地 6 个，聘任教练员 10 人。

地市级开展残疾人体育健身活动 56 次，参加人数 0.7 万人，残疾人体育示范点 19 个，残疾人体育健身指导员 974 人。

九、组织建设

2013 年，全省各级残联顺利圆满完成换届任务，一大批新生力量加入残疾人工作者队伍。省级残联和 12 个省辖市残联领导班子中配备了残疾人理事长或副理事长；90 个县级残联机关配备了残疾人干部；已建乡镇（街道）残联 2355 个，选聘残疾人专职委员 2387 名；已建社区（村）残协 4.7 万个，选聘残疾人专职委员 4.9 万名。

全省志愿者服务工作稳步发展，截止 2013 年底，登记注册的助残志愿者 40.8 万人，受助残疾人 436.7 万人次。

全省各级残联实有人员已达 0.8 万人。各级残联共举办培训班 1200 余期，培训机关干部、协会干部及残疾人专职委员 2.3 万人次。

全省共建省级以下各类残疾人专门协会 880 个，各专门协会已建比例为 100%。

十、信息化

统计队伍建设进一步加强，各级残联共有 197 名专、兼职统计人员从事残疾人事业统计工作，统计人员业务素质培养普遍得到重视，省级残联举办培训班 1 期，参加培训的人员达到 50 人次；地市级举办培训班 19 期，参加培训的人员达到 305 人次。

地方残联全面推进网站建设，目前 1 个省级残联已全部开通了公众服务网站，有 10 个地市级残联网站和 17 个县级残联网站也已开通。2013 年各级残联开设网站技术培训班 19 期，培训各级残联信息员达 381 人次。

各级残联共有 235 名专业技术人员从事信息化工作；省残联建立局域网 1 个。

十一、服务设施

大力加强基层残疾人服务设施建设，截至 2013 年底，已竣工并投入使用的各级残疾人综合服务设施 134 个，总建设规模 17.8 万平方米，总投资 28293.8 万元；已竣工并投入使用的各级残疾人康复设施 6 个，总建设规模 4.5 万平方米，总投资 9304.0 万元；已竣工并投入使用的各级残疾人托养服务设施 2 个，总建设规模 0.5 万平方米，总投资 100 万元。

2013 年湖北省残疾人事业发展统计公报

2013 年，在省委省政府的坚强领导下，在中国残联和省直各部门的大力支持下，省残联党组理事会认真贯彻落实党的十八大和十八届三中全会精神，以党的群众路线教育实践活动为契机，抢抓历史发展机遇，紧紧围绕解决残疾人“三最”问题，提高残疾人“两个体系”建设水平中心任务，改善残疾人生活状况，提高残疾人服务水平，全省残疾人事业在新的历史起点上实现了良好开局。

一、康复

一年来，湖北省康复工作，紧紧围绕残疾人“人人享有康复服务”战略目标，认真组织实施“十二五”残疾人事业发展纲要及配套康复实施方案所下达的各项工作任务，完成了“十二五”国家七彩梦儿童项目任务、省 0-6 岁贫困残疾儿童救助项目任务及中央和省残疾人常规康复项目年度任务等工作。康复处全体同志克难奋进，开拓创新，扎实工作，圆满地完成了年度各项工作计划。

在 39 个市辖区和 59 个县（市）开展了社区康复工作，累计已建社区康复站的社区总数 4683 个，配备 8875 名社区康复协调员。

48 个县（市、区）的 70 个医疗卫生机构陆续开展残疾儿童筛查工作，年度新诊断 0-6 岁残疾儿童 1835 人。

开展视力残疾康复机构总数达到 17 个，完成白内障复明手术 30428 例；为 12576 名贫困白内障患者免费施行复明手术；为 6074 名低视力患者配用助视器，培训低视力儿童家长 10170 名，有效开展家庭康复训练。对 6080 名盲人进行定向行走训练。

推进听力语言康复机构规范化管理，完善基层服务网络。已建设省级听力语言康复机构 1 个，基层听力语言康复机构 35 个。年度新收训聋儿 833 名，在训聋儿 1053 名；规范聋儿家长学校，开展家庭训练，共培训聋儿家长 1178 名；开展各级各类听力语言康复专业技术人员培训，共培训专业人员 50 人；开展成年听力语言康复技术服务数 649 人次；训练后走向共 207 名；机构内在岗专业人员 269 名。

开展肢体残疾康复训练服务机构达 47 个，其中，省级康复机构 1 个，地市级、县级康复机构 46 个；培训各级各类肢体残疾康复人员 291 人次；全省共对 12328 肢体残疾者实施康复训练；实施救助项目资助 2058 名脑瘫儿童进行机构康复训练，资助 275 名贫困肢体残疾儿童实施矫治手术。

开展智力残疾康复训练服务的机构 49 个，其中，省级康复机构 1 个，地市级、县级康复机构 48 个；培训各级各类智力残疾康复人员 246 人次；全省共对 5437 名智力残疾人进行康复训练；实施救助项目资助 899 名智力残疾儿童进行机构康复训练，同时培训儿童家长。

大力推广“社会化、综合性、开放式”精神病防治康复工作。在 92 个县（市、区）开展精神病防治康复工作，对 346615 名重性精神病患者进行综合防治康复，监护率达到 65.1%，显好率达到 40.6%，社会参与率达到 30.6%，肇事率 0.01%；解除关锁 218 人；对 91176 名贫困精神病患者进行医疗救助。

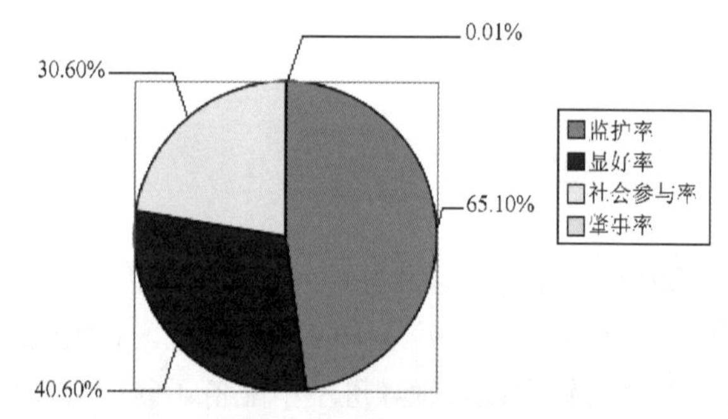

图 1　重性精神病患者

建立了 1 个省级和 31 个地市级及以下孤独症儿童康复训练机构；586 名孤独症儿童在各级机构进行了康复训练。　加强残疾人辅助器具服务体系建设，深入开展辅助器具供应服务，为残疾人减免费用供应辅助器具 43117 件，其中装配假肢 1311 例、矫形器 786 例，验配助视器 5863 件。

二、教育

2013 年，残疾人受教育权得到了更好保障，进一步提高了残疾人素质和平等参与社会的能力。

残疾人事业专项彩票公益金助学项目，为全省家庭经济困难的残疾儿童享受普惠性学前教育提供资助 632 名。各地也积极多渠道争取资金支持，对 25 名残疾儿童给予学前教育资助。

已开办特殊教育普通高中班（部）8 个，在校生 334 人；其中聋高中 7 个，在校生 334 人。残疾人中等职业学校（班）8 个，在校生 160 人，毕业生 76 人，其中 41 人获得职业资格证书。全省有 305 名残疾人被普通高等院校录取。

截至 2013 年底，全省有未入学适龄残疾儿童少年 2461 人，其中视力残疾儿童 178 人，听力残疾儿童 204 人，言语残疾儿童 125 人，肢体残疾儿童 799 人，智力残疾儿童 654 人，精神残疾儿童 102 人，多重残疾儿童 399 人。

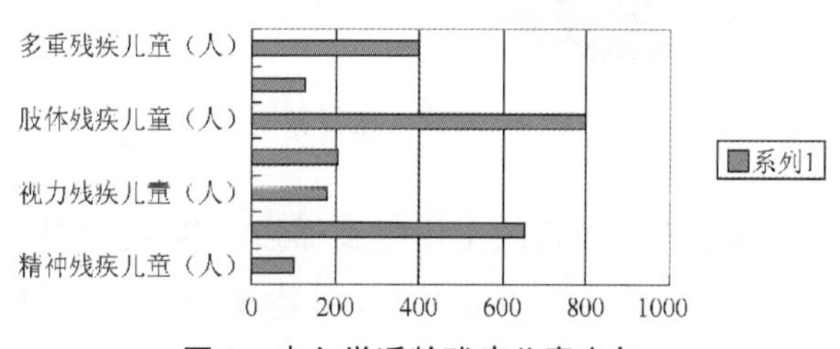

图 2　未入学适龄残疾儿童少年

三、就业

2013 年，残疾人就业取得新进展。城镇新就业残疾人 33322 人，其中，集中就业残疾人 57781 人，按比例安排残疾人就业 43231 人，公益性岗位就业 4563 人，个体就业及其它形式灵活就业 122324 人，辅助性就业 2079 人。全国城镇就业人数 229978 人；902868 名农村残疾人在业，其中 686380 名残疾人从事农业生产劳动。

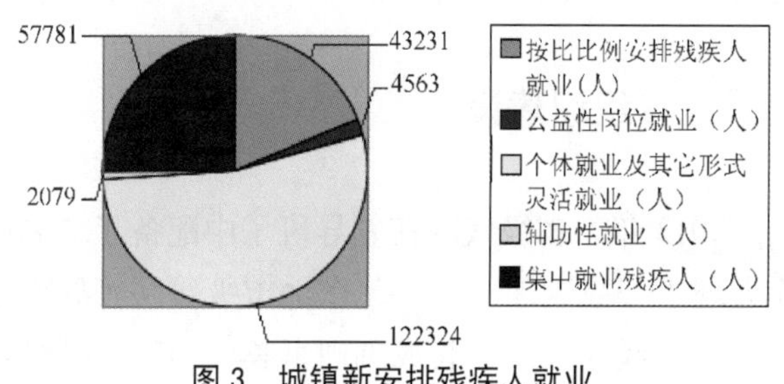

图 3　城镇新安排残疾人就业

全省残疾人职业培训基地达到 269 个，其中残联兴办 205 个，依托社会机构兴办 64 个，10749 人次城镇残疾人接受了职业培训。

盲人按摩事业稳定发展，按摩机构迅速增长。2013 年度培训盲人保健按摩人员 671 名、盲人医疗按摩人员 286 名；保健按摩机构达到 790 个，医疗按摩机构达到 49 个；在专业技术职务资格评审中，有 14 人通过医疗按摩人员初级职称评审。

四、社会保障

2013 年新型农村和城镇居民社会养老保险进一步扩大覆盖面，已有 225319 人城镇残疾人参加了城镇居民社会养老保险，参保率 61.2%。在 60 岁以下的参保残疾人中有 56087 名重度残疾人，其中 44831 名得到了政府的参保扶助，代缴补贴比例达到 79.9%。有 104365 名非重度残疾人也享受了全额或部分代缴的优惠政策。

新型农村社会养老保险方面，共有 849036 名残疾人参加了新型农村社会养老保险，参保率 68.8%。在 60 周岁以下的参保残疾人中有重度残疾人 153168 人，其中 133304 人得到了政府的参保扶助，代缴补贴比例达到 87.03%。有 153168 名非重度残疾人也享受了全额或部分代缴的优惠政策。

城镇残疾职工参加社会保险人数达到 81117 人，城镇残疾居民参加基本医疗保险达到 303029 人，城镇 184621 名和农村 530260 名残疾人纳入最低生活保障范围；城镇集中供养残疾人和农村五保供养残疾人分别达到 12331 人和 41474 人；201418 名和 3148 名符合条件的城乡残疾人分别享受了稳定的生活补贴和护理补贴。93067 城乡残疾人得到了其他救助救济。

残疾人托养服务工作规范推进，残疾人托养服务机构达到 209 个，共为 20914 名残疾人提供了托养服务。其中寄宿制托养服务机构 62 个；日间照料机构 124 个；综合性托养服务机构 23 个。接受居家托养服务的残疾人达到 13970 人。

五、扶贫开发

2013 年，残疾人扶贫开发成效显著，贫困残疾人生产生活状况得到进一步改善。111745 名贫困残疾人得到扶持，其中 59644 人通过扶贫开发实际脱贫；接受实用技术培训的残疾人达到 55040 人次。

康复扶贫贴息贷款扶持 3473 名农村残疾人，1526 个单位和 8301 个人对贫困残疾人开展结对帮扶。残疾人扶贫基地达到 100 个，安置 2665 名残疾人就业，扶持带动11169名残疾人。完成1200户农村贫困残疾人危房改造，各地投入危房资金9467500元，1525名残疾人受益。

六、宣传文化

2013年，省残联宣文处全体同志根据《2013年湖北省残疾人宣传文体工作目标责任书》的要求，团结一心，勤奋工作，目标责任制规定的11项职能目标基本完成。全年中央级媒体采用稿件24件；全省主要新闻媒体刊播稿件省级1450件，地市级1840件；报纸专版省级22个，地市级120个。截至2013年底，全省共有省级残疾人专题广播节目2个，电视手语栏目1个；地市级残疾人专题广播节目15个，电视手语栏目4个。

残疾人文化生活更加丰富活跃，残疾人受到社会广泛关注并更加全面地参与到社会生活当中。省残联出台了本地加强残疾人文化的意见，17个地市（州）制定了本地实施意见；公共图书馆盲文及盲人有声读物图书室七、体育省级达到11个，地市级20个；残疾人文化周省级举办17场次，地市级举办56场次；残疾人文化艺术类的比赛及展览省级进行18次，地市级54次；残疾人艺术团队省级达到19个，地市级6个。

2013年，残疾人体育工作以提高残疾人体育健身服务能力和残疾人体育运动水平为着力点，全面实施“自强健身工程”，不断提高竞技水平。

举办第三届残疾人健身周活动，残疾人群众体育健身活动省级举办24场次，地市级211场次；

残疾人群众体育健身活动参加人省级2500人次，地市级13165人次；残疾人群众体育活动示范点省级达到25个，地市级63个；全省累计培养审批了671名残疾人体育健身指导员。在全省举办残疾人体育比赛1次，参赛残疾人运动员100人次；残疾人体育训练基地10个，残疾人体育训练基地在编人员10人，聘任教练员24人。

八、维权

各级残联维权组织建设得到加强，残疾人事业法律法规体系进一步完善，残疾人维权工作全面开展。

2013年，制定或修改了关于残疾人的专门法规、规章地市级2件件；制定或修改保障残疾人权益的规范性文件地市级2件、县级11件。全省县级以上人大进行《残疾人保障法》执法检查和专题调研39次；政协进行视察和专题调研36次。全省开展普法宣传教育活动182次，38159人参加；举办法律培训班64个，3219人参加。

截至2013年底，全省成立残疾人法律救助工作协调机构83个，建立残疾人法律救助工作站38个，办理案件698件，建立残疾人法律援助中心（工作站）95个，办理案件1369件，有力地促进了法律救助和法律援助工作。

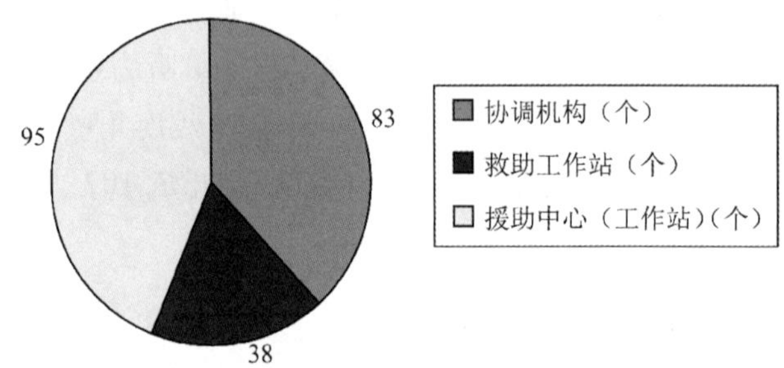

图4 残疾人法律救助工作

残疾人参政议政工作得到加强，各级残联协助人大代表、政协委员提出议案、建议、提案128件，办理议案、建议、提案81件。

无障碍建设法规、标准进一步完善。全省共出台了6个地市、县级无障碍建设与管理法规、规章和规范性文件；76个市、县系统开展无障碍建设；全省开展无障碍建设检查189次，无障碍培训263人次；为2467个贫困残疾人家庭实施了无障碍改造；为45654名残疾人发放了残疾人机动轮椅车燃油补贴。

全省各级残联共处理残疾人群众来信2509件，接待残疾人群众来访24561人次，其中集体访174批次、2498人次。

九、组织建设

2013年，省级残联在领导班子中配备了2名残疾人理事长或副理事长；5个地市级残联领导班子中配备了残疾人理事长或副理事长；47个县级残联机关配备了残疾人干部；已建乡镇（街道）残联1251个，已建率达到97.6%，选聘残疾人专职委员1872名；已建社区（村）残协23176个，已建率达到94.5%，选聘残疾人专职委员13942名。

全省地市县乡残联实有人员已达3507人。各级残联共举办培训班 196 期，培训机关干部、协会干部及残疾人专职委员 7030 人次。

全省共建立市级以下各类残疾人专门协会 539 个，市级专门协会已建比例为 91.7%，市辖区专门协会已建比例 97.1%；县（含县级市）级专门协会已建比例为 93.0%。

十、服务设施建设

残疾人服务设施建设得到全面发展。截至 2013 年底，全省已竣工并投入使用、筹建、在建的各级残疾人综合服务设施 93 个，总建设规模 211766.6 平方米，总投资 530649.8 万元；已竣工并投入使用、筹建、在建的各级残疾人康复设施 21 个，总建设规模 148239.03 平方米，总投资 27187.33 万元；已竣工并投入使用、筹建、在建的各级残疾人托养服务设施 35 个，总建设规模 62257.6 平方米，总投资 9259.5 万元。

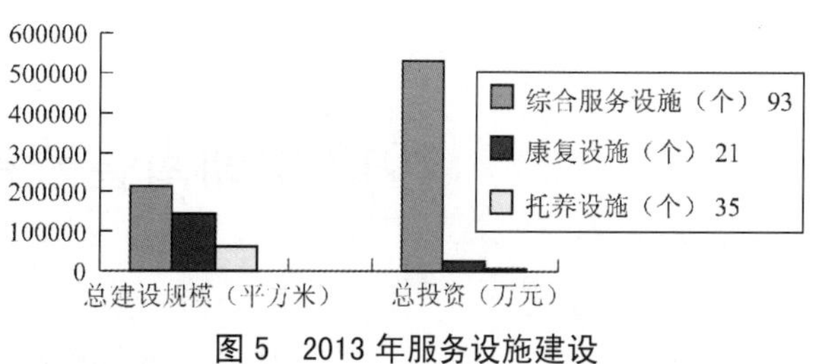

图 5　2013 年服务设施建设

十一、信息化建设

2013 年，省残联网站年度访问量达到 92 万多次，刊发各级残联稿件超过 2000 篇，内容更新总量达到 3000 条。全省 16 个地市级残联和 104 个县级残联开通网站，比 2012 年增加 80 个。全省所有残联实现网上信息报送与审核。首次将网站无障碍纳入中国残联网站绩效评估范围。

截至 2013 年底，全省残疾人人口基础信息数据库累计采集、收录持证残疾人 1097151 人。结合全省农村贫困残疾人扶贫调查，采集农村贫困残疾人扶贫需求信息 80 余万条。

2013年湖南省残疾人事业发展统计公报

2013年湖南省残疾人工作完成各项任务指标，残疾人各项工作全面发展，残疾人得到不同程度的服务和保障。综合2013年度残疾人事业统计数据及实际情况，公报如下：

一、残疾人康复

2013年我省残疾人康复工作全面提升，康复工作以围绕2015年初步实现“人人享有康复服务”为目的，以突破残疾儿童康复、辅助器具服务和残疾预防工作为重点，加快康复机构建设，并以康复机构为依托，认真实施各类康复救助项目，全面推进社区康复。

截止到2013年底，在全省14个市州所属125个县区13270个社区村开展社区康复服务，已建成5368个社区康复站，有13210名各级社区康复协调员，本年度新增社区康复协调员2611名。到2013年底全省共建立45所家长学校，已登记家长学员5176名，增强了社区康复力量。

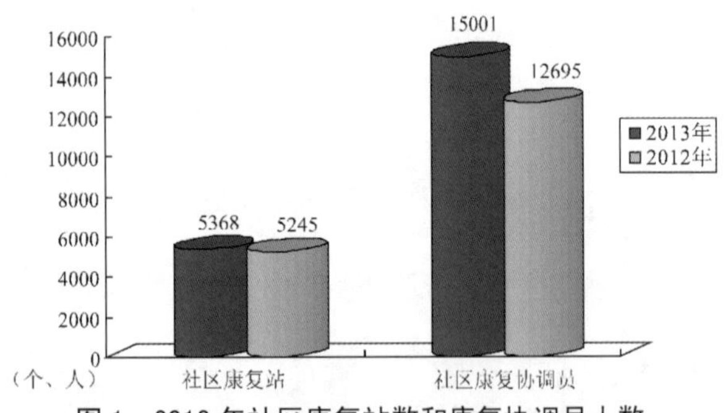

图1　2013年社区康复站数和康复协调员人数

2013年共完成白内障复明手术29456例，为14242名贫困白内障患者免费施行复明手术；为6605名低视力患者配用助视器，培训低视力儿童家长2313名。对5567名盲人进行定向行走训练。

全省共建立听力语言康复机构55个，新收训聋儿917名，在训聋儿1618名；规范聋儿家长学校，开展家庭训练，共培训聋儿家长1780名；开展各级各类听力语言康复专业技术人员培训，培训专业人员311人；为526名贫困成年听力残疾人免费验配助听器，提供技术服务880人次。

全省开展肢体残疾康复训练服务机构54个，比2012年增加14个，培训各级各类肢体残疾康复人员351人次；全省共对12788名肢体残疾者实施康复训练；对515名脑瘫儿童实施国家康复救助项目，资助378名贫困肢体残疾儿童实施矫治手术；为麻风畸残者实施免费矫治手术100例。

开展智力残疾康复训练服务机构50个，全省共对7462名智力残疾人进行康复训练；500名智力残疾儿童得到了“国家彩票公益金”救助，实施地方救助项目资助500名智力残疾儿童进行机构康复训练。

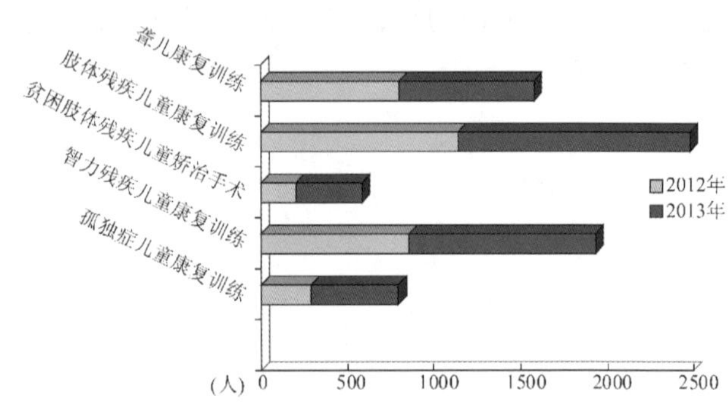

图2　2013年残疾儿童康复机构训练情况

全省120个县（市、区）开展精神病防治康复工作，覆盖总人口6460.38万人，75887名精神病贫困患者接受救助。2013年，加大了精神残疾康复机构建设，省级共投入200万元，支持精神康复工、农、娱疗站的建设项目。现有各级精神康复机构110个，机构内精神病人19786名。建立孤独症儿童康复机构44个，501名孤独症儿童在各级机构接受康复训练，其中245名贫困孤独症儿童得到康复救助。

2013年，累计建立辅助器具供应机构96个，其中市级14个，县级82个，建成了省市县三级辅助器具配发服务网络。为残疾人减免费用供应辅助器具6.6万件，其中装配假肢2373例、矫形器1062例，验配助视器5646件。

二、残疾人教育

2013年，残疾人教育工作取得新进展，残疾人受教育权利得到了更好保障。

实施专项彩票公益金助学项目，资助学前残疾儿童400名，资助新入园儿童254名。

全省有特殊教育普通高中学校（班）14个，在校生335人。残疾人中等职业学校（班）21个，在校生1091人，381人毕业，其中136人获得职业资格证书。全省有268名残疾人被普通高等院校录取，120名残疾人进入特殊教育学院学习。

截止到2013年底，全省有未入学适龄残疾儿童少年5839名，其中视力残疾儿童276人，听力残疾儿童232人，言语残疾儿童327人，肢体残疾儿童2114人，智力残疾儿童1595人，精神残疾儿童163人，多重残疾儿童1132人。

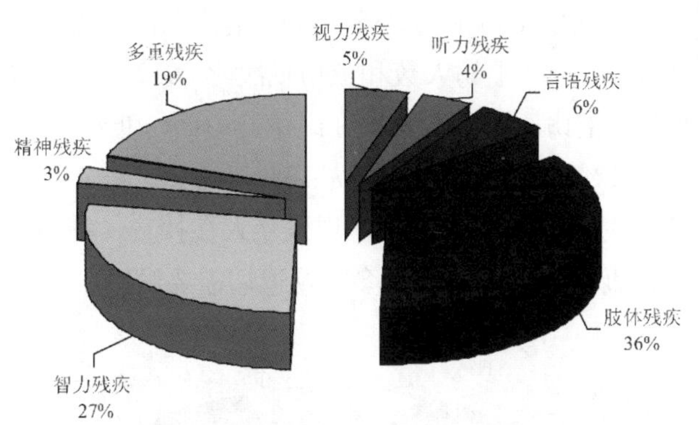

图3 2013年未入学残疾儿童情况

三、残疾人就业

残疾人就业稳步增长。2013年，城镇新增13735名残疾人就业，其中，集中就业4110人，按比例就业2330人，个体及其他形式灵活就业6091人，公益性岗位就业955人，辅助性就业249人。全省城镇就业人数27.88万，93.06万名农村残疾人实现就业，其中68.26万人从事农业生产劳动。

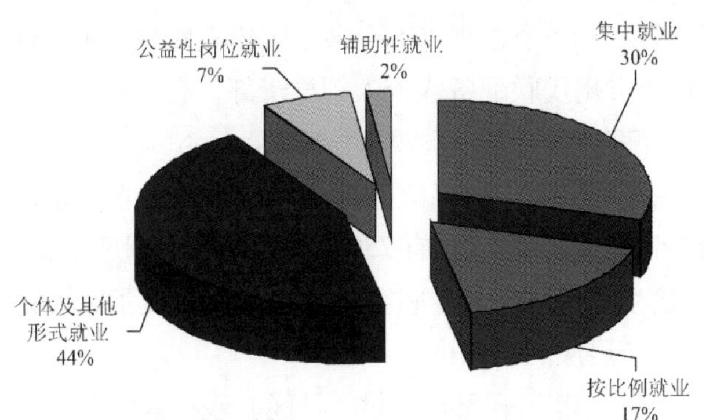

图4 2013年城镇残疾人新增就业情况

全省残疾人职业培训基地达到185个，其中残联兴办75个，依托社会机构兴办110个，6368人次城镇残疾人接受了职业培训。

2013年度培训盲人保健按摩和医疗按摩人员1496名，全省盲人保健按摩机构达到531个，盲人医疗按摩机构达到17个，本年度培训的盲人中已有1202人就业；在专业技术职务资格评审中，有41人通过医疗按摩人员初级职称评审。

四、残疾人扶贫

2013年，残疾人扶贫开发进一步深化，贫困残疾人生产生活状况得到进一步改善。86949名贫困残疾人得到扶持，其中43646人通过扶贫开发实际脱贫，接受实用技术培训的残疾人达14904人次。

中央康复扶贫贴息贷款项目扶持1959名农村残疾人，省级康复扶贫贴息贷款项目支持37家农村残疾人转移就业集中的企业，稳定2136名残疾人就业。1631个单位和9636名个人对贫困残疾人开展结对帮扶。残疾人扶贫基地达到184个，安置4529名残疾人就业，扶持带动10878名残疾人。

对7639户农村贫困残疾人实施危房改造，各地投入危房改造资金5241.55万元，8430名残疾人受益。

基层党组织助残扶贫项目帮扶1519名农村贫困残疾人，“万村千乡市场工程”助残扶贫项目帮扶490名贫困残疾人就业。

五、残疾人社会保障

2013年残疾人社会保障状况保持平稳。残疾人参加新型农村和城镇居民社会养老保险实现了基本全覆盖。

已有200802名城镇残疾人参加了城镇居民社会养老保险。在60岁以下的参保残疾人中有58641名重度残疾人，其中57030得到了政府的参保扶助；有21665非重度残疾人也享受了全额或部分代缴的优惠政策；领取养老金待遇的人数达到132283人。

新型农村社会养老保险方面，共有1304675名残疾人参加了新型农村社会养老保险。在60周岁以下的参保残疾人中有重度残疾人230322人，其中227316人得到了政府的参保扶助（全部代缴183633人，部分代缴43683人）；有43960名非重度残疾人也享受了全额或部分代缴的优惠政策；享受养老金待遇的人数达到 498922 人。

城镇残疾职工参加社会保险人数达到 200802 人，城镇残疾居民参加基本医疗保险达到 301479 人。

城乡 866748 名残疾人纳入最低生活保障范围，城镇集中供养残疾人和农村五保供养残疾人分别达到 7773 名和 67985 名，160625 名城乡残疾人获得其他救助救济，121722 名符合条件的城乡残疾人分别享受了稳定的生活补贴。

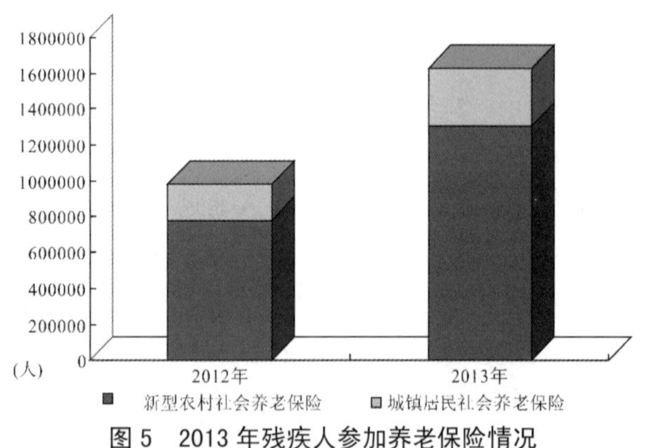

图 5　2013 年残疾人参加养老保险情况

残疾人托养服务工作稳步推进。残疾人托养服务机构达到 111 个，为 3499 名残疾人提供托养服务。接受居家托养服务的残疾人达到 19853 人。

六、残疾人宣传文体

残疾人事业宣传紧密围绕事业大局，大力弘扬人道主义，营造了良好的舆论范围。2013 年中央媒体采用稿件 12 件，主要新闻媒体刊登稿件 155 件，开设电视手语栏目 2 个，电视公益广告片 22 个。省级公共图书馆及盲人有声读物图书室 6 个，举办残疾人文化周 3 场次。

大力加强体育后备人才选拔培养，全年举办两次青少年残疾人体育选拔赛。全省残疾人体育训练基地 8 个，省级举办 3 次残疾人体育比赛，有 512 名残疾人运动员参赛，地市本年度举办 121 次残疾人体育活动，共有 8675 名残疾人参加体育活动。数据显示，我省在残疾人文化及体育方面的投入远远不能满足残疾人参与文化及体育活动的要求，这也制约了我省残疾人体育发展。

七、残疾人维权

维护残疾人权益是残疾人工作的出发点和落脚点。2013 年加大对残疾人保障法执法检查和监督力度，加强法律服务和法律救助，推动无障碍设施建设。

截止 2013 年底，全省共建立各级残疾人法律救助协调机构 71 个，残疾人法律救助工作站 72 个，共办理案件 368 件，残疾人法律援助中心 118 个，共办理案件 753 件。

各级残联协助人大代表、政协委员提出议案、建议、提案 79 件，办理议案、建议、提案 53 件。

全省共有 6 个市系统开展无障碍建设，共开展无障碍建设检查 52 次，无障碍培训 373 人次；为 1861 户贫困残疾人家庭实施了无障碍改造；为 50150 名残疾人发放了残疾人机动轮椅车燃油补贴。

2013 年省残联接收残疾人来信 80 封，来访 954 人次，其中个体上访 885 人次，集体上访 6 批次，从数据上看，上访人数和上访批次比 2012 年呈下降趋势，上访原因主要集中在以下几方面：康复 17%，教育 6%，就业 16%，扶贫 13%，社会保障 24%，机动轮椅车 10%，数据体现残疾人在扶贫、社会保障、康复等方面还有很多问题迫切需要解决。

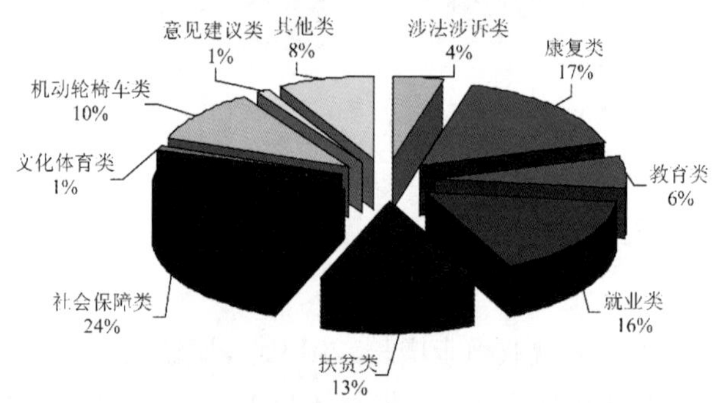

图 6　2013 年残疾人来访（人次）情况

八、残疾人组织

截止 2013 年底，市、县、乡残联实有工作人员 5519 人，14 个市州 125 个县市区建立残联，其中有 11 个市州残联配备残疾人领导干部，有 73 个县区残联配备了残疾人干部。

全省 2413 个乡镇已有 2407 个乡镇成立残联，有 2381 名工作人员，有 750 个乡镇配备专职理事长，已建乡镇残联中有专职委员 2421 名，形成了比较完善、多层次的组织机构。

全省建立了 39688 村（社区）残疾人协会，配备了 34420 名残疾人专职委员，建立了 22882 个残疾人活动室。

全省共有注册志愿者 209447 名，受助残疾人达

565672 人次。

九，残疾人服务设施

残疾人服务设施建设得到全面发展。截至 2013 年底，全省已竣工并投入使用的各级残疾人综合服务设施 93 个，总建设规模 12.16 万平方米，总投资 2.34 亿元；已竣工并投入使用的各级残疾人康复设施 32 个，总建设规模 1.66 万平方米，总投资 3245.5 万元；已竣工并投入使用的各级残疾人托养服务设施 18 个，总建设规模 2.86 万平方米，总投资 3384.1 万元。

十、残疾人信息化

残疾人事业数据统计工作稳步推进，做到数据支撑有公信力，为出台残疾人政策决策提供可靠数据。全省各级有 157 名统计员，其中有统计从业登记证书的 43 人，举办一次统计业务培训班，221 人接受培训。

2013 年，湖南省残疾人工作紧紧围绕省委省政府《关于促进残疾人事业发展的实施意见》下功夫，残疾人工作呈稳步上升态势，残疾人“两个体系”的建设正在完善，但是，发展中我们也还有很多需要解决的问题，残疾人康复远不能满足残疾人的需求，残疾人还不能完全平等享受到教育的权利，残疾人就业总会遇到歧视，少数残疾人生活仍得不到保障，支撑残疾人事业发展的法律法规和政策需要进一步配套和完善。我们将进一步增强信心，努力解决我省残疾人工作在发展路上出现的问题，相信在 2015 年我省残疾人都能“人人享受到康复服务”，“人人享受有适度保障”，就业更加充分，有学习能力的残疾儿童接受义务教育比例达到 85%，实现“政策法规体系完善，保障机制健全，服务体系完备，参与环境和谐，残疾人全面发展”。

2013 年广东省残疾人事业发展统计公报

2013 年是全面实施残疾人事业"十二五"规划承上启下的关键年，一年来，广东省残疾人事业发展紧扣残疾人保障与服务两个体系建设的主线，全面推进了残疾人康复、教育、就业、社会保障、权益保障、信息助残等专项服务工作，残疾人事业取得一定成绩。

一、残疾人康复

1. 残疾儿童筛查：截至 2013 年底，全省共 41 个县，169 个医疗卫生机构陆续开展残疾儿童筛查工作，年度新诊断 0-6 岁残疾儿童 3175 人，并进行了免费康复训练。

2. 社区康复：全省 91.97%的市辖区、县（市）开展了社区康复工作，61.13%的村（社区）开展了社区康复工作，新增社区康复站 198 个，累计已建社区康复站的社区总数为 7892 个，配备社区康复协调员 1.84 万名。

3. 视力残疾康复：开展视力残疾康复机构总数达到 72 个，完成白内障复明手术 9.19 万例，为 2769 名低视力患者配用助视器，培训低视力儿童家长 918 人，盲人定向行走训练 6838 人。

4. 听力言语康复：开展听力语言康复机构 78 个，年度新收训聋儿 1019 人，在训聋儿 2350 人，培训聋儿家长 3723 人次，培训基层听力语言康复专业技术人员 1058 人次。

5. 肢体残疾康复：开展肢体残疾康复训练服务机构 243 个，康复训练肢体残疾人 32972 人，其中救助脑瘫儿童机构康复训练 3381 人，肢体残疾人社区家庭康复 29591 人。免费为 57 名贫困肢体残疾儿童实施矫治手术，装配矫形器并进行术后康复训练。培训基层肢体残疾康复训练人员 1973 人次。

6. 智力残疾康复：开展智力残疾康复训练服务的机构 251 个，康复训练智力残疾人 9738 人，其中救助智力残疾儿童进行机构康复训练 3177 人，智力残疾人社区家庭康复 6561 人。培训各级各类智力残疾康复管理、技术人员 678 人次。

7. 精神残疾康复：129 个县（市、区）开展精神病防治康复工作，对 38.95 万名精神病患者进行综合防治康复，监护率达到 78.64%，显好率达到 67.78%，社会参与率达到 49.91%，肇事率 0.21%。解除关锁精神残疾 537 人，救助贫困精神病患者 10.31 万人。

8. 孤独症儿童康复：各级孤独症儿童康复训练机构共 118 个，康复训练孤独症儿童 3000 人，其中救助贫困孤独症儿童 1581 人。

9. 辅助器具适配：全省省级以下辅助器具适配机构 82 个，为各类残疾人供应辅助器具 54505 件，其中国家彩金项目免费装配假肢 2599 例、免费装配矫形器 3834 例、免费验配助视器 3831 件、免费其他基本型辅助器具 2353 件。

二、残疾人教育

1. 学前教育阶段：本年度残疾人事业专项彩票公益金资助学前教育残疾儿童 550 人，其他助学项目资助学前教育残疾儿童 444 人。

2. 义务教育阶段：截止到 2013 年底，全省特殊教育学校 94 所（其中盲人学校 3 所，聋人学校 9 所，培智学校 42 所，其他学校 40 所），比上年增加 14 所；全省特殊教育学生 24485 人，比上年减少 537 人，减少 2.1%，其中在特殊教育学校就读的学生 10669 人，比上年增加 1312 人，增长 14%，在普通学校特教班就读的学生 192 人，在普通学校随班就读的学生 13624 人。全省未入学适龄残疾儿童少年登记在册 4303 人，其中视力残疾 154 人、听力残疾 160 人、言语残疾 180 人、智力残疾 1546 人、肢体残疾 1123 人、精神残疾 346 人、多重残疾 794 人。

3. 高中教育阶段：全省开办特殊教育普通高中班（部）8 个，在校生 140 人；残疾人中等职业学校（班）8 个，在校生 855 人；2013 年高中阶段教育毕业 224 人，其中 134 人获得职业资格证书。

4. 高等教育阶段：全省共 37 名残疾人进入特

殊教育学院学习，342 名残疾人进入普通高等院校学习。

三、残疾人培训、就业与扶贫

1. 全省建立残疾人职业培训、就业、扶贫基地共 285 个。

2. 残疾人培训：全省城镇职业培训 1.3 万人，培训盲人保健按摩人员 896 人，医疗按摩人员 282 人。

3. 残疾人就业：本年度城镇在业残疾人数 20.18 万，其中新安排残疾人就业 1.98 万；农村残疾人在业 61.38 万，其中 50.19 万残疾人从事农业生产劳动。

4. 残疾人扶贫：本年度扶持贫困残疾人 4.66 万人次，接受实用技术培训的残疾人达到 1.73 万人次，截至年底共安置残疾人就业 3506 人，扶持带动残疾人 5158 户。全年完成 1486 户农村贫困残疾人危房改造，受益残疾人 1655 人。

四、残疾人社会保障与托养

1. 社会保障：2013 年底城镇残疾职工与居民参加社会保险人数达到 44.26 万人，纳入最低生活保障 9.19 万人，集中供养和其他救助救济残疾人 3.67 万人；农村残疾居民参加社会保险人数达到 153.5 万人，纳入最低生活保障 27.8 万人。五保供养和其他救助救济残疾人 6.85 万人。全省 102 个县（市区）出台并实施残疾人生活补贴政策文件，36.2 万残疾人人享受了生活补贴。96 个县（市区）出台并实施残疾人护理补贴制度，29.9 万残疾人享受了护理补贴。

2. 残疾人托养：全省残疾人托养服务机构达到 385 个，共为 12828 残疾人提供了托养服务。其中寄宿制托养服务机构 20 个，托养残疾人 881 人；日间照料机构 328 个，托养残疾人 9684 人；综合性托养服务机构 37 个，托养残疾人 2263 人。接受居家托养服务的残疾人达到 1.96 万人。

五、残疾人宣传文化与体育

1. 残疾人宣传：本年度省级主要新闻媒体刊播残疾人事业活动稿件 85 件，省级共有残疾人事业报刊专版 4 个，残疾人专题广播节目 1 个，电视手语新闻栏目 1 个，残疾人事业新闻宣传促进会 1 个；地市级主要新闻媒体刊播稿件 2564 件，地市级共有报刊专版 37 个，残疾人专题广播节目 24 个，电视手语新闻栏目 9 个，建立地市级新促会 22 个。

2. 残疾人文化：省级和地市级公共图书馆设立盲文及盲人有声读物阅览室已达到 41 个，举办残疾人文化周活动 98 次，举办残疾人文化艺术类比赛及展览 27 次，已成立残疾人艺术团队 12 个。

3. 残疾人体育：省级举办残疾人群众健身活动 8 次，残疾人参加活动 1130 人次，举办残疾人体育比赛 8 次，残疾人运动员参加比赛 430 人次；地市级举办残疾人体育健身活动 96 次，参加人数 1.08 万人次。

六、残疾人法制建设与维权

1. 残疾人法规体系建设：2013 年全省各级残联参与、制定、修改有关残疾人的法规、规章、政策性文件共 12 个，其中地市级 5 个，县区级 7 个。开展人大政协执法检查与专题调研 33 次，其中地市级 15 次，县区级 18 次。协助人大代表、政协委员提出议案、提案与建议共 59 件，其中省级 2 件，地市级 26 件，县区级 31 件。

2. 残疾人法律宣传与救助：全省各级残联组织普法宣传教育活动 258 次，2.42 万人次参加；组织残疾人工作者法律培训班 64 期，4022 人次参加。地市级建立法律救助工作站和法律援助中心（工作站）25 个，全年办理案件 83 件，县区级建立法律救助工作站和法律援助中心（工作站）113 个，全年办理案件 450 件。

3. 无障碍建设：截至年底，全省各级残联共颁发无障碍建设与管理法规、政府令 30 个，系统开展无障碍建设的地级市 10 个，县区 55 个；贫困残疾人家庭无障碍改造 6560 户；发放残疾人机动轮椅车燃油补贴 29087 人。

4. 残疾人信访工作：全年各级残联信访部门共处理残疾人来信 3208 件，其中省级 53 件，地市级 310 件，县区级 2845 件；各级残联接待残疾人群众来访 11579 人次，其中集体访 62 批次、724 人次。

七、残疾人事业组织建设

截至 2013 年底，省市县乡残联实有人员 6850

人。全省有 13 个地级市残联配备了残疾人领导，47 个县（市、区）残联配备了残疾人干部；已建乡镇（街道）残联 1605 个，已建率达到 99.69%，选聘残疾人专职委员 1612 名；已建社区（村）残协 2.31 万个，已建率达到 92.89%，选聘残疾人专职委员 2.29 万名。各级残联共举办培训班 1144 期，培训机关干部、协会干部及残疾人专职委员 31821 人次。共建立省级以下各类残疾人专门协会 719 个，建设率为 100%。

八、残疾人事业统计与信息化

截至 2013 年底，全省县区级以上残联有专兼职统计工作人员 171 人，其中有统计从业资格 36 人，占 21.1%，地级以上市举办统计人员培训班 22 期，476 人参加培训。全省共有各级残联门户网站 81 个，其中省级 1 个、地市级 21 个、县区级 59 个；举办信息化工作培训班 23 期，685 人参加培训；省级残联网站全年发稿量 2838 篇。2013 年全省各级残联信息化建设共投入 942 万，其中硬件投入占 48.2%、软件投入占 37.0%、系统运行维护费占 14.8%。各级残联共有信息化专业技术人员 281 名。

九、残疾人服务设施建设

截至 2013 年底，已竣工并投入使用的各级残疾人综合服务设施 85 个，总建设规模 34.26 万平方米，总投资 10.94 亿元；已竣工并投入使用的各级残疾人康复设施 49 个，总建设规模 9.06 万平方米，总投资 2.58 亿元；已竣工并投入使用的各级残疾人托养服务设施 33 个，总建设规模 4.53 万平方米，总投资 0.88 亿元。

2013 年广西壮族自治区残疾人事业发展统计公报

2013 年，广西残疾人工作深入贯彻落实中央、自治区关于促进残疾人事业发展重大部署，全面推进残疾人社会保障和服务体系建设，创新残疾人工作，夯实残疾人工作基础，促进残疾人事业迈上新台阶。

一、全面开展社区康复工作，大力推进城市和农村残疾人“人人享有康复服务”目标的实现

在 36 个市辖区和 75 个县（市）开展了社区康复工作，累计已建社区康复站的社区总数 0.24 万个，配备 1.20 万名社区康复协调员。

48 个县的 32 个医疗卫生机构陆续开展残疾儿童筛查工作，年度新诊断 0-6 岁残疾儿童 2373 人。

开展视力残疾康复机构总数达到 6 个，完成白内障复明手术 23172 例；为 11，775 名贫困白内障患者免费施行复明手术；为 7697 名低视力患者配用助视器，培训低视力儿童家长 305 名，有效开展家庭康复训练。对 2493 名盲人进行定向行走训练。

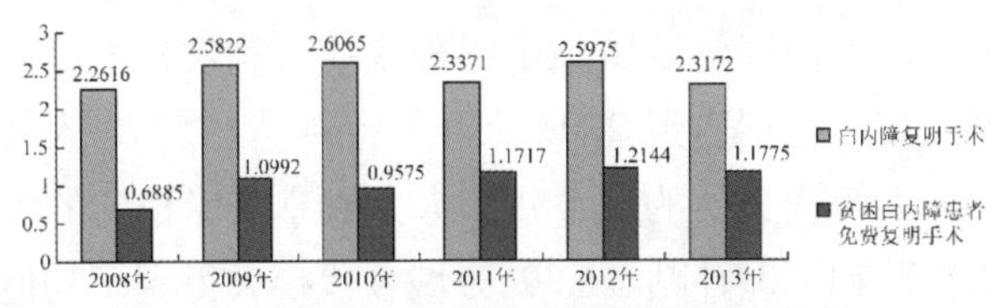

图 1　2008-2013 年广西白内障复明手术人数情况（单位：万人）

推进听力语言康复机构规范化管理，完善基层服务网络。已建设省级听力语言康复机构 1 个，基层听力语言康复机构 28 个。年度新收训聋儿 545 名，在训聋儿 919 名；规范聋儿家长学校，开展家庭训练，共培训聋儿家长 1099 名；开展各级各类听力语言康复专业技术人员培训，共培训专业人员 68 人。

大力推广“社会化、综合性、开放式”精神病防治康复工作。在 92 个市县开展精神病防治康复工作，对 12.42 万重性精神病患者进行综合防治康复，监护率达到 77.41%，显好率达到 68.49%，社会参与率达到 53.34%，肇事率 0.48%；解除关锁 30 人；对 11238 名贫困精神病患者进行医疗救助。

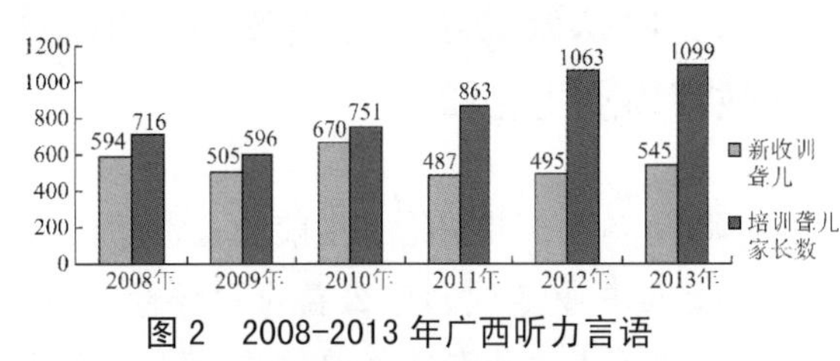

图 2　2008-2013 年广西听力言语康复训练情况（单位：人）

建立了 1 个省级孤独症儿童康复训练机构；399 名孤独症儿童在各级机构进行了康复训练。

开展肢体残疾康复训练服务机构达 19 个，其中，省级康复机构 1 个，地市级、县级康复机构 18 个；培训各级各类肢体残疾康复人员 324 人次；全区共对 7845 肢体残疾者实施康复训练，其中肢体残疾儿童社区、家庭康复训练数为 1519 人，成年肢体残疾人社区、家庭康复训练数为 5712 人；实施救助项目资助 614 名脑瘫儿童进行机构康复训练，资助 203 名贫困肢体残疾儿童实施矫治手术。

图 3　2008-2013 年广西肢体残疾康复训练情况（单位：人）

开展智力残疾康复训练服务的机构 20 个，其中，省级康复机构 1 个，地市级、县级康复机构 19 个；培训各级各类智力残疾康复人员 143 人次；全区共对 3582 名智力残疾人进行康复训练；实施救助项目资助 559 名智力残疾儿童进行机构康复训练，同时培训儿童家长。

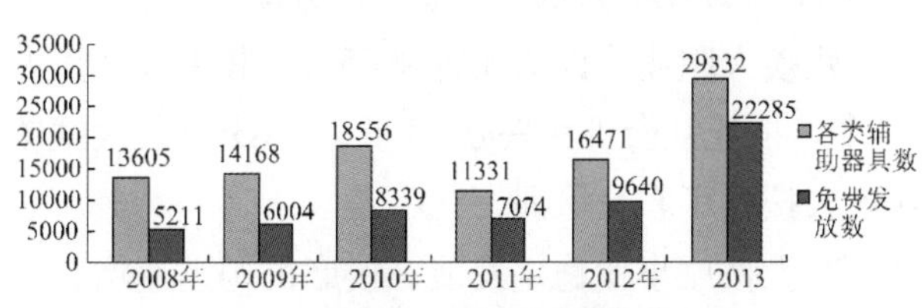

图 4　2008-2013 年广西辅助器具供应情况（单位：人）

加强残疾人辅助器具服务体系建设，深入开展辅助器具供应服务，为残疾人供应辅助器具 29332 件，供应品种为 200 种，免费发放的辅助器具件数为 22285 件。全年装配假肢 1224 例、矫形器 213 例，验配助视器 9674 件。

二、以扶残助学为"引擎"，推动我区特殊教育事业上台阶

对 850 名残疾儿童给予学前教育资助，其中，接受残疾人事业专项彩票公益金助学项目资助为 440 人，残疾人事业专项彩票公益金助学项目资助新入园为 316 人，其他残疾儿童学前教育助学项目资助 94 人。

已开办特殊教育普通高中班（部）11 个，在校生 261 人；其中聋高中 7 个，在校生 221 人；盲高中 3 个，在校生 40 人。残疾人中等职业学校（班）7 个，在校生 169 人，盲人 3 人，聋人 77 人，肢残 89 人；毕业生 77 人，聋人 38 人，肢残 39 人。有 201 名残疾人被普通高等院校录取。

截止到 2013 年底，全区未入学适龄残疾儿童少年有 4804 人，其中视力残疾儿童 228 人，听力残疾儿童 240 人，言语残疾儿童 386 人，智力残疾儿童 1302 人，肢体残疾儿童 1395 人，精神残疾儿童 144 人，多重残疾儿童 1109 人。

三、贯彻落实《残疾人就业条例》，促进就业工作迈出新步伐

贯彻落实《残疾人就业条例》，进一步完善政策法规体系，提高就业服务水平，全面推动残疾人就业工作纵向发展。2013 年，城镇新增就业残疾人 5278 人，其中，集中就业 1106 人，按比例安排就业 1794 人，公益性岗位就业 574 人，个体就业及其它形式灵活就业 1456 人，辅助性就业 348 人。城镇就业人数 77329 人；639664 万农村残疾人在业，其中 509175 万残疾人从事农业生产劳动。

残疾人职业培训基地达到 65 个，其中残联兴办 28 个，依托社会机构兴办 37 个，0.63 万人次城镇残疾人接受了职业培训。

盲人按摩事业稳定发展，按摩机构迅速增长。2013 年度培训盲人保健按摩人员 609 名、盲人医疗按摩人员 64 名；保健按摩机构达到 155 个，医疗按摩机构达到 7 个；在专业技术职务资格评审中，有 9 人通过医疗按摩人员初级职称评审。

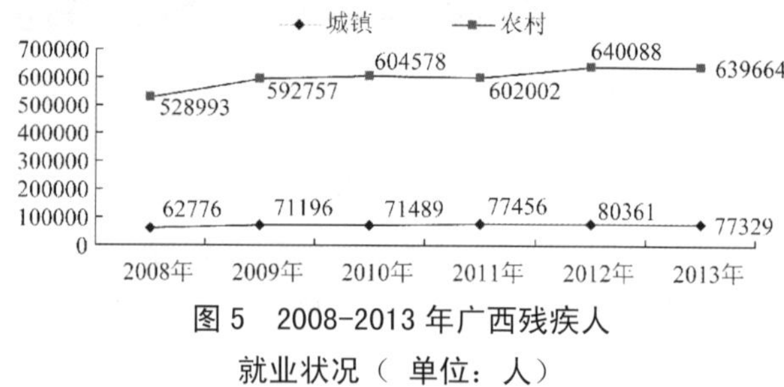

图 5 2008-2013 年广西残疾人就业状况（单位：人）

2013 年 17.87 万城镇残疾人参加了城镇居民社会养老保险，参保率 79.40%。在 60 岁以下的参保残疾人中有 1.53 万重度残疾人，其中 1.37 万得到了政府的参保扶助，代缴补贴比例达到 89.27%。有 1.23 万非重度残疾人也享受了全额或部分代缴的优惠政策。领取养老金待遇的人数达到 9.14 万人。

新型农村社会养老保险方面，共有 72.73 万残疾人参加了新型农村社会养老保险，参保率 56.53%。在 60 周岁以下的参保残疾人中有重度残疾人 11.30 万，其中 10.52 万得到了政府的参保扶助，代缴补贴比例达到 93.07%。有 5.34 万非重度残疾人也享受了全额或部分代缴的优惠政策。享受养老金待遇的人数达到 33.97 万人。

城镇残疾职工参加社会保险人数达到 4.62 万，城镇残疾居民参加基本医疗保险达到 16.88 万人；7.04 万城镇残疾人和 40.60 万农村残疾人纳入最低生活保障范围；城镇集中供养残疾人和农村五保供养残疾人分别达到 2009 人和 41664 人；5310 人和 220 人符合条件的城乡残疾人分别享受了稳定的生活补贴和护理补贴。6.32 万城乡残疾人得到了其他救助救济。

残疾人托养服务工作规范推进，残疾人托养服务机构达到 30 个，共为 1151 残疾人提供了托养服务。其中寄宿制托养服务机构 3 个；日间照料机构 24 个；综合性托养服务机构 3 个。接受居家托养服务的残疾人达到 1.94 万人。

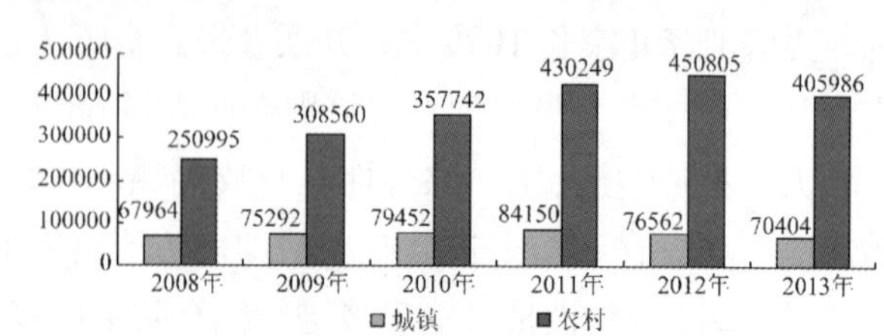

图 6 2008-2013 年广西残疾人纳入最低生活保障情况（单位：人）

四、以新农村建设为契机，探索扶贫工作新模式

结合建设社会主义新农村，大力推进残疾人扶贫开发；把残疾人扶贫纳入“整村推进”范围，加大“帮包带扶”工作力度；开展以农村实用技术为主的培训，提高贫困残疾人生产劳动能力和技能。

2013年，4.84万贫困残疾人得到扶持，其中3.55万人通过扶贫开发实际脱贫；接受实用技术培训的残疾人达到3.22万人次。

康复扶贫贴息贷款扶持587农村残疾人，5654个单位和9128个人对贫困残疾人开展结对帮扶。残疾人扶贫基地达到133个，安置2315残疾人就业，扶持带动13471残疾人。

2013年完成7853户农村贫困残疾人危房改造，各地投入危房资金6，225.56万元，9303名残疾人受益。

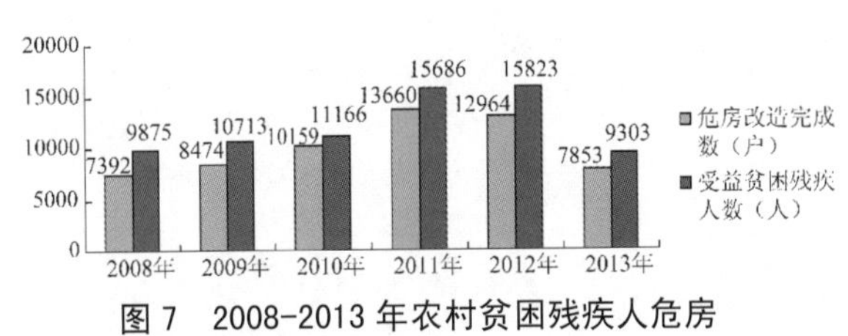

图7 2008-2013年农村贫困残疾人危房改造情况（单位：户、人）

五、以丰富残疾人文化生活为出发点，提升宣传文体工作活力

主要新闻媒体刊播稿件数112件，报刊专版4个，残疾人专题广播节目1个，电视手语新闻栏目1个，省级残疾人事业新闻宣传促进会1个。

地市级主要新闻媒体刊播稿件数524件，报刊专版18个，残疾人专题广播节目12个，建立地市级新促会1个。

省级和地市级公共图书馆设立盲文及盲人有声读物阅览室已达到1和6个，举办残疾人文化周1和26个，举办残疾人文化艺术类比赛及展览分别是2和7个，已成立残疾人艺术团队4个。

省级残疾人体育健身活动1次，参加人数0.01万人，残疾人体育示范点2个，残疾人体育健身指导员46人，残疾人体育比赛1次，参与的残疾人运动员272人次，残疾人体育训练基地1个，聘任教练员11人。

地市级残疾人体育健身活动30次，参加人数0.36万人，残疾人体育示范点13个，残疾人体育健身指导员192人。

六、深入实施“扶残维权工程”，加强维权工作力度

各级残联维权组织建设得到加强，残疾人事业法律法规体系进一步完善，残疾人维权工作全面开展。

2013年制定或修改保障残疾人权益的规范性文件地市级2件。县级以上人大进行《残疾人保障法》执法检查和专题调研8次；政协进行视察和专题调研4次。开展普法宣传教育活动235次，11.15万人参加；举办法律培训班49个，0.32万人参加。

截至2013年底，成立残疾人法律救助工作协调机构18个，建立残疾人法律救助工作站26个，办理案件149件，建立残疾人法律援助中心（工作站）119个，办理案件606件，有力地促进了法律救助和法律援助工作。

残疾人参政议政工作得到加强，各级残联协助人大代表、政协委员提出议案、建议、提案32件，办理议案、建议、提案20件。

无障碍建设法规、标准进一步完善。共出台了11个省、地市、县级无障碍建设与管理法规、规章；125个市、县、区系统开展无障碍建设；开展无障碍建设检查182次，无障碍培训0.05万人次；为0.38万个贫困残疾人家庭实施了无障碍改造；为1.88万残疾人发放了残疾人机动轮椅车燃油补贴。

各级残联共处理残疾人群众来信1916余件，接待残疾人群众来访17030人次，其中集体访21批次、543人次。

七、规范基层残疾人组织建设

加强基层残疾人组织规范化建设。全区1237个乡（镇、街道）建立健全了残联组织，配备专职理事长170名、兼职理事长702名、残疾人专职委员1456名；全区15785个社区（村）都已建立残协，共选聘15846名残疾人专职委员。

省市县乡残联实有人员已达0.30万人。各级残联共举办培训班0.09万期，培训机关干部、协会干

部及残疾人专职委员2.27万人次。县（市、区）残联全部实现了规范化建设。

专门协会工作日益受到重视，协会在推动"三个活跃"中的作用日益显现。共建立省级以下各类残疾人专门协会620个，市级专门协会已建比例为100%，市辖区专门协会已建比例100%；县（含县级市）级专门协会已建比例为100%。

八、信息化建设稳步推进

统计队伍建设进一步加强，各级残联共有140名专、兼职统计人员从事残疾人事业统计工作，统计人员业务素质培养普遍得到重视，省级残联举办培训班1期，参加培训的人员达到150人次；地市级举办培训班11期，参加培训的人员达到142人次。

地方残联全面推进网站建设，目前1个省级残联已全部开通了公众服务网站，有14个地市级残联网站和102个县级残联网站也已开通公众服务网站。2013年省级及地市级残联开设网站技术培训班12期，培训各级残联信息员达288人次。

各级残联共有202名专业技术人员从事信息化工作；省级残联共建立局域网1个，网上办公（OA）系统1个。

九、基础服务设施建设力度进一步加大

截至2013年底，全区已竣工并投入使用的各级残疾人综合服务设施94个，在建项目共计9个，其中已竣工并投入使用的各级残疾人综合服务设施总建设规模12.99万平方米，总投资21，962.37万元；已竣工并投入使用的各级残疾人康复设施1个，在建9个，其中已竣工并投入使用的各级康复设施总建设规模0.07万平方米，总投资125.00万元；已竣工并投入使用的各级残疾人托养服务设施2个，在建8个，其中已竣工并投入使用的各级残疾人托养服务设施总建设规模0.09万平方米，总投资70.20万元。

2013年海南省残疾人事业发展统计公报

2013年在海南省委、省政府的领导和中国残联的指导下，我们以残疾人为本，落实科学发展观，用党的十八大、十八届三中全会和中国残联六代会以及省残联六代会精神统领残疾人事业发展全局。以各级残联换届为契机，结合党的群众路线教育实践活动，密切联系群众，以全新的面貌，务实清廉的作风，完成残疾人各民生项目，推动全省残疾人事业再上新的台阶。

一、康复服务

我省围绕残疾人“人人享有康复服务”目标，加强残疾人康复服务与残疾预防工作，通过实施国家、省康复项目工程，使各类残疾人得到不同程度的康复。

截止2013年底，已在全省各市县、乡镇开展了社区康复工作，建立一批社区康复站，为残疾人社区康复创造便捷的服务条件，全省累计配备了1373名社区康复协调员，有6794名残疾人得到不同程度的康复服务。在全社会的积极参与下，全省实施白内障复明手术2894例，其中，为贫困白内障患者免费手术1651例，占手术完成总数的二分之一以上；为2927名低视力患者配用助视器，开展家庭康复训练，培训低视力儿童家长11名；对997名盲人进行定向行走训练。继续推进听力语言康复机构建设，累计已建听力语言康复机构省级1个，县级3个；本年度新收训聋儿108名，在训聋儿160名，培训聋儿家长157名；实施贫困聋儿人工耳蜗、助听器抢救性康复项目，完成国家“七彩梦”聋儿抢救性康复“人工耳蜗”26名、“助听器”30名的项目任务。完成2013年省委省政府为民办实事适应症贫困残疾儿童人工耳蜗植入手术60例。开展“成人助听行动”，为465名成年人免费验配助听器。开展智力残疾康复训练服务省级机构2个。培训智力残疾康复人员28人次；对762名智力残疾人进行康复训练；实施救助项目资助70名智力残疾儿童进行机构康复训练，同时培训儿童家长。大力推广“社会化、综合性、开放式”精神病防治康复试点工作。在13个市县开展精神病防治康复工作，对1.58万重性精神病患者进行综合防治康复，监护率达到69.94%，显好率达到20.94%，社会参与率达到11.97%，肇事率0.13%；解除关锁65人；对1886名贫困精神病患者进行医疗救助。新增了2个省级孤独症儿童康复训练机构；7名孤独症儿童在各级机构进行了康复训练，并对家长开展培训。通过机构、社区、家庭相结合的方式对1152名肢体残疾人进行了康复训练，其中，脑瘫儿童系统康复训练50人，肢体残疾儿童社区、家庭康复418人，成年肢体残疾人社区、家庭康复684人。深入开展辅助器具供应服务，为残疾人减免费用供应辅助器具5866件，其中装配假肢464例、矫形器6例，验配助视器2387件。

二、教育助学

加大残疾人受教育的保障力度。全省已开办特殊教育普通高中班（部）8个，在校生610人；残疾人中等职业学校（班）有2个，部分毕业生取得了职业资格证书；接受残疾人事业专项彩票公益金助学项目资助的残疾儿童有122人次；开展各教育阶段残疾学生或贫困残疾人子女学生资助工作，全省共有1295名贫困残疾学生及低保残疾人子女学生受益。

三、就业培训

采取优惠和扶持保护措施，多渠道、多层次、多种形式促进残疾人实现就业。2013年，全省城镇新增2133名残疾人就业。其中，集中就业残疾人309名，按比例安排残疾人就业1114名，公益性岗位安排就业残疾人12名，个体就业及其它形式灵活就业残疾人678名，辅助性就业20人；全省城镇实际在业人数12356人；有66939名残疾人在农村实现就业，其中，56461人从事农业生产劳动。截止2013年底，全省残疾人职业培训基地有12个，其中残联自办 3 个，依托社会机构创办 9 个，全年有 2322 人次城镇残疾人接受了职业培训。2013 年度培训盲人保健按摩人员 195 名、盲人医疗按摩人员 30 名；保健按摩机构达到 146 个，医疗按摩机构达到 2 个；出台《海南省盲人医疗按摩人员从事医疗按摩资格证书管理实施细则》，全年为 50 名盲人按摩人员进行保健按摩师资格鉴定。培训盲人保健、医疗按摩师以及扶持特困盲人按摩师实现就业达 225 人。

四、社会保障

我省残疾人社会保障状况明显改善。残疾人新型农村和城镇居民社会养老保险工作继续推进。由于我省残疾人社会保障工作起步晚，残疾人社会保障在供给与需求上矛盾仍然突出。2013 年，全省有 5.21 万城镇残疾人参加了城镇居民社会养老保险，参保率 74.53%。60 岁以下的参保残疾人中有 0.81 万重度残疾人，其中 0.74 万得到了政府的参保扶助，代缴补贴比例达到 91.20%。有 0.07 万非重度残疾人也享受了全额或部分代缴的优惠政策。领取养老金待遇的人数达到 1.8 万人。新型农村社会养老保险方面，有 12.77 万残疾人参加了新型农村社会养老保险，参保率 88.36%。60 岁以下的参保残疾人中有重度残疾人 2.65 万，其中 2.56 万得到了政府的参保扶助，代缴补贴比例达到 96.45%。有 0.08 万非重度残疾人也享受了全额或部分代缴的优惠政策。享受养老金待遇的人数达到 4.48 万人。城镇残疾职工参加社会保险人数达到 0.81 万，城镇残疾居民参加基本医疗保险达到 5.03 万人，城镇 1.44 万和农村 4.61 万残疾人纳入最低生活保障范围；城镇集中供养残疾人和农村五保供养残疾人分别达到 326 人和 2135 人；享受贫困残疾人生活补贴和重度残疾人生活护理补贴分别达到 1679 人和 30438 人。城乡 2 万残疾人得到了其他救助救济。残疾人托养服务工作规范推进，残疾人托养服务机构达到 6 个，共为 410 残疾人提供了宿制托养服务，接受居家托养服务的残疾人达到 1.18 万人。实施“阳光家园”计划，残疾人托养服务工作取得成效，三亚市残联被中国残联授予首批“阳光家园”全国示范机构。

五、扶贫开发

残疾人扶贫工作有所进展，贫困残疾人生产生活状况得到进一步改善。2013 年，0.7 万贫困残疾人得到扶持，其中 0.16 万人通过扶贫开发实际脱贫；接受实用技术培训的残疾人达到 0.52 万人次。在三亚、琼中、保亭等市县建立残疾人扶贫基地 9 个，安置 127 名残疾人就业，扶持带动 644 户残疾人家庭发展生产。残疾人居住环境不断改善，完成 2622 户农村贫困残疾人危房改造，各地投入危房资金 1,950.45 万元，2724 名残疾人受益。

六、法制维权

各级残联维权组织建设得到加强，残疾人事业法律法规体系进一步完善，残疾人维权工作全面开展。2013 年全省县级以上人大进行《残疾人保障法》执法检查和专题调研 4 次；政协进行视察和专题调研 2 次。开展普法宣传教育活动 17 次，0.24 万人参加。截至 2013 年底，成立残疾人法律救助工作协调机构 1 个，建立残疾人法律救助工作站 2 个，办理案件 2 件，建立残疾人法律援助工作站 17 个，办理案件 75 件，各级残联协助人大代表、政协委员提出议案、建议、提案 8 件，办理议案、建议、提案 10 件。2013 年全省有 600 户贫困残疾人家庭得到无障碍改造；投入改造资金 198 万元；为 900 名残疾人发放残疾人机动轮椅车燃油补贴 196 万元。

全省各级残联共处理残疾人群众来信 191 余件，接待残疾人群众来访 2658 人次。

七、宣文体育

大力宣传残疾人事业，反映残疾人生活，宣传扶残助残先进典型，全省共刊播残疾人事业新闻稿件共 196 篇（条），大力营造有利于残疾人事业发展的社会环境。搭建“海南省公共卫生联播网残疾人事业宣传平台”，加大了扶残助残宣传力度，普及残疾预防等知识。截止 2013 年底，全省已开设残疾人专题广播节目 4 个，电视手语栏目 3 个；建立省级盲人有声读物图书室 1 个；地市级盲人有声读物图书室 1 个；设立残疾人文化艺术基地 1 个；设立残疾人文化进社区示范点 40 个。开展形式多样的社区文化活动，丰富残疾人文化娱乐生活。开展残疾人体育工作，组织开展省级残疾人体育健身活动 3 次，参加人数 280 人；培训残疾人体育健身指导员 40 人；

举办全省性残疾人体育比赛 1 次，参与的残疾人运动员 167 人次。

八、组织建设

残疾人基层组织规范化建设进一步完善，全省已建乡镇(街道)残联 227 个，已建率达到 100.00%，选聘残疾人专职委员 255 名；已建社区（村）残协 0.26 万个，已建率达到 86.29%，选聘残疾人专职委员 0.27 万名。各级残联队伍不断充实，工作队伍人数已达 0.06 万人。加强残联干部培训工作，举办各式各样培训班共 106 期，培训机关干部、协会干部及残疾人专职委员 2184 人次，残联系统干部队伍素质有所提升。全省乡（镇、街道）和村（社区）志愿者实名登记注册人数有 7458 人。截止 2013 年底，成立的省级以下各类残疾人专门协会达 120 个，其中，盲人协会 24 个、聋人协会 24 个、肢残人协会 24 个、智力残疾人及亲友协会 24 个、精神残疾人及亲友协会 24 个。市级专门协会已建比例为 100%，市辖区专门协会已建比例 100%；县（含县级市）级专门协会已建比例为 100%。

九、信息化建设

统计队伍建设进一步加强，各级残联共有 23 名专、兼职统计人员从事残疾人事业统计工作。统计人员业务素质培养普遍得到重视，省级残联举办培训班 1 期，参加培训的人员达到 31 人次。各级残联全面推进网站建设，省残联门户网站同时进行无障碍改造，为更多的残疾人提供信息服务。2013 年省残联开设网站技术培训班 1 期，培训各级残联信息员达 50 人次。

十、综合服务设施

各级残疾人综合服务设施项目建设有所进展，但部分已建成的残疾人综合服务设施存在局限性，如建筑面积不足、功能单一、硬件设施陈旧等，还不具备综合服务能力。截止 2013 年底，全省已投入使用和累计投入使用的项目有 7 个，有 4 个在建项目，6 个项目正在筹建。

2013 年重庆市残疾人事业发展统计公报

2013 年，重庆市残疾人工作认真贯彻落实党的十八大、十八届三中全会和中国残联第六次全国代表大会、市委四届三次、四次全会精神，按照市残联第四次代表大会确定的“12345”工作总目标，着眼于让残疾人生活更加殷实、精神更加丰富、人格更有尊严，以加快建设残疾人“两个体系”为重点，把保障和改善残疾人民生摆在更加突出位置，为实现残疾人同步小康奠定了坚实基础。

一、残疾人康复工作

加大残疾人康复救助力度，进一步扩大康复服务范围。为 17429 名白内障患者实施复明手术（其中，免费手术 7320 名），为 2611 名低视力患者配用助视器，对 1141 名盲人进行定向行走训练；对 443 名聋儿、2554 名智力残疾人、329 名孤独症儿童、7301 名肢体残疾人进行康复训练；对 221 名贫困肢体残疾儿童实施矫治手术；对 11610 名贫困精神病患者进行医疗救助；为残疾人装配普及型假肢 232 例、矫形器 104 例，供应其它辅助器具 14164 件。

完善康复政策，推进落实《将部分医疗康复项目纳入医疗保险基金支付范围的通知》。制定《重庆市防盲治盲工作规划（2012—2015 年）》、《关于印发重庆市社区康复站建设管理规范的通知》等政策文件。完成国家残疾儿童康复救助“七彩梦行动计划”项目任务。规范康复机构建设，在全国率先实施国家残疾儿童康复救助项目定点机构标准化建设及评估工作。新建 100 个残疾人康复示范社区，5 个区县辅具展示厅。在 10 个区县开展居家康复服务试点，完成 7 个区县“人人享有康复服务”市级初评。

二、残疾人教育工作

残疾人特殊教育不断加强。2013 年，残疾人事业专项彩票公益金助学项目，共为 194 名家庭经济困难的残疾儿童享受普惠性学前教育提供了资助。全市也积极多渠道争取资金支持，对 64 名残疾儿童给予学前教育资助。

全市共开办特殊教育普通高中 2 所，在校生 201 人；其中聋高中 1 所，在校生 8 人；盲高中 1 所，在校生 193 人。残疾人中等职业教育机构 5 个，在校生 247 人。有 194 名残疾人被普通高等院校录取，20 名残疾人进入特殊教育学院学习。

三、残疾人就业工作

残疾人就业覆盖面不断扩大。2013 年全市通过多种形式新安排城镇残疾人就业 6937 人，其中，集中就业 2659 人，按比例安排就业 1391 人，公益性岗位就业 157 人，个体就业及其它形式灵活就业 2354 人，辅助性就业 376 人。全市城镇实际在业人数 13.8 万；50.1 万农村残疾人稳定实现就业，其中 40.5 万残疾人从事农业生产劳动。

开展残疾人职业技能培训，共兴办职业培训基地 32 个，其中残联兴办 5 个，依托社会机构兴办 27 个，0.5 万城镇残疾人接受了职业培训。

盲人按摩事业稳定发展，按摩机构迅速增长。2013 年度培训盲人保健按摩人员 298 名、盲人医疗按摩人员 143 名；保健按摩机构达到 703 个，医疗按摩机构达到 9 个。

四、社会保障工作

2013 年新型农村和城镇居民社会养老保险进一步扩大覆盖面，已有 13.3 万城镇残疾人参加了城镇居民社会养老保险，参保率 77.9%。在 60 岁以下的参保残疾人中有 2.4 万重度残疾人，其中 2.4 万得到了政府的参保扶助，代缴补贴比例达到 100%。有 4 万非重度残疾人也享受了全额或部分代缴的优惠政策。领取养老金待遇的人数达到 5.3 万人。

新型农村社会养老保险方面，共有 30.1 万残疾人参加了新型农村社会养老保险，参保率 73.7%。

在 60 周岁以下的参保残疾人中有重度残疾人 6.1 万，其中 6.1 万得到了政府的参保扶助，代缴补贴比例达到 100%。有 6.7 万非重度残疾人也享受了全额或部分代缴的优惠政策。享受养老金待遇的人数达到 13.2 万人。

城镇残疾职工参加社会保险人数达到 7.3 万，城镇残疾居民参加基本医疗保险达到 17.5 万人，城镇 6.3 万和农村 12.8 万残疾人纳入最低生活保障范围；城镇集中供养残疾人和农村五保供养残疾人分别达到 3696 人和 18072 人；7604 人和 8065 人符合条件的城乡残疾人分别享受了稳定的生活补贴和护理补贴。8.5 万城乡残疾人得到了其他救助救济。

残疾人托养服务工作规范推进，残疾人托养服务机构达到 97 个，共为 2034 残疾人提供了托养服务。其中寄宿制托养服务机构 19 个；日间照料机构 52 个；综合性托养服务机构 26 个。接受居家托养服务的残疾人达到 1.5 万人。

五、残疾人扶贫开发工作

2013 年全市加大扶持残疾人力度，贫困残疾人生产生活状况得到进一步改善。全市共扶持贫困残疾人 4.7 万人，其中 2.3 万人通过扶贫开发实际脱贫；接受实用技术培训的残疾人达到 1.3 万人次。

康复扶贫贴息贷款扶持 1352 名农村残疾人，1209 个单位和 13904 人对贫困残疾人开展结对帮扶。残疾人扶贫基地达到 100 个，安置 1378 名残疾人就业，扶持带动 2097 人。

全市加大资金投入，完成 3355 户农村贫困残疾人危房改造，共投入危房资金 5772.8 万元，3655 名残疾人受益。

六、残疾人宣传文化体育工作

加大宣传工作力度。2013 年，市级中央媒体采用稿件 40 件，主要新闻媒体刊播稿件 280 件，报刊专版 8 个，残疾人专题广播节目 1 个，电视手语新闻栏目 1 个，市级残疾人事业新闻宣传促进会 1 个；区级主要新闻媒体刊播稿件 800 件，报刊专版 66 个，残疾人专题广播节目 12 个，电视手语新闻栏目 10 个，建立区级新促会 1 个。

全市公共图书馆设立盲文及盲人有声读物阅览室已达到 20 个，举办残疾人文化周 109 场，举办残疾人文化艺术类比赛及展览 38 次，已成立残疾人艺术团队 9 个。

举办市级残疾人体育健身活动 3 次，参加人数 1780 人次，残疾人体育示范点 10 个，残疾人体育健身指导员 85 人，残疾人体育比赛 1 次，参与的残疾人运动员 65 人次，残疾人体育训练基地 5 个，聘任教练员 15 人。

举办区级残疾人体育健身活动 336 次，参加人数 3.2 万人，残疾人体育示范点 104 个，残疾人体育健身指导员 427 人。

七、残疾人维权工作

继续完善残疾人法律法规，开展法律服务、法律援助和法制宣传，维护残疾人合法权益。2013 年，全市制定或修改保障残疾人权益的规范性文件 1 件。县级以上人大进行《残疾人保障法》执法检查和专题调研 21 次；政协进行视察和专题调研 29 次。开展普法宣传教育活动 191 次，7.1 万人参加；举办法律培训班 43 个，0.4 万人参加。

截至 2013 年底，成立残疾人法律救助工作协调机构 41 个，建立残疾人法律救助工作站 15 个，办理案件 676 件，建立残疾人法律援助中心（工作站）41 个，办理案件 1271 件，有力地促进了法律救助和法律援助工作。

残疾人参政议政工作得到加强，各级残联协助人大代表、政协委员提出议案、建议、提案 71 件，办理议案、建议、提案 64 件。

无障碍建设法规、标准进一步完善。全市共出台了 6 个无障碍建设与管理法规、规章；38 个区县系统开展无障碍建设；开展无障碍建设检查 64 次，无障碍培训 1072 人次；为 3952 个贫困残疾人家庭实施了无障碍改造；为 4258 名残疾人发放了残疾人机动轮椅车燃油补贴。

各级残联共处理残疾人群众来信 279 余件，接待残疾人群众来访 4291 人次。

八、残疾人组织建设工作

2013 年，全市基层残疾人组织规范化建设逐步完善，县（区）、乡（镇、街道）、村（社区）三级网络整体推进。全市已建乡镇（街道）残联 1012 个，已建率达到 100%，选聘残疾人专职委员 946 名；已建社区（村）残协 1.1 万个，已建率达到 100%，选聘残疾人专职委员 10255 名。

各级残联实有人员已达 0.2 万人。举办培训班 7514 期，培训机关干部、协会干部及残疾人专职委员 1.6 万人次。

建立各类残疾人专门协会 190 个，市辖区专门协会已建比例 94.3%；县级专门协会已建比例为 95.8%。

九、残疾人综合服务设施建设

残疾人综合服务设施建设得到进一步发展。截止到 2013 年底，全市已竣工并投入使用的各级残疾人综合服务设施 28 个，总建设规模 8.54 万平方米，总投资 25，116.24 万元；已竣工并投入使用的各级残疾人康复设施 4 个，总建设规模 0.46 万平方米，总投资 1，200 万元；已竣工并投入使用的各级残疾人托养服务设施 1 个，总建设规模 0.01 万平方米，总投资 197.89 万元。

十、残疾人事业统计与信息化建设

统计队伍建设进一步加强，全市共有 49 名专、兼职统计人员从事残疾人事业统计工作，统计人员业务素质培养普遍得到重视，举办培训班 1 期，参加培训的人员达到 50 人次。

全面推进网站建设，目前市残联和 37 个区县残联已开通网站。开设网站技术培训班 1 期，培训各级残联信息员达 55 人次。

2013 年四川省残疾人事业发展统计公报

2013 年，在残疾人事业“十二五”期间蓬勃发展的契机下，在省委、省政府的领导下，在中国残联的指导和支持下，在全社会的关爱下，我省残疾人事业延续了良好的发展势头，各方面工作取得了新进步、新成效，残疾人得到了更多的实惠。现根据我省 2013 年度残疾人事业统计数据和实际情况，进行分析，并公报如下：

一、康复

1. 积极推进残疾人社区康复工作。截至 2013 年底，共在 31 个市辖区和 100 个县（市）开展了社区康复工作，累计已建社区康复站的社区总数达 7000 个，配备 1.53 万名社区康复协调员。

2. 进一步完善视力康复机构，通过实施一批重点康复工程，使各类视力残疾人得到不同程度的康复。截至年底，开展视力残疾康复机构总数达到 23 个，完成白内障复明手术 3.78 万例；为 2.44 万名贫困白内障患者免费施行复明手术；为 5640 名低视力患者配用助视器，培训低视力儿童家长 565 名，有效开展家庭康复训练；对 6878 名盲人进行了定向行走训练。

3. 大力推进听力语言康复机构规范化管理，完善基层服务网络。已建设省级听力语言康复机构 1 个，基层听力语言康复机构 31 个。年度新收训聋儿 859 名，在训聋儿 1305 名；规范聋儿家长学校，开展家庭训练，共培训聋儿家长 1563 名；开展各级各类听力语言康复专业技术人员培训，共培训专业人员 168 人。

4. 肢体残疾康复工作成效显著。截至年底，全省开展肢体残疾康复训练服务机构达到 57 个，其中，省级康复机构 1 个，地市级、县级康复机构 56 个；培训各级各类肢体残疾康复人员 1360 人次；全国共对 2.23 万名肢体残疾者实施康复训练；实施救助项目资助 5285 名脑瘫儿童进行机构康复训练，资助 556 名贫困肢体残疾儿童实施矫治手术。

5. 稳步推进智力残疾康复工作。截至年底，全省开展智力残疾康复训练服务的机构达到 50 个，其中，省级康复机构 1 个，地市级、县级康复机构 49 个；培训各级各类智力残疾康复人员 1008 人次；全国共对 6110 名智力残疾人进行康复训练；实施救助项目资助 1100 名智力残疾儿童进行机构康复训练，同时培训儿童家长。

6. 大力推广“社会化、综合性、开放式”精神病防治康复工作。2013 年，共在 143 个市县开展精神病防治康复工作，对 40.12 万重性精神病患者进行综合防治康复，监护率达到 78.92%，显好率达到 61.66%，社会参与率达到 34.86%，肇事率 0.43%；解除关锁 316 人；对 18815 名贫困精神病患者进行医疗救助。

7. 加强残疾人辅助器具服务体系建设，深入开展辅助器具供应服务。全年共为残疾人减免费用供应辅助器具 8.09 万件，其中装配假肢 1597 例、矫形器 608 例，验配助视器 5532 件。

8. 加大残疾儿童筛查工作力度。共有 71 个县的 82 个医疗卫生机构陆续开展了残疾儿童筛查工作，年度新诊断 0-6 岁残疾儿童 4256 人。

二、教育

2013 年，我省残疾人受教育权得到了更好地保障，进一步提高了残疾人整体素质和平等参与社会的能力。

1. 本年度，残疾人事业专项彩票公益金助学项目共为我省家庭经济困难的残疾儿童享受普惠性学前教育提供资助 805 人次；全省各地也积极多渠道争取资金支持，对 1107 名残疾儿童提供了学前教育资助。

2. 截至 2013 年底，全省已开办特殊教育普通高中班（部）13 个，在校生 219 人；其中聋高中 5 个，在校生 161 人；盲高中 1 个，在校生 58 人。残疾人中等职业学校（班）10 个，在校生 249 人，毕业生 65 人，其中 9 人获得职业资格证书。有 295 名残疾人被普通高等院校录取。

3. 截至2013年底，全省未入学适龄残疾儿童总数为4436人，其中视力残疾儿童381人，听力残疾儿童310人，言语残疾儿童322人，智力残疾儿童1295人，肢体残疾儿童1548人，精神残疾儿童105人，多重残疾儿童475人。

三、就业

1. 2013年，全省残疾人就业工作取得稳步进展。城镇新增就业残疾人3.19万人，其中，集中就业1.06万人，按比例安排就业6692人，公益性岗位就业1082人，个体就业及其它形式灵活就业1.26万人，辅助性就业871人。城镇就业残疾人数达到26.91万人；农村残疾人在业人数达到180.51万，其中143.66万残疾人从事农业生产劳动。

2. 截至2013年底，全省残疾人职业培训基地达到517个，其中残联兴办240个，依托社会机构兴办277个，3.12万人次城镇残疾人接受了职业培训。

3. 盲人按摩事业稳定发展。全年共培训盲人保健按摩人员1064名、盲人医疗按摩人员58名；保健按摩机构达到1381个，医疗按摩机构达到42个。

四、社会保障

2013年度全省残疾人社会保障状况保持平稳，残疾人参加新型农村和城镇居民社会养老保险工作取得新进展。

1. 截至2013年底，已有26.41万城镇残疾人参加了城镇居民社会养老保险，参保率71.40%。在60岁以下的参保残疾人中有4.41万重度残疾人，其中4.37万得到了政府的参保扶助，代缴补贴比例达到98.98%。有2.08万非重度残疾人也享受了全额或部分代缴的优惠政策。领取养老金待遇的人数达到7.15万人。

2. 新型农村社会养老保险方面，共有145.76万残疾人参加了新型农村社会养老保险，参保率79.02%。在60周岁以下的参保残疾人中有重度残疾人24.82万，其中24.80万得到了政府的参保扶助，代缴补贴比例达到99.91%。有8.25万非重度残疾人也享受了全额或部分代缴的优惠政策。享受养老金待遇的人数达到33.89万。

3. 城镇残疾职工参加社会保险人数达到13.26万，城镇残疾居民参加基本医疗保险达到33.66万，有15.97万城镇残疾人和73.80万农村残疾人纳入了最低生活保障范围；城镇集中供养残疾人和农村五保供养残疾人分别达到了8141人和5.29万人；4.43万城镇残疾人和1.29万农村人分别享受了稳定的生活补贴和护理补贴。此外还有21.99万城乡残疾人得到了其他救助救济。

4. 残疾人托养服务工作规范推进。全省残疾人托养服务机构达到177个，其中寄宿制托养服务机构39个；日间照料机构106个；综合性托养服务机构32个。接受居家托养服务的残疾人达到4.80万人。

五、扶贫

2013年，全省残疾人扶贫开发工作进一步推进，贫困残疾人生产生活状况得到进一步改善。

1. 本年度共扶持贫困残疾人25.39万名，其中12.12万人通过扶贫开发实际脱贫；11.15万人接受了实用技术培训。

2. 通过康复扶贫贴息贷款扶持农村残疾人3031名；已建立结对帮扶单位4962个，全年共结对帮扶残疾人2.69万名；已建立残疾人扶持基地343个，全年共安置5.3万残疾人就业。

3. 2013年，全省共完成3046户农村贫困残疾人危房改造，各地投入危房资金5238.37万元，使得3660名残疾人受益。

六、维权

2013年，全省残疾人维权组织建设得到加强，残疾人事业法律法规体系得以进一步完善。

1. 2013年，制定或修改了关于残疾人的专门法规、规章省级1件、地市级1件；制定或修改保障残疾人权益的规范性文件省级3件、地市级4件。县级以上人大进行《残疾人保障法》执法检查和专题调研41次；政协进行视察和专题调研60次。全省共开展普法宣传教育活动644次，有11.37万人参加；举办法律培训班121个，有6600人参加。

2. 截至2013年底，全省已建残疾人法律救助工作协调机构86个，残疾人法律救助工作站44个，全年共办理案件240件，已建残疾人法律援助中心（工作站）139个，全年共办理案件1074件，有力地促进了法律救助和法律援助工作。

3. 残疾人参政议政工作得到加强，一年来，各级残联协助人大代表、政协委员提出议案、建议、提案 102 件，办理议案、建议、提案 73 件。

4. 无障碍建设法规、标准进一步完善。共出台了 23 个省、地市、县级无障碍建设与管理法规、规章；全省有 35 个市、县、区系统开展无障碍建设；开展无障碍建设检查 263 次，无障碍培训 4000 人次；为 1.27 万个贫困残疾人家庭实施了无障碍改造；为 2.83 万残疾人发放了残疾人机动轮椅车燃油补贴。

5. 2013 年，全省各级残联共处理残疾人群众来信 5569 余件，接待残疾人群众来访 3.59 万人次，其中集体访 43 批次、874 人次。

七、宣传文化

2013 年，全省残疾人宣传工作实现了进一步发展，残疾人事业的社会影响力和关注度得到更大提升，营造了有利于残疾人事业发展的舆论环境。残疾人文化生活更加丰富活跃，残疾人受到社会广泛关注并更加全面地参与到社会生活当中。

1. 一年来，省级中央媒体采用稿件 15 件，主要新闻媒体刊播稿件数 100 件。截至年底，省级宣传残疾人事业的报刊专版已有 15 个，残疾人专题广播节目达到 5 个，电视手语新闻栏目达到 5 个，省级残疾人事业新闻宣传促进会 1 个。地市级主要新闻媒体刊播稿件数 2294 件，报刊专版已有 94 个，残疾人专题广播节目 62 个，电视手语新闻栏目 5 个。

2. 全省公共图书馆设立盲文及盲人有声读物阅览室已达到 38 个，举办残疾人文化周 70 个，举办残疾人文化艺术类比赛及展览 79 场次，已成立残疾人艺术团队 4 个。

八、体育

1. 2013 年，共组织省级残疾人体育健身活动 5 次，参加人数 4000 人；已建省级残疾人体育示范点 5 个，残疾人体育健身指导员 31 人；举办省级残疾人体育比赛 1 次，参与的残疾人运动员 72 人次；省级残疾人体育训练基地达到 5 个，聘任教练员 33 人。

2. 共组织地市级残疾人体育健身活动 74 次，参加人数 5000 人；已建地市级残疾人体育示范点 113 个，残疾人体育健身指导员达到 1604 人。

九、组织建设

1. 截至 2013 年，省级残联领导班子均配备了残疾人理事长或副理事长；有 10 个地市级残联在领导班子中配备了残疾人理事长或副理事长；96 个县级残联机关配备了残疾人干部。

2. 全省已建乡镇（街道）残联 4302 个，已建率达到 92.46%，选聘残疾人专职委员 4026 名；已建社区（村）残协 4.36 万个，已建率达到 85.24%，选聘残疾人专职委员 3.18 万名。

3. 2013 年，各级残联共举办培训班 5600 期，培训机关干部、协会干部及残疾人专职委员 7.89 万人次。

4. 全省已建立省级以下各类残疾人专门协会 933 个，市级专门协会已建比例为 100%，市辖区专门协会已建比例 99.56%；县（含县级市）级专门协会已建比例为 87.54%。

十、信息化

1. 2013 年，全省统计队伍建设进一步加强。全省各级残联共有 185 名专、兼职统计人员从事残疾人事业统计工作，统计人员业务素质培养普遍得到重视；共举办地市级培训班 30 期，参加培训的人员达到 651 人次。

2. 全面推进网站建设，省级残联已开通无障碍公众服务网，有 17 个地市级残联网站和 91 个县级残联网站也已开通；全省各级残联共开设网站技术培训班 30 期，培训各级残联信息员达 892 人次。

3. 截至 2013 年底，全省各级残联共有 283 名专业技术人员从事信息化工作。

十一、服务设施建设

全省残疾人服务设施建设工作稳步推进。

截至 2013 年底，全省已竣工并投入使用的残疾人综合服务设施达到了 82 个，总建设规模 18.57 万平方米，总投资 52203.40 万元；已竣工并投入使用的残疾人康复设施 25 个，总建设规模 11.25 万平方米，总投资 55821.00 万元；已竣工并投入使用的残疾人托养服务设施 9 个，总建设规模 2.07 万平方米，总投资 4214.74 万元。

2013年贵州省残疾人事业发展统计公报

2013年，在贵州省委、省政府的领导下，在中国残联的指导下，在相关部门的支持下，省残联以残疾人"两个体系"建设为主线，按照突出重点、全面推进的工作思路，扎实开展党的群众教育实践活动、重点推动事关残疾人事业发展全局性、根本性和基础性工作，着力实施一系列民生项目，全面完成各项工作任务，为新起点上推进残疾人事业发展打下了良好基础。根据残疾人事业统计数据和实际情况公报如下:

一、康复工作

与省卫生厅等部门共同印发了《残疾人事业专项彩票公益金康复项目贵州省实施方案》，与省卫生厅共同印发了《贫困精神病患者服药救助项目贵州省配套实施办法》和《贫困精神病患者住院医疗救助项目贵州省配套实施办法》。2013年，继续实施"百万贫困白内障患者复明工程"、"七彩梦行动计划"、 国家和省彩票公益金等项目，19个县的8个医疗卫生机构陆续开展残疾儿童筛查工作，年度新诊断0-6岁残疾儿童534人。完成白内障复明手术1.57万例；为9，220名贫困白内障患者免费施行复明手术；为3807名低视力患者配用助视器，培训低视力儿童家长228名，有效开展家庭康复训练。对2275名盲人进行定向行走训练。已建设省级听力语言康复机构1个，基层听力语言康复机构20个。年度新收训聋儿381名，在训聋儿578名；规范聋儿家长学校，开展家庭训练，共培训聋儿家长759名；开展各级各类听力语言康复专业技术人员培训，共培训专业人员96人。全省共对1813肢体残疾者实施康复训练；实施救助项目资助398名脑瘫儿童进行机构康复训练，资助218名贫困肢体残疾儿童实施矫治手术。 建立了1个省级孤独症儿童康复训练机构；309名孤独症儿童在各级机构进行了康复训练。为残疾人减免费用供应辅助器具19289件，其中装配假肢813例、矫形器223例，验配助视器5527件。

二、教育就业工作

已开办特殊教育普通高中班（部）6个，在校生212人。有339名残疾人被普通高等院校录取。有未入学适龄残疾儿童少年4427人，其中视力残疾儿童666人，听力残疾儿童564人，言语残疾儿童424人，智力残疾儿童1006人，肢体残疾儿童1026人，精神残疾儿童240人，多重残疾儿童501人。

城镇新就业残疾人5928人，其中，集中就业1149人，按比例安排就业1379人，公益性岗位就业176人，个体就业及其它形式灵活就业3214人，辅助性就业10人。城镇就业人数8.05万；79.15万农村残疾人在业，其中62.46万残疾人从事农业生产劳动。

三、社会保障工作

2013年9.40万城镇残疾人参加了城镇居民社会养老保险，参保率68.65%。在60岁以下的参保残疾人中有1.22万重度残疾人，其中1.14万得到了政府的参保扶助，代缴补贴比例达到93.87%。有0.71万非重度残疾人也享受了全额或部分代缴的优惠政策。领取养老金待遇的人数达到5.92万人。新型农村社会养老保险方面，共有42.74万残疾人参加了新型农村社会养老保险，参保率62.12%。在60周岁以下的参保残疾人中有重度残疾人6.77万，其中6.77万得到了政府的参保扶助，代缴补贴比例达到99.93%。有2.29万非重度残疾人也享受了全额或部分代缴的优惠政策。享受养老金待遇的人数达到20.63万人。城镇残疾职工参加社会保险人数达到3.86万，城镇残疾居民参加基本医疗保险达到10.81万人，城镇5.39万和农村44.69万残疾人纳入最低生活保障范围；城镇集中供养残疾人和农村五保供养残疾人分别达到1800人和12688人。

四、扶贫工作

2013年7月，省人民政府通过贵州省农村贫困残疾人扶贫开发规划（2011—2020 年）。8 月，会同省住建厅联合下发了《关于优先支持农村贫困残疾人家庭危房改造的通知》，在新一轮的农村危房改造中贫困残疾人将享受更加优惠的政策。10.69 万贫困残疾人得到扶持，其中 6.89 万人通过扶贫开发实际脱贫；接受实用技术培训的残疾人达到 1.37 万人次。康复扶贫贴息贷款扶持 454 农村残疾人，585 个单位和 18442 个人对贫困残疾人开展结对帮扶。残疾人扶贫基地达到 134 个，安置 975 残疾人就业，扶持带动 3548 残疾人。完成 2306 户农村贫困残疾人危房改造，各地投入危房资金 1，224.74 万元，3226 名残疾人受益。

五、维权工作

县级以上人大进行《残疾人保障法》执法检查和专题调研 19 次；政协进行视察和专题调研 7 次。开展普法宣传教育活动 242 次，3.23 万人参加。各级残联协助人大代表、政协委员提出议案、建议、提案 43 件，办理议案、建议、提案 20 件。为 1.67 万残疾人发放了残疾人机动轮椅车燃油补贴。各级残联共处理残疾人群众来信 2052 余件，接待残疾人群众来访 8468 人次，其中集体访 30 批次、404 人次。

六、宣传文化工作

贵州电视台手语新闻共播出 50 期，广播电台《同在蓝天下》专题节目全年共播出 96 期，《贵州日报》刊发专版 3 次、各类残疾人事业发展新闻 40 余条，在“发扬人道主义，发展残疾人事业”专栏共刊发相关文章 50 余篇。同时编辑完成《贵州残联》杂志 6 期、简报 15 期、贵州残联网站发布消息 960 余条，编印了《发展中的贵州残疾人事业》宣传画册。成功举办第八届贵州省残疾人艺术汇演，共产生金奖 8 个，银奖 12 个，铜奖 16 个。组团参加第八届全国残疾人艺术汇演（甘肃赛区），我省选送的 12 个参赛节目共获得一等奖 4 个、二等奖 5 个、三等奖 2 个，获得创作奖 6 个，并以团体总分排名第三的优异成绩荣获团体二等奖。

七、体育工作

与省体育局、省教育厅、省人社厅联合下发了《关于切实解决优秀残疾人运动员就学和就业工作的实施意见》，为我省解决残疾人运动员特别是优秀残疾人退役运动员的就学、就业工作提供了政策支持。在第二十二届夏季听障奥林匹克运动会羽毛球女子双打比赛中，我省选手获得亚军；在 2013 年世界轮椅与截肢人运动会上，我省运动员夺得 2 金 2 银；在亚洲青年残疾人运动会中，我省运动员获得 1 金 1 银，还和另一名中国选手配对夺得 1 银。2013 年组织我省残疾人运动员参加了全国残疾人游泳、羽毛球、田径、举重等单项赛事，共获金牌 25 枚、银牌 27 枚、铜牌 14 枚。

八、组织建设工作

认真抓好残联系统班子换届工作，全省 9 个市（州）残联全部召开了换届会议，领导班子已全部配备残疾人领导干部；83 个县（市、区）完成的换届工作。部分县（市、区）将残疾人专职委员纳入公益性岗位，大部分县（市、区）将残疾人专职委员的补贴纳入县级财政预算；创新工作方式，采取整村推进、上门办证等措施方便残疾人办证，目前，全省第二代残疾人证办证率达 34%。

九、信息化工作

2013 年，在仁怀市、遵义县启动了盲人读屏软件补贴工作；完成了省残联机关协同办公 OA 建设，为机关办公自动化搭建了重要平台；完成了省残联网站无障碍改造及改版招投标。我省残疾人工作主要数据指标继续编入省统计局、国家统计局贵州调查总队编制的《贵州省统计年鉴》；继续开展统计工作评价，推动全省统计工作机制的建立和数据质量的提高。

2013年云南省残疾人事业发展统计公报

2013年，云南省残联认真贯彻落实党的十八大、十八届三中全会精神和云南省委第九届七次会议精神、中国残联第六次全国代表大会精神，在云南省委、省政府的坚强领导下，省残联新一届领导班子全心全意为群众，聚精会神抓工作，开拓创新谋发展。全省残疾人事业按照省委、省政府确定的“翻两番、增三倍、促跨越、奔小康”的总体部署，以党的群众路线教育实践活动为动力，着力推进残疾人社会保障体系和服务体系建设，切实维护残疾人的合法权益，不断改善残疾人的生产生活状况，各项工作取得显著成绩。

一、残疾人康复

2013年云南省残疾人康复工作紧紧围绕省政府三件惠民实事，实施了3万例白内障患者复明手术的“光明工程”、救助8.3万民精神病患者的“重性精神病患者治疗康复救助”和救助2600名残疾儿童的“康复工程”，使这三件惠民实事深入民心，让残疾人朋友得到了切实的实惠和帮助。

2013年全省共实施“光明工程”免费白内障复明手术35327例，完成任务数的118%，该项工程全省各级残联紧密合作，云南省残联主要负责白内障患者的筛查和转运工作，筛查任务为36000例，完成初筛眼疾患者77299人，复筛合格人数42915人，完成率为119%，全面超额完成了“光明工程”白内障患者筛查任务。开展重性精神病患者治疗康复救助，全省在专科医院、社区、居家康复患者85916人，完成目标任务的103.5%；实施0-6岁残疾儿童康复工程救助3202人，完成任务数的123%。确保了省政府惠民实事任务目标的完成，给贫困白内障患者带来了实实在在的利益。

截止到2013年底，全省已有11个市辖区、117个县（市）中的13683个社区开展了残疾人社区康复工作，全省共有11649名社区康复协调员接受培训，建立了42.85万人的康复服务档案，有14.42万人接受社区康复服务，上述数据相比2012年均有大幅增长，其中接受社区康复服务人数增长128%，社区康复覆盖面进一步扩大。

图1　2009-2013年云南省白内障复明手术完成情况（例）

围绕初步实现残疾人“人人享有康复服务”的目标。将常规康复工作与康复重点项目有机融合，将对外合作交流康复项目融入到常规康复工作中，统筹安排，不断扩大残疾人康复的受益面。全省培训社区康复员11649名；为低视力者配用助视器6126件；对2910名盲人进行盲人定向行走训练；对9182名成年肢体残疾人开展社区家庭康复训练；为15271名贫困精神病人提供医疗救助，监护精神病患者100203名。完成辅助器具配发46816件，为2102名残疾人装配假肢、矫形器。

加强省级聋儿康复机构建设，完善聋儿康复网络。共对675名聋儿进行了听力语言康复训练，规范聋儿家长学校，开展家庭训练，共培训聋儿家长1135名。

大力推广“社会化、综合性、开放式”精神病防治康复工作。2013年，在全省123个市县开展精神病防治康复工作，覆盖人口4179.08万人，对15.24万重度精神病患者进行综合防治康复，监护数10.02万，监护率达到65.74%，显好数6.08万，显好率达到39.9%，社会参与率达到32.7%，肇事率0.14%；解除关锁71人；对15271名贫困精神病患者进行医疗救助。

深入开展辅助器具供应服务，全面推进普及型假肢装配，截止到2013年底，累计建立辅助器具供应服务机构51个，为残疾人免费供应辅助器具

46816 件，其中装配普及型假肢 1228 例，装配矫形器 874 例。

全年开展肢体残疾康复训练服务的机构达到 32 个，对 406 名贫困肢体残疾儿童实施矫治手术、装配了矫形器等辅助器具，进行了术后康复训练；对 11409 名肢体残疾人进行了康复训练，其中：脑瘫儿童系统康复训练 492 人，肢体残疾儿童社区、家庭康复 1735 人，成年肢体残疾人社区、家庭康复 9182 人。

全年开展智力残疾康复训练服务的机构达到 21 个；对 3800 名 0-14 岁的智力残疾儿童进行了康复训练，不同程度地开展了智力残疾儿童早期康复训练与服务。

二、残疾人教育

云南省残疾人教育工作有新的发展。残疾儿童少年义务教育稳步发展。全省特教学校发展到 53 所，在校接受义务教育的残疾学生 1.7 万余人，入学率达 88%。参加高考的残疾学生 455 名，录取 360 名，录取率达 79%。开创我省残疾人高等教育新局面，启动与云南开放大学联合创办“华夏特教学院”的工作。2013 年 9 月，我省首个特殊教育本科专业在昆明学院开班招生，45 名学生将成为我省特殊教育的骨干。努力做好扶残助学工作，继续争取“通向明天——交通银行残疾青少年助学计划”及彩票公益金助学项目资金，完成“交通银行大学生励志奖”、“交通银行特教园丁奖”相关工作。

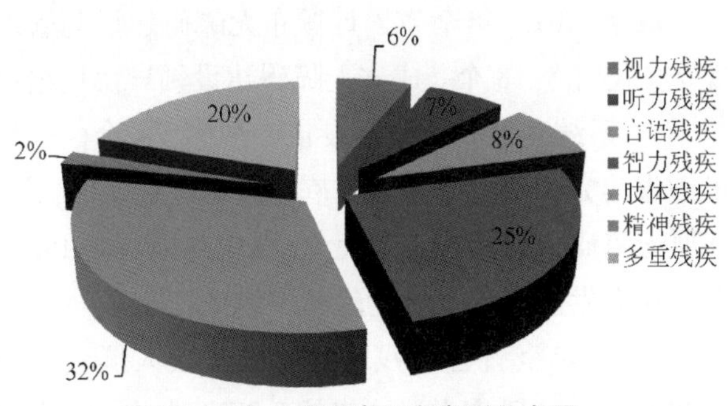

图 2　未入学残疾儿童类型分布图

未入学适龄残疾少年儿童总数 4878 人，其中视力残疾 306 人，听力残疾 316 人，言语残疾 392 人，智力残疾 1241 人，肢体残疾 1577 人，精神残疾 95 人，多重残疾 951 人。

2013 年全省有 429 名残疾学生达到普通高等院校录取分数线，其中录取 413 人，录取率为 96.27%。

全省残疾人中等职业教育机构有 5 个，在校生 580 人，毕业生 245 人，其中获得职业资格证书 90 人。

三、残疾人就业与扶贫

2013 年云南省积极推进《云南省残疾人就业规定》立法相关工作。强化 2013 年按比例安排残疾人就业工作，残疾人就业保障金征收工作进一步规范。全省征收就业保障金 3.36 亿元。开展 2013 年就业援助月活动。建立残疾人就业培训申报审核制度。城镇残疾人实际在业 76222 人，当年新增就业 4485 人，接受职业培训 8451 人。福利企业招用残疾职工 16618 人。农村残疾人从事农业生产劳动 841889 人，其他形式就业 130627 人。

培训盲人保健按摩 597 人；医疗按摩人员 88 人，保健按摩机构达到 656 个，医疗按摩机构达到 11 个；有 56 人通过医疗按摩人员初级职称评审；扶持特困盲人按摩师就业 373 人。

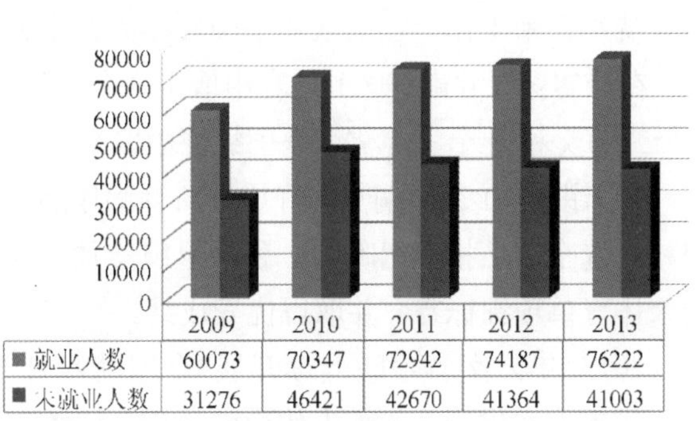

	2009	2010	2011	2012	2013
■就业人数	60073	70347	72942	74187	76222
■未就业人数	31276	46421	42670	41364	41003

图 3　2009-2013 年云南省城镇残疾人就业情况表（人）

城镇残疾职工参加社会保险人数达到 5.78 万人，其中参加养老保险人数 3.80 万人，参加医疗保险人数 3.49 万人；城镇残疾居民参加医疗保险达到 11.50 万人；城乡 65.35 万名残疾人纳入最低生活保障范围；城镇已纳入最低生活保障 8.07 万人，城镇集中供养和其他救助救济 2.09 万人；农村已纳入最低生活保障 57.28 万人。

寄宿制托养机构 17 个，托养残疾人 674 人；日间照料和综合托养机构合计 26 个，托养残疾人 766 人；本年度享受居家托养服务残疾人 20382 人。

2013 年度扶持贫困残疾人户 5.95 万户，扶持 8.42 万人，脱贫 3.30 万人，返贫 1.59 万人，接受实用技术培训的残疾人 4.37 万人次。

结对帮扶单位2199个,结对帮扶个人24839人;建立残疾人扶贫基地184个,安置残疾人就业2371人,扶持带动残疾人16921人。

完成6435户农村贫困残疾人危房改造,受益残疾人7270人。

四、残疾人宣传文化体育

2013年全省各级残联广泛依托省、州（市）级报刊、广播电台、电视台、网站等公共媒体，广泛宣传残疾人事业，为残疾人"两个体系"建设营造良好的社会环境。以"全国助残日"、"国际残疾人日"、"残疾人文化周"、省残联六次代表大会等为契机，精心组织协调主要媒体开展系列主题宣传活动；注重实效，加强基层残疾人文化建设。以开展城市社区和农村乡镇残疾人文化活动为主要形式，积极协调当地文化部门共同在残疾人相对集中的社区、残疾人服务机构、特殊教育学校、福利企业以及各种公共文化服务场所因地制宜地组织残疾人开展活动；认真组织第七届全省残疾人艺术汇演，加强残疾人特殊艺术工作。在第八届全国残疾人艺术汇演中，在分赛区（甘肃赛区）比赛中取得3个一等奖、4个二等奖和3个三等奖，全国综评中取得2个金奖、3个银奖和2个铜奖的好成绩；舞蹈作品《心恋》入选全国汇报演出晚会。积极组织参加全国残疾人体育单项锦标赛，并取得优异成绩。

2013年云南省残联继续开展"全国助残日"活动、残疾人文化周、残疾人体育健身周、残疾人文化进社区等群众性残疾人文化体育活动，推进残疾人体育健身指导员培训和自强健身示范点建设。文山、怒江等地积极开展富有地方特色的残疾人文化体育活动。

2013年省级主要新闻媒体刊播残疾人事业稿件数237件，报刊专版14个，残疾人专题广播栏目1个，电视手语新闻栏目1个，电视公益广告片1个，建立省级新促会1个；地市级主要新闻媒体刊播稿件数1，179件，报刊专版42个，残疾人专题广播栏目14个，电视手语新闻栏目7个，建立地市级新促会9个。

省级和地市级公共图书馆设立盲文及盲人有声读物阅览室已达到13个，举办残疾人文化周72场次，举办残疾人文化艺术类比赛及展览12个，已成立残疾人艺术团队11个。

省残联开展残疾人体育健身活动2次，参加人数1，237人，残疾人体育示范点8个，残疾人体育健身指导员95人，聘任教练员18人。

地市级残联开展残疾人体育健身活动39次，参加人次1，469人，建立残疾人体育示范点12个，培训残疾人体育健身指导员43人。

五、残疾人维权

2013年积极指导各州（市）健全维权机构。177名残疾人、残疾人亲友和残疾人工作者进入县级以上人大、政协参政议政，共提出议案提案49件，办理议案提案30件。认真办理省人大代表建议、省政协委员的提案和其他信访案件，争取残疾人合理诉求得到满足。全省批准建立6个州（市）、6个县（区）省级残疾人法律救助站。完成云南省2013年度全国残疾人状况监测相关工作。省级安排完成400户贫困残疾人家庭无障碍改造，每户补贴6000元；配套国家完成400户贫困残疾人家庭无障碍改造，每户配套2500元。

2013年全省各级残联开展普法宣传教育活动261次，参加人数2.79万人；开展法律培训班46次，参加人数2574人。

国家批准建立在我省的2个残疾人法律救助工作站，2013年办理案件10件；全省累计建立残疾人法律援助中心（工作站）134个，2013年办理案件836件。

截至2013年全省累计颁布无障碍建设与管理规定、政府令18个，成立无障碍建设领导协调组织37个，系统开展无障碍建设市、县达74个。2013年全省共完成贫困残疾人家庭无障碍改造1241户，开展无障碍建设检查145次；2013年各地共向19376名残疾人发放残疾人机动轮椅车燃油补贴。

2013年全省各级残联共受理残疾人群众来信3699件，接待残疾人群众来访2.27万人次，其中集体访77批次，582人次。

六、残疾人组织建设

全省2013年各级残联共有工作人员3532人；所有的县级残联均已计划单列并实现规范化建设达

标；全省建有乡（镇、街道）残联 1360 个，共配备乡镇、街道残联理事长和选聘残疾人专职委员数 1919 人；在 12668 个村和 1440 个社区建立残协 14012 个，选聘残疾人专职委员 13132 人。

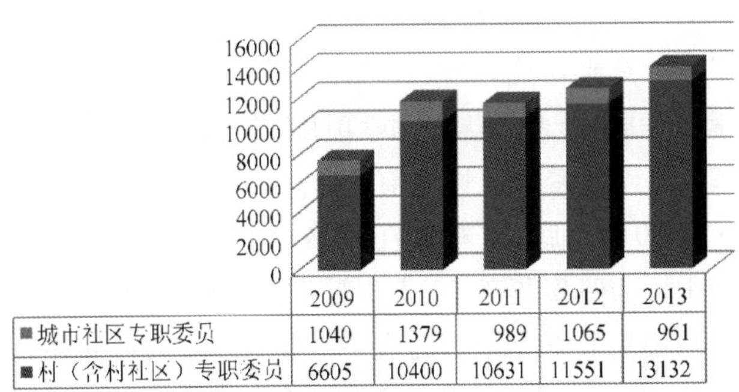

	2009	2010	2011	2012	2013
■城市社区专职委员	1040	1379	989	1065	961
■村（含村社区）专职委员	6605	10400	10631	11551	13132

图 4　2009-2013 年城乡社区（村）专职委员聘用情况（人）

全省共建立各类残疾人专门协会 680 个，其中盲人协会 135 个、聋人协会 135 个、肢残人协会 137 个、智力残疾人及亲友协会 130 个、精神残疾人及亲友协会 130 个。

七、信息化建设工作

2013 年云南省残联加大了各地残联门户网站的建设力度，规范基础信息使用管理，积极推动建立与横向政府部门之间信息共享机制。启动了全省残联信息化建设规划和一期项目科研报告编制工作，在信息化建设上力争做到真正惠及云南省广大残疾人和残疾人家庭，有特色、有优势，计划用五年左右的时间建成以“一个数据中心、两个信息资源库、三个应用平台、四级业务覆盖”为基本框架的信息化体系，实现残疾人事业的科学化、规范化、精细化管理，为残疾人两个体系建设提供重要支撑。

统计队伍建设进一步加强，2013 年全省各级残联共有 217 名专、兼职统计人员从事残疾人事业统计工作，统计人员业务素质培养普遍得到重视，省残联举办培训班 1 期，参加培训人员 50 人次；地市级举办培训班 13 期，参加人员 256 人次。

全省各级残联全面推进网站建设，截止到 2013 年底，全省各级残联共计建设网站 48 个。2013 年，全省各级残联共举办网站技术培训班 14 期，培训人员 306 人次。各级残联共有 217 名专业技术人员从事信息化工作。截至 2013 年底，各级残联配备了 1792 台计算机，投入信息化建设经费达 379.41 万元。

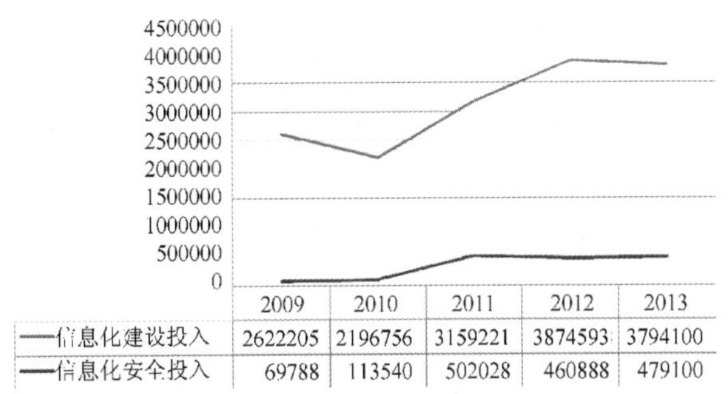

	2009	2010	2011	2012	2013
—信息化建设投入	2622205	2196756	3159221	3874593	3794100
—信息化安全投入	69788	113540	502028	460888	479100

图 5　2009-2013 年信息化建设资金投入情况（元）

2013 年，虽然全省残疾人工作取得了较大的进展，但是与广大残疾人的需求相比，仍然存在很大的差距。在工作中还存在不少困难和问题：一是残疾人事业由于基础较薄弱，在总体上与全省经济社会的快速发展还有不相适应的地方。二是基层组织建设和服务能力仍然比较薄弱，部分县级残联由于经费投入不足，许多工作难以有效开展。三是残疾人康复服务需求量较大，其中多数为贫困残疾人，由于康复经费投入始终处在较低水平，使残疾人得不到切实的康复服务。四是信息化建设工作急需加强，以适应残疾人事业发展需要。这些问题，都有待我们在今后的工作中努力加以解决。

2014 年是深入学习贯彻党的十八届三中全会和省委九届七次全会精神，全面落实中国残联和省残联“六代会”工作部署的开局之年。全省残联系统将按照为民务实清廉的总要求，全心全意为残疾人服务，推动残疾人事业不断发展，为实现全面建成小康社会的宏伟目标做出新的更大的贡献。

2013年西藏自治区残疾人事业发展统计公报

2013年，在自治区党委、政府的正确领导下，在中国残联的大力指导下，全区残疾人工作以构建残疾人社会保障体系和服务体系基本框架为重点，深入实施残疾人事业“十二五”发展纲要，残疾人生活状况得到改善，重点、难点工作有了新的突破。

一、康复

以“人人享有康复服务”为目标，继续实施康复人才培养百千万工程、贫困残疾儿童抢救性康复工程、贫困肢体残疾儿童矫治手术工程、百万贫困白内障患者复明工程等项目，全面完成了中国残联下达的2013年度康复工作各项指标和《西藏自治区残疾人康复“十二五”实施方案》中2013年度的任务。

社区康复：截至2013年底，在1个市辖区和11个县开展了社区康复工作，培训社区康复协调员16人；10个县陆续开展残疾儿童筛查工作，视力残疾康复：2013年度新诊断0-6岁残疾儿童78人；全年完成白内障复明手术909例，为290名贫困白内障患者免费施行复明手术，为20名低视力患者配用助视器，对281名盲人进行定向行走训练；听力语言残疾康复：年度新收训聋儿13名，在训聋儿15名；开展家庭训练，共培训聋儿家长13名。肢体残疾康复：培训各级各类肢体残疾康复人员16人次；全年共对504肢体残疾者实施康复训练；实施救助项目资助90名脑瘫儿童进行机构康复训练，资助25名贫困肢体残疾儿童实施矫治手术。智力残疾康复训练：全年共对176名智力残疾人进行康复训练；实施救助项目资助5名智力残疾儿童进行机构康复训练。辅助器具供应服务：加强残疾人辅助器具服务体系建设，深入开展辅助器具供应服务，为残疾人减免费用供应辅助器具275件，其中装配假肢60例，验配助视器20件。

二、教育

继续开展残疾人特殊教育和残疾儿童随班就读工作，分别在拉萨市、日喀则地区、那曲地区特殊学校开展“彩票公益金助学项目”为家庭经济困难的残疾儿童享受普惠性学前教育提供资助30人次。截止到2013年底，有未入学适龄残疾儿童少年178人，其中视力残疾儿童20人，听力残疾儿童13人，言语残疾儿童26人，智力残疾儿童10人，肢体残疾儿童74人，精神残疾儿童7人，多重残疾儿童28人。

三、就业、扶贫

2013年，城镇新就业残疾人164人，其中，集中就业77人，按比例安排就业53人，公益性岗位就业11人，个体就业及其它形式灵活就业23人。城镇就业人数1530人；1.93万农村残疾人在业，其中1.87万残疾人从事农业生产劳动。盲人按摩事业稳定发展，按摩机构迅速增长。2013年度培训盲人保健按摩人员13名、盲人医疗按摩人员13名；保健按摩机构达到17个，有8人通过医疗按摩人员中级职称评审。

2013年，401名贫困残疾人得到扶持，其中108人通过扶贫开发实际脱贫；接受实用技术培训的残疾人达到165人次。56个单位和169个人对贫困残疾人开展结对帮扶。完成74户农村贫困残疾人危房改造，各地投入危房资金34.32万元，69名残疾人受益。

四、社会保障

2013年0.21万城镇残疾人参加了城镇居民社会养老保险，参保率31.96%。在60岁以下的参保残疾人中有0.03万重度残疾人，其中0.03万得到了政府的参保扶助，代缴补贴比例达到92.95%。有0.04万非重度残疾人也享受了全额或部分代缴的优惠政策。领取养老金待遇的人数达到0.13万人。

新型农村社会养老保险方面，共有1.49万残疾人参加了新型农村社会养老保险，参保率20.04%。在60周岁以下的参保残疾人中有重度残疾人0.15

万，其中0.13万得到了政府的参保扶助，代缴补贴比例达到88.62%。有0.50万非重度残疾人也享受了全额或部分代缴的优惠政策。享受养老金待遇的人数达到0.70万人。城镇残疾职工参加社会保险人数达到0.72万，城镇残疾居民参加基本医疗保险达到0.44万人，城镇0.09万和农村1.57万残疾人纳入最低生活保障范围；城镇集中供养残疾人和农村五保供养残疾人分别达到26人和425人；2617人和24人符合条件的城乡残疾人分别享受了稳定的生活补贴和护理补贴。0.14万城乡残疾人得到了其他救助救济。接受居家托养服务的残疾人达到0.67万人。

五、维权

各级残联维权组织建设得到加强，残疾人事业法律法规体系进一步完善，残疾人维权工作全面开展。2013年，修订《残疾人保障法》地方实施办法1件。县级以上人大进行《残疾人保障法》执法检查和专题调研1次。开展普法宣传教育活动65次，0.82万人参加。截至2013年底，建立残疾人法律援助中心（工作站）8个，有力地促进了法律救助和法律援助工作。残疾人参政议政工作得到加强，各级残联协助人大代表、政协委员提出议案、建议、提案2件，办理议案、建议、提案3件。为0.02万个贫困残疾人家庭实施了无障碍改造；为0.24万残疾人发放了残疾人机动轮椅车燃油补贴。各级残联共处理残疾人群众来信394余件，接待残疾人群众来访411人次。

六、组织建设

2013年，2个地市级残联在领导班子中配备了残疾人理事长或副理事长；1个县级残联机关配备了残疾人干部；省市县乡残联实有人员已达204人。

七、信息化与事业统计

利用残联门户网站和残联微博等电子信息手段，不断加大残疾人工作信息宣传力度，信息量有了大幅度增长，信息质量显著提升，公开发布信息62条，在各类新闻媒体上积极刊登关于残疾人工作的新闻报道67篇，扩大了残疾人工作影响面；统计队伍建设进一步加强，各级残联共有16名专、兼职统计人员从事残疾人事业统计工作，统计人员业务素质培养普遍得到重视，省级残联举办培训班1期，参加培训的人员达到20人次；地市级举办培训班3期，参加培训的人员达到21人次。在各地（市）残联和各驻村工作队的协助下，在全区5451个行政村开展的《西藏自治区残疾人基本信息调查表》统计工作已基本结束，目前正在开展数据录入工作。

2013年陕西省残疾人事业发展统计公报

2013年，省残联坚持以"科学发展、富民强省"为主题，认真贯彻落实党的十八大精神，按照"三个依托、两个整合"的总体思路，扎实推进残疾人"两个体系"建设，全面完成了年度目标任务，全省残疾人事业呈现出重点突破、协调推进、全面发展的良好势头，在全面建成小康社会进程中迈出了新步伐。

一、康复

2013年，通过实施一批重点康复工程，为残疾人提供了有效的康复服务。大力加强残疾人社区康复示范站建设；做好儿童残疾预防，起草了《关于开展0-6岁残疾儿童抢救性康复工作的意见》；积极推进残疾人康复机构规范化建设；加强康复人才队伍建设，大力宣传和普及康复知识。

社区康复工作实现全覆盖，累计建立社区康复站1282个，配备社区康复协调员8769名。

23个县的29个医疗卫生机构陆续开展残疾儿童筛查工作，年度新诊断0-6岁残疾儿童1018人。

开展视力残疾康复机构总数达到49个，全年完成白内障复明手术14302例；为9020名贫困白内障患者免费施行复明手术，全年为2497名低视力患者配用助视器，培训低视力儿童家长55名；对3764名盲人进行定向行走训练。

推进听力语言康复机构规范化管理，完善基层服务网络。已建设省级听力语言康复机构1个，市级听力语言康复机构11个，县级听力语言康复机构24个。年度机构新收训聋儿626名，在训聋儿951名；规范聋儿家长学校，开展家庭训练，共培训聋儿家长1264名；开展各级各类听力语言康复专业技术人员培训，共培训专业人员108人。

开展肢体残疾康复训练服务机构达97个，其中，省级康复机构4个，地市级、县级康复机构93个；培训各级肢体残疾康复管理、技术人员52人次；全省共对9422名肢体残疾者实施康复训练；实施救助项目资助421名脑瘫儿童进行机构康复训练，资助323名贫困肢体残疾儿童实施矫治手术。

开展智力残疾康复训练服务的机构达到21个，其中，省级康复机构2个，地市级、县级康复机构19个；培训各级智力残疾康复管理、技术人员256人次；全省共对3357名智力残疾人进行康复训练；实施救助项目资助610名智力残疾儿童进行机构康复训练。

大力推广"社会化、综合性、开放式"精神病防治康复工作。全省精神病防治康复工作已经实现全覆盖，对20.27万名重性精神病患者进行综合防治康复，监护率达到58.18%，显好率达到66.73%，社会参与率达到55.24%，肇事率0.12%；解除关锁病人138人；对16543名贫困精神病患者进行了医疗救助。

建立了2个省级孤独症儿童康复训练机构，省级机构对282名孤独症儿童进行了康复训练。

全面启动"关爱重残 共享阳光"重度残疾人辅助器具适配项目，深入开展辅助器具供应服务，为残疾人减免费用供应辅助器具55396件，其中装配普及型假肢1371例，装配矫形器782例，验配助视器3100件。

二、教育

实施残疾人事业专项彩票公益金助学项目，为家庭经济困难的残疾儿童享受普惠性学前教育提供资助200人次。各地也积极多渠道争取资金支持，对67名残疾儿童给予学前教育资助。

已开办特殊教育普通高中班（部）3个，在校生106人；其中聋高中2个，在校生98人；盲高中1个，在校生8人。残疾人中等职业学校（班）8个，在校生1399人，毕业生1223人，其中997人获得职业资格证书。有291名残疾人被普通高等院校录取，30名残疾人进入特殊教育学院学习。

三、就业

认真落实《省级残疾人就业保障金支持集中安

置残疾人就业企业（基地）申报指南》，会同省民政厅、省财政厅等 9 部门出台了《关于加快推进残疾人就业工作的指导意见》，提出了 17 条促进残疾人就业举措。城镇新安排 7866 名残疾人就业。其中，集中就业残疾人 2135 人，按比例安排残疾人就业 2289 人，公益性岗位就业 680 人，个体就业及其它形式灵活就业 2710 人，辅助性就业 52 人。城镇就业人数 10.63 万人；70.51 万农村残疾人在业，其中从事农业生产劳动 53.43 万人。

残疾人职业培训基地达到 80 个，其中残联兴办 21 个，依托社会机构兴办 59 个，12337 人次城镇残疾人接受了职业培训。

盲人按摩事业稳定发展，按摩机构迅速增长。2013 年度培训盲人保健按摩人员 1016 名、盲人医疗按摩人员 85 名；保健按摩机构达到 304 个，医疗按摩机构达到 79 个；有 15 人通过医疗按摩人员初级职称评审。

四、社会保障

城乡残疾人社会养老保险实现全覆盖。省残联协调省财政厅出台了关于《陕西省残疾人生活补贴实施意见》的补充通知，规定自 2014 年 1 月 1 日起对 18 周岁以下生活困难的三级以上残疾儿童，生活补贴标准提高至每人每月 100 元。

8.94 万城镇残疾人参加了城镇居民社会养老保险，参保率 33.99%。在 60 岁以下的参保残疾人中有 1.73 万重度残疾人，全部得到政府的参保扶助，代缴补贴比例达到 100%。有 2.69 万非重度残疾人也享受了全额或部分代缴的优惠政策。领取养老金待遇的人数达到 3.33 万人。

34.52 万残疾人参加了新型农村社会养老保险，参保率 33.23%。在 60 周岁以下的参保残疾人中有重度残疾人 7.87 万，其中 7.37 万得到政府的参保扶助，代缴补贴比例达到 93.61%。10.62 万非重度残疾人也享受了全额或部分代缴的优惠政策。享受养老金待遇的人数达到 9.67 万人。

城镇残疾职工参加社会保险人数达到 6.73 万，城镇残疾居民参加基本医疗保险达到 19.99 万人；城镇 7.19 万和农村 31.69 万残疾人纳入最低生活保障范围；城镇集中供养残疾人和农村五保供养残疾人分别达到 3123 人和 21218 人；76.92 万和 447 名符合条件的城乡残疾人分别享受了稳定的生活补贴和护理补贴。39.73 万城乡残疾人得到了其他救助救济。

残疾人托养服务工作规范推进，开展了“阳光家园”示范创建活动。残疾人托养服务机构达到 128 个，共为 8192 名残疾人提供了托养服务。其中寄宿制托养服务机构 61 个；日间照料机构 20 个；综合性托养服务机构 47 个。接受居家托养服务的残疾人达到 1.75 万人。

五、扶贫开发

会同省财政厅下发《陕西省农村残疾人扶贫示范基地项目申报指南》，确定每年在全省建立省级扶贫基地不少于 20 个、县级基地不少于 30 个的目标，省财政分别补贴省级 30 万元、县级 15 万元。协调省住建厅下发《关于优先支持农村贫困残疾人家庭危房改造的通知》。

23.72 万贫困残疾人得到扶持，其中 8.62 万人通过扶贫开发实际脱贫；接受实用技术培训的残疾人达到 16653 人次。

康复扶贫贴息贷款扶持 13750 名农村残疾人，1166 个单位和 6167 名个人对贫困残疾人开展结对帮扶。残疾人扶贫基地达到 198 个，安置 3632 名残疾人就业，扶持带动 10022 名残疾人。

完成 4432 户农村贫困残疾人危房改造，各地投入危房资金 4042.73 万元，5675 名残疾人受益。

六、宣传文化

省残联首次联合省文化厅举办全省残疾人文化建设培训会，提出了“一纳入三依托”的工作思路，即将残疾人文化工作纳入全省文化工作范围同步实施，依托全省文化资源优势发展残疾人文化事业、依托全省文化机构阵地健全残疾人文化服务网络、依托社会力量开展残疾人各项文化活动。省残联联合省教育厅、省民政厅、省文化厅、省广播电影电视局举办第八届全省残疾人文艺汇演，300 多名残疾人演员进行了 4 类 72 个节目的展示，艺术形式之广泛、演出质量之高堪为历届之最。我省代表团在第八届全国残疾人艺术汇演中荣获一等奖、二等奖各三个，三等奖六个，团体总分二等奖，创历届最好成绩。省残联协调省广播电视台首次对省“两会”进行了电视手语同步直播。

省级中央媒体采用稿件 214 件，主要新闻媒体刊播稿件 403 件，电视手语新闻栏目 1 个，省级残疾人事业新闻宣传促进会 1 个。

地市级主要新闻媒体刊播稿件数 1088 件，报刊专版 11 个，残疾人专题广播节目 8 个，电视手语新闻栏目 9 个，建立地市级新促会 3 个。

省级和地市级公共图书馆设立盲文及盲人有声读物阅览室已达到 18 个，省、市共举办残疾人文化周 36 次，举办残疾人文化艺术类比赛及展览 16 个，成立残疾人艺术团队 5 个。

七、体育

我省运动员在国内外多项体育赛事中获得金牌 28 枚、银牌 9 枚、铜牌 17 枚。其中，在我省首次派员参加的第二十二届夏季听障奥运会上，我省运动员汪子翔夺得男子游泳 1 金、1 银、2 铜的好成绩。

省级残疾人体育健身活动 43 次，参加人数 3800 人，残疾人体育示范点 25 个，残疾人体育健身指导员 189 人，残疾人体育比赛 8 次，参与的残疾人运动员 213 人次，残疾人体育训练基地 25 个，聘任教练员 12 人。

地市级残疾人体育健身活动 64 次，参加人数 3149 人，残疾人体育示范点 28 个，残疾人体育健身指导员 83 人。

八、维权

各级残联维权组织建设得到加强，残疾人事业法律法规体系进一步完善，残疾人维权工作全面开展。起草了《陕西省<无障碍环境建设条例>实施办法》，多次与省法制办协调，将《办法》列入 2014 年立法计划。配合省发改委编写了《陕西省基本公共服务体系“十二五”规划》残疾人基本公共服务专章。

县级以上人大执法检查或专题调研 12 次，政协视察和专题调研 12 次。开展普法宣传教育活动 144 次，参加人数 2.01 万人；开展法律培训班 27 次，参加人数 2169 人。

全省建立残疾人法律救助协调机构 25 个；建立残疾人法律救助工作站 4 个，办理案件 5 件，建立残疾人法律援助中心（工作站）107 个，办理案件 646 件，有力地促进了法律救助和法律援助工作。

残疾人参政议政工作得到加强，各级残联协助人大代表、政协委员提出议案、建议、提案 28 件，办理议案、建议、提案 33 件。

无障碍建设法规、标准进一步完善。共出台了无障碍建设与管理法规、规章 13 个；系统开展无障碍建设市、县 43 个；开展无障碍建设检查 30 次，无障碍培训 80 人次；为 1091 名贫困残疾人家庭实施了无障碍改造；为 19697 名残疾人发放了机动轮椅车燃油补贴。

各级残联共处理残疾人群众来信 447 件，接待残疾人群众来访 1.76 万人次，其中集体访 10 批次，134 人次。

九、组织建设

省残联联合省财政厅下发了《关于落实残疾人专职委员工作补贴经费省级补贴有关事项的通知》，规定“从 2013 年元月起，对全省残疾人专职委员施行工作补贴，标准为每人每月不低于 100 元”。基层残疾人组织更加规范，队伍更加稳定。注重培养、推广先进典型，在全省 20 个县（区）、102 个乡镇（街道）、1009 个村（社区）开展创建“全省残疾人工作示范点”活动，为全省残疾人工作树立了一批看得见、摸得着、学得到的典型。

9 个地市级残联的领导班子配备了残疾人理事长或副理事长；61 个县级残联机关配备了残疾人干部；已建乡镇（街道）残联 1543 个，已建率达到 99.49%，选聘残疾人专职委员 1663 名；已建社区（村）残协 28156 个，已建率达到 99.64%，选聘残疾人专职委员 28746 名。

省市县乡残联实有人员已达 4640 人。各级残联采取多层次、多渠道、多形式的分级分类培训形式举办培训班 1721 期，培训机关干部、协会干部及残疾人专职委员 2.61 万人次。

省级以下共建立各类残疾人专门协会 587 个，市级专门协会已建比例为 100%，市辖区专门协会已建比例 100%；县（含县级市）级专门协会已建比例为 99.28%。

十、服务设施建设

截止2013年底，已竣工并投入使用的各级残疾人综合服务设施76个，总建设规模14.69万平方米，总投资31195.31万元；已竣工并投入使用的各级残疾人康复设施19个，总建设规模2.90万平方米，总投资4492.66万元；已竣工并投入使用的各级残疾人托养服务设施37个，总建设规模9.33万平方米，总投资12396.30万元。

十一、事业统计与信息化建设

统计队伍建设进一步加强，各级残联共有134名专、兼职统计人员从事残疾人事业统计工作，统计人员业务素质培养普遍得到重视，省级残联举办培训班1期，参加培训的人员达到44人次；地市级举办培训班12期，参加培训的人员达到301人次。

全面推进网站建设。省级残联已开通了公众服务网站。10个地市级残联及杨陵区、韩城市残联全部建成网站，51个县级残联网站也已开通。各级残联共有160名专业技术人员从事信息化工作。2013年省级及地市级残联开设网站技术培训班13期，培训各级残联信息员达325人次。

2013 年甘肃省残疾人事业发展统计公报

2013 年，是全省残疾人事业发展历程中具有重要意义的一年，也是残疾人工作取得丰硕成果的一年。在省委省政府的坚强领导下，在中国残联的有力指导和社会各界的大力支持下，全省各级残联组织围绕建设幸福美好新甘肃、帮助残疾人实现同步小康的工作大局，凝心聚力、乘势而为，顺利完成了各项年度工作任务，残疾人基本状况进一步改善，残疾人事业呈现亮点纷呈、多极突破、强劲发展的良好势头。

一、康复

全省 86 个县（区、市）的 4955 个村（社区）开展了社区康复工作，累计建成社区康复站 1249 个，社区康复协调员达到 7863 人，38 万残疾人接受了社区康复服务。

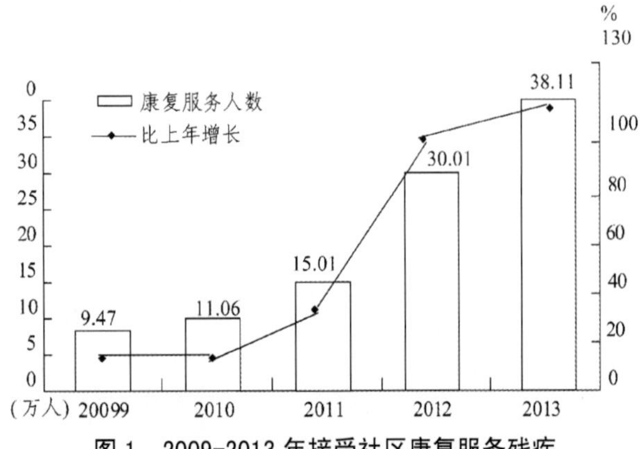

图 1　2009-2013 年接受社区康复服务残疾人数及增长速度

开展视力残疾康复机构 15 个，实施白内障复明手术 10755 例，其中贫困白内障患者免费手术 7331 例；为 3127 名低视力患者配用了助视器；培训低视力儿童家长 580 名，对 2126 名盲人进行了定向行走训练。

已建省级听力语言康复机构 1 个，市、县级听力语言康复

机构 17 个。年度新收训聋儿 396 名，在训聋儿 571 名。全年培训聋儿家长 454 名。

开展肢体残疾康复训练机构 24 个，实施肢体残疾儿童矫治手术 414 人，有 5176 名肢体残疾人接受了康复训练。肢体残疾儿童社区、家庭康复 865 人，成年肢体残疾人社区、家庭康复 3872 人。

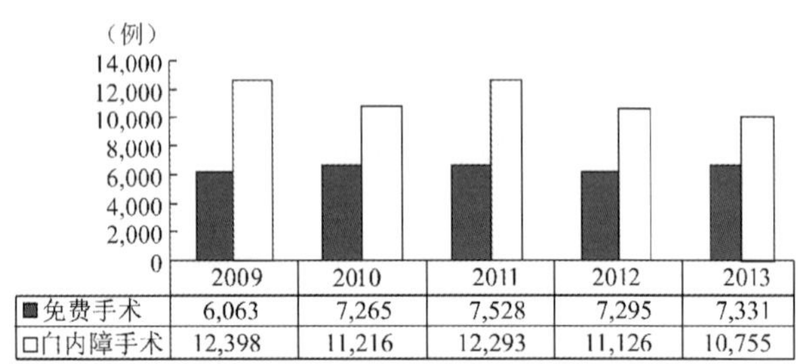

图 2　2009-2013 年全省实施白内障手术数量

开展智力残疾康复训练机构 22 个，有 1969 名智力残疾人接受了康复训练，社区、家庭康复 1497 人，成年智力残疾人社区、家庭康复 80 人。

有 60 个县（区、市）开展了精神病防治康复工作，有精神病康复机构 32 个，对 12 万精神病患者进行了综合治疗康复。监护 10.3 万人，监护率达 86%；显好 7.2 万人，显好率达 60%；参与社会 5.6 万人，社会参与率达 47%；肇事 68 人次，解除关锁 23 人。有 1.4 万精神病患者接受了治疗，有 3260 名精神病患者接受了康复训练。对 2.1 万贫困精神病患者进行了医疗救助。

建立 15 个孤独症儿童康复训练机构，有 68 名孤独症儿童在康复训练机构接受治疗，对 84 名孤独症儿童进行了救助。

各级辅助器具服务机构为残疾人供应各类辅具 18385 件，其中装配假肢 726 例，装配矫形器 349 例，其他辅助器具 17310 件。

表 1　2013 年康复训练服务机构（个）

级　别	类别				
	视力	听力语言	肢体	智力	辅助器具
省　级	1	1	1	1	1
市州级	4	11	6	9	8
县　级	10	6	17	12	58
合　计	15	18	24	22	66

二、教育

残疾人事业专项彩票公益金助学项目，为全省

家庭经济困难的残疾儿童享受普惠性学前教育资助300多人次。各地多渠道积极争取资金对253名学前残疾儿童给予了学前教育资助。

截至2013年底，全省有未入学适龄残疾儿童3137人，其中视力残疾儿童194人，听力残疾儿童186人，言语残疾儿童170人，肢体残疾儿童1106人，智力残疾儿童829人，精神残疾儿童123人，多重残疾儿童529人。

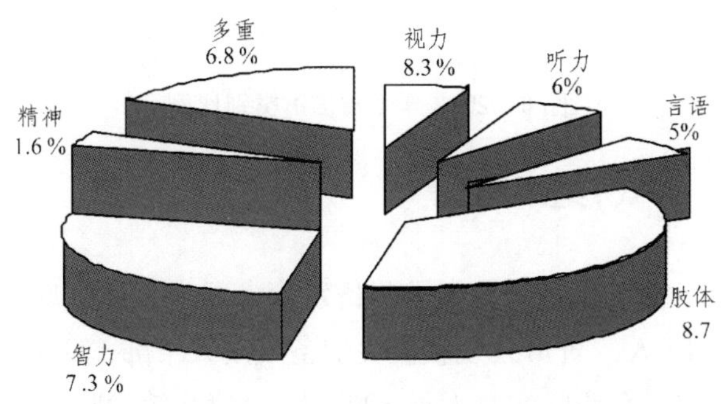

图3 2013年全省未入学适龄残疾儿童类别比例

全省开办特殊教育普通高中学校（班）3个，在校生165人，毕业40人。开办残疾人中等职业学校（班）4个，在校生45人，毕业41人，获得职业资格证书4人。全省有247名残疾考人生被普通高等院校录取。

三、就业

认真贯彻《甘肃省残疾人就业办法》落实有关优惠政策，残疾人就业工作取得新进展。全省城镇残疾人就业106012人。其中按比例就业20183人，集中就业24599人，个体及其他形式就业54602人，公益性岗位就业5853人，辅助性就业775人；农村残疾人就业53.8万人。其中从事农业生产劳动44.8万人，其他形式就业9万人。

全省有残疾人职业培训基地42个。其中残联兴办19个，依托社会机构兴办23个。接受了职业培训的残疾人达1.9万人。

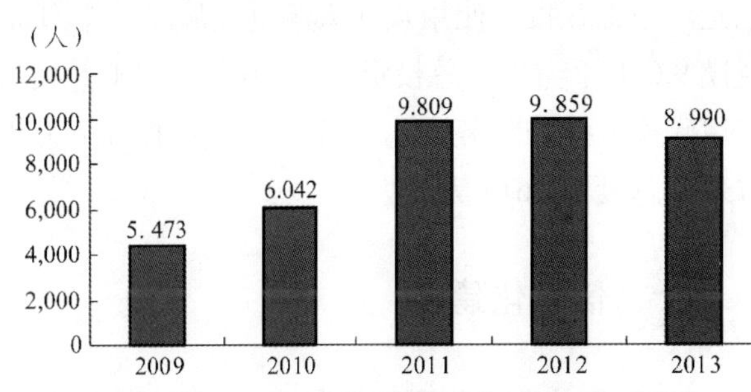

图4 2009—2013年城镇残疾人新增就业人数

全省有医疗按摩机构28个，培训盲人医疗按摩人员112名；有保健按摩机构209个，培训保健按摩人员371名；盲人医疗按摩就业56人，盲人保健按摩就业227人。在专业技术职务资格评审中有6人通过了中级职称评审，16人通过了初级职称评审。

四、社会保障

已有12.6万城镇残疾人参加了城镇居民社会养老保险，参保率86.5%。60岁以下的参保残疾人中，有3.9万重度残疾人享受了政府全额或部分代缴的优惠政策。

新型农村社会养老保险方面，有79.3万残疾人参加新型农村社会养老保险，参保率86%。60岁以下的参保残疾人中，有17.6万重度残疾人享受了政府全额或部分代缴的优惠政策。

1.8万城镇残疾职工参加养老保险，1.9万参加医疗保险。

城镇、农村分别有11.4万和33.4万残疾人纳入最低生活保障。

城镇集中供养残疾人和农村五保供养残疾人分别为0.1万人和1.8万人；城镇和农村残疾人获得其他救助救济分别为1.3万人和8.9万人；1.9万人和5.7万人分别享受了生活补贴和护理补贴。

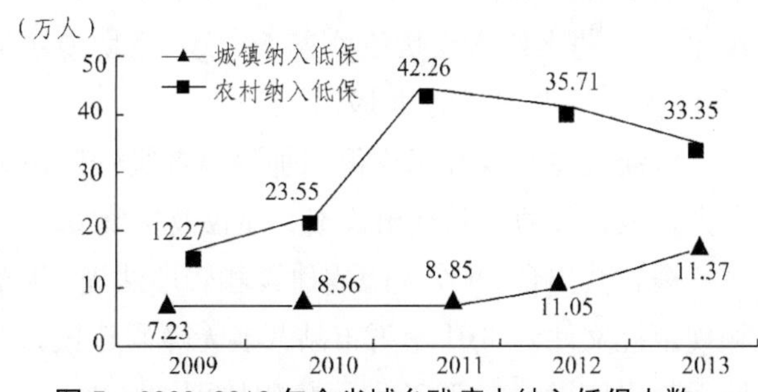

图5 2009-2013年全省城乡残疾人纳入低保人数

残疾人托养机构达到47个，为2.8万残疾人提供了托养服务。其中寄宿制托养服务机构21个；日间照料机构7个；综合托养服务机构19个。接收居家托养服务的残疾人达到2.5万人。

五、扶贫

2013年残疾人扶贫开发工作成效显著，贫困残疾人生产生活状况得到进一步改善。11.6万贫困残疾人得到扶持。其中9.7万贫困残疾人实际脱贫；

接受实用技术培训的残疾人达 4.5 万人次。落实中央康复扶贫贷款项目资金 3702 万元，有 1566 名贫困残疾人得到扶持。

已建残疾人扶贫基地 44 个，扶持带动残疾人户 2124 户，单位结对帮扶残疾人 7.3 万人。

全省共投入资金 1.2 亿元，实施农村贫困残疾人危房改造 1 万户。

六、宣传文体

宣传文化：全年省市主要新闻媒体刊播残疾人事业稿件 3005 条，专题广播节目 45 个，电视手语栏目 10 个。有 1 个省级和 2 个市级残疾人艺术团队，举办残疾人文化艺术比赛及展览 49 场次。建立省市盲人有声读物图书室 11 个。

体育活动：建立省级群众体育活动示范点 18 个，组织残疾人群众体育健身活动 2 次，参加人数 3000 人次；建立市级残疾人体育活动示范点 16 个，参加人数 6.4 万人次。举办省级体育比赛 4 次，参赛运动员 148 人。

七、维权

全省制定或修改了关于残疾人的专门法规、规章 5 件，制定或修改保障残疾人权益的规范性文件 70 件。全省各级人大执法检查 56 次，政协专题调研 43 次，举办普法活动 191 次。

残疾人参政议政工作得到加强，各级残联协助人大代表、政协委员提出议案、建议及提案 62 件。

全省共出台 39 个无障碍建设和管理法规、规章和规范性文件； 101 个省市县开展无障碍建设，开展无障碍建设检查 72 次，无障碍培训 289 次。

表 2　2013 年全省各级残疾人法律救助情况

级　别	法律救助协调机构（个）	法律救助		法律援助	
		工作站（个）	办理案件（件）	工作站（个）	办理案件（件）
省　级	1	1	209	1	2
市州级	15	15	33	15	72
县　级	61	61	262	79	865
合　计	77	77	504	95	939

全省建立残疾人法律救助工作协调机构 77 个。建立残疾人法律救助工作站 77 个，办理案件 504 件；建立残疾人法律援助中心 95 个，办理案件 939 件。

各级残联接待残疾人来信来访 8465 人次。其中来信 1793 件，来访 6672 人次。为 1218 户贫困残疾人家庭进行了无障碍改造，为 1.5 万残疾人发放机动轮椅车燃油补贴。

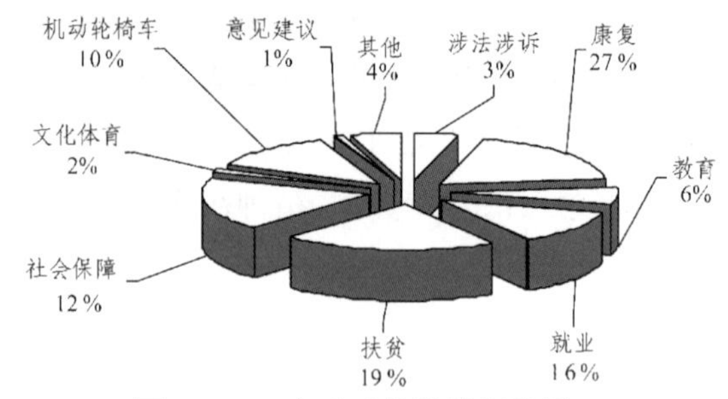

图 6　2013 年全省信访类别比例

八、组织建设

省市残联领导班子配备残疾人理事长或副理事长 15 人。省市县残联机关配备残疾人干部 173 人。省市县乡残联实有人员 3993 人。已建乡镇残联 1369 个，已建村残协 17214 个，选聘残疾人专职委员 18625 人。

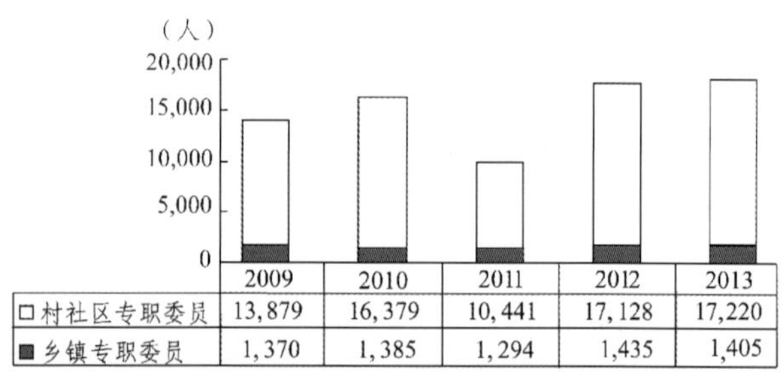

	2009	2010	2011	2012	2013
□村社区专职委员	13,879	16,379	10,441	17,128	17,220
■乡镇专职委员	1,370	1,385	1,294	1,435	1,405

图 7　2009-2013 年全省专职委员数量

全省各级残联举办培训班 239 期，培训机关干部、协会干部及残疾人专职委员 3365 人次。2832 名优秀残疾人被收入残疾人人才库。全省各级专门协会全部建立。

九、服务设施建设

全省残疾人服务设施截至 2013 年底竣工并投入使用 99 个，建筑规模 10.4 万平方米，总投资 1.8 亿元；竣工并投入使用残疾人康复设施 7 个，建筑规模 9.6 万平方米，总投资 2320 万元；竣工并投入使用残疾人托养服务设施 6 个，建筑规模 1.7 万平方米，总投资 2614 万元。

十、信息化建设

2013 年甘肃省残联网站年度访问量达到 60 多

万次。刊登残联系统信息稿件2588篇，较往年增长6.7%，14个市级残联和20个县级残联开通残联网站。省市级残联举办各类信息统计、网络技术培训班16期，培训信息化工作干部310人。全年投入信息化建设资金162万元。

截至2013年底，全省残疾人人口基础数据库共采集到61万残疾人的基础数据信息，采集率为33.6%。完成“甘肃省残联残疾人综合业务数据库”软件研发工作。

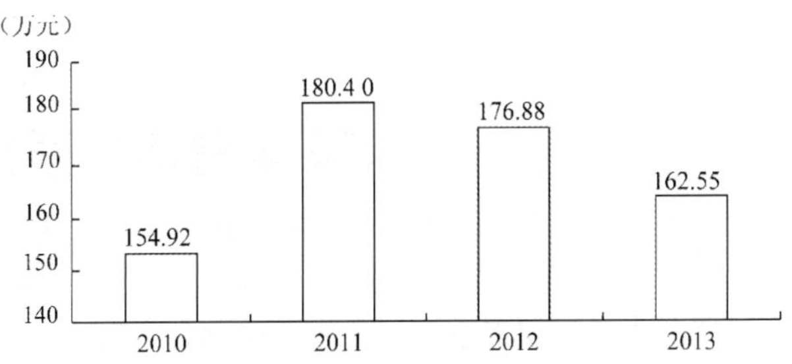

图8 2010-2013年全省残联信息化建设资金

2013年青海省残疾人事业发展统计公报

2013年，在省委、省政府的坚强领导和中国残联的有力指导下，青海省残联以残疾人社会保障和服务体系建设为核心任务，全力推进《青海省残疾人事业"十二五"规划》和年度计划，全面完成了各项业务指标，残疾人生产生活状况进一步改善，残疾人事业实现新发展。

一、康复

在4个市辖区和42个县（市）开展了社区康复工作，累计已建社区康复站的社区总数484个，配备2120名社区康复协调员。

16个县的42个医疗卫生机构陆续开展残疾儿童筛查工作，年度新诊断0-6岁残疾儿童255人。

开展视力残疾康复机构总数达到4个，完成白内障复明手术3613例；为3505名贫困白内障患者免费施行复明手术；为1927名低视力患者配用助视器，培训低视力儿童家长87名，有效开展家庭康复训练。对1157名盲人进行定向行走训练。

推进听力语言康复机构规范化管理，完善基层服务网络。已建设省级听力语言康复机构1个，基层听力语言康复机构5个。年度新收训聋儿132名，在训聋儿180名；规范聋儿家长学校，开展家庭训练，共培训聋儿家长196名；开展各级各类听力语言康复专业技术人员培训，共培训专业人员64人。

开展肢体残疾康复训练服务机构达10个，其中，省级康复机构1个，地市级、县级康复机构9个；培训各级各类肢体残疾康复人员222人次；全国共对1261肢体残疾者实施康复训练；实施救助项目资助147名脑瘫儿童进行机构康复训练，资助93名贫困肢体残疾儿童实施矫治手术。

开展智力残疾康复训练服务的机构9个，其中，省级康复机构1个，地市级、县级康复机构8个；培训各级各类智力残疾康复人员192人次；全国共对607名智力残疾人进行康复训练；实施救助项目资助112名智力残疾儿童进行机构康复训练，同时对残疾儿童家长进行了培训。

大力推广"社会化、综合性、开放式"精神病防治康复工作。在34个市县开展精神病防治康复工作，对3655名重性精神病患者进行综合防治康复，监护率达到60.44%，显好率达到50.16%，社会参与率达到34.22%；解除关锁3人；对1500名贫困精神病患者进行医疗救助。

建立了1个省级孤独症儿童康复训练机构；161名孤独症儿童在各级机构进行了康复训练。

加强残疾人辅助器具服务体系建设，深入开展辅助器具供应服务，为残疾人供应配发辅助器具20909件，其中装配假肢719例、矫形器591例，验配助视器1741件。

二、教育

通过残疾人事业专项彩票公益金助学项目资助家庭经济困难的残疾儿童74人次，通过其他项目争取资金对279名残疾儿童给予学前教育资助。

已开办特殊教育普通高中班（部）2个，在校生54人；其中聋高中2个，在校生54人。残疾人中等职业学校（班）2个，在校生29人。有75名残疾人被普通高等院校录取。

截止2013年底，有未入学适龄残疾儿童少年928人，其中视力残疾儿童61人，听力残疾儿童61人，言语残疾儿童51人，智力残疾儿童296人，肢体残疾儿童309人，精神残疾儿童15人，多重残疾儿童135人。

三、就业

城镇新就业残疾人1415人，其中，集中就业602人，按比例安排就业157人，公益性岗位就业109人，个体就业及其他形式灵活就业439人，辅助性就业108人。城镇就业人数6467名；4.69万农村残疾人在业，其中3.97万残疾人从事农业生产劳动。

残疾人职业培训基地达到28个，其中残联兴办15个，依托社会机构兴办13个，2131人次城镇残疾人接受了职业培训。

培训盲人保健按摩人员 266 名、盲人医疗按摩人员 68 名；保健按摩机构达到 203 个，医疗按摩机构达到 3 个；在专业技术职务资格评审中，分别有 9 人和 17 人通过医疗按摩人员中级和初级职称评审。

四、社会保障

8242 名城镇残疾人参加了城镇居民社会养老保险，参保率 68.67%。60 岁以下的参保残疾人中，1325 名重度残疾人全部得到了政府的参保扶助，代缴补贴比例达到 100%。由于部分地区政策扩面，144 名非重度残疾人也享受了全额或部分代缴的优惠政策。领取养老金的人数达到 5845 人。

新型农村社会养老保险方面，共有 4.18 万残疾人参加了新型农村社会养老保险，参保率 92.58%。60 周岁以下的参保残疾人中，重度残疾人 1.05 万全部得到了政府的参保扶助，代缴补贴比例达到 100%。由于部分地区政策扩面，340 名非重度残疾人也享受了全额或部分代缴的优惠政策。享受养老金的人数达到 2.83 万人。

城镇残疾职工参加社会保险人数达到 4966 人，城镇残疾居民参加基本医疗保险达到 1.28 万人，城镇 0.57 万和农村 2.28 万残疾人纳入最低生活保障范围；城镇集中供养残疾人和农村五保供养残疾人分别达到 717 人和 1670 人；19268 名符合条件的城乡残疾人享受了稳定的生活补贴，29 名符合条件的城乡残疾人享受了护理补贴。6438 名城乡残疾人得到了其他救助救济。

残疾人托养服务工作规范推进，残疾人托养服务机构达到 41 个，共为 603 名残疾人提供了托养服务。其中寄宿制托养服务机构 24 个；日间照料机构 4 个；综合性托养服务机构 13 个。接受居家托养服务的残疾人达到 1.53 万人。

五、扶贫开发

1.32 万贫困残疾人得到扶持，其中 6990 人通过扶贫开发实际脱贫；接受实用技术培训的残疾人达到 6711 人次。

康复扶贫贴息贷款扶持 546 名农村残疾人，340 个单位和 954 个人对贫困残疾人开展结对帮扶。残疾人扶贫基地达到 29 个，安置 350 名残疾人就业，扶持带动 390 户残疾人。

完成 2554 户农村贫困残疾人危房改造，各地投入危房改造资金 3,178.55 万元，2621 名残疾人受益。

六、维权

各级残联维权组织建设得到加强，残疾人事业法律法规体系进一步完善。

县级以上人大进行《残疾人保障法》执法检查和专题调研 9 次；政协进行视察和专题调研 9 次。开展普法宣传教育活动 87 次，7664 人参加；举办法律培训班 24 个，578 人参加。

截至 2013 年底，成立残疾人法律救助工作协调机构 55 个，建立残疾人法律援助中心（工作站）55 个，办理案件 154 件，有力地促进了法律救助和法律援助工作。

残疾人参政议政工作得到加强，各级残联协助人大代表、政协委员提出议案、建议、提案 12 件，办理议案、建议、提案 9 件。

无障碍建设法规、标准进一步完善。出台了 1 个县级无障碍建设与管理法规、规章；11 个市、县、区系统开展无障碍建设；开展无障碍建设检查 22 次；为 1160 个贫困残疾人家庭实施了无障碍改造；为 7703 名残疾人发放了残疾人机动轮椅车燃油补贴。

各级残联共处理残疾人群众来信 183 余件，接待残疾人群众来访 440 人次。

七、宣传文化

省残联全年中央媒体采用稿件 12 件、主要新闻媒体刊播稿件 765 件、开办残疾人专题广播节目 1 个、设立电视手语新闻栏目 1 个，现有残疾人事业新闻宣传促进会 1 个。

地市级残联全年主要新闻媒体刊播稿件数 172 件、报刊专版 35 个、残疾人专题广播节目 15 个。

省级和地市级公共图书馆设立盲文及盲人有声读物阅览室已达到 1 和 4 个，举办残疾人文化周 2 和 15 个，举办残疾人文化艺术类比赛及展览分别是 2 和 4 个，地市级已成立残疾人艺术团队 1 个。

八、体育

省残联组织残疾人体育健身活动 8 次，参加人数2000人，残疾人体育示范点4个，残疾人体育健身指导员70人，残疾人体育比赛5次，参与的残疾人运动员800人次，残疾人体育训练基地1个，聘任教练员6人。

地市级级残联组织残疾人体育健身活动5次，参加人数220人，残疾人体育示范点1个，残疾人体育健身指导员2人。

九、组织建设

2个地市级残联在领导班子中配备了残疾人理事长或副理事长；14个县级残联机关配备了残疾人干部；已建乡镇（街道）残联404个，已建率达到100%，选聘残疾人专职委员528名；已建社区（村）残协4515个，已建率达到98.73%，选聘残疾人专职委员2975名。

省市县乡残联实有人员已达1196人。各级残联共举办培训班134期，培训机关干部、协会干部及残疾人专职委员4402人次。

共建立省级以下各类残疾人专门协会270个，市级专门协会已建比例为100%，市辖区专门协会已建比例100%；县（含县级市）级专门协会已建比例为100%。

十、服务设施建设

截至2013年底，已竣工并投入使用的各级残疾人综合服务设施31个，总建设规模1.79万平方米，总投资4011.16万元；已竣工并投入使用的各级残疾人康复设施3个，总建设规模0.41万平方米，总投资973.00万元。

十一、信息化建设

统计队伍建设进一步加强，各级残联共有62名专、兼职统计人员从事残疾人事业统计工作，统计人员业务素质培养普遍得到重视，省级残联举办培训班1期，参加培训的人员达到80人次；地市级举办培训班8期，参加培训的人员达到124人次。

地方残联全面推进网站建设，目前1个省级残联已全部开通了公众服务网站，有4个地市级残联网站和3个县级残联网站也已开通。2013年省级及地市级残联开设网站技术培训班11期，培训各级残联信息员达234人次。

各级残联共有70名专业技术人员从事信息化工作；省级残联共建立局域网1个。

2013年宁夏回族自治区残疾人事业发展统计公报

2013年，全区残疾人工作在自治区党委、政府的正确领导下和中国残联的精心指导下，认真贯彻六代会精神，实施“五大圆梦工程”、实现“十个全覆盖”为契机，经过各级残联的共同努力，全面完成了年度工作任务，取得了新成就。

一、康复

2013年，通过实施一批重点康复工程，使各类别残疾人得到不同程度的康复。

1．视力残疾康复。本年度完成白内障复明手术2780例，其中为2120名贫困白内障患者免费施行复明手术。全年为1077名低视力患者配用助视器，培训低视力儿童家长261名，有效开展家庭康复训练。对1219名盲人进行定向行走训练。

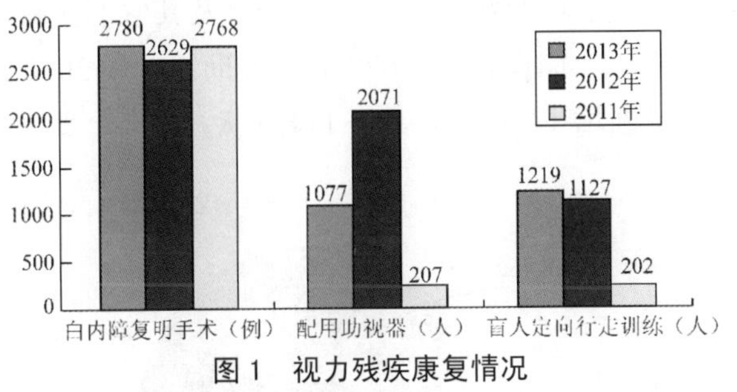

图1　视力残疾康复情况

2．听力言语残疾康复。建立各级聋儿康复机构建设6个，共对167名聋儿进行了听力语言康复训练。规范聋儿家长学校，开展家庭训练，共培训聋儿家长199名；培养各类专业人员40人。

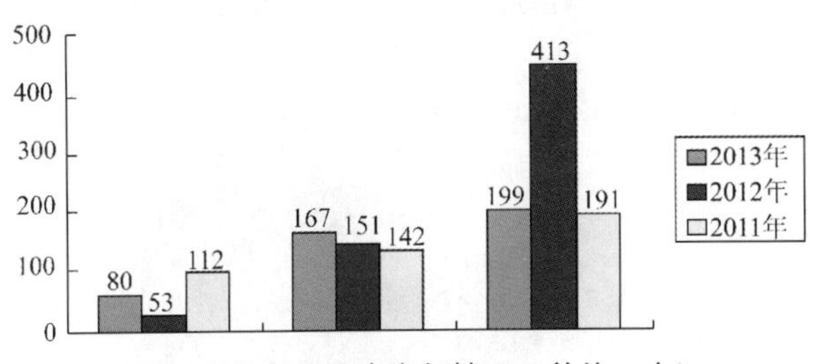

图2　听力言语残疾康复情况（单位：人）

3．精神残疾康复。大力推广“社会化、综合性、开放式”精神病防治康复工作。2013年，在21个市、县（区）开展精神病防治康复工作，对3.57万精神病患者进行综合防治康复，监护率达到90.72%，显好率达到63.99%，社会参与率达到52.23%，肇事率0.26%，解除关锁1人。对4438名贫困精神病患者进行医疗救助。

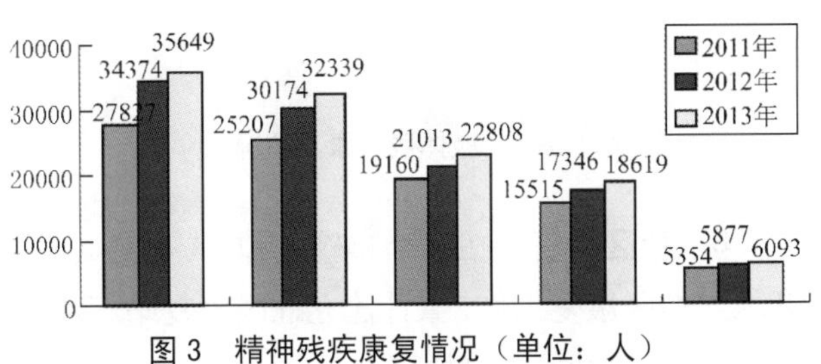

图3　精神残疾康复情况（单位：人）

全区建立了15个孤独症儿童康复训练机构，机构内在训儿童163名，有45名贫困孤独症儿童得到了康复救助。

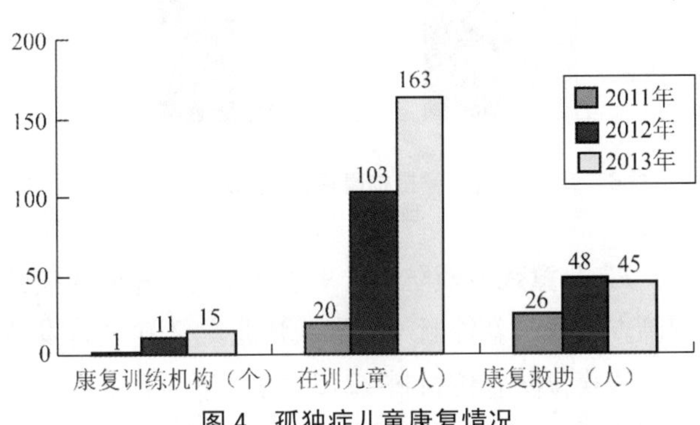

图4　孤独症儿童康复情况

4．肢体残疾康复。全年开展肢体残疾康复训练服务的机构达到13个，对72名贫困肢体残疾儿童实施矫治手术、装配了矫形器等辅助器具，进行了术后康复训练；对5238名肢体残疾人进行了康复训练，其中：脑瘫儿童机构康复训练175人，肢体残疾儿童社区、家庭康复233人，成年肢体残疾人社区、家庭康复4830人。

深入开展辅助器具供应服务，全面推进普及型假肢装配，截止到2013年底，累计建立辅助器具供应服务机构5个，为残疾人减免费用装配普及型假肢285例，装配矫形器183例，供应各类辅助器具23090件。

5．智力残疾康复。全年开展智力残疾康复训练服务的机构达到14个；对646名智力残疾儿童进行了康复训练，不同程度地开展了智力残疾儿童早期康复训练与服务。

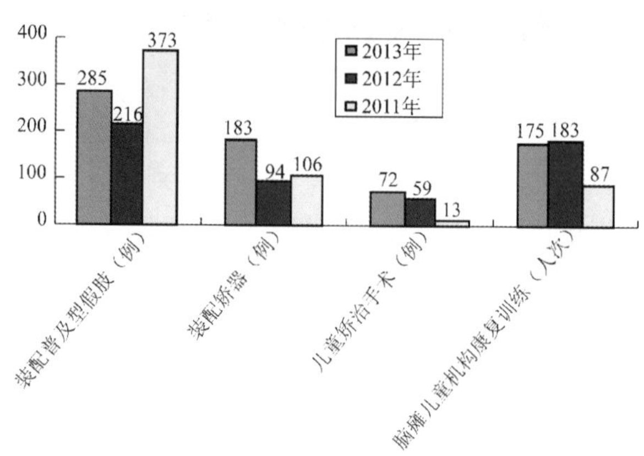

图 5　肢体残疾康复情况

6．**社区康复**。在 9 个市辖区和 13 个县（市）开展了社区康复工作，累计建立社区康复站 524 个，配备 1478 名社区康复协调员。

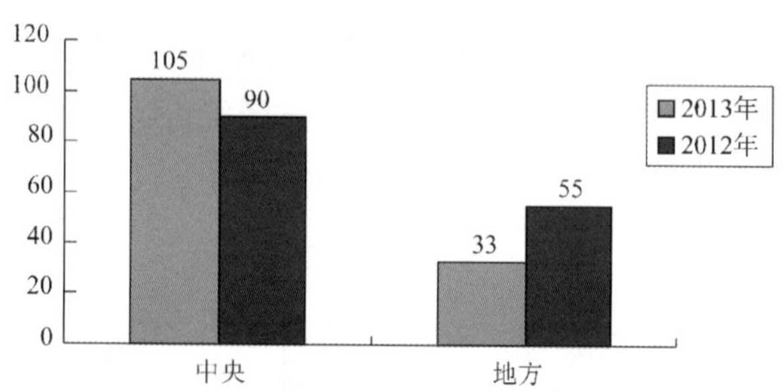

图 6　智力残疾儿童机构康复训练情况（单位：人）

7．**儿童残疾预防**。在 9 个县（区）开展残疾儿童筛查工作，新诊断 0-6 岁残疾儿童 210 名，发放儿童残疾预防宣传材料 32150 份，举办儿童残疾预防宣传活动 25 次。

8．**康复人才培训**。区市县康复机构在岗人员 360 人，本年度举办康复管理人员培训班 10 期，康复业务人员培训班 8 期，社区康复协调员培训班 17 期，共培训 957 人。

二、教育

学前教育阶段，本年度接受残疾人事业专项彩票公益金助学项目资助 60 人，新入园 34 人；其他残疾儿童学前教育助学项目资助 69 人。

义务教育阶段，未入学适龄残疾儿童少年总数 1021 人，其中视力残疾 72 人，听力残疾 46 人，言语残疾 56 人，肢体残疾 262 人，智力残疾 383 人，精神残疾 37 人，多重残疾 165 人。

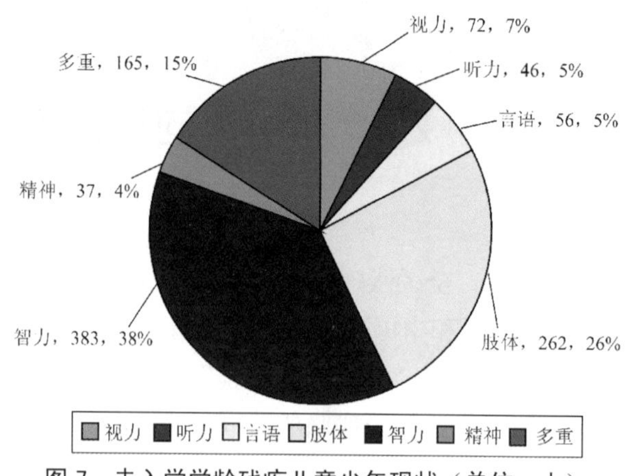

图 7　未入学学龄残疾儿童少年现状（单位：人）

高等教育情况，开办特殊教育普通高中学校 1 所，在校生 281 人；残疾人中等职业教育学校 1 所，在校生 15 人；普通高等院校录取残疾考生 121 人。

三、就业

城镇残疾人就业状况。在业人数 23602 人，其中，集中就业 5054 人，本年度新增 218 人；按比例就业 6475 人，本年度新增 425 人；公益性岗位就业 439 人，本年度新增 128 人；个体及其它形式就业 11604 人，本年度新增 679 人；辅助性就业 30 人，本年度新增 12 人；未就业 11128 人。

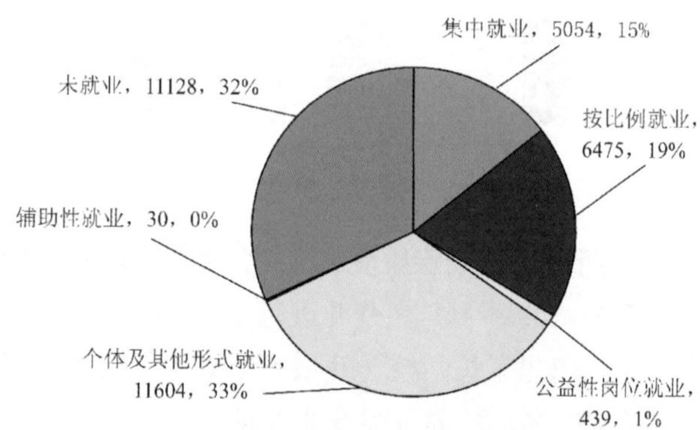

图 8　城镇残疾人就业状况（单位：人）

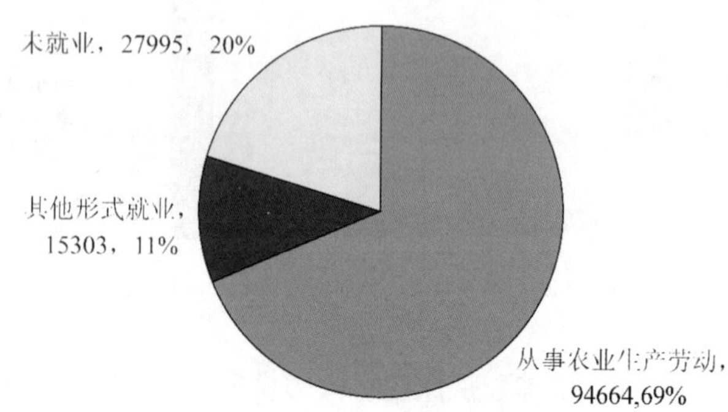

图 9　农村残疾人就业状况（单位：人）

农村残疾人就业状况。实际就业 109967 人，其中从事农业生产劳动 94664 人，其他形式就业 15303 人。未就业 27998 人。

累计建立残疾人职业培训基地 31 个，其中残联兴办 3 个，依托社会机构兴办 28 个。本年度城镇职业培训 2861 人次。

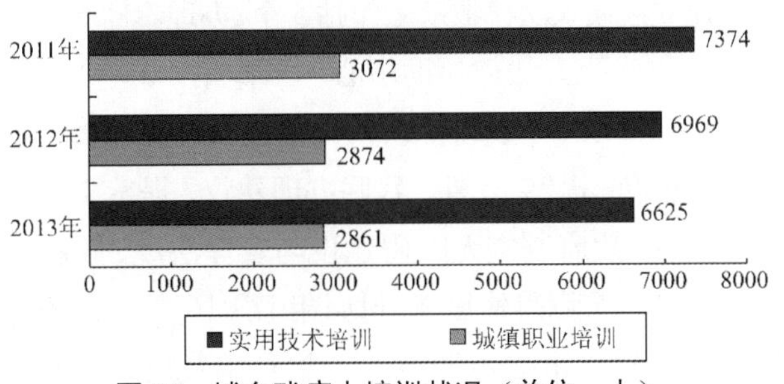

图 10 城乡残疾人培训状况（单位：人）

本年度培训盲人保健按摩 174 人，培训医疗按摩 60 人；开办保健按摩机构达到 117 个，医疗按摩机构 1 个；有 10 人通过医疗按摩专业技术中级和初级资格评审。从事保健和医疗按摩就业 206 人。

四、社会保障

城镇残疾职工参加社会保险人数达到 9029 人，其中参加养老保险人数 7722 人，参加医疗保险人数 6252 人；城镇残疾居民参加社会保险 86791 人；其中参加医疗保险 48109 人，参加养老保险 48930 人，参保率 86%。

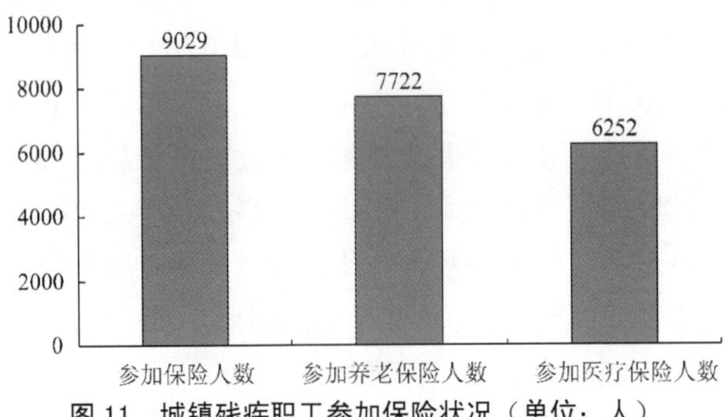

图 11 城镇残疾职工参加保险状况（单位：人）

农村居民参加社会保险 204649 人，其中参加新型农村合作医疗 180270 人，参加新型农村社会养老保险 139654 人，参保率 80%。

城乡 87856 名残疾人纳入最低生活保障范围。城镇已纳入最低生活保障 14749 人，城镇集中供养和其他救助救济 6407 人；农村已纳入最低生活保障 73107 人，五保供养和其他救助救济 12017 人。

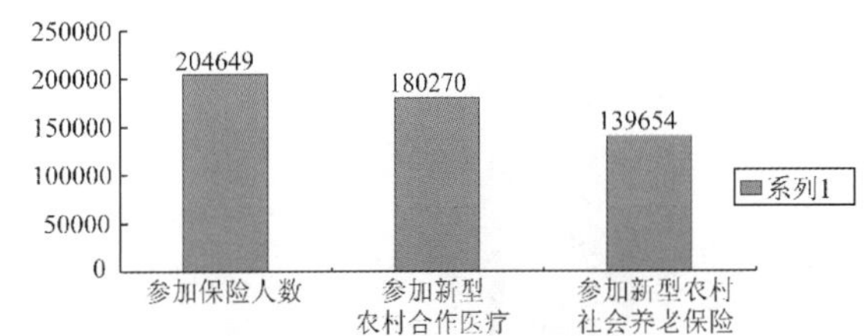

图 12 农村残疾居民参加社保保险状况（单位：人）

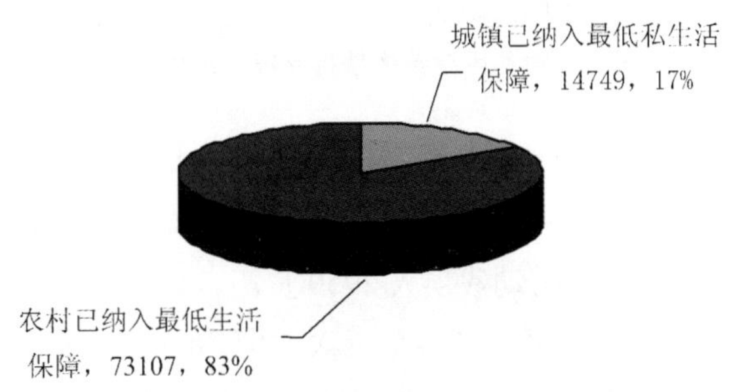

图 13 城乡残疾人纳入最低生活保障状况（单位：人）

建立寄宿制托养机构 5 个，托养残疾人 204 人；兴办日间照料托养服务机构 34 个，托养残疾人 1197 人；建立综合托养服务机构 5 个，托养残疾人 160 人。本年度享受居家托养服务残疾人 14127 人。

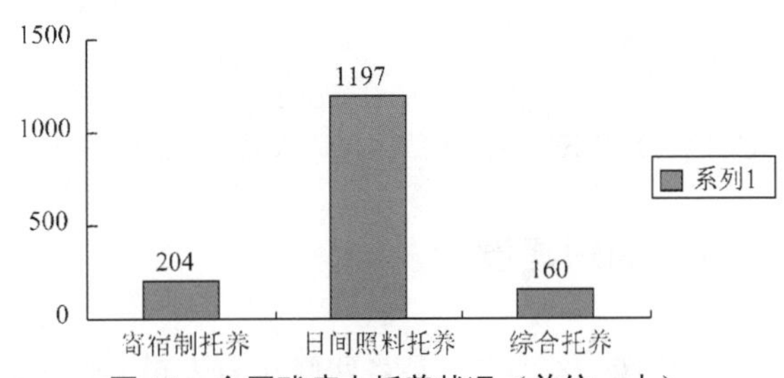

图 14 全区残疾人托养状况（单位：人）

五、扶贫

农村现有贫困残疾人户 73893 户，本年度扶持 14166 户，扶持率达 19%；农村现有贫困残疾人 97661 人，本年度扶持 15457 人，扶持率达 16%。本年度脱贫残疾人 12554 人，返贫 1693 人，接受实用技术培训 6625 人次，投入培训经费 429.38 万元。

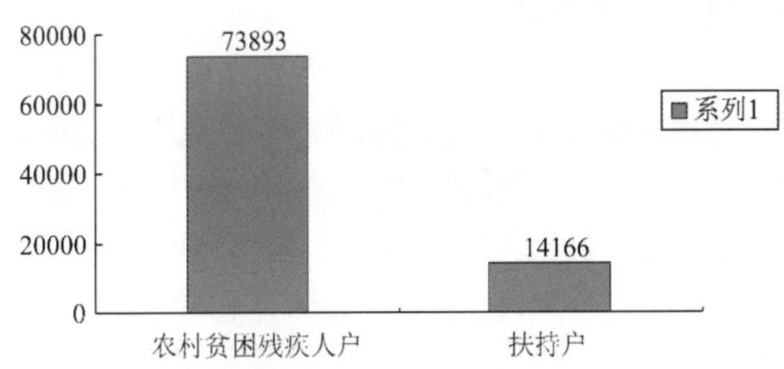

图 15 农村贫困残疾人户扶持状况（单位：户）

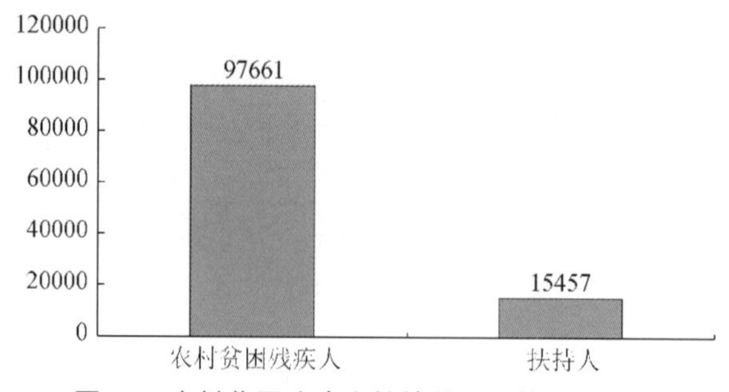

图 16　农村贫困残疾人扶持状况（单位：人）

建立结对帮扶单位 244 个，结对帮扶个人 957 人；共建立残疾人扶持基地 26 个，安置残疾人就业 686 人，扶持带动残疾人 2950 户。

本年度康复扶贫贴息贷款 2405.36 万元，项目贷款扶持残疾人 653 人，到户贷款扶持残疾人 472 人。

本年度完成农村贫困残疾人危房改造 283 户，投入危房改造资金 140.8 万元，受益残疾人 311 人。

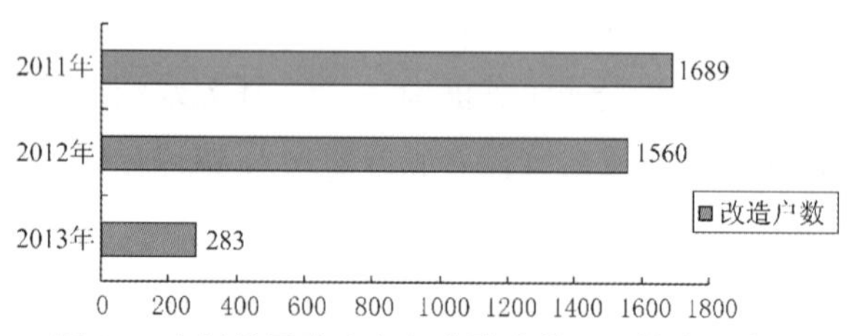

图 17　农村贫困残疾人危房改造状况（单位：户）

六、组织建设

2013 年，区、市、县乡残联实有人员 689 人，编制 503 人；5 个地市级残联中，有 4 个地市级残联的领导班子配备了残疾人理事长或副理事长；21 个县级残联，其中有 10 个县级残联机关配备了残疾人干部。

在残疾人专职委员选聘方面，225 个乡镇（街道）中，选聘残疾人专职委员 240 名；2428 个社区（村）中，选聘残疾人专职委员 1668 名。

各级残联干部队伍培训工作取得较好成绩，较往年有大幅度的提升。

各市、县（区）应建立各类残疾人专门协会 135 个，已建各类残疾人专门协会 94 个，已建率达 70%，全部没有进行社团登记。其中盲人协会 19 个、聋人协会 19 个、肢残人协会 19 个、智力残疾人及亲友协会 18 个、精神残疾人及亲友协会 18 个。

七、维权

本年度地市级政府制定或修改了关于残疾人的专门法规、规章 2 件，县级以上人大执法检查或专题调研残疾人工作 6 次，政协视察和专题调研 6 次。

全区开展普法宣传教育活动 40 次，参加人数 2388 人；

开展法律培训班 18 次，参加人数 451 人；

建立残疾人法律救助工作协调机构 8 个；

建立残疾人法律救助工作站 5 个，办理案件 61 件；

建立残疾人法律援助中心（工作站）25 个，办理案件 372 件；　残联协助人大代表、政协委员提出议案、建议、提案 13 件；残联办理建议、提案 13 件。

各级政府制定无障碍建设与管理法规、政府令 5 个；成立无障碍建设领导协调组织 16 个；系统开展无障碍建设市、县 23 个；开展贫困残疾人家庭无障碍改造 1162 户，组织无障碍检查 36 次，无障碍培训 148 人次，发放残疾人机动轮椅车燃油补贴 16193 人。

各级残联共处理残疾人群众来信 11 件，比上年减少 2 件；接待残疾人群众来访 407 人次，比上年减少 11 人次。

八、宣传文化

中央级媒体采用稿件 1 件，主要新闻媒体刊播稿件 560 件，报纸专版 2 个，广播电台残疾人专题节目 1 个，电视手语栏目 1 个，自治区残疾人事业新闻宣传促进会 1 个。

地市级主要新闻媒体刊播稿件 413 件，报纸专版 15 个，广播电台残疾人专题节目 6 个，电视手语栏目 3 个，电视公益广告片 6 个，报纸公益广告 5 个。自治区和地市级公共图书馆设立盲文及盲人有声读物阅览室已达到 1 和 5 个，举办残疾人文化周 1 和 11 个，举办残疾人文化艺术类比赛及展览分别是 1 和 30 个，已成立残疾人艺术团队 0 和 2 个。

九、体育

自治区举办残疾人群众体育健身活动 1 次，参加人数 750 人；设立残疾人群众体育示范点 9 个，聘任残疾人体育健身指导员 104 人；建立残疾人体育训练基地 2 个，聘任教练员 5 人。

地市级举办残疾人体育健身活动 9 次，参加人数 458 人，设立残疾人群众体育示范点 19 个，聘任残疾人体育健身指导员 51 人。

十、综合服务设施

截止到 2013 年底，已竣工并投入使用的各级残疾人综合服务设施共计 17 个，在建项目 1 个，筹建项目 2 个。其中已竣工并投入使用的各级残疾人综合服务设施总建设规模达 2.98 万平方米，总投资 6957 万元。

各级康复设施在建项目共计 3 个，建设规模 4.13 万平方米，总投资 2.08 亿元。

十一、信息化

统计队伍建设进一步加强，各级残联共有 24 名专、兼职统计人员从事残疾人事业统计工作，其中有 9 名持有统计从业资格证书。统计人员业务素质培养普遍得到重视，本年度自治区残联举办统计培训班 1 期，参加培训 87 人次；地市级举办业务培训班 6 期，参加培训 179 人次。

各级残联全面推进网站建设。自治区残联建立局域网，全部开通了公众服务网站，网上信息服务覆盖全区。有 4 个地市级残联和 8 个县级残联开通网站，这为今后残联系统网站集群服务奠定了基础。

各级残联共有 37 名专业技术人员从事信息化工作。自治区及地市级残联举办信息工作培训班 6 期，培训各级残联信息员 209 人次。

2013年新疆维吾尔自治区残疾人事业发展统计公报

2013年按照中央和自治区党委关于开展群众路线教育实践活动的统一部署，自治区残联党组加强组织领导，贯彻整风精神，按照"照镜子、正衣冠、洗洗澡、治治病"的总要求，以为民务实清廉为主要内容，把政治上强作为检验所有党员干部的第一标准，坚持边学边查边整边改，扎实推进教育实践活动，在残联系统上下进行了一次深刻的思想政治洗礼。通过深入开展党的群众路线教育实践活动，残联系统对"全心全意为残疾人服务"的宗旨有了更加深刻的理解，为残疾人服务的能力和水平有了较高的提升，干部职工在推动残疾人事业向前发展的积极性、主动性和创造性方面明显增强。通过自治区组织民生工程中的富民安居工程、儿童康复救助、白内障复明、阳光家园托养工程和自治区残联大力实施扶贫就业基地建设、光明工程、农村基层党组织助残扶贫、爱心天使助学基金、贫困残疾人康复救助关爱、社区康复建设、儿童助听、阳光助行、肢体残疾假肢装配、残疾人驾驶机动燃油补贴等惠残工程，改善了残疾人的生存状况；残疾人康复、教育、就业、扶贫、社会保障、文化宣传体育、权益保障、无障碍环境建设、基层设施建设、慈善捐助、信息化建设、理论研究和援疆工作都取得了新成绩。现根据2013年度残疾人事业统计数据和实际情况，进行分析，并公报如下：

一、康复

全疆在11个市辖区和80个县（市）开展了社区康复工作，累计已建社区康复站的社区总数0.15万个，配备0.37万名社区康复协调员。

8个县的9个医疗卫生机构陆续开展残疾儿童筛查工作，年度新诊断0-6岁残疾儿童134人。

2013年，通过实施一批重点康复工程，使各类别残疾人得到不同程度的康复。开展视力残疾康复机构总数达到28个，完成白内障复明手术1.36万例；为7009名贫困白内障患者免费施行复明手术；为6163名低视力患者配用助视器，培训低视力儿童家长309名，有效开展家庭康复训练。对1641名盲人进行定向行走训练。

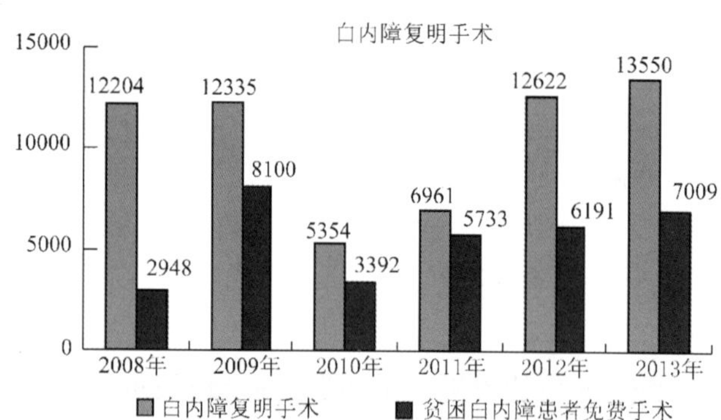

图1 白内障患者复明手术开展情况（单位：例）

推进听力语言康复机构规范化管理，完善基层服务网络。已建设省级听力语言康复机构1个，基层听力语言康复机构15个。年度新收训聋儿220名，在训聋儿349名；规范聋儿家长学校，开展家庭训练，共培训聋儿家长449名；开展各级各类听力语言康复专业技术人员培训，共培训专业人员45人。

开展肢体残疾康复训练服务机构达73个，全部为地市级、县级康复机构；培训各级各类肢体残疾康复人员406人次；全国共对4972肢体残疾者实施康复训练；实施救助项目资助586名脑瘫儿童进行机构康复训练，资助78名贫困肢体残疾儿童实施矫治手术。

开展宣传普及教育，为麻风患者回归社会营造良好社会氛围。

开展智力残疾康复训练服务的机构23个，其中，省级康复机构1个，地市级、县级康复机构22个；培训各级各类智力残疾康复人员44人次；全国共对2165名智力残疾人进行康复训练；实施救助项目资助410名智力残疾儿童进行机构康复训练，同时培训儿童家长。

大力推广"社会化、综合性、开放式"精神病防治康复工作。在69个市县开展精神病防治康复工作，对2.34万重性精神病患者进行综合防治康复，监护率达到66.59%，显好率达到49.87%，社会参与率达到32.55%，肇事率0.01%；解除关锁4人；对4820名贫困精神病患者进行医疗救助。

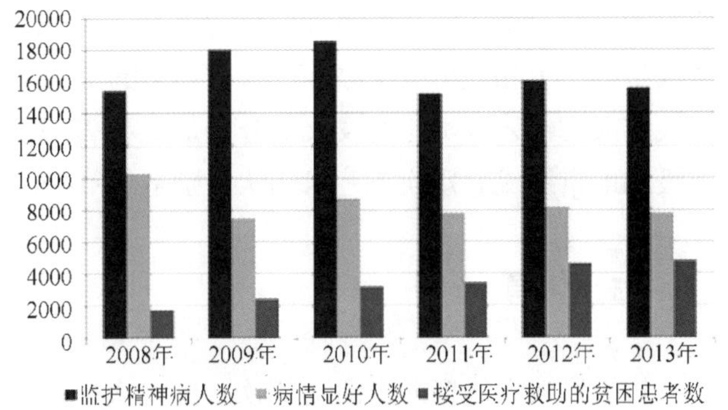

图 2　精神病防治康复工作情况（单位：人）

建立了 1 个省级孤独症儿童康复训练机构，5 个地市级以下孤独症儿童康复训练机构；406 名孤独症儿童在各级机构进行了康复训练。

加强残疾人辅助器具服务体系建设，深入开展辅助器具供应服务，由于援疆工作进展良好，为残疾人减免费用供应辅助器具 37829 件，其中装配假肢 523 例、矫形器 506 例，验配助视器 6662 件。

二、教育

为家庭经济困难的残疾儿童享受普惠性学前教育提供资助 200 人次。各地也积极多渠道争取资金支持，对 4 名残疾儿童给予学前教育资助。

已开办特殊教育普通聋高中班（部）1 个，在校生 57 人。残疾人中等职业学校（班）2 个，在校生 530 人，毕业生 144 人，其中 111 人获得职业资格证书。有 241 名残疾人被普通高等院校录取。

截止到 2013 年底，有未入学适龄残疾儿童少年 4183 人，其中视力残疾儿童 224 人，听力残疾儿童 177 人，言语残疾儿童 279 人，智力残疾儿童 1304 人，肢体残疾儿童 1171 人，精神残疾儿童 224 人，多重残疾儿童 804 人。

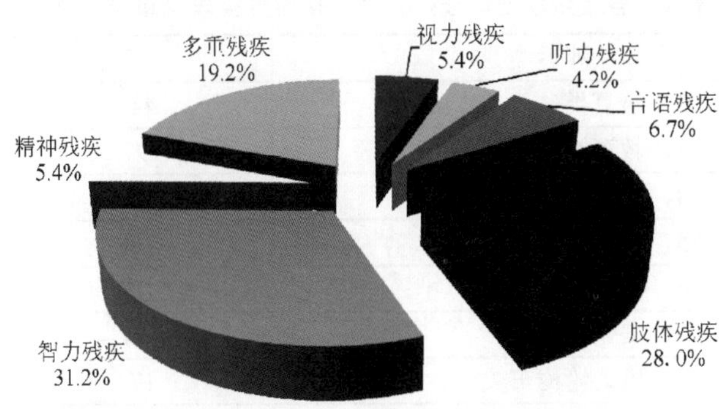

图 3　未入学残疾儿童中各类残疾儿童所占比例

三、就业

2013 年，城镇新就业残疾人 5882 人，其中，集中就业 1787 人，按比例安排就业 1876 人，公益性岗位就业 216 人，个体就业及其它形式灵活就业 1833 人，辅助性就业 170 人。城镇就业人数 7.24 万；22.98 万农村残疾人在业，其中 20.01 万残疾人从事农业生产劳动。

残疾人职业培训基地达到 370 个，其中残联兴办 96 个，依托社会机构兴办 274 个，0.93 万人次城镇残疾人接受了职业培训。

盲人按摩事业稳定发展，按摩机构迅速增长。2013 年度培训盲人保健按摩人员 196 名、盲人医疗按摩人员 90 名；保健按摩机构达到 102 个，医疗按摩机构达到 18 个；在专业技术职务资格评审中，有 15 人通过医疗按摩人员初级职称评审。

四、社会保障

2013 年 8.16 万城镇残疾人参加了城镇居民社会养老保险，参保率 62.21%。在 60 岁以下的参保残疾人中有 0.98 万重度残疾人，其中 0.94 万得到了政府的参保扶助，代缴补贴比例达到 96.50%。有 1.7 万非重度残疾人也享受了全额或部分代缴的优惠政策。领取养老金待遇的人数达到 2.08 万人。

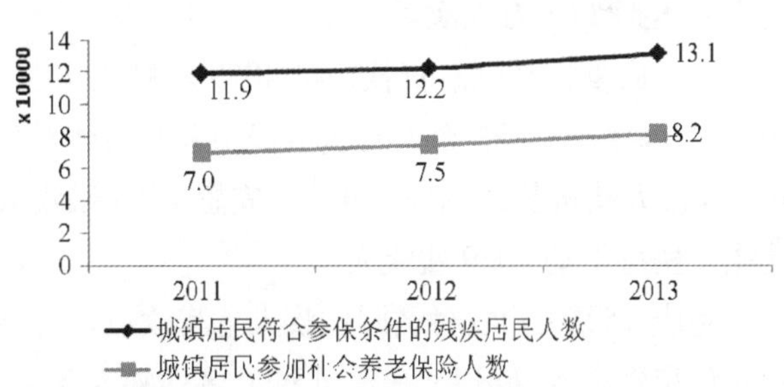

图 4　城镇居民参加社会养老保险情况（单位：万人）

新型农村社会养老保险方面，共有 16.75 万残疾人参加了新型农村社会养老保险，参保率 73.88%。在 60 周岁以下的参保残疾人中有重度残疾人 3.66 万，其中 3.15 万得到了政府的参保扶助，代缴补贴比例达到 86.02%。有 5.3 万非重度残疾人也享受了全额或部分代缴的优惠政策。享受养老金待遇的人数达到 5.38 万人。

城镇残疾职工参加社会保险人数达到 5.63 万，城镇残疾居民参加基本医疗保险达到 9.53 万人，城镇 5.79 万和农村 14.73 万残疾人纳入最低生活保障范围；城镇集中供养残疾人和农村五保供养残疾人分别达到 890 人和 2737 人；10277 人和 7852 人符合条件的城乡残疾人分别享受了稳定的生活补贴和护理补贴。1.9 万城乡残疾人得到了其他救助救济。

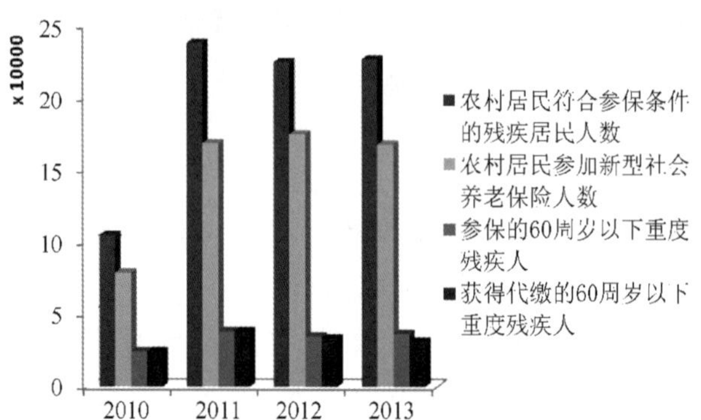

图 5　农村居民参加新型社会养老保险情况（单位：万人）

残疾人托养服务工作规范推进，残疾人托养服务机构达到 110 个，共为 2031 残疾人提供了托养服务。其中寄宿制托养服务机构 16 个；日间照料机构 88 个；综合性托养服务机构 6 个。接受居家托养服务的残疾人达到 2.31 万人。

五、扶贫

2013 年，3.53 万贫困残疾人得到扶持，其中 1.12 万人通过扶贫开发实际脱贫；接受实用技术培训的残疾人达到 2.03 万人次。

康复扶贫贴息贷款扶持 4079 农村残疾人，2040 个单位和 6521 个人对贫困残疾人开展结对帮扶。残疾人扶贫基地达到 114 个，安置 2263 残疾人就业，扶持带动 4029 残疾人。

完成 15280 户农村贫困残疾人危房改造，各地投入危房资金 6，748.13 万元，15490 名残疾人受益。

六、宣传文化

省级中央媒体采用稿件 60 件，主要新闻媒体刊播稿件数 260 件，报刊专版 7 个，残疾人专题广播节目 1 个，电视手语新闻栏目 1 个，省级残疾人事业新闻宣传促进会 1 个。

地市级主要新闻媒体刊播稿件数 1472 件，报刊专版 15 个，残疾人专题广播节目 35 个，电视手语新闻栏目 5 个，建立地市级新促会 3 个。

省级和地市级公共图书馆设立盲文及盲人有声读物阅览室分别达到 3 和 5 个，举办残疾人文化周省级举办 2 个和地市级举办 63 个，省级和地市级举办残疾人文化艺术类比赛及展览分别是 3 和 22 个，省级和地市级成立残疾人艺术团队分别是 1 和 4 个。

七、体育

省级残疾人体育健身活动 2 次，参加人数 0.02 万人，残疾人体育训练基地 5 个，聘任教练员 12 人。

地市级残疾人体育健身活动 18 次，参加人数 0.3 万人，残疾人体育示范点 4 个，残疾人体育健身指导员 26 人。

八、维权

各级残联维权组织建设得到加强，残疾人事业法律法规体系进一步完善，残疾人维权工作全面开展。

2013 年，制定或修改了关于残疾人的专门法规、规章地市级 1 件；县级以上人大进行《残疾人保障法》执法检查和专题调研 14 次；政协进行视察和专题调研 11 次。开展普法宣传教育活动 238 次，6.09 万人参加；举办法律培训班 37 个，0.14 万人参加。

截至 2013 年底，成立残疾人法律救助工作协调机构 50 个，建立残疾人法律救助工作站 21 个，办理案件 178 件，建立残疾人法律援助中心（工作站）87 个，办理案件 751 件，有力地促进了法律救助和法律援助工作。

残疾人参政议政工作得到加强，各级残联协助人大代表、政协委员提出议案、建议、提案 39 件，办理议案、建议、提案 17 件。

表 1　各级残联处理残疾人群众来信分类表（单位：件）

类别	件数
1、涉法涉诉类	22
2、康复类	417
3、教育类	97
4、就业类	159
5、扶贫类	188
6、社会保障类	104
7、文化体育类	34
8、机动轮椅车类	174
9、意见建议类	112
10、其他类	76
合计	1383

无障碍建设法规、标准进一步完善。共出台了10个省、地市、县级无障碍建设与管理法规、规章；2个市、县、区系统开展无障碍建设；开展无障碍建设检查97次，无障碍培训0.05万人次；为0.17万个贫困残疾人家庭实施了无障碍改造；为2.05万残疾人发放了残疾人机动轮椅车燃油补贴。

各级残联共处理残疾人群众来信1383余件，接待残疾人群众来访12873人次，其中集体访3批次、17人次。

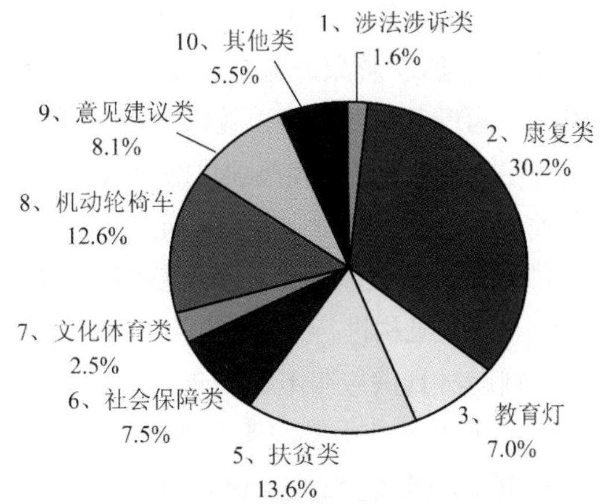

图6　残疾人群众来信分类占比情况图

九、组织建设

2013年，省级残联、地（州、市）、县（市、区）、乡（镇、街道）残联，分别召开了代表大会和主席团会议，选举产生了新一届主席团和领导班子。通过换届，12个地市级残联在领导班子中配备了残疾人理事长或副理事长；58个县级残联机关配备了残疾人干部；已建乡镇（街道）残联1016个，已建率达到96.49%，选聘残疾人专职委员1379名；已建社区（村）残协0.76万个，已建率达到76.74%，选聘残疾人专职委员0.5万名。

省市县乡残联实有人员已达0.28万人。各级残联共举办培训班0.06万期，培训机关干部、协会干部及残疾人专职委员1.04万人次。

共建立省级以下各类残疾人专门协会526个，市级专门协会已建比例为100%，市辖区专门协会已建比例100%；县（含县级市）级专门协会已建比例为95.71%。

十、信息化

统计队伍建设进一步加强，各级残联共有101名专、兼职统计人员从事残疾人事业统计工作，统计人员业务素质培养普遍得到重视，省级残联举办培训班1期，参加培训的人员达到25人次；地市级举办培训班12期，参加培训的人员达到180人次。

地方残联全面推进网站建设，目前1个省级残联已全部开通了公众服务网站，有10个地市级残联网站和25个县级残联网站也已开通。2013年省级及地市级残联开设网站技术培训班6期，培训各级残联信息员达93人次。

各级残联共有137名专业技术人员从事信息化工作；省级残联共建立局域网1个。

十一、基础设施

截至2013年底，全区已竣工并投入使用的各级残疾人综合服务设施68个，总建设规模17.78万平方米，总投资48768.63万元；已竣工并投入使用的各级残疾人康复设施8个，总建设规模0.53万平方米，总投资1657万元；已竣工并投入使用的各级残疾人托养服务设施7个，总建设规模1.03万平方米，总投资2326万元。

2013 年新疆生产建设兵团残疾人事业发展统计公报

2013 年，兵团残疾人事业深入贯彻落实党的十八大、十八届三中全会精神，按照《兵团残疾人事业"十二五"发展纲要（2011-2015 年）》（新兵发〔2011〕55 号）年度目标任务，紧紧围绕残疾人社会保障体系和服务体系建设，以改善残疾人基本生活为重点，扎实工作，各项工作有了新的起色，兵团残疾人事业发展取得新进展。

一、康复

通过实施一批重点康复工程，使各类别残疾人得到不同程度的康复。围绕"人人享有康复服务"的工作目标，充分发动和利用社会资源，积极推进社区康复示范团场创建活动。有 11 个师直单位和 127 个团场开展了社区康复工作，已建立社区康复站的社区有 0.01 个，配备 0.03 名社区康复协调员。42 个医疗卫生机构在 127 个团场陆续开展残疾儿童筛查工作，年度新诊断 0-6 岁残疾儿童 385 人。

全年完成白内障复明手术 0.18 例；为 694 名贫困白内障患者免费施行复明手术；为 1026 名低视力患者配用助视器，培训低视力儿童家长 194 名，对 121 名盲人进行定向行走训练。

开展听力语言康复工作，年度新收训聋儿 31 人，在训聋儿 78 人；培训聋儿家长 100 名；为成年听力语言残疾人提供康复技术服务 1056 人次。

开展肢体残疾康复训练服务机构 1 个，其中，省级康复机构 1 个；培训各级各类肢体残疾康复人员 2 人次；共对 2124 名肢体残疾患者实施康复训练；实施救助项目资助 25 名脑瘫儿童进行机构康复训练；资助 54 名贫困肢体残疾儿童实施矫治手术。

开展智力残疾康复训练服务的机构 1 个，其中，省级康复机构 1 个；对 805 名智力残疾患者进行不同程度的康复训练与服务；实施救助项目资助 19 名智力残疾儿童进行机构康复训练；智力残疾儿童社区、家庭康复训练 253 人；成年智力残疾人社区、家庭康复训练 533 人。

大力推广"社会化、综合性、开放式"精神病防治康复工作。在 6 个师开展精神病防治康复工作，对 1.00 万重性精神病患者进行综合防治康复，监护率达到 71.21%，显好率达到 65.26%，社会参与率达到 51.41%，肇事率 0.14%；对 3051 名重度精神病患者进行综合防治康复，对 2033 名贫困患者进行医疗救助，其中，通过"彩票公益金康复项目"资助 797 名贫困精神病患者免费服药，救助 165 名重症患者得到免费住院治疗，接受其他项目医疗救助 1071 名贫困患者，各级投入经费 208 万多元。

建立了 1 个省级孤独症儿童康复训练机构；24 名孤独症儿童在机构进行了康复训练。

开展辅助器具供应服务，全年供应各类残疾人辅助器具 4996 件，其中装配普及型假肢 102 例、矫形器装配 36 例，验配助视器 1284 件。

二、教育

残疾人受教育权得到了更好保障，残疾儿童少年九年义务教育全面普及，学前教育阶段本年度接受残疾人事业专项彩票公益金助学项目资助 30 人，自筹资金资助 5 人。认真做好残疾学生参加高考工作，有 33 名残疾学生被疆内外普通高等院校录取。

截止到 2013 年底，有未入学适龄残疾儿童少年 49 人，其中视力残疾儿童少年 4 人，听力残疾儿童少年 1 人，言语残疾儿童少年 2 人，肢体残疾儿童少年 16 人，智力残疾儿童少年 14 人，精神残疾儿童少年 5 人，多重残疾儿童少年 7 人。

三、就业

城镇新安排 1769 名残疾人就业。其中，集中就业残疾人 255 人，按比例安排残疾人就业 460 人，个体及其它形式就业 195 人，公益性岗位就业 70 人，辅助性就业 789 人，全兵团城镇实际在业人数 1.79 万人；职业培训基地 2 个，其中，残联兴办 1 个，依托社会机构兴办 1 个，0.08 万人次接受了城镇职业培训。

培训盲人保健按摩人员 18 人，保健按摩机构共 26 个，医疗按摩机构 7 个；在专业技术职务资格评审中，分别有 7 人和 5 人通过医疗按摩人员中级和初级职称评审。

四、社会保障

有 0.90 万城镇残疾人参加了城镇居民社会养老保险，参保率 64.17%。在 60 周岁以下的参保残疾人中有 0.31 万重度残疾人，其中 0.26 万得到了政府的参保扶助，代缴补贴比例达到 83.23%。有 0.14 万非重度残疾人也享受了全额或部分代缴的优惠政策。领取养老金待遇的人数达到 0.30 万人。

城镇残疾职工参加社会保险人数合计 1.41 万人，城镇残疾居民参加城镇居民医疗保险人数为 2.28 万人，城镇已纳入最低生活保障 2.08 万人，城镇集中供养和其他救助救济 0.81 万人。

残疾人托养服务工作进一步推进，残疾人托养机构达 27 个，共为 670 残疾人提供托养服务。其中寄宿制托养机构 23 个，日间照料托养机构 2 个，综合性托养服务机构 2 个。本年度接受居家托养服务残疾人达到 0.64 万人。

五、扶贫

2.00 万贫困残疾人得到扶持，其中 0.22 万人通过扶贫开发实际脱贫；接受实用技术培训的残疾人达到 1.24 万人次。

中央彩票公益金康复扶贫贴息贷款扶持 606 名贫困残疾人； 1192 个单位和 2876 个人对贫困残疾人开展结对帮扶；残疾人扶贫基地达到 18 个，安置 328 名残疾人就业，扶持带动 808 残疾人（户）。

将残疾人住房建设纳入兵团保障性住房建设年度计划，完成 3407 户贫困残疾人危房改造，各级投入危房资金 9617.50 万元， 3428 名残疾人受益。

六、维权

各级开展普法宣传教育活动 205 次， 6.40 万人次参加；截至 2013 年底，成立残疾人法律救助工作协调机构 4 个， 建立残疾人法律救助工作站 3 个，办理案件 30 件； 建立残疾人法律援助中心（站、点）166 个，办理案件 339 件，有力地促进了法律援助和法律服务工作。

无障碍建设领导协调组织 4 个，贫困残疾人家庭无障碍改造 0.02 万户，为 0.49 万名残疾人发放了机动轮椅车燃油补贴。

各级残联共处理残疾人群众来信 347 件，接待残疾人群众来访 2750 人次。

七、宣传文体

省级主要新闻媒体刊播稿件数 485 件，电视手语新闻栏目 1 个，电视公益广告片 4 个，报纸公益广告 15 个；地市级主要新闻媒体刊播稿件数 1196 件，报刊专版 5 个。

有 1 个地级公共图书馆设立盲文及盲人有声读物图书室；省级和地市级举办残疾人文化周 2 和 20 个，举办残疾人文化艺术类比赛及展览分别是 1 和 5 次。

省级残疾人体育健身活动 2 次，参加人数 0.02 万人，残疾人体育健身指导员 3 人，聘任教练员 2 人；地市级残疾人体育健身活动 16 次，参加人数 0.15 万人，残疾人群众体育活动示范点 2 个，残疾人体育健身指导员 87 人。

八、组织建设

残联领导班子中配备残疾人或副理事长情况：省级残联领导班子中配备有 1 名残疾人，1 个地级残联在领导班子中配备了残疾人，3 个县级残联配备了残疾人干部，已建乡镇（街道）残联 7 个，选聘残疾人专职委员 9 人。兵团残联系统实有人员 0.03 万人，省级以下共建立各类残疾人专门协会 64 个。

九、信息化建设

统计队伍建设进一步加强，各级残联共有 179 名兼职统计人员从事残疾人事业统计工作，统计人员业务素质培养普遍得到重视，省级残联举办培训班 1 期，参加培训的人员 65 人次；地市级举办培训班 8 期，参加培训的人员 144 人次。

推进网站建设，目前有 1 个省级 1 个地市级残联开通了公众服务网站。省级网站发稿量 507 篇，各级残联共有 184 名兼职人员从事信息化工作。

十、服务设施建设

截至2013年底，已竣工并投入使用的各级残疾人综合服务设施10个，总建设规模0.70万平方米，总投资968.00万元；已竣工并投入使用的各级残疾人康复设施2个，总建设规模0.66万平方米，总投资2128.50万元；已竣工并投入使用的各级残疾人托养服务设施27个，总建设规模4.53万平方米，总投资6629.90万元。

2013 年黑龙江垦区残疾人事业发展统计公报

2013 年是执行《中国残疾人事业“十二五”计划发展纲要》的攻坚年，在农垦总局党委的高度重视下，在中国残联的正确领导下，在全垦区残疾人工作者和广大残疾人的共同努力下，农垦总局残联全面完成了年初制定的工作目标，团结和带领全垦区残疾人在康复、教育、就业、扶贫、文化等各个方面取得了巨大的进步。现将 2013 年各项业务工作指标完成情况统计分析报告如下：

一、康复工作

紧紧围绕“人人享有康复服务”的目标，充分利用、整合资源，积极推进残疾人社区康复工作，使更多的残疾人享有康复服务并受益。

截止 2013 年底，全垦区共有 38 个农牧场开展社区康复服务，已开展康复服务的社区达 43 个，社区康复协调员累计达 161 人。已建社区康复服务档案人数 37604 人，占辖区内残疾人总数的 41.44%，接受社区康复的人数累计达 1774 人，其中，本年度新增接受社区康复的人数为 402 人。

2013 年，通过实施一批重点康复工程，使各类别残疾人得到不同程度的康复。全年完成白内障复明手术 444 例，为 152 名贫困白内障患者免费施行复明手术。低视力者配用助视器 140 人，培训低视力儿童家长 60 人，盲人定向行走训练 140 人。

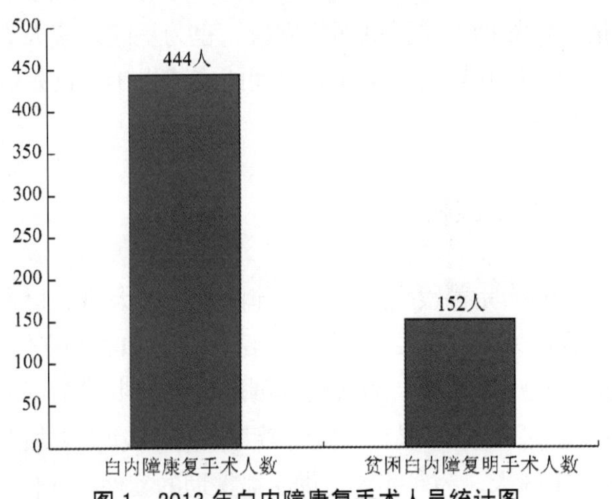

图 1　2013 年白内障康复手术人员统计图

大力推进精神病防治康复工作，按照“低水平覆盖”的要求，在全垦区范围内开展精神病防治康复工作，覆盖总人口 163 万余人，精神病总人数 14455 人，监护精神病人数 6516 人，显好精神病人数 2370 人。接受治疗的精神病患者 2556 人，精神病康复机构 3 家，在其中康复的精神病人数为 627 人。年度累计投入 89 万余元，其中，农场级年度经费投入 80 余万元，管理局级年度经费投入 9.4 万元。

积极开展智力残疾人康复救助工作，为 52 名智力残疾儿童提供机构康复训练，为 118 名轻度智力残疾儿童提供社区、家庭康复训练。

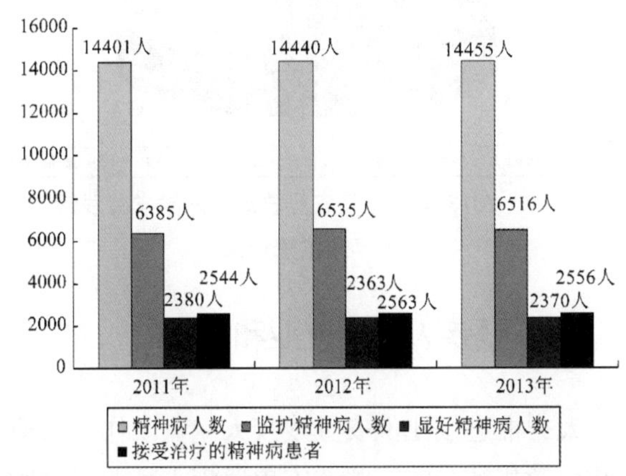

图 2　2011-2013 年度垦区精神残疾人康复工作一览

加强肢体康复训练工作，共为 317 名肢体残疾人提供训练，其中肢体残疾儿童机构训练 27 人，肢体残疾人社区、家庭训练 290 人。

加强对听力残疾儿童的康复训练，2013 年，为 16 名听力残疾儿童提供家庭康复训练，新培训听力残疾儿童家长 32 名。

为了使残疾人出行方便，2013 年共为 58 名残疾人装配了大腿假肢.为 88 名残疾人装配了小腿假肢，为各类残疾人免费配发辅助器具 2352 件，其中为重度残疾人配发辅具 8 件，使更多的残疾人得以恢复和改善肢体功能。

加大对残疾儿童的筛查和救助力度，目前有 103 个农场开展残疾儿童筛查工作，开展儿童筛查的医疗机构有 8 所，新诊断的 0-6 岁残疾儿童有 6 人。发放残疾儿康预防宣传材料 1405 份，举办残疾儿童预防宣传活动 15 次。

为了更好的服务残疾人，2013 年开展康复人才培训活动，培训康复管理人员 45 人，康复业务人员 46 人，培训社区康复协调员 144 人，极大程度的缓解了康复人才不足的情况。

二、教育工作

在有关部门的共同努力下，残疾人教育事业取得了良好的成绩，目前，未入学的学龄残疾儿童少年共 166 人，其中视力残疾人 2 人，听力残疾人 5 人，言语残疾 11 人，肢体残疾人 53 人，智力残疾人 78 人，精神残疾人 6 人，多重 11 人。20 名学龄前儿童接受彩票公益金助学资助。

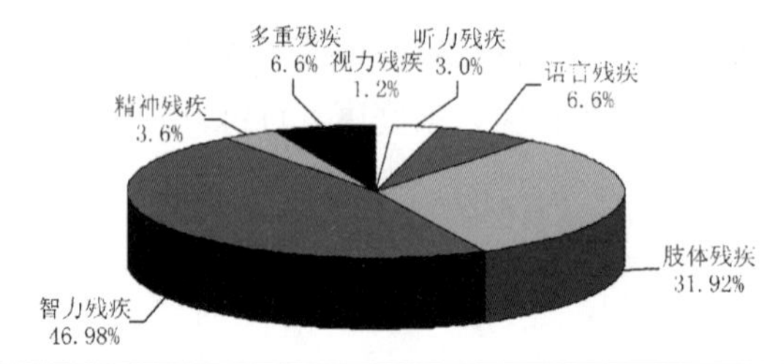

图 3　2013 年黑龙江农垦总局未入学学龄残疾少年儿童统计图

三、残疾人劳动就业和扶贫

大力推进按比例安置残疾人就业工作，采取集中和分散相结合的方法，安置残疾人就业。鼓励有能力的残疾人自主创业。截至目前，残疾人就业人数 15801 人，其中集中就业 52 人，按比例就业 5460 人，个体及其他形式就业 9949 人，公益岗位就业 295 人。

为了更好的解决残疾人的实际困难，动员全社会的力量，开展“帮包带扶”工作。垦区目前有特困残疾人 11427 人，低收入残疾人 16622 人。本年度扶持贫困残疾人 4291 户，共 5343 人，脱贫 1502 人。为 2141 名残疾人提供实用技术培训。为 600 户贫困残疾人进行危房改造。全年参与扶贫的结对帮扶单位 108 个，帮扶个人 695 人，物资和资金投入 24.3 万元。

四、盲人按摩

卫生部、人力资源和社会保障部、国家中医药管理局和中国残疾人联合会联合制定了《盲人医疗按摩管理办法》出台后，垦区的盲人按摩有了更迅速的发展。目前，盲人医疗按摩机构 1 个，保健按摩机构 2 个，盲人医疗按摩人员中级的 4 人，初级的 5 人，盲人保健按摩人员 5 人。

五、社会保障

残疾人社会保障工作是当前残疾人工作的重点，这项工作残疾人受益面广，解决残疾人的实际困难比较彻底、稳定。2013 年城镇残疾职工参加社会保险人数为 8207 人，残疾居民参加城镇医疗保险人数 55889 人，城镇个体就业参加社会保险人数 5786 人，其中，个体就业参加城镇居民养老保险人数 3438 人，参加医疗保险人数 3752 人。全年纳入最低生活保障范围的 30568 人，集中供养 111 人，其他救济 4171 人。机构托养残疾人 371 人，其中智力残疾 41 人，精神残疾 276 人，其他类别残疾人 54 人，享受居家托养服务残疾人 1542 人。

六、宣传文化

2013 年残疾人事业的社会宣传力度得到进一步加强，社会舆论环境得到进一步改善。在主要新闻媒体刊播稿件数 213 件，在残疾人文化周举办残疾人艺术作品展，共收到刺绣、书法、绘画、摄影等艺术作品 300 余件，极大程度的丰富残疾人的文化生活。完善北大荒新月网站的各项工作，开设网上办公、法律援助、新月论坛、残疾人热线、整合残疾人数据库，建立覆盖垦区的电子数据传输平台，建立黑龙江垦区精神病人社会化服务管理系统，为精神病救助工作提供网络支持，也为垦区残疾人事业的发展和残疾人工作者之间的交流提供了良好的平台。

七、维权

继续完善残疾人事业法律法规，加大执法检查和监督力度，开展法律服务、法律援助和法制宣传，维护残疾人权益，为残疾人创造文明进步的无障碍环境。全年共开展普法宣传教育活动 61 次，参加人数 3138 人，为残疾人提供法律援助的案件 133 件。为推进垦区的无障碍建设，垦区共成立无障碍建设领导协调组织9个，共印发无障碍宣传材料300余份。为150名贫困残疾人家庭进行无障碍改造。为1618名残疾人发放机动轮椅车燃油补贴。

信访工作的开展，有力的维护了残疾人的合法权益。全年共处理各类信访案件133件，其中康复类10件，教育类34件，就业类30件，扶贫类32件，社会保障类27件。全年接待来访1222人次，无一起集体上访案件发生。整体上看，问题主要集中在就业、优惠政策方面，这说明残疾人的就业、生活问题仍然是我们迫切要解决的重大问题。

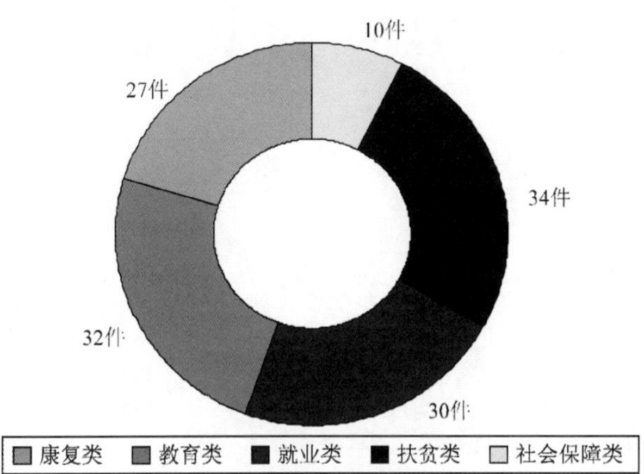

图4 2013年处理各类信访案件图

八、组织建设

残疾人组织是政府联系残疾人的纽带和桥梁，是做好残疾人工作的重要保证。全垦区共有各类残疾人97000人，持证残疾人有35427人，占残疾人总数的36.5%。全垦区有专兼职残疾人工作者210人，其中行政编制65人，事业编制135人。配备残疾人专职委员109人。举办省级综合培训班2次，参加人数247人；地市级干部培训班1次，参加人数13人。

九、综合服务设施

截止到2013年底，已竣工并投入使用的各级残疾人综合服务设施共计6个，筹建项目共计3个，综合服务设施的投入使用将会给残疾人带来更大的方便。

十、信息化建设

统计队伍建设进一步加强，共有113名专、兼职统计人员从事残疾人事业统计工作，其中省级1人，地市级9人，县级103人。统计人员业务素质培养普遍得到重视，省级、管理局级统计人员均持证上岗。省级残联举办培训班1期，参加培训的人员40人次；地市级举办培训班2期，参加培训的人员达到51人次。

全面推进网站建设，有门户网站1个，发稿量900篇。信息化建设投入资金约29万余元，系统维护费3.6万元，信息化专业人才126人，为垦区残联信息化建设提供保障。

十一、存在的问题和不足

2013年，黑龙江农垦总局的残疾人工作较好地完成了各项计划任务，但由于经济和体制等原因，从工作整体来看，黑龙江农垦的残疾人事业发展与中国残联的要求还有一定的差距：一是贫困残疾人的医疗、康复、教育、就业、社会保障等方面还存在着一定的困难，不能完全满足残疾人的需求；二是改善残疾人社会保障体系还不够健全；三是残疾人无障碍建设环境还存在不足，尤其是信息无障碍建设还处在起步阶段。因此，2014年垦区各级残联将紧紧围绕中央7号文件和国办19号文件精神，全面推进"两个体系"建设，提高服务能力和保障能力，在保障民生等方面加大扶持力度，完善工作机制，保障残疾人的基本需求。

附录

Appendix

关于使用 2010 年末全国残疾人总数及各类、不同残疾等级人数的通知

残联〔2012〕25 号

各省、自治区、直辖市及计划单列市残联，新疆生产建设兵团残联，黑龙江农垦总局残联：

根据第六次全国人口普查我国总人口数，及第二次全国残疾人抽样调查我国残疾人占全国总人口的比例和各类残疾人占残疾人总人数的比例，推算了 2010 年末我国残疾人总人数及各类、不同等级的残疾人数，现通知如下：

全国残疾人总数为 8502 万人。

各类残疾人的人数分别为：视力残疾 1263 万人；听力残疾 2054 万人；言语残疾 130 万人；肢体残疾 2472 万人；智力残疾 568 万人；精神残疾 629 万人；多重残疾 1386 万人。

各残疾等级人数分别为：重度残疾 2518 万人；中度和轻度残疾人 5984 万人。

以上数据可在工作中使用并对外公开。

中国残疾人联合会

二〇一二年三月五日

第二次全国残疾人抽样调查残疾标准

（国务院 2005 年 11 月 4 日批准）

视力残疾标准

一、视力残疾的定义

视力残疾，是指由于各种原因导致双眼视力低下并且不能矫正或视野缩小，以致影响其日常生活和社会参与。

视力残疾包括盲及低视力。

二、视力残疾的分级

类别	级别	最佳矫正视力
盲	一级	无光感-＜0.02；或视野半径＜5 度
	二级	0.02-＜0.05；或视野半径＜10 度
低视力	三级	0.05-＜0.1
	四级	0.1-＜0.3

〔注〕

1. 盲或低视力均指双眼而言，若双眼视力不同，则以视力较好的一眼为准。如仅有单眼为盲或低视力，而另一眼的视力达到或优于 0.3，则不属于视力残疾范畴。

2. 最佳矫正视力是指以适当镜片矫正所能达到的最好视力或针孔视力。

3. 以注视点为中心，视野半径＜10 度者，不论其视力如何均属于盲。

听力残疾标准

一、听力残疾的定义

听力残疾，是指人由于各种原因导致双耳不同程度的永久性听力障碍，听不到或听不清周围环境声及言语声，以致影响日常生活和社会参与。

二、听力残疾的分级

听力残疾一级：

听觉系统的结构和功能方面极重度损伤，较好耳平均听力损失≥91 dB HL，在无助听设备帮助下，不能依靠听觉进行言语交流，在理解和交流等活动上极度受限，在参与社会生活方面存在极严重障碍。

听力残疾二级：

听觉系统的结构和功能重度损伤，较好耳平均听力损失在 81-90 dB HL 之间，在无助听设备帮助下，在理解和交流等活动上重度受限，在参与社会生活方面存在严重障碍。

听力残疾三级：

听觉系统的结构和功能中重度损伤，较好耳平均听力损失在 61-80 dB HL 之间，在无助听设备帮助下，在理解和交流等活动上中度受限，在参与社会生活方面存在中度障碍。

听力残疾四级：

听觉系统的结构和功能中度损伤，较好耳平均听力损失在 41-60dB HL 之间，在无助听设备帮助下，在理解和交流等活动上轻度受限，在参与社会生活方面存在轻度障碍。

言语残疾标准

一、言语残疾的定义

言语残疾，是指由于各种原因导致的不同程度的言语障碍，经治疗一年以上不愈或病程超过两年者,而不能或难以进行正常的言语交往活动，以致影响日常生活和社会参与（3 岁以下不定残）。

言语残疾包括：

1. 失语：是指由于大脑言语区域以及相关部位损伤所导致的获得性言语功能丧失或受损。

2. 运动性构音障碍：是指由于神经肌肉病变导致构音器官的运动障碍，主要表现为不会说话、说话费力、发声和发音不清等。

3. 器官结构异常所致的构音障碍：是指构音器官形态结构异常所致的构音障碍。其代表为腭裂以及舌或颌面部术后造成的构音障碍。主要表现为不能说话、鼻音过重、发音不清等。

4. 发声障碍（嗓音障碍）：是指由于呼吸及喉存在器质性病变导致的失声、发声困难、声音嘶哑等。

5. 儿童言语发育迟滞：指儿童在生长发育过程中其言语发育落后于实际年龄的状态。主要表现不会说话、说话晚、发音不清等。

6. 听力障碍所致的语言障碍：是指由于听觉障碍所致的言语障碍。主要表现为不会说话或者发音不清。

7. 口吃：是指言语的流畅性障碍。常表现为在说话的过程中拖长音、重复、语塞并伴有面部及其他行为变化等。

二、言语残疾的分级

言语残疾一级：

无任何言语功能或语音清晰度≤10%，言语表达能力等级测试未达到一级测试水平，不能进行任何言语交流。

言语残疾二级：

具有一定的发声及言语能力。语音清晰度在11%-25%之间，言语表达能力等级测试未达到二级测试水平。

言语残疾三级：

可以进行部分言语交流。语音清晰度在26%-45%之间，言语表达能力等级测试未达到三级测试水平。

言语残疾四级：

能进行简单会话，但用较长句或长篇表达困难。语音清晰度在46%-65%之间，言语表达能力等级测试未达到四级测试水平。

肢体残疾标准

一、肢体残疾的定义

肢体残疾，是指人体运动系统的结构、功能损伤造成四肢残缺或四肢、躯干麻痹（瘫痪）、畸形等而致人体运动功能不同程度丧失以及活动受限或参与的局限。

肢体残疾包括：

1. 上肢或下肢因伤、病或发育异常所致的缺失、畸形或功能障碍；

2. 脊柱因伤、病或发育异常所致的畸形或功能障碍；

3. 中枢、周围神经因伤、病或发育异常造成躯干或四肢的功能障碍。

二、肢体残疾的分级

肢体残疾一级：不能独立实现日常生活活动。

1. 四肢瘫：四肢运动功能重度丧失；
2. 截瘫：双下肢运动功能完全丧失；
3. 偏瘫：一侧肢体运动功能完全丧失；
4. 单全上肢和双小腿缺失；
5. 单全下肢和双前臂缺失；
6. 双上臂和单大腿（或单小腿）缺失；
7. 双全上肢或双全下肢缺失；
8. 四肢在不同部位缺失；
9. 双上肢功能极重度障碍或三肢功能重度障碍。

肢体残疾二级：基本上不能独立实现日常生活活动。

1. 偏瘫或截瘫，残肢保留少许功能（不能独立行走）；
2. 双上臂或双前臂缺失；
3. 双大腿缺失；
4. 单全上肢和单大腿缺失；
5. 单全下肢和单上臂缺失；
6. 三肢在不同部位缺失（除外一级中的情况）；
7. 二肢功能重度障碍或三肢功能中度障碍。

肢体残疾三级：能部分独立实现日常生活活动。

1. 双小腿缺失；
2. 单前臂及其以上缺失；
3. 单大腿及其以上缺失；
4. 双手拇指或双手拇指以外其他手指全缺失；
5. 二肢在不同部位缺失（除外二级中的情况）；
6. 一肢功能重度障碍或二肢功能中度障碍。

肢体残疾四级：基本上能独立实现日常生活活动。

1. 单小腿缺失；
2. 双下肢不等长，差距在5厘米以上（含5厘

米);

3. 脊柱强（僵）直;

4. 脊柱畸形，驼背畸形大于 70 度或侧凸大于 45 度;

5. 单手拇指以外其他四指全缺失;

6. 单侧拇指全缺失;

7. 单足跗跖关节以上缺失;

8. 双足趾完全缺失或失去功能;

9. 侏儒症（身高不超过 130 厘米的成年人);

10. 一肢功能中度障碍或两肢功能轻度障碍;

11. 类似上述的其他肢体功能障碍。

智力残疾标准

一、智力残疾的定义

智力残疾，是指智力显著低于一般人水平，并伴有适应行为的障碍。此类残疾是由于神经系统结构、功能障碍，使个体活动和参与受到限制，需要环境提供全面、广泛、有限和间歇的支持。

智力残疾包括：在智力发育期间（18 岁之前)，由于各种有害因素导致的精神发育不全或智力迟滞；或者智力发育成熟以后，由于各种有害因素导致智力损害或智力明显衰退。

二、智力残疾的分级

级别	分级标准			
	发展商（DQ）0-6 岁	智商（IQ）7 岁及以上	适应性行为（AB）	WHO-DAS Ⅱ分值 18 岁以上
一级	≤25	<20	极重度	≥116 分
二级	26-39	20-34	重度	106-115 分
三级	40-54	35-49	中度	96-105 分
四级	55-75	50-69	轻度	52-95 分

精神残疾标准

一、精神残疾的定义

精神残疾，是指各类精神障碍持续一年以上未痊愈，由于存在认知、情感和行为障碍，以致影响其日常生活和社会参与。

二、精神残疾的分级

18 岁以上（含）的精神障碍患者根据《世界卫生组织残疾评定量表Ⅱ》（WHO-DASⅡ）分数和下述的适应行为表现，18 岁以下者依据下述的适应行为的表现，把精神残疾划分为四级：

精神残疾一级：

WHO-DASⅡ值≥116 分，适应行为严重障碍；生活完全不能自理，忽视自己的生理、心理的基本要求。不与人交往，无法从事工作，不能学习新事物。需要环境提供全面、广泛的支持，生活长期、全部需他人监护。

精神残疾二级：

WHO-DASⅡ值在 106-115 分之间，适应行为重度障碍；生活大部分不能自理，基本不与人交往，只与照顾者简单交往，能理解照顾者的简单指令，有一定学习能力。监护下能从事简单劳动。能表达自己的基本需求，偶尔被动参与社交活动；需要环境提供广泛的支持，大部分生活仍需他人照料。

精神残疾三级：

WHO-DASⅡ值在 96-105 分之间，适应行为中度障碍；生活上不能完全自理，可以与人进行简单交流，能表达自己的情感。能独立从事简单劳动，能学习新事物，但学习能力明显比一般人差。被动参与社交活动，偶尔能主动参与社交活动；需要环境提供部分的支持，即所需要的支持服务是经常性的、短时间的需求，部分生活需由他人照料。

精神残疾四级：

WHO-DASⅡ值在 52-95 分之间，适应行为轻度障碍；生活上基本自理，但自理能力比一般人差，有时忽略个人卫生。能与人交往，能表达自己的情感，体会他人情感的能力较差，能从事一般的工作，学习新事物的能力比一般人稍差；偶尔需要环境提供支持，一般情况下生活不需要由他人照料。

多重残疾

存在两种或两种以上残疾为多重残疾。多重残疾应指出其残疾的类别。多重残疾分级按所属残疾中最重类别残疾分级标准进行分级。

中国残联统计调查项目目录

审批项目一览表

统计调查项目名称	批准文号	有效期截止时间
中国残疾人事业统计年报报表制度	国统制[2014]76 号	2016-08
中国残疾人事业统计年报快报制度	国统制[2014]76 号	2016-08
中国残疾人事业统计台账制度	国统制[2014]76 号	2016-08
全国残疾人状况监测问卷	国统制[2013]81 号	2015-7

中国残疾人联合会文件

残联发[2006]1 号

关于印发《中国残联系统统计工作管理办法》的通知

各省、自治区、直辖市及计划单列市残联，新疆生产建设兵团残联、黑龙江农垦总局残联:

为了加强统计工作的管理,规范统计调查行为，提高统计调查的整体效益，充分发挥统计工作的服务和监督作用，中国残联依据《中华人民共和国统计法》、《中华人民共和国统计法实施细则》、《部门统计调查管理暂行办法》，结合工作实际，对原有的《中国残联系统统计工作暂行规定》、《中国残联系统专项业务统计调查项目管理暂行办法》、《中国残联机关统计资料管理暂行办法》等进行了修订和整合，制定了《全国残联系统统计工作管理办法》，现予以印发，请遵照执行。

中国残疾人联合会

二〇〇六年一月三日

中国残联系统统计工作管理办法

一、总 则

第一条 为了科学、有效地组织全国残联系统统计工作，规范统计调查行为，提高统计调查的整体效益，充分发挥统计工作的服务和监督作用，依据《中华人民共和国统计法》(以下简称《统计法》)、《中华人民共和国统计法实施细则》(以下简称《实施细则》)、《部门统计调查管理暂行办法》，结合工作实际，制定本办法。

第二条 全国残联系统统计工作的基本任务是：对全国残疾人事业的发展状况和残联系统的业务工作进行统计调查、统计分析、统计预测和统计监督，为国家和各级人民政府制定与残疾人事业相关的政策、法规提供依据，为领导运筹决策和残联系统工作的发展提供有效的服务。

第三条 全国残联系统统计工作由：中国残疾人事业统计年报制度、中国残疾人事业统计快报制度、中国残疾人事业基础统计台账制度、专项业务统计调查工作组成。

第四条 各级残联应加强统计现代化建设，积极利用信息技术手段，使残疾人事业统计数据更加科学、准确、及时，逐步实现残疾人事业统计数据的电子化和统计数据的社会共享与服务。

二、统计机构、职责和统计人员

第五条 全国残联系统统计工作实行统一领导、分级负责。中国残联负责全国残疾人事业统计工作的组织、协调与管理，并对地方残联统计工作进行指导，具体由中国残联设置的统计机构负责组织实施。地方各级残联的统计工作由地方各级残联设置的统计机构或统计主管部门负责管理和组织实施，并接受上级残联统计机构和同级人民政府统计部门的指导、监督与管理。

第六条 中国残联的统计机构设在中国残联信息中心，负责组织、协调和管理全国残联系统的统计工作。其主要职责是：制定残疾人事业统计调查计划和项目，制定统计标准；组织协调各级残联搜集、整理、提供统计资料，管理统计资料的发布，开展统计分析、统计预测和统计监督工作；指导、检查全国残联系统统计工作，组织统计业务经验交流，开展全国残联系统统计科学研究；做好统计人员培训工作；制订全国残联系统统计工作现代化规划。

各省级残联应设置统计机构或明确统计主管部门并设专职统计人员，负责指导本行政区域内各级残联统计工作，组织管理本级残联的统计工作。其主要职责是：在完成好中国残联和上级残联下达的各项统计调查工作的同时，为本级残疾人事业提供各项统计数据，并开展统计调查活动。

各地级市残联应明确统计主管部门并设专（兼）职统计人员，其主要职责是：在完成好中国残联和上级残联下达的各项统计调查工作的同时，为本级残疾人事业提供各项统计数据，并开展统计调查活动。

各县级残联应明确统计工作主管部门或主管负责人，确定兼职统计人员。其主要职责是：做好基础数据工作，建立统计台账，完成好中国残联和上级残联下达的统计调查任务，为本级残疾人事业提供各项统计数据，并开展统计调查活动。

第七条 各级残联统计人员应保持相对稳定。统计人员的调动，应当征得本级统计主管部门或统计工作负责人的同意；省级专职统计人员的调动，应当征得中国残联统计机构的同意。统计人员调动工作或离职，应当由经过统计业务培训、能够胜任统计业务工作的人员接替，并办理交接手续。各级残联的统计人员应取得同级人民政府统计机构颁发的统计上岗证，具有残联系统业务知识和计算机操作能力。

三、统计报表制度的编制、修改与审批

第八条 中国残疾人事业统计年报、快报制度和统计台账制度中的指标、指标涵义、调查范围、

分类目录、计算方法和统计报表表式、统计编码以及报送时间，由中国残联统一规定，按照国家统计局的要求报送国家统计局进行审批备案。按规定程序经国家统计局批准或备案的统计报表，在报表的右上角标明制表机关名称、表号、批准或备案机关名称及其批准文号。被调查的部门、人员应当准确、及时地按报表规定填报。

不符合前款规定的统计报表（包括以搜集数字为主的调查提纲）是非法报表，被调查的部门可以拒绝填报。

第九条 中国残疾人事业统计年报、快报和统计台账应根据中国残疾人事业发展的需要及时进行调整和补充。中国残联各业务部门因工作需要，调整和补充有关指标时，应进行充分论证并与中国残联统计管理部门联系与协商，经中国残联理事会批准后，报国家统计局批准或备案。

四、统计台账管理

第十条 为了规范中国残联系统统计工作，做到依法统计，发挥统计服务和监督作用，根据《中华人民共和国统计法》和国家相关统计工作的规定，中国残联将制定中国残疾人事业统计台账制度，加强统计台账的管理与数据的报送。

第十一条 中国残疾人事业统计台账（卡）充分利用电子网络化的方式、将科学合理、准确实用的动态管理，与中国残疾人事业统计报表制度相衔接。台账填写内容要符合法律法规政策的要求，填写对象真实、准确；先填卡，后建帐，做到由台账中提取统计数字。

第十二条 各级残联必须依据中国残疾人事业统计台账（卡）中的数据，报送中国残疾人事业统计快报、年报和各项专项业务统计调查的统计报表，做到填报统计报表的数据全面、准确、及时、数出一门。

第十三条 中国残疾人事业统计台账在统一格式、统一软件下实施，由各级地方残联统计人员协调业务部门和人员用计算机或纸质台账、台卡方式进行专门管理。统计人员发生变动时，要严格履行交接手续。

第十四条 省级、地（市）级残联都应建立电子化台账。有条件的县级残联也要实行电子化台账，各级残联应积极推动电子化台账建设，加强统计台账的管理工作。在没有实行全面电子化台账之前，将实行电子化台账和纸质台账、台卡的同时保存。

第十五条 中国残疾人事业统计台账、台卡按中国残疾人事业统计报表逐级汇总上报。

五、专项业务统计调查管理

第十六条 中国残联和地方各级残联开展的专项业务统计调查，以及残联各业务部门与其他部门或单位联合组织实施的统计调查，其调查的统计指标与中国残联年报、快报指标交叉重复或需要对外公布统计数据的统计调查，均属于专项业务统计调查管理范畴。

第十七条 中国残联系统各级统计机构统一管理和协调本级业务部门专项业务统计调查。

第十八条 专项业务统计调查项目必须符合国家统计局《部门统计调查项目管理暂行办法》的基本原则与要求。专项业务统计调查项目的立项必须有充分的理由。调查要有明确的目的和资料使用范围。调查项目应当与中国残联职能范围和各项业务工作相对应。

第十九条 中国残联系统各级统计机构通过建立审批备案制度、调查项目公布制度、跟踪检查制度、举报制度，对会内专项业务统计调查进行管理。

第二十条 专项业务统计调查项目中的统计标准和分类必须与政府综合统计机构规定使用的标准和分类相一致。涉及政府综合统计机构规定以外的专业标准和分类，要与国家有关标准或行业标准相一致。尚无国家标准和行业标准的，必须严格按照标准化及分类科学的原则进行归纳和设计，并在使用前征求政府综合统计机构的意见。

第二十一条 中国残联新增设的统计调查项目在制定好统计调查方案后，须提交中国残联统计机构审核，报国家统计局批准后统一组织实施。

地方残联新增设的统计调查项目，由本级残联统计机构统一管理，报上级残联统计机构和同级人民政府统计局批准后组织实施。地方残联制发的统计调查表内容、指标涵义、计算方法、完成期限等，均不得与中国残联制发的有关统计调查表相抵触。

六、统计资料的管理与发布

第二十二条 残联系统统计资料实行归口管理。全国性残联系统 统计资料，由中国残联统计机构统一管理；地方性残联系统统计资料，由地方残联统计机构或统计人员统一管理。统计机构和统计人员必须建立统计工作责任制和统计资料整理、审查、管理制度，不断提高工作质量和工作效率，保证残联系统统计资料的准确、及时。

各级残联的文件、报告、简报、情况反映、信息等引用综合性的统计数字，必须经本级统计机构或统计人员复核。对外提供和公布的统计资料，必须经本级统计机构或统计人员统一复核和办理并由主管理事长批准。任何部门和个人不得擅自公开和使用未经正式公布的残联系统统计资料。

第二十三条 各级残联统计机构、统计人员必须建立健全统计资料档案，对原始记录、统计台账和综合分析等统计资料，按有关规定保管，不得损坏。对于属于国家秘密的残联系统统计资料，要按照《中华人民共和国保守国家秘密法》、国家统计局《统计资料保密管理办法》等有关规定，妥善保管。

七、奖励和惩罚

第二十四条 各级残联对有下列表现之一的残联统计机构或者人员，给予表扬或奖励:

一、在改革和完善残联系统统计制度、统计方法等方面，有重要贡献的;

二、在完成规定的残联系统统计调查任务，保障残联系统统计资料的准确性、及时性方面，做出显著成绩的;

三、在进行残联系统统计分析、统计预测和统计监督方面取得重要成绩的;

四、在运用和推广现代化信息技术方面，有显著效果的;

五、在残联系统统计科学研究方面有所创新的;

六、坚持实事求是，依法办事，同违反统计法规和本办法的行为作斗争，表现突出的。

第二十五条 各级残联对有下列行为之一的机构或者人员，给予批评或处分:

一、虚报、瞒报、拒报残联系统统计资料的;

二、伪造、篡改残联系统统计资料的;

三、无故迟报残联系统统计资料的;

四、侵犯统计机构、统计人员行使统计法规及本办法所规定的职权或打击报复统计人员的;

五、违反统计法规及本办法，未经批准，自行编制发布残联系统统计报表的;

六、违反统计法规及本办法，未经核定批准，擅自对外提供或公布残联系统统计资料的。

八、附 则

第二十六条 本办法由中国残联负责解释。

第二十七条 本办法自发布之日起试行。

中华人民共和国统计法

（1983 年 12 月 8 日第六届全国人民代表大会常务委员会第三次会议通过 根据 1996 年 5 月 15 日第八届全国人民代表大会常务委员会第十九次会议《关于修改〈中华人民共和国统计法〉的决定》修正 2009 年 6 月 27 日第十一届全国人民代表大会常务委员会第九次会议修订）

第一章　总　则

第一条　为了科学、有效地组织统计工作，保障统计资料的真实性、准确性、完整性和及时性，发挥统计在了解国情国力、服务经济社会发展中的重要作用，促进社会主义现代化建设事业发展，制定本法。

第二条 本法适用于各级人民政府、县级以上人民政府统计机构和有关部门组织实施的统计活动。

统计的基本任务是对经济社会发展情况进行统计调查、统计分析，提供统计资料和统计咨询意见，实行统计监督。

第三条 国家建立集中统一的统计系统，实行统一领导、分级负责的统计管理体制。

第四条 国务院和地方各级人民政府、各有关部门应当加强对统计工作的组织领导，为统计工作提供必要的保障。

第五条 国家加强统计科学研究，健全科学的统计指标体系，不断改进统计调查方法，提高统计的科学性。

国家有计划地加强统计信息化建设，推进统计信息搜集、处理、传输、共享、存储技术和统计数据库体系的现代化。

第六条 统计机构和统计人员依照本法规定独立行使统计调查、统计报告、统计监督的职权，不受侵犯。

地方各级人民政府、政府统计机构和有关部门以及各单位的负责人，不得自行修改统计机构和统计人员依法搜集、整理的统计资料，不得以任何方式要求统计机构、统计人员及其他机构、人员伪造、篡改统计资料，不得对依法履行职责或者拒绝、抵制统计违法行为的统计人员打击报复。

第七条 国家机关、企业事业单位和其他组织以及个体工商户和个人等统计调查对象，必须依照本法和国家有关规定，真实、准确、完整、及时地提供统计调查所需的资料，不得提供不真实或者不完整的统计资料，不得迟报、拒报统计资料。

第八条 统计工作应当接受社会公众的监督。任何单位和个人有权检举统计中弄虚作假等违法行为。对检举有功的单位和个人应当给予表彰和奖励。

第九条 统计机构和统计人员对在统计工作中知悉的国家秘密、商业秘密和个人信息，应当予以保密。

第十条 任何单位和个人不得利用虚假统计资料骗取荣誉称号、物质利益或者职务晋升。

第二章　统计调查管理

第十一条　统计调查项目包括国家统计调查项目、部门统计调查项目和地方统计调查项目。

国家统计调查项目是指全国性基本情况的统计调查项目。部门统计调查项目是指国务院有关部门的专业性统计调查项目。地方统计调查项目是指县级以上地方人民政府及其部门的地方性统计调查项目。

国家统计调查项目、部门统计调查项目、地方统计调查项目应当明确分工，互相衔接，不得重复。

第十二条　国家统计调查项目由国家统计局制定，或者由国家统计局和国务院有关部门共同制定，报国务院备案；重大的国家统计调查项目报国务院审批。

部门统计调查项目由国务院有关部门制定。统计调查对象属于本部门管辖系统的，报国家统计局备案；统计调查对象超出本部门管辖系统的，报国家统计局审批。

地方统计调查项目由县级以上地方人民政府统计机构和有关部门分别制定或者共同制定。其中，由省级人民政府统计机构单独制定或者和有关部门共同制定的，报国家统计局审批；由省级以下人民政府统计机构单独制定或者和有关部门共同制定的，报省级人民政府统计机构审批；由县级以上地方人民政府有关部门制定的，报本级人民政府统计机构审批。

第十三条　统计调查项目的审批机关应当对调查项目的必要性、可行性、科学性进行审查，对符合法定条件的，作出予以批准的书面决定，并公布；对不符合法定条件的，作出不予批准的书面决定，并说明理由。

第十四条　制定统计调查项目，应当同时制定该项目的统计调查制度，并依照本法第十二条的规定一并报经审批或者备案。

统计调查制度应当对调查目的、调查内容、调查方法、调查对象、调查组织方式、调查表式、统计资料的报送和公布等作出规定。

统计调查应当按照统计调查制度组织实施。变更统计调查制度的内容，应当报经原审批机关批准或者原备案机关备案。

第十五条　统计调查表应当标明表号、制定机关、批准或者备案文号、有效期限等标志。

对未标明前款规定的标志或者超过有效期限的统计调查表，统计调查对象有权拒绝填报；县级以上人民政府统计机构应当依法责令停止有关统计调查活动。

第十六条　搜集、整理统计资料，应当以周期性普查为基础，以经常性抽样调查为主体，综合运用全面调查、重点调查等方法，并充分利用行政记录等资料。

重大国情国力普查由国务院统一领导，国务院和地方人民政府组织统计机构和有关部门共同实施。

第十七条　国家制定统一的统计标准，保障统计调查采用的指标涵义、计算方法、分类目录、调查表式和统计编码等的标准化。

国家统计标准由国家统计局制定，或者由国家统计局和国务院标准化主管部门共同制定。

国务院有关部门可以制定补充性的部门统计标准，报国家统计局审批。部门统计标准不得与国家统计标准相抵触。

第十八条　县级以上人民政府统计机构根据统计任务的需要，可以在统计调查对象中推广使用计算机网络报送统计资料。

第十九条　县级以上人民政府应当将统计工作所需经费列入财政预算。

重大国情国力普查所需经费，由国务院和地方人民政府共同负担，列入相应年度的财政预算，按时拨付，确保到位。

第三章　统计资料的管理和公布

第二十条　县级以上人民政府统计机构和有关部门以及乡、镇人民政府，应当按照国家有关规定建立统计资料的保存、管理制度，建立健全统计信息共享机制。

第二十一条　国家机关、企业事业单位和其他组织等统计调查对象，应当按照国家有关规定设置原始记录、统计台账，建立健全统计资料的审核、签署、交接、归档等管理制度。

统计资料的审核、签署人员应当对其审核、签署的统计资料的真实性、准确性和完整性负责。

第二十二条　县级以上人民政府有关部门应当及时向本级人民政府统计机构提供统计所需的行政记录资料和国民经济核算所需的财务资料、财政资料及其他资料，并按照统计调查制度的规定及时向本级人民政府统计机构报送其组织实施统计调查取得的有关资料。

县级以上人民政府统计机构应当及时向本级人民政府有关部门提供有关统计资料。

第二十三条　县级以上人民政府统计机构按照国家有关规定，定期公布统计资料。

国家统计数据以国家统计局公布的数据为准。

第二十四条　县级以上人民政府有关部门统计调查取得的统计资料，由本部门按照国家有关规定公布。

第二十五条　统计调查中获得的能够识别或者推断单个统计调查对象身份的资料，任何单位和个人不得对外提供、泄露，不得用于统计以外的目的。

第二十六条　县级以上人民政府统计机构和有关部门统计调查取得的统计资料，除依法应当保密的外，应当及时公开，供社会公众查询。